Biographical sketches of the graduates of Yale College with annals of the college history

Franklin Bowditch Dexter

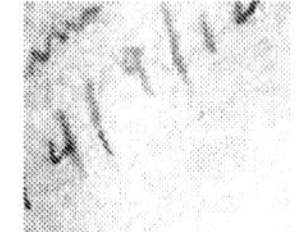

BIOGRAPHICAL SKETCHES

OF THE

GRADUATES OF YALE COLLEGE

WITH

Annals of the College History

VOL. VI

SEPTEMBER, 1805—SEPTEMBER, 1815

BY

FRANKLIN BOWDITCH DEXTER, LITT.D.

NEW HAVEN
YALE UNIVERSITY PRESS
1912

TO

SIMEON E. BALDWIN, LL.D.

GOVERNOR OF CONNECTICUT

AND

TRACY PECK, LL.D.

EMERITUS PROFESSOR OF LATIN IN YALE UNIVERSITY

THIS VOLUME IS INSCRIBED

AS A GRATEFUL MEMORIAL

OF THE INTIMATE ASSOCIATION AND FRIENDSHIP

FOR OVER HALF A CENTURY

OF THREE MEMBERS OF THE CLASS OF 1861, YALE COLLEGE

Parvula (nam exemplo est) magni formica laboris
Ore trahit quodcunque potest atque addit acervo
Quem struit haud ignara ac non incauta futuri.

Horace, Sat., I, i, 33–35.

In this work, when it shall be found that much is omitted, let it not be forgotten that much likewise is performed.

Samuel Johnson, Preface to the English Dictionary.

Claudite iam rivos, pueri: sat prata biberunt.

Vergil, Bucol., Ecl. iii, 111.

Finis coronat opus.

PREFACE

With the present volume this series is necessarily, by personal limitations, brought to a close. After 1815, Class Records are mainly available, and the "Obituary Records" which have been printed annually since 1860 cover much of the ground.

A supplementary volume has also been prepared, to be published in a few months, which contains brief sketches of all deceased graduates of the Academical Department since 1815, who are not included in the "Obituary Records"; so that, in the present volumes, the "Obituary Records," and the proposed Supplement, biographies of all deceased graduates of the College will be at command.

As the present series thus becomes one item in a much longer series, it has not seemed desirable to add (as had been intended) any statistical summary of these six volumes.

YALE UNIVERSITY LIBRARY,
June, 1912.

CONTENTS

BIOGRAPHICAL SKETCHES

AND

ANNALS OF YALE COLLEGE

Annals, 1805-06

The class entering College as Freshmen in November, 1805, was unusually small, only thirty-five in number at the date of printing the annual Catalogue of students; in the list of this year, for the first time, the places where the students room are given.

At the beginning of June, 1806, Professor Silliman returned from Europe, and almost at once began lecturing to the Senior Class.

At Commencement in September, 1806, Tutors Stedman and Hoadly, both of the Class of 1801, retired from the tutorship; and their places were supplied by the election of Sereno E. Dwight and Mills Day, both of the Class of 1803.

At this Commencement the first public steps were taken towards the establishment of a chair of medicine and the creation of a medical department, by the appointment of a committee to report on the subject.

The Yale Library has an interesting collection of silhouettes of twenty-six members of the graduating class of this year, the earliest class pictures known to be extant; included in the list is one of James Fenimore Cooper, a non-graduate member.

Sketches, Class of 1806

*Daniel Adams, A.M	*1812
**Jason Allen*	*1835
*Curtis Atwood	*1854
*David Bacon	*1823
*Clark Bissell, LL D 1847, Reip Conn Gubern. et Cur. Supr. Jurid , Socius ex officio, Jurispr. Prof	*1857
*Edmundus Bliss	*1821
*Georgius Whitefield Bolles, A M	*1858
*Ichabod Brewster	*1813
*Rawlins Lowndes Brown	
*Thomas Bull	*1850
*Henricus Judson Canfield	*1856
*Henricus Carleton, Reip. Ludovic. Cur. Supr. Jurid.	*1863
*Benjamin Smith Carnes	
**Rufus Chandler,* A M.	*1837
*Nathanael Chauncey, A M.	*1865
*Johannes Clark	*1854
**Simeon Colton,* S T D Del 1846, Coll. Mississ Praeses	*1868
*Samuel Shepard Conner, e Congr.	*1819
*Johannes Paris Cunningham	*1809
*Johannes Darrington	*1855
*Samuel Huntington Devotion	*1862
**Carolus Johannes Doughty,* A M	*1844
**Josephus Edwards*	*1863
*Isaacus Mills Ely, A M	*1845
*Henricus Fish, A M., M.B. Dartm 1810, M.D. 1826	*1850
*Royal Fowler, M.D Schol. Med. Berks 1826	*1849

*Jacobus Gadsden, A.M. 1815, ad Rempubl. Mexic. Legatus *1858
*Thomas Ruggles Gold *1829
*Georgius Goodwin *1878
*Shubael Flagg Griswold *1826
*Carolus Horatius Havens *1829
*Johannes Hazen *1843
*Alfredus Hennen, A.M. 1826, in Univ. Ludov. Jurispr. Prof. *1870
*Johannes Mauritius Heron *1833
*Lyman Hicock *1816
*Russell Hubbard, A.M. *1810
*Jabez Williams Huntington, e Congr, Reip. Conn. Cur. Supr. Jurid., Rerumpubl. Foed. Sen. *1847
**Nathanael Gilbert Huntington,* A.M. 1833 *1848
*Timotheus Langdon, A.M. *1811
*Edmundus Law *1829
*Jacobus Lockwood *1864
*Carolus Marvin *1838
*Ludovicus Mitchell *1826
*Homerus Moore *1811
*Carolus Moseley, A.M. *1815
*Daniel Mulford, A M *1811
*Hemanus Norton *1847
*Chauncaeus Pettibone *1838
*Sethus Pierce *1881
**Caleb Pitkin,* A M. *1864
**Royal Robbins* *1861
*Jacobus Root *1875
*Hezekias Rudd, A.M. *1868
*Josephus Silliman *1850
**Lucius Smith* *1847
*Henricus Strong, A.M., LL.D. 1848, Tutor, Socius ex officio *1852
*Johannes Strong, A M. *1834
*Johannes McCurdy Strong *1806
*Josias Bartlett Strong *1850

*Gulielmus Todd, A M. *1831
*Phineas Lyman Tracy, e Congr *1876
*Leverett Hubbard Trumbull *1807
*Gulielmus Tully, A M., M.D. 1819, in Acad Med. Cast. Med. Theor. et Prax. Prof. et ejusd. Praeses, Mat. Med. et Therap. Prof. *1859
**Hezekias Gold Ufford,* A M. 1820 *1863
**Guilielmus Fowler Vaill,* A.M. *1865
*Thomas Glasby Waterman *1862
*Martinus Welles, A.M., Socius ex officio *1863
*Willard Welton *1866
*Robertus Wilkinson, A.M. 1842 *1849
*Ebenezer Young, Socius ex officio, e Congr. *1851

DANIEL ADAMS, the fifth son of Cornelius Adams, of Canterbury, Connecticut, and a brother of graduates of 1800, 1801, and 1803, was born in Canterbury on March 6, 1783. Like his brothers, he was prepared for College by John Adams (Yale 1795), but he did not enter until after the opening of the Freshman year.

After graduation he studied divinity, and subsequently law.

He died in New York City on May 23, 1812, in his 30th year.

AUTHORITIES

Adams (Henry and John) History, 324.

JASON ALLEN, the seventh child and fourth son of Jason Allen, a farmer of Montville, New London County, Connecticut, and grandson of Jason and Mary (Atwell) Allen, was born in Montville on May 30, 1781 His mother was Lydia, only child of John Allen, of Montville, and her husband's first cousin. He entered College after the opening of Freshman year.

After graduation he studied theology in Norwich, and was licensed to preach by the New London Association of Ministers in 1808.

Early in 1810 he was called to the pastorate of the Congregational Church in Woodbridge, and he was ordained and installed there by the Western Consociation of New Haven County on April 11, 1810 The sermon on that occasion was preached by President Dwight.

After sixteen years of faithful labor, he was dismissed at his own request on April 25, 1826. There had been about a hundred additions to the church during his pastorate, but a secession of disaffected parishioners to form a new Union Society had made his later years uncomfortable.

Mr Allen soon removed to Central New York, where he connected himself with the Oneida Presbytery He did not settle again in the ministry, but occupied himself mainly with teaching.

He lived for some years in or near Utica, but was teaching and also supplying the Congregational Church in Lenox, in the northeastern corner of Madison County, at the time of his death there, from typhus fever, after a brief illness, on March 1, 1835, in his 54th year

One of his successors in the pastorate at Woodbridge describes him as "a man of culture and refinement, of athletic proportions, and of great strength."

He first married Nancy, the eldest child of Othniel and Hannah (Tomlinson) DeForest, of Stratford, who was nearly five years his junior. One of her sisters married his classmate, Rudd

By her he had three daughters, born in Woodbridge in 1812–18, all of whom grew up and married. She died in Utica, after a brief illness, on February 9, 1828, in her 42d year

After her death he married Lydia White, by whom he had two daughters

AUTHORITIES

Baker, Hist of Montville, 433-34. Conn. Magazine, X, iv. The DeForests of Avesnes, 233 *Marvin,* 150th Anniversary Sermon, Woodbridge, 20-21. N. Y. Observer, March 28, 1835. *Orcutt,* Hist. of Stratford, ii, 1193, Tomlinsons in America, 53-54.

CURTIS ATWOOD, the eldest son of Noble Atwood, of Woodbury, Connecticut, and grandson of Elijah and Anna (Jocelyn) Atwood, of Woodbury, was born on April 10, 1783. His mother was Margaret, daughter of Stephen and Lydia (Warner) Judd, of Woodbury.

After a short period of teaching, he studied medicine, and settled early in South Carolina, where he married and had children

He died in South Carolina, in October, 1854, in his 72d year.

AUTHORITIES

Cothren, Hist of Woodbury, i, 493

DAVID BACON, the youngest son of Asa Bacon, of Canterbury, Connecticut, and a brother of Asa Bacon (Yale 1793) and John Bacon (Yale 1796), was born in Canterbury on July 2, 1785. He did not enter College until after the opening of the Freshman year.

He studied medicine after graduation, but early fell a victim to intemperate habits

He died in New York City, from general debility, on January 13, 1823, in his 38th year He was unmarried.

AUTHORITIES

Francis B Trowbridge, MS Letter, July, 1908

CLARK BISSELL, the eldest of four sons of Joseph William and Betsey (Clark) Bissell, of Lebanon, Connecticut, and grandson of Joseph Bissell (Yale 1751), was born in Lebanon on September 7, 1782.

His father was a farmer in straitened circumstances, and his preparation for College was mainly by himself. While at Yale he gained a part of his support by teaching; at graduation he delivered an Oration on National Faith.

In the fall of 1806 he went to the Eastern Shore of Maryland, and there spent about a year as tutor in the family of a Mr. Singleton.

On his return to Connecticut, he taught school for a year in Saugatuck, now Westport, pursuing meanwhile the study of the law under the instruction of the Hon. Samuel B. Sherwood (Yale 1786). In 1808, having succeeded in paying off his College debts, he entered the office of the Hon. Roger M. Sherman (Yale 1792), of Fairfield, where he completed his preparation, and in 1809 was admitted to practice. In June of that year he settled in Norwalk, where by unwearied industry and scrupulous fidelity he rose steadily in his profession.

In 1829 he was a Representative in the Legislature, and at that session he was elected a Judge of the Supreme Court of Errors and of the Superior Court, and held that office until 1839, when he resigned, — the salary being entirely inadequate.

In 1841 he was sent again as a Representative; in 1842 and 1843 was a member of the State Senate; and in April, 1847, and April, 1848, successively, was elected by the Whigs as Governor.

In August, 1847, he accepted the appointment of Professor in the Yale Law School (in succession to Professor Townsend), and a year later he also succeeded Judge Daggett as Kent Professor of Law in the College; and continued to discharge the duties of both positions until compelled by ill health and the infirmities of advancing age to resign in July, 1855. He also represented Norwalk once more in the Legislature in 1850, when a matter of special local importance was pending. The honorary degree of Doctor of Laws was conferred on him by Yale in 1847.

After his retirement from office in the College, he spent his closing years at his home, occupied mainly in reading and in association with his family, until his peaceful death, after a gradual decline, in Norwalk, on September 15, 1857, at the age of 75. The sermon delivered at his funeral by his pastor, the Rev. William B Weed (Yale 1830), was afterwards published

He married, on April 29, 1811, Sally, second daughter of the Hon. Samuel B. Sherwood (Yale 1786), of Westport,.who died on February 27, 1856

The Yale Law School owns a copy of a portrait of Governor Bissell; reproductions are given in Hurd's *History of Fairfield County,* and in Norton's *Governors of Connecticut.*

His children were four sons, of whom one died in youth, and two daughters The eldest son was graduated at Yale in 1830, and one daughter married the Hon. Orris S. Ferry (Yale 1844).

As a lawyer Governor Bissell maintained a high reputation; and as a Judge his learning, probity, impartiality, and courtesy reflected honor on the Bench. As Governor, his sound judgment and purity of purpose won universal respect. His Christian character was consistent and humble.

His publications were mainly confined to the requirements of official duty. Two only need be specified:

1. Speech of His Excellency Clark Bissell, Governor of Connecticut, to the Legislature of the State, May, 1847 Hartford, 1847. 8°, pp 16. [*Y. C.*

2. Speech to the Legislature May, 1848 New Haven, 1848. 8°, pp 16. [*Y. C.*

AUTHORITIES

Crosby, Annual Obit Notices, 1857, 38–39 *Hurd,* Hist of Fairfield County, 556–58 *Norton,* Governors of Conn., 207–12 Norwalk Gazette, Sept 22, 1857. *Stiles,* Hist. of Windsor, 2d ed, ii, 78 Ward Family Genealogy, 113

EDMUND BLISS, the only son of Alexander Bliss, a tanner, of Springfield, Massachusetts, by his first wife, Margaret Warner, and grandson of Jedediah and Miriam (Hitchcock) Bliss, of Springfield, was born on February 20, 1786. Moses Bliss (Yale 1755) and Aaron Bliss (Yale 1766) were half-brothers of his father, and Alexander Bliss (Yale 1812) was a half-brother of his own.

In College he was regarded by his classmates as eccentric, but gifted with a remarkable ability for argument.

He settled as a lawyer in his native place, and died there, unmarried, on April 16, 1821, in his 36th year.

AUTHORITIES.

Bliss Family, 88. *Bridgman*, Northampton Epitaphs, 111.

GEORGE WHITEFIELD BOLLES, the son of Deacon John Bolles, a leading Baptist of Hartford, Connecticut, and grandson of Enoch and Hannah (Moore) Bolles, of New London, was born in Hartford on January 25, 1787. His mother was Lydia Taber, of New London.

For several years after graduation he was an assistant in an academic school in Hartford kept by George J. Patten. He afterwards began the study of medicine with Dr. Mason F. Cogswell (Yale 1780), of Hartford.

He practiced his profession to some extent in Hartford, and was also for some time an apothecary there. Some of the later years of his life were spent in Ohio.

About 1855 he returned, in failing health, to the residence of a brother in Hartford, where he died, from congestion of the lungs, on May 21, 1858, in his 72d year. He was never married.

AUTHORITIES.

Hinman, Genealogy of the Puritans, 286.

ICHABOD BREWSTER, the third son of Ichabod Brewster, a farmer of Lebanon, Connecticut, and grandson of Ichabod and Lydia (Barstow) Brewster, of Lebanon, was born on April 17, 1784 His mother was Lucy, daughter of Deacon Moses and Mehitable (Bridges) Clark of Lebanon. He spent the first two years of his College course in Williams College.

He studied medicine with Dr John S Peters, of Hebron, and later with Drs. Archer and Randolph, of Amelia County, Virginia. He received a license to practice from the Medical Society of the State of New York in 1810.

About June, 1811, he settled for the practice of his profession on John's Island, about twelve miles west of Charleston, South Carolina, where he continued with growing success, until his death on September 11, 1813, in the 30th year of his age. His estate was appraised at less than $3,000. He was never married

---

AUTHORITIES

Jones, Brewster Genealogy, 1, 147

RAWLINS LOWNDES BROWN, commonly known as LOWNDES BROWN, was a native of Charleston, South Carolina, the only child of Joseph Brown, of Georgetown, who married in November, 1784, Harriet, the fourth child of Judge Rawlins Lowndes, President of the Province in 1778–79, and Mary (Cartwright) Lowndes. His father died before he entered College

After graduation, he wished to become a planter, but his mother opposed the plan; so that when in 1812 he desired to join the army, she felt debarred from objecting.

In March, 1812, he was appointed First Lieutenant of Artillery; was promoted to the rank of Captain in 1817; and resigned from the service in September, 1819.

On December 23, 1819, he was married by the Rt. Rev. John Henry Hobart to Margaretta, daughter of John R. and Eliza (McEvers) Livingston, of Redhook, and New York City.

By this marriage he had one child, a daughter, who married Baron Solwyns, of the Belgian diplomatic service, but left no issue.

He remained at the North after his marriage, and probably died about 1845.

AUTHORITIES.

Heitman, Hist. Register of U. S. Army, i, 253. N. E. Hist. and Genealogical Register, xxx, 152. *Holgate,* Amer. Genealogy, 182.

THOMAS BULL, the eldest child of Thomas Bull, a merchant of Hartford, Connecticut, and grandson of Captain Caleb and Martha (Cadwell) Bull, was born in Hartford on November 9, 1787. His mother was Ruth, daughter of Moses and Sarah (Howard) Butler, of East Hartford. His eldest sister married Richard E. Goodwin, of the next class.

He was occupied after graduation in his father's store until he came of age, in November, 1808, when he sought his fortune in the Western Reserve of Ohio.

About 1824 he became Secretary of the Manhattan Insurance Company in New York, and he continued for many years to be engaged in the insurance business in that city, with his residence in Brooklyn, where he died on April 1, 1850, aged 62½ years.

He married Sarah Parsons Clark, the second daughter of Russell Clark, Junior, and Content (Ward) Clark, of New Haven, who was born in June, 1786, and survived him.

AUTHORITIES.

Hinman, Genealogy of the Puritans, 396.

Henry Judson Canfield, son of Judge Judson Canfield (Yale 1782), of Sharon, Connecticut, was born in Sharon on January 21, 1789.

After graduation he studied law in the Litchfield Law School, and was admitted to the bar in 1810

His father had large landed interests in Mahoning County, in Northeastern Ohio, where the town of Canfield had been named for him in 1798. Thither the son removed early, to take the care of his father's property; and there the rest of his life was spent.

He died in Canfield, on November 27, 1856, in his 68th year.

AUTHORITIES

Kilbourne, Litchfield Bench and Bar, 234

Henry Carleton, born Henry Carleton Cox, had attended the University of Georgia before entering Yale from Athens, Georgia, in Junior year. The following sketch of his life was written by his grandson, the Hon. Carleton Hunt.

Judge Carleton was born in Virginia, passed his life to manhood in Georgia, then emigrated to Mississippi, from whence he came to New Orleans, Louisiana, and served honorably as a Lieutenant of Infantry under General Jackson, in the campaign which terminated January 8, 1815

May 29, A.D. 1815, Mr. Carleton married a French lady from the West India Islands, Aglaé Pauline Robertine Valentine D'Avezac de Castera, sister of Louise, wife of Edward Livingston and of Auguste D'Avezac, late United States Chargé d'Affaires to The Hague The issue of this marriage was Aglaé Marie, only child of Mr. Carleton, afterwards the wife of Dr. Thomas Hunt, founder of the Medical College of Louisiana, leading advocate of university education in that State

Throughout his professional life, Mr. Carleton maintained a close intimacy with Edward Livingston, of whose legal attainments he entertained an exalted opinion, and whose success in public life he watched with brotherly affection.

Soon after he went to Louisiana, Mr. Carleton undertook and executed, in conjunction with the late Jurisconsult Louis Moreau Lislet, a translation of "Las Siete Partidas" of Alfonso the Wise. That translation is the only one in English in existence, and, in preparing it, Mr. Carleton rendered service to law and to learning, and, at the same time, erected for himself an enduring monument.

Mr. Carleton was appointed District Attorney for the Eastern District of Louisiana in 1832, vice John Slidell removed by General Jackson. April 1, 1837, Mr. Carleton was appointed a Judge of the Supreme Court of Louisiana, but resigned on account of ill health in 1839. He was a laborious student, and was well known for his impartiality and learning, both as a lawyer and a judge. Ardent love of country was perhaps his chief characteristic. A Southern man by birth and by residence of many years, he adhered throughout the Civil War without wavering to the cause of the Union, as the palladium of American civil rights and liberties

Judge Carleton visited Europe several times and traveled in search of health, until about twelve years previous to his death, when he finally settled in Philadelphia. He was in London, June 2, 1851; in Dinar, France, on the 20th April, 1852. He was in New York on the 3d October, 1858 He was subsequently in Europe for more than a year, which he seems to have passed in the Island of Jersey. After a long widowerhood, he was married a second time, while abroad, to Mrs. Maria (Vanderburgh) Wiltbank, who survived him

In his retirement, he became a great student of the Bible, Biblical literature, and mental philosophy. He was a loyal alumnus of Yale College He kept up his acquaintance with the classics. His regular habit was to read the New Testament in the original Greek. He was familiar with the writings of all metaphysicians, with many of whom he had corresponded and compared opinions. He published, in 1857, a carefully prepared volume entitled, "Liberty and Necessity." His thirst for knowledge was insatiable

Judge Carleton died on Saturday, March 28, 1863, in his 78th year The cause of his demise was an acute and painful attack of congestion of the lungs, which lasted but twenty-four hours Death arrested him, as it might take the smith, at the anvil Around his death-bed were scattered his well-read Bible, his carefully corrected manuscripts, and the books on philosophy he loved so dearly. With his last breath, he cried aloud in prayer to Christ to have mercy on his soul, and straightway was no more.

He published:

Liberty and Necessity, in which are considered the Laws of Association of Ideas, the meaning of the word Will, and the true intent of Punishment Philadelphia, 1857. 12°, pp xii, 9–165
[*B Publ. Br Mus Harv. Y C*
Based on James Mill's *Analysis of the Phenomena of the Mind.*

He also communicated to the American Philosophical Society, of which he was a member from October, 1859, several papers on the same subject (1860–63), the latest of which, read seven weeks before his death, was printed, with the title, *Liberty and Necessity,* in the *Proceedings* of the Society, vol. 9, pp. 130–39.

Another most important task which he accomplished was the translation, in conjunction with L Moreau Lislet, of the following:

The Law of Las Siete Partidas, which are still in force in the State of Louisiana New Orleans, 1820 2 vols. 8° [*B Publ.*

Published at the expense of the State. The translators had already published on their own responsibility, in 1818 (8°, pp 197), Number 1 of such a translation

BENJAMIN SMITH CARNES came to College from Charleston, South Carolina, entering after the opening of the Freshman year. He was the son of Captain Patrick Carnes, of Ashepoo, South Carolina, who died in 1786, and of Susannah, daughter of Benjamin and Ann (Loughton) Smith, and widow of Barnard Elliott.

He became dissipated, and died about 1810 His name last appears in the Charleston directory in 1809, and is first starred as deceased in the Triennial Catalogue of our graduates issued in 1814

AUTHORITIES

Miss I DeSaussure, MS Letter, May, 1911

RUFUS CHANDLER, the third son of Lieutenant Joseph and Olive (Backus) Chandler, of Pomfret, Connecticut, and grandson of Joseph and Elizabeth (Sumner) Chandler, of Pomfret, was born on May 26, 1785

After graduation he went to Hanover County, near Richmond, Virginia, as a school teacher.

He remained there until his marriage, on October 1, 1812, to Nancy, daughter of Thomas and Susanna (Pleasants) Trevilian, of Caroline County

Through his wife he became the owner of a small plantation at Oxford, about thirty miles north of Richmond, where he established in 1815 a private school which he called "Little Yale." He continued thus, occupied as a teacher and farmer, for several years, until the partial failure of his health, when he gave up his school

He was ordained to the Baptist ministry on June 13, 1830, and preached statedly at Burruss, in the vicinity.

Elder Chandler died at "Little Yale," on July 18, 1837, in his 53d year

His widow died in January, 1857, in her 73d year.

They had seven children, of whom the two eldest died in infancy. Four sons and one daughter survived their parents

AUTHORITIES

Chandler Family, 2d ed, 290, 527–28

NATHANIEL CHAUNCEY, the youngest of five children of the Hon Charles and Abigail (Darling) Chauncey, of New Haven, was born here on February 27, 1789. His two brothers were graduated at Yale in 1792 and 1796, respectively. On account of his youth, he did not enter College until after the opening of the Junior year Although the youngest member of his class, he stood in the first rank in scholarship, and was offered a tutorship in 1808, but declined it.

He studied law, for two years with his father, and later in Philadelphia, where both of his brothers had settled; and was admitted to the Philadelphia bar, but his constitution, never robust, had been enfeebled by close application as an undergraduate, and he found himself unable to prosecute so confining a profession. He therefore soon retired from practice, and engaged for a short time in commercial pursuits, but these were not to his taste, and he then returned about 1819 to his father's house in New Haven, to minister to him in his old age.

After the death of his father, in April, 1823, he passed five years in Europe, in travel and in literary pursuits. During this time he occupied himself in part with investigations into the history of the Chauncey family, and thus strengthened a love for the study of genealogy, which continued through his life.

He returned to the United States in the fall of 1828, and made his home in Philadelphia.

On June 8, 1836, he was married to Elizabeth, the eldest child of Samuel and Nancy (Gardner) Salisbury, of Boston, who was eighteen years his junior. She had previously been engaged to Henry E. Dwight (Yale 1815), the youngest son of President Dwight, who died in 1832.

She died on May 21, 1850, aged 43 years. Besides an infant, who died a few days after his mother, she left two sons,—graduates of Harvard University in 1859 and 1861, respectively.

Mr. Chauncey died in Philadelphia on February 9, 1865, at the age of 76; and was buried, by his own desire, in New Haven beside his parents.

He was "distinguished by guileless purity of purpose, a nice sense of right and honor, benevolent feeling and large charity, — an embodiment and exemplar of the Christian gentleman."

A portrait by Sully is in the possession of his family.

A sketch of his character is given in a paper by his second cousin, Professor William Chauncey Fowler (Yale 1816), which was read before the New England Historic-Genealogical Society in March, 1866, and published separately.

He published:

1. An Oration, delivered before the Washington Association of Philadelphia, and the Washington Benevolent Society of Pennsylvania, on the Fourth of July, 1815. Philadelphia, 1815. 8°, pp. 22.
[*B. Publ. N. Y. Publ. Libr. U. T. S. Y. C.*

A Federalist note of triumph on the close of the war.

2. An Address delivered before the New England Society of Philadelphia, on the Fourth of May, 1818. Philadelphia, 1818. 8°, pp. 11. [*Y. C.*

On the late President Dwight.

In 1820 he contributed three papers to *The Microscope*, a semi-weekly periodical, edited by Cornelius Tuthill (Yale 1814). The first and third articles, signed *Azrael* (vol. i, pp. 25–30; ii, 17–24), relate to the occupations and acquirements of Angels; the second, signed *Concinnus* (vol. i, pp. 153–60), gives an account of the New-Haven Dandy Club.

He was also the author of an anonymous article in the monthly *Christian Spectator* for February, 1823 (vol. 5, pp. 57–65), signed F C, and entitled:—

Christian Courtesy.

An obituary notice of his friend, Henry E. Dwight (Yale 1815), in 1832, contributed to the *Philadelphia Daily Advertiser,* is reprinted in the *Religious Intelligencer,* New Haven, vol 17, p. 255

AUTHORITIES

Fowler, Chauncey Memorials, 116, 151–53; Conditions of Success in Genealogical Investigations. *Salisbury,* Family Memorials, 1, 54–56

JOHN CLARK, a son of Ebenezer Clark, of Washington, Connecticut, and a brother of the Rev. Jehu Clark (Yale 1794), was born in Washington in 1787 His preparation for College was completed under Sereno E. Dwight (Yale 1803) in New Haven, and he entered at the opening of the Junior year.

After graduation he studied theology, and was licensed to preach by the Fairfield East Association of Ministers on May 29, 1810. His health, however, failing, he relinquished the profession and devoted some years to teaching.

He married, on April 3, 1817, Lucy, eldest child of Ward and Dorcas (Porter) Peck, of Waterbury, Connecticut, and widow of Captain Ansel Porter of Waterbury.

After his marriage he lived in the house formerly belonging to Captain Porter, and employed himself in farming, though continuing through life to devote much time to teaching. He became involved in 1823 in a personal quarrel with his pastor, the Rev. Daniel Crane (Princeton 1797), which resulted in Mr Crane's dismissal in 1825.

He died in Waterbury, from disease of the heart, on April 25, 1854, aged 77 years. His widow died on May 15, 1865, in her 81st year.

His children were four sons and a daughter

AUTHORITIES.

Anderson, Hist. of Waterbury, i, 192, 215; iii, 582. 628-31, Appendix, 37, 101, 104; ii, 75.

SIMEON COLTON, the eldest child of Jabez Colton (Yale 1775), was born in Somers, Connecticut, where his father was then teaching, on January 8, 1785. The Hon. Roger S. Baldwin (Yale 1811) was his first cousin. His father settled permanently in Longmeadow, Massachusetts, his native town, adjoining Somers on the north, about 1790. His College course was interrupted by school-teaching during two winters, mainly for the purpose of earning money.

Early in November, 1806, he took charge of the Academy just founded in Monson, Massachusetts, but remained for only a single year. Thence he went to the Academy in Leicester, where he was the principal preceptor from October, 1807, to February, 1809.

He then went to Wilbraham, to assist the Rev. Ezra Witter (Yale 1793) in the instruction of private pupils, and at the same to receive instruction in theology; but owing to some unforeseen embarrassment in Mr. Witter's circumstances, he remained with him for only two months. Then he went to Northampton, and taught for three months a school for young ladies; and thence to Salem, as an attendant to John Pickering (Harvard 1759), a brother of Timothy Pickering, who was afflicted with epilepsy.

He now entered fully upon the study of theology, under the direction of the Rev. Dr. Samuel Worcester (Dartmouth Coll. 1795); and joined the First Church in Salem, on profession of his faith, in December, 1809. He had been reared under strict religious influences, but was altogether indifferent to the subject until the sudden death, from scarlet fever, of Isaac Welton, his classmate and roommate at College, in February, 1806.

He was licensed to preach at North Danvers by the Salem Association of Ministers on May 8, 1810, and in January, 1811, began to preach on probation in the Congregational Church in Palmer, where he was called to the pastorate in April, on a salary of $450, and was ordained and installed on the 19th of June.

On September 3, 1812, he married Lucretia, eldest child of Captain Gideon and Lucretia (Woodworth) Colton, of Longmeadow, who died in Palmer on July 14, 1821, in her 33d year.

Some opposition to his ministry began to be expressed in the spring of 1821; and after his home was broken up by his wife's death, he was led to ask a dismission, which was granted on November 13. One hundred and twenty members had been added to the church during his pastorate,—largely the fruits of a revival in 1819.

While settled in Palmer he had been a Trustee of Monson Academy, and now he went back to his old position as Principal there, and served in that office for nine years. By his efforts, and those of others, new life was infused into the institution, and his labors and sacrifices in its behalf were rewarded with marked success.

On August 9, 1823, he married Susan, daughter of Isham Chapman, of Tolland, Connecticut.

In 1830 he went to Amherst, and for three years had charge of the Academy there with gratifying results

He then went by invitation to Fayetteville, Cumberland County, North Carolina, and took charge in January, 1834, of Donaldson Academy, an institution just founded by the Fayetteville Presbytery. He held this position until the close of 1839, when difficulties connected the division of the Presbyterian Church into the Old and New Schools caused him to resign He continued, however, to teach a private school in Fayetteville until July, 1846

He then accepted a call to the presidency of Mississippi College, at Clinton, in Hinds County, Mississippi, under the patronage of the New School branch of the Presbyterian Church. He found that the so-called College was little more than a respectable Academy, and that the efforts to build it up required larger means than its friends could command; after encountering many difficulties and receiving an invitation to return to North Carolina, he resigned his place on July 28, 1848.

The honorary degree of Doctor of Divinity had been conferred on him by Delaware College in 1846.

He then became Principal of Cumberland Academy, just founded by the Fayetteville Presbytery at Summerville, in what is now Harnett County, and entered on his duties in January, 1849. Here again there was a failure, through the want of union and concentrated action on the part of the Presbytery; and he resigned his place in November, 1853.

His wife died in Summerville on November 24, 1850; and he was married for the third time, on December 21, 1851, to Catharine E., widow of Jones Fuller, of Fayetteville.

In January, 1854, he removed to Ashboro, in Randolph County, where he taught an Academy for about seven years, and then, owing to the increasing infirmities of age, closed his regular teaching.

He died in Ashboro on December 27, 1868, aged 84 years, and was buried in Summerville. His wife survived him.

By his first wife he had one daughter, and by his second wife three sons and three daughters. All his children survived him, except one daughter by the second marriage. The second son was graduated at the University of North Carolina in 1855, and became a minister; four of his sons have been graduated at Yale.

Dr. Colton was an excellent teacher and a strict disciplinarian. He had at different times about two thousand pupils under his instruction, who were benefited and inspired by his enthusiasm and moral earnestness. He was also a practical chemist and surveyor, and gave much attention to mineralogy and geology.

Although mainly engaged in teaching, he did not neglect his commission as a minister. After leaving Palmer he continued, until within a few months of his death, to preach quite regularly as an assistant or occasional supply.

His portrait is reproduced in the *Monson Academy Centennial Souvenir.*

He published:

1 The Gospel a message of glad tidings. A Sermon [from Acts xiii, 32] preached before the Union Charitable Society, at their first annual meeting in Monson, September 8, 1818 Hartford, 1818 8°, pp 16 [*C. H. S.*

2 Masonry founded on the Bible.—A Sermon [from Eph ii, 20], delivered at Amherst, Mass. June 26, A L 5826, at the Festival of Saint John the Baptist Amherst, 1826 8°, pp 31 [*A. A S M. H. S.*

3 The Claims of Anti-Masonry, and Duty of Masons. An Address delivered before the Central Lodge of Free-Masons, in Dudley, Mass June 24, A. L. 5830 Southbridge, 1830 8°, pp 24 [*A A. S*

4 An Address to all persons connected with Presbyterian Churches and Congregations 1839

This able pamphlet consisted of six letters, signed *Presbuteros,* and relating to the disruption of the Presbyterian Church in 1837 He wrote as an adherent of the New School, and was in consequence presented to the Synod of North Carolina for trial by the Fayetteville Presbytery The Synod decided against him, but confined themselves to requiring from him merely a statement that he had not intended to offend the Presbytery The pamphlet was reprinted (pp 1–18), with an Appendix containing his Defence before the Presbytery (pp 19–53), by the Presbytery, in

Documents connected with the Trial of the Rev Simeon Colton Fayetteville, 1839 8°, pp xii, 107

5 An Address delivered at Wake Forest College.

6. Speech, delivered at the Celebration of the Semi-Centennial Anniversary of Monson Academy, July 19th, 1854.

In Discourses and Speeches, delivered at the Celebration. New-York, 1855. 8°, pp. 75–80.

After his death selections from his manuscripts were printed, in the *Historical Magazine*, vol. 6, second series, pp. 233–38, 282–85 (October–November, 1869), with the title:

Extracts from the Records of the Town of Palmer, and Minutes of the History of the Town.

AUTHORITIES.

Rev. James H. Colton, MS. Letter, April, 1869. Longmeadow Centennial, pt. 2, 37, 40. Semi-Centennial Anniversary of Monson Academy, 17–27, 75–80. *Temple*, Hist. of Palmer, 219, 230–32.

Samuel Shepard Conner was born in New Hampshire in 1785 or 1786, and entered Yale from Exeter in that State, after the opening of the Freshman year. He had been prepared for College at the Phillips Academy, Exeter. At graduation he delivered an Oration on the Policy and Necessity of exciting a Martial Spirit among the Citizens of the United States.

He settled in Waterville, in the District of Maine, as a lawyer, in 1810.

He entered the United States Army as Major of the 21st Infantry in March, 1812, served as aide-de-camp to General Henry Dearborn in the beginning of 1813, and was Lieutenant Colonel of the 13th Infantry from March, 1813, until his resignation in July, 1814, when he resumed the practice of the law in Waterville.

Later in 1814 he was elected a Representative in Congress from Massachusetts, and served from December, 1815, to March, 1817.

In 1819 he was appointed Surveyor-General of the Ohio land district. While engaged in the duties of this position, he died among strangers in Covington, Kentucky, on December 25, 1819, aged 33 years.

He married Elizabeth, daughter of Isaac and Eleanor Denniston, of Albany, New York, who died in Albany on February 8, 1865, aged 76 years.

AUTHORITIES

Heitman, Hist Register of U S Army, i, 321. *Munsell,* Annals of Albany, iii, 185; Collections of Hist of Albany, iii, 232 National Intelligencer, February 1, 1820

JOHN PARIS CUNNINGHAM came to College from Charleston, South Carolina, entering after the opening of Freshman year.

He returned to Charleston, and died in 1809

JOHN DARRINGTON entered College from the High Hills of Santee, Sumter County (about eighteen miles South of Camden, and thirty miles East of Columbia), South Carolina, after the opening of Freshman year.

He spent his life in Alabama, and died on his large and valuable estate near Grovehill, Clarke County, on September 12, 1855.

SAMUEL HUNTINGTON DEVOTION, the youngest son of Judge Ebenezer Devotion (Yale 1759), of Scotland, then part of Windham, Connecticut, was born in Scotland on February 18, and was baptized on June 8, 1783.

He entered College after the opening of the Sophomore year At graduation he delivered an Oration on Theoretical Opinions.

He studied law with Judge Zephaniah Swift (Yale 1778), of Windham, and was admitted to the bar there on December 9, 1808 A little later he removed to Boston, where an elder brother (Yale 1785) was living, and where he was admitted to the bar in April, 1810 The elder brother died on July 1; and soon after the younger one removed to New Orleans, where he was admitted to the bar on May 1, 1811. His stay there also was brief, as in August, 1814, he was admitted to the bar in Pittsburgh, Pennsylvania.

This was his last effort in professional life; and about 1815 he returned to his father's house, carefully shutting himself in from society for the remainder of his life. No reason for his singular conduct was known.

He died in Scotland on May 7, 1862, in his 80th year.

He is believed to have been married, and to have lost his wife early.

AUTHORITIES.

Rev. S. G. Willard, MS. Letters, 1862.

CHARLES JOHN DOUGHTY, a son of John Doughty, long and honorably known as town clerk and as chief of the fire department of Brooklyn, New York, and grandson of John Doughty, a butcher, of Brooklyn, was born in Brooklyn on January 11, 1784. He entered College after the opening of the Freshman year.

He studied law in New York City after graduation, and was in practice there from 1811 to 1820.

He married a Miss Stanton.

In 1821 the followers of Swedenborg in New York purchased a house of worship for the New Jerusalem Church, and Mr. Doughty, who had for some time previously officiated as reader or preacher in their meetings, was elected pastor and duly ordained.

In September, 1838, by mutual consent his connection with the congregation was dissolved. A Second Church was formed in September, 1841, of which Mr. Doughty served as pastor, until his death, in New York, on July 19, 1844, aged 60½ years. His estate was administered by a son of the same name.

AUTHORITIES.

Greenleaf, Hist. of N. Y. Churches, 371-72.

Joseph Edwards was born in Middletown, Connecticut (probably in that part which is now Cromwell), on August 27, 1783.

He did not enter College until after the opening of the Freshman year.

He began the study of theology upon graduation with the Rev. Asahel Hooker (Yale 1789), of Goshen, at the same time conducting an academy there.

On October 4, 1809, he was ordained and installed as pastor of the Congregational Church in West Stockbridge, Massachusetts, where he remained until June 23, 1812.

After other engagements in preaching, he removed in the fall of 1826 to Greenfield, in Huron County, Ohio, and in March, 1828, to a farm of 900 acres in Ripley, in the same county, about sixty miles southwest of Cleveland. Here he spent the rest of his life, highly respected and useful, preaching occasionally, but without any stipulated salary

He died at his home in Ripley on April 30, 1863, in his 80th year

He was twice married His second wife survived him His children were six daughters, and a son (Oberlin College 1840) who entered the ministry.

AUTHORITIES

Firelands Pioneer, iv, 61–64. *Rudd,* MS. Letter, March, 1865 *H. Williams,* Hist. of the Fire Lands, 320, 323.

Isaac Mills Ely, the youngest son of the Rev. Dr David Ely (Yale 1769), of Huntington, Connecticut, was born in Huntington on April 6, 1787. He was named for a maternal uncle (Yale 1786), and the name was perpetuated in the next generation by a nephew (Yale 1843). At graduation he delivered an Oration on the Profession of Law.

He then studied law, and began practice in New York City about 1811. He had a superior mind in acuteness, and brilliancy, and an amiable disposition, and was a favorite in society. He early gave promise of eminence at the bar; but owing to some excesses his health became impaired, and for many years he withdrew almost entirely from the practice of his profession and from general society.

In April, 1845, he was stricken with paralysis and apoplexy, and died in New York, firm in Christian belief, on the 25th of that month, aged 58 years.

He was never married.

AUTHORITIES.

Ely Ancestry, 115. N. Y. Observer, May 3, 1845. *Orcutt*, Hist. of Stratford, ii, 1197.

Henry Fish was born in Hartford, Connecticut, on October 15, 1788, being a son of Miller Fish, a merchant of Hartford, and his wife, Catharine Corning.

He studied medicine under Dr. Nathan Smith in Hanover, New Hampshire, and received the degree of Bachelor of Medicine in 1810 from Dartmouth College.

He then settled in New York City in medical practice.

In October, 1812, he married Rebecca Birch, of Salisbury, Connecticut, and about 1819 or 1820 he removed to Salisbury, where he remained in practice for about twenty-five years. The honorary degree of M.D. was conferred on him by Yale College in 1826.

He then removed to Lee, in Berkshire County, Massachusetts, where he died on December 22, 1850, in his 73d year.

AUTHORITIES.

Hist. of Litchfield County, 1881, 537.

Royal Fowler was born in Pittsfield, Massachusetts, on December 16, 1785, the youngest son of Stephen Fowler, and a brother of Bancroft Fowler (Yale 1796). He spent the first two years of his course at Williams College.

He studied medicine after graduation with Dr. Horatio Jones, of Stockbridge, and began practice in 1811 in Great Barrington.

Dr. Jones died in April, 1813; and Dr. Fowler being invited by the town of Stockbridge to take his place, soon removed thither, and remained in practice until about 1845. He proved to be a peculiarly careful physician, and was much confided in by his patients. The honorary degree of M.D. was conferred on him by the Berkshire Medical Institution in 1826.

He died in Stockbridge on September 20, 1849, in his 64th year.

He married, in September, 1812, Frances, second daughter of Stephen and Elizabeth (Owen) Dewey, of Sheffield, by whom he had one daughter and three sons; one son was graduated at Williams College in 1847.

The widow died at the house of her second son, a Presbyterian clergyman in Auburn, New York, on December 27, 1869, in her 81st year.

AUTHORITIES.

Descendants of Ambrose Fowler, *E. F Jones*, Stockbridge, 237. 14 Dewey Family Hist., 899, 945

James Gadsden, the third child of Philip Gadsden, of Charleston, South Carolina, was born in Charleston on May 15, 1788, and entered College after the opening of the Freshman year, having been prepared at the Associated Academy of Charleston Two brothers were graduated in 1804.

He went into commercial life in Charleston, and in December, 1812, entered the United States Army as Second Lieutenant of Engineers, undergoing active service on the Canada border.

After the close of the war he was detailed to accompany General Jackson in the capacity of an engineering expert, on the expedition to examine and report on the forts and other military defences of the Gulf of Mexico and the Southwestern frontier. Jackson was so pleased with his appearance that he at once made him his confidential aide-de-camp.

In the fall of 1816, owing to delicate health, he was desirous of retiring from the army, but his devotion to General Jackson kept him at his post, and he was appointed by President Madison in conjunction with General Simon Bernard to review the examination of the defences in which he had taken part the year before.

In 1818, still as Jackson's aid, he took a distinguished part in the campaign against the Seminoles, at the end of which he was promoted to a captaincy and appointed Collector of the port of Pensacola.

He then had charge of the construction of works for the defence of the Gulf frontier, and while thus engaged was made (in October, 1820) Inspector General of the Southern division of the army, with the rank of Colonel.

When the army was reduced in 1821, he was employed as Adjutant General, but the Senate twice refused (April–May, 1822) to confirm President Jackson's nomination of him for this office, and his appointment therefore expired; but he assisted Calhoun, then Secretary of War, for several months.

He then settled in Florida as a planter, and became a member of the Territorial Council. Under a commission (April, 1823) from President Monroe he effected a treaty in September, 1823, for the removal of the Seminoles from middle to southern Florida; and in this connection crossed the peninsula from the Atlantic to the Gulf (being the first white man to do so), and presented a report on the topography of the region.

In 1831–32 he served as Assistant Engineer of the Territory, and in the spring of 1836 was Quartermaster General of the Florida Volunteers.

Later he returned to his native State, and was engaged in commerce and in extensive rice-culture.

He was also President of the South Carolina railroad.

In the summer of 1853 President Pierce sent him to Mexico as Minister Plenipotentiary; and on December 30 of that year he negotiated the treaty known by his name, by which a new boundary between the two countries was established. A tract of about twenty million acres, constituting the southern part of what is now New Mexico and Arizona, was thus secured. Before all details were adjusted he was superseded as minister (in 1856), and then retired to private life in Charleston, where he died on December 25, 1858, in his 71st year, after a brief illness.

He married, after August, 1825 (when she is mentioned in her father's will as unmarried), Susannah Gibbes, daughter of William Hort, of Charleston, by his first wife, Alice Gibbes, and a half-sister of Benjamin S. Hort (Yale 1808).

She died shortly before him They left no children

An oil-painting of General and Mrs. Gadsden, by J. B Flagg, is still preserved

He published:

Sketches of the Life and Public Services of General Andrew Jackson. Charleston, 1824

Originally published in the *Charleston Mercury.*

Six of his letters to Calhoun (1829–47) are printed in Jameson's edition of Calhoun's Correspondence.

AUTHORITIES

Brady, The True Andrew Jackson, 411–12 *Crosby,* Annual Obit Notices, 1858, 121–23 *Miss I. DeSaussure,* MS Letter, May, 1911. *Heitman,* Hist Register of U S Army, 411 *Parton,* Life of Jackson, ii, 360, 503

Thomas Ruggles Gold, the eldest son of Deacon Benjamin Gold, a farmer and merchant of Cornwall, Connecticut, and grandson of the Rev. Hezekiah Gold (Yale 1751), was born in Cornwall on March 25, 1787, and was named after his father's brother (Yale 1786). His mother was Eleanor, daughter of Solomon and Eleanor (Pierce) Johnson, of Cornwall. A brother was graduated here in 1834; and another brother was the inventor of the Gold steam-heater. One sister married the Rev. Cornelius B. Everest (Williams 1811), and a second married the Rev. Herman L. Vaill, M.A. (honorary Yale 1824).

He remained in Cornwall after graduation, and distinguished himself as a teacher of the Hebrew and other languages on a system of his own. Meantime he was licensed to preach by the Litchfield North Association on September 29, 1815.

He died in Washington, while on a visit, sustained by Christian hope, on December 30, 1829, in his 43d year. He was never married.

AUTHORITIES.

Conn. Courant, January 12, 1830. *Gold*, Hist. of Cornwall, 292.

George Goodwin, the third son in a family of twelve children of George Goodwin, of Hartford, Connecticut, and grandson of Samuel and Laodamia (Merrill) Goodwin, of Hartford, was born in Hartford on April 23, 1786. Two brothers were graduated at Yale, in 1807 and 1823 respectively.

Soon after graduation he went into the grocery business in his native city in company with Spencer Whiting in the firm of Whiting & Goodwin; and afterwards continued the same business, from about 1810 to 1815, in company with one of his younger brothers.

On November 25, 1809, he married Maria, second daughter of Andrew and Mary (Osborn) Kingsbury, of Hartford.

In 1815 the firm of Hudson & Goodwin, to which his father had belonged, was dissolved, and the firm of George Goodwin & Sons succeeded to the business of bookselling, printing and publishing, the leading interest then being the *Connecticut Courant,* which they retained until 1836; and for this and their other publications they made the paper at their mills in East Hartford.

In order to give more attention to paper-making, which gradually became their leading business, he removed his residence, in 1821, to Burnside, in East Hartford. Here he became at once a leading man in all that concerned the welfare of the town, taking strong ground in favor of temperance, morality, and religion. He passed an active and useful life until 1861, when the company failed in business, and the mills passed into other hands

Soon after his sight began to fail, and in 1868 he became totally blind. He died, from old age, in Burnside, on February 8, 1878, in his 92d year.

Although unsuccessful as a business man, he was industrious, honorable, and liberal, as a Christian, humble and retiring, but utterly conscientious and faithful

He represented East Hartford in the State Legislature in 1829, 1834, and 1856.

His wife died in Burnside on March 6, 1851, in her 63d year.

Their children were seven daughters, one of whom died in infancy, and two sons. George G. Williams, Ph.B. (Yale 1880), is a grandson.

AUTHORITIES.

The Goodwins of Hartford, 645, 367–70 *Walworth,* Hyde Genealogy, 650–52 Kingsbury Genealogy, 288, 1, 678.

SHUBAEL FLAGG GRISWOLD, the eldest child of Shubael Griswold, of East Hartford, Connecticut, and grandson of Captain Shubael and Abigail (Stanley) Griswold, of Torrington, was baptized on January 19, 1789. His mother was a daughter of Dr. Samuel Flagg, of East Hartford, and a sister of Hezekiah Flagg (Yale 1800).

He studied law with the Hon. Chauncey Goodrich, of Hartford, and in the Litchfield Law School; and after his admission to the bar he practiced in Hartford from 1810 to about 1820.

He was a victim of intemperate habits, and died at his home in East Hartford, on May 29, 1826, in his 39th year, leaving an insolvent estate.

CHARLES HORACE HAVENS, third son of John Havens, of Moriches, on the south shore, in the township of Brookhaven, Long Island, and grandson of Jonathan and Patience (Tuthill) Havens, of Shelter Island, was born on December 4, 1784. His mother was Abigail, eldest child of Merriday and Mary (Strong) Bostwick, of Greenwich, Connecticut. His mother died in 1801, and his father in June, 1810.

He did not enter College until after the opening of the Sophomore year.

He studied medicine after graduation, and served as a surgeon in the State militia during the War of 1812.

He was Clerk of Suffolk County from 1812 to 1820, and was afterwards Assistant Health Officer at the Quarantine Ground, on Staten Island.

He married Betsey, second daughter of Recompence and Naomi (Burnham) Sherrill, of Easthampton, Long Island, who died on June 20, 1848, in her 66th year.

Their children were one son and two daughters.

After a lingering illness he died in his native town on July 18, 1829, aged 46 years. His residence was still on Staten Island, and administration was taken out on his estate there by a brother.

AUTHORITIES

Mallmann, Shelter Island, 164.
N Y. Spectator, July 24, 1829 Ster-
rill Family, 1894, 39.

JOHN HAZEN was born in Franklin, then part of Norwich, Connecticut, on February 7, 1780, the son of Jacob and Abigail (Burnham) Hazen, and grandson of Jacob and Mary (Brett) Hazen.

He studied medicine, and practiced his profession in Franklin, Delaware County, New York, where he died on July 14, 1843, in his 64th year

---

ALFRED HENNEN was born on the 17th of October, 1786, in Elkridge, a suburb of Baltimore, Maryland He was the elder son of Dr James Hennen; who was the son of a doctor in Castlebar, County Mayo, in Northwestern Ireland, and the brother of Dr. John Hennen, the author of a well-known treatise on the Principles of Military Surgery.

His father settled in 1795 in Nashville, Tennessee, where the son received the rudiments of his classical education at the first grammar school ever established in that part of the State. He was then indentured to a merchant in Philadelphia, but showed himself so bent on study that in 1801 his father placed him in the school of Robert Rogers (Brown Univ. 1775), of Newport, Rhode Island, and in 1803 he entered the Sophomore Class at Yale. He was already a member of the Presbyterian Church, and was intending to enter the ministry.

He won the Berkeley Scholarship at graduation, and remained in residence for two years,—at the same time studying law under Judge Charles Chauncey.

Returning to Nashville in 1808, he was licensed to practice, but removed early in 1809 to New Orleans, where he was admitted to the bar of the Territory on May 1.

When Louisiana was invaded in 1814, he enlisted in the company of cavalry which formed the life-guard of General Jackson, and honorable mention of his services as Corporal in this company was made in the despatches of the General.

He practiced in the courts of New Orleans from 1809 until his death in 1870, interrupted only by a two years' residence within the Confederate lines during the occupation of New Orleans by United States troops. He bore the hardships and reverses of the war with cheerful patience, and returned at its close with renewed zeal to earnest work in his profession.

He was universally respected as a learned and conscientious lawyer, and admired for his great dignity and grace of manner. He was several times offered a seat on the bench, but declined.

His scholarly interests extended far beyond the requirements of his profession, and he was especially proficient in Oriental and Biblical studies. His library was one of the largest private libraries in the South.

For many years before his death he was Professor of Common and Constitutional Law in the University of Louisiana.

Prior to the introduction of Presbyterianism into New Orleans, he was a vestryman in the Episcopal Church; and subsequently, from 1828 until his death, a ruling elder in the First Presbyterian Church.

After an illness of only ten days, he died in New Orleans, on January 19, 1870, in his 84th year. A Discourse on the occasion of his death, by his pastor, the Rev. Dr. Benjamin M. Palmer, was afterwards published (New Orleans, 1870, 8°, pp. 31).

He married, in August, 1809, Anna Maria Nicholson, who died in 1818.

Of her three children, two died in infancy, and the third became a lawyer of some eminence in New Orleans, and was long Clerk of the District Court.

He next married, in May, 1819, Ann Maria Davison, who survived him.

She had twelve children, eight of whom survived their father. One son was a member of the Class of 1842 at Yale.

Besides legal compositions, the only article of Mr. Hennen's which I have noticed in print is a brief characterization, written in 1854, of his former pastor, the Rev. Sylvester Larned (Middlebury Coll 1813), in Sprague's *Annals of the American Pulpit,* vol. 4, pp. 567–68.

John Maurice Heron, also known as Maurice Heron, was a son of 'Squire William Heron, a native of Cork, Ireland, who settled in Redding, Connecticut. before the Revolution. A sister married the Rev. Bethel Judd (Yale 1797).

He did not enter College until after the opening of the Sophomore year

He studied law after graduation, and settled in his native town, but does not appear to have engaged to any extent in practice.

He was by birth and training a devoted Episcopalian, and being under appointment as a delegate from the parish of Christ Church in Redding to the diocesan Convention to be held at Norwich on October 9, 1833, he took passage from New York the day before on the steamboat *New England,* of the Connecticut River Steamboat Company, and was killed by the explosion of the steamer at 3 o'clock in the morning of the 9th, at Essex, on the Connecticut River, within a mile of his landing place.

He left no will, and his small estate was distributed among his brothers and sisters.

AUTHORITIES.

Todd, Hist. of Redding, 2d ed., 104.

LYMAN HICOCK, the eldest child of Captain Joseph Hicock, Junior, and Currence (Richards) Hickok, of Southbury, Connecticut, was born in Southbury (then part of Woodbury), on July 21, 1785.

After graduation he studied law with the Hon. Noah B. Benedict (Yale 1788), of Woodbury, and subsequently with the Hon. Asa Chapman (Yale 1792), of Newtown. But before his admission to the bar his health failed.

He died in Southbury from consumption on August 31, 1816, in his 32d year. He was never married.

AUTHORITIES.

Cothren, Hist. of Woodbury, i, 565. *Hon. R. D. Smyth,* MS. Letters, September, 1860.

RUSSELL HUBBARD, the eldest son of Deacon and General John and Martha Hubbard, of Hamden, Connecticut, and grandson of the Rev. John Hubbard (Yale 1744), of Meriden, was born in Hamden, then part of New Haven, on October 18, 1784. His mother was the second daughter of Phineas and Martha (Sherman) Bradley, of Litchfield. He did not enter College until after the opening of the Freshman year.

He is said to have studied for the ministry after graduation, but a fondness for travel drove him abroad. He is reported to have made several voyages, and finally, in November or December, 1810, in his 27th year, to have been lost at sea, with his next younger brother, on board the brig *Triton,* on a voyage from New Haven to the West Indies

AUTHORITIES

Davis, Hist. of Wallingford, 226 Dickerman Ancestry, 498.

JABEZ WILLIAMS HUNTINGTON, the younger son of General Zachariah Huntington, a merchant and one of the principal inhabitants of Norwich, Connecticut, and a nephew of General Ebenezer Huntington (Yale 1775), was born in Norwich on November 8, 1788 His mother was Hannah, second daughter of Thomas Mumford, of Groton, and sister of Benjamin M. Mumford (Yale 1790). At graduation he spoke on the Extent of Liberal Education in Connecticut.

After graduation he became a teacher for about a year in the Academy kept in Litchfield South Farms, by James Morris (Yale 1775).

He then studied law in the Litchfield Law School, and remained in Litchfield for the practice of his profession. He won the confidence and esteem of the community and the reputation of a sound and able lawyer

In 1828 he was one of the representatives of the town in the State Legislature. From 1829 to 1834 he served as a representative in Congress In 1832–33 he assisted Judge Gould in the conduct of his Law School

He was married, on May 22, 1833, to Sally Ann, the youngest daughter of his first cousin, Joseph Huntington, and his wife, Eunice (Carew) Huntington, of Norwich.

In May, 1834, he was appointed a Judge of the Superior Court and of the Supreme Court of Errors of Connecticut, and resigned his seat in Congress at the end of the current session, in June, and in the following October he removed his residence to Norwich.

On the death in April, 1840, of the Hon. Thaddeus Betts (Yale 1807), a Senator in the United States Congress from Connecticut, Judge Huntington was appointed for the remainder (1840–45) of the unexpired term, and thereupon resigned his judgeship. When this term closed, he was elected for another term; but he died in the midst of his labors, in Norwich, from inflammation of the bowels, after a brief but severe illness, on November 1, 1847, at the age of 59.

Two sermons occasioned by his death were published,—one by his pastor, the Rev. Dr. Hiram P. Arms, of the First Congregational Church, and one by the Rev. Dr. Alvan Bond, of the Second Congregational Church. Both emphasize his consistent Christian character.

At the time of his death he was living in the house of his wife's mother, and his widow continued to reside there for a few years, but died at the house of her sister, the widow of Judge Huntington's classmate and first cousin, the Hon. Henry Strong, in Norwich, on June 26, 1861, in her 51st year. They had no children.

In the *Norwich Courier* the following tribute is paid to him:

A statesman of more unbending integrity, or more unwavering fidelity to the interests of the Union, never occupied a seat in the Senate of the United States; and the records of that body, during the last eight years, bear ample testimony to the untiring industry, energy, and distinguished ability with which he discharged the responsible duties assigned him by his native State.

He is elsewhere commended as a clear and accurate advocate, a sound constitutional lawyer, of pleasing and popular manners.

He published:

1. Speech, on the bill to provide for the Removal of the Indians West of the Mississippi. Delivered in the House of Representatives, May 18, 1830. 8°, pp. 28. [*U. T. S. Y. C.*

Also, in Speeches on the passage of the Bill for the Removal of the Indians. [Edited by Jeremiah Evarts.] Boston, 1830. 12°, pp. 179–212.

2 Speech, on the subject of the Removal of the Deposites, delivered in the House of Representatives, January, 1834. Washington, 1834. 8°, pp 32
[*A A S. B. Publ. M. H. S. U T. S Y. C.*

3 Speech, on the Prospective Pre-emption Bill Delivered in the Senate of the United States, January 7, 1841. Washington, 1841. 8°, pp 8 [*A. A. S Y. C*

4 Speech, on the amendment to the bill "To incorporate the subscribers to the fiscal Bank of the United States," requiring the assent of the Legislatures of the States to the establishment of offices of discount and deposit within their respective territorial limits Delivered in the Senate of the United States, July 3, 1841. Washington, 1841 8°, pp 15
[*A. A. S Columbia Univ M. H. S. U. S. Y C.*

5. Speech, upon the Resolutions of Mr. Clay, delivered in the Senate of the United States, March 21, 1842 Washington, 1842 8°, pp. 18.
[*A. A. S. B Ath Br Mus M H. S. Y. C.*
In favor of a higher tariff.

6 Speech, on the Bill to provide further Remedial Justice in the Courts of the United States Delivered in the Senate of the United States May 11, 1842 Washington, 1842. 8°, pp 26
[*A A. S. Br Mus. N. Y. Publ. Y. C.*

7. Speech, in favor of electing Representatives by Districts throughout the U. States Delivered in the Senate of the United States, May 31, 1842 Washington, 1842 8°, pp 8
[*A. A. S B. Ath Br Mus Y C.*

8 Speech, on the resolution for the annexation of Texas to the United States, and its admission as a State, into the Union — Delivered in the Senate of the United States, February 21 and 22, 1845 8°, pp 16
[*A. A S Columbia Univ M H. S Y C*

9. Speech, on the Oregon Question · delivered in the Senate of the United States, April 13, 1846 Washington, 1846 8°, pp 15.
[*A. A S. A C. A. M. H S Y C*

AUTHORITIES

Boardman, Lights of the Litchfield Bar, 35 Huntington Family Memoir, 249, 326 *Kilbourne,* Bench and Bar of Litchfield County, 29, 64–65, 86, 183, 190, 256 *Perkins,* Old Norwich Houses, 263. *O. H. Smith,* Early Indiana Trials, 615–16.

NATHANIEL GILBERT HUNTINGTON, the eldest son of Deacon Josiah Huntington, a farmer of Rocky Hill Parish, in Wethersfield, Connecticut, and grandson of Deacon Samuel and Hannah (Metcalf) Huntington, of Lebanon, was born at Rocky Hill on October 30, and baptized on November 6, 1785. His mother was Abigail Gilbert, of Goshen Parish in Lebanon. He was a third cousin of his classmate, Jabez W. Huntington. He was prepared for College by the Rev. Dr. Nathan Perkins, of West Hartford. During his Junior year he became a Christian, and resolved to fit himself for the ministry.

He studied theology with Dr. Perkins, and was licensed to preach by the Hartford North Association of Ministers on June 7, 1809.

In the following October he began to preach in the Second Congregational Church in Woodbridge, New Haven County (Bethany Parish), where he was ordained and installed on August 22, 1810.

He was of delicate frame, and had early been threatened with pulmonary disease; but by reason of equable temperament, strict regularity of life, and careful husbanding of his strength, he was able to retain acceptably and successfully his pastoral office until March, 1823, when, in consequence of repeated hemorrhages from the lungs and increasing debility, he was compelled to take a dismission.

He removed in 1840 to Orange, in the same County, where he prolonged his life by superintending the cultivation of a small farm, so far as he was able. He died in Orange on February 20, 1848, in his 63d year.

He married in 1812, Betsy, daughter of Zephaniah and Sarah Tucker, of Derby, who survived him to extreme old age. Their children were two daughters and two sons, all of whom survived him.

He published:

A System of Modern Geography... Hartford, 1833 12°, pp 304; and Atlas 4°. [*U. S.*

The same. Revised and improved. Hartford, 1835 12°, pp 306; and Atlas 4° [*Br. Mus N H Col. Hist Soc. U S*

He is also said to have been a contributor to the *Christian Spectator*

AUTHORITIES.

Huntington Family Memoir, 186-219. *Stiles,* Hist of Wethersfield, ii, 87, 271 *Sharpe,* Hist of Seymour, 458

TIMOTHY LANGDON, the eldest child of the Rev Timothy Langdon (Yale 1781), of Danbury, Connecticut, was born in Danbury on May 19, 1788. His mother died in 1794, and his father in 1801, and he did not enter College until after the opening of Freshman year A brother was graduated in 1809

He died, unmarried, in West Hartford, on March 19, 1811, in his 23d year.

AUTHORITIES.

Farnam, Whitman Family, 628.

EDMUND LAW, the youngest son of Thomas Law, chief magistrate of the district of Behar, India, was born in India in 1790. His father was the fifth son of the Rt Rev Edmund Law (Cambridge University 1723), Bishop of Carlisle, England, and Mary (Christian) Law, and a brother of Edward, first Baron Ellenborough, lord chief justice of England Thomas Law was obliged by ill-health to leave India in 1791, with a fortune of £50,000, but in 1794 he emigrated to New York, in consequence of ill-treatment by the East India Company and the general political situation. In 1796 he married Miss Custis, a granddaughter of Mrs. Washington, and settled in Washington City His eldest son was graduated at Harvard in 1804, and shortly after Edmund Law entered the Junior Class at Yale.

After graduation he took charge of some of his father's affairs in Washington, and also practiced law. In 1812, 1813, and 1814, he was a member of the Common Council of the city.

When the Territory of Florida was organized, in the spring of 1822, he was appointed by President Monroe a member of the Legislative Council, and became in September its President.

He was hardly embarked in this attractive situation, when the death of his only surviving brother, on October 4, 1822, recalled him to Washington to assist his father.

He mingled largely in gay society, and was connected with the militia, holding the rank of Lieutenant. He was again a member of the Common Council in 1825.

In April, 1826, when Commodore David Porter went to Mexico, to enter the service of that country as commander-in-chief of the navy, Lieutenant Law accompanied him, as his secretary, but was obliged to return in 1827 by the condition of his health.

He was re-elected to the Common Council in 1828, but died in Washington, after a protracted illness, on June 23, 1829, in his 39th year.

An engraving from a portrait executed about 1824 is given in Clark's *Greenleaf and Law in the Federal City*.

By Mary Robinson, who long survived him, he left one son.

AUTHORITIES.

A. C. Clark, Greenleaf and Law in the Federal City, 304–05, 309–12, 322, 348.

JAMES LOCKWOOD, the son of James Lockwood, a farmer of New Canaan, Connecticut, was baptized in New Canaan, on February 9, 1784.

He was prepared for College in his native town, and entered after the opening of the Freshman year.

After graduation he studied medicine in Westport, with Dr. David Richmond; and in 1808 married Nancy Pearsall, of Westport

In 1809 he began practice in Cross River, a village in the township of South Salem (or Lewisborough), Westchester County, New York, just north of his native town, where he continued to reside for more than half a century, in the faithful discharge of his duties, universally beloved and respected. He was esteemed, both as an upright citizen and as an unusually skillful physician.

He found time amid his extensive practice to keep pace with medical science, and also to retain his familiarity with the Greek and Latin classics.

In 1862 he had a slight paralytic shock, and the occurrence of other shocks caused his death, in Cross River, on September 30, 1864, in his 81st year.

His wife outlived him Their children were two sons and a daughter, of whom only a son, who followed his father's profession, survived him

---

AUTHORITIES

Dr James D Lockwood, MS Letter, March, 1865

CHARLES MARVIN, the youngest in a family of twelve children of Colonel Ozias Marvin, of Norwalk, Connecticut, and grandson of Matthew and Elizabeth (Clark) Marvin, of Norwalk, was born on February 9 (or 21), 1786. His mother was Sarah, daughter of Joseph and Rebecca (Rogers) Lockwood, of Norwalk. He was prepared for College by the Rev. Dr. Matthias Burnet, of Norwalk, but did not enter until Junior year.

He studied medicine, and practiced his profession in Oneida County, New York,—at one time in the town of Paris, perhaps also in Clinton

He died, unmarried, in the Retreat for the Insane in Hartford, Connecticut, on February 1, 1838, at the age of 52

AUTHORITIES

Hall, Hist of Norwalk, 242. Lockwood Family, 221. Marvin Family, 345 *Selleck,* Norwalk, 191

Lewis Mitchell, the fifth son of Chief Justice Stephen Mix Mitchell (Yale 1763), of Wethersfield, Connecticut, was born in Wethersfield on September 22, 1787, and was baptized on the following day. In his Senior year he acted as President Dwight's amanuensis. He delivered the Salutatory Oration at graduation.

Two years after graduation he was offered a tutorship in College, but declined it.

He studied law in the Litchfield Law School, and practiced his profession with success in Troy, New York.

His industrious devotion to business brought on disease, which caused his death, after about three years' illness, at his father's house in Wethersfield, on June 30, 1826, in his 39th year. He was never married.

Judge Gould, his preceptor, pronounced him to have one of the finest legal minds that he had ever known. In, professional knowledge, skill, and acumen he was not surpassed by any of his contemporaries, and his personal character and private virtues were equally to be commended.

AUTHORITIES.

Conn. Courant, July 31, 1826. *Salisbury,* Family Histories, i, 180. *Stiles,* Hist of Wethersfield, ii, 507. *Tillotson,* Wethersfield Inscriptions, 91

Homer Moore, the eldest of eight children of Captain Roger Moore, a Revolutionary officer, and grandson of Lieutenant Joseph and Mary (Stevens) Moore, of that part of Simsbury, Connecticut, which is now Granby, was born on July 23, 1787. His mother was Rosetta, second daughter of Silas and Hannah (Holcomb) Hayes, of Granby. His father's farm was on the border line between Granby and Southwick (in Massachusetts). In the Yale Catalogue of Students in his Freshman year his residence is given as Granby; in the subsequent years as Southwick. A brother was graduated here in 1827 His classmate Pettibone was a second cousin.

He studied law after graduation in Hartford, and was admitted to the bar in August, 1810.

In February, 1811, he took a journey to Ohio, with the design of settling there for the practice of his profession On July 5 he arrived at the house of Edward Phelps (whose wife was his father's first cousin), in Worthington, Franklin County, a few miles north of the present city of Columbus, where he was seized with a fever on August 8, which raged for over three weeks, until his death on September 1, in his 25th year. He was buried in the graveyard of the Episcopal Church at Worthington.

A notice of his death describes him as "of good natural talents and handsome acquirements, conciliatory in his manners, interesting in his conversation, generous and benevolent in his disposition, and discreet, virtuous, and amiable in his whole deportment and character."

AUTHORITIES

Andrew Moore of Windsor and his Descendants, 45 Conn Courant, Oct. 2, 1811 *Davis,* Hist Sketch of Westfield, 35. Hayes Family, 31.

CHARLES MOSELEY, the only child of William Moseley (Yale 1777), by his wife Laura Wolcott, was born in Hartford, Connecticut, in 1786 or 1787.

He studied law after graduation, and began practice in his native city; but died there on March 27, 1815, at the age of 28. He was never married.

AUTHORITIES

Moseley Family, 26. Wolcott Memorial, 149

DANIEL MULFORD, son of Jonathan Mulford, and grandson of Captain Jonathan and Esther (Conklin) Mulford, of New Providence, near Elizabeth, New Jersey, was born on September 17, 1781. His mother was Deborah, daughter of Jeremy and Elizabeth (Dodge) Ludlow

His father died in December, 1792, and he was trained as a shoemaker. He showed, however, a desire for higher privileges, and after the death of his mother in April, 1801, finding himself in control of a small property, he attended the select school kept by the Rev. Samuel Whelpley in Morristown.

In March, 1803, he obtained a place as clerk in New York City; but returned to Morristown in December, and resumed school work. By his acquaintance with Henry Ford (Yale 1803), of Morristown, he was led to prepare himself for admission to the Junior Class at Yale in November, 1804.

He had already shown alarming symptoms of pulmonary disease, but was able to finish the course with credit

After graduation he began the study of law in the office of Sylvester D. Russell, of Morristown, but in June, 1807, was induced to take charge of the Morristown Academy, where he showed much aptitude as a teacher. His health was always precarious, and in October, 1808, he went South in the hope of recovery. One of his friends was practicing law in Georgia, and that led him to take a horseback journey to that State, where he was admitted to practice law, in Savannah, and remained for about two years. From January, 1811, he was in partnership with Thomas E. Lloyd.

He returned to New Jersey, to die there (probably in Morristown), from consumption, on October 26, 1811, in his 31st year. He was buried in New Providence. He was never married.

He was regarded as a young man of great promise, and a pleasing writer, both of prose and poetry A Pindaric ode, called "The Ale fair, or Reynard's decease," written by him, was printed anonymously in March, 1807.

An interesting manuscript diary, which he kept from 1801 to 1808, and many letters of his are owned by the Yale Library

AUTHORITIES.

Littell, Family Records of Passaic Valley, 298

HEMAN NORTON, son of Nathaniel and Mary, or Patty (Beebe) Norton, of Goshen, Connecticut, and grandson of Ebenezer and Elizabeth (Baldwin) Norton, of Goshen, was born on September 13, 1785. His father removed to a farm in East Bloomfield, Ontario County, New York, in 1789.

On graduation he settled in East Bloomfield as a farmer, and he married on August 23, 1807, Julia, third daughter of Elisha and Mary (Beebe) Strong, of Windsor, Connecticut, and sister of Elisha B. Strong (Yale 1809)

In 1819 he removed to Canandaigua, in Ontario County, where Elisha B Strong had previously settled, and where he went into business as a merchant.

In 1825 he again followed his brother-in-law to Rochester, in Monroe County, and engaged in the forwarding business. In 1829 he was a member of the State Legislature.

In 1830 he removed to New York City, where he was a commission merchant until his death, on April 29, 1847, in his 62d year.

His widow died in Plainfield, New Jersey, on September 12, 1863, in her 77th year.

Their children were three sons and three daughters, all of whom grew to maturity. The second son was graduated at West Point in 1831, and was for many years Professor of Civil Engineering in the Sheffield Scientific School. Nathaniel Norton (Yale 1860) is a grandson.

AUTHORITIES.

Dwight, Strong Family, i, 107–08 Hist of Ontario County, 207.

CHAUNCEY PETTIBONE, the eldest child of General Chauncey Pettibone, of Granby, Connecticut, and grandson of Colonel Ozias Pettibone, of Simsbury, was born on July 17, 1787. His mother was Theodosia, second daughter of Deacon and Captain Samuel and Rosanna (Holcomb) Hayes, of Granby.

He became a lawyer, and after a brief sojourn in Indiana, settled in practice in New Orleans.

He soon after removed to Wilkinson County, in the southwestern corner of Mississippi, where he married, on June 20, 1822, Susan, daughter of Gerard C and Dorothy (Nugent) Brandon, and an aunt of Robert L. Brandon (Yale 1856).

He remained in Wilkinson County for the rest of his life, settling on an estate inherited by his wife, about five miles from Fort Adams, where he died, on June 14, 1838, in his 51st year.

He is remembered as a handsome man, of artistic tastes. Two children survived him, a son and a daughter.

AUTHORITIES

A C Bates, MS Letter, November, 1911 Hayes Family, 27. *Mrs Mary P Wall,* MS Letter, November, 1911

SETH PIERCE, son of Captain Seth Pierce, a wealthy farmer of Cornwall, Connecticut, and grandson of Lieutenant Joshua and Hopestill Pierce, of Pembroke, Massachusetts, and Cornwall, was born in Cornwall on May

16, 1785. His mother was Amy, elder daughter of Lieutenant John and Hannah (Gould) Hart, of Cornwall. He entered College after the opening of the Freshman year.

A lifelong disease of the eyes compelled him at graduation to defer, and ultimately to abandon, all hope of entering a profession. He accordingly found occupation in the care of his father's large farm, of over a thousand acres, though his life was an isolated one, and his chief solace lay in continuing, so far as his infirmity allowed, the studies which had been the interest of his youth. Through all his maturer years his Greek Testament was an almost constant companion.

He had no taste for public business; but once (1828) he consented to represent Cornwall in the Legislature, and for a number of years he was one of the board of school visitors of the town. He also attained the rank of Major in the militia Through an unusually prolonged life he retained the entire respect of the community, and was widely known for his cheery ways and native shrewdness.

He died in Cornwall, after a brief illness, on August 6, 1881, in his 97th year, being the last survivor of his Class, and for the last five years of his life the oldest living graduate of the College

He was never married.

Of great mildness of temper, deliberation of manner, and firm integrity, he was always a lover of learning and a liberal supporter of Christian institutions.

He held a high estimate of the value of his own education, and always spoke of the College in the highest terms of gratitude. He enjoyed his last visit to Commencement, in 1879, when over 94 years of age.

AUTHORITIES.

Gold, Hist. of Cornwall, 2d ed, 245, 448.

CALEB PITKIN, the eldest child of Deacon Stephen Pitkin, of New Hartford, Connecticut, who afterwards removed to Rootstown, Ohio, and grandson of Caleb and Damaris (Porter) Pitkin, of New Hartford, was born in New Hartford on February 27, 1781. His mother was Jemima, daughter of Abiel and Jemima (Richards) Tyler, of New Hartford. He labored on his father's farm until he came of age, and then devoted himself to study, with a view to the ministry

After graduation he took a brief theological course with the Rev Asahel Hooker (Yale 1789), of Goshen, and was licensed to preach by the Litchfield North Association of Ministers on June 10, 1807

He was married on June 15, 1807, to Anna, daughter of James and Anna (Cook) Henderson, of New Hartford, and then spent a few months in the supply of the vacant pulpits in Derby and in Oxford.

On March 6, 1808, he was ordained and installed as pastor of the Second (or Plymouth) Congregational Church in Milford, where he remained until his dismission on October 22, 1816.

The succeeding winter he spent as a missionary in Ashtabula and Portage Counties, in the Connecticut Western Reserve of Ohio; and on April 23, 1817, he was installed as pastor of the church in Charlestown, Portage County. Here he continued about ten years, spending one half of the time in traveling extensively over the Reserve as a missionary. During the early part of this time, he received under his instruction a few young men who were preparing for the ministry.

In 1822 he was the chairman of a committee of the Portage Presbytery which prepared and published the following:

An Address to the Public, on the subject of establishing a Literary and Theological Institution, in the Connecticut Western Reserve 8°, pp 16 [*Y. C.*

As a result of this *Appeal,* and of personal efforts, a charter was secured for Western Reserve College, at Hudson, in February, 1826, and Mr. Pitkin was named as one of the Board of Trustees.

Henceforward the College was the principal object of his attention He was the first President of the Trustees, and as such delivered a Latin address at the laying of the corner-stone of the first building. In 1828 he removed to Hudson, and remained there until his death From January, 1826, to August, 1843, he seems to have been almost exclusively employed in soliciting funds for the institution, with most hearty and self-sacrificing devotion

He also continued to preach in destitute places, as long as strength permitted

He died in Hudson on February 5, 1864, at the age of 83, being at that time the only remaining member of the original Board of Trustees of the College. Mrs. Pitkin died on December 5, 1882, in her 99th year.

Their children were two daughters (both of whom died before their father) and three sons. An adopted daughter, the wife of the Rev. Daniel Vrooman, a missionary in China, also died before him. The eldest daughter married the Rev. Charles M. Preston (Western Reserve Coll 1830) Two of the sons — one a lawyer, and one a minister—were graduates of Western Reserve College, in 1834 and 1836, respectively.

A copy of Mr. Pitkin's portrait is given in the *Pitkin Genealogy*

Besides his share in the *Appeal* above mentioned, he was the author of:

A Statistical Report of the settlement and the longevity of the first settlers and other inhabitants of Hudson In Proceedings of the fifty-sixth Anniversary of the Settlement of Hudson. Akron, 1875. 8°, pp 4-9

AUTHORITIES

Cutler, Hist of Western Reserve College, 9-11, 14-18, 26, 44. *Rev Dr H L Hitchcock,* MS Letter, June, 1864 Panoplist, xiv, 143 Pitkin Genealogy, 39, 75.

ROYAL ROBBINS, the eldest in a family of eleven children of Captain Elisha and Sarah (Goodrich) Robbins, of Wethersfield, Connecticut, and nephew of the Hon. Asher Robbins (Yale 1782), was born in Wethersfield on October 21, 1787. He was a roommate in College of his classmate Pitkin and his becoming a Christian is believed to have been due to Pitkin's instrumentality.

The first two years after graduation were spent in teaching,—in Hadley, Massachusetts, and in Wethersfield and Glastonbury, Connecticut. He then spent a year in the study of law with his uncle Asher, in Newport, Rhode Island; to which succeeded several years of teaching in Wethersfield, which were interrupted by an interval of theological study under the Rev. Dr. David Porter, of Catskill, New York

Finally, perhaps late in 1812, he began in earnest to prepare himself for the ministry, under the direction of the Rev. Andrew Yates (Yale 1794), of East Hartford, and was licensed to preach by the Hartford North Association on February 1, 1814

During the next two years he supplied in various places, such as East Hartford, East Granby, Clinton and Bloomfield.

He finally accepted a call to settle as colleague pastor with the Rev. Dr. Benoni Upson (Yale 1776) in Kensington Parish, in Berlin, where he was ordained and installed on June 26, 1816

The senior pastor died in November, 1826, and Mr. Robbins continued in office until relieved of duty in June, 1859. He then devoted himself anew to literary pursuits, and just before his death was engaged in the preparation of a historical discourse for the centennial anniversary of the completion of the Brick Church in Wethersfield.

He died in Kensington, after a brief but somewhat painful illness, from a bilious disorder, with fever, on

March 26, 1861, in his 74th year. A memorial pamphlet, including the sermon delivered at his funeral, was afterwards published.

He married, on November 7, 1816, Martha, eldest daughter of Captain Ashbel Wright, of Wethersfield, who died on December 15, 1837, in her 42d year. He next married, on October 17, 1839, Elizabeth Bourne, the eldest child of Captain John Willard and Nancy (Smith) Russell, of Bristol, Rhode Island, who survived him.

By his first marriage he had three daughters and five sons; all these survived him, except the eldest daughter and the youngest son, both of whom died in infancy. The eldest son was graduated at Yale in 1843

Though without any gifts as an orator, he was a laborious and faithful minister, of blameless life. The most striking traits in his character were his purity, disinterestedness, and benevolence

His literary taste, his power of expression, and his facility of composition, were far beyond the common standard, and enabled him to add materially to a scanty professional income. It was unfortunate that the one of his works which had the largest sale, his *Outlines of Ancient and Modern History,* was bought outright by the publisher, who in his turn realized a considerable sum from it He published

1. Religious Institutions dear to the People of God —A Sermon [from Ps cxxxvii, 5-6], delivered in Berlin, Kensington, on the day of the Public Thanksgiving, December 9, 1824. Hartford, 1825. 8°, pp 21 [*A C A Br Mus. C. H S Y C*

2 The Legend of Mount Lamentation In *The Token* Boston, 1828 12°, pp. 351-63.

The story of an adventure of Leonard Chester, of Wethersfield, in Berlin, in 1636.

3 Critical and biographical notice of James Gates Percival In S Kettell's *Specimens of American Poetry,* vol. 3 Boston, 1829 12°, pp 24-37

Percival was a native of Kensington Parish

4. Outlines of Ancient History, on a new plan Embracing Biographical Notices of Illustrious Persons . Hartford, 1830 12°, pp. 228.

And, bound with the above

Outlines of Modern History, on a new plan Embracing Biographical Notices of Illustrious Persons. ... Hartford, 1830. 12°, pp. 396 [*B. Publ. Harv. U. S. Y C*

Several editions. This was extensively used in schools.

The same work was issued, by other publishers, with the title:

The World displayed, in its History and Geography; embracing a History of the World, from the Creation to the Present Day New York, 1830. 12°, pp 408 + 30 pl [*Harv*

5 Encouragement to Holy Effort —A Sermon [from I Cor. xv, 58], delivered at the Funeral of the Rev. Samuel Goodrich, late Senior Pastor of the Church in Worthington (Berlin), Conn, who died April 19th, 1835 Hartford, 1835. 8°, pp. 28 [*A C. A. Br. Mus Y. C*

6 Historical Sketches of English and American Literature . By Robert Chambers and Rev Royal Robbins Hartford, 1837. 12°, pp. 329

In this volume Mr. Robbins revised the work of Mr. Chambers, adding the American portion.

7. Memoir of the Life of John G C Brainard Prefixed to The Poems of John G C Brainard A new and authentic collection Hartford, 1842 16°, pp xi–lx

8 The happiness of a long and useful life —A Sermon [from Acts ix, 39] delivered at the Funeral of Mrs Ruth Hart, Relict of General Selah Hart, of Kensington (Berlin), Conn, who died January 15th, 1844, in the one hundredth and second year of her age. Hartford, 1844. 8°, pp 16. [*B Publ. Br Mus U. T S Y C*

9 Christian Sympathy —A Discourse [from II Tim i, 4], occasioned by the death of Ashbell Welles, Esq., delivered in the South Congregational Church in New Britain, January 8, 1854 Hartford, 1854 8°, pp 23. [*M. H S*

10. God's Ways with his People —A Discourse [from Job xxiv, 13], preached on the first Sabbath of the year; including Remarks on the Death and Character of Deacon Roswell Moore Hartford, 1857. 8°, pp 19 [*A. C. A*

11. John Smalley, D.D. In W. B Sprague's *Annals of the American Pulpit,* vol. 1 New York, 1857. 8°, pp 562–65

12 Discourse on Benjamin Allen 1859

He also contributed largely to the following works, among others

C A. Goodrich·—The Universal Traveller. Hartford, 1843, 12°.

S. G. Goodrich:—A Pictorial History of America, embracing both the Northern and Southern Portions of the New World. Hartford, 1844 8°.

C. A Goodrich.—Great Events in the History of North and South America .. Hartford, 1849. 8°

S. G. Goodrich —A History of all Nations.. Boston, 1849–51. 2 vols 8°

He is said to have published an edition of *Blair's Outlines of Chronology*

He was a frequent contributor to the (monthly) *Christian Spectator,* and the following is believed to be a nearly complete list of his articles.

Volume 2, pp. 180–86, 235–40 (April–May, 1820): A moral estimate of Paradise Lost [This enjoyed the unusual distinction of being reprinted in the (London) *Christian Observer,* vol. 22 (April–May, 1822)]

Volume 4, pp. 393–400 (August, 1822): On Early Religious Education; pp 460–66 (September, 1822). Christianity not promoted in the world by the existence of different denominations.

Volume 5, pp 76–82 (February, 1823): On Miscellaneous Reading

Volume 6, pp. 337–41 (July, 1824). A Comparative Estimate of the Religion of the Bible with other Religious Systems.

Volume 7, pp. 497–501 (October, 1825): The Influence of the Private Devotions of Ministers on their Preaching.

Volume 8, pp 113–20 (March, 1826): On Encomiums bestowed upon Unsanctified Genius

Volume 9, pp 534–53 (October, 1827) The Prose Works of Milton.

In the *Quarterly Christian Spectator*

Volume 1, pp. 246–67 (June, 1829). Review of Dunallan

Volume 3, pp. 227–52 (June, 1831). Review of the Life of Reginald Heber, D D; pp 393–417 (September, 1831)· Review of Memoirs of Howard; pp 433–41: Review of [C. A Goodrich's] Outlines of Ecclesiastical History; pp 576–97 (December, 1831) Review of Dr Miller's Introductory Lecture

Volume 4, pp. 34-53 (March, 1832): Remains of the late Rev. Charles Wolfe; pp. 375-401 (September, 1832): Moral Influence of Manufactures; pp. 418-38: Natural History of Enthusiasm and Saturday Evening; pp. 598-614 (December, 1832): The Rectory of Valehead.

Volume 5, pp. 193-207 (June, 1833): Moral Characteristics of the Nineteenth Century; pp. 568-90 (December, 1833): Character and Genius of Cowper.

Volume 6, pp. 36-53 (March, 1834): Means enjoyed by this Country for Promoting the Highest Interests of Mankind; pp. 118-40: Fanaticism; pp. 308-31 (June, 1834): Memoir of Rev. Elias Cornelius; pp. 632-54 (December, 1834): General Improvement of Society; pp. 655-72: Memoirs of Hannah More.

Volume 7, pp. 127-51 (March, 1835): Character and Writings of Hannah More; pp. 445-81 (September, 1835): Spiritual Despotism; pp. 597-629 (December, 1835): Wayland's Elements of Moral Science (in part by Dr. N. W. Taylor).

Volume 8, pp. 205-25 (June, 1836): Sketch of the Life and Character of the Hon. Stephen Mix Mitchell, LL.D.; pp. 505-19 (December, 1836): The Dangers of our Country; pp. 643-63: Physical Theory of Another Life.

Volume 9, pp. 134-50 (March, 1837): Comparative View of the Divine Mercies.

Volume 10, pp. 18-36 (February, 1838): Goldsmith and his Writings; pp. 257-80 (May, 1838): A Critical and Moral Estimate of the Night Thoughts; pp. 353-70 (August, 1838): On Dueling.

Of his papers in other periodicals may be mentioned:

In the *American National Preacher:*

A sermon on The Spirit of the Bible, from Ps. cxix, 156, in vol 13, pp. 113-24 (August, 1839).

The guidance needed by youth, from Jer. iii, 4, in vol. 16, pp. 206-16 (September, 1842).

In the *New Englander:*

Volume 6, pp. 24-41 (January, 1848): Webster's Dictionary revised by Prof. Goodrich.

Volume 9, pp. 531-44 (November, 1851): The Puritan Element in the American Character.

In the *American Quarterly Review:*

Volume 7, pp. 337-61 (June, 1830): Wheaton's Travels in England.

Volume 20, pp 351–66 (December, 1836): Colton's Visit to Constantinople.

AUTHORITIES.

Spring, Memorial of R. Robbins 578–80, 606, 864. *Trumbull,* Hist. of *Stiles,* Hist of Wethersfield, ii, 575, Hartford County, ii, 17–18

JAMES ROOT, the second son of Ephraim Root (Yale 1782), of Hartford, Connecticut, was born in Hartford on April 23, 1787. A brother entered College with him, but was graduated a year later.

About the time of his graduation his father met with reverses of fortune, and transferred to him, as his patrimony, a tract of land in the Western Reserve. He made his way thither on horseback, and for about thirty years lived alone, in a log cabin, in what became Rootstown, Portage County, Ohio, about thirty miles southeast of Cleveland. He was an active participant in the War of 1812, and underwent many hardships of pioneer life

Eventually his land appreciated in value, and after he returned to Hartford (or East Hartford) in middle life, he became by this means possessed of a large fortune.

On his return he married Lucy Ann Olmstead, of New Hartford, Connecticut, who died on June 29, 1843, aged 33 years

They had one child, who married Austin C Dunham (Yale 1854).

Mr Root died in Hartford, after a few days' illness, on April 17, 1875, at the age of 88

He was regarded as somewhat eccentric, but was generous with his wealth in directions which appealed to him.

AUTHORITIES

Dwight, Strong Family, i, 327 Root Genealogy, 191, 259

HEZEKIAH RUDD, the third son and seventh child of Deacon Jonathan Rudd, of Scotland Parish in Windham, Connecticut, and grandson of Jonathan and Esther

(Tyler) Rudd, of Windham, was born in Scotland on February 2, 1781. His mother was Mary, younger daughter of Deacon Simon and Elizabeth (Hyde) Tracy, of Norwich. He worked on his father's farm, with intervals of school-teaching in the winter, until he came of age, and was then prepared for the Sophomore Class by John Adams (Yale 1795) at the Plainfield Academy. Huntington was his roommate for the three years of his residence here.

He married on September 24, 1809, Maria, daughter of Othniel and Hannah (Tomlinson) DeForest, of Huntington, one of whose sisters married his classmate Allen.

Early in 1810 he succeeded his old preceptor, Mr. Adams, as principal of Bacon Academy in Colchester, where he remained for three years.

After a brief interval of teaching in Stratford, he took the DeForest homestead in Huntington, and for thirty years maintained there a classical school. Most of the youth of the town of both sexes for two generations were his pupils, thus securing advantages which the greater part of them could not otherwise have enjoyed. His house was also usually well filled with boarding pupils,—including many from the Middle and Southern States who were preparing for College.

His wife died in Huntington on January 12, 1828, in her 38th year; and he married on the 4th of the following September, Mary Eliza Coggeshall, of Colchester, daughter of Nathaniel and Margaret (Rudd) Coggeshall, of Newport, Rhode Island, who survived him.

When he retired from teaching he removed to Brooklyn, New York, where he resided for thirteen years at the house of one of his sons. The remainder of his life was passed with other members of his family, latterly with a nephew in Norwich, Connecticut, where he died on September 11, 1868, in his 88th year.

He had a fine literary taste, and considerable poetic talent.

By his first marriage he had four daughters, of whom two died in infancy, and one son The youngest daughter married Professor George N. Allen (Oberlin Coll 1841), and was the mother of Frederic DeForest Allen, late Professor at Yale and at Harvard.

By his second marriage he had three sons, of whom one died in infancy, and two daughters

AUTHORITIES

Rev. Dr. H. P Arms, MS Letter, September, 1868 DeForest Family, 233 Geneal Hist of Conn, i, 328 *Orcutt*, Hist of Stratford, ii, 1314, Tomlinson Family, 54. *Chas D. Rudd*, MS Letter, December, 1868 *Walworth*, Hyde Genealogy, i, 157, ii, 718-20.

JOSEPH SILLIMAN, the eldest child of Dr Joseph Silliman, of New Canaan, Connecticut, and his wife, Patty Leeds, of New Canaan, was baptized on October 1, 1786 A brother was graduated in 1808

He studied no profession, but spent his life as a farmer on his paternal estate in New Canaan

He acted with the Whigs in politics, and served as a Representative in the Legislature in 1835 and 1850.

He died in New Canaan on October 22, 1850, in his 65th year.

LUCIUS SMITH, a son of General David and Ruth (Hitchcock) Smith, of Plymouth, then part of Watertown, Connecticut, and a brother of Junius Smith (Yale 1802), was born on April 9, 1784

He began life as a merchant in Litchfield, but eventually studied for the Episcopal ministry, and was ordained Deacon by Bishop Hobart on January 12, 1819

His entire ministerial life was spent in Western New York. From 1819 to 1823 he was rector of St. Peter's Church, in Auburn, though during the later portion of that time he was absent as an agent for obtaining funds for Geneva College, which received its charter in April, 1822.

From Auburn he removed to St. James's Church, in Batavia, where he spent ten years. In 1834 he entered as missionary in charge of Trinity Church, in Fredonia, in the township of Pomfret, in Chautauqua County, where he labored until physical disability constrained him to retire from active duty in 1843.

He then returned to Batavia, where his strength yielded to repeated attacks of disease, and his death occurred, while he was still in unimpaired mental vigor, on January 17, 1847, in his 63d year.

He was a trustee of Hobart College (the successor of Geneva College) from its beginning in 1825 to 1836.

He is remembered as very hospitable, and the impersonation of cheerfulness and good nature.

Several children survived him.

AUTHORITIES.

Anderson, Hist. of Waterbury, i, Appendix, 127. *Brainard,* Hist. of St. Peter's Church, Auburn, 30-31. Cayuga County Hist. Society's Collections, vi, 74, 114-15. Hitchcock Family, 224. Journal of Convention of the Prot. Episc. Church in Western N. Y., 1847, 28.

HENRY STRONG, the younger son of the Rev. Dr. Joseph Strong (Yale 1772), of Norwich, Connecticut, was born on August 23, 1788. He was a first cousin of his classmates Jabez W. Huntington and John McCurdy Strong; and third cousin of his classmate John Strong.

He was prepared for College by his father, and spent a portion of the first two years of the course at home. At graduation he delivered an Oration on Distinctions in Society.

For two years after graduation he conducted a small school for young ladies in Norwich, while studying law with James Stedman (Yale 1801). He then filled a tutorship at Yale for two years; and meanwhile completed his law studies with Judge Charles Chauncey.

He was admitted to the bar in New Haven in November, 1810, but spent his life in the practice of his profession in his native city, attaining distinction and being regarded as the equal of any of his contemporaries in the State.

He uniformly declined all overtures of political preferment, and only reluctantly consented to serve as a State Senator in 1840 and 1841, and again in 1845 as a Representative in the Legislature. As Senator he was *ex officio* a member of the Yale Corporation in 1841–42. He also declined to be considered as a candidate for a professorship in the Yale Law School.

The honorary degree of LL D was conferred on him at Yale in 1848

After suffering for many weeks in an almost helpless state from a paralytic affection, he died in Norwich on November 12, 1852, in his 65th year A Discourse by the Rev. Dr. Hiram P. Arms on the occasion of his death was afterwards published.

An engraved portrait is given in the *Strong Family Genealogy,* and in the *History of Norwich.*

His argument in defence of Miss Prudence Crandall, of Canterbury, for teaching colored persons not natives of Connecticut, is printed in the

Report of the Trial Brooklyn, 1833 8°, pp. 14–18. [*Y. C*

He married on July 7, 1825, Eunice Edgerton, the second daughter of Joseph and Eunice (Carew) Huntington, of Norwich, who died in Norwich on June 19, 1865, in her 68th year.

Their only child surviving infancy was a daughter who married Dr. Daniel F. Gulliver (Yale 1848).

AUTHORITIES

Caulkins, Hist of Norwich, 544, 630–31. *Dwight,* Strong Family, i, 749, 751–52. Huntington Family, Memoir, 167, 326 *Perkins,* Old Houses of Norwich, 290–91.

John Strong, the only son of Lieutenant John and Sarah (Walker) Strong, of Woodbury, Litchfield County, Connecticut, and grandson of Preserved and Esther (Stoddard) Strong, of Woodbury, was born on December 21, 1786.

He studied law after graduation, and was admitted to the bar of his native county in December, 1808. He then opened an office in Woodbury, and continued in the active discharge of his professional duties until his death there on November 1, 1834, in his 48th year.

He was a member of the State Legislature in May, 1813, in 1825, and in 1826, and Judge of Probate for the Woodbury District in 1816, 1817, and 1834.

He was a man of strict integrity and unsullied purity. He had a clear and acute mind, and his clients reposed unbounded confidence in him; his modesty and unobtrusive manners prevented his attainments receiving wider recognition.

He married, in June, 1810, Flora, elder daughter of Jehiel and Anna (Terrill) Preston, of Woodbury, who long survived him.

Their children were two daughters and five sons, all of whom, except the youngest son, lived to maturity. A grandson, J. Preston Strong, was for many years employed as a trusted accountant in the Yale Treasury.

AUTHORITIES.

Cothren, Hist. of Woodbury, i, 397, 665, 705, 707. *Dwight*, Strong Family, i, 535-36.

John McCurdy Strong, the only child of the Rev. Dr. Nathan Strong (Yale 1769), of Hartford, Connecticut, by his second wife, Anna McCurdy, was born in Hartford on August 12, 1788.

During the Senior vacation preceding Commencement he had begun the study of law in the office of the Hon.

Chauncey Goodrich (Yale 1776), of Hartford. He received his degree at New Haven on Wednesday, September 10, and then returned home by way of Norwich. On the evening of Tuesday, September 16, he started on horseback across the Connecticut River to Hartford on the ferry-boat His horse became frightened and jumped overboard, and so much time elapsed before the body of Mr Strong was recovered that life was extinct He had just entered on his 19th year.

The sermon preached at his funeral the next day by the Rev. Dr. Abel Flint (Yale 1785), of Hartford, was afterwards published

He was a young man of great personal attractions and of brilliant mental endowments, though of a naturally feeble constitution.

AUTHORITIES

Dwight, Strong Family, i, 745 *Salisbury,* Family Histories, i, 74-75. *Sprague,* Annals of the Amer Pulpit, ii, 36 *Walker,* Hist of First Church, Hartford, 342.

Josiah Bartlett Strong, the third son of Deacon Daniel Strong, of Lebanon, Connecticut, and grandson of Daniel and Esther (Chappell) Strong, of Lebanon, was born on May 21, 1782. His mother was Desire, daughter of Ichabod and Desire (Otis) Bartlett. His next elder brother, Daniel Strong, died about a month before his expected graduation here in 1801.

He studied law with Judge Zephaniah Swift (Yale 1778), of Windham, and afterwards for a short time with the Hon. Charles Marsh (Dartmouth Coll 1786), of Woodstock, Vermont.

In 1809 he settled in Northfield, Washington County, Vermont, as a lawyer. In 1820-21 he represented the town in the State Legislature In 1820-22 he was Associate Judge of the County Court.

In 1826 he removed about twenty miles to the northwest, to Huntington, in Chittenden County, and in 1828 from there, about ten miles to the southwest, to Starksboro, in Addison County, where the rest of his life was spent.

He died in Starksboro, from paralysis, on June 27, 1850, in his 69th year.

He married, on April 26, 1809, Clarissa, eldest child of Colonel Isaiah and Sibyl (Prior) Loomis, of Lebanon. She died on May 26, 1844, in her 63d year.

They had five daughters and four sons, all of whom married and had issue, except one daughter and one son, who died in youth.

AUTHORITIES.

Dwight, Strong Family, ii, 775, 777. *L. Hebard*, MS. Letter, April, 1853. Loomis Genealogy, 1875, 132. Loomis Female Branches, ii, 791-92, 891.

William Todd, the only child of Dr. Jonathan Todd, of East Guilford, now Madison, Connecticut, by his second wife, Ruth Bishop, and grandson of Timothy Todd (Yale 1747), of East Guilford, was born on January 3, 1785.

Jeremiah Evarts (Yale 1802) and the Rev. Dr. John Todd (Yale 1822) were his first cousins. He did not enter College until after the opening of the Freshman year.

He studied law and was admitted to the bar in 1809, and practiced his profession for upwards of twenty years in Guilford, securing the confidence and esteem of his fellow-citizens, and being remembered as an ornament to society and a pillar of the church.

He was sent as a delegate to the State Constitutional Convention in 1818; and was a representative of the town in the Legislature in the session of October, 1818, and in eight later years between 1819 and 1829.

He died in Guilford on October 8, 1831, in his 47th year.

He married, on July 6, 1814, Sarah, eldest daughter of Dr. Jared and Sarah (Chittenden) Redfield, of Guilford, who died in 1892, in her 97th year. They had no children.

AUTHORITIES

N E. Hist. and Geneal Register, lxii, 50 Redfield Genealogy, 147 *Steiner*, Hist of Guilford, 149, 277, 454, 473, 516 *Talcott*, Chittenden Family, 145

PHINEAS LYMAN TRACY, the eldest child of Philemon Tracy, M D (honorary, Yale 1817), a distinguished physician of Norwich, Connecticut, and grandson of Dr Elisha Tracy (Yale 1738), was born in Norwich on December 25, 1783. His mother was Abigail, second daughter of Jonathan and Lydia (Proctor) Trott, of Norwich A brother was graduated from the Yale Medical School in 1816, and a nephew, Albert H. Tracy, from the College in 1854 He did not enter College until after the opening of Sophomore year.

After graduation he was for a year the preceptor of the Woodstock Academy, and he spent a second year in teaching in his native town

He then entered the law office of the Hon. John Woodworth (Yale 1788), at Albany. In 1811, he was admitted to the bar in Utica, where he had completed his studies, and settled in Madison Village, in Madison County; but between three and four years later, he removed to Batavia, in Genesee County, where he passed the rest of his life.

He immediately entered into an extensive and lucrative practice which continued to occupy him until the fall of 1827, when he was elected to Congress to fill a vacancy. He was at this time a prominent Anti-Mason

On March 1, 1815, he had married Harriet, daughter of John Lay (Yale 1780), of Clinton, and some years subsequently her younger brother, George W Lay (Hamilton Coll. 1817), had become associated with him in partnership.

He remained a member of Congress until March, 1833, when his partner succeeded him.

He was a Presidential Elector for Harrison in 1840; and in January, 1841, was appointed Chief Judge of the Genesee County Court, and held that office until January, 1846, when he retired from public life. He was highly esteemed as a conscientious and upright judge, of distinguished courtesy, learning, and integrity.

He died in Batavia on December 22, 1876, within three days of completing his 90th year.

Mrs. Tracy died in Batavia, after a protracted illness, on May 18, 1872, in her 80th year. They left no children.

Judge Tracy had for many years been vestryman or warden of St. James's Church in Batavia, over which his classmate, Lucius Smith, was long settled.

AUTHORITIES.

Caulkins, Hist. of Norwich, 544. *Hammond,* Hist. of Madison County, 612. *Perkins,* Old Houses of Norwich, 392–93, 577. *Salisbury,* Family Histories, i, 340. *P. L. Tracy,* MS. Letter, July, 1868. *Walworth,* Hyde Family, ii, 1088.

Leverett Hubbard Trumbull, the younger son of the Hon. John Trumbull (Yale 1767), of Hartford, Connecticut, was born in Hartford on July 10, 1788, and was named for his maternal grandfather (Yale 1744).

His health failed after graduation, and he died tranquilly at his home in Hartford, on May 7, 1807, in his 19th year.

He was a young man of uncommon personal charm and of brilliant intellect.

The epitaph written by his father for his grave was as follows:

CARISSIMO SUO
LEVERFTT HUBBARD TRUMBULL,
JOHANNIS FILIO, IN COLL. YAL A.B
JUVENI CUI, FORMAE, ORIS, VULTUSQUE GRATIA ET VENUSTATE,
MORUM SUAVITATE, CASTITATE, ELEGANTIA,
ARDORE STUDII, INGENII VIGORE,
IN OMNIGENA LITERATURA ET INGENIIS ARTIBUS SOLERTIA,
VIRTUTIS ET VERAE PIETATIS AMORE, CULTU, REVERENTIA,
INTER AETATIS SUAE SODALES VIX ALIUS PRAECELLUIT;
QUI HARTFORDIAE NATUS
JULII 10MO MDCCLXXXVIII,
MAIAE 7MO MDCCCVII OBIIT,
HOC MARMQR MOERENS ET ORBUS MULTAGEMENS PATER POSUIT.

AUTHORITIES

Conn Courant, May 13, 1807. *Farnam,* Whitman Family, 628

WILLIAM TULLY, the only child of William Tully, of (Old) Saybrook, Connecticut, and grandson of William and Elizabeth (Lay) Tully, of Saybrook, was born at Saybrook Point on November 18, 1785. His mother was Eunice, younger daughter of Elias and Mercy (Pratt) Tully, of Saybrook, and a first cousin of her husband He was prepared for College, very imperfectly, by his pastor, the Rev. Frederick W Hotchkiss (Yale 1778).

He taught a district school in Saybrook during the winter after graduation, and in the spring of 1807 began the study of medicine with Dr Mason F. Cogswell (Yale 1780), of Hartford. For the last three months of 1808 he attended the lectures of Dr. Nathan Smith in Hanover, New Hampshire; and the Yale Library has an interesting manuscript diary of his experiences there.

He then returned to Dr. Cogswell's office; but in October, 1809, went back to Hanover, to attend a second course of lectures. At the close of the term he studied for a time with Dr Samuel Carter, of Saybrook, but in March, 1810, entered the office of Dr Eli

Ives (Yale 1799) in New Haven, and while with him gave particular attention to botany. In October he was licensed to practice by the Connecticut Medical Society.

After this he taught again at home for five months, but in May, 1811, went by invitation to Enfield, to settle in practice; he was soon, however, attacked with typhus fever, and on his recovery was summoned to attend his father in his last illness.

In March, 1812, he returned to Enfield, but removed thence to Milford, in March, 1813. Dissatisfied with his situation there, he settled in November, 1815, in Middletown Upper Houses, now Cromwell, whence he went, in September, 1818, to the city of Middletown.

The honorary degree of M.D. was conferred on him by Yale College in 1819, and the next year he began his career as an author. He had formed an intimate friendship with Dr. Thomas Miner (Yale 1796), of Middletown, one result of which was the volume of *Essays* issued by them jointly in 1823. The vigor with which new and startling opinions, especially in advocacy of the "stimulating" practice, were advanced, subjected the authors to bitter criticism, which Dr. Tully at least resented as personal opposition.

In June, 1822, he removed to East Hartford, and in July, 1824, he was appointed President and Professor of Theory and Practice in the Vermont Academy of Medicine, at Castleton,—the latter position involving attendance during an autumn session of fourteen weeks. He accepted the appointment, and after some friction (due perhaps, in part, to his distant residence) he removed in January, 1826, to Albany, about 75 miles from Castleton, where he formed a partnership with Dr. Alden March, who was one of his colleagues in Castleton, and had become an intimate friend. In his new location he had more professional business than ever before, but on account of frequent illness in his family he still found difficulty in performing his duties as Professor.

It was therefore with much satisfaction that he received in March, 1829, the suggestion that he should remove to New Haven to fill the professorship of materia medica and therapeutics in the Yale Medical School, as in that place his family could be safely left among friends

In June, on the occasion of a vacancy in the professorship of materia medica in the Castleton school, he received the additional appointment of lecturer in that branch, the effect of which was to require of him two lectures a day instead of one

In September he received the appointment of Professor of materia medica and therapeutics at Yale, and in May, 1830, he removed his family to New Haven, where his distinguished reputation secured him many friends and a reasonable share of professional business. He also continued his duties at Castleton until his resignation in 1838

In September, 1833, he had the opportunity of taking a professorship in the Medical College of South Carolina, at Charleston, but declined.

For a time his relations with his colleagues were satisfactory; but eventually he was dissatisfied with his compensation, and imagined that there was a conspiracy to slander him, so that he ceased giving his lectures in the spring of 1841. His resignation of his professorship was not accepted until August, 1842

Subsequently he spent nearly a year in South Carolina, without his family

In the spring of 1851 he removed to Springfield, Massachusetts, where he died on February 28, 1859, in his 74th year. During his later years his professional occupation was mainly in consultation, and his circumstances were sadly straitened He was buried in New Haven.

He married, in January, 1813, Mary, the youngest child of the Rev Elam Potter (Yale 1765), of Enfield, who died after years of ill-health on September 8, 1853, in her 63d year

They had ten children, of whom two daughters and a son survived them.

A portrait of Dr. Tully was given to the College in 1906 by his last surviving child.

A Biographical Notice by Dr. Tully's successor in his chair at Yale, Dr. Henry Bronson, was published in the *Proceedings* of the Connecticut Medical Society for 1860, pp. 109–15, was reprinted in volume 65 of the *Boston Medical and Surgical Journal*, for August 22, 1861, pp. 54–60, and separately. This is a striking tribute to Dr. Tully's remarkable personality. A few sentences may be quoted:

> Dr. Tully was doubtless the most learned and thoroughly scientific physician of New England. .. His knowledge of Botany was extensive and very accurate. Chemistry, particularly organic and pharmaceutical Chemistry, he understood probably better than any one in this country. .. He knew Latin and Greek well, at least so far as these languages are employed in natural science.. Dr. Tully was an intelligent and discriminating practitioner. He investigated his cases thoroughly, usually arrived at a correct diagnosis, drew inferences cautiously, and grounded his opinions on the facts before him. His unrivaled knowledge of Materia Medica, particularly indigenous Materia Medica, and his familiarity with all the new remedies, especially the new organic compounds, gave him a great advantage in prescription. His resources, in a difficult case, were, so far as I know, unparalleled. .. In talking as in writing, he was magisterial, exuberantly, if not ambitiously, learned, discursive and diffuse. ... Sum up all his imperfections, and deduct them from his merits, and there is enough left to make a man of—a whole man, and (may I not add?) a great man. .. In his mind was combined great love of detail with extraordinary powers of generalization—an unusual combination.

His costly library of scientific, medical, and miscellaneous books, comprising some 2,000 volumes, was sold at auction in New York in the October following his death.

He published:

1. On the Ergot of Rye.
In the *American Journal of Science*, vol. 2, 1820, pp. 45–53.

2. Scutellaria-laterifolia Scull-cap.

In the *Middlesex Gazette,* Middletown, Nov 30, 1820 On the supposed use of this plant in cases of Hydrophobia

3. Diversity of the two sorts of Datura found in the United States

In the *American Journal of Science,* vol. 6, 1823, pp. 254–58

4. Essays on Fevers, and other medical subjects.—By Thomas Miner, M D, and William Tully, M D. Middletown, 1823 8°, pp. 484. [*B. Publ. C. H S Surg. Gen'l's. Office. Y. C.*

Part 1, pp. 13–287, is credited to Dr. Miner; part 2, pp. 289–484, to Dr. Tully. The latter contains three papers on the Fevers of Middletown and Chatham, and an analysis of Miller's Account of an Epidemic Fever of Virginia.

5 An Examination of the Strictures in the New-England Journal for October, 1823, and in the North-American Review for October, 1823, on Essays on Fevers, etc.—By Thomas Miner, M D, and William Tully, M.D Middletown, 1823 8°, pp. 32

[*B. Ath B. Publ. Harv N Y. H S Surg. Gen'l's. Office Y. C.*

6 An Essay, Pharmacological and Therapeutical, on Sanguinaria-Canadensis.

In the *American Medical Recorder,* vol 13, pp. 1–48, 249–84, + pl. (January and April, 1828).

This obtained a prize offered by the *Recorder* for the best essay on the indigenous materia medica; it is distinguished by original observation and elaborate scholarship.

7. Catalogue of the Phenogamous Plants and the Ferns growing without cultivation, within five miles of Yale College.

From E Baldwin's *History of Yale College,* 1831; written in conjunction with Dr. Eli Ives and Dr. M C Leavenworth. Also published separately New Haven, 1831. 8°, pp. 38.

8 Results of Experiments and Observations on Narcotine, and Sulphate of Morphine.

In the *American Journal of Science,* vol 21, 1832, pp 39–55

9. On the Medicinal Powers of Sanguinarine and its Salts;

On the Chlorite of Potassa;

On Congestion

In the *Boston Medical and Surgical Journal,* vol. 6, 1832, pp. 245–48; 325-32; 341–48; 357–66.

10. Actæa racemosa.
In the same, vol. 8, 1833, pp. 133–44, 149–55.

11. Materia Medica or Pharmacology and Therapeutics. Springfield, 1852–58. Vol. 1, parts 1, 2. 8°, pp. 1534.
[*B. Ath. Surg. Gen'l's. Office. U. S. Y. C.*

What is here published was but a fragment of the work as planned. The Introduction, only, occupies 365 pages; and the remainder is discursive to a fault, but encyclopedic in its contents. Besides the topics indicated on the title-page, the work is equally concerned with medical theory and practice.

Dr. Tully furnished the definitions of the terms of anatomy, physiology, medicine, botany, and some other branches of natural history, for the editions of Webster's *Dictionary*, published in 1840 and 1847.

AUTHORITIES.

Conn. Med. Society's Proceedings, 1860, 109–15; 1892, 566–68. Conn. Valley Hist. Society's Papers, ii, 170–74. *Field*, Centennial Address at Middletown, 197. N. E. Hist. and Geneal. Register, iii, 162. *W. L. Kingsley*, Yale College, ii, 74–76.

Hezekiah Gold Ufford, the third son of Samuel Ufford, of Stratford, Connecticut, and grandson of Ebenezer and Jane (Moss) Ufford, of Stratford, was born in Stratford on April 14, 1779. His mother was Abigail, daughter of the Rev. Hezekiah Gold (Harvard Coll. 1719), pastor in Stratford, and sister of the Rev. Hezekiah Gold (Yale 1751). He was prepared for College by the Rev. Ira Hart (Yale 1797), of Middlebury, and entered after the opening of Freshman year. At graduation he delivered a poem, on Patronage indispensable to the cultivation of the muse. He was the oldest in his class.

He studied theology with President Dwight, and having united with the College Church in July, was licensed to preach by the Fairfield East Association of Ministers on October 15, 1807. As it proved, however, after two or three years, that his strength of voice was not sufficient for public speaking, he accepted an invitation to become the principal of an academy in Bloomingdale, in the upper part of New York City; and subsequently he spent many years in the work of a classical teacher in New York (from 1814), and in his native town (after 1830).

He retained in active exercise his scholarly tastes and habits, and the reading of Greek was the amusement of his leisure during the last months of his life Though debarred from his chosen profession, he labored much in kindred ways, aiding feeble churches, gathering the neglected into Sunday Schools, and giving Bible-class instruction

He died in Stratford, very suddenly, on January 23, 1863, in his 84th year.

He married on March 19, 1812, Julia, elder daughter of Moses and Susannah (Woodruff) Hine, of Woodbridge, Connecticut, who died on May 5, 1864, in Stratford, after a brief illness, aged 76 years

Their children, two daughters and two sons, survived him Alexander U. McAlister, a graduate of the Sheffield Scientific School in 1866, was a grandson

He published

An Elementary Treatise on Logic New-York, 1823. 12°, pp. 192 [*Harv* *N Y Publ* *Y C*

AUTHORITIES

Hine Genealogy, 95–96 *A McAlister,* MS Letter, July, 1863. *Orcutt,* Hist of Stratford, ii, 1320

William Fowler Vaill, son of the Rev Joseph Vaill (Dartmouth Coll. 1778), for over fifty years pastor of the Congregational Church in Hadlyme, in the township of Lyme, Connecticut, and grandson of Captain Joseph and Jerusha (Peck) Vaill, of Litchfield, was born in Hadlyme on June 7, 1783. His mother was Sarah, eldest daughter of the Rev. Joseph Fowler (Yale 1743), of East Haddam. A brother was graduated here in 1811. He was prepared for College by his father, and had united with the church before coming to Yale.

After graduation, while pursuing theological study with his father, he assisted him in the work of instructing pupils, and then spent a short time with the Rev. Asahel Hooker (Yale 1789), of Goshen. He was licensed to preach by the Middlesex Association of Ministers on September 15, 1807.

On December 21, 1808, he was ordained and installed as pastor of the Congregational Church in North Guilford, where he did faithful and efficient service in the work of the ministry and in teaching private pupils until 1820.

He then offered himself to the United Foreign Missionary Society in New York for a mission which they were about to establish among the Osage Indians in what is now Oklahoma. Being dismissed from his pastoral charge by the Consociation on April 12, and appointed Superintendent of the new mission, he left for his distant field the same month.

He was stationed on the west side of the Grand or Neosho River, about twenty-five miles north of its junction with the Arkansas, and the reports of his work there are printed in the volumes of the *American Missionary Register,* issued by the Society which commissioned him.

In the summer of 1826 his mission, with others of the United Foreign Missionary Society, was taken over by the American Board of Commissioners for Foreign Missions.

In 1834 the station was abandoned, in consequence of the unsettled condition of the Osages; and Mrs. Vaill's health being impaired, the family returned during that summer to Connecticut, where she died.

About 1837 Mr. Vaill accepted a commission as a missionary at Wethersfield, in Henry County, northwestern Illinois. For seven years his labors were mainly confined to Wethersfield, as stated pastor of the Congregational Church; but afterwards he gave himself to missionary service over a wider area, in which he was occupied up to the very end. He was intently devoted to his work, and labored unremittingly.

He died in Wethersfield, after five days' illness, on February 24, 1865, in his 82d year.

He married early in life, at North Guilford, Asenath Selden, by whom he had two sons and four daughters. One son was graduated at Amherst College in 1840, and became a minister.

He had also three children by a second marriage who survived him.

AUTHORITIES

Congregational Quarterly, vii, 422-24 *Parsons,* Memoir of Rev J Vaill, 57-58, 82-85, 171-80 *Steiner,* Hist of Guilford, 297

THOMAS GLASBY WATERMAN, a son of David Waterman, of New York City, himself a non-graduated student at Yale, was born in New York on January 23, 1788, and while a child removed with his parents to Salisbury, Connecticut, where his father established valuable and extensive iron works

After graduation he studied law in the Litchfield Law School, and in Salisbury, and subsequently with the Hon. Samuel Sherwood, in Delhi, Delaware County, New York In 1809 he was admitted to the bar in the city of New York, but he remained with Mr. Sherwood until 1812, when he went for a few months to Owego, and thence to Binghamton, where he resided until his death.

He married, on August 22, 1813, Pamela, eldest daughter of General Joshua and Rhoda (Jewell) Whitney, of Binghamton

He attained eminence in his profession, and served for one year (1822–23) as District Attorney for Broome County. At a later date he served as an associate judge of the County Court of Common Pleas.

He was also to some extent in public life. In 1824 he was a member of the State Assembly, and from 1827 to 1830 a member of the Senate. While in the Senate he was particularly active in promoting the proposed revision of the Statutes of the State, enacted in 1827–28. In 1824 he attained the rank of Brigadier General in the militia, and was subsequently usually known by that title.

Although then comparatively a young man, and at the head of his profession, he retired from practice about 1830, and was afterwards chiefly engaged in lumbering and milling enterprises and in land operations, amassing a large fortune.

He was remarkable for his liberal contributions to the charitable and religious undertakings of his vicinity, and for his increasing kindness to the poor and unfortunate.

A published notice at the time of his death commemorates him as "a model of truth, probity, and honor, kind, amiable, and benevolent, yet full of decision and firmness, with a clear, good judgment, a strong sense of duty, and a laborious and indefatigable spirit in discharging its obligations."

He was a personal friend of Jackson and VanBuren, and a strong Democrat, until Jackson's bank policy drove him into the Whig ranks. Later, he acted with the Republicans.

He died in Binghamton on January 7, 1862, at the age of 74.

His widow died on October 1, 1864, in her 71st year.

A son was graduated at Yale in 1844.

He published:

The Justice's Manual; or, a Summary of the Powers and Duties of Justices of the Peace in the State of New York... Albany, 1828. 8°.

The same Second edition, adapted to the Revised Statutes Albany, 1829 8°, pp. 294 [*B. Publ.*

The same. Third edition

AUTHORITIES

Lawyer, Binghamton, 91–92, 335–36 *Pierce,* Whitney Genealogy, 385–86 *Wilkinson,* Annals of Binghamton, 164–65

MARTIN WELLES, the eldest child of General Roger Welles (Yale 1775), of Newington Parish, in Wethersfield, Connecticut, was born on December 7, 1787, and was baptized on January 27, 1788, by the name of his maternal grandfather, Captain Martin Kellogg.

He studied law after graduation with Samuel Cowles, of Farmington, and after his admission to the bar opened an office there. In September, 1809, he married Frances (or Fanny), daughter of Reuben S. and Levia Norton, of Farmington.

In 1813 he was admitted to the bar of New York State, and began practice in Newburgh, in Orange County. Thence he removed about 1817 to New York City; but in 1820 failing health compelled his return to Wethersfield, and for some years he retired from professional life.

He was, however, sent by his fellow-townsmen to the General Assembly as a representative in six sessions (1824–27, 1831–32), and was also elected to the State Senate in 1827, 1828, and 1829. He served as Clerk of the Lower House in 1824–26, and as Speaker in 1831–32, presiding with marked dignity and ability. As one of the senior Senators, he was a Fellow of the Yale Corporation for two years (1828–30). He was a pronounced Whig in politics.

He was an associate Judge of the Hartford County Court from 1824 to 1830

While in the Legislature in 1827, the new State Prison was, largely through his strenuous efforts, located in Wethersfield, and he planned and superintended the erection of the buildings.

In 1850 he resumed practice in Hartford, with energy and devotion.

He had made large investments in land in Ottawa County, in northern Ohio, where the town Martin was named for him. While attending to business there, he died in Martin, on January 19, 1863, in his 76th year. He was buried in Newington.

His children were four sons, and a daughter who died in infancy. The two elder sons were graduates of Yale, in 1830 and 1834, respectively, but both died before him.

A copy of his portrait is given in the *History of Wethersfield.*

Of unimpeachable integrity, powerful and acute intellect, deep knowledge of the law, fearless independence and forcible diction in asserting the claims of his clients, he was an advocate not easy to encounter. With great dignity of deportment he united in his family life the tenderest sympathies and warmth of heart.

AUTHORITIES.

Conn. Reports, xxx, 607–08. Kelloggs in the New World, i, 194. *Stiles,* Hist. of Wethersfield, i, 185, 630; ii, 770–72. *Trumbull,* Hist. of Hartford County, i, 127–28; ii, 334. *R. Welles,* Annals of Newington, 98.

WILLARD WELTON, the oldest son of Benjamin Welton, a farmer in limited circumstances, of Watertown, Connecticut, and grandson of Oliver and Margaret (Warner) Welton, of Waterbury, was born in Watertown, on January 14, 1782. His mother was Agnes, daughter of Nathaniel and Sarah (Smith, Candee) Gunn, of Waterbury. He entered College at the opening of the Sophomore year, after having prepared himself with difficulty.

After graduation he studied law in Hudson, New York.

In 1808 he married, and in October, 1810, was admitted to the bar and began practice in Sherburne, Chenango County, New York He had been brought up in the Episcopal Church, but here attended Presbyterian worship.

In the spring of 1819 he gave up the law, and removed about twenty miles northward, to a farm in the town of Madison, in Madison County, where he lived until his wife's death in 1832. Here he became a member of the Congregational Church, and took a special interest in the Bible Class and Sunday School.

About the time of his second marriage, in the spring of 1835, he removed to Hamilton village, a few miles distant, where his latter years were spent.

He died in Hamilton on August 11, 1866, in his 85th year

Two sons survived him

He was a consistent member of the Congregational Church in Hamilton. He was an extreme opponent of slavery, and very earnest and even arbitrary in the advocacy of his views

---

AUTHORITIES.

Anderson, Hist of Waterbury, i, Appendix, 149

ROBERT WILKINSON was one of triplets born to John and Content Wilkinson, of Beekman, Duchess County, New York, on November 25, 1786, and a grandson of Captain William Wilkinson, of South Kingston, Rhode Island. His mother was a daughter of Dr. William and Mary (Palmer) Moore, of Stonington, Connecticut. While taking this son to College for examination for admission in June, 1802, his father was killed by the giving way of a part of the bridge, as he was crossing the Housatonic river at New Milford.

His scholarship was excellent, and he was assigned the Valedictory oration at graduation.

He studied law in Poughkeepsie, and settled in practice at first in Glens Falls, where he held the office of Surrogate of Warren County from March, 1813, to February, 1815. Later, perhaps about 1825, he removed to Poughkeepsie, in his native county, where he attained eminence, both as a lawyer, and as a finished orator.

He held the office of Surrogate of Duchess County from February, 1840, to February, 1844.

In 1827, when over forty years of age, he became for the first time a professor of religion, and thenceforwards was active in Christian work. He also held office as a ruling elder in the Presbyterian Church.

He died, after a severe illness, from fever, in Poughkeepsie, on August 13, 1849, in his 63d year.

He married, on February 15, 1809, Phebe, fourth daughter of Jesse Oakley, and sister of Judge Thomas B. Oakley (Yale 1801) and of Jesse Oakley (Yale 1814). She died on May 25, 1866, aged 80 years.

Their children were two sons and a daughter. Robert Wilkinson (Yale 1895) is a grandson.

AUTHORITIES.

Bockée Family, 72. N. Y. Evangelist, August 23, 1849. Peters Lineage, 101-02. Wilkinson Family, 561-64.

Ebenezer Young was born in Killingly, Windham County, Connecticut, on December 25, 1783, the son of Elijah and Bethiah (Slack) Young.

He studied law after graduation, and settled in practice in that part of his native town which was then known as Westfield, now Danielson. He was also successfully engaged in cloth-manufacture at Chestnut Hill in East Killingly.

Very early he became prominent in local politics, and in October, 1810, he was sent to the General Assembly as a Federalist Representative from Killingly. He filled the same office at the sessions in May, 1811, October, 1816, and May, 1817.

In 1823, 1824, and 1825, he was a member of the State Senate, and as one of the seniors in that body he served as an *ex-officio* Fellow of the Yale Corporation for the year 1825–26.

In 1827 and 1828 he was again sent to the Lower House of the Legislature, and in both years was chosen Speaker.

In 1828 he was elected to the House of Representatives in the United States Congress, and was twice re-elected, serving until March, 1835.

He was also very actively interested in the promotion of social reforms, more especially peace and temperance.

He died at his residence in (West) Killingly, on August 19, 1851, at the age of sixty-seven.

He married, on January 25, 1810, Anna Burnett, of Windham.

A daughter married the Hon. Thomas Backus (Brown Univ. 1819).

He published:

Speech on the bill to reduce and otherwise alter the Duties on Imports.—Delivered in the House of Reps. in Committee of the Whole, Jan. 28, 1833. Washington, 1833. 8°, pp. 13. [*Y. C.*

AUTHORITIES.

F. M. Peck, MS. Letter, July, 1852. *Larned,* Hist. of Windham County, ii, 433, 540. *Miss A. M. Young,* MS. Letter, January, 1912.

Annals, 1806-07

At Commencement in September, 1807, the resignation of the Rev Dr. Levi Hart (Yale 1760), of Preston, now Jewett City, as a member of the Corporation, on account of extreme infirmity, was accepted; and the Rev. Dr. Andrew Lee (Yale 1766), of Hanover Society, now Sprague, was elected in his stead.

At the same time Seth Norton, of the Class of 1804, was elected to a tutorship, in place of John Hall (Yale 1802), resigned.

This date also marks the acquisition of the valuable cabinet collected by Benjamin D. Perkins, of the Class of 1794, and the gift of two thousand dollars from the Hon Oliver Wolcott (Yale 1778), which was assigned to the use of the Library.

The year 1806–07 witnessed the publication of the earliest Yale periodical, which under the title of *Literary Cabinet* began its bi-weekly issue on November 15, 1806, under the editorial care of Wales, Grimké, and Sutherland, of the Senior Class, it was an octavo sheet of eight pages, and appeared throughout the current year.

Sketches, Class of 1807

---

*Guilielmus Weston Adams, et Car. Austr. 1808 *1831
*Joel Adams, et Car. Austr. 1808 *1859
**Samuel Rogers Andrew,* 1817, A M 1817, Socius, Secretarius *1858
*Guilielmus Atwater *1833
*Johannes Morse Austin *1863
*Abrahamus Dudley Baldwin, Soc ex officio *1862
**Johannes Bartlett,* A.M *1866
*Benjamin Bassett *1858
*Josephus Bennett, A.M. 1812 *1837
*Thaddaeus Betts, Reip. Conn Vice-Gub., Socius ex off., Rerumpubl. Foed. Sen. *1840
*Johannes Boyle *1810
*Aristarchus Champion *1871
*Henricus Guilielmus Channing, A.M. *1866
*Eleutheros Dana Comstock, A.M. *1859
*Holbrook Curtis, A.M. *1858
*Sheldonus Clark Curtiss, A.M. 1812 *1836
*Johannes Paine Cushman, A.M. Conc 1816, e Congr. *1848
*Leonardus Augustus Daggett, A M *1867
*Johannes Denniston *1810
**David Raymond Dixon* *1861
*Guilielmus Dubose, et Car. Austr. 1808, Reipubl. Car. Austr. Vice-Gubern. *1855
*Johannes Dunwody *1858
*Henricus Field
*Jacobus Fowler, A M *1873
*Robertus Smith Gardiner *1824

*Richardus Edwards Goodwin, A.M. *1838
*Thomas Smith Grimké, LL.D. 1830 *1834
*Ebenezer Grosvenor *1817
*Amos Potter Hall, et Guil. 1807 *1813
*David Hanford *1844
**Lutherus Hart,* A.M., Socius *1834
*Jacobus Howard *1811
**Araetius Bevil Hull,* A.M., Tutor *1826
**Daniel Huntington,* 1816, A.M. 1816 *1858
*Guilielmus Jay, LL.D. Ken. 1858 *1858
*Algernon Sidney Jones *1858
*Johannes Kell *1828
*Ezra Kellogg *1812
*Leonellus Henricus Kennedy, A.M. 1811 *1847
*Lester Kimberly *1811
*Guilielmus Coit Leffingwell, A.M. 1811 *1833
*Stephanus Lockwood *1827
**Amasa Loomis* *1824
*Justus McKinstry *1849
*Darius Mead, M.D. Univ. Penns. 1809, Socius ex officio *1864
**Samuel Thomas Mills,* A.M. 1811 *1853
*Isaacus Hubbell Osborn *1843
*Guido Richards *1873
*Samuel Root, A.M. *1868
*Augustus Sherrill, et Guil. 1807 *1853
*Guilielmus Stebbins, 1826, A.M. 1826 *1858
*Alexander Hodgdon Stevens, M.D. Univ. Penns. 1811, LL.D. Univ. Nov. Ebor. Reg. 1849, in Coll. Med. et Chir. Nov. Ebor. Chirurg. Prof. et ejusd. Praeses, in Coll. Rutg. Chirurg. Prof., Reip. Nov. Ebor. et Rerump. Foed. SS. Med. Praeses *1869
**Henricus Pierce Strong,* A.M. Viridim. 1817 *1835
*Jahacobus Sutherland, LL.D. Columb. 1836, Reip. Nov. Ebor. Cur. Supr. Jurid. *1845
*Carolus Wiley Taylor *1865

**Nathanael Gulielmus Taylor,* A M , S T D Conc 1823, Theol. Didact Prof	*1858
**Johannes Ludovicus Tomlinson*	*1853
*Jonathan Georgius Washington Trumbull	*1853
**Jacobus Wakefield Tucker,* A M	*1819
*Leonardus Eugenius Wales, A M.	*1823
*Curtiss Warner	*1813
*Ely Warner, A.M.	*1872
*Guilielmus Avery Whelpley, A M	*1828

JOEL ADAMS, the son of Joel and Grace (Weston) Adams, was born in Richland District, South Carolina, on March 6, 1784, his father having removed from Virginia to South Carolina a few years before He and a younger brother joined the Class at the opening of the Junior year

After graduation he studied law in the office of Judge Abraham Nott (Yale 1787), in Columbia, the county seat of Richland District, as well as the capital of the State.

He was admitted to the bar in 1810, but soon abandoned the profession, and devoted himself with eminent success to the life of a planter on his paternal estate, about fifteen miles southeast of Columbia, on the Congaree River.

In politics he was a strict constructionist. He was a member of the State Legislature in 1812 and 1813, and again in 1832, when the Convention was called which passed the ordinance of Nullification.

He died in May 1, 1859, in his 76th year, at his homestead in Richland.

He married in the spring of 1809, Mary G Hopkins, of Richland District, who survived him

They had a family of twelve children One son was graduated here in 1831.

He was a useful citizen, respected by all for his kind and charitable disposition, his public spirit, his integrity, and love of justice

AUTHORITIES

J P. Adams, MS Letter, July, 1860

William Weston Adams was a younger brother of the last-named graduate, and entered College with him

He became a physician and practiced for some time in what is known as the Fork Section, in Richland County, South Carolina.

He married a Miss Goodwyn, by whom he had several children. Two sons and two daughters settled in Alabama, and he is believed to have removed to that State before his death, which occurred at the age of 45, in May, 1831.

AUTHORITIES

Miss I. DeSaussure, MS Letter, October, 1911

Samuel Rogers Andrew, the only son of Samuel Andrew, a farmer in the northern part of Milford, Connecticut, and grandson of Jonathan and Elizabeth (Smith) Andrew, of Milford, was born on May 6, 1787. Rector Andrew (Harvard 1675) was his great-grandfather. His mother was Charlotte Rogers, of Milford

His College course was interrupted, presumably by illness, in his Senior year, and he did not receive his degree until 1817.

He at first studied law, and then spent a few years at the South, where he was engaged in editing a newspaper and in teaching

Finally he studied theology in Milford with the Rev. Dr Bezaleel Pinneo (Dartmouth Coll. 1791), was licensed to preach by the New Haven West Association of Ministers on September 26, 1815, and on October 8, 1817, was ordained and installed as pastor of the South Congregational Church in Woodbury ·

On June 5, 1821, he married Mary, third daughter of Captain Henry Daggett (Yale 1771), of New Haven.

After a long pastorate of eminent usefulness, he was compelled by failing health to resign his charge on July 8, 1846, and later in the same year he removed his residence to New Haven.

In August, 1837, he had been chosen a Fellow of Yale College, and in October, 1846, he was elected by his associates to the office of Secretary of the Corporation He accepted the office, but at the following Commencement resigned his seat in the Board of Fellows, it being then understood that County representation was desirable, and his residence being now removed from Litchfield County.

He performed the duties of Secretary with punctilious care and great efficiency, until his very sudden death, in New Haven, on May 26, 1858, just after entering on his 72d year. He had also continued during these years to preach as opportunity offered

The *New-York Observer* gives this estimate of his mental endowments.

> His intellect was strong, clear, comprehensive, and discriminating. His judgment was pre-eminently sound and wise. His taste was pure and classical His style in writing and in conversation was lucid, chaste, and often elegant. -His sensibilities were exquisitely susceptible to beauty in nature, in literature, and in character His thoughts were always just, and often rich and original

He was an independent thinker in theology, and a man of excellent sense. His nature was modest and retiring, and his temper mild and amiable.

His wife died in New Haven on August 14, 1875, in her 83d year

His children were three sons and two daughters. The eldest son was graduated here in 1843, but died in early manhood, leaving a son, who is a graduate of the College in 1871. The elder daughter married the Rev. William Aitchison (Yale 1848), and the younger married the Rev. James A. Gallup (Yale 1851).

He was a frequent and valued contributor to the *Quarterly Christian Spectator;* and the following, among other articles by him, may be specified:

Volume 1, pp 453–64 (September, 1829). Review of James on Christian Charity

Volume 2, pp. 16–43 (March, 1830): Review of Memoir of Mrs. Judson, pp 281–99 (June, 1830): Review of the Lives of Mather and Henry, pp. 449–59 (September, 1830). Review of Advice to a Young Christian; pp 598–608 (December, 1830): On the Fear of God, as an essential principle of true religion

Volume 3, pp 531–51 (December, 1831). Review of the Writings and Character of Sir Matthew Hale

Volume 4, pp 89–109 (March, 1832): Assurance of their piety peculiarly the duty of Christians at the present day, pp 513–28 (December, 1832): On Religious Joy.

Volume 5, pp 87–108 (March, 1833), Works of Leighton; pp 291–313 (June, 1833): Memoir of James Brainerd Taylor; pp 657–72 (December, 1833): What is the Real Difference between the New-Haven Divines and those who oppose them?

Volume 6, pp. 73–88 (March, 1834): [Review of] Eternity Realized, pp 381–405 (September, 1834): A Memoir of Miss Mary Jane Graham.

Volume 7, pp. 76–89 (March, 1835) Man's Dependence on the Grace of God, for Holiness of Heart and Life

Volume 8, pp 22–43 (March, 1836): Memoir of Rev. John H. Rice, D.D

He also contributed one sermon to the *National Preacher* Whether it is right to use Intoxicating Drinks at the present day, Tried and Settled; from II Cor v, 10 In vol 14, pp 17–32 (February, 1840)

AUTHORITIES

Amer Congregational Year Book, 1859, 118. *Cothren*, Hist of Woodbury, i, 305–06, ii, 1355–56 Doggett-Daggett Genealogy, 141, 180 N Y Observer, June 10, 1858 Prescott Memorial, 133–35

WILLIAM ATWATER, the only son of the Rev. Noah Atwater (Yale 1774), of Westfield, Massachusetts, was born in Westfield on January 30, 1786. His father died the year before he entered College

He studied medicine under Dr. Nathan Smith in Hanover, New Hampshire, and settled in practice in his native town in 1810

He married on December 20, 1810, Harriet, youngest daughter of Lemuel and Eunice (Lyman) Pomeroy, of Southampton, and niece of the Rev Seth Pomeroy (Yale 1753). She died on October 17, 1824, in her 38th year.

Dr. Atwater died in Westfield, on February 7, 1833, aged 47 years He enjoyed an extensive practice, and was esteemed as a learned physician, and an interesting and witty companion.

His children were two daughters and four sons The eldest son died in infancy, the youngest son followed his father's profession

In 1821 he was a Representative of the town in the State Legislature

AUTHORITIES

American Ancestry, ix, 232 Atwater Hist. and Genealogy, 175, 243-44 *Coleman*, Lyman Family, 351 Westfield Bicentennial, 168-69.

JOHN MORSE AUSTIN, the second son of Judge Eliphalet Austin, of New Hartford, Connecticut, and a first cousin of Ralsaman C Austin (Yale 1801), was born in New Hartford in 1783. His mother was Sibyl (or Isabella), younger daughter of Daniel and Elizabeth (Goodrich) Dudley, of Guilford In 1799 his father removed with his family to the Western Reserve of Ohio, where he founded the town of Austinburg, in what is now Ashtabula County The son entered Yale at the opening of the Junior year, from Williams College, where he had spent two years.

He studied law for two years after graduation with Judge Henry Baldwin (Yale 1797), then of Pittsburgh, Pennsylvania, and after being admitted to the bar practiced in Pittsburgh for about three years.

In 1812 he married Priscilla Stevens, who was then twenty years of age, and removed to Uniontown, in Fayette County, about forty miles south of Pittsburgh, where he continued to practice with reputation for over thirty years, and accumulated a handsome fortune. He retired from active service about fifteen years before his death, which occurred in Uniontown on April 8, 1863, when he was nearly 80 years of age. His wife survived him.

Their children were four daughters and six sons. Two sons became lawyers, and one a Baptist clergyman.

AUTHORITIES.

R. S. Austin, MS. Letter, June, 1870. Dudley Family, 1077–78.

Abraham Dudley Baldwin, the only child of Dudley Baldwin (Yale 1777), and a nephew of the Hon. Abraham Baldwin (Yale 1772), was born at Greenfield Hill, in Fairfield, Connecticut, on April 15, 1788. His father died in 1794, and his mother in 1795. He did not enter College until after the opening of the Freshman year.

He studied law after graduation, but preferred not to enter on its practice, and resided through life on his estate at Greenfield Hill, chiefly engaged in agricultural pursuits. He was a representative in the State Legislature in the sessions of 1821, 1822, 1826, and 1829; and a member of the State Senate in 1830, 1838, and 1840. As one of the six senior Senators, he was *ex-officio* a Fellow of the Yale Corporation in 1838–39, and 1840–41. He was also High Sheriff of Fairfield County from 1831 to 1837, and held the rank of Captain in the militia.

He died at Greenfield Hill on June 8, 1862, in his 75th year.

He first married Mary Grant, of Greenfield Hill, by whom he had one son and one daughter. She died on September 6, 1814, aged 23½ years.

He married, secondly, in 1815, Henrietta, daughter of Joel and Grace (Perry) Jennings, of Fairfield, who bore him three sons and four daughters; the second daughter married the Rev. Philo Canfield (Williams Coll. 1836). Mrs Baldwin died on June 4, 1867, aged 83 years.

Captain Baldwin inherited no small share of the talent for which his family were distinguished, and was a most worthy, influential, and honorable man.

AUTHORITIES

Baldwin Genealogy, i, 431, 450. Greenfield Church 150th Anniversary, 38. Jennings Genealogy, ii, 416

JOHN BARTLETT, third son of Deacon John Bartlett, of Exeter Parish, Lebanon, Connecticut, and a brother of the Rev. Shubael Bartlett (Yale 1800), was born in Lebanon on August 16, 1784 As a boy he sang in the church choir at a funeral service in memory of Washington

After graduation he remained at the College for two years in the office of Butler, and at the same time pursued the study of theology under President Dwight. He was licensed to preach by the Hartford North Ministerial Association on February 7, 1810, and later in that year was preaching statedly to a congregation in Wapping in South Windsor.

In 1811 Judge David Golden, of that part of Warren, Herkimer County, New York, which is now Columbia, applied to President Dwight to recommend a minister for a Congregational meeting-house which he had just built; and as a result Mr. Bartlett was ordained and installed on September 26 as pastor of that Church, his brother preaching the sermon.

He was married on September 12, 1812, by his brother to Jane, daughter of Judge David Vandewater and Mary (Chesney) Golden of Columbia.

Receiving a call to a more promising field of labor, he was dismissed from this charge and was installed on February 15, 1815, as pastor of the Congregational Church in Wintonbury Society, now Bloomfield, Connecticut, where he remained for sixteen years.

On account of ill health he was then dismissed, on May 19, 1831, and for four years served as an agent of the American Bible Society.

He was again installed, on October 28, 1835, over the First Congregational Church in (West) Avon, of which he was pastor until October, 1847, when he resigned on account of failing health.

For six or eight years longer he continued to preach in various neighboring churches, until laid aside by bodily infirmity.

In 1849 he removed to the house of a son-in-law, in East Avon, where he died suddenly on April 25, 1866, in his 82d year. His wife died in Avon on December 3, 1869, in her 73d year.

They had five daughters and three sons who grew to maturity, besides three children who died in infancy. One son, David W. Bartlett, became known as an author.

Four grandsons are graduates: John P. Bartlett, Ph.B. 1878, Philip G. Bartlett, B.A. 1881, Francis B. Kellogg, B.A. 1883, and Alexis P. Bartlett, B.A. 1894.

He was a man of handsome features and uncommon musical gifts; brilliant in conversation, highly esteemed as a preacher, and open-minded to new ideas in theology, and to modern reforms.

He published:

A Sermon [from Ps. lxxv, 1], preached in Wintonbury Meeting-House, Windsor; on the occasion of the Annual Thanksgiving, December 6th, A.D. 1821. Hartford, 1822. 8°, pp. 19.
[*Br. Mus. Y. C.*

AUTHORITIES.

Miss E. S. Bartlett, MS. Letter, Dec., 1911. *M. H. Bartlett,* MS. Letter, May, 1866. Loomis Genealogy, Female Branches, ii, 690–91. *Stiles, Hist.* of Windsor, 2d ed., ii, 65–66. *Trumbull,* Hist. of Hartford County, ii, 11.

BENJAMIN BASSETT, a son of Benjamin and Mary (Hinman) Bassett, of Derby, Connecticut, and a brother of the Rev. Archibald Bassett (Yale 1796), was born in Derby on December 10, 1782.

He began the study of medicine after graduation with Dr. Eli Ives (Yale 1799), of New Haven, and continued it under Dr. Benjamin Rush in Philadelphia.

After brief periods of practice in Redding and in Milford, and elsewhere, he settled in 1826 in Yorktown, in Westchester County, New York, and removing thence to the adjoining township in 1829, was successfully employed in Peekskill for the remainder of his life.

He was the President of the County Medical Society in 1846 and 1847.

He died in Peekskill on March 21, 1858, in his 76th year.

He married Sally Hanly, by whom he had two sons.

Of his contributions to periodicals only two have been traced:

1. On Epidemic Dysentery and Intermittent Fever.
In the *New York Medical Journal,* May, 1831.

2. An Address to the Westchester County Medical Society, on the Laws of Epidemics, as exhibited in those that have prevailed in that county during the last twenty years.
In the *New York Journal of Medicine, and the Collateral Sciences,* vol. 9, pp. 183–92, Sept., 1847.

AUTHORITIES.

Orcutt, Hist. of Derby, 697–98. *Scharf,* Hist. of Westchester County, i, 570, 576–77.

JOSEPH BENNETT, son of Thomas Bennett, Junior, and Anna (Warnock) Bennett, was born in Charleston, South Carolina, on December 25, 1788. His father was a leading builder and architect in Charleston, and the owner of a lumber-mill, who built the Circular Church and many houses in that city. A younger brother was graduated here in 1810, and an elder brother was Governor of South Carolina from 1820 to 1822.

He did not enter College until the Sophomore year, his preparation having been completed in New Haven under Jeremiah Evarts (Yale 1802).

He studied law with the Hon. Langdon Cheves, of Charleston, and was admitted to the bar in May, 1810.

He was married by President Dwight to Emilia, the youngest child of Colonel William and Lois (Mansfield) Lyon, of New Haven, on September 9, 1810.

He practiced his profession in Charleston until 1832, being at one time Comptroller of the city.

In 1832 he removed to New Haven, where he died on July 3, 1837, in his 49th year. His widow died here on March 4, 1869, at the age of 82.

Their children were two sons, who survived him, and three daughters who died in early life. Three sons of the younger son, Judge Thomas Bennett, are Yale graduates.

AUTHORITIES.

Miss S. J. Bennett, MS. Letter, January, 1911. Mansfield Family, 52.

THADDEUS BETTS, the second son of Judge William Maltby Betts, an able lawyer of Norwalk, Connecticut, and grandson of Dr. Thaddeus Betts (Yale 1745), was born in Norwalk on February 4, 1789. His mother was Lucretia, only daughter of Captain Jabez and Mercy (St. John) Gregory, of Norwalk. He did not enter College until after the opening of the Sophomore year.

He studied law after graduation, and was admitted to the bar in 1810.

He was one of the representatives of the town in the State Legislature in May, 1815, and after a long interval of devotion to his profession, he was again sent to the Legislature, as a Whig, in 1830. In 1831 he was a member of the State Senate, and in 1832, and again in 1834, was elected Lieutenant Governor. On March 4, 1839, he began a six years term as United States Senator, but he died in Washington, of a fever, on April 7, 1840, in his 52d year

He married Antoinette, third daughter of Dr. John and Sarah (St John) Cannon, of Norwalk, who died on February 26, 1864, in her 75th year. Three sons and a daughter also survived him.

Senator Betts was distinguished for acuteness of intellect, vigor of understanding, and soundness and probity of life.

AUTHORITIES

J Q Adams, Diary, x, 257 *Alexander,* St John Genealogy, 149-50. *Hall,* Hist of Norwalk, 260, 275 *Hinman,* Early Puritan Settlers, 206 *Hurd,* Hist of Fairfield County, 875 *Selleck,* Norwalk, 189, 231-32, 299, 410. Thomas Betts and his Descendants, 97.

JOHN BOYLE entered College from Cambridge, in Dorchester County, on the Eastern shore of Maryland, at the beginning of the Junior year,—having previously been, during a part of the Junior year, a member of the Class of 1806, from which he was dropped in June, 1805, on account of a fight with his classmate, James Fenimore Cooper.

He was considered a young man of considerable energy of mind, of much political information, and strongly attached to Republican principles.

He died before the close of the year 1810.

AUTHORITIES

J H Trumbull, MS Letter, May, 1874.

Aristarchus Champion, one of twin sons of General Henry Champion, of Westchester Society in Colchester, Connecticut, and grandson of Colonel Henry and Deborah (Brainard) Champion, of Westchester, was born on October 23, 1784. His mother was Abigail, daughter of Sylvanus and Abigail (Olmsted) Tinker, of East Haddam.

After graduation he studied law in New London, but instead of settling in practice found occupation in the management of his father's large interests in lands in the Western Reserve of Ohio and in Western New York. In 1826 he took up his residence in Rochester, New York, where he invested largely in real estate, while the place was as yet a mere village. There he spent the rest of his life, occupied with the care of his property and with labors of local and public beneficence. He was the wealthiest citizen of Rochester, and his systematic munificence toward religious and philanthropic objects had at that time rarely been equaled in this country.

He was a Vice-President of the American Bible Society from 1844 until his death, and President of the American Home Missionary Society from 1858 to 1860.

He died at his residence in Gates township, outside the city limits, on September 18, 1871, aged nearly 87 years.

He was never married. His property was largely left to religious and charitable societies, and in particular to the American Bible Society and the Presbyterian Board of Foreign Missions. He had also been a large benefactor of Yale College, especially in connection with the founding of the professorship of the Pastoral Charge in the Divinity school in 1839.

His portrait is given in the *Champion Genealogy*.

AUTHORITIES.

Trowbridge, Champion Genealogy, 282.

Henry William Channing, the eldest child of the Rev. Henry Channing (Yale 1781), and of Sally (McCurdy) Channing, of New London, Connecticut, was born in New London on August 5, 1788, and entered College at the opening of the Junior year.

After his graduation he began the study of law in the Litchfield Law School, and continued it in Albany, in the office of the Hon. Harmanus Bleecker.

He was admitted to the bar in New York City in 1811, and settled there in practice

For a brief period during the war of 1812 he served as a volunteer with the rank of Major, under the command of General Jacob Brown; and at the battle of Sacket's Harbor, where, according to the official report, he acquitted himself with great bravery and gallantry, he was severely wounded.

He continued to practice in New York for upwards of fifty years, early acquiring and always maintaining a high professional reputation

He died in New York on January 24, 1866, in his 78th year

He married in 1827 Adeline D'Anville Cook of Boston, who died on June 15, 1833.

Their children were three sons, of whom two died in infancy, and the third survived his father, following the same profession.

AUTHORITIES

Munsell, Annals of Albany, i, 299 *Salisbury,* Family Histories and Genealogies, i, 84 *Walworth,* Hyde Genealogy, ii, 753

Eleutheros Dana Comstock, a son of Dr Daniel Comstock, of Danbury, Connecticut, and grandson of David and Rebecca (Grumann) Comstock, of Norwalk, was born in 1790. His mother was Mary (or Polly), daughter of George and Margaret (Clark) Dana, of

Ashburnham, Massachusetts, and a niece of the Rev. Dr. James Dana (Harvard 1735), of Wallingford and New Haven. This son was named for a son of Dr. Dana who had died shortly before in early manhood; and he was brought up in Dr. Dana's family as a child of the house. Professor James D. Dana (Yale 1833) was a first cousin.

About 1814 he went into business in New York City as a merchant, and his residence continued there through life.

While on his return to the East from the Pacific coast, he took his own life by jumping overboard on the passage from Sacramento to San Francisco, on the evening of the 17th of August, 1859, when he was in his 70th year.

AUTHORITIES.

A. Comstock, MS. Letter, February, 1865.

HOLBROOK CURTIS, son of Zalmon and Esther Curtis, of Newtown, Fairfield County, Connecticut, and grandson of Nehemiah and Martha (Clark) Curtis, of Newtown, was born on July 14, 1787. His mother was a daughter of Captain John and Esther (Nichols) Holbrook, of Seymour, then part of Derby.

When he was twelve years old, he was placed by his parents in the family of the Rev. Dr. Daniel Burhans, the Episcopal Rector in Newtown, to be fitted for College; but his final preparation for the Junior Class was conducted by that accomplished classical scholar, Judge Asa Chapman (Yale 1792).

On graduation he returned to his native town and studied law with Judge Chapman, being admitted to the bar at Fairfield in 1809.

He pursued the practice of his profession in Newtown until 1813. In consequence of the death of Samuel W. Southmayd (honorary M.A. Yale 1809), a lawyer of

Watertown, in Litchfield County, in March of that year, he was invited by several gentlemen to remove thither, and accepted the invitation, making that his home for the rest of his life.

During his long professional career he received the confidence and esteem of the community, and pursued an honorable, high-minded, liberal course in the performance of his duties as a lawyer, as a citizen, and as a man.

He served as a Representative of the town in seven sessions of the State Legislature between 1821 and 1845; was Judge of Probate for the Watertown District from its establishment in 1834 to 1850; and Judge of the County Court from 1847 to 1849. He was also repeatedly a delegate to the General Conventions of the Episcopal Church, in which he had been trained and to which he was devotedly attached.

He was a man of constant and extensive reading, was well versed in the Latin poets, and had made some progress in modern languages. He was warm and social in his feelings, and possessed of an immense fund of anecdote.

He died in Watertown on February 21, 1858, from apoplexy, in his 71st year

He first married Eliza, or Elizabeth Stone, second daughter of Younglove and Dothee (Stone) Cutler, of Watertown, who died in Watertown on August 27, 1819, in her 27th year.

He next married, on October 7, 1822, Elizabeth P, eldest daughter of Judge William Edmond (Yale 1777), of Newtown, by his second wife, Elizabeth Payne.

His eldest son by his second marriage (Trinity Coll 1843) was a lawyer and Judge of distinction in New York City; and Dr H. Holbrook Curtis (Yale Ph.B 1877) is a grandson

A portrait of Judge Curtis is engraved in the *History of Litchfield County*

AUTHORITIES

Cothren, Hist. of Woodbury, i, 534, 543; ii, 1489 Cutler Memorial, 77. *Hurd*, Hist. of Litchfield County, 31-32 *Kilbourne*, Bench and Bar of Litchfield County, 94-95, 142, 239 *Orcutt*, Hist of Derby, 730.

SHELDON CLARK CURTISS, the eldest son of Sheldon Curtiss, of Derby, Connecticut, and grandson of Oliver and Hannah (Clark) Curtiss, of Derby, was born on August 31, 1788. His mother was Lois, daughter of Isaac Nichols, of Derby. A sister married John Humphreys (Yale 1796).

Soon after graduation he began the study of the law in the office of the Hon. Nathan Smith, of New Haven. He was admitted to the bar of New Haven County on March 29, 1810, and settled in practice in Derby.

On October 11, 1812, he was married by the Rev. Amos Pardee (Yale 1793) to Hannah, elder daughter of Joel and Lucy (Dewey) Bradley, of Lebanon, Connecticut, and Lanesborough, Berkshire County, Massachusetts, who was born in November, 1791.

He continued in his profession at Derby until 1817, but active life was not agreeable to his retiring nature, and he then removed to Lanesborough, where in a rich agricultural district he devoted himself to the care and superintendence of a farm, while his leisure hours were spent in his well-stored library.

After more than three years of disease and helpless confinement he died in Lanesborough on February 1, 1836, in his 48th year

His wife died shortly before him

Of their two daughters, one married the Hon David L. Seymour (Yale 1826).

Mr. Curtiss was a devoted member of the Episcopal Church.

AUTHORITIES

Columbian Register, February 13, 1836. *Orcutt*, Hist. of Derby, 715 *Palmer*, Hist. of Lanesborough, i, 86, 89, 115

JOHN PAINE CUSHMAN, the younger son of Judge Isaac Cushman, of Pomfret, Connecticut, and grandson of Isaiah and Sarah (Ring) Cushman, of Plympton, Massachusetts, and Pomfret, was born on March 8, 1784. His mother was Sarah, second daughter of Seth and Mabel (Tyler) Paine, of Brooklyn Parish in Pomfret. Two of her brothers were graduates of Harvard College, and the elder had a distinguished career in Vermont

He was prepared for College at the Plainfield Academy by John Adams (Yale 1795), and entered with the Class of 1806, but after many discouragements, from serious inflammation of the eyes, he was finally obliged after the beginning of the Senior year to retire permanently from the Class and take a rest of an entire year

After graduation he began the study of law with Judge Zephaniah Swift (Yale 1778), of Windham, whence he went in 1808 to the Litchfield Law School In 1809, after a brief stay in the office of Abraham Van Vechten, in Albany, he settled permanently in Troy, New York, at first in the office of William M. Bliss (Yale 1790).

In 1812 he married Maria Jones, eldest daughter of Colonel Benjamin Tallmadge (Yale 1773), of Litchfield.

A few years after his marriage a new and vitalizing religious experience led him to unite (in 1816) with the Presbyterian Church; and in this connection he was led to reconsider the question of a profession, with the possibility of entering the ministry, but he found himself too fully committed in various directions to make any change He served as a Ruling Elder in the First Presbyterian Church from 1818.

He was a member of Congress for one term (December, 1817–March, 1819), but though unanimously renominated declined to stand again, from a desire to resume his professional business as a means of livelihood

In 1834 he received the appointment of Recorder of the city, which office he held until he was made Judge of the Circuit Court in February, 1838.

He was also a Regent of the State University from April, 1830, to April, 1834, and a Trustee of Union College from 1833 until his death

He retained his judicial position with credit until disqualified by age (in 1844); and subsequently devoted himself to the care and improvement of his large real-estate interests, and to projects for extending and beautifying the city. While still busily occupied he suffered, in November, 1847, a slight attack of paralysis He recovered partially, but a gradual failure of strength set in, and his death followed, in Troy, on September 16, 1848, in his 65th year.

His widow died in Troy on March 19, 1878, at the age of 88.

Their children were four sons and four daughters Three sons were graduated at Union College, in 1834, 1836, and 1851, respectively; the eldest daughter and the youngest son died in infancy.

A lithographed portrait of Judge Cushman at the age of 35 is given in the *Cushman Genealogy*.

He was "distinguished for his industry and abilities as a lawyer; widely known and respected as an eminent jurist; and in all the walks of life loved and honored for his unbending integrity and his moral and religious qualities."

It is believed he printed nothing, except a notable speech, delivered in Congress in 1818 on Internal Improvements

---

AUTHORITIES

Cushman Genealogy, 318–34, 540
Woodruff, Geneal Register of Litchfield, 219

LEONARD AUGUSTUS DAGGETT, the third child and eldest son of the Hon David Daggett (Yale 1783), of New Haven, was born on April 30, 1790

He read law in his father's office for a year after graduation, and then spent two or three years in New York City to qualify himself for mercantile pursuits, in which he was for several years engaged in New Haven.

He was married by his classmate and pastor, the Rev. Dr. Nathaniel W. Taylor, on September 12, 1819, to Jennette, daughter of Timothy and Susanna (Macomber) Atwater, of New Haven, who died on June 19, 1825, in her 27th year

From 1819 to 1823 he was a teacher in New Haven, and for the next ten years was engaged in foreign commerce in this city He then resumed the occupation of teaching a select school, in which he continued until 1850 After that date he was not actively engaged in any pursuit. As a teacher he was methodical, thorough, and practical.

On May 13, 1853, he was married in New York, by the Rev. Dr. Gardiner Spring, to Julia, an elder sister of his former wife, and the widow of George Raymond, of New York.

In 1862 he was attacked with paralysis, from the effects of which he suffered until his death.

He died in New Haven on April 26, 1867, aged 77 years. His widow died here on July 6, 1883, in her 89th year.

By his first wife he had two sons and two daughters. The younger son died in infancy, and the elder was graduated at Yale in 1839, and in turn left three sons who were graduates

---

AUTHORITIES

Atwater Hist, 144, 195. Doggett-Daggett Family, 154, 202-03.

JOHN DENNISTON, a grandson of Alexander Denniston, who emigrated from Longford, Ireland, in 1731, to the village of Little Britain, in New Windsor, Orange County, New York, was born in New Windsor on December 14, 1778, and was at graduation the oldest in his class. He united with the Presbyterian Church just before entering College.

At the time of graduation he was in feeble health, but as far as health would permit he devoted himself to a course of study for the ministry

He died at his home on January 13, 1810, in his 32d year, and was buried in the churchyard of Bethlehem meeting-house, in the adjoining township of Cornwall His death was the first in the class.

DAVID RAYMOND DIXON, son of Major Joseph Dixon, of Manchester, Vermont, and grandson of Archibald Dixon, of Pomfret and Bethlehem, Connecticut, was born in Manchester on July 4, 1783 A brother was graduated here in 1813. Their mother was Mercy Raymond, of Kent, Connecticut

In 1795 his family removed to Sherburne, in Chenango County, New York, and he was prepared for admission to the Junior Class at Yale by the Rev. Robert Porter (Yale 1795), in the Academy which afterwards became Hamilton College

A year or two after graduation he opened a school in Utica, New York, which proved very successful He married there, on November 13, 1809, Nancy Taft, two of whose sisters had already married in Utica.

She died in 1811, leaving a son, who survived both parents.

While teaching, Mr. Dixon was also chosen an elder in the Presbyterian Church, and pursued theological studies under the direction of the pastor, the Rev James Carnahan (Princeton Coll 1800)

He left Utica in 1813, and on October 6 married Elizabeth, daughter of the Rev John Sergeant, Junior, the Indian missionary of the neighboring town of Vernon.

About this date he was licensed to preach, and went as a missionary to Oswego County, where he was ordained and installed in 1815 as pastor of the Presbyterian Church in Mexico This relation existed for nearly twenty years, during which period he performed a great amount of pioneer missionary labor. After a brief interval of similar labor in the Province of Ontario, Canada, he removed to Tipton, in Southern Michigan, and a few years later to Unadilla, about twenty-five miles north of Tipton, where he remained until his death. During nearly all this latter portion of his life he was an industrious colporteur of the American Tract Society. On the division of the Presbyterian Church, he united with the New School

After the death of his second wife he married, in October, 1848, Mrs R. Joslin

He died from paralysis, after a brief illness, in Unadilla, on June 24, 1861, at the age of 78

By his second marriage he had two daughters and two sons, of whom only one son, a graduate of Hamilton College in 1837, survived him

He was a man of good common sense, of sound learning, and of most estimable religious character.

AUTHORITIES.

Bagg, Pioneers of Utica, 268 *J R. Dixon,* MS Letter, September, 1861 *Hatch,* Hist. of Sherburne, 64. Presbyterian Historical Almanac, 1863, 295

WILLIAM DUBOSE was born in St Stephen's Parish, South Carolina, in 1787 His father, Samuel Dubose, a planter in that parish, about forty miles north of

Charleston, was descended from a Huguenot refugee. He was prepared for College by the Rev Dr. David Ely (Yale 1769), of Huntington, Connecticut His youngest brother was graduated here in 1825

He was admitted to an *ad eundem* Bachelor's degree at the South Carolina College in 1808

He spent his life on his plantation, and would have preferred to avoid public life. He was, however, repeatedly a member of both houses of the State Legislature, and in 1836–37 Lieutenant Governor. He repeatedly declined to accept a nomination for Congress

He died at St. Stephen's after a protracted illness, on February 24, 1855, in his 68th year

---

JOHN DUNWODY, one of twin sons of Dr. James Dunwody, or Dinwiddie, of Liberty County, Georgia, and a descendant of John Dinwiddie, of Londonderry, Ireland, was baptized on January 15, 1786 He entered College at the opening of Sophomore year. His father died in the year of his graduation. His mother was Esther Dean, widow of Benjamin Splatt. An elder sister married the Hon. John Elliott (Yale 1794)

He settled in Midway in Liberty County as a planter, and married very early Jane, daughter of Captain James and Ann (Irvine) Bulloch

He was a deacon in the Midway Congregational Church from 1836 until his removal a year or two later to Cobb County in the northern part of the State.

His home was in Roswell, a few miles north of Atlanta, where he aided in 1839 in organizing a Presbyterian Church, of which he was for seventeen years a Ruling Elder; he was also Superintendent of the Sabbath School.

He died in Roswell, on June 6, 1858, in his 73d year, after a protracted and painful illness.

His wife died about two years before him.

AUTHORITIES

Bulloch, Stewart, Elliott and Dunwody Families, 21 Midway Church Records, 117. *Stacy*, Hist of Midway Church, 262

Henry Field, of Newburgh, New York, entered College at the opening of the Junior year. He was probably born in 1788.

Nothing is known of his later history.

James Fowler, the eldest child of the Hon. Samuel Fowler (Yale 1768), of Westfield, Massachusetts, by his second wife, Jemima Lyman, was born in Westfield, on January 4, 1789.

After graduation he began to read law with the Hon. Jonathan Leavitt (Yale 1785), of Greenfield, and in 1808 continued his studies with John Ingersoll (Yale 1790), of Westfield, and in the Litchfield Law School. Finally he spent a short time in the office of Elijah Bates (Yale 1794), of Westfield, and was admitted to the Hampshire County Bar in the fall of 1810 He practiced his profession, however, but little, preferring agricultural pursuits.

He was originally a Democrat, but eventually became a Republican. Besides being repeatedly a member of the lower house of the State Legislature, he was sent to the Senate in 1822, 1823, 1824, 1828, 1829, and 1840, and was also one of the Governor's Council for two years (1825 to 1827).

He was especially interested in the promotion of education, and from 1826 to 1838 served as a Trustee of Amherst College. He and his wife opened and conducted the first evening school in Westfield.

He was very active in securing the transfer of the State Normal School to Westfield in 1844, giving the land on which the buildings were to stand. He also gave a public park to the town.

He was the first President of the Hampden Bank. He was known as a staunch advocate of temperance, and was in every way respected for his worth and integrity. At the Bi-centennial Celebration in Westfield, in 1869, although then an octogenarian, he presided with great dignity.

He survived all his classmates, dying in Westfield on October 18, 1873, in his 85th year.

He married on February 9, 1820, Lucy, daughter of Major Thomas James Douglas, of Westfield

She died on July 16, 1840, in her 49th year; and he next married, on October 6, 1841, Charlotte, daughter of Captain Silas and Mamre (Bradley) Whitney, of Stockbridge. She was born in September, 1804.

By his first marriage he had one son, who was graduated at Yale in 1839, and one daughter

AUTHORITIES

Boltwood, Noble Genealogy, 585-86 *Coleman,* Lyman Family, 453. *Pierce,* Whitney Genealogy, 170

ROBERT SMITH GARDINER, the only son of Dr Nathaniel Gardiner, of East-Hampton, Long Island, and grandson of Colonel Abraham and Mary (Smith) Gardiner, was born on September 10, 1786 His mother was Elizabeth, only daughter of Thomas and Mary (Sylvester) Dering, of Shelter Island, and sister of Henry Packer Dering (Yale 1784) Dr Nicoll H. Dering (Yale 1813) was a first cousin

He died on January 19, 1824, in his 38th year He was never married.

AUTHORITIES.

Hedges, Hist. of East-Hampton, 281 *Mallmann,* Shelter Island, 177

RICHARD EDWARDS GOODWIN, the eldest son of George and Mary (Edwards) Goodwin, of Hartford, Connecticut, and a brother of George Goodwin of the previous Class, was born in Hartford on December 7, 1782, and was prepared for the Sophomore Class at the Hartford Grammar School.

On graduation he became associated with the firm of Hudson & Goodwin, of which his father was a member. In 1815 this firm was succeeded in the bookselling, printing and publishing business by the new firm of George Goodwin & Sons.

He died in Hartford on February 18, 1838, in his 56th year.

He married, on December 29, 1810, Ruth, eldest daughter of Thomas Bull, of Hartford, and sister of Thomas Bull, of the previous Class She died in Hartford on July 25, 1835, in her 46th year.

Their children, three sons and two daughters, all lived to maturity.

He was Major of the Foot Guards from 1816 to 1819, and a remarkably handsome man, of genial manners and social nature.

AUTHORITIES.

Goodwin Family, 645-47 *Hinman,* Early Puritan Settlers of Conn, 396

Thomas Smith Grimké, the second in a family of fourteen children of Judge John Faucheraud Grimké, of Charleston, South Carolina, and grandson of John Paul Grimké, was born on September 22, 1786. The Grimké family were German by descent, and his paternal grandmother's family was French Huguenot. His mother was Mary (or Polly), second daughter of Thomas and Sarah (Moore) Smith, of Charleston, and a descendant of Thomas Smith, one of the early Landgraves of Carolina A brother was graduated here in 1810, and a sister married the Rev Thomas D. Frost (Yale 1813).

He completed the course in the Charleston College, and in 1804 entered on the study of law in the office of John Julius Pringle, then Attorney General of South

Carolina. Here he met two recent Yale graduates, and was so much struck with their advancement that he suspended his law studies and prepared for entrance into the Junior Class here in the fall of 1805.

On his return from Yale he desired to study for the ministry, but yielded to his father's wishes, and continued his preparation for the bar

After his admission to the bar, in May, 1809, he practiced his profession in Charleston with distinguished success

He was also prominent in political life, and a member of the State Senate in 1826–30

He was a pioneer in the temperance reformation, and one of the most prominent members of the American Peace Society Though a sound classical scholar himself, he was opposed to the domination of the classics in education, and urged the substitution of the Bible as a text-book. He was one of the earliest advocates of reformed spelling, as a means of simplifying education, and used his method in his own publications after 1833.

In the interest of these and kindred reforms he was lavish in the use of his time and his means, and benevolence and piety may be named as his most marked characteristics His strength was given without stint to the advancement of Christian principle as he viewed it

In the fall of 1834 he went to Ohio to fulfil several engagements for addresses, and to visit his brother On October 10 he left Cincinnati to meet his brother at his residence in Columbus; but was attacked with the cholera on the 11th, and was taken from the stage, when about twenty-four miles from his destination, to the house of a Mr. Anderson at Gwynn's Farm, where he died the following morning, at the age of 48 He was buried in Columbus. A sermon occasioned by his death and preached in Charleston (probably by Bishop Gadsden, Yale 1804) was printed in the *Gospel Messenger*, volume 11, December, 1834.

He married, on January 25, 1810, Sarah Daniel Drayton, of Charleston, who died on July 23, 1867

Their children were six sons The second became an Episcopal clergyman, and the third a physician.

An engraving from his portrait is given in Donald G. Mitchell's *American Lands and Letters*

The honorary degree of Doctor of Laws was conferred on him by Yale in 1830

He published

1. Oration on the Character of the accomplished Orator, before the Charleston Moot Society, 28th January, 1809. Charleston, 1809. 8°, pp 32.

2 An Oration delivered in St Philip s Church, before the Inhabitants of Charleston, on the 4th of July, 1809, by the appointment of the South-Carolina State Society of Cincinnati, and published at the request of that Society, and of the American Revolution Society Charleston, 1809 8°, pp. 53

[*A A S A C. A B Ath B. Publ Columbia Univ M H. S. N Y. Publ Y. C.*

On the absolute necessity of Union, and the folly and madness of disunion.

For a second edition, see below, No 9

3 Report to Vestry of St Philip's on the establishment of a Monument Fund 1825

4. An Oration, on the Practicability and Expediency of reducing the whole body of the law to the simplicity and order of a Code: Delivered in the City-Hall, before the South-Carolina Bar Association on Saturday, the 17th March, 1827, being the Anniversary Charleston, 1827. 8°, pp 31

[*B. Ath M H. S N Y Publ U T S Y C*

5 An Address, on the Character and Objects of Science and, especially, the Influence of the Reformation on the science and literature, past, present and future, of Protestant Nations. delivered in the First Presbyterian Church, on Wednesday the 9th of May, being the Anniversary of the Literary and Philosophical Society of South-Carolina Charleston, 1827. 8°, pp. 80

[*A A. S A C. A B Ath B Publ Harv Y C*

6. Report.—South-Carolina. To the Honorable the President, and other Members of the Senate of the said State. . . —On the practicability and expediency of a Code of the Statute and Common Law of this State. . Columbia, 1827. 8°, pp. 26.

[*A. A. S. B. Ath. B. Publ. Harv. Y. C.*

Signed by Thos. S. Grimké, Chairman Pro Tem. Dated November 7, 1827.

7. Report on the Bank of the State of South-Carolina. December, 1827. Columbia. 8°, pp. 8.

8. Origin of Rhyme.

Two articles, in the *Southern Review*, vol. 2, pp. 31–72, and vol. 3, pp. 156–92 (August, 1828, and February, 1829).

9. Speech of T. S. Grimké, one of the Senators from St. Philip's and St. Michael's, delivered in the Senate of South Carolina, in December, 1828, during the debate on Sundry Resolutions, of the Senate and House of Representatives, respecting the Tariff.

Prefixed to this speech is a reprint of the author's Oration, delivered on 4, July, 1809. Charleston, 1829. 8°, pp. 32 + 120.

[*A. C. A. B. Ath. M. H. S. U. S. Y. C.*

Included are, also, his Protest against the Report and Resolutions of the Special Committee appointed 27th Nov., 1827, and his Resolutions submitted to the Senate, 12th December, 1828, bearing on the relations of the State to the Federal Government.

10. Address at the Dedication of the building in Chalmers Street, designed as a depository for Bibles, Tracts, and Sunday School Books, and for the Anniversary Celebrations of Religious Societies, delivered on Wednesday evening, April 8, 1829. Charleston. 8°, pp. 32 + 1.

[*A. A. S. A. C. A. B. Ath. Harv. M. H. S. Y. C.*

11. Address on the expediency and duty of adopting the Bible as a Class Book: in every science of education, from the Primary School to the University: delivered at Columbia, S. C., in the Presbyterian Church, on Friday Evening, 4th of December, 1829, before the Richland School. Charleston. 8°, pp. 96.

[*A. A. S. A. C. A. B. Ath. B. Publ. Columbia Univ. Harv. M. H. S. Y. C.*

12. Oration on the Advantages, to be derived from the Introduction of the Bible, and of Sacred Literature, as essential parts of all education, in a literary point of view merely, from the Pri-

mary School, to the University: delivered before the Connecticut Alpha of the Φ B K Society, on Tuesday, September 7, 1830 New Haven, 1830 8°, pp. 76

[*A A S A. C. A B Ath B. Publ. Harv. M H. S Philad. Libr. Co. U T S Y. C.*

13 Address, at a Meeting in Charleston, South Carolina, held March 29, 1831, to consider the resolution of the American Sunday School Union, respecting Sunday Schools in the Valley of the Mississippi Philadelphia, 1831. 8°, pp. 15.

[*A A S A. C A. B Ath. Br Mus. Harv. U. T. S. Y. C*

14 Sunday School Jubilee.—Address at the Celebration of the Sunday School Jubilee or the 50th year from the Institution of Sunday Schools, by Robert Raikes delivered at Charleston, S C., in the Hall of the Sunday School Depository, on Wednesday Evening, 14th of September, 1831 Charleston, 1831 8°, pp 20

[*A A. S. B. Ath C H S. Harv N. Y. H. S Y C.*

The same Philadelphia, 1832. 8°, pp 20 [*B Ath Y. C*

15 Reflections on the Character and Objects of all Science and Literature, and on the relative excellence and value of Religious and Secular Education, and of Sacred and Classical Literature: in two Addresses and an Oration with additions and improvements With an Appendix containing a letter, on the study of the Bible, to the Committee appointed by the Literary Convention, held at New York, Oct 20, 1830, and an address, delivered at Charleston (S. C.), at the dedication of a building designed as a depository for Bibles, Tracts and Sunday School Books, and for anniversary celebrations of Religious Societies New Haven, 1831. 12°, pp xii, 201.

[*A A. S. A C A. B. Ath. B. Publ. Br. Mus Columbia Univ. Harv U. T. S. Y C.*

Including a reprint of Nos 5, 10, 11, and 12.

16 A Letter to the Honorable John C Calhoun, Vice-President of the United States, Robert Y. Hayne, Senator of the United States, George McDuffie, of the House of Representatives of the United States, and James Hamilton, Jr., Governor of the State of South Carolina. Philadelphia, 1832 8°, pp. 17.

[*A A S B. Publ Br. Mus. N. Y. Publ. Libr. Y. C.*

The same. Second edition Charleston, 1832 8°, pp. 15

[*B. Ath Harv M. H S. N Y Publ Libr. Y. C.*

17. Address on the truth, dignity, power and beauty of the Principles of Peace, and on the unchristian character and influence of War and the Warrior: delivered in the Centre Church at New-Haven, during the session of the Legislature of Connecticut, at the request of the Connecticut Peace Society, on Sunday Evening, the 6th of May, 1832 Hartford, 1832. 8°, pp. 56.

[*A A S. A. C. A. B. Ath. B. Publ Br Mus. C. H. S. Columbia Univ. Harv M. H S U S. U. T. S. Y. C.*

Also, Philadelphia, 1834

18. Oration on the duties of youth, to instructors and themselves: on the Importance of the Art of Speaking, and of Debating Societies. delivered by appointment, before the Euphradian Society of the College of Charleston, on Monday, 13th August, 1832, in the College Chapel Charleston, 1832 8°, pp 28

[*A C A B. Ath. B. Publ. Harv. M H. S Y C.*

19. A Letter to the People of South-Carolina Charleston, 1832. 8°, pp 16

[*A. A S. B. Ath M. H S N Y H. S. U S Y. C*

Inside title, To the People of the State of South-Carolina

There are two editions, differing slightly in arrangement

A solemn remonstrance against nullification

20. Correspondence on the Principles of Peace, Manual Labor Schools, &c Charleston, 1833 8°, pp. 16 [*B Ath. Y C.*

21. Address on the patriot character of the Temperance Reformation· delivered before the Charleston Temperance Society, and the Young Men's Temperance Society of Charleston, on Tuesday Evening, 26th February, 1833, in the First Presbyterian Church, Charleston Charleston, 1833 8°, pp 35.

[*A. C. A M. H. S N. Y H. S Philad Libr Co. Y. C.*

22. Letter, to a friend in Albany, on Temperance [1833] 8°, pp. 10 [*B. Ath. Y. C.*

23 An Essay on the appropriate use of the Bible, in common education Prepared for the American Lyceum Charleston, 1833. 8°, pp 16.

[*A A. S. A C. A B Ath. B. Publ Harv. M. H. S. Y. C.*

24. Oration on the Principal Duties of Americans; delivered before the Washington Society, and other citizens of Charleston;

in the Second Presbyterian Church, on Thursday the 4th of July ... Charleston, 1833. 8°, pp 39.

[*A. C. A B Ath B Publ Harv N. Y Publ Philad Libr Co U T. S Y C*

25 The Temperance Reformation the Cause of Christian Morals—An Address delivered before the Charleston Temperance Society and the Young Men's Temperance Society, of Charleston, on Tuesday Evening, February 25th, 1834, in St Stephen's Chapel Charleston, 1834 8°, pp 26

[*B. Ath. Columbia Univ M H S U T S. Y C*

26 Address on the power and value of the Sunday School System in evangelizing heathen and re-constructing Christian communitys, by an improvement of the religion and morals, the education and literature, and the social, civil and political institutions of evry people, and on the Southern enterprise of the American Sunday School Union Delivered in the Lutheran Church, City of Charleston, on Monday Evening, March 17, 1834 Philadelphia, 1834. 8°, pp 34

[*A C A B. Ath Columbia Univ Harv Y C*

27 Argument, delivered in the Court of Appeals of the State of South-Carolina, before the Hon David Johnson & William Harper; on the 2d and 3d April, 1834 in the case of the State, ex relatione Edward McCrady, against Col B. F Hunt; on the Constitutionality of the Oath in the Act for the Military Organization of this State, passed 19th December, 1833 With . Statement of the Case Charleston, 1834 8°, pp 28

[*A A S B Publ U T S. Y C*

An argument against the imposition of a special oath of allegiance to the State of South Carolina, as subversive of the oath to the United States

28 Address of the Literary and Philosophical Society of South-Carolina, to the People of the State, on the Classification, Character, and Exercises, or the Objects and Advantages of the Lyceum System, with a view to its general introduction into our Towns, Villages, and the Country at large Charleston, 1834 8°, pp 56

[*B. Ath Y C.*

Signed by a committee of three persons, of whom Mr. Grimké was chairman

The three following articles were furnished by the author for the press, but were not published until after his death:

29 Oration on the comparative elements and dutys of Grecian and American Eloquence. Delivered before the Erodelphian Society of Miami University, at Oxford, Ohio, on the 23d of September, 1834· being their ninth anniversary celebration, with notes Cincinnati, 1834 8°, pp 58

[*B Ath. Br Mus Columbia Univ Harv. M H. S N Y H. S U S. Y. C.*

30 Oration on American Education, delivered before the Western Literary Institute and College of Professional Teachers, at their fourth annual meeting, October, 1834. Cincinnati, 1835 8°, pp 43

[*A. A S. B Ath Columbia Univ Harv. Y C.*

The special subject is, "that neither the classics nor the mathematics should form part of a scheme of general education in our country"

31 Defensive War

In the *Calumet,* vol 2, pp 140–51, 165–80, January–April, 1835.

In his Senior year in College he was one of the editors of the *Literary Cabinet* (see above, p 83); but his contributions have not been identified

He translated from the French Merle d'Aubigné's *Discourse on the study of the History of Christianism,* Charleston, 1833, 8°, pp 24, and he edited, with Notes, Dymond's *Inquiry into the Accordancy of War with the Principles of Christianity,* published by his sisters after his death, Philadelphia, 1834, 12°

AUTHORITIES

The Calumet, ii, 129–56 *Fraser,* Reminiscences of Charleston, 79–80 *Mitchell,* Amer Lands and Letters, ii, 122–26 *O'Neall,* Bench and Bar of S C, ii, 378–89 S C Hist and Geneal Magazine, iv, 50, 68 *J H Smith,* Eulogium on T S Grimke

---

Ebenezer Grosvenor, third son and child of Lemuel and Eunice (Avery) Grosvenor, of Brooklyn or Pomfret, Connecticut, was born on July 26, 1788.

He entered College at the opening of the Sophomore year

He studied law, and settled in practice in Pomfret.

He died on November 10, 1817, in his 30th year, and was buried in Trinity churchyard, Brooklyn.

AMOS POTTER HALL, of Lanesborough, Massachusetts, probably a son of Joseph and Dorcas (Potter) Hall, was a member of Williams College for the first three years of the course. He also received an *ad eundem* degree from Williams College in 1807

He practiced law in his native town, and died, very suddenly, in Rutland, on June 13, 1813, aged 27 years The notice of his death states that he was dancing at a ball the night before.

AUTHORITIES

Columbian Centinel, June 23, 1813

DAVID HANFORD, son of Stephen Hanford, of that part of Norwalk now included in Westport, Connecticut, and grandson of Phineas and Hannah (Comstock) Hanford, of Norwalk, was born on July 16, 1786 His mother was Phebe, daughter of Elijah and Phebe (Smith) Fitch, of Norwalk. He did not enter College until after the opening of the Sophomore year.

Upon graduation he studied medicine, and settled in 1810 in the village of Middletown, in the southern part of the township of Walkill, Orange County, New York, where he enjoyed an extensive practice, until his death there on October 13, 1844, in his 59th year.

He was for many years a Ruling Elder in the Presbyterian Church

He married in 1812, Margaret, daughter of Captain Daniel Bailey, of Phillipsburg, in the same township. Several children survived him

AUTHORITIES

Hall, Hist. of Norwalk, 296 N Y Observer, Nov 9, 1844. *Ruttenber and Clark*, Hist of Orange County, 167–68 *Selleck*, Norwalk, 262.

Luther Hart, son of David Hart, a house-carpenter, of Wallingford and Goshen, Connecticut, was born in Goshen on July 27, 1783 His mother was Hannah Hudson, from Long Island. In his boyhood the family removed to the adjoining town of Torrington, and in 1799 he became interested in personal religion and joined the Congregational Church About the end of 1802 he began his preparation for College under his pastor, the Rev Alexander Gillet (Yale 1770) At graduation he delivered an Oration on Originality.

The first year after graduation, he spent as teacher in James Morris's Academy in Litchfield South Farms He then began his theological studies under the direction of the Rev. Dr. Ebenezer Porter (Dartmouth Coll. 1792), of Washington

In September, 1808, the Theological Seminary at Andover was opened, and Mr. Hart spent the greater part of the first year there. He was licensed to preach by the Essex Middle Association, and after a short interval, he was invited to preach in Plymouth, Connecticut, and was ordained and installed there, on September 5, 1810,—the sermon on that occasion being preached by Dr. Porter. His annual salary was fixed at $500, in 1832 it was raised to $600

On September 18, 1811, he married Minerva, only daughter of General Daniel Potter (Y. C. 1780), of Plymouth.

His preaching was simple, clear, and sententious, and was accompanied by four or five general revivals of religion About 420 members were added to the church during the twenty-four years of his ministry

In September, 1829, he was elected a Fellow of Yale College.

After a week's illness from lung fever, he died at his home in Plymouth, on April 25, 1834, in his 51st year. The sermon preached at his funeral by the Rev. Noah

Porter (Yale 1803) was substantially printed in the *Quarterly Christian Spectator* for the following September.

Mrs Hart died in 1882, at the age of 92 Their only child, a son, died in infancy

A portrait of Mr. Hart is reproduced in Atwater's *History of Plymouth,* and in Griggs's *Reminiscences of Elam Fenn*

The inscription placed over his grave says:

As a Preacher he was discriminating in doctrine, vivid in illustration, pungent in application as a Pastor, watchful, active, and faithful in reproof, yet rejoicing rather to bind up the broken-hearted Among the clergy, wise in counsel, efficient in action: in the common relations of life affectionate and modest, respected and beloved

Dr Porter says of him·

Together with rich and various learning, and habits strictly intellectual, he had an uncommon measure of native sagacity,—a kind of intuitive discernment of character,—and quick sense of propriety He had also a lovely temper, and a warm, tender, and generous heart . The quality, however, which, more than almost any other, was prominent in him, and will most readily suggest itself to his acquaintances with the mention of his name, was his sprightliness of fancy, his aptness for pleasant and humorous associations, and delicately keen and pithy satire

He published:

1 Salvation for lost men a Christmas Sermon [from Matt xviii, 11], preached December 25th, 1817 Hartford, 1818 8°, pp 32

[*A C A Br Mus C H S. N Y Publ Y C*

2 Plain Reasons for relying on Presbyterian Ordination. In a letter to a friend. [New-Haven, 1818] 12°, pp 43

[*C. H S U T S. Y C*

Anonymous, with signature Z A., being No 3 of *Tracts, designed to illustrate and enforce the most important Doctrines of the Gospel* Answered, anonymously, by the Rev Bethel Judd

3 The Gospel Ministry a display of Divine Benevolence—A Sermon [from Eph iv, 11-12], delivered at Watertown, Con, at

the Installation of the Rev Darius O Griswold, January 19, 1825. Hartford, 1825 8°, pp. 28
[*A. C. A Br. Mus C. H. S N Y Publ U. T S. Y C.*

4 A Sermon [from Ps xlvi, 10], delivered at Torrington, Lord's Day, Jan 22, 1826, at the Funeral of the Rev. Alexander Gillett: together with a Memoir of his life and character New-Haven, 1826 8°, pp. 41 [*Br Mus Y C*

5. A Memoir of the life of the Rev Amos Pettengill, late Pastor of the Congregational Church in Waterbury (Salem), Con — Written for the Massachusetts Sabbath School Society . Boston, 1834. 12°, pp, 264 [*A C A Harv.*

The series of *Tracts* referred to above, under No. 2, led to the establishment of a monthly periodical at New Haven, in 1819, called the *Christian Spectator*, in which Mr. Hart took a lively interest, and to some of the first volumes of which he was a principal contributor. This was succeeded, in 1829, by the *Quarterly Christian Spectator*, for which he furnished a number of important articles; of these may be specified, an important series on the religious declensions and revivals in New England, as follows

Review on the Early History of the Congregational Churches of New-England, vol 2, pp. 321–38 (June, 1830).

Review of Bellamy's True Religion Delineated, same, pp 397–424; Review of Bellamy on the Permission of Sin, pp 529–40 (September, 1830).

A View of the Religious Declension in New England, and of its Causes, during the latter half of the eighteenth Century, vol 5, pp. 207–37 (June, 1833).

Character and Writings of Dr Strong; same. pp 337–63 (September, 1833).

AUTHORITIES

Atwater, Hist of Plymouth, 30, 40–41 *Bronson*, Hist of Waterbury, 303–96 *Davis*, Hist. of Wallingford, 526–27. *Griggs*, Reminiscences of E. Fenn, 19–20, 36–38 *Hibbard*, Hist of Goshen, 198–201 Litchfield County Consociation Centennial, 124–27 *E. Lyman*, Farewell Sermon, 18–20, 38–39 *Orcutt*, Hist of Torrington, 43, 471–73, 544–47 Quarterly Christian Spectator, vi, 475–96 *Sprague*, Annals of the Amer Pulpit, ii, 523–26 Tuttle Family, 68

JAMES HOWARD, Junior, the eldest child of James Howard, of Hampton, Windham County, Connecticut, and grandson of John and Sarah (Bennett) Howard, of Hampton, was born on October 25, 1783. His mother was Sarah, daughter of Deacon Benjamin Chaplin, Junior, and Mary (Paine, Ross) Chaplin, of Mansfield. He was prepared for College under John Adams (Yale 1795) in the Plainfield Academy.

After graduation he studied law, and settled in his native town, where at the time of his early death he had already given promise of eminence at the bar.

He represented the town in the General Assembly at the session of October, 1810; but died on the 11th of the following February, in Hampton, in his 28th year. He was unmarried.

AUTHORITIES.

Howard Genealogy (1884), 191-92.

ARÆTIUS BEVIL HULL, the only surviving child of Dr. Amzi Hull, of Woodbridge, Connecticut, and grandson of Captain Miles and Eunice (Hull) Hull, of Cheshire, was born on October 12, 1788. His mother was Mary Ann, youngest daughter of Janus and Margaret (Dixon) Kasson, of Bethlehem. Dr. Hull died in 1795, and his widow married in 1800 Captain Gideon Leavenworth, of Huntington, where her son was prepared for College by the Rev. Dr. David Ely (Yale 1769). His course was overshadowed by pecuniary embarrassments, and by a first attack of pulmonary disease in his Senior year.

He taught in Wethersfield for a short time after graduation, but was then obliged on account of threatening consumption to seek a Southern climate.

Returning with improved health in the fall of 1810, he accepted a tutorship in the College, which he held with credit for six years. At the end of this period, he was licensed to preach by the New Haven West Association of Ministers, on October 8, 1816, and was married by his classmate Taylor, on May 5, 1817, to Abigail Elizabeth, daughter of Dr Joseph Darling (Yale 1777), of New Haven.

He found occupation as a preacher for longer or shorter periods in various places, as in Brookfield, Connecticut, from October, 1819, to October, 1820

Early in 1821 he was invited with substantial unanimity to the pastorate of the First Church in Worcester, Massachusetts, where he was ordained and installed on May 23, 1821. His classmate Taylor preached the sermon on this occasion.

In May, 1825, a return of his former disease interrupted his labors, and his death followed, in Worcester, on May 17, 1826, in his 38th year. The sermon delivered at his funeral by the Rev. John Nelson (Williams Coll. 1807), of Leicester, was afterwards published.

Mrs. Hull returned to New Haven, where her husband was buried, and died at her son's residence in Brooklyn, New York, on January 9, 1860, at the age of 70.

Their children were four sons and two daughters.

The eldest child was graduated at Yale in 1837, and became a clergyman. The youngest (posthumous) son died in infancy. Charles A Hull (Yale 1869) is a grandson

A monument was erected to Mr. Hull's memory in Worcester, and the inscription is, in part, as follows:

He endeared himself to the people of his charge by his affectionate and assiduous devotion to his ministerial and pastoral duties, while the sauvity of his manners, the purity of his life, and the sincerity and earnestness of his efforts in advancing the cause of education, and in the promotion of the general interests of the community, commanded its respect and gratitude.

He was a scholar of refined taste, and the style of his discourses was unusually chaste and perspicuous, earnest and direct, harmonizing with the tenor of his life, and being rendered yet more impressive, during the greater part of his ministry, by his conscious and evident nearness to the grave.

Accustomed to the best forms of polished life, he was dignified without display, and courteous without dissimulation, constantly manifesting in his private intercourse and his public labours, that for himself and others he sought first the Kingdom of Heaven

The Rev. Dr. William B. Sprague, who was in College during a part of Mr. Hull's tutorship, speaks of his courtly and polished manners, and adds:

He was a person of an uncommonly attractive exterior,—small but well-formed, with a face expressive of great intelligence, and manners that combined simplicity and dignity in an unusual degree He had a highly cultivated taste, and wrote in a classical and elegant style

The only composition of his which I have seen in print is.

The Providence of God a Sermon [from Matth. x, 29], delivered to the First Church in Worcester. .

In E Smalley's *Worcester Pulpit*, 1851, pp. 205–19.

AUTHORITIES

Centennial Commemoration of 1st Parish Meeting House, Worcester, 72, 95, 97–99 Leavenworth Family, 105, 107 *Lincoln and Hersey*, Hist of Worcester, 162–63 *Smalley*, Worcester Pulpit, 198–219 *Sprague*, Annals of the Amer Pulpit, ii, 593–94 Tuttle Family, 507.

DANIEL HUNTINGTON, the third son of General Jedidiah Huntington (Harvard 1763), of Norwich, Connecticut, and a younger brother of the Rev Joshua Huntington (Yale 1804), was born in Norwich on October 17, 1788, but his family removed to New London in his infancy, and he was prepared for College by John Adams (Yale 1795) at Bacon Academy, in Colchester His College residence was interrupted in his Freshman year, and he was subsequently for a time a member of Brown University; but he was admitted to a degree here and ranked with his Class in 1816.

He united by profession of faith with the First Church of New London in February, 1809, and after a course of theological study, chiefly with the Rev. Dr Joel Benedict, of Plainfield, he was licensed to preach by the New

London Association of Ministers in 1811, and then spent several months in the Andover Theological Seminary as a Resident Licentiate.

Early in the spring of 1812 he began to supply the pulpit of the North or Fourth Congregational Church in Bridgewater, Massachusetts, and received a unanimous call from the church on July 13 His salary was fixed at $700, and on July 21 he was married to Mary Hallam, daughter of Captain Gurdon and Hannah (Sage) Saltonstall, of New London

He accepted the call on September 14, and was ordained and installed over the Church in the parish of North Bridgewater on October 28. In 1821 the precinct became the town of North Bridgewater, the name of which was changed to Brockton in 1874

His wife died in June, 1822, and he next married, on October 28, 1823, Alma, daughter of Benjamin and Sally French, of Boston.

He continued at his post with growing acceptableness, until obliged to retire by the state of his health, which had failed gradually from overwork during an unusual religious interest extending over two or three years. He was dismissed by a council on March 27, 1833 The church had received two hundred and fifty-three members under his ministry.

He removed in May, 1833, to New London, and soon undertook the instruction of successive classes of young ladies in the higher branches, in the Female Academy there.

He also in 1835 resumed occasional preaching, and after having during two years supplied in part the Second Congregational Church of New London, an offshoot from the First Church, which was organized in 1835, he was hoping to become their pastor, when his plans were overthrown by the death of his wife on June 3, 1837.

As returning health permitted him to engage again in preaching, he was glad to accept, in November, 1839, an earnest call, on a salary of $600, from a new church which had been organized in the southern portion of his former field, in the district known as Campello, where he was installed on January 1, 1840, and where he spent some fruitful and happy years He saw reason, however, for offering his resignation in May, 1851, but was induced to withdraw it.

He was again married, on November 1, 1841, to Sarah Sayr Rainey, of New London.

In April, 1853, the parish requested his resignation, and he was accordingly dismissed, to the great grief of the most of his flock, on May 11

During the remainder of his life while living in New London, he continued to preach occasionally, down to the last.

He died in New London, after a painful illness, on May 21, 1858, in his 70th year His wife survived him.

By his first marriage he had three daughters, of whom the eldest died early. The second daughter married Alfred Hebard (Yale 1832). By his second marriage he had two sons and three daughters; two daughters died in infancy.

A portrait is given in the *History of North Bridgewater.*

The historian of North Bridgewater describes him as

> a man of refined sensibilities, generous sympathies, unfeigned humility, and extreme modesty, that imposed a restraint on the putting forth of his native genius. of pleasant aspect, voice, and manner, of genial humor, and gifted with good judgment . As a pastor, he had few equals, being eminently kind, sympathizing, prudent, and studious

He was a man of fine musical talent, and did much to elevate the standard of church music in the first part of his ministry.

He published:

1. A Sermon [from Ps. xxv, 16], delivered in the North Meeting-House in Bridgewater, May 12, 1812, at the Funeral of Mr.

Alpheus Packard, who died at Cohasset, May 10, 1812, being the day appointed for his marriage. Boston, 1812. 8°, pp. 14

[*A. A S B Publ M. H. S.*

2 A Discourse [from Phil. i, 21], delivered at Braintree, on Thursday, April 9, 1818, at the Funeral of Mrs Sarah Strong Storrs, wife of the Rev. Richard S Storrs. Boston, 1818. 8°, pp. 24. [*A. A. S A C. A B. Ath C. H. S. Y. C.*

3 A Poem, on the Pleasures and Advantages of True Religion, delivered before the United Brothers' Society, in Brown University, on their Anniversary, August 31, 1819 Providence, 1819. 12°, pp. 23.

[*B. Ath B Publ Brown Univ C H. S. M H. S U S Y. C.*

4 A Discourse [from Ps. xliv, 1-3], delivered in the North Meeting-house in Bridgewater, on Friday, Dec 22, 1820. Being the Second Centurial Anniversary of the Landing of the Pilgrims at Plymouth. Boston, 1812. 8°, pp 24

[*A. A S A. C. A B Publ. Y. C*

Largely occupied with the religious history of the town

5. A Discourse [from II Pet. 1, 5-8] delivered at the organization of the Trinitarian Congregational Church, in Taunton, Mass — Aug. 16, 1821 Boston, 1821 8°, pp 16.

[*A A. S. B. Ath B. Publ Br. Mus C H S U. T. S Y. C*

6 A Memoir of Mary Hallam Huntington Philadelphia (American Sunday School Union).

7. The Duty of Christians to the Jews — A Sermon [from Rom xi, 30-31], delivered at the annual meeting of the Palestine Missionary Society, in Halifax, Ms. June 18, 1823. Boston, 1823. 8°, pp 22, x

[*A. A. S. A C. A. B Publ Br Mus C. H. S. Y C*

8 A Sermon [from John xvii, 3], delivered before the Massachusetts Society for Promoting Christian Knowledge, on their Anniversary, May 26, 1824 Boston, 1824. 8°, pp 32.

[*A A. S A C. A. B Ath. B Publ Br Mus M H S U. T. S.*

The sermon occupies pp. 1-18

9 Religion and the Triumphs of Faith: Poems.—Delivered before Literary Societies Boston, 1830 12°, pp 40.

[*A. C A. Br Mus Brown Univ*

10 Address delivered at the Consecration of the Union Cemetery, at Oak Grove, North Bridgewater, Mass, May 21, 1849 8°, pp 8. [*A C A Br. Mus Harv*

11 Memoir of Loenza Howard. of North Bridgewater, Mass — Prepared for the Massachusetts Sabbath School Society Boston, 1850 12°, pp 36 [*A C. A*

12 Discourse [from Ez. xxxiii, 33] delivered at the Funeral of the Rev. Philip Colby, late Pastor of the Congregational Church, in North Middleborough, Mass March 3d, 1851 New Bedford, 1851. 8°, pp 18 [*A C A Harv.*

13 A Discourse [from Acts xxvi, 22] delivered in the South Church of North Bridgewater, October 31, 1852, being the fortieth anniversary of his Ordination Boston, 1853 8°, pp 24 [*A C. A B Ath B Publ*

He also published in the *Boston Recorder* for June 10, 1817, an Account of the Revival in Bridgewater in 1816

In Sprague's *Annals of the American Pulpit* are his brief reminiscences of the Rev Samuel Niles (Princeton Coll. 1769), vol 1, pp 715–16, and of his own brother Joshua, vol 2, pp 502–03.

AUTHORITIES

Blake, Early Hist of 1st Church, New London, 300–02 *Caulkins,* Hist. of N London, 623 *Crosby,* Annual Obit Notices, 1858, 173–74 *Everest,* Poets of Conn, 163–68. *Hill,* Hist of Old South Church, Boston, ii, 375 Huntington Family Memoir, 245–46, 324–25 *Kingman,* Hist of North Bridgewater, 28–34, 58–61, 137–39, 309, 329. Saltonstall Ancestry, 3, 41, 243–44 Starr's Repository, 1, 107, 111

WILLIAM JAY, of Huguenot descent, the second son of Chief-Justice John Jay (Columbia Coll. 1766), of New York City, and grandson of Peter and Mary (VanCortlandt) Jay, of New York, was born in New York on June 16, 1789 His mother was Sarah VanBrugh, eldest daughter of Governor William Livingston (Yale 1741), of Elizabeth, New Jersey

At an early age he was placed under the care of the Rev. Thomas Ellison (Oxford Univ. 1781), of Albany, for classical instruction, and at a later date Henry Davis

(Yale 1796) prepared him in New Haven for admission to the Freshman Class at Yale in January, 1804. On his entrance he occupied a room with Horace Holley (Yale 1803), then a student of theology. At graduation he delivered an Oration on Enthusiasm.

He injured his eyesight during Junior year by early morning study, and although after graduation he began the study of law in Albany, in the office of John B. Henry, the difficulty with his eyes interfered seriously, so that he was compelled to abandon his work in August, 1809.

On September 3, 1812, he married Hannah Augusta, the second daughter of John McVickar, a merchant of New York City, and his wife, Ann Moore.

During the period of his enforced retirement he resided at his father's country-seat, Bedford, in Westchester County, and there he entered on that career of active philanthropy which largely employed his time and thoughts for the next forty years. His earliest efforts were in behalf of temperance, in connection with the organization of the Society for the Suppression of Vice in Bedford

Another movement which enlisted his active support resulted in the formation of the American Bible Society in 1816

In May, 1818, he was appointed by Governor Tompkins an associate justice of the Westchester County Court, and two years later he was commissioned by Governor Clinton as Presiding Judge of the same court. Early in 1823, the adoption of the new State constitution terminated his tenure of office; but in response to a general demand, Governor Clinton recommissioned him as Judge, and he served until displaced in 1843 by Governor Bouck at the demand of pro-slavery democrats.

His father died in May, 1829, and the most of Judge Jay's leisure for the next four years was occupied in the preparation of the elder Jay's *Life and Writings*, published in 1833

In October, 1832, President Jackson appointed him a commissioner for the adjustment of all unsettled matters with the Western Indians; but he declined the appointment.

By this time he had become known as a vigorous opponent of slavery, and he emphasized his position by contributing to the first number (May 1, 1833) of the *Emancipator,* a new anti-slavery organ, a notable letter on the policy of the party. He held back, at first, from sympathy with the formation of anti-slavery societies, but in 1834 he consented to take office in the American Anti-Slavery Society, and in February, 1835, he published a powerful argument in their favor. Later he withdrew from the support of the Society, on account of its entanglement with new doctrines, and in 1840 he joined in the organization of the American and Foreign Antislavery Society, with a more limited scope. He declined in 1840 to allow the use of his name as candidate of the Liberty Party for the office of Governor of New York, though at a later date he supported that party, and in 1845 was their candidate for the Senate.

On his release from judicial duties in 1843 he made a long visit to Europe and Egypt for the benefit of his health He made another briefer visit to England in 1856

In the later period of his life the question of slavery and the promotion of peace were his chief interests He was the President of the American Peace Society from 1848 until his death.

After some two years of failing health from disease of the heart, he died at his residence in Bedford on October 14, 1858, in his 70th year.

His wife died on April 26, 1857, at the age of 67. Their children were five daughters and two sons The only surviving son, the Hon. John Jay, was graduated at Columbia College in 1836 Alexander Jay Bruen (Yale 1878) and William Livingston Bruen (Yale 1879) are grandsons.

Three portraits of Judge Jay are reproduced in Tuckerman's *William Jay and the Constitutional Movement for the Abolition of Slavery* (New York, 1893),—the only biographical volume which has been published. A eulogy delivered by Frederick Douglass in 1859 before the colored citizens of New York, and a discourse delivered by the Rev Dr George B Cheever before the American Peace Society, also deserve to be mentioned

He received the honorary degree of Doctor of Laws from Kenyon College in 1858

He was an able Judge, a skilful writer, fearless and keen in controversy, and a model of personal excellence.

He published:

1. On the Profession of Law

Nine articles, signed Coke, in the *Literary Cabinet,* a College bi-weekly periodical, published at New Haven in 1806–07: pp 11–14, 17–20, 27–30, 35–38, 41–43, 50–51, 59–61, 67–68, 83–84.

2. Circular Letter from the Committee of the Society for the Supression of Vice in the Town of Bedford, to the Venders of Ardent Spirits in the Town of Bedford and its immediate vicinity. [Dated May 1, 1815, and signed by Ebenezer Grant, President, and William Jay, Secretary] 8°, pp. 8. [*N. Y. H S.*

3. Address to Grocers and Venders of Ardent Spirits, in the City of New-York. [New-York, 1815.] 12°, pp 8. [*Y. C.*

Anonymous. Issued by the New-York State Temperance Society.

4. An Answer to Bishop Hobart's Pastoral Letter on the subject of Bible and Common Prayer-Book Societies —By an Episcopalian New-York, 1815. 8°, pp 16 [*B. Publ*

5. Memoir on the subject of a General Bible Society for the United States of America. By a Citizen of New York New Jersey, 1816 8°, pp 16

6. An Appeal to the Christians of America, in behalf of the American Bible Society, including a Defence of its Constitution: a number of facts, proving the necessity of its establishment: and an Answer to the Objections which have been made against it —By a Lay Member of the Convention which formed the Society. New-York, 1816. 8°, pp. 54. [*Y. C*

7. Dialogue between a Clergyman and a Layman on the subject of Bible Societies. By a Churchman. 1817.

8. Remarks on a Petition to the Legislature praying for the Repeal of the Acts for improving the Agriculture of this State. By a Westchester Farmer. 1821.

9. A Letter to the Right Reverend Bishop Hobart, occasioned by the Strictures on Bible Societies, contained in his late Charge to the Convention of New-York.—By a Churchman of the Diocese of New-York. New-York, 1823. 8°, pp. 80.

[*B. Ath. B. Publ. Br. Mus. Columbia Univ. N. Y. Publ. Y. C.*

This anonymous Letter was answered by Bishop Hobart in a much more acrimonious anonymous pamphlet.

10. A Letter to the Right Rev. Bishop Hobart, in reply to the Pamphlet addressed by him to the Author, under the signature of Corrector. New-York, 1823. 8°, pp. 33.

[*B. Ath. B. Publ. Br. Mus. Columbia Univ. Harv. N. Y. H. S. U. T. S. Y. C.*

This Letter, published over Mr. Jay's name, was again replied to anonymously by the Bishop.

11. A Reply to a Second Letter to the author; from the Right Rev. Bishop Hobart, with Remarks on his hostility to Bible Societies, and his mode of defending it. ... New-York, 1823. 8°, pp. 32.

[*B. Ath. Columbia Univ. N. Y. Publ. Y. C.*

This pamphlet appears to have closed the controversy.

12. Essay on the Importance of the Sabbath considered merely as a Civil Institution. 1826.

Written in response to an offer of the Presbyterian Synod of Albany of a prize for an essay on this subject.

13. Essay on the Perpetuity and Divine Authority of the Sabbath.

A second prize essay. This essay was printed, with another by the Rev. Samuel Nott, Junior, in a pamphlet in 1827. Albany. 8°, pp. 3-35.

[*A. C. A. B. Ath. Br. Mus. Columbia Univ. N. Y. H. S. U. T. S. Y. C.*

14. Remarks on the proposed changes in the Liturgy and Confirmation Service. 1827.

15. The Office of Assistant Bishop inconsistent with the Constitution of the Protestant Episcopal Church. 1829.

16. An Essay on Duelling. New-York, 1830. 8°, pp 29
[*N. Y. H S. Y. C.*

This anonymous essay was honored with a medal from an anti-duelling society in Savannah.

17 The Life of John Jay .. By his son New York, 1833. 2 vols. 8°, pp. viii, 520 + pl.; iii, 502.
[*A. A S. A. C A. B Ath. B. Publ Br Mus. Columbia Univ. Harv. M. H. S. N Y. H. S. N. Y. Publ. U. S Y C*

18 An Address to the inhabitants of West Chester County, New-York New-York, 1834. 8°, pp. 16. [*Y. C.*

On temperance, in his capacity as President of the County Temperance Society

19. An Inquiry into the Character and Tendency of the American Colonization and American Anti-Slavery Societies New-York, 1835. 12°, pp 202 [*B. Ath B Publ. Br. Mus. Y. C.*

The same. Second edition New-York, 1835. 12°, pp 206
[*B. Ath. N. Y. Publ. U. S. Y. C.*

Also, other editions, including one published in London, with the title, Slavery in America

In opposition to the Colonization scheme.

20. Addresses to the Westchester County Auxiliary Bible Society, 1836, 1839, 1841, 1845, etc.

21 A View of the Action of the Federal Government, in behalf of Slavery. New York, 1839. 12°, pp 217.
[*B Ath. Br Mus Harv N Y. H. S.*

The same. Second edition. New York; published by the American Anti-Slavery Society, 1839 12°, pp 240
[*B Publ. Br. Mus. Harv. U. T S. Y. C.*

The same Utica, 1844. 12°, pp 112
[*Br. Mus. Harv U. S. Y. C.*

Without the author's Introduction and Appendix, but with an Appendix (pp 95–112) by Joshua Leavitt (Yale 1814).

22 The Condition of Free People of Color in the United States. New York, 1839 8°, pp. 24.

Anonymous

23 Address to the Friends of Constitutional Liberty, on the Violation by the United States House of Representatives of the Right of Petition. 1840.

24. Address before the New York Female Bible Society. 1840.

25. War and Peace: the evils of the first, and a plan for preserving the last. New-York, 1842. 12°, pp. 101
[*B Ath. B Publ Columbia Univ Harv N Y. H S U. T. S*

The same London, 1842 8°, pp iv, 48
[*B. Publ. Br. Mus Harv U. S.*

This little book is notable for its proposal of stipulation by treaty for international arbitration

26. Caste and Slavery in the American Church By a Churchman New-York and London, 1843 8°, pp 51. [*B. Publ*

In part published in the *New World* newspaper of March and April, 1843.

27. Letter to Hon. Theodore Frelinghuysen. New York, 1844. 8°, pp 8 [*Br Mus U T S.*

Mr. Frelinghuysen was a candidate for the Vice-Presidency and had written a letter, expressing the view that Congress had no right to interfere with slavery.

28 An Address delivered before the American Peace Society, at its annual meeting, May 26, 1845 Boston, 1845 8°, pp. 31.
[*A. A. S. A. C. A B Publ Br. Mus. Columbia Univ. Harv M H. S N Y Publ U. T S*

Devoted mainly to an inquiry whether the Society is at variance with God's will. In the foot-notes are severe comments on Bishop Onderdonk, of New York

29. Trial by Jury in New York. 1846

30. Introductory Remarks, in volume entitled:

A Reproof of the American Church, by the Bishop of Oxford. Extracted from a "History of the Protestant Episcopal Church in America," by Samuel Wilberforce. With an Introduction by an American Churchman New York, 1846. 8°, pp 59.
[*B. Publ N Y. H S. Y. C.*

The introduction occupies pp. 3–44: it is a sharp rebuke of the conduct of the American Episcopal Church in respect to slavery

31 A Letter to the Right Rev. L Silliman Ives, Bishop of the Protestant Episcopal Church in the State of North Carolina, occasioned by his late Address to the Convention of his Diocese By a Protestant Episcopalian. Washington [1846] 8°, pp. 15.

The same Second edition. New York, 1848 12°, pp. 32

The same By William Jay Third edition. New York, 1848 8°, pp. iii, 32. [*B Publ. Br Mus Harv U. T. S Y. C.*

A severe arraignment of the Bishop for his justification of slavery.

32. Address to the Inhabitants of New Mexico and California, on the omission by Congress to provide them with Territorial Governments, and on the social and political evils of Slavery. New York, 1849. 12°, pp. 56 [*B. Ath Br. Mus Harv. Y. C.*

Written by Mr. Jay, and signed by him and twenty other members of the American and Foreign Anti-Slavery Society, August, 1849.

33. A Review of the Causes and Consequences of the Mexican War. Boston, 1849 12°, pp 333.

[*A. C. A. B Ath. B Publ. N Y. H S. U S. U. T. S Y. C*

Also, several later editions: and a translation into Spanish, published in Cadiz.

34. Table of the Killed and Wounded in the War of 1812 Compiled during the War.

In the *Collections* of the New York Historical Society, Second Series, vol 2, pp. 447–66 1849

35. The Calvary Pastoral, with Comments a Tract for the Times New York, 1849 8°, pp. 44 [*U T S.*

An anonymous criticism of a pastoral letter, issued by the Rector of Calvary Church, the Rev Samuel L. Southard, and exhibiting high-church tendencies.

36 Letter to Hon William Nelson, M C, on Mr. Clay's Compromise. New-York, 1850. 12°, pp 22.

[*A. A S B. Publ. Br. Mus Harv. Y C.*

37. Letter to Hon William Nelson, M C, on Mr. Webster's Speech New-York, 1850. 12°, pp. 12.

[*B. Ath. B Publ. N. Y. Publ. Y. C.*

The same Boston, 1850. 8°, pp. 12.

[*B Ath. B Publ Br Mus. M. H S. N Y. H S.*

38 A Letter to the Hon Samuel A. Eliot, Representative in Congress from the city of Boston, in reply to his apology for voting for the Fugitive Slave Bill By Hancock Boston, 1851 8°, pp 57 [*B. Ath. B. Publ. Harv. M. H S. Y. C.*

39 Reply to Remarks of Rev. Moses Stuart, . on Hon John Jay, and an Examination of his Scriptural Exegesis, contained in his recent pamphlet entitled, "Conscience and the Constitution" New-York, 1850 8°, pp. 22.

[*A A S. A C A B Ath B. Publ. Br Mus Columbia Univ Harv. M. H. S U. T S Y C*

A spirited rebuke of Professor Stuart.

40 The Kossuth Excitement a Letter Boston, American Peace Society, 1852 8°, pp 8

[*A. A. S. B. Publ Br Mus Harv. U. S. Y C.*

41 The Bible against Slavery. Adrian, Mich., 1852

42. An Address to the Anti-Slavery Christians of the United States New-York, 1852 8°, pp. 16. [*Y. C.*

An appeal in behalf of the American and Foreign Anti-Slavery Society, signed by a number of clergymen and others, May, 1852.

43. Letters respecting the American Board of Commissioners for Foreign Missions, and the American Tract Society. New-York, 1853 8°, pp 16.

[*A. A S A C. A B. Publ Br. Mus Harv U T. S.*

These two letters are also included in a pamphlet published in 1854 (New-York, 12°, pp. 60) with the title:

American Slavery in connection with American Christianity

In this edition they are entitled Indian Missions; and, Letter on the Reasons assigned by the American Tract Society for its silence in regard to American Slavery

44. Petition of the American Peace Society to the United States Senate in behalf of Stipulated Arbitration 1853.

45. Miscellaneous Writings on Slavery Boston, 1853 12°, pp 670 + portrait

[*B. Publ. Br Mus. Columbia Univ Harv M. H S N. Y. Publ. U S Y C*

Containing Nos 19, 21, 22, 30, 31, 32, 36, 38, 42

46. An Examination of the Mosaic Laws of Servitude .. New York, 1854. 8°, pp 56

[*A C. A B. Publ Harv M H. S U. T. S Y. C.*

The motto on the title-page is, "The statutes of the Lord are right."

47 The Eastern War an Argument for the Cause of Peace. An Address before the American Peace Society, at its twenty-seventh anniversary, May 28, 1855 Boston, 1855 8°, pp. 36
[*A. C. A. B Publ M. H. S.*

48 A Letter to the Rev. William Berrian, D.D., on the Resources, Present Position, and Duties of Trinity Church: occasioned by his late pamphlet "Facts against Fancy" New-York, 1856. 8°, pp. 20
[*B. Publ Columbia Univ. M H. S. N Y. Publ U T S. Y. C.*

49. A Letter to the Committee chosen by the American Tract Society, to inquire into the Proceedings of its Executive Committee, in relation to Slavery. [1857] 8°, pp. 38.
[*A. C. A B Publ Columbia Univ Harv M. H. S. U. T S. Y. C*

Judge Jay left in manuscript an elaborate Commentary on the Old and New Testaments, the work of many years

AUTHORITIES

Baird, Hist of Rye, 484. *Crosby,* Annual Obit Notices, 1858, 177-80 Historical Magazine, II, 349-50 *Holgate,* Amer Genealogy, 238 McVickar Family Tree *Partridge,* Memorial of W Jay *Tuckerman,* Wm. Jay and the Abolition of Slavery *Van Rensselaer,* New Yorkers of the XIX century, 28, 36.

ALGERNON SIDNEY JONES, the fifth son of Isaac Jones (Yale 1757) and his wife Sibyl (Benjamin) Jones, of New Haven, was born in New Haven on June 9, 1786. He did not enter College until after the opening of the Freshman year.

After graduation he was for a few years an apothecary in New Haven; and while living here was married in Hartford, on June 28, 1812, by the Rev. Philander Chase, to Frances Farnham S, daughter of Richard Jennys, of Nassau, New Providence, Bahama Islands.

From New Haven he removed to Huntington, in Fairfield County, where he practiced medicine for some years

He finally settled in Williamsburg, a suburb of New York City, where he continued to practice his profession for some years, and where he died on February 23, 1858, in his 72d year.

AUTHORITIES.

Rev. Isaac Jones, MS Letter, May 1, 1848. N. Y. Geneal. and Biogr. Record, xlii, 43 *Russell,* Hist. of Christ Church, Hartford, ii, 244.

JOHN KELL entered College from Sunbury, Georgia.

His later residence is said to have been in Darien, Georgia

He is believed to have died in 1828.

EZRA KELLOGG, the youngest son of Epenetus Kellogg, a farmer of Norwalk, Connecticut, and grandson of Epenetus and Jemima (Rogers) Kellogg, of Norwalk, was born on October 15, 1789. His mother was Rebecca, daughter of John and Rebecca (Fitch) Richards, of Darien Parish, in Stamford.

He studied medicine after graduation, but is said to have died in Maryland, unmarried, in September, 1812, in his 23d year.

AUTHORITIES

Kelloggs in the New World, i, 165

LIONEL HENRY KENNEDY was a son of Lieutenant James and Mary Eliza Kennedy, of Charleston, South Carolina.

He returned home after graduation, and studied law, being admitted to the bar in Charleston in 1809.

He held a prominent position in the city, and for many years served as a Representative in the Legislature. He was also an active member and officer of the State Society of the Cincinnati (his father having been an officer in the Revolution), and held the rank of Major in the Palmetto Regiment.

In 1837 or 1838 he removed to Spartanburg, where he died on January 17, 1847, aged about 60 years.

He married Mary Ann Jane, daughter of Captain Jervis Henry Stevens, of Charleston, who survived him for many years, with one daughter.

On July 4, 1813, he delivered on Oration before the Society of the Cincinnati in Charleston.

He published:

An Official Report of the Trials of sundry Negroes, charged with an attempt to raise an Insurrection in the State of South-Carolina: preceded by an Introduction and Narrative, and in an Appendix, a report of the trials of Four White Persons, on indictments for attempting to incite the slaves to insurrection. Prepared and Published at the request of the Court—By L H Kennedy & Thomas Parker, Members of the Charleston Bar, and the Presiding Magistrates of the Court Charleston, 1822, 8°, pp 188, x, 4
[*B Publ. Harv. N Y Publ. Y. C.*

AUTHORITIES

Miss I DeSaussure, MS Letter, October, 1911.

LESTER KIMBERLY, a son of Captain Silas Kimberly, of West Haven, then part of New Haven, and a grandson of Nathaniel Kimberly, of West Haven, was born on January 20, 1787. His mother was Sarah, daughter of Jonathan and Mary Smith, of New Haven. His father died a few months before he entered College. General Dennis Kimberly (Yale 1812) was a brother.

He was living in New Haven in 1809, but died on October 13, 1811, in his 25th year. His estate was not settled, however, until 1826, when his widow was still alive.

William Coit Leffingwell, the second son of William Leffingwell (Yale 1786), was born in Norwich, Connecticut, on December 25, 1788. In his infancy the family removed to New York City, and in 1809 to New Haven.

He settled in New Haven, and was married in New York on September 3, 1816, to Sarah S., daughter of David Dunham, of New York He was engaged in mercantile business in New York for some years, while his residence continued in New Haven.

He died in New Haven on January 5, 1833, at the age of 44. His widow died here on December 13, 1862, in her 65th year. They had six sons and three daughters, of whom three sons died in early life. The fourth son received the degree of M.D. at Yale in 1847.

AUTHORITIES.

Leffingwell Record, 81, 114 *Perkins*, Old Houses of Norwich, 519. Tuttle Family, 204.

Stephen Lockwood, the second son of Stephen Lockwood, of Norwalk, Connecticut, and grandson of Joseph and Rebecca (Rogers) Lockwood, of Norwalk, was born on June 1, 1789 His mother was Sarah, daughter of Dr Thaddeus Betts (Yale 1745), of Norwalk. He was thus a first cousin of his classmate Betts. He was prepared for the Sophomore Class in College by the Rev. Dr Matthias Burnet, of Norwalk.

He remained in New Haven as a resident graduate for nearly a year, and then became a teacher in a Female Academy in New London. In 1811 he settled in New York City as a dry-goods merchant. He was also very earnest in city missionary work

From 1817 until his death he was an Elder in the Brick Presbyterian Church; and on Thursday, March 22, 1827, he was returning from attendance at an ecclesiastical council in company with his pastor, the Rev. Dr. Gardiner Spring (Yale 1805), on board the steamboat *Oliver Ellsworth* bound from Hartford to New York. The boiler of the boat exploded when they were about seven miles from Saybrook, and Mr. Lockwood was so severely scalded that he died in consequence two days later, in his 38th year.

He married, on September 5, 1811, Sally, an elder sister of his classmate Richards, who survived him.

Their children were four daughters and one son

AUTHORITIES

Dolbeare Family, 18. *Hall,* Hist. of Norwalk, 291 *Holden and Lockwood,* Lockwood Family History, 220, 367–68. *Knapp,* Hist. of Brick Presbyterian Church, N. Y., 197, 517 *Morse,* Richards Family, 99, 103 Religious Intelligencer, xi, 751.

AMASA LOOMIS, Junior, the eldest child of Deacon Amasa Loomis, of South Windsor, Connecticut, and grandson of Deacon Amasa and Hannah (Hurlbut) Loomis, of East Windsor, was born on October 10, 1785, and baptized on February 19, 1786. His mother was Priscilla, daughter of Captain Jonathan and Priscilla (Hammond) Birge,—his mother's mother having become in 1784 the second wife of his father's father He entered College at the opening of the Junior year.

After graduation he studied theology, and was licensed to preach on February 5, 1811, by the Hartford North Association of Ministers. For the next two years he preached in various localities, until his ordination and installation, in May, 1813, as pastor of the Congregational Church in New Salem Society in Colchester, now the township of Salem.

He was dismissed from this charge in January, 1817, and then went to the Western Reserve in Ohio, where he was settled over the Presbyterian Church in Painesville from 1818 to 1823. His health then failed, and he died at his father's house, in South Windsor, on January 31, 1824, in his 39th year.

He married on August 31, 1819, Frances, daughter of Captain George and Mabel (Olmsted) Pitkin, of East Hartford, Connecticut, who died in 1840, aged 48 years.

Their only child died in infancy.

AUTHORITIES

Loomis Family, 167 Pitkin Genealogy, 53, 108 *Stiles*, Hist of Windsor, 2d ed, ii, 447.

JUSTUS MCKINSTRY, the second son of Charles McKinstry, of Hillsdale, Columbia County, New York, and grandson of Captain John McKinstry, a native of Armagh, Ireland, and an immigrant to Londonderry, New Hampshire, and Hillsdale, was born on October 27, 1785. His mother was Tabitha Patterson, of Hillsdale.

He studied law, and was admitted to the bar of Columbia County in 1810. From that date until his death he practiced his profession in Hudson in the same county, and held the respect of his fellow-citizens

For three years from November, 1822, he held the office of Clerk of the County Courts.

He died from cholera at the Astor House in New York City on May 20, 1849, in his 64th year. He left no immediate family, and his estate was divided among the representatives of his brothers and sisters

AUTHORITIES

N. Y Spectator, May 24, 1849 *Willis*, McKinstry Genealogy, 23

DARIUS MEAD, the youngest child of Joshua Mead, of Round Hill, in the northwestern part of Greenwich, Connecticut, by his first wife, Rachel Knapp, and grandson of Nathaniel and Prudence (Wood) Mead, of Greenwich, was born in that town on July 9, 1787, and was prepared for College by the Rev. Dr Isaac Lewis (Yale 1765), of Greenwich.

He studied medicine in the University of Pennsylvania under Dr. Benjamin Rush, and was graduated with the degree of M D. in 1809

For a few months after receiving his diploma he practiced medicine in New York City, but in 1810 returned to Greenwich, settling at first within the limits of the Old Society, in the eastern part of the town, but soon removing to the Second or West Society, where he resided, engaged in active practice, until his death, which occurred on January 28, 1864, after a painful illness of eight weeks, in his 77th year. The funeral sermon, by the Rev Samuel B. S. Bissell (Yale 1830), was afterwards published, and included a photograph of Dr. Mead.

He married, in 1809, Lydia K, daughter of Dr. Elisha Belcher, of Round Hill, who died on January 15, 1848, in her 61st year.

Their children were four daughters and two sons The youngest daughter married Philander Button (Yale 1839)

Dr. Mead attained a high reputation as a physician, and was skilful and successful in an extensive and laborious practice He was a man of stern integrity and consistent piety.

In 1845 and 1846 he represented the Twelfth Senatorial District in the State Senate, being nominated by his fellow-citizens without his knowledge of their intentions. For the second year of his service, as one of the six senior Senators, he was *ex officio* a member of the Yale Corporation.

He was essentially public-spirited; and was the most energetic promoter of the foundation of the Greenwich Academy in 1827, and also of the new cemetery near his home

---

AUTHORITIES

Bissell, Memorial of D. Mead. Hist of Greenwich, 293. Mead Family, 116-19, 377-78. *Mead,*

Samuel Thomas Mills, one of twin sons of the Rev Samuel Mills (Yale 1776), was born in Wethersfield, Connecticut, on March 6, and baptized on March 13, 1785 In his infancy his father became the pastor of the Congregational Church in Chester, then a parish of Saybrook

He did not enter College until after the opening of the Sophomore year.

After graduation he was for one year a tutor in the family of Isaac Bronson, of New York City and Greenfield Hill, Connecticut, and then for two years studied theology in the Andover Seminary. He was licensed to preach by the Middlesex (Connecticut) Association of Ministers on October 2, 1810.

On October 11, 1811, he was ordained and installed as pastor of the Presbyterian Church in Litchfield, Herkimer County, New York, where he continued about five years

On February 6, 1817, he was installed over the Presbyterian Church in Onondaga Hollow, but remained only until September 2, 1818, when he became the first preceptor of the Utica Female Academy. His health, however, was infirm, and this compelled his resignation after a year had expired.

A little later he undertook service as a home missionary in the employ of the Female Missionary Society of Oneida, and had been acting as pastor of the Presbyterian Church in Moscow, Livingston County, when he was installed in 1825 as pastor in the village of Peterborough, in the township of Smithfield, Madison County, where he remained for the next ten years.

He was then installed, on July 16, 1835, over the church which his father had formerly served, in Chester, Connecticut. His ministry here was fruitful and acceptable, but he was dismissed at his own request on April 11, 1838.

He returned soon after to New York State, and in 1840–41 was acting pastor of the New School Presbyterian Church in Oswego. After that he went to Ohio, and for three or four years taught in Columbus, serving also for a part of the time as Chaplain of the State Penitentiary. In 1845 he retired from active service, and resided in Cleveland until his removal in 1852 to New York City, where he died on February 27, 1853, at the age of 68.

He was married on October 15, 1810, by the Rev. Joab Brace (Yale 1804), of Newington, Connecticut, to Harriet M. Belden, who died soon, leaving no children.

He next married Charlotte, daughter of Colonel Gerrit G and Maria (Antill) Lansing, of Oriskany, Oneida County, New York, by whom he had four sons and two daughters.

AUTHORITIES.

Bagg, Pioneers of Utica, 469. *Chesebrough,* Sketch of Chester Church, 17; *MS. Letters, 1892–93. *Hotchkin,* Hist. of Western N Y, 308. *Robinson,* Memoir of Rev W. Robinson, 204. *Stiles,* Hist. of Wethersfield, ii, 504. *Talcott,* N. Y. and N. E. Families, 137.

Isaac Hubbell Osborn, son of Jeremiah Osborn, of Easton, Fairfield County, Connecticut, was baptized on October 8, 1786. He entered at the opening of the Junior year, having been prepared by Bennet Tyler (Yale 1804) in the Weston Academy

He is reported to have died in Fulton, Oswego County, New York, in 1843; no trace of the settlement of his estate in that county is found

---

Guy Richards, the tenth child in a family of twelve children of Guy Richards, a merchant of New London, Connecticut, and grandson of Guy and Elizabeth (Harris) Richards, of New London, was born on January 8, 1788. His mother was Hannah, the youngest daughter of George and Mary (Sherwood) Dolbeare, of Montville. A sister married William P. Cleaveland (Yale 1793). The Rev. George Richards (Yale 1840) was a nephew; as also Charles A. and George R. Lewis (Yale 1829).

After graduation he began the study of law, but soon left this profession, and for several years followed the sea, rising in a short time to the position of Master.

In 1820 he entered on a business career in New York City, to which he devoted himself with great zeal, and from which he retired many years before his death with the ample rewards of an industrious life. He was admired and loved for his honor, his generosity, his frankness, and his genial courtesy.

He made a profession of religion at the age of eighty.

He died in New York City on March 26, 1873, in his 85th year.

He was married on January 23, 1822, by the Rev. Dr. Gardiner Spring to Mary Ivers, of New York City.

After her death he was married by Dr. Spring on March 28, 1848, to her sister, Bouquet Ivers, who died in January, 1854, aged 67 years.

He had no children.

AUTHORITIES.

Baker, Hist. of Montville, 336. Dolbeare Family, 18. *Knapp,* Hist. of the Brick Presbyterian Church, N. Y., 202. *Morse,* Richards Family, 99.

SAMUEL ROOT, the youngest son of Ephraim Root (Yale 1782), of Hartford, Connecticut, and a brother of James Root (Yale 1806), was born in Hartford on March 22, 1789. He entered College with his elder brother, but soon withdrew, to join the next Class.

After graduation he read law in the office of Seth P. Staples (Yale 1797), of New Haven, and was admitted to the bar; but owing to some dislike to the practice, he abandoned it after a few years, and retired to a farm in West Hartford, where he passed an uneventful life.

He was a good scholar and a great reader, and endowed with refined and delicate feelings, but never aspired to make any show in society.

After many years of failing health, he died in West Hartford on May 21, 1868, in his 80th year. He left a wife and three sons.

AUTHORITIES.

Dwight, Strong Genealogy, i, 327. *E. Gleason,* MS. Letter, June, 1868. *James Root,* MS. Letter, June, 1868. Root Genealogy, 191, 259.

AUGUSTUS SHERRILL, the second son of Henry Sherrill, of East Hampton, Long Island, who removed to Richmond, Berkshire County, Massachusetts, during the Revolution, and grandson of Henry and Jane (Conkling) Sherrill, of East Hampton, was born in Richmond, on March 26, 1789. His mother was Lois Chidsey, of Richmond. He spent the earlier part of the College course at Williams College, where he received an *ad eundem* Bachelor's degree in 1807.

After graduation he studied law, and settled in Ithaca, New York.

Here he enjoyed to a marked degree the confidence of the community, as a painstaking and accurate practitioner.

After a Reformed Dutch Church was organized in the village, in 1830, he was chosen one of the Elders.

He died in Ithaca on January 6, 1853, in his 64th year.

He married Clarissa Whiton, by whom he had one daughter.

AUTHORITIES.

Selkreg, Landmarks of Tompkins County, 68, 187, 197. Sherrill Family, 1894, 25, 43.

William Stebbins, the eldest son of the Rev. Stephen Williams Stebbins (Yale 1781), of Stratford, Connecticut, was born in Stratford on June 26, 1786

He was prostrated by a severe illness near the close of his Senior year, and though he was permitted to graduate with his Class, his plans for studying theology were broken up.

His father removed to the pastorate of the Congregational Church in West Haven in 1815, and for many years the son's only active occupation was that of a teacher in that parish

From May, 1834, down to about 1850 he had the charge of a Depository for Sunday-School books and tracts in New Haven.

He died in Colchester, the residence of his daughter, on June 28, 1858, at the age of 72.

He married in May, 1817, Lucretia, daughter of Deacon Samuel Raynolds, of Somers, by whom he had three sons, one of whom died in youth, and a daughter. The Rev. Charles N. Ransom (Yale 1880) is a grandson.

AUTHORITIES

Orcutt, Hist. of Stratford, ii, 1294 Street Genealogy, 118

Alexander Hodgdon Stevens, the third son of General Ebenezer and Lucretia (Ledyard, Sands) Stevens, was born in New York City on September 4, 1789. Three of his brothers were Yale graduates, in 1805, 1811, and 1813, respectively. He was prepared for College by John Adams (Yale 1795) at the Academy in Plainfield, Connecticut.

Having selected medicine as his profession, he entered after graduation the office of Dr. Edward Miller, Professor in the College of Physicians and Surgeons of New York, and attended one course of lectures in that institution. He took his second year's course in the

University of Pennsylvania, where he received the degree of Doctor of Medicine in April, 1811.

He was then connected for seven months with the surgical service of the New-York Hospital, prior to his sailing, about the beginning of 1812, for a period of further study abroad. He spent one season in London, in attendance on the lectures of Abernethy and Sir Astley Cooper, and then for a shorter time attended the clinics of Boyer and Larrey in Paris. On his voyage to London and again on his return, he was captured by English seamen and detained for a short time in prison at Plymouth.

On his arrival in New York he learned of the death of his preceptor, Dr Miller, with whom he had been expecting to enter into partnership; and he settled in general practice in his native city, while also accepting an appointment as surgeon in the army, which he held through the war.

In 1813 he married Mary Jane, daughter of John Murray and Margaret (Carrick) Bayard, of Millstone, New Jersey.

In 1814 he accepted an appointment as Professor of Surgery in Rutgers College, but delivered lectures there for two years only, though he nominally retained the chair for ten years longer. His wife died in 1817, and in the same year he was appointed one of the surgeons of the New York Hospital, and for twenty-two years faithfully discharged the duties of that office, introducing there most successfully the practice of clinical instruction.

In 1820 he was elected a Trustee of the College of Physicians and Surgeons, and he retained that office until 1826, when, in the very height of professional success, he was chosen Professor of the Principles and Practice of Surgery in the same institution. Meantime, he was married, at Morrisania, on April 19, 1825, to Catharine, daughter of James and Helen (Van Cortlandt) Morris, and sister of James VanCortlandt Morris (Yale 1816).

For many years he devoted himself assiduously to the duties of his chair, the private instruction of office-pupils, and to hospital service. In 1831 a six-months' visit to Europe renewed his health and vigor.

During the cholera epidemic of 1832, Dr. Stevens was made by the Board of Health the President of the special council which superintended the public medical service, and conducted that service with great efficiency.

In the spring of 1834, his health beginning to fail, he took Dr. John Watson into partnership, and soon resigned to him the whole of his lucrative practice, restricting himself to consultation. About the same time he purchased a small estate at Hallett's Cove, now Astoria, Long Island, where he erected a fine residence, devoting himself to horticulture in the summer, and dispensing an elegant hospitality to his city friends.

In 1837 he exchanged his chair of surgery in the College of Physicians and Surgeons for a new chair of Clinical Surgery; but two years later he laid down the burden of instruction, his later connection with the Faculty being only as Emeritus Professor, and as President from 1843 to 1855.

His wife died in Astoria on July 16, 1838, and he was next married in New York on May 29, 1841, by the Rev. Dr. Manton Eastburn, to Phebe, daughter of John N. Lloyd (Yale 1802), of Lloyd's Neck, Long Island.

In 1842 an association for the Relief of Widows and Orphans of Medical Men was organized in New York, in which Dr Stevens took a deep interest; and at one of its annual dinners a project was started by him which resulted in the foundation, in 1847, of the New York Academy of Medicine, in which he took great interest.

The American Medical Association was also founded in 1847, and Dr. Stevens chosen a Vice-President. At the second meeting, in 1848, he was unanimously elected

President. In the same year he was elected President of the New York State Medical Society, and was re-elected (a rare compliment) in 1849.

In June, 1849, he received the honorary degree of Doctor of Laws from the Regents of the State University.

About 1851 he retired to his country residence at Lloyd's Neck, where he spent the greater part of the year in the cultivation of his farm and the education of his children.

In 1867 he returned to the city, where he spent the last two winters of his life After a brief illness,—not over two days in duration,—he died in New York on March 30, 1869, in his 80th year.

By his second wife he had three daughters, two of whom died early, and the third married the Rev. James J. Bowden (Columbia Coll. 1813). By his third wife he had three sons and two daughters. One son was graduated at Yale in 1864.

His portrait was painted by Inman in 1849 for the New York Hospital, and a copy was presented to the College of Physicians and Surgeons in 1869. A photographic likeness is prefixed to the *Memorial Discourse* by Dr Adams.

As an operating surgeon, Dr. Stevens was deliberate and cautious, and remarkable for his ready resources in meeting unexpected complications. As a lecturer and teacher, he was familiar in style, clear, comprehensive, and often quaint in his expressions. As a citizen, he was strictly upright. He was a firm believer in the truths of Christianity.

He published:

1 A Dissertation on the Proximate Cause of Inflammation, with an Attempt to establish a rational plan of cure Submitted to the examination of John Andrews, D. D. Provost, the Trustees, and Medical Professors of the University of Pennsylvania, on the twenty-fifth of April, 1811. For the Degree of Doctor of Medicine. Philadelphia, 1811. 8°, pp. 37

[*Br. Mus Surg.-Gen'l's. Office. Y. C.*

2. Familiar instructions for the prevention of cholera, prepared for a family about leaving the city, 5th July, 1832. New York, 1832. 8°, pp. 8. [*Surg.-Gen'l's Office*

3 A clinical Lecture on the Primary Treatment, of Injuries, delivered at the New-York Hospital, November 22d, 1837. New-York, 1837 8°, pp. 34.
[*B. Ath B. Publ Surg -Gen'l's. Office. U S.*

4. Lectures on Lithotomy, delivered at the New-York Hospital, December, 1837. New-York, 1838 8°, pp 93 + 5 pl.
[*M. H. S Surg.-Gen'l's. Office. U S*

5. An Address to the Class of Graduates of the College of Physicians and Surgeons of the University of the State of New-York, delivered at the Commencement, March 11th, 1847. New-York, 1847. 8°, pp. 16.
[*B. Ath B. Publ Br Mus. Surg. Gen'l's. Office.*

6 Address, delivered before the State Agricultural Society, Members of the Legislature, and of the Medical Society of the State of New-York, at the Capitol in Albany, February, 1848, on the Food of Plants. Albany, 1848. 8°, pp 22
[*B. Publ Surg. Gen'l's Office. U T S.*

7. The Plea of Humanity in behalf of Medical Education the Annual Address delivered before the New York State Medical Society, and Members of the Legislature, at the Capitol, February 6, 1849.—Published by the Society. Albany, 1849. 8°, pp 20.
[*A. A. S M H. S. N. Y. H. S Surg. Gen'l's Office. Y C.*

The same, with title· A Plea [etc.] .. —Printed by order of the Assembly. Albany, 1849 8°, pp 28.
[*Br. Mus Surg Gen'l's. Office Y. C.*
Also, in the *Transactions* of the Medical Society for 1849.

The same 4th edition. New-York, 1849. 8°, pp 44.
[*A. A S B. Ath B Publ. Br. Mus. Surg.-Gen'l's. Office. U. S.*

8 Communication, on the subject of the removal of the Quarantine Establishment. In Documents of the New York State Assembly, March 9, 1849 8°, pp. 11

9 Clinical Lecture on Tumors. 1850.

10 Annual Address delivered before the New-York State Medical Society. Albany, 1850. 8°, pp. 31.

[*B. Publ Br. Mus. Surg.-Gen'l's. Office.*

From the Transactions of the Society, on the Public Health.

He also made many contributions to medical and surgical journals.

He was one of the editors of *The Medical & Surgical Register* consisting chiefly of Cases in the New-York Hospital; vol. 1, New-York, 1818-20, containing fifteen articles by him, and of the *New York Medical and Physical Journal*, vol 7. 1828-29.

He edited, with Notes·

The first lines of the Practice of Surgery ... —By Samuel Cooper—From the fourth London edition. New-York, 1822 2 vols, 8°.

He translated from the French, with notes, and an appendix.

A Treatise on Surgical Diseases, and the operations suited to them. By Baron Boyer. New-York, 1815-16. 2 vols, 8°.

AUTHORITIES.

J G Adams, Memorial Discourse Amer Historical Magazine (1906), i, 325 *Dwight*, Strong Genealogy, i, 636 Medical and Surgical Reporter, xiii, 5-7 Medical Record, iv, 117-18 N. Y - Geneal. and Biogr. Record, v, 19; xvi, 71

Henry Pierce Strong, the youngest son of Colonel Adonijah Strong, of Salisbury, Connecticut, and a brother of the Rev. William Lightbourn Strong (Yale 1802), was born in Salisbury on February 23, 1785.

After graduation he studied theology,—for part of the time (less than two years, 1808-10) in the new Andover Seminary,—and in 1810 he began to preach to a new and feeble congregation, in Elizabeth Street, New York City, which developed in April, 1811, into a Presbyterian Church, over which he was installed pastor on September 4.

He married in Danbury, Connecticut, on November 6, 1810, Laura, daughter of Captain James Clark, and sister of Adam Stoddard Clarke (Yale 1788).

The Elizabeth Street Church so dwindled that it was dissolved in October, 1813, and on May 25, 1814, he was installed pastor of the Congregational Church in Woodbury, Connecticut, where he did not, however, escape criticism. He was said to be too much engrossed with outside cares, and was in consequence dismissed in January, 1816

His next settlement was over the Congregational Church in St. Albans, Vermont, where he was installed on January 22, 1817. Here he was regarded as a preacher of great ability, and of personal excellence, but he took a dismission on October 3, 1821

From November 10, 1824, to May 10, 1831, he was pastor of the Presbyterian Church in Phelps, Ontario County, New York Finally, in 1832, he removed about fifteen miles southwestwards to the Presbyterian Church in the village of Rushville, partly in Ontario and partly in Yates County, where he died of a fever on August 28, 1835, aged 50½ years

He had nine sons, of whom three died in infancy, and a daughter, who also died early. Two sons were graduated at Yale, in 1838, and 1842, respectively.

Mrs. Strong died at the house of one of her sons in Rockford, Illinois, on February 9, 1861, in her 75th year.

He published:

1. A Sermon [from Jer xxiii, 28], preached September 8, 1811, at the Presbyterian Church in Elizabeth Street, New-York; being the Sabbath after the author's ordination, and installation as pastor of the church in that place New-York, 1811. 8°, pp. 24.
[*A. C A B Publ. Br. Mus. Y. C*

2 A Sermon [from Titus, ii, 15], delivered June 24, 1830, at the Installation of the Rev Silas C. Brown, A.M as Pastor of the Presbyterian Church, in West-Bloomfield Rochester, 1830 8°, pp. 24. [*A C. A Br. Mus*

The sermon occupies pp 1-11.

AUTHORITIES.

Cothren, Hist of Woodbury, i, 304-05 *Dwight*, Strong Family, ii, 1042, 1050-51. *Greenleaf*, Hist. of N. Y Churches, 144-45. *Hemenway*, Vermont Gazetteer, ii, 332-33. *Hotchkin*, Hist of Western N. Y., 380

JACOB SUTHERLAND entered College from Poughkeepsie, New York, in 1802, and spent three years with the Class of 1806. He was born in Poughkeepsie about 1787, the only surviving son of Solomon Sutherland, who died in 1803. His mother was a sister of the Hon. Smith Thompson (Princeton Coll. 1788)

In his Senior year he was one of the editors of the *Literary Cabinet.*

After graduation he studied law in the office of Harmanus Bleecker, in Albany, and then settled in practice in Poughkeepsie.

On September 5, 1811, he married Frances, third daughter of Chancellor John and Cornelia (Bogart) Lansing, of Albany.

In 1818 he removed to North Blenheim, in Schoharie County, to look after the large landed possessions in that vicinity which belonged to Chancellor Lansing and himself. In November, 1819, he was appointed United States District Attorney for the county, and in 1821 he was sent as a delegate to the State Constitutional Convention.

He also held the position of District Attorney, until in January, 1823, he was appointed a Justice of the Supreme Court, when he accepted the post and removed to Albany, though obliged in consequence to forego the acceptance of the office of State Senator, to which he had just been elected

In October, 1835, he resigned his judgeship, to accept the clerkship of the same Court, as a better paid office. He now removed his residence to Geneva.

In 1836 he was a Presidential Elector, and in the same year he received the honorary degree of LL.D. from Columbia College.

The winter of 1844–45 he spent in the West Indies on account of his health, and while on his return home he died in Albany, at the house of Rensselaer Westerlo, whose wife was a sister of Mrs. Sutherland, on May 13, at the age of 58.

He had a family of eight daughters and one son.

AUTHORITIES.

Munsell, Annals of Albany, i, 299; x, 248, 363. *Simms,* Hist of Schoharie County, 615. *Talcott,* N. Y and N. E Families, 135, 146.

CHARLES WILEY TAYLOR, the youngest of seven sons of Ahijah Taylor, a farmer of that part of Norwalk which is now included in Westport, Connecticut, and of Isabella (Wiley) Taylor, was born on January 11, 1786, and died in Westport, in the house in which he was born, on December 5, 1865, aged nearly 80 years.

He did not enter College until after the opening of Sophomore year.

After graduation he studied medicine with Dr. David Richmond, of Saugatuck village, now Westport, and began practice in his native place.

About 1811 he removed to Florida, in Warwick township, Orange County, New York, where he taught school, and also practiced his profession. He lived in the family of Dr. Samuel S Seward, and had as a pupil Dr Seward's son, afterwards the distinguished Hon. William H. Seward.

His health, however, becoming impaired, he returned in 1814 or 1815 to his native town, where he followed agricultural pursuits (mainly) for the rest of his life.

He was one of the representatives of Norwalk in the State Legislature in 1829 and 1835; and held other prominent town-offices.

About two years before his death, one of his arms was broken by the kick of a horse, in consequence of which he was afterwards confined to his bed.

He was never married.

AUTHORITIES.

D M. Marvin, MS Letter, December, 1866

NATHANIEL WILLIAM TAYLOR, the second son of Nathaniel Taylor, a farmer and tradesman, of New Milford, Connecticut, and grandson of the Rev. Nathanael Taylor (Yale 1745), was born in New Milford on June 23, 1786. His mother was Anne, younger sister of Amos Northrop (Yale 1762), of New Milford.

He bore the names of his grandfather and of his uncle (Yale 1785).

Having been prepared by the Rev Azel Backus (Yale 1787), of Bethlehem, he entered Yale in 1800, but was soon attacked with an affection of the eyes which compelled him to leave. A year later he resumed his studies, and remained with the Class of 1805 until some time in Sophomore year, when his course was again arrested, for the same cause. Finally he returned and completed Junior and Senior years with the Class of 1807. At graduation he delivered an Oration on the Advantages of National Adversity.

During the year after graduation he was the private tutor of a son of General Stephen Van Rensselaer, of Albany, and spent several months in the city of Montreal, where he acquired the French language.

He then became a student of theology with President Dwight, and for two years lived in his family and acted as his amanuensis, writing down from his dictation many of the sermons which compose his theological system.

He was licensed to preach by the Western Association of Ministers of New Haven County on August 21, 1810, and on October 15 married Rebecca Maria, daughter of Major Beebe and Lois (Northrop) Hine, of New Milford, whose mother was his first cousin. In the previous month he had declined an election to a College tutorship.

After having preached in other pulpits, and having once declined a call to this church, he accepted, reluctantly and only in consequence of the almost imperative advice of President Dwight, a second call to the First Church of New Haven, where he was ordained and installed on April 8, 1812 The sermon preached on that occasion by Dr. Dwight was afterwards published.

For ten years he filled this pulpit with conspicuous success, enjoying frequent revivals among his people, and promoting like results in other congregations. He was early recognized as one of the most powerful preachers of his generation, and the effect of his message was aided by a presence of great dignity and a countenance of uncommon beauty.

In September, 1822, the Yale Divinity School was founded and Mr. Taylor was appointed Professor of Didactic Theology. This professorship had been suggested by a proposed gift from the eldest son of President Dwight, chiefly that it might be filled by his admired friend, Mr. Taylor; and the Theological Department was organized at this time with the expectation of making him a teacher of theology, in consequence of the success which had attended him in his ministry and in the exposition of systematic divinity.

His connection with his church was dissolved in December, 1822. In 1823 he received the honorary degree of Doctor of Divinity from Union College.

The period of his pastorate had been an active and exciting one; but that of his professorship was yet more stirring and momentous.

His first published utterance in reply to adverse criticism of his doctrinal teaching as Arminian and Pelagian, was the *Concio ad Clerum,* on human depravity, preached at Commencement in 1828, and from that date for a score of years he was the center of a flood of controversy.

As a teacher, in his prime, he was enthusiastic and confident in his message, and magnetically fascinating and stimulating to his students. His intellectual vigor remained unbroken, after the gradual failure of his physical powers He continued to teach until within five or six weeks of the end, and died in New Haven on March 10, 1858, in his 72d year. The memorial sermons delivered by Dr. Leonard Bacon, Dr. Samuel W. S. Dutton, and Professor George P. Fisher, were subsequently published.

Mrs. Taylor died in New Haven on August 26, 1868, at the age of 79.

Their children were five daughters, the youngest of whom died in infancy, and one son (Yale 1844).

The eldest daughter married President Noah Porter (Yale 1831), the second married the Rev. Dr. Samuel G Buckingham (Yale 1833); the third married Dr. A. B. Robeson (Yale 1837); and the fourth married Walter T. Hatch (Yale 1837).

The University owns three portraits and a marble bust of Dr. Taylor.

He published·

1 Regeneration the beginning of holiness in the human heart A Sermon [from I John, ii, 29]. New-Haven, 1816. 8°, pp. 19.
[*A C. A. Br. Mus Y. C.*

2 Man, a free agent without the aids of Divine Grace [New-Haven, 1818.] 12°, pp. 18. [*Y C*

Designed to refute the Methodist notion of gracious ability; being No. 2 of Tracts designed to illustrate and enforce the most important Doctrines of the Gospel.

3. Review of Norton's Inaugural Discourse. In the *Christian Spectator,* February, 1821, vol. 3, pp 74–83

Anonymous.

4 Review of Professor Norton's Views of Calvinism—From the *Christian Spectator* for April, 1823 New-Haven. 8°, pp. 30. [*Y. C.*

Anonymous

5 A Sermon [from Isa. lix, 14], addressed to the Legislature of the State of Connecticut, at the Annual Election in Hartford, May 7, 1823 Hartford, 1823. 8°, pp 43. [*Br. Mus Y. C.*

The same Second edition. New-Haven, 1823. 8°, pp 40. [*B. Publ. Y. C.*

The object of the sermon is to show that a corrupt public opinion on the subject of morals destroys the efficacy of civil government

6 Concio ad Clerum—A Sermon [from Eph ii, 3] delivered in the Chapel of Yale College, September 10, 1828. New Haven, 1828. 8°, pp. 38
[*A A. S B. Publ Br Mus. Harv. U. T S. Y. C*

The same New Haven, 1842 8°, pp. 40.
[*A. C. A. B. Publ. Br. Mus. U. T. S. Y. C.*

On human depravity. The sermon was reviewed by the Rev. Joseph Harvey (Yale 1808), and led the way to prolonged controversy

7. Essays on the Means of Regeneration, first published in the Quarterly Christian Spectator, for 1829 New Haven, 1829. 8°. [*A. C A. Y. C.*

Anonymous These Essays originally appeared in vol 1 of the *Spectator*, pp 1–40, 209–34, 481–508, 692–712, in the form of a review of Gardiner Spring's *Dissertation*, and are here republished with the same paging They brought Dr Bennet Tyler (Yale 1804) into the field, as an opponent of Dr. Taylor

8 An Inquiry into the Nature of Sin, as exhibited in Dr. Dwight's Theology. A Letter to a Friend, by Clericus [With remarks on an Examination of Dr. Taylor's and Mr Harvey's Views on the same subject] New Haven, 1829 8°, pp 43
[*A. C. A. U. T. S. Y. C.*

9. Review of Dr. Tyler's Strictures upon an article in the Christian Spectator, on the Means of Regeneration—First published in the Christian Spectator for March, 1830 .. New-Haven, 1830. 8°, pp. 56 [*A. C A. Y. C.*

Anonymous

10 A Review of Dr. Woods' Letters to Dr. Taylor, on the Permission of Sin Together with remarks on Dr Bellamy's Treatise, on the same subject—First published in the Quarterly Christian Spectator, for September, 1830 New-Haven, 1830 8°, pp. 50
[*A. C. A. U T. S. Y. C*

Anonymous; pp. 40–50, the remarks on Bellamy, were contributed by the Rev Luther Hart. Dr Taylor's essay was in reply to *Letters* addressed to him in July, 1830, by Professor Leonard Woods, of Andover

11 Case of the Rev Mr Barnes [Biblical Repertory on Imputation]

In the *Quarterly Christian Spectator* for June, 1831, vol 3, pp. 292–336. Anonymous.

12. The Biblical Repertory on the Doctrine of Imputation

In the *Quarterly Christian Spectator* for September, 1831, pp 497–512 Anonymous

13. Correspondence between Rev Dr. Taylor and Rev Dr Hawes.—From the Connecticut Observer [1832] 8°, pp. 8
[*A C A U. T. S Y C.*

Dr Taylor's letter was a response to Dr Hawes' request for a statement of his views respecting the doctrines of the Bible, and was first printed in the *Observer,* a Hartford newspaper of February 20, 1832; it was also reprinted in the *Spirit of the Pilgrims* for March, 1832, vol. 5, pp. 173–79

14 Reply to Dr. Tyler's Examination Boston, 1832 8°, pp 24. [*A. C A U. T. S Y. C*

From the *Spirit of the Pilgrims* for August, 1832, vol 5, pp 425–48 In reply to Remarks on No. 13, above, by Dr Bennet Tyler, published in the same periodical for June Dr. Tyler made a rejoinder to this Reply, in the same periodical for September and October

15 Remarks on Propagated Depravity, and Sin as the necessary means of the greatest good. First published in the Quarterly Christian Spectator, for September, 1832, as a review of Dr Tyler's Remarks on Dr Taylor's Letter. New-Haven, 1832 8°, pp. 40
[*A C A. Y. C*

Anonymous.

16 Reply to Dr Tyler [on the Doctrine of Decrees, the Doctrines of Propagated Depravity, etc , and the Doctrine of Irresistible Grace].

In the *Spirit of the Pilgrims* for December, 1832, and January and February, 1833, vol 5, pp 669–94, and vol. 6, pp 5–18, 65–84

17 Review of Spring's Dissertation on Native Depravity —First published in the Quarterly Christian Spectator New Haven, 1833. 8°, pp. 20 [*Y C*

Anonymous From the *Spectator* for June, 1833

18 A Letter, on the subject of his late discussion with Rev Dr. Tyler.—First published in the Quarterly Christian Spectator, for September, 1833. New-Haven 8°, pp. 24 [*Y C.*

19 He was also the author of the Reply to the President (pp 5–12), in the following.

The New-Haven Memorial to the President, protesting against the use of the United-States Army to enforce the bogus laws of Kansas, the Answer of President Buchanan, and the Reply of the Memorialists. [New Haven, 1857.] 8°, pp 12 [*Harv. Y C*

After his death were published.

20. Practical Sermons. New York, 1858 8°, pp. 455. [*A. C A. B. Publ U. T. S. Y C.*

Containing thirty-two sermons, written during his early ministry

21 Lectures on the Moral Government of God. New York, 1859 2 vols, 8°, pp xiii, 417, viii, 423. [*A C A. U. T S Y C*

With Introduction by his son-in-law, President Porter

22. Essays, Lectures, etc., upon select topics in Revealed Theology New York, 1859 8°, pp viii, 480 [*A C. A. B. Publ U T. S. Y. C*

23 An Address delivered at the funeral of Dr Noah Webster, May 31st, 1843.

In Professor William C Fowler's *Essays*, Hartford, 1876 8°, pp. 62–71.

He was a large contributor to the (Monthly) *Christian Spectator*, but only the two articles above mentioned (Nos 3, 4) have been identified, and probably other articles than those specified in the *Quarterly Christian Spectator* were from his pen He was thus in part (jointly with Noah Porter, Junior) the author of a review of Wardlaw's Christian Ethics, in vol 7, September, 1835; and with Royal Robbins the author of a review of Wayland's Elements of Moral Science, in the same volume for December

A letter descriptive of President Dwight, written in 1844 to the Rev. William B Sprague, is printed in Sprague's *Annals of the American Pulpit,* vol 2, pp. 161–64

AUTHORITIES

Bacon, Hist. Discourses at New Haven, 281–83 Congregational Quarterly, ii, 245–66 *Dwight,* Memories of Yale Life and Men, 253–58 *Fowler,* Essays, 47–71 *Kilbourne,* Biogr Hist. of Litchfield County, 261–62 *W L Kingsley,* Yale College, ii, 28–36. Memorial of Dr Taylor *Orcutt,* Hist of New Milford, 625–28, 775 Semi-Centennial Anniversary of the Divinity School, 16–18, 79, 91–103.

JOHN LEWIS TOMLINSON, the son of Captain John Lewis Tomlinson, of Derby, Connecticut, and a nephew of the Rev. Daniel Tomlinson (Yale 1781), was born in Derby in 1786. His mother was Deborah, daughter of Captain Samuel Bassett, of Derby, and he was a first cousin of his classmate Bassett.

After graduation he studied law, and settled in Derby During the war of 1812 he saw some service in the militia, with the rank of Lieutenant.

While he was president of the Derby Bank, in 1824–25, by some loose management heavy losses were incurred, as a result of which, and of consequent criticism, he relinquished in 1827 his profession, and in 1832 left Derby

Having studied theology, he was ordained to the ministry in connection with the Presbyterian Church about 1836, and had charge of a small congregation in Adrian, Michigan, from about 1838 to 1842.

For a few years longer he remained in missionary service in Michigan, and then removed to Ohio, where the rest of his life was spent in similar employment. For a part of the time his residence was in Cleveland, where he died suddenly, on March 18, 1853, in his 67th year

He bore an excellent and exemplary reputation.

A daughter survived him

AUTHORITIES

Orcutt, Hist of Derby, 277–78, 300–01, 599, 662; Tomlinson Family, 72, 117.

Jonathan George Washington Trumbull, the youngest child of David and Sarah (Backus) Trumbull, of Lebanon, Connecticut, and grandson of Governor Jonathan Trumbull (Harvard 1727), was born in Lebanon on October 3, 1789. His brother Joseph was graduated here in 1801. He was educated at the expense of Governor Jonathan Trumbull, Junior (Harvard 1759), who was his father's brother, and whose wife was his mother's half-sister,—they having no sons

After graduation he studied law, but never entered on practice

He settled in Norwich, where he was engaged to some extent in mercantile and manufacturing business. He married, on November 14, 1815, Jane Eliza, the eldest child of Daniel Lathrop (Yale 1787), of Norwich, who died in Norwich on October 21, 1843, at the age of 48.

He died in Norwich, just after midnight, on September 5, 1853, aged nearly 64 years He had been in declining health from paralysis for about sixteen months, and for the last few months almost helpless.

One son survived him.

AUTHORITIES.

American Ancestry, v, 33–34. *Hine*, Early Lebanon, 102 *Huntington*, Lathrop Family Memoir, 146 *Perkins*, Old Houses in Norwich, 512. *Walworth*, Hyde Genealogy, ii, 1083

James Wakefield Tucker, a son of Deacon Thomas Tucker, a school-teacher of Danbury, Connecticut, and Anna (Dibble) Tucker, was born in Danbury on April 19, 1787.

He studied theology after graduation with the Rev Moses Stuart (Yale 1799), of New Haven, and was licensed to preach by the Western Association of Ministers of New Haven County on May 30, 1809.

His first settlement in the ministry was in Rowley, Essex County, Massachusetts, where he was ordained and installed over the First Congregational Church on June 24, 1812, with a salary of $600. As his family increased, he found his salary inadequate, and was reluctantly forced to ask a release

He was accordingly dismissed, after five years' service, on June 24, 1817. During his ministry twenty-three persons were added to the church.

On August 4, 1818, he was installed over the Presbyterian Church in Springfield, New Jersey, and for six months he devoted himself zealously to the work. He died there, after an acute illness of forty-eight hours, from bilious colic, on February 11, 1819, in his 32d year.

He married on October 18, 1809, Harriet, fourth daughter of Timothy Atwater, of New Haven, and a sister of the wife of his classmate Daggett.

She returned after his death to New Haven, with her children, four daughters and one son, and died in New York City on October 1, 1844, in her 55th year.

The son was graduated at Yale in 1836 One daughter married the Rev Lorenzo L Langstroth (Yale 1831), and another married a son of her father's classmate Hull, and was the mother of Charles A Hull (Yale 1869).

Mr. Tucker is credited with a clear and discriminating mind and correct literary taste. He was explicit and direct in the pulpit, and fervently interested in the duties of his profession. In his brief ministry in Springfield he took special interest in the Sunday Schools which had just been begun, and was regarded as showing remarkable pulpit ability

AUTHORITIES

Amer Quarterly Register, vii, 253, 259 Atwater Hist, 1901, 144, 407. Christian Spectator, i, 106–08. *Gage,* Hist of Rowley, 29 *Chas A Hull,* MS Letter, April, 1911 *Ricord,* Hist of Union County, 497.

LEONARD EUGENE WALES, the youngest son of the Rev. Dr. Samuel Wales (Yale 1767), the Professor of Divinity in Yale College, was born in New Haven in

1788. He first entered as Freshman in 1802 His College career was distinguished, and he delivered the Valedictory Oration at graduation, besides being one of the editors of the *Literary Cabinet,* a periodical published by his classmates in their Senior year.

He studied law, and entered on practice in his native city, where he was unusually successful He held the office of City Attorney from 1819 to 1821.

His career was cut short by his death here, from typhus fever, after an illness of about two weeks, on September 14, 1823, at the age of 35

He was unmarried. His estate shows a valuable library.

The notice of his death in the public prints describes him as possessed of a vigorous and highly cultivated mind, united with a fine classical taste. He enjoyed a high reputation as a lawyer, and was deeply lamented His Christian character was abundantly manifested.

AUTHORITIES

Conn Journal, Sept. 16, and Dec. 30, 1823

CURTISS WARNER, a son of Noadiah and Polly (Curtiss) Warner, of Southbury, Connecticut, was born on January 24, 1787 His scholarship in College was eminent, and he delivered the Salutatory Oration at graduation

In 1810 he took charge of a grammar-school in Winchester, which he conducted acceptably until his death there on April 18, 1813, in his 26th year.

AUTHORITIES

Boyd, Hist of Winchester, 403 *Cothren,* Hist of Woodbury, iii, 450

ELY WARNER, the second son and fourth child of Jonathan Warner, of Chester, then a parish in Saybrook,

Connecticut, and grandson of Jonathan and Elizabeth (Selden) Warner, was born in Chester on May 24, 1785. His mother was Hephzibah, daughter of Joseph and Rebecca (Selden) Ely, of Hadlyme.

After graduation he taught for a year or more, and then entered the Litchfield Law School. As a witness to his faithful attendance he left at his death three manuscript volumes, containing the lectures which he heard, written out from his own stenographic notes.

He was admitted to the bar at Middletown about 1811, and began practice in Saybrook, but in 1816 settled in Haddam.

He represented Haddam in the State Legislature in 1825 and 1831. In 1829 he was appointed Chief Judge of Middlesex County Court, and served until 1835. Subsequently he became cashier of the East Haddam Bank, but in 1837 returned to Chester, and resided on his farm there for the rest of his life.

In 1855 he was appointed one of the County Commissioners for Middlesex County, and he held that office for two years. He was also for over fifty years actively engaged as a County Surveyor.

He died, from paralysis, at his residence in Chester, on October 23, 1872, in his 88th year, being at that time the oldest practicing lawyer in the State.

Judge Warner was married, on November 11, 1817, to Sarah Ward, eldest daughter of John and Mehitable (Clark) Warner, of Chester, who survived him.

Their children were five sons and three daughters, of whom all but two sons survived him.

One son was graduated at Yale in 1854, but died the next year.

He was a pure minded man, an able pleader, an intelligent citizen, and died without an enemy.

AUTHORITIES.

Ely Ancestry, 121, 224–25. *Andrew E. Warner,* MS. Letter, May, 1873.

WILLIAM AVERY WHELPLEY was a grandson of Samuel and Hannah (Olmsted) Whelpley, who removed from Wilton Parish in Norwalk, Connecticut, to the northeastern part of Stockbridge, on the borders of Lenox, Massachusetts, in 1766 His father, William Whelpley, resided within the limits of Lenox, where he was born about 1785, he was prepared for admission to Yale at the opening of the Junior year, by his uncle, the Rev Samuel Whelpley, then the principal of a select school in Morristown, New Jersey

After graduation he returned to Morristown to teach, and in 1809 succeeded his uncle in his place in Morristown, and as the head of the school approved himself as an excellent scholar, a faithful teacher, and a true gentleman. In the fall of 1810 he declined an election to a tutorship in College.

He also studied medicine, and settled in practice in Morristown, where he died in 1828—(probably on August 6, from consumption).

His widow, Mrs. Sarah Whelpley, died in Morristown, on April 21, 1869.

AUTHORITIES.

Barnard's Amer Journal of Education, xvi, 740

Annals, 1807-08

Seth Norton, of the Class of 1804, entered on the tutorship at the beginning of this year, but resigned at its close; as did also the Senior Tutor, Noyes Darling, of the Class of 1801, and Tutor Mills Day, of the Class of 1803. At Commencement in 1808 Thomas Hopkins Gallaudet and Edward Hooker, of the Class of 1805, and Louis Mitchell, Henry Stone, and Nathaniel Chauncey, of the Class of 1806, were elected to tutorships

At the same Commencement the Senior Fellow, the Rev. Enoch Huntington, of Middletown, of the Class of 1759, resigned his office, on account of greatly enfeebled health; and his example was followed by the Rev Dr Nathan Williams, of Tolland, of the Class of 1755 Their places were filled by the election of the Rev. Dr. Joseph Strong, of Norwich, of the Class of 1772, and the Rev Achilles Mansfield, of Killingworth, of the Class of 1770.

A remarkable revival of religion was experienced in the College, in April, 1808.

Sketches, Class of 1808

*Ebenezer Baldwin, A M. *1837
*Milton Barlow *1867
*Carolus Isaacus Battell, Reip. Ind Cur Super Jurid *1868
*Timotheus Phelps Beers, A.M., M.D. 1824, Obstetr. Prof. *1858
*Josephus Hart Bellamy, A.M *1848
*Burr Bradley *1849
*Johannes Brainard, A.M. *1851
*Henricus Brown *1849
*Johannes Chandler *1875
**Jonathan Edwards Chaplin,* A.M *1847
**Noachus Coe,* A.M. *1871
**Jonathan Cone,* A M. *1850
*David Ludovicus Daggett *1810
*Josephus Delafield *1875
**Matthaeus Rice Dutton,* A.M., Tutor, Math et Philos. Nat et Astron. Prof. *1825
*Justinus Dwinell, e Congr. *1850
*Erastus Edgerton *1809
*Daniel Fuller *1856
*Henricus Guilielmus Gibbs, A.M.
*Guilielmus Miller Gibson
*Timotheus Jones Gridley, A.M., M.D. Dartm. 1812 et Coll. Med Viridim. 1839 *1852
*Carolus Griswold, A M *1839
**Guilielmus Hanford* *1861
**Josephus Harvey,* A.M., S.T.D Amh. 1835 *1873
**Nathanael Hewit,* S.T.D. Amh. 1830 *1867
*Jacobus Abrahamus Hillhouse, A.M. *1841

*Benjamin Simmons Hort *1825
*Radulphus Isaacs Ingersoll, e Congr., apud Aul. Russ. Legatus *1872
*Preserved Jennings *1837
*Johannes Thomas Jones *182–
*Jonathan Knight, A.M., M D 1818, Tutor, Anat. et Physiol etiam Chirurg. Prof., Rerumpubl. Foed Soc. Med Praeses *1864
*Garrick Mallery, LL.D. Lafay. 1840 *1866
*Josias Hinman Minor *1820
*Johannes Bates Murdock *1815
*Amasa Parker, A.M. *1855
**Jacobus Hill Parmelee,* A.M. Neo-Caes. 1814 *1872
*Guilielmus Seward Pierson, A M., M D Dartm. 1813 *1860
*Theodorus Pomeroy, M.D Schol Med Berks. 1849 *1860
**Lyman Spencer Rexford,* A.M. Hamilt. 1819 *1843
*Silas Webster Robbins, A.M. 1845, Reip. Kentuck. Cur. Super Jurid *1871
*Carolus Fox Roberts *1836
*Henricus Guilielmus Rogers *1819
*Guilielmus Silliman *1861
*Abrahamus Miller Smith *1839
*Guilielmus Mason Smith, A M. 1815 et Hamilt 1815 *1838
*Job Staples *1861
**Timotheus Tuttle,* A M. *1864
*Septimius Tyler, A.M. 1813 *1817
*Carolus Wheeler, A M. 1827 *1858
**Comfort Williams,* A M *1825

EBENEZER BALDWIN, the eldest son of the Hon. Simeon Baldwin (Yale 1781), of New Haven, was born in New Haven on May 20, 1790.

He studied law with Harmanus Bleecker in Albany, New York, was admitted to the bar in 1813, and settled there in practice, attaining distinction in the literary and political circles of the city.

He was successively Master in Chancery, County Surrogate (from July, 1819, to February, 1821), Alderman, City Recorder (to February, 1826), and military aid to Governor DeWitt Clinton, with the rank of Colonel.

On account of broken health he returned about 1828 to his father's house, and with unquenched mental vigor occupied himself as he was able with literary work

The fruits of his leisure were.

1 Annals of Yale College, in New Haven, Connecticut, from its foundation, to the year 1831 With an Appendix, containing statistical Tables, and exhibiting the present condition of the Institution New Haven, 1831 8°, pp viii, 324

[*A A S B Publ. Br. Mus Columbia Univ. Harv M.H S U S U T S Y C*

After his death appeared

The same, Second edition, with title

Annals of Yale College, from its foundation, to the year 1831 To which is added, an Appendix, bringing it down to 1838 New Haven, 1838 8°, pp viii, 343

[*A. C. A. B Ath. B Publ Br Mus U S U. T. S Y C*

A valuable compilation, not even now entirely superseded Although the second edition did not appear until 1838, the Appendix appears to be mainly the work of the author, and prepared before his last illness

2. Observations on the physical, intellectual, and moral qualities of our Colored Population with remarks on the subject of Emancipation and Colonization New Haven, 1834. 8°, pp 52

[*B Ath B Publ. Y C*

He also contributed to several biographical collections then in course of publication in New York and Philadelphia; and in January, 1836, issued the first number of a monthly magazine, entitled:

The American Historical Magazine, and Literary Record 8°
Six numbers only were issued (without his name) but about the time of the publication of the last number, in June, 1836, his health failed so completely as to prevent further exertion

After lingering in feebleness for six months, he died in New Haven, on January 26, 1837, in his 47th year He was never married A medallion portrait is owned by the family

AUTHORITIES

Baldwin Genealogy, i, 278. *Munsell,* Annals of Albany, i, 299; viii, 143, Collections, ii, 433, 447, 450-51, 470 N. Y Geneal and Biogr. Record, xlii, 43

MILTON BARLOW, the son of Thomas and Amy Barlow, of Amenia, Duchess County, New York, was born in Amenia on May 3, or 4, 1784 He came to Yale from Williams College at the opening of the Senior year.

He studied law, and was admitted to the bar of Duchess County in 1811, but never practiced. He spent an indolent and uneventful life in his native State, and died in East Chester, Westchester County, on October 26, 1867, in his 83d year He was buried in Amenia He was unmarried

AUTHORITIES

H Barlow, MS Letter, August, 1868 *VanAlstyne,* Burying Grounds of Sharon and Amenia, 129

CHARLES ISAAC BATTELL, the youngest son of William and Sarah Battell, of Milford and Torringford, Connecticut, and grandson of John and Mehitable (Sherman) Battell, of Dedham, Massachusetts, was born in Torringford on July 25, 1789. His mother was a sister of Judge Gideon Buckingham (Yale 1765), of Milford. The Hon Robbins Battell (Yale 1839) was a nephew

He studied law in Catskill, and the earlier years of his professional life were spent in Western New York.

In 1819 he removed to Indiana, taking up his residence at first in Springfield, which he represented in the State Legislature in two sessions (November, 1820–January, 1822).

In 1823 he removed to Evansville, on the southern border of the State, where he had a long and honorable career He filled acceptably various important public positions He was thus a member of the State Senate for two sessions (December, 1833–February, 1835), and Judge of the State Circuit Court.

He was affiliated politically with the Whigs and Republicans.

In 1866 he went to reside in the family of a niece, the wife of Cortland L. Latimer (Yale 1832), in Cleveland, Ohio, where he died on April 12, 1868, in his 79th year He was never married

Judge Battell was a man of sterling integrity, pure life, and intelligent Christian faith

---

AUTHORITIES.

Chapman, Buckingham Family, 23 *Orcutt,* Hist. of Torrington, 159, 649

Timothy Phelps Beers, the second son of Deacon Nathan Beers, of New Haven, and grandson of Nathan and Hannah (Nichols) Beers, of Stratford and New Haven, was born on December 25, 1789. His mother was Mary, second daughter of Judge John and Mary (Richardson) Phelps of Stafford Springs, and a sister of Timothy Phelps (Yale 1780). One of his sisters married Dr. Eli Ives (Yale 1799), a second married Dr. John Titsworth (Yale 1814), and a third married Dr Charles Hooker (Yale 1820) A brother was graduated here in 1817.

He was prepared for College by Thomas Adams (Yale 1800).

After graduation he began the study of medicine in New Haven with his brother-in-law, Dr. Ives, and in the winter of 1811–12 he attended lectures in the University of Pennsylvania, at Philadelphia

In the spring of 1812 he began practice in his native place In the summer of 1813 he accepted duty as Surgeon of a regiment of militia, and was stationed for several months at New London. The rest of his life was devoted unselfishly to the performance of his professional duties in New Haven. In 1824 the honorary degree of M.D was conferred on him by Yale College, on the recommendation of the State Medical Society

In 1830 he was appointed a Professor in the Medical Institution of Yale College, and he filled acceptably the chair of Obstetrics until his resignation in July, 1856.

After a brief but distressing illness of one week, from a disease of the kidneys, he died in New Haven on September 22, 1858, in his 69th year. The addresses delivered at his funeral by his colleague and classmate, Dr Knight, and by his pastor, the Rev. Dr. S. W S. Dutton, were subsequently published. Dr. Knight describes him as "an upright, truthful, benevolent man, a kind-hearted, intelligent physician, and a sincere Christian."

His portrait, painted by Nathaniel Jocelyn about 1830, is owned by the Medical School.

He first married his first cousin, Caroline, eldest daughter of Judge Isaac Mills (Yale 1786), of New Haven, who died on August 11, 1826, in her 34th year

He was married, secondly, on January 2, 1827, in New York, by the bride's brother-in-law, the Rev. Dr. Gardiner Spring (Yale 1805), to Mary Ann, daughter of Captain Hanover and Phebe (Wolcott) Barney, of New Haven, and formerly the wife of George Ingersoll Whiting, of New Haven. She died in New Haven on February 26, 1893, in her 94th year.

By his first wife he had three daughters (one of whom died before him) and two sons. One son was graduated at the Yale Medical School in 1847. One daughter married General William S. Pierson (Yale 1836), a son of a classmate, and another was the mother of the Rev. Isaac Peck (Yale 1879).

AUTHORITIES

Conn. Medical Society's Proceedings, 1859, 85–89. Historical Magazine, ii, 348 *W. L. Kingsley,* Yale College, ii, 74 Memorial of Dr Beers N Y. Geneal and Biogr. Record, xliii, 44 Phelps Family, i, 306–07, 533

JOSEPH HART BELLAMY, the only child of 'Squire David Bellamy, of Bethlehem, Connecticut, and grandson of the Rev. Dr Joseph Bellamy (Yale 1735), was born in Bethlehem in 1788 His mother was Silence, daughter of David Leavitt, of Bethlehem He was prepared for College by his pastor, the Rev. Dr. Azel Backus (Yale 1787).

After graduation he studied in the Litchfield Law School, and settled in his native town, where he spent his life, partly engaged in agriculture He never cared for an extensive practice, but was much employed in public business. He represented the town in the General Assembly in October, 1818, 1819, 1821, 1826, and 1827, and was a member of the State Senate in 1841. He was a County Commissioner in 1839 and 1840.

Through life he maintained an irreproachable character, and was held in the highest esteem

He died in Bethlehem, after a short but painful illness, on November 2, 1848, aged 60 years

He married, on November 4, 1813, Sarah Griswold, second daughter of Judge John Griswold Hillhouse, and Elizabeth (Mason) Hillhouse, of Montville, Connecticut, who was born on January 31, 1790.

Their children were two sons, who died young, and two daughters. The elder daughter married the Rev. Nathan W. Munroe (Harvard 1830), and the younger married the Rev. Aretas Loomis (Williams Coll. 1815).

AUTHORITIES.

Baker, Hist. of Montville, 557–58. *Cothren,* Hist. of Woodbury, i, 355–57. *Hinman,* Early Puritan Settlers of Conn., 185. *Kilbourne,* Bench and Bar of Litchfield County, 95. N. E. Hist. and Geneal. Register, lxi, 340. *Walworth,* Hyde Genealogy, ii, 927.

BURR BRADLEY was prepared for College by James Burnet (Yale 1798), of Norwalk, Connecticut, and entered from Fairfield,—perhaps from that portion of the town now included in Westport,—where he was born in 1789.

He studied medicine after graduation, and finally settled in Warsaw, Hancock County, Illinois, on the Mississippi River, about thirty miles north of Quincy. Here he was much esteemed as a physician, and also highly valued for his Christian character. He was a Ruling Elder for many years in the Presbyterian Church.

Warsaw was visited by the cholera in the late summer of 1849, and Dr. Bradley was one of the early victims, at the age of 60.

He was survived by a wife and children.

AUTHORITIES.

Home Missionary, xxii, 196.

JOHN BRAINARD, the eldest son of Colonel John Brainard, a farmer of Haddam, Connecticut, and grandson of Captain Jabez and Hannah (Clark) Brainard, of Haddam, was born on April 5, 1782. His mother was Hannah, daughter of Thomas and Hannah (Snow) Hubbard. He was prepared for College by the Rev. Dr. Nathan

Perkins, of West Hartford, and entered after the opening of the Freshman year

For three or four years after graduation he taught school,—in Wethersfield, and in Albany; and he then went into business in Pittsburgh, Pennsylvania, in partnership with a distant kinsman, Edward Selden, Junior (Yale 1811)

Mr. Selden died in 1823, and at that time or earlier Mr. Brainard removed to New Orleans, where the rest of his life was spent

He was for some years an officer in the Custom House in New Orleans.

He died in New Orleans on November 22, 1851, in his 70th year. He was unmarried

AUTHORITIES.

Brainard Genealogy, 231 Brainerd-Brainard Genealogy, pt 6, 56.

HENRY BROWN, the youngest son of Daniel and Anna (Phelps) Brown, of Hebron, Connecticut, and a brother of Daniel Bishop Brown (Yale 1800), was born in Hebron on May 13, 1789. He entered Yale from Williams College at the beginning of the Senior year

After graduation he began the study of law with Abram VanVechten, of Albany, New York, and continued it with John Gregg, of Canandaigua, and with his own brother, Daniel B. Brown, in Batavia.

Being admitted to the bar about 1813, he settled in practice in Springfield, Otsego County Later he removed to Stark, in Herkimer County, where he was placed on the bench, and served as Chief Judge of the County Court from February, 1823, to March, 1825. He made large outlays in Stark, in the establishment of mills and other industries.

He returned again to Otsego County, and practiced in Cooperstown until his removal to Chicago in 1836.

There he took a leading position at once, and for two years from May, 1837, held the office of Justice of the Peace.

He was elected City Attorney for the year 1842 and again filled that position for the latter half of the next year, during an accidental vacancy.

He then occupied himself with the preparation of his *History of Illinois*, which appeared in the latter part of 1844; and in 1845 he resumed the regular practice of his profession, in partnership with his only son, then 25 years of age.

The cholera visited Chicago in 1849, and he was the first victim, dying on March 16, in his 60th year. He was buried with Masonic honors, and was survived by his wife and four daughters, besides his son.

Judge Brown was eminently kindly and cordial in intercourse, and devoid of all pretension. He was very industrious in his habits, and took a leading position in Chicago as an historical and literary authority, being an extensive reader and a ready writer and speaker.

He was originally a Democrat and entertained ex-President VanBuren on his southwestern tour in 1842. He became a Free-Soiler in 1848; but was too transparent to be a successful politician.

He was of imposing stature, and of dignified appearance, weighing over two hundred pounds.

1. A Narrative of the Anti-Masonick Excitement, in the Western part of the State of New-York, during the years 1826, '7, '8, and a part of 1829. Batavia, 1829. 12°, pp. 6, 244.

[*A. A. S. B. Ath. B. Publ. Br. Mus. U. S. U. T. S. Y. C.*

Giving the Masonic view of the abduction and fate of William Morgan.

2. A History of Illinois, from its First Discovery and Settlement, to the present time. New-York, 1844. 8°, pp. x, 492 + map.

[*A. A. S. B. Ath. B. Publ. Br. Mus. Harv. U. S. U. T. S. Y. C.*

After his death appeared, in Fergus' *Historical Series,* No 9, Chicago, 1876, 8°, pp 1–18:

3 The Present and Future Prospects of Chicago an Address delivered before the Chicago Lyceum, January 20, 1846

AUTHORITIES

Andreas, Hist of Chicago, i, 184, 431–32, 501–02 *Hardin,* Hist of Herkimer County, 353 Phelps Family, i, 237.

JOHN CHANDLER, the eldest child of John and Mary (Campfield) Chandler, was born in Elizabeth, New Jersey, on December 30, 1784. He spent his Freshman year at Princeton College.

After graduation he studied theology, and was for a part of the year 1809–10 a member of the Andover Seminary.

He received a license to preach, and continued for some twenty years a licentiate under the care of the Presbytery of Elizabeth, but his delicate health and feeble vocal powers prevented his undertaking active service.

He married on September 16, 1818, Margaret, daughter of James Chapman, of Elizabeth, and widow of James C Mulford, and settled in Newark From January, 1829, until his death he held the office of Elder in the Third Presbyterian Church, of which he was one of the earliest and most devoted members He was well known in Newark as a quiet citizen and Christian gentleman

His wife died in 1861, and he died at the residence of a son-in-law in Brooklyn, New York, on December 1, 1875, aged nearly 91 years, being the last survivor of his Class

He had four children, one of whom died before him.

AUTHORITIES.

T C Chandler, MS Letter, May, 1876

Jonathan Edwards Chaplin, the youngest son of Benjamin Chaplin (Yale 1778) and Sarah (Edwards) Chaplin, of that part of Mansfield which is now Chaplin, Connecticut, and a great-grandson of Jonathan Edwards (Yale 1720), was born in Mansfield on April 30, 1789, one month after his father's death. His mother married Captain Daniel Tyler, of Brooklyn, Connecticut, in 1790; and his grandfather Chaplin, who died in 1795, left provision for this grandson's liberal education. He entered College at the opening of the Sophomore year from the Woodstock Academy, of which Seth Norton (Yale 1804) was then the preceptor. A half-sister married the Rev. Samuel P. Williams (Yale 1796).

After graduation he studied law, and practiced for a short time in Pomfret, but soon removed to Buffalo, New York, where he was admitted to the bar in September, 1811.

During the War of 1812 he was appointed aide-de-camp to General Porter, of the Northwestern army. His army experience was disastrous and almost fatal to him, as it laid the foundation for a habit of intemperance which continued for many years.

In 1818 he removed to Urbana, Champaign County, Ohio, where he resumed the practice of his profession, and soon acquired the reputation of being an astute and able lawyer. In 1820 he married Harriet, daughter of Abishai and Lucinda Hoisington, of Wayne, now Woodstock, in that County, who had removed from Windsor, Vermont, to Ohio, three years before.

With great versatility, ready wit, and an immense fund of anecdote, he kept a sort of popularity, though degraded by his habits. At the beginning of 1830, however, under peculiar circumstances he experienced a radical change, broke off from his intemperance, and united with the Methodist Church. In 1831 he became convinced that it was his duty to preach the gospel, and accordingly received license as a local preacher.

He now abandoned the law, and in November, 1833, became Principal of a Seminary just established under the auspices of the Methodist Episcopal Church in Norwalk, Huron County, where he continued until 1838, when he entered on pastoral work, at first in Elyria, and then in Tiffin, where his wife died, on January 27, 1840, at the age of 42

He was then stationed at Maumee, in Lucas County, where he married on May 20, 1841, Abigail, daughter of Colonel Thomas Hunt, of the United States Army, and Eunice (Wellington) Hunt, and widow of Colonel Josiah Snelling, who died in 1829.

In the fall of 1842 he was transferred to the Michigan Conference, and appointed Principal of a branch of the State University of Michigan, at White Pigeon, on the Southern border of the State. For four years he was occupied with the duties of this office, and gave good satisfaction He also continued to take constant ministerial duty, and found the combination too exhausting

He had therefore determined to resign his position as Principal, but before this was accomplished he died in White Pigeon, after a painful illness of eight weeks, on September 15, 1846, in his 58th year

His wife survived him, as also his two sons by his first marriage.

He was a good classical scholar and an admirable teacher. As a preacher he was especially marked by his powers of analysis and condensation. He was genial and social in his nature, and an entertaining companion, full of anecdote and good-humor. He took an active interest in politics, and in 1845 was the unsuccessful Whig candidate for Governor.

AUTHORITIES

Dimock, Mansfield Records, 41. *Edwards,* Descendants of Timothy Edwards, 31, 33 Hunt Genealogy, 318-19 *Sprague,* Annals of the Amer Pulpit, VII, 797-802. *Williams,* Hist of Huron and Erie Counties, 151

Noah Coe, the eldest child of Charles Coe, a farmer, of Durham, Connecticut, and grandson of Abel and Prudence (Rossiter) Coe, of Durham, was born in Durham on May 24, 1786. His mother was Hannah, daughter of James and Mary (Curtis) Bates, of Durham.

He studied theology after graduation, for a part of the years 1809–10 in the Andover Seminary, and was licensed to preach by the New Haven East Association of Ministers on June 12, 1810.

His first pastoral charge was in Chester, Orange County, New York, where he was ordained and installed by the Presbytery of Hudson on July 3, 1811. He was dismissed from Chester in 1813, and in June, 1814, was installed over the Presbyterian Church of New Hartford, Oneida County, where he was highly respected and beloved, and where he remained until February, 1835.

He then returned to New Haven, Connecticut, and for about a year supplied the vacant pulpit in Woodbridge.

In 1836 he began to supply the Second Congregational Church in Greenwich, which called him to a settlement on March 30, 1837. He was accordingly installed as pastor on May 23, and had on the whole a successful ministry.

Dissatisfaction, however, arose in the church, his critics claiming that his labors were inadequate to the needs of the parish, and that his usefulness was gone.

The Church and Society in April, 1845, requested him to join with them in calling the Fairfield West Consociation. He declined to be a party to their action, but the Consociation met on May 20, and voted his dismission; they stated in their result that the charge of inadequate service was wholly unfounded, but that his usefulness and comfort had been brought to an end by the hasty and censurable proceedings of a portion of his people.

About two hundred persons had been added to the Church during his ministry.

He was not again a settled pastor, but for ten or fifteen years labored almost continually in other forms of ministerial service. From 1848 to 1854 he was engaged as a city missionary in New York and Brooklyn.

He then removed to New Haven, where he resided until his death. From November, 1854, to February, 1856, he was the stated supply of the Congregational Church in Northfield parish, in Litchfield; and for the following year supplied the Congregational Church at New Preston Hill, in Washington. A prayer which he made at a Fast-Day service in Woodbury, in January, 1861, with a scathing reference to President Buchanan, is still remembered.

He died suddenly, at his daughter's house in New Haven, on May 9, 1871, at the age of 85

He married, on October 25, 1810, Elizabeth, second daughter of the Rev. Samuel Goodrich (Yale 1783), of Berlin, Connecticut, who died in New Haven on March 10, 1864, in her 77th year Their children were two daughters and three sons.

The second son was graduated here in 1837, and the third son (who became a minister) in 1838; but both died before their parents. The younger daughter married the Rev. Chauncey Goodrich (Yale 1837); the elder daughter died in infancy

He was, with the Rev. Moses Gillett (Yale 1804), one of the editors of the following:

A Narrative of the Revival of Religion, in the County of Oneida, particularly in the bounds of the Presbytery of Oneida, in the year 1826. Utica, 1826. 8°, pp. 88. [*Y. C*

AUTHORITIES

Bartlett, Coe Family, 188, 277–78. *Cothren*, Hist of Woodbury, ii, 1102–03 *Fowler*, Hist of Durham, 126–27, 401 Goodrich Family, 129 *P. Jones*, Annals of Oneida County, 277. *Mead*, Hist. of Greenwich, 262–63. 150th Anniversary of 2d Church, Greenwich, 38. *Ruttenber and Clark*, Hist. of Orange County, 618

Jonathan Cone, the only son in a family of six children of Deacon Cephas Cone, of Westchester Parish, in Colchester, Connecticut, and grandson of Jonathan and Ann (Chapman) Cone, of East Haddam, was born in Westchester on July 12, 1785. His mother was Sarah, daughter of John Gates, of East Haddam. His youngest sister married Dr. Andrew F. Warner (Yale 1812). He was prepared for admission to the Junior Class at Yale by John Adams (Yale 1795), at Bacon Academy in Colchester. He united with the College Church on profession of his faith in July, 1808.

He studied theology after graduation, and was for more than one year (in 1809–10) a member of the Andover Seminary. He was licensed to preach by the Middlesex Association of Ministers in March, 1810; and on May 22, 1811, he was ordained and installed as pastor of the Congregational Church in Bristol. His early ministry there was successful; but about 1822 difficulties, involving charges against his moral character, arose. Mr. Cone wielded church discipline unsparingly, but after long-continued recriminations he was dismissed without censure on March 19, 1828. Three hundred and eleven persons had been added to the Church during his pastorate.

He spent the next two years in Colchester, and was then installed on June 16, 1830, over the Presbyterian Church in Durham, Greene County, New York, where he remained until 1848.

He then established his residence in New Haven, where he died, after a very painful illness, on January 4, 1850, in his 65th year.

He married on January 27, 1810, Abigail Cleveland, third daughter of Dr. Robert and Anna (Cone) Usher, of Chatham, Connecticut, who died in New Haven on August 30, 1871, in her 84th year.

Their children were five sons, one of whom died in infancy, and six daughters. The eldest son was graduated at the Yale Medical School in 1837, the second son at the New York University in 1842, and the two youngest at Yale in 1847 and 1851, respectively. The eldest daughter married the Rev. Orlando L. Kirkland (Hamilton College 1822), and the fifth daughter married the Rev Lewis Thompson (Centre Coll. 1836). Two sons became ministers

He published:

The salvation of sinners, the result of God's gracious purpose — A Sermon [from II Tim, i, 9], delivered in Lisbon, Hanover Society, May 17, 1829 Norwich, 1830 8°, pp 28

[*U. T. S Y C*

AUTHORITIES.

Bristol, or "New Cambridge," 1875, 13-14 Cone Family, 22, 170, 1907, 191. Bristol Church Manual, 183-84 *T Robbins,* Diary, i, 994-95

DAVID LEWIS DAGGETT, son of the Hon. David Daggett (Yale 1783), was born in New Haven on February 8, 1792, and was at graduation the youngest member of the Class During his Senior year he served as President Dwight's amanuensis.

He died in New Haven, after a short but distressing illness, on October 2, 1810, in his 19th year

His epitaph, besides recording his Christian faith, thus describes him:

Ardent in the pursuit of knowledge, and possessed of a sound and discriminating mind, he gave pleasing hopes of future usefulness and distinction Candour, frankness, a love of truth, and an amiable disposition, endeared him to all, who knew him

His father, throughout his prolonged life, is said never to have ceased lamenting the loss of this, his best beloved son

AUTHORITIES

Alden, Amer Epitaphs, i, 269 Conn Journal, Oct 4, 1810 Doggett-Daggett Family, 154

Joseph Delafield, the second of nine sons of John Delafield, who emigrated from England in 1783, and in 1784 married Ann, third daughter of Joseph and Elizabeth (Hazard) Hallett, of Hallett's Cove, later Astoria, Long Island, was born in his father's house on the site of the present Battery in New York, on August 22, 1790. A brother was graduated here in 1812. His father was one of the wealthiest merchants of New York, and his preparation for College was completed in New Haven under Henry Davis (Yale 1796).

He studied law in the office of Josiah Ogden Hoffman, of New York, and was admitted to the bar in 1811.

In 1810, while still a student, he received a commission as Lieutenant in the Fifth Regiment of the Militia, and in February, 1812, was advanced to the rank of Captain. When war was declared, in the spring of that year, he raised a full company of volunteers, and joined Colonel Hawkins's command. After being quartered at Sandy Hook for a year, he helped to recruit a regiment (the 46th Infantry) for the regular army, of which he was commissioned Major in April, 1814. The regiment, however, saw no active service, being kept in garrison on Governor's Island, and he was honorably discharged in June, 1815.

In 1816 Major Delafield became the Secretary to the Agent employed by the Commissioners (under the treaty of Ghent) for the settlement of the Northwestern boundary. Subsequently he was appointed on the commission, and was employed in this capacity (and ultimately as the sole commissioner) until 1828. During this period, his winters were spent in Washington, and his summers on the northwestern border, where he began a collection of minerals which occupied much of his later time and came to be ranked as one of the best in private hands in this country.

In later years he was not engaged in active business, but devoted most of his time to the cultivation of the sciences and to kindred pursuits

In 1827 he was elected the President of the New York Lyceum of Natural History, and he retained that office until 1866, when he declined a re-election

He was married, on December 12, 1833, to Julia, eldest daughter of Maturin and Margaret (Lewis) Livingston, of New York, and thenceforth divided his time between his residence in New York and his country seat in Yonkers, on the Hudson.

On his grounds in the country he built a lime-kiln so constructed as to burn continuously, on a plan until then unknown in this country; for several years the works yielded large profits

He was a Trustee of the College of Physicians and Surgeons from 1832; and a Trustee of the Society Library from 1842 to 1855.

He died in New York, of acute pneumonia, on February 12, 1875, in his 85th year. His wife died on June 23, 1882, at Rhinebeck, in her 81st year.

Their children were three sons, one of whom died young.

He published, in the *Annals* of the Lyceum of Natural History of New-York, volume 1, pp. 79–81, September, 1823·

Notice of new Localities of simple Minerals along the north coast of Lake Superior, and in the Indian Territory NW. from Lake Superior to the river Winnepec. Read January 19, 1824

AUTHORITIES

Heitman, Hist. Register of U. S. Army, i, 365. *Holgate,* Amer Genealogy, 183 N Y. Geneal and Biogr. Record, vi, 111; vii, 91 *VanRensselaer,* New Yorkers of the xix. century, 14

Matthew (Royce or) Rice Dutton, the eldest son of Thomas and Tenty (Punderson) Dutton, of Watertown, Connecticut, and a nephew of the Rev. Aaron Dutton (Yale 1803), was born in Watertown on June 30, 1783. A brother was graduated here in 1818.

When about thirteen years old, he removed with his family to Northfield, a small parish of Litchfield, where his father kept a small country store, and he was employed, when not otherwise engaged, as a clerk. In the summer of 1799 he kept a school in Northfield, and the next winter in the adjoining town of Harwinton. At seventeen he entered the law office of Ephraim Kirby, of Litchfield; but in consequence of weak eyes and broken health, from an attack of measles, he was soon obliged to abandon his studies. Some years followed, of rest, of further teaching, and of private study, until he decided to endeavor to obtain a College education, substantially by his own efforts. His final preparation for the Junior Class was made under James Morris (Yale 1775), of Litchfield South Farms.

He graduated with the highest honors which could be allotted to one who had entered so late, and at Commencement he delivered an Oration on Enthusiasm.

Before graduation he had begun to teach in Farmington, and he went thence to the Fairfield Academy, where he had already taught. The year 1809–10 he spent in the Andover Theological Seminary, to which succeeded four years of a College tutorship. At Commencement in 1811 he delivered a Master's Oration on Popularity; and the same year he was licensed to preach by the Litchfield South Association of Ministers.

Throughout his tutorship he suffered severely with his eyes, and was dependent, in great measure, on the voluntary aid of students, even in preparing himself for his daily duties. During the last year of his tutorship he declined, on account of imperfect health, an urgent call from the First or North Church in Portsmouth, New Hampshire, in succession to the Rev. Dr. Joseph Buckminster (Yale 1770).

On September 24, 1814, he was ordained and installed as pastor of the Congregational Church in Stratford, Connecticut, the sermon on that occasion being preached by President Dwight.

He remained in Stratford, universally beloved, until his election, in September, 1822, after the death of Professor Alexander M Fisher (Yale 1813), to the chair of Mathematics and Natural Philosophy at Yale. Mathematics was a favorite study, and he excelled in it; so that he was tempted to accept the appointment, and was dismissed from his pastoral charge in October, 1822.

He entered on his duties with alacrity and ardor; but his constitution, always delicate, was not equal to the effort His physical powers were soon prostrated, and he died in New Haven, partly from general debility and partly from pulmonary affection, on July 17, 1825, at the age of 42 His funeral sermon was preached by Professor Fitch.

He married, soon after his ordination, Maria, daughter of Dr Asa and Abigail (Burnham) Hopkins, of Hartford, who long survived him.

Their children were two sons, of whom the elder was graduated at Yale in 1837.

Professor Dutton was respected and loved, both as a teacher and preacher With simple, winning manners, and a well-balanced, symmetrical character, his memory was cherished by his friends with unaccustomed reverence.

He published:

1 An elementary Treatise on Conic Sections, Spherical Geometry, and Spherical Trigonometry.—Being the Fifth and Sixth Parts of a course of Mathematics adapted to the method of instruction in American Colleges. New-Haven, 1824 8°, pp. 408 + 1 + 3 + 16 pl. [*B Ath. Br Mus. Y. C.*

In continuation of a series of text-books begun by President Day

2 He also contibuted to the (Monthly) *Christian Spectator;* the only article which has been identified is:

Review of Andrews Norton on True and False Religion, vol 4, pp 299-318 (June, 1822).

AUTHORITIES.

Anderson, Hist. of Waterbury, i, Appendix, 47. *Bronson*, Hist. of Waterbury, 389. *Orcutt*, Hist. of Stratford, i, 413. Religious Intelligencer, x, 126–27. *Sprague*, Annals of the Amer. Pulpit, ii, 592–95.

JUSTIN DWINELL, a son of Stephen Dwinell, of Coventry, Rhode Island, and Shaftsbury, Vermont, and grandson of Stephen and Abigail (Harris) Dwinell, of Topsfield, Massachusetts, and Coventry, was born in Shaftsbury in 1785. His mother was Susanna, daughter of Henry Olin, of East Greenwich, Rhode Island. The first three years of his College course were spent in Williams College.

After graduation he studied law, and in 1811 began practice in Cazenovia, Madison County, New York.

He was a member of the State Legislature during two sessions, from November, 1820, to April, 1822.

In February, 1823, he was appointed Chief Judge of the County Court and held that office for ten years.

In the meantime he was also a member of the Congress of the United States for one term, December, 1823, to March, 1825.

He was District Attorney for Madison County from 1837 to 1845.

Subsequently he was withdrawn from active duties by the condition of his health for a few years, and died in Cazenovia, after a prolonged and painful illness, on September 17, 1850, aged 65 years.

By his wife, Louisa Whipple, he had seven sons, two of whom died in infancy, and two daughters. One son became a lawyer, and two, physicians.

Judge Dwinell was a man of superior intelligence, of most uncompromising integrity, of great purity of character, and a sincere Christian.

AUTHORITIES.

Dunnel and Dwinell Genealogy, 30, 47.

ERASTUS EDGERTON, the third son of Captain Daniel Edgerton, of Norwich and Tolland, Connecticut, by his second wife, Mary Edgerton, was born in Tolland on November 8, 1786 His mother was the eldest daughter of Dr. Samuel and Hannah (Bicknell) Cobb, of Tolland, and widow of Reuben Chapman. He united with the College Church on profession of his faith in May of the Senior year, and delivered the Valedictory Oration at graduation.

He was of promising talents and acknowledged piety. During the year after graduation he lost his reason, and while insane took his own life in Tolland, on April 24, 1809, in his 23d year. He was the first in the Class to die

---

AUTHORITIES

Conn Journal, May 4, 1809. *Waldo*, Early Hist. of Tolland, 99

DANIEL FULLER entered College from Hampton, Connecticut, at the opening of the Sophomore year, having been prepared for admission by Seth Norton (Yale 1804), the Preceptor of Woodstock Academy. He was born in Hampton on February 14, 1789, and was the youngest child of Joseph Fuller, of Hampton, and grandson of John, of Ipswich, Massachusetts, and Hampton His mother was Mary, second daughter of Joshua and Mary (Abbot) Holt, of Hampton

He became a real-estate broker in Philadelphia, and is believed to have died in December, 1855, in his 67th year.

HENRY WILLIAM GIBBS, son of Reuben and Sally Gibbs, of Litchfield South Farms, now Morris, Connecticut, and grandson of Henry and Abigail (Martin) Gibbs, of Litchfield, was born about 1784.

He was for a time after graduation in the Litchfield Law School, and later a resident in the neighborhood of Easton, Maryland.

In 1815–16 he was for a short time a merchant in New York City, in connection with the firm of Gibbs & Hall, of which his younger brother James was a member.

On September 2, 1816, he was married in New York to Celia Dean, of that city, an orphan girl of 19.

In 1823 he was living in Litchfield in destitute circumstances; but although he was then the only surviving son, his father was so dissatisfied with his character and conduct as to be unwilling to help him.

He left Litchfield in 1826. He is said to have been resident in Syracuse, New York, about 1840 to 1850.

AUTHORITIES.

Woodruff, Litchfield Genealogical Register, 90.

WILLIAM [MILLER] GIBSON entered College from Washington, Wilkes County, Georgia, during the Freshman year, having received his final preparation in New Haven at the hands of Jeremiah Evarts (Yale 1802). He was born about 1787.

He remained here as a graduate student for one year.

He became a lawyer in his native State, being located some forty years after graduation in Warrenton, Warren County.

TIMOTHY JONES GRIDLEY, a son of Isaac Gridley (Yale 1773), of Middletown Upper Houses, now Cromwell, Connecticut, was baptized on November 23, 1788. His mother was Elizabeth, daughter of Captain John Smith, of Cromwell.

He studied medicine, in part under Dr. Nathan Smith, in Hanover, New Hampshire, and received the degree of M.D. from Dartmouth College in 1812. (The same degree was given him, in an honorary way, by the Castleton, Vermont, Medical School in 1839.)

He settled for the practice of his profession in Amherst, Massachusetts, and in a long service there acquired a reputation second to that of no other physician in that part of the State Besides his professional usefulness, he was prominent in all the public affairs of the town In 1820, 1826, 1844, and 1846, he represented Amherst in the State legislature He was also a member of the Governor's Council for one year (1849–50)

After a year of serious ill-health, he died in Amherst on March 10, or 11, 1852, in his 65th year.

He married, April 20, 1815, Dorothy Smith, second daughter of General Ebenezer Mattoon (Dartmouth 1776), of Amherst, who died on February 16, 1820, aged 34, leaving two daughters and a son

He married for his second wife, in Enfield, Connecticut, on November 27, 1823, Eliza, daughter of Grove and Elizabeth (Robbins) Lawrence, of Paris, New York, and widow of Henry Olmsted, of Norfolk, Connecticut, who died in October, 1814. She was a niece of the Rev Francis LeB. Robbins, at whose house she was married.

She died in Amherst on July 6, 1850, in her 58th year. Her children were two daughters, the younger of whom married Dr George S Woodman (Amherst 1846)

AUTHORITIES

Carpenter, Hist. of Amherst, 189 Dickerman Family, 547. *Dudley,* Hist of Cromwell, 24 *Field,* Centennial Address at Middletown, 250 *T Robbins,* Diary, i, 385, 941, 946, ii, 61, 418, 813, 981, 1039 *Stockwell,* LeBaron Descendants, 150.

CHARLES [CHANDLER] GRISWOLD, the second son of Governor Roger Griswold (Yale 1780), was born in Norwich, Connecticut, on February 8, 1791. The family removed to Lyme in 1798. After graduation he was Preceptor of the Chelsea Grammar School in Norwich

He settled at Black Hall in Lyme as a lawyer, and held the rank of Colonel in the State Militia. He was a Deacon in the First Congregational Church from 1829 until his death.

He represented the town in four sessions of the State Legislature in 1813–15; and for the last year of his life was Judge of Probate for the Lyme district.

He was active in all religious and other public enterprises in the town, and one long existent monument of his taste and public spirit was the graceful Congregational meeting-house erected in Lyme in 1817, modeled indirectly from a London prototype, by Wren, which he had admired in his early travels in England.

He had great interest in intellectual and scientific pursuits, and was especially devoted to mineralogy.

He died in Lyme, on August 7, 1839, aged 48½ years.

He married, on November 14, 1820, Ellen Elizabeth, younger daughter of Judge Elias Perkins (Yale 1786), of New London, who died on February 26, 1877, in her 78th year.

Their children were two daughters and six sons. The eldest daughter married Dr. Shubael F. Bartlett (Yale 1833). Two sons died in infancy, and three were graduated at Yale, in 1848, 1851, and 1857, respectively.

AUTHORITIES.

Magazine of Amer. Hist., xi, 327–28. *Mitchell,* Woodbridge Record, 108. *Perkins,* Chronicles of a Conn. Farm, 156, 166–67. *Salisbury,* Family-Histories and Genealogies, ii, 105–06. *Walworth,* Hyde Genealogy, ii, 888–89.

WILLIAM HANFORD, the youngest son in a family of twelve children of John Hanford, of Norwalk, Connecticut, and grandson of Elnathan and Sarah (St. John) Hanford, of Norwalk, was born on November 11, 1787. His mother was Mehitabel, daughter of Nathan and Bethia (Strong) Comstock, of Wilton Parish, then part of Norwalk. He was a great-great-grandson of the Rev. Thomas Hanford, the first minister of the town. He was prepared for the Junior Class mainly by his pastor, the Rev Dr. Matthias Burnet.

After an interval of school-teaching in Jamaica, Long Island, he began in 1810 the study of theology in the Andover Seminary, where he completed the course in 1813. Having accepted an appointment from the Missionary Society of Connecticut as missionary to the Western Reserve of Ohio, he was ordained as an evangelist in North Stamford, on October 13, 1813

After nearly two years of itinerant service, he was called to be the first pastor of the Congregational Church in Hudson, Summit County, on July 5, 1815, and was installed on August 17.

In October, 1817, he married Amelia, daughter of 'Squire Elizur Wright (Yale 1781) and Rhoda (Hanmer) Wright, of Tallmadge, in the same county

Infirm health rendering him, in his own opinion, incapable of discharging his arduous duties, he was dismissed from the church in Hudson on September 7, 1831, to accept a call to the Presbyterian Church in Windham, Portage County, where he was installed on the 12th of the following month.

Increasing infirmity compelled him to lay down this pastorate in 1840, and he soon retired to Tallmadge, which was his residence for the rest of his life.

For seven or eight years he was able to supply the churches in the vicinity, and especially one at Middlebury village, in the township of Tallmadge, but he was for many years a great sufferer from dyspepsia complicated with other disorders. He died in Tallmadge on May 31, 1861, in his 74th year.

His wife survived him They had no children.

Mr. Hanford was a wise, faithful, and laborious pastor, a judicious and safe counselor, and a benevolent and upright citizen. He was known as a consistent opponent of slavery. His preaching was clear and practical, and his prayers peculiarly impressive.

The only specimen of his authorship which I have noticed in print is:

A Biographical Sketch of Elizur Wright. In Tallmadge Semi-Centennial Commemoration. Akron, 1857. 8°, pp. 82–85.

AUTHORITIES.

Congregational Quarterly, iii, 330; xv, 309–11. *Hall,* Hist. of Norwalk, 280. *Lane,* Akron and Summit County, 820–21. *Selleck,* Norwalk, 99. *Wilson,* Presbyterian Almanac, 1862, 185.

JOSEPH HARVEY, of East Haddam, Connecticut, on the borders of Lyme (Hadlyme Parish), was born on March 1, 1787. He was the eldest child of Deacon Ithamar Harvey, and a grandson of Captain Ithamar and Anna (Cone) Harvey, of East Haddam. His mother was Electa, the youngest child of the Rev. Joseph Fowler (Yale 1743), of East Haddam. He was prepared for College by his pastor, the Rev. Joseph Vaill (Dartmouth Coll. 1778), whose wife was his mother's sister. During part of the College course he served as an amanuensis for President Dwight. In the fall of 1807 he united with the College Church on profession of his faith. At graduation he delivered an Oration on the Advantages of moderate Talents.

After graduation he studied theology with the Rev. Dr. Ebenezer Porter (Dartmouth Coll. 1792), then pastor in Washington, Connecticut, and was licensed to preach by the Litchfield South Association of Ministers, in June, 1809.

The Rev. Asahel Hooker (Yale 1789) was dismissed from his pastorate over the Congregational Church of Goshen, in Litchfield County, on June 12, 1810; and Mr. Harvey thereafter supplied the pulpit with such favor that he was unanimously called to the vacant place.

Having accepted the call, he was married, on September 20, in Hadlyme, to Catharine Desire, the third child of Colonel Richard Ely Selden and Desire (Colt) Selden, a sister of Richard Ely Selden (Yale 1818).

On October 24 he was ordained and installed in Goshen, where he labored faithfully and acceptably for fifteen years His ministry there was memorable on several accounts, including his active interest in education and in missions

In 1814 Henry Obookiah and another Hawaiian boy were taken into his family for instruction, and this circumstance, in connection with the formation (in 1812) of the Foreign Mission Society of Litchfield County, which was due largely to his initiation, brought him into the intensest sympathy with the missionary movement.

He also, during this period of his ministry, had a succession of pupils, both those preparing for College and students of theology.

In 1816, when the Foreign Mission School was established largely through his influence, in the adjacent town of Cornwall, he was appointed to the office of Principal, but his people refused to allow him to accept the position.

In 1820, a remarkable revival of religion began in his parish, which continued for about a year. His labors in this connection were exhausting, and in fact his constitution never fully recovered from the strain of this period

He struggled on in his work until September, 1825, when he resigned to accept the position of General Agent of the American Education Society, whose office was in Boston. During his pastorate one hundred and thirty-nine members had been added to the church.

In Boston he suffered from ill health, and was also disappointed with the character of his duties, so that he insisted on retiring in July, 1826.

He then returned to his native place, in miserable health and sadly depressed. But he improved sufficiently to accept a call from the Congregational Church in Westchester Society, in Colchester, Connecticut, where he was installed on January 17, 1827.

Here also his ministry was rewarded with seasons of revival, but his interest was also largely absorbed by the theological controversy of those days. He was one of the founders of the Theological Institute at East Windsor Hill, and of the *Evangelical Magazine* supported in the same interest, of which he acted as editor in 1834-35 The honorary degree of Doctor of Divinity was given him by Amherst College in 1835.

On December 13, 1835, he was dismissed from his pastoral charge, and he removed soon after to South Windsor, and was occupied for the next three years with the editorship of *The Watchman,* a weekly religious paper, which was published in Hartford in place of the *Evangelical Magazine.* He also served for one year (1837) as acting pastor of the South Windsor Congregational Church.

In the latter part of 1838 he was engaged to preach statedly in the little village of Thompsonville, in Enfield The result of his labors soon led the people to desire a church organization; and as they decidedly preferred connection with the Presbyterian body, and Dr. Harvey did not disapprove their choice, he joined the Presbytery of New York, and that Presbytery constituted the church of eighty-two members in Thompsonville the first Presbyterian Church in Connecticut on July 5, 1839, and installed him as pastor five days later

He held this charge with fidelity and success for nearly eighteen years, during which he received one hundred and eighteen persons into the church After having reached the age of seventy, he resigned his charge on April 28, 1857.

In the spring of 1858 he removed with his wife and two daughters to the village of Harvey in the suburbs of Marquette, on the upper peninsula of Michigan, where his youngest son was in business, and where he continued for fourteen years longer, as enabled by the bracing influence of that climate, to teach a small village school on week-days and to preach on Sundays, for a meagre compensation.

His wife died in Harvey on August 5, 1865, in her 77th year, and his own death occurred there, after eight days' illness, on February 4, 1873, at the age of 86 years, lacking twenty-four days.

Of their seven children, three died in infancy or early youth, and only two daughters and a son survived them.

Dr. Harvey had strong intellectual powers, and is remembered with esteem in the churches which he served His theological outlook was somewhat rigid and narrow, and he was remarkably persistent in his advocacy of his views. A typical instance of his attitude is seen in his attack on his long-time associate, Dr. Tyler, in his old age, for lack of orthodoxy.

He published:

1 A Sermon [from Rev xi, 15], preached at Litchfield, before the Foreign Mission Society of Litchfield County, at their annual meeting, February 15, 1815 New-Haven, 1815 8°, pp 28.

[A C A B Ath Br Mus C. H S U. T. S. Y. C.

On the prophetic supremacy of the kingdom of Christ.

This Society was the first organized auxiliary of the American Board The author expects quite confidently the beginning of the millennium in another half-century, *i. e*, about 1866.

2. The Banner of Christ set up A Sermon [from Ps. xx, 5], delivered at the Inauguration of the Rev. Herman Daggett, as Principal of the Foreign Mission School in Cornwall, Connecticut, May 6, 1818. New-Haven, 1818. 12°, pp 34.

[A. C A B. Ath B. Publ Br. Mus. Harv U. T S Y C.

3. A Reply to the statements of Mr. Daniel Parker, in a late publication, entitled "Proscription Delineated." Hartford, 1819. 8°, pp 112.

[A C A. B Publ Br. Mus. C. H S. Harv. U T S Y. C.

Mr. Parker was graduated at Yale in 1798

4 Revival in Goshen
In the *Christian Spectator,* vol 4, pp 497–501 (September, 1822)

5 A Review of a Sermon, delivered in the Chapel of Yale College, September 10, 1828. By Nathaniel W Taylor, D.D. Hartford, 1829. 8°, pp 40.
[*A. C. A. B Publ. Br Mus C. H. S. U. T S. Y C.*

6 An Examination of a Review of Dr. Taylor's Sermon on Human Depravity, and Mr. Harvey's Strictures on that Sermon Hartford, 1829. 8°, pp. 53. [*A. C. A C H. S. Y. C.*
Anonymous. The Review (published in the *Quarterly Christian Spectator* for June, 1829) was written jointly by Professor Chauncey A. Goodrich (Yale 1810) and the Rev Dr Noah Porter (Yale 1803)

7. An Inquiry concerning the Obligations of Believers to the Visible Church New-Haven, 1830. 12°, pp. 248
[*B. Ath U. T S Y C.*

8 An Appeal to Christians, on the immorality of using or vending Distilled Liquors, as an article of luxury or diet Delivered before the Temperance Society in East-Hampton, Conn, May 5th, 1831 Middletown, 1831. 8°, pp 31.
[*A. C. A Br Mus. C. H S. U T. S.*

9 Letters, on the present state and probable results of Theological Speculations in Connecticut—By an Edwardean. 1832. 8°, pp 44
[*A C. A B Publ. Br. Mus. U T S Y C*
Supposed to be written chiefly by Mr. Harvey

10 An Examination of the Pelagian and Arminian theory of Moral Agency as recently advocated by Dr. Beecher in his "Views in Theology." New York, 1837. 12°, pp. 223
[*A C. A. B. Publ. Br. Mus. U T S. Y. C*

11 Remarks at a County Meeting. 1837.
On temperance.

12 An Eulogy on the Life and Public Services of the late Daniel Webster, delivered at Thompsonville, November 23, 1852 Hartford, 1852. 8°, pp 24. [*Br Mus Y. C.*

13 A letter to the Rev Dr. Tyler, in reply to his Discourse on Human Ability and Inability. Springfield, 1855. 8°, pp 32
[*A. A. S. A. C A. B Publ. Br. Mus. U T. S Y. C.*

14 A Second Letter to the Rev Dr Tyler on Human Ability and Inability. Hartford, 1855 8°, pp. 16
[*A C A B Publ. Y C.*

15 Discourses on the Scriptural Basis of Ministerial and Christian Fellowship Springfield, 1856. 8°, pp. 72.
[*A C A. Br Mus. Y. C*

He was one of the projectors of the following, and the responsible editor of volumes 3 and 4

The Evangelical Magazine Hartford, July, 1832–June, 1836. 4 volumes 8° [*Y C*

A monthly. Succeeded by:

The Watchman, a weekly religious paper Hartford

AUTHORITIES

Harvey Book, 146, 195–98 *Hibbard,* Hist of Goshen, 92, 270–73, 316–20 *Lee,* Memorial of Dr Harvey *T Robbins,* Diary, ii, 328, 456–57.

NATHANIEL HEWIT, the eldest child of Nathaniel and Sarah Hewit, of New London, Connecticut, and grandson of Joseph and Sarah (Babcock) Hewit, was born in New London on August 28, 1788. His mother was the sixth daughter of Colonel Christopher and Eunice (Prentice) Avery, of Groton. He was prepared for admission to the Sophomore Class by John Adams (Yale 1795), at Bacon Academy in Colchester

After graduation he at first determined to pursue the legal profession, and entered the office of the Hon. Lyman Law (Yale 1791), of New London, but soon altered his plans.

He was for a time preceptor of the Plainfield Academy, and while there studied theology with the Rev Dr. Joel Benedict (Princeton Coll. 1765). He was licensed to preach by the New London County Association of Ministers on September 24, 1811, and effectively supplied various congregations in Vermont and elsewhere.

He became convinced, however, that he needed more thorough preparation before assuming permanent responsibilities, and accordingly spent about six months, in 1813–14, in Andover Seminary.

He then, in the spirit of true missionary zeal and self-sacrifice, accepted a call to the Presbyterian church in Plattsburg, New York, on the shore of Lake Champlain, which was then little more than a military outpost, in a comparatively new country. He was ordained and installed there by the Presbytery of Champlain on July 5, 1815; and was married in New Haven, on September 26, 1816, by the Rev Nathaniel W Taylor, to Rebecca Woolsey, the youngest sister of his classmate Hillhouse.

The severity of the climate at Plattsburg was so injurious to his health that he was compelled to seek a milder region, and was dismissed from his charge on October 2, 1817

He was soon after invited to supply for a Sunday the vacant pulpit of the Congregational Church in Fairfield, Connecticut, and gave such satisfaction that the church and society speedily united in calling him, and he was installed there on January 14, 1818.

His ministry in Fairfield was a notable one, especially perhaps for his prominence as one of the early advocates of the temperance reformation. His effectiveness as an orator led, after the formation of the American Temperance Society, to his employment as their agent for five months in 1827.

So much was accomplished in this temporary service, that he was urged to resign his pastoral charge and give himself wholly and permanently to this work.

He reluctantly consented to take up the task for three years; and was accordingly dismissed from the church in Fairfield on December 18, 1827.

He labored with fidelity and eminent success in this difficult field, until his physical powers were much exhausted and his nervous and digestive system greatly depressed Just at this date the Second Congregational Church in Bridgeport, adjoining Fairfield, was organized, and on August 28, 1830, they gave him a unanimous call to the pastorate, which he gladly accepted. He was installed on December 1, the sermon preached by the Rev. Dr Leonard Woods, of Andover Seminary, being afterwards published. The honorary degree of Doctor of Divinity was conferred on him by Amherst College in 1830

His wife died in Bridgeport on January 4, 1831, in her 37th year. In the following May he was invited to go to England to assist in giving an impulse to the movement for temperance reform in that country His mission was successful, but was cut short by the news of the death of his eldest child, a daughter, at the age of 14, at the close of July

Soon after his return he was married again, on November 14, to Susan Eliot, one of his Fairfield parishioners, the daughter of the Rev. Andrew Eliot (Harvard 1762), one of his predecessors in the Fairfield pulpit, and sister of the Rev Andrew Eliot (Yale 1799)

In 1833 he was prominent among the founders of the East Windsor Theological Institute and subsequently bitterly opposed the New Haven theology

His ministry in Bridgeport was in the main prosperous and peaceful for twenty years, though persistently marked by arbitrary conduct. In November, 1851, he proposed the settlement of a colleague-pastor; characteristically nominating the person to be chosen He was then depressed and ill; but as his health improved, he withdrew, in July, 1852, his offer The Church, however, challenged his method of procedure, and as the result of a bitter quarrel he presented his resignation, and his dismission was ratified by the Fairfield West Consociation on September 20, 1853.

The Church, which consisted at his settlement of one hundred and twenty-eight members, and to which three hundred and seventy-three had been added in his pastorate, now numbered two hundred and thirty-eight.

A minority of seventy-eight members, who sympathized with his attitude, were dismissed on October 9, and formed a new organization in connection with the Old School Presbyterians, over which he was installed on October 31.

He ministered to this church without assistance for nine years When he reached the age of seventy, in the fall of 1858, he tendered his resignation, but it was not accepted. On April 1, 1862, on account of increasing infirmities he released his salary and an associate pastor was settled in the ensuing summer

He died in Bridgeport on February 3, 1867, in his 79th year.

His wife died, after years of suffering from cancer, on May 1, 1857, in her 67th year.

By his first marriage he had two daughters and four sons Two sons died in infancy; of the others one was graduated at Amherst College in 1839, and became a Roman Catholic priest of some distinction; the remaining son received the degree of M.D from the New York University in 1847. The younger daughter married Dr. William S Bowen (Princeton Coll 1821). By his second marriage he had one daughter, who died in childhood

An engraving from his portrait is given in Orcutt's *History of Stratford and Bridgeport.*

Dr. Hewit was a man of marked intellectual power and of sweeping eloquence But the pen was irksome to him, and he left no adequate memorials of his ability

He published:

1. An Address, to the Congregational Churches in Connecticut, on the present state of their religious concerns By an Observer. Hartford, 1833 8°, pp 58 [*A. C. A Br Mus Y C*

An attack on the New Haven theology.

2 The Wine question [Address, to the Friends of Temperance in Connecticut; with Introduction] [New York,] 1839 8°, pp. 16. [*B Ath Br. Mus. U T. S Y. C*

Extracted from volume 6 of the *Literary and Theological Review*, pp. 206–21.

The Address was written in 1836 by Dr Hewit, as the Chairman of a Committee appointed by a Temperance Convention held in Hartford in September of that year

3. The Moral Law the essential element of American Liberty. The substance of a Lecture, to the Bridgeport Lyceum, read April 19, 1839. Bridgeport, 1839 8°, pp. 12 [*B. Ath* ·

4. A Discourse [from Eph iv, 3–6], delivered before the General Association of Connecticut, at its annual meeting, New-Haven, June, 1840 By Nathaniel Hewitt [*sic*], D D Hartford, 1840 8°, pp 26

[*A A S. A C A Br. Mus C. H S U T S Y C*

The preacher desires to insist on the old-school Calvinistic doctrines, in opposition to New Haven theology

5. Discourse at the funeral solemnities, observed at Bridgeport, under the direction of the City Authorities, April 19th, 1841, commemorative of the Decease of William Henry Harrison, President of the United States Bridgeport, 1841. 8°, pp. 13.

[*B Publ Br. Mus*

6. Documents relating to the Dismission of the First Pastor of the Second Congregational Church in Bridgeport, Sept 21, 1853 Bridgeport, 1853 12°, pp 69. [*Y C.*

Compiled by Dr Hewit

He also prepared for publication the following

First Annual Report of the Executive Committee of the American Society for the Promotion of Temperance —For the year ending Nov 1827 Andover, 1828 8°, pp 68

He contributed three articles (besides one above mentioned) to the *Literary and Theological Review,* as follows

Reply to Professor Pond's Article on Voluntary Associations, volume 5, pp 1–38 (March, 1838).

The Nature of the Kingdom of Christ, same, pp 193–206 (June, 1838)

On the Nature of Sin, same, pp 418–27 (September, 1838)

Also, one sermon to the *National Preacher*

Christ freely offered to sinners indiscriminately, from John iv, 10. In vol 32, pp 270–78 (September, 1858).

AUTHORITIES.

Atwater, Memorial of Dr. Hewit *Blake,* Early Hist of First Church, New London, 302-04. *Child,* An old New England Church, 100-04; Prime Ancient Society of Fairfield, 31-34 Dwight Genealogy, ii, 1092-93 N Y Geneal and Biogr Record, iv, 146. *Orcutt,* Hist of Stratford, i, 644-45, 648-50 Religious Intelligencer, xv, 543. *Sweet,* Averys of Groton, 70 *Walworth,* Hyde Genealogy, ii, 930 *Wildey,* Chesebrough Family, 415-16

JAMES ABRAHAM HILLHOUSE, the eldest child of the Hon. James Hillhouse (Yale 1773), and the namesake of his father's uncle (Yale 1749), was born in New Haven on September 26, 1789 He first entered College with the Class of 1806, but remained with them for only a part of Freshman year. He held a high rank in College, particularly in English composition. At graduation he delivered an Oration on the Utility of Imagination.

On taking his second degree in 1811 he delivered a Master's Oration on the Education of a Poet, which led to his receiving the appointment to give the Poem before the Phi Beta Kappa Society in 1812.

Meantime he had spent some three years in Boston in preparation for a mercantile career, but the outbreak of the war with Great Britain interfered with his plans

In 1819 he visited England and was admitted to some of the best society. Zachary Macaulay, the father of Lord Macaulay, is on record as saying that he considered him the most accomplished young man with whom he was acquainted.

On his return he went into business as a hardware merchant in New York City, where he was married, on November 23, 1822, to Cornelia Ann, eldest daughter of Isaac Lawrence, a wealthy merchant of New York, and of Cornelia, daughter of the Rev. Dr. Abraham Beach (Yale 1757), who performed the marriage ceremony. The Hon William Beach Lawrence (Columbia Coll. 1818) was a brother, and a sister married the Rt. Rev. William Ingraham Kip (Yale 1831), Bishop of California.

Soon after his marriage he retired from business and removed to New Haven, where he erected the stately mansion still standing on Pierson-Sage Square, in which the rest of his life was spent in literary leisure, with the exception of an annual winter visit of a few months to New York.

As he reached middle life symptoms of consumption appeared, in the fall of 1839, and his health gradually failed. In the autumn of 1840 he went to Boston for a visit to old friends, but after his return his disease assumed, about the first of January, an alarming form, and he died at home on January 5, 1841, in his 52d year.

His widow died in New Haven on September 20, 1874.

Their children were three daughters and a son. The latter died in infancy. Two daughters died unmarried, and the eldest, who married her first cousin, Dr. William Hillhouse (honorary M A. Yale 1849), left no issue.

The College owns Mr. Hillhouse's portrait, which is engraved in Donald G. Mitchell's *American Lands and Letters* Mr Mitchell was able to recall the poet's prim, lithe figure, as it appeared in his last years on the city streets

The prevalent character of his writing was grace rather than strength, and a certain spirit of refined elegance and chasteness.

He published·

1 Percy's Masque a Drama, in five acts. London, 1819 12°, pp. vii, 112 [*Y. C.*

The same—From the London Edition, with alterations New-York, 1820 12°, pp. 150.
[*A. A S B Ath. B Publ Harv. Y. C.*

Anonymous.

2 The Judgment, a Vision By the Author of Percy's Masque. New-York, 1821. 8°, pp 46.
[*B Ath B. Publ Br. Mus. Columbia Univ Harv Y. C.*

Originally delivered as the annual poem before the Phi Beta Kappa Society, at New Haven, in September, 1812

3. Hadad, a dramatic poem. New-York, 1825. 8°, pp. 209.
[*B Ath B Publ Br. Mus Columbia Univ. Harv N. Y. H. S U. S. U. T. S. Y. C.*

This is considered the author's best achievement; written in 1824.

4. An Oration pronounced at New-Haven, before the Society of Phi Beta Kappa, September 12, 1826 On some of the considerations which should influence an Epic or a Tragic writer, in the choice of an era. New-Haven, 1826. 8°, pp. 32
[*A. A S A. C. A. Br Mus Columbia Univ. Harv M. H S Y. C.*

5. An Oration, pronounced at New Haven, by request of the Common Council, August 19, 1834, in commemoration of the life and services of General Lafayette New Haven, 1834. 8°, pp. 40.
[*B. Ath B. Publ Br. Mus. Harv. M H S U T S. Y. C*

6. Sachem's-Wood: a short poem, with notes. New Haven, 1838. 8°, pp. 30 [*B Publ Y. C.*

Anonymous Written just after the bi-centennial celebration of the founding of New Haven, in honor of his father and of the family estate, at first called Highwood

7. Dramas, Discourses, and other pieces. Boston, 1839. 2 v, 12°, pp. xiv, 296; iii, 249.
[*B Ath B Publ. Br Mus. Columbia Univ. Harv Y C.*

These volumes contain his previously published pieces; and also *Demetria,* a romantic play of early composition, and a discourse on *The Relations of Literature to a Republican Government,* which was delivered before the Brooklyn Lyceum in 1836, and repeated, on occasion of an accidental vacancy, as the Phi Beta Kappa Oration at Yale, later in the same year

AUTHORITIES.

Duyckinck, Cyclopedia of Amer. Literature, i, 816–20. Dwight Genealogy, ii, 1092. *Everest,* Poets of Conn, 169–86 *Griswold,* Poets and Poetry of America, 129–39 *Holgate,* Amer. Genealogy, 219 Lawrence Genealogy, 1858, 93. *Mitchell,* Amer. Lands and Letters, i, 275–77 New Englander, xvi, 705–41. N. Y Geneal. and Biogr. Record, iv, 146; v, 14. Southern Lit. Messenger, vii, 329–35. *Walworth,* Hyde Genealogy, ii, 929.

Benjamin Simmons Hort, the eldest child of William Hort, of Charleston, South Carolina, a native of

Barbadoes, by his second wife, Catharine Simons, was born in Charleston on April 6, 1791. His preparation for College was completed under the Rev. Dr. Azel Backus (Yale 1787), of Bethlehem, Connecticut.

He returned home after graduation, and died there on September 8, 1825, in his 35th year.

His wife, Mary D. Hort, died in Charleston on March 9, 1821, aged 30 years They had one daughter, who died in infancy, and three sons, who survived their parents.

AUTHORITIES.

Miss I. DeSaussure, MS Letter, May, 1911

RALPH ISAACS INGERSOLL, the eldest son of the Hon. Jonathan Ingersoll (Yale 1766), of New Haven, and a grandson of Ralph Isaacs (Yale 1761), was born in this city on February 8, 1789, and was prepared for College by Stephen Twining (Yale 1795), of New Haven.

After his graduation he read law for two years with Seth P Staples (Yale 1797), of New Haven, and on admission to the bar in December, 1810, began practice in his native city.

The opportunity for entrance into political life came with the upheaval in 1817–18, when the Democrats and Tolerationists assumed the government. Mr Ingersoll took sides with the Democrats, and in 1818 was an unsuccessful candidate for Congress. In April, 1819, at the first elections under the new State Constitution, he was chosen by a slender majority as one of the representatives in the General Assembly. For this first year he was made one of the Clerks of the Assembly, and being re-elected to that body in the six subsequent years, he came to be recognized as the ablest member on his side of the House In 1824 he served as Speaker, and in 1825 his seat was vacated by his being at the same election chosen as a Representative in the United States Congress.

He continued in Congress for four terms, or until 1833, when he declined a re-election. He was an industrious and able member, and for the last four years served on the most important Committee of the House, that of Ways and Means In the meantime he served one year (June, 1830—May, 1831) as Mayor of New Haven.

In the Spring of 1833 he resumed his place at the bar, and was at once made State's Attorney for New Haven County, and held that post with fidelity and ability until 1845, when he declined further reappointment. He was again a candidate for the General Assembly in April, 1834, but was defeated by the Whigs, on account of the popular revolt against Jackson's bank policy.

In December, 1835, Governor Edwards selected him to fill the vacancy in the United States Senate caused by the death of the Hon Nathan Smith, but he declined the offer. He also repeatedly refused to accept the nomination of his party for the governorship

In August, 1846, President Polk, who had known him intimately in Congress, unexpectedly nominated him as Envoy Extraordinary and Minister Plenipotentiary to Russia, and the Senate unanimously confirmed the appointment. He accepted in September, and served the government faithfully and ably until September, 1848, when he was recalled at his own repeated request

He then gladly returned to his profession, and practiced it with unabated vigor for sixteen years longer. His practical retirement in his eightieth year was hastened by an unfortunate accident, causing a fracture of the hip-joint, by which he was confined to the house for many months and from which he never fully recovered. He was able, however, for years longer, with the support of a cane, to visit his office daily. The fracture of an arm by a fall, early in 1872, confined him to the house, and his death followed, on August 31, in his 84th year

He was married on February 10, 1814, by the Rev Samuel F. Jarvis (Yale 1805), to Margaret Catharine Eleanora VandenHeuvel, of New York, a sister of Jacob A VanHeuvel (Yale 1804), who died in New Haven on December 23, 1878, aged 90 years.

One son was graduated at Yale in 1840, and was the Governor of the State from 1873 to 1877 Another son was a Member of Congress from 1851 to 1855

Mr. Ingersoll was eminent as an advocate and a highly successful public speaker His life was pure and exemplary, and his manner admirably courteous and winning.

He published:

1. Speech, on the Proposition to amend the Constitution of the United States, respecting the Election of President and Vice President. Delivered in the House of Representatives, March 6, 1826. 12°, pp 32 [*A A S*

2 Speech on the Bill reported by the Committee of Ways and Means to reduce the Tariff.—Delivered in the House of Representatives, Jan 10, 1833 Washington, 1833 8°, pp 22. [*Y. C*

3 His Speech on being conducted to the Chair, at a Democratic Convention, at Hartford, in 1839, was widely circulated, and was replied to by Judge W. W Boardman (Yale 1812).

4. Speech, December 24, 1850. In the Proceedings of the Union Meeting, held at Brewster's Hall New Haven, 1851 8°, pp. 19–27.

AUTHORITIES

Bronson, Sketch of R. I. Ingersoll. Conn Reports, xxxix, 596–601 Geneal Hist. of Conn, i, 278–79 New Haven City Year Book, 1864, 75–77 *Polk,* Diary, ii, 152; iii, 479–80 *Royall,* Black Book, iii, 126

PRESERVED JENNINGS was born on November 11, 1788, in Greens Farms, then in Fairfield, now Westport, Connecticut, and was prepared for admission by James Burnet (Yale 1798), of Norwalk. He united with the College Church on profession of faith in the May before graduation.

In November, 1810, he entered the Andover Theological Seminary, but very soon returned home disabled. Protracted confinement in a darkened room, on account of ophthalmia, resulted in insanity, which continued through his life.

He died by his own hand, in Westport, on November 27, 1837, at the age of 49.

AUTHORITIES.

Congregational Quarterly, xv, 309.

JOHN THOMAS JONES was born in New York City in 1789, and entered College at the opening of Sophomore year from the tuition of the Rev. Dr. David Ely (Yale 1769), of Huntington, Connecticut. His father, Dr. Thomas Jones, who died in 1798, was a son of Dr. Evan Jones, a native of Wales, and a brother of John Jones, M.D. (honorary, Columbia Coll. 1768), Professor of Surgery in Columbia. His mother was Margaret, daughter of the Hon. Philip Livingston (Yale 1737). One of his sisters married Judge David S. Jones (Columbia 1796); and another married the Hon. DeWitt Clinton (Columbia 1786).

He was connected for some years with the New York Society Library (then commonly called the City Library), of which his father had been a Trustee.

He probably died about 1825.

JONATHAN KNIGHT, the elder son of Dr. Jonathan Knight, of Norwalk, Connecticut, who was a native of Lisbon, and a Surgeon's mate in the Revolution, was born in Norwalk on September 4, 1789. His mother was

Ann, daughter of Dr. Asahel Fitch, of Redding. His brother was graduated at the Yale Medical School in 1822. He was prepared for admission to the Sophomore Class by his pastor, the Rev. Dr. Matthias Burnet.

For the year after graduation he was the Preceptor of the Chelsea Grammar School in Norwich, and for a second year taught in the Union School in New London, and then entered on a College tutorship He had already pursued medical studies, when in 1811 the plan of a Medical School at Yale was determined on, and Professor Silliman suggested to President Dwight that young Mr Knight would make a good teacher of Anatomy, after due preparation.

He was accordingly encouraged to resign his tutorship at the Commencement in 1811, having already been licensed to practice by the State Medical Society in August; and he spent the following winter in attendance on medical lectures in the University of Pennsylvania In April, 1812, Dr. Cogswell of Hartford (Yale 1780) was invited to the chair of Anatomy and Surgery, and Dr. Knight was offered the position of Assistant Professor. He returned to Philadelphia the next winter for a second course of lectures, and in August, 1813, after Dr. Cogswell's name had been dropped, and Dr. Nathan Smith had been secured for the chair of Surgery, Dr. Knight was appointed to a full professorship, and the subjects of Anatomy and Physiology assigned to him.

He was married, in Greenwich, in October, 1813, by the Rev. Dr Isaac Lewis (Yale 1765), to Elizabeth, daughter of the late James Lockwood (Yale 1766), who died in New Haven on January 21, 1844, at the age of 56

The honorary degree of Doctor of Medicine was conferred on him by the College in 1818

He retained his chair of instruction for a quarter of a century, and in 1838, on the death of Dr. Thomas Hubbard, was transferred to the Chair of Surgery, which he held for another like period, retiring in May, 1864, with mental activity unimpaired. Besides his duties in the Medical Institution, he had for many years given a brief annual course of lectures on Anatomy and Physiology to the Senior Class in the Academical Department. He was also for fifty years engaged in extensive private practice.

In 1846 and 1847 he was President of the Convention which formed the American Medical Association, and in 1853 was President of the Association itself.

He died in New Haven, after a painful illness of about twelve days, from peritonitis, on August 25, 1864, aged nearly 75 years. The Discourse delivered on the occasion of his interment, by his pastor, the Rev. Dr. Leonard Bacon (Yale 1820), was afterwards printed.

His portrait, painted by Nathaniel Jocelyn in 1828, is in the Medical School, as also a bust, executed by Truman H. Bartlett in 1865. A photograph of the portrait is given in Kingsley's *Yale College.*

His eldest daughter married the Rev. William T. Bacon (Yale 1837).

Dr. Knight was exceedingly modest and retiring in manner, and a conservative in opinions and practice. He was of extraordinary mental clearness and balance, based on sound religious principle.

He published:

1. An Eulogium on Nathan Smith, M.D., late Professor of the Theory and Practice of Physic and Surgery, in the Medical Institution of Yale College; pronounced at his funeral. New-Haven, 1829. 8°, pp. 28.

   [*A. C. A. B. Ath. B. Publ. Br. Mus. Columbia Univ. C. H. S. Harv. M. H. S. Surg. Gen'l's. Libr. Y. C.*

2. A Lecture, introductory to the course of instruction in the Medical Institution of Yale College, delivered Nov. 2, 1838. New Haven, 1838. 8°, pp. 27.

   [*B. Publ. C. H. S. M. H. S. U. S. Y. C.*

Delivered at the entrance on his duties as Professor of Surgery, and devoted to biographical sketches of Drs. Eneas Munson, Mason F. Cogswell, Nathan Smith, and Thomas Hubbard.

3 On the Propagation of Communicable Diseases—An Introductory Lecture to the course of 1849–50, in the Medical Institution of Yale College. New Haven, 1849. 8°, pp. 20.
[*B Ath. B. Publ. M. H. S. Surg Gen'l's. Libr Y C.*

4. A Lecture, introductory to the course of lectures in the Medical Institution of Yale College, September 29, 1853 New Haven, 1853. 8°, pp 19. [*Surg. Gen'l's Libr. Y C*
Mainly occupied with an historical sketch of the Institution

5. Address at the funeral of Timothy Phelps Beers, M.D., late Professor in the Medical Institution of Yale College, in the North Church, New Haven, September 24, 1858. With the Address of Dr. Dutton. New Haven, 1858. 8°, pp 3–8.
[*Harv Surg. Gen'l's Libr. Y. C*

6 A biographical sketch of Prof. Timothy P. Beers, M.D, and A biographical sketch of Bela Farnham, M D, of East Haven.
In *Proceedings* of the Conn Medical Society, 1859, pp. 85–94.

He was requested by the State Medical Society to prepare a history of surgery in Connecticut from 1800 to 1850, but gave up the attempt from the difficulty of procuring material.

AUTHORITIES

Bacon, Discourse at interment of Dr. Knight. Conn Med Society's Proceedings, 1854, 8–9; 1867, 147–51. *Hall,* Hist. of Norwalk, 258 *Kingsley,* Yale College, ii, 72–73 *Selleck,* Norwalk, 211.

GARRICK MALLERY, son of Garrick and Hannah (Minor) Mallery, of Middlebury, then part of Woodbury, Connecticut, was born on April 17, 1784. His mother was probably a daughter of Deacon Josiah and Jerusha (Mitchell) Minor, of Woodbury

He was prepared for College by his pastor, the Rev. Ira Hart (Yale 1797). During his Junior year his family removed to Rutland, in Jefferson County, New York.

After graduation he studied in the Litchfield Law School, and later found employment as Principal of the Academy in Wilkes-Barré, Pennsylvania, where he also read law with Judge Roswell Welles (Yale 1784), then the leader of the bar in that Judicial District. He was admitted to practice in Luzerne County in August, 1811. A little later he became a partner of Judge Welles.

In 1827 he was elected to the State Legislature, without party nomination, and was re-elected in the three following years From his position as Chairman of the respective Committees, he was largely instrumental in establishing the Internal Improvement and Penitentiary systems of Pennsylvania

In 1831 he was appointed by Governor Wolf presiding Judge of the Third Judicial District of the State, which position he resigned in 1836, and in November of the same year removed to Philadelphia to resume the active practice of his profession, in which he was eminently successful. At the time of his death he was the oldest active member of the bar in the city, and retained his vigor so fully that only six weeks before the end he conducted an important and hotly contested jury trial, lasting more than a week. For some years before his death he held the office of Master in Chancery for the Supreme Court.

In 1840 he received the honorary degree of Doctor of Laws from Lafayette College

He died in Philadelphia on July 6, 1866, in his 83d year

He first married, in June, 1811, Sylvina Pierce, second daughter of Colonel Lord and Mary (Pierce) Butler, of Wilkes-Barré, who died in March, 1824, aged 30 years. By her he had three sons and two daughters. One daughter married Justice William Strong (Yale 1828).

He married, secondly, on June 30, 1830, Catharine Julia, younger daughter of Dr. Henry and Esther Harris (Maclay) Hall, of Harrisburg, by whom he had one son. She died on July 17, 1832, in Reading, Pennsylvania, at the age of 28.

He married, thirdly, on June 27, 1838, Jeannette, daughter of Dr John Conrad Otto (Univ. of Pa. 1796)

and Eliza (Tod) Otto, of Philadelphia, by whom he had two daughters and two sons.

The child of his second wife (Yale 1850), and one daughter and the sons of his last wife, survived him.

AUTHORITIES

Egle, Pennsylvania Genealogies, 367, 378–79. *Kulp,* Families of Wyoming Valley, iii, 1083–85

JOSIAH HINMAN MINOR, the youngest of eight children of Deacon Josiah Minor, of Woodbury, Connecticut, and grandson of Deacon Clement and Sarah (Crissey) Minor of Woodbury, was baptized on December 6, 1789. His father died in 1801. He was probably a half-brother of the mother of his classmate Mallery.

He is said to have studied law, but died in 1820, aged 31 years; no settlement of his estate in the Woodbury probate court can be found, though he is buried there.

AUTHORITIES.

Cothren, Hist. of Woodbury, i, 649, iii, 172

JOHN BATES MURDOCK, son of the Rev. Jonathan Murdock (Yale 1766), of Bozrah, Connecticut, and of his wife, Keziah Murdock, was baptized on January 28, 1787, and was prepared for admission to the Sophomore Class by John Adams (Yale 1795), at the Bacon Academy in Colchester. His father died in 1813, and his mother in 1820.

In March, 1812, he enlisted in the United States army, and was assigned to the 25th regiment of infantry with the rank of 1st Lieutenant He was promoted to a captaincy in April, 1813, and to the rank of brevet Major in July, 1814, for distinguished service at the battle of Lundy's Lane.

In May, 1815, he was transferred to the 6th infantry, and he died on the 6th of the following September, at Fort Lewis, on Long Island, in New York harbor, in his 28th year. He was unmarried

AUTHORITIES

Caulkins, Hist. of Norwich, 435. *Heitman,* Hist. Register of U. S Army, i, 737 National Intelligencer, Sept. 21, 1815.

Amasa Parker, a brother of the Rev Daniel Parker (Yale 1798), and son of Amasa and Deidamia (Parmelee) Parker, of Washington, Connecticut, was born in Washington on October 28, 1784, and spent the first three years of his course in Williams College

After graduation he began the study of law in the Litchfield Law School, and continued it in Kinderhook, New York, in the office of Judge Peter VanSchaack (Columbia Coll. 1768)

About 1812 he settled in Delhi, Delaware County, where he was admitted to practice in 1814.

He was in partnership with the Hon. Samuel Sherwood from 1817 to 1827, when Mr. Sherwood removed, and then with Amasa J. Parker, his nephew, until the latter was promoted to the bench in 1844 For the remainder of his life his son Robert was associated with him.

He attained the rank of Colonel in the State Militia in 1819, and was commonly known by that title. From 1832 to 1841 he held the office of Surrogate of Delaware County. In 1847 he is said to have declined the offer of a nomination for the position of Justice of the Supreme Court of the State.

He was a man of powerful build, over six feet in height, of engaging manners, of pure character, and of high standing in his profession He was for many years Senior Warden of St. John's Church in Delhi

He died suddenly, from apoplexy, in Delhi, on March 1, 1855, in his 71st year.

He married on July 23, 1812, Rebecca Pardee, of Ellsworth Society in Sharon, Connecticut, where his brother was then pastor. After her death he married on August 24, 1841, Mrs. Phebe Moore

AUTHORITIES.

Cothren, Hist of Woodbury, 1, 453-54 *Gould,* Hist of Delaware County, 380 *Munsell,* Hist. of Delaware County, 166 *Hon A J. Parker,* M S Letter, Dec, 1911

JAMES HILL PARMELEE, the youngest son of Captain Ezra Parmelee, of Killingworth, now Clinton, Connecticut, and Newport, New Hampshire, and grandson of Ezra and Jemima (Bushnell) Parmelee, of Clinton, was born in Newport on May 15, 1783 His mother was Sibyl, eldest child of James and Hannah (Nettleton) Hill, of Clinton. He entered Yale (probably from Dartmouth College) at the opening of the Senior year.

After graduation he taught in Newbern, North Carolina, for two years or more, and in August, 1812, at the opening of the Princeton (New Jersey) Theological Seminary, joined the first class matriculated there. Earlier in the same year he had united with the First Presbyterian Church in Baltimore. He remained at the Seminary between two and three years, and in the meantime served for one year (1813-14) as a Tutor in the College.

He was licensed to preach by the Presbytery of New Brunswick, in April, 1815, and for a short time supplied the Presbyterian Church in Trenton

In 1816 he was married in Baltimore to Priscilla Horne, a native of Birmingham, England, with whose assistance he carried on for about four years a classical school for young ladies in Baltimore, which was very successful, until the condition of Mrs. Parmelee's health obliged them to relinquish it in 1820. He then removed to Zanesville, Ohio, where his wife died in 1822.

In 1823 he was ordained as an evangelist by the Lancaster (Ohio) Presbytery, and gave himself for many years mainly to the work of a home missionary and colporteur. He also edited for some years the *Zanesville Gazette*. In 1836 he married Catharine F. Barker, probably a daughter of General Samuel A. Barker (Yale 1772), of Lagrange, Duchess County, New York, who died in 1844. About 1845 he removed to Duncan Falls, about nine miles below Zanesville, on the Muskingum River, where his residence continued till his death.

About 1846 he married Hannah Wilson, who survived him.

He died, of pneumonia, at Duncan Falls, on April 6, 1872, in his 89th year.

His only child, a son by his first marriage, died in opening manhood.

AUTHORITIES.

Carter, N. Hampshire Native Ministry, 572. Hall, Hist. of Presbyterian Church, Trenton, 368. *Ezra P. Prentice*, MS. Letter, May, 1873. *Wheeler*, Hist. of Newport, N. H., 493, 497, 499.

William Seward Pierson, the only son of Deacon Abraham Pierson, of Killingworth, now Clinton, Connecticut, and grandson of Deacon Dodo and Mary (Seward) Pierson, of Clinton, was born on November 17, 1787, and received his name in memory of his great-grandfather. Rector Pierson was his great-great-grandfather. His mother was Lydia, third daughter of Captain Peleg and Sarah (Dudley) Redfield, of Clinton. He was prepared for College by the Rev. Dr. John Elliott (Yale 1786), of East Guilford, now Madison.

After graduation he taught in Springfield, Massachusetts, for two years, until his health failed. After his recovery he studied medicine at Dartmouth College, and received the degree of M.D. there in August, 1813.

He began practice in Clinton, but in April, 1814, Dr. Lyman Norton, the physician resident in Durham, was removed by death; and Dr. Pierson was thereupon formally invited by the inhabitants of that town to settle among them, and accepted the invitation.

On May 30, 1814, he married Nancy, daughter of Captain Jacob and Olive (Paine) Sargeant, of Hartford.

In 1818 he received a request from the people of Windsor to remove to that place. He removed thither in December of that year, and enjoyed an eminently successful professional career, until about 1836, when he was prostrated with a painful and protracted illness, after which he never re-entered on practice to any considerable extent

He died, after a distressing illness of about one week, in Windsor on July 16, 1860, in his 73d year.

His widow died on September 17, 1863, in her 75th year.

Their children were four sons and five daughters. Three sons and one daughter died in infancy or early youth. The eldest son was graduated at Yale in 1836. The eldest daughter married the Hon. Rufus P. Spalding (Yale 1817), and another married the Rev. Samuel H. Allen (Amherst Coll. 1841).

Dr Pierson was distinguished for his remarkably tender sensibilities, his ready tact, his excellent judgment, and strict integrity.

AUTHORITIES.

American Ancestry, x, 5. Conn Med. Society's Proceedings, 1860, 133–41 *Fowler*, Hist of Durham, 193 Pierson Genealogy, 15 Redfield Family, 38. *Stiles*, Hist of Windsor, 2d edition, i, 459, ii, 607.

THEODORE POMEROY was born in Southampton, Massachusetts, on March 14, 1785, the youngest son of Captain Lemuel Pomeroy, Junior, and of Eunice, daughter of Deacon Elias and Anne (Phelps) Lyman.

He was prepared for College by the Rev. Enoch Hale (Yale 1773), of Westhampton

After graduation he pursued medical studies with Dr. James, of Albany, and Dr. Chester, of Hudson, New York. He also attended a course of lectures at the Berkshire Medical College in Pittsfield, Massachusetts, and at first settled in practice in Cooperstown, New York, where he married Mary, daughter of Dr. Thomas Fuller

In 1821 he succeeded to the practice of Dr Amos G Hull, of Utica, who remained for a short time in partnership with him. Subsequently Edward Aiken (Middlebury Coll. 1815) studied with him, and in 1824 became his partner; he soon removed on account of health, and his place was taken in 1828 by John P Batchelder, M D. (Harvard 1815).

About 1830 Dr Pomeroy's practice greatly declined,—partly on account of a peculiarly fatal epidemic which prevailed among his patients, and partly on account of his becoming absorbed in business pursuits, which eventually engrossed his entire time. Most important among these was the management of a factory for making oil-cloth.

The honorary degree of M.D. was conferred on him by the Berkshire Medical Institution in 1849.

After the death of his first wife he married Cornelia Voorhees, of New Brunswick, New Jersey, who survived him.

He died while on a visit to one of his sons in St. Anthony, Minnesota, on June 26, 1860, in his 76th year

By his first marriage he had two sons and a daughter. His eldest son was graduated at Union College in 1835, and became a physician. By his second marriage he had four sons and a daughter.

AUTHORITIES.

Bagg, Pioneers of Utica, 520–22 *Coleman,* Lyman Genealogy, 350, 352

LYMAN SPENCER REXFORD, son of Joel and Rhoda (Spencer) Rexford, of Mount Carmel Society, in Hamden, and Barkhamsted, Connecticut, and grandson of Daniel and Desire (Hotchkiss) Rexford, of Mount Carmel and Barkhamsted, was born in Barkhamsted on April 24, 1784. His father was a farmer, and removed about 1795 to what is now Smyrna, then part of Sherburne, Chenango County, New York. He was prepared for admission to the Senior Class by the Rev. Timothy M. Cooley (Yale 1792), of East Granville, Massachusetts.

After graduation he studied law, and was licensed to practice in the Court of Common Pleas in October, 1811. He practiced law for about seven years, for most of the time in Sherburne.

He married Mary Wells, of Oneida County; and the loss of a son in 1818 brought about such a change in his purposes and views that he began the study of theology with the Rev. John Truair, of Sherburne, and was licensed to preach by the Union (Congregational) Association, probably in 1820. He received an honorary degree of M.A from Hamilton College in 1819 Mr. Truair left the Sherburne Church in September, 1820, and Mr. Rexford served as Stated Supply for two years. He was ordained to the ministry by a Congregational council on September 18, 1822

He then preached for a short time in Burlington, Otsego County, and going thence to the Presbyterian Church in Carlisle, Schoharie County, was received into membership in the Presbytery of Albany in January, 1824.

Late in 1827 he removed to Norwich, in Chenango County, and thence in 1829 to Sherburne, his permanent home Later in 1829 he joined the Presbytery of Chenango, with which he remained in connection until his death

About 1830, on account of difficulty with his throat, he was obliged to give up regular preaching, and thereafter served only as an occasional supply.

He engaged for a few years in the 'thirties in business, but was not successful.

In 1842 he was married, for the second time, to Mrs Amanda Lush, by birth Miss Keeler, of Albany.

He died in Sherburne on November 8, 1843, in his 60th year.

By his first marriage he had two sons, both of whom died early.

Mr Rexford was a man of ability and of varied information He was fond of theological discussion, and was especially effective in elocution and very critical of others in that regard.

AUTHORITIES

C. R. Johnson, Hist of Congregational Church, Norwich, 52–53 Rexford Genealogy, 40, 51–52

SILAS [WEBSTER] ROBBINS, the eldest son of Jacob Robbins, of Rocky Hill, in Wethersfield, Connecticut, by his second wife, Eunice Webster, was born at Rocky Hill on August 24, and baptized on December 18, 1785. His mother is said to have been a niece of Noah Webster (Yale 1778). He was a first cousin of Levi Robbins (Yale 1796), and assumed a middle name after graduation.

In 1808 he entered the Litchfield Law School, and in 1811 emigrated to Kentucky and began the practice of his profession in Winchester.

About the 1st of November, 1811, he was married to Caroline, youngest daughter of Hon. Uriah Tracy (Yale 1778), of Litchfield

He soon became prominent at the bar, and for one term, 1824–29, was Circuit Judge of the Eleventh District.

In 1824–26, when the Judges of the Supreme Court, were unsuccessfully assailed for upholding the obligation of contracts, as against the paper-money delusion, he was one of the Circuit Judges who consistently supported the authority of the higher court.

His wife died in Mount Sterling, Montgomery County, on January 26, 1836, in her 44th year, and in 1838 he removed to Springfield, Illinois, where he resumed the practice of law.

In 1858 he retired from active life to his farm in the township of Springfield, about four miles northwest of the city, where he died on June 19, 1871, in his 86th year.

He was twice married after the death of his first wife, and left a widow.

His only surviving child was one of three daughters by his first marriage.

Judge Robbins was an excellent public speaker, and active as such in politics as well as in the temperance cause and in all the benevolent movements of the day. He was a valued member of the Second Presbyterian Church in Springfield.

AUTHORITIES.

W. Corkle, MS. Letter, May, 1872.
Stiles, Hist. of Wethersfield, ii, 558.
Woodruff, Geneal. Register of Litchfield, 221.

CHARLES FOX ROBERTS, of Philadelphia, entered the Class at the opening of Sophomore year, his final preparation having been conducted by Henry Davis (Yale 1796), in New Haven.

He died at Pine Grove, Schuylkill County, on October 3, 1836, in his 46th year. He had inherited a large estate, and led rather a gay life.

HENRY WILLIAM ROGERS was a native of Long Island, but entered College from Norwich, Connecticut, at the opening of the Sophomore year, having been prepared by John Adams (Yale 1795), at the Bacon Academy in Colchester.

He studied law, but finally migrated to South Carolina, where hè was admitted to the bar in the Charleston district in 1818, and established himself in practice in Beaufort. He died in Beaufort on October 11, 1819, at the age of 31 years

---

WILLIAM SILLIMAN, the second child of Dr. Joseph and Patty (Leeds) Silliman, of New Canaan, Connecticut and a brother of Joseph Silliman (Yale 1806), was born in New Canaan on January 17, and baptized on March 30, 1788 He was prepared for the Sophomore Class by his pastor, the Rev. Justus Mitchell (Yale 1776).

After leaving College he studied law, and from the time of his admission to the bar until his death, he was a successful practitioner in the City of New York, chiefly in the courts of Chancery.

He died at East Chester, in Westchester County, New York, on October 24, 1861, in his 74th year

---

ABRAHAM MILLER SMITH, son of Platt and Polly Smith, of East Hampton, Long Island, was born in 1790. His mother was a daughter of Judge Abraham Miller, of East Hampton. A niece married Dr. Frederick W. Lord (Yale 1821).

He became a merchant in Newburgh, New York. He had purchased Western lands, and while on a visit to them died in Prairie du Chien, Wisconsin Territory, on June 19, 1839, aged 49 years.

He was never married

AUTHORITIES.

H P. Hedges, Hist of East-Hampton, 306, MS Letter, June, 1870

William Mason Smith was born in Charleston, South Carolina, in 1788 His father was the Rev Robert Smith, a native of the County of Norfolk, England, and a graduate of Cambridge University in 1753, who emigrated to Charleston in 1757, was made Bishop of South Carolina in 1795, and died in 1801. His mother was Anna Maria, daughter of Colonel Edward and Elizabeth (Chew) Tilghman, of Wye, Maryland, and widow of Charles Goldsborough, of Talbot, Maryland. His elder brother was graduated at Harvard in 1805, and received an *ad eundem* degree at Yale This son was named for an English Member of Parliament, who had been an influential friend of his father He was prepared for College by Robert Rogers (Brown Univ. 1775), in Newport, Rhode Island.

He was for a short time a midshipman in the United States Navy.

He married Susanna, daughter of the Hon. John Julius and Susannah (Reid) Pringle, of Charleston. His brother had previously (on January 2, 1818) married her sister Elizabeth Mary Pringle.

He owned a large plantation, called Smithfield, on Combahee River, some thirty miles west of Charleston, and built a handsome town house on Meeting Street These residences were centres of culture and refinement; but beyond the ordinary duties of a wealthy citizen he took no part in public life. He was a vestryman of St. Philip's Church, and on the committee for its rebuilding after the fire of 1835.

He died without issue on August 7, 1838, at the age of fifty. His wife placed an elegant mural monument to his memory, by Sir Francis Chantrey, in St Philip's Church, of which his father was long Rector

She died in the city of Charleston on May 18, 1846, in her 58th year

AUTHORITIES

Miss I DeSaussure, MS. Letter, May, 1911 *Hanson*, Old Kent, 254 *D E. Huger Smith*, MS Letter, June, 1911.

JOB STAPLES, the eighth child and fifth son of the Rev. John Staples (Princeton 1765) and of Susannah (Perkins) Staples, of Westminster Parish, in Canterbury, Connecticut, was born on August 23, 1786 Two brothers were graduated here in 1797 and 1809 respectively. His father died some months before he entered College

He taught school for a short time in Chester, Orange County, New York

In 1816 he settled in Cranberry, a township in the southwestern corner of Butler County, Pennsylvania, about fifteen miles northwest of Pittsburgh, where the rest of his life was spent on a farm.

He died in Cranberry, in September or October, 1861, in his 76th year.

By his wife, Susan, a native of the vicinity, he had five sons and eight daughters.

AUTHORITIES

Perkins Family, pt 3, 38

TIMOTHY TUTTLE, the youngest of eight children of Joseph Tuttle, a farmer of East Haven, Connecticut, and grandson of Noah and Rachel (Hoadley) Tuttle, of East Haven, was born on November 21, 1781. His mother was Mary, daughter of Daniel Grainger (Yale 1730), a woman of great energy and decision, joined to fervent piety. In the spring of 1799 the family removed to Durham. He fitted himself to teach school, and while thus engaged in 1803 became a Christian and united with the village church His pastor, the Rev. David Smith (Yale 1795), encouraged him to prepare for College, and he accomplished the task in ten months' time. At graduation he delivered a Dissertation on the Progress of Reason. He was the oldest member of the Class.

After graduation he taught for a short time, and then began the study of theology with Mr. Smith He was licensed to preach in May, 1809, and on February 15, 1810, married Mary, only daughter of Stephen and Mary (Merwin) Norton, of Durham, to whom he had long been attached.

In April, 1810, he began to preach in Groton, which had long been without a settled ministry. As one result of his labors the extinct church in the North part of the town was re-organized in December, 1810, and on August 14, 1811, he was ordained and installed as pastor over the parent church in Groton and the new church, seven miles distant, on a salary of $450, and for over twenty years he preached in the two churches on alternate Sundays In 1822 he consented to a reduction of his salary to $400

On April 2, 1834, he was dismissed from the South or original church, and thenceforwards devoted himself to the parish of North Groton, which later became the town of Ledyard, with a stipend of $300.

His wife died on February 14, 1856, in her 73d year She was survived by her two daughters The husband of the elder was a clergyman, and after 1859 he lived in Ledyard and gave some assistance to Mr. Tuttle, who remained full pastor until his death there, on June 6, 1864, in his 83d year.

The sermon preached at his funeral by his neighbor, the Rev. Thomas L Shipman (Yale 1818), was afterwards published.

He was a man of few words and of marked simplicity of character. He was eminently faithful and devoted to his people, in a difficult post.

His portrait is reproduced in Avery's *History of Ledyard.*

He published:

1 Concio ad Clerum a Sermon [from Acts ix, 15], delivered in the Chapel of Yale College, on the evening of August 15, 1832

In the *Evangelical Magazine*, vol. 1, pp 281–90, February, 1833

On Ministers as chosen vessels unto God

2 A Dissertation on Infant Baptism Norwich, 1833 8°, pp 18 [*A C A*

3 A Sermon [from Haggai, ii, 9]: preached at the Dedication of the new Congregational Church, in Ledyard. Dec 6, 1843 Norwich, 1844. 8°, pp. 12 [*B Publ C H S Y. C*

Historical

4. A Sermon [from Deut viii, 2], preached August 14, 1851, it being the fortieth anniversary of his ordination Norwich, 1851 8°, pp. 16 [*B Publ.*

5. Two Sermons [from Eph. vi, 4, and I Thess iv, 12], preached at Ledyard, the first, May 30, 1852, and the other, October 3, 1852 Norwich, 1853 8°, pp 18 [*A. C A.*

The first treats of the duty of Parents in regard to the Moral and Religious Training of their Children, and the second of the duty of Professors of Religion to act Honestly in reference to persons out of the Church

6. Sketches of History of the Congregational Church and Society in Ledyard. Delivered [from Ps lxxvii, 5] Aug 14th, 1859, being the 48th anniversary of the present pastorate Norwich, 1859 8°, pp 23. [*A. C. A. B. Publ U T. S. Y C.*

7. Semi-Centennial—A Sermon [from III John, 4], preached August 14, 1861 It being the fiftieth anniversary of his ordination Norwich, 1861 8°, pp 15
[*A. C A. B. Publ U. T S. Y. C.*

8 A permanent ministry

In *Contributions to the Ecclesiastical History of Connecticut,* New Haven, 1861, 8°, pp 239–45

9 History and Reminiscences of the Monthly Meeting of the Congregational Ministers of New London County, Ct.

In the *Congregational Quarterly,* vol. 3, pp 331–37, October, 1861.

With shrewd and kindly personal comments

He is also said to have printed a Discourse commemorative of the Massacre at Fort Griswold (1781)

AUTHORITIES.

Avery, Hist of Ledyard, 35–37 Congregational Quarterly, vi, 301 *Fowler,* Hist of Durham, 127–28 N London County Hist. Society's Papers, ii, 37–38 *Shipman,* Sermon at Mr. Tuttle's Funeral Tuttle Family, 300–06

SEPTIMIUS TYLER, a son of Daniel Tyler (Harvard 1771) and of Mehitabel (Putnam) Tyler, of Brooklyn, Connecticut, was born in Brooklyn in 1789, and was prepared for admission to the Sophomore Class by Rinaldo Burleigh (Yale 1803) in the Plainfield Academy

After graduation he taught school in Virginia, and meantime studied law, so that he was admitted to practice in that State in 1811.

In September, 1814, he enlisted in the United States Army, and served with the rank of Captain until honorably discharged in June, 1815

In the summer of 1817 he was employed by the United States Government to proceed to Hayti, in connection with some claims of American citizens on the black governments there. Not meeting with success he was obliged to return in the same vessel, the frigate *Congress,* and he died upon the passage home, on September 16, aged 28 years

AUTHORITIES.

J Q Adams, Diary, iv, 12 *Heitman,* Hist Register of U S Army, i, 977. *Larned,* Hist of Windham County, ii, 262.

CHARLES WHEELER was born in Philadelphia in 1787.

At graduation he delivered an Oration on Ridicule.

After graduation he studied law at home with Charles Chauncey (Yale 1792), and was admitted to the bar in 1812. His life was spent in his native city, in the practice of his profession. He enjoyed the respect of his fellow-citizens for an upright and honorable character, and died in Philadelphia, a sincere and hopeful Christian, on June 16, 1858, aged 71 years.

He married, on September 14, 1822, Eliza, fourth daughter of Captain Samuel and Eleanor (Ledlie) Bowman, of Wilkes-Barré, and aunt of Samuel S. Bowman (Yale 1845). She died on May 23, 1848, in her 55th year.

Their children were four daughters and two sons.

AUTHORITIES

Bond, Hist of Watertown, 699

COMFORT WILLIAMS, the eighth in a family of ten children of Eliel Williams, of Rocky Hill, in Wethersfield, Connecticut, and grandson of Captain Elias and Prudence (Robbins) Williams, of Rocky Hill, was born on January 23, and baptized on April 27, 1783 His mother was Comfort, daughter of John and Sarah (Robbins) Morton, of Wethersfield. He united with the College Church in May, 1808.

After graduation he studied theology for two years, during the second of which he was in Andover Seminary; and he was licensed to preach by the New Haven East Association of Ministers on June 12, 1810

On May 20, 1811, he married Lucy Williams, of Rocky Hill.

In 1812 he went to New York State under the employ of the Missionary Society of Connecticut, and labored as a home missionary in Oneida County and elsewhere for the next three years. He was conducting a classical school in Clinton in 1813; was ordained as an evangelist by the Presbytery of Oneida in February, 1813, and early in 1814 was laboring in Ogdensburg, St. Lawrence County.

In the summer or fall of 1814 he was employed to preach for a few months in the village which afterwards became the city of Rochester, and in August, 1815, a Presbyterian Church of sixteen members (the first religious Society in that place) was organized, over which on January 17, 1816, he was installed by the Presbytery of Geneva as pastor.

He was dismissed from this charge by his own request on June 6, 1821 His residence continued in Rochester, and he preached in various neighboring communities, until his death, in Rochester, on August 26, 1825, in his 43d year.

His wife died in the latter part of the year 1824

They had three sons and one daughter, all of whom lived to maturity.

AUTHORITIES

T Edwards, Thanksgiving Discourse, 1836, 38 *Hotchkin,* Hist of Western N. Y., 489. *Stiles,* Hist. of Wethersfield, ii, 833-35

Annals, 1808-09

At Commencement in 1809 the Rev. Dr. Nathan Strong (Yale 1769), of Hartford, resigned his place in the Corporation; and the vacancy was filled by the election of the Rev. Benoni Upson (Yale 1776), of Kensington Society in Berlin.

Late in 1808 Smibert's picture of Bishop Berkeley and his family was presented to the College by Isaac Lothrop, of Plymouth, Massachusetts.

Sketches, Class of 1809

**Burr Baldwin*, A M 1814	*1880
**Daniel Banks*, A M	*1827
*Samuel Brown Barrell, A.M.	*1858
*Jahacobus Bockee	*1810
*Garrett Garnsey Brown	*1870
*Johannes Burch	
*Hezekias Bradley Chaffee, A M. 1817	*1864
*Carolus Ezra Clarke, e Congr.	*1863
*Sanctus-Georgius Deane, A.M 1813	*1834
**Edvinus Wells Dwight*, A.M.	*1841
*Theodorus Eames, A.M.	*1846
*Howland Fish	*1862
*Josias Willard Gibbs, A M. et Harv. 1818, LL.D. Neo-Caes 1853, Tutor, Biblioth., Litt Sacr Prof.	*1861
*Alfredus Heyliger	*1863
*Samuel Johnson Hitchcock, A M , LL.D. 1842, Tutor	*1845
*Guilielmus Hungerford, LL D 1856	*1873
**Philo Judson*	*1874
**Johannes Langdon*, A M , Tutor	*1830
*Gurdonus Guilielmus Lathrop	*1832
**Jonathan Lee*	*1866
*Edvardus Blake Lining, A M.	*1849
**Benjamin Clark Meigs*, A M. 1814	*1862
**Alfredus Mitchell*	*1831
**Asahel Nettleton*, S T D. Hampd -Sidn. 1839 et Jeff. Penns 1839	*1844
*Carolus Goodrich Olmsted	*1865

*Johannes Still Winthrop Parkin *1866
**Philander Parmele* *1822
*Lemuel Purnell *1818
*Johannes Parker Rice, A.M *1875
*Hugo Robinson *1855
*Hezekias Booth Sanford, A M. 1817
*Benjamin French Shelton *1826
*Moses Aaron Simons *1822
**Carolus Smith* *1836
*Ebenezer Smith *1830
*Sophos Staples *1826
*Elisaeus Beebe Strong *1867
*Henricus Matson Waite, LL.D. 1855, Reipubl Conn Cur. Supr. Jurid Princ. *1869
*Samuel Dexter Ward *1871
*Gaylord Welles, M.D. 1827 *1870
*Guilielmus Henricus Winthrop *1860
*Alexander Wolcott *1830
**Simeon Woodruff*, A.M. 1815 *1839

BURR BALDWIN, the eldest child of Dr. Gabriel Baldwin, of that part of Weston, Connecticut, which in 1845 became Easton, and grandson of Jared and Damaris (Booth) Baldwin, of Newtown and New Milford, was born in Weston on January 19, 1789 His mother was Sarah, daughter of Zechariah and Martha (Burr) Summers, of Redding. Two brothers were graduated at the Yale Medical School in 1825: He was prepared for the second term, Sophomore year, by Henry Sherman (Yale 1803), then Principal of Staples Academy. He united with the College Church in August of the Junior year.

A few weeks after graduation he took charge of the classical department in the Newark (New Jersey) Academy, and remained there, in the absence of the Principal. William Woodbridge (Yale 1780), until the spring of

1810 He then took a position in the school which Mr. Woodbridge was conducting in Greenwich village, as it was then called, in what is now the heart of New York City In the following winter he taught again in Newark, and in the spring of 1811 entered the Andover Theological Seminary, in the Class of 1813.

In the spring of 1812 he was accepted for appointment as a missionary by the American Board, and in the following autumn he took a long horseback excursion to bid farewell to his friends, which brought on a species of dyspepsia, which so reduced him that he was obliged to return home in the spring of 1813. His friends then supposed him to be rapidly declining; but he recovered sufficiently to go back to Andover for a part of the ensuing winter.

In the autumn of 1814, not being well enough to preach, he became the Principal of the Newark Academy, and so continued until the spring of 1816.

His health was then so much improved that he secured on May 11 a license to preach from the Litchfield (Connecticut) South Association of Ministers, preparatory to serving as a missionary of the New Jersey Mission Society in Ohio and Western Virginia for one year. For the following year he was employed by the Female Missionary Society of New York to labor in that city; and about this time, with the prospect of never attaining vigorous health, he was honorably discharged by the American Board from their list of candidates

He left New York in May, 1818, as the climate appeared not to agree with him, and then labored for a year as a missionary in the northeastern part of New Jersey.

On June 2, 1819, he was ordained as an evangelist by the Litchfield South Association, and he was employed as an agent of the Presbyterian Education Society until the spring of 1820, in eastern New Jersey and New York State. He was foremost in these early years in the establishment of Sunday-school instruction, and in the religious training of colored youth.

He was married, on November 17, 1820, to Cornelia C., daughter of Jonathan Keen, of Newark.

He next served as an agent of the United Foreign Missionary Society until May, 1821; and then as stated supply of two small Presbyterian churches, in the northern part of Sussex County, New Jersey, until obliged to leave by poor health in the autumn of 1823

He then went as a missionary to northeastern Pennsylvania, and in the spring of 1824 accepted a call from the Presbyterian Church in Montrose, Pennsylvania, but his installment was deferred until the meeting of the Presbytery in September. His ministry was at first remarkably successful, but when some disaffection arose, he took a dismission in May, 1829.

On February 17, 1830, he was installed as the first pastor of the North Congregational Church in New Hartford, Connecticut, where he remained until February 6, 1833.

He then supplied various pulpits in Rhode Island, Connecticut, and Western Massachusetts, until he was installed over the Congregational Church in Ashfield Massachusetts, on April 20, 1836.

He was dismissed from Ashfield in September, 1838, and, in order to secure better education for his children, returned to Newark, where he established a school, which occupied him until the autumn of 1847

He then spent eight months in building up destitute congregations within the limits of the Presbytery of Montrose; and subsequently was similarly occupied in other parts of the State, and again in the vicinity of Montrose His wife died on October 2, 1854, in Montrose, in her 60th year.

From the autumn of 1856 to the summer of 1857 he spent in missionary work in Texas, under the auspices of the Southern Aid Society, and then labored again for two years in the Presbytery of Montrose. He was then for sixteen months similarly employed in the Genesee valley, New York

In July, 1862, he was appointed post-chaplain at Beverly, West Virginia, and served until late in 1863.

After a few months' leisure, he spent over a year in missionary labor in Delaware County, New York, but from April, 1866, lived in retirement in Montrose.

On the last Sunday of 1879 he fell while on his way to church, and his death occurred, in Montrose, on January 23, 1880, at the age of 91.

A second wife, Mrs Charlotte A Beach, whom he married on April 25, 1857, survived him

By his first wife he had two daughters and six sons The eldest daughter married the Rev. Eliphalet Whittlesey (Williams Coll 1840) One son (who changed his name by adoption) was graduated at Rutgers College in 1849

Mr. Baldwin was the last survivor of his Class

AUTHORITIES

Baldwin Genealogy, i, 369, 388–90; iii, 1078 *Rev B Baldwin*, MS Letter, June, 1867. *Blackman*, Hist. of Susquehanna County, 340–43. Ward Family Genealogy, 112, 182

DANIEL BANKS, of Weston, Connecticut, was prepared for admission to the Sophomore Class by Henry Sherman (Yale 1803), the Principal of Staples Academy He was a son of Daniel Banks, of Weston, and was baptized on October 29, 1786.

During the year after graduation he taught in the Academy in North Salem, Westchester County, New York, under the principalship of the Rev. Herman Daggett (Brown Univ. 1788).

He meantime studied theology, and was licensed to preach by the Fairfield West Association of Ministers on October 9, 1810.

He found employment as a missionary in Jefferson County, in northern New York; and on July 29, 1814, he was invited to become the first pastor of a Congregational Church in Watertown. He accepted the call, and was installed there on October 25, 1815, retaining also the charge for half the time of another small Congregational church in Rutland, eight miles to the southeastwards, where he was previously laboring. The Watertown church became Presbyterian in January, 1821, and he retired from service in the following month.

He removed to Potsdam, St. Lawrence County, where he died in 1827, at the age of 41.

His wife, Mrs. Harriet Banks, died while on a visit to her father, in Clinton, New York, on October 4, 1820, from consumption, after a long and distressing illness, in her 25th year.

AUTHORITIES.

Emerson, Hist. of Jefferson County, 798, 842–43. *Haddock,* Centennial Hist. of Jefferson County, 239. Religious Intelligencer, v, 399–400.

Samuel Brown Barrell, son of Joseph Barrell, a wealthy merchant of Boston and Charlestown, Massachusetts, was born in Boston on June 1, 1790. A half-brother was graduated at Harvard College in 1783. His father died in October, 1804. His mother was probably Sarah, eldest daughter of Joseph and Mehitable (Nott) Webb, of Wethersfield, Connecticut, and widow of John Simpson, of Boston.

He studied law after graduation in the office of the late Peter O. Thacher (Harvard 1796), of Boston, and followed the practice of his profession in that city until 1824, when he removed to Washington City, District of Columbia.

His chief business in Washington was connected with the obtaining from Congress the settlement of claims against the Government held by individuals.

Mr. Clay, when Secretary of State in 1827, appointed him as Commissioner to proceed to New Brunswick to effect if possible an adjustment of the difficulties with relation to the boundary line He returned to Washington from this mission in February, 1828.

At a later date he was extensively engaged in land business in Maryland and Tennessee

He returned to Boston in August, 1854, and spent the rest of his life in that city, where he died on March 22, 1858, in his 68th year

He married, in Boston, on November 16, 1824, Catharine Maria Ward, a sister of a classmate, who survived him until 1877.

He left no children.

AUTHORITIES.

J Q. Adams, Diary, vii, 428 *Dr. Joseph Palmer,* MS Letter, August, 1858. *Ward,* Hist. of Shrewsbury, 463

Jacob Bockee, of Amenia, Duchess County, New York, was born on November 12, 1788, and was prepared for admission to the Sophomore Class by Henry Davis (Yale 1796), in New Haven. He was the third son of Captain Jacob Bockee, of Amenia, and grandson of Abraham and Maria (Kaar) Bockee, of New York City and Amenia His mother was Catharine, daughter of Isaac and Margaret (Platt) Smith, of Hempstead.

After graduation he began the study of medicine under Dr. Brodhead, of Columbia County, but on account of his health he was obliged to return home.

He died in Amenia, from consumption, supposed to be the result of over-study, on November 24, 1810, aged 22 years This was the earliest death in the Class.

AUTHORITIES

Abm. Bockee, MS Letter, November, 1862 *Flint,* Bockée Family, 51, 87.

GARRETT GARNSEY BROWN, son of David and Philena Brown, was born in Bethlehem, Connecticut, on February 13, 1785, and was prepared for admission to the second term of Sophomore year by James Morris (Yale 1775), of Litchfield South Farms. He united with the College Church in May of his Junior year.

After graduation he taught school in Milford for one term, and then began a course of study in the Andover Theological Seminary, where he continued until licensed to preach by the New Haven East Association of ministers, on December 27, 1811.

He preached as a candidate in various places for the next five or six years, but finally gave up the idea of a settlement, and for nearly fifty years he wandered over the Southern and Southwestern States, teaching in private families and in schools, and preaching, but scarcely remaining a year in any one place.

In 1854 he went to the Hawaiian Islands and taught a private school there for about a year; but he met with losses, and returned in 1855 to the Southwest.

After the outbreak of the Civil War he came back to his native place; but he was entirely without property, and was at length obliged to take refuge in the almshouse in Woodbury, where the town of Bethlehem supported him. He died there, after a brief illness, on October 1, 1870, in his 86th year.

He was never married.

His mental powers were sufficiently good, but overpowering indolence was fatal to him. He retained the full use of his faculties to the last.

AUTHORITIES.

Rev. G. W. Banks, MS. Letter, April, 1871. *Cothren,* Hist. of Woodbury, ii, 1422–23.

JOHN BURCH entered College from Powelton, Hancock County, Georgia, about fifty miles west of Augusta. He was born about 1785, and his preparation for College was completed under Jeremiah Evarts (Yale 1802) in New Haven

His name is first marked as deceased in the Triennial Catalogue of Graduates issued in 1844

HEZEKIAH BRADLEY CHAFFEE, son of Dr. Hezekiah Chaffee, Junior, of Windsor, Connecticut, and grandson of Dr. Hezekiah and Lydia (Griswold, Phelps) Chaffee, of Windsor, was born on March 3, and baptized on June 28, 1789. His mother was Charlotte, daughter of Hezekiah and Abigail (Sherwood) Bradley, of Green's Farms, in Fairfield, now Westport. His younger brother was graduated in 1810. He was prepared for College by Nathan Johnson (Yale 1802)

He began the study of law with Gideon Tomlinson (Yale 1802), at Greenfield Hill, in Fairfield, but when war with England was declared he went to Jefferson County, New York, and saw active service for a year or two in the militia.

After the peace he began a mercantile life in Hartford, in connection with his brother In 1823 he undertook a commercial enterprise in Mexico, and spent two years in travel in that country About 1852 or 1853 he retired to Windsor, to live with a widowed sister, and he died there from congestion of the lungs, on December 13, 1864, in his 76th year He was never married

---

AUTHORITIES

Chaffee Genealogy, 205 *Hinman*, Early Puritan Settlers, 517 *O B.* *Stiles*, Hist of Windsor, 2d ed, ii, 143
Loomis, MS Letter, August, 1865

Charles Ezra Clarke, the second son of Captain Ezra Clarke, of Saybrook, Connecticut, was born in Saybrook on October 16, 1789. His mother was Elizabeth, second daughter of Ambrose and Elizabeth (Tully) Whittlesey, of Saybrook. He was prepared for admission by his pastor, the Rev. Frederick W. Hotchkiss (Yale 1778).

After graduation he studied law in Greene County, New York, and in 1815 established himself in Watertown, Jefferson County, in the practice of his profession, in which he was constantly engaged for about twenty years, and partially till near the close of his life. From about 1826 to 1848 his younger brother (honorary M.A. Yale 1840) was associated with him.

In 1825 he purchased a farm and mill-seat, at Great Bend village, in the township of Champion, about a dozen miles east of Watertown; and as he devoted much of his attention to milling enterprises and became a skillful agriculturalist, he gradually withdrew from his profession.

He was elected to the State Assembly for two terms, in 1839–40, and to the 31st session of the United States Congress, in 1849–51,—serving in both these stations with distinguished ability. As a lawyer he stood at the head of the profession in the vicinity, and was long remembered for his wit and eloquence.

He married, on April 22, 1852, Hannah (or Anna) Sanford, eldest daughter of Eliada and Hannah (Sanford) Tuttle, of North Haven, Connecticut, and widow of Pinney Kelsey, who died in October, 1847.

Mr. Clarke died in Champion, after a long and painful illness, on December 8, 1863, in his 57th year.

His wife survived him, with four of their five children.

He published:

1. Speech on the Admission of California Delivered in the House of Representatives, May 13, 1850 Washington, 1850 8°, pp 16 [*Harv.* *M. H. S* *Y. C.*

2. Speech on the Bill establishing the Boundary between Texas and New Mexico Delivered in the House of Representatives, August 30, 1850 Washington, 1850 8°, pp 15 [*B. Publ*

3. To the Capitalists of Boston An Address before a meeting of the Sackets Harbor and Saratoga Railroad Company, Saratoga Springs, November 13, 1850 Boston, 1851 8°, pp. 12. [*B Publ*

4 A Letter on the Construction of Plank Roads
In W. Kingsford's History, Structure, and Statistics of Plank Roads, in the United States and Canada Philadelphia, 1851 8°, pp. 36-39. [*Harv.* *U. S.* *Y C.*

5. An Argument on the Expediency of Constructing a Railroad from Sacket's Harbor to Saratoga Boston, 1851 8°, pp 25 [*B. Ath* *B Publ.* *M. H. S*

AUTHORITIES

J Clarke, MS. Letter, June, 1864
Emerson, Jefferson County, 189-90
Haddock, Centennial Hist of Jefferson County, 264
Tuttle Family, 254
Whittlesey Genealogy, 92.

St George Deane, the eldest son of Michael Deane, a native of Bermuda, and of Rebecca (Perinchief) Deane, was born in Bermuda on April 21, 1789.

He returned to Bermuda after his graduation, and was engaged there for some time in the business of instruction.

He afterwards went to Nassau, in the Bahama Islands, and had charge of an academy there. Subsequently he was appointed by the Governor as general Superintendent of a district or village. His duties consisted of providing instruction, and promoting, as far as possible, the welfare of the community. While thus engaged he was attacked by fever, conveyed to Nassau, and died there on December 22, 1834, in his 46th year.

AUTHORITIES.

A. T Deane, MS Letter, May, 1885

Edwin Welles Dwight, the second son and child of Henry Williams Dwight, of Stockbridge, Massachusetts, and grandson of General Joseph and Abigail (Williams, Sergeant) Dwight, of Great Barrington, was born in Stockbridge, on November 17, 1789. His mother was Abigail, daughter of Ashbel and Abigail (Kellogg) Welles, of West Hartford, Connecticut. A younger brother was graduated at Yale in 1813. His grandmother was a half-sister of Colonel Ephraim Williams, the founder of Williams College, and he spent the first three years of his College course in that institution.

He remained in New Haven after graduation and in 1809 befriended Henry Obookiah, the native of Hawaii whose memoirs he afterwards wrote. For a few months in 1812 he served as Rector of the Hopkins Grammar School.

In 1813 he began the study of theology with the Rev. Dr. Andrew Yates (Yale 1794), of East Hartford, and when Dr. Yates in August, 1814, removed to Union College, in Schenectady, New York, he seems to have gone to Litchfield to study under the Rev. Dr. Lyman Beecher (Yale 1797).

He was licensed to preach by the South Association of Litchfield County ministers on October 17, 1815, and then made Schenectady his headquarters for further study under Dr. Yates.

In 1816 he did some missionary service in Western New York, and later was preaching in Woodbury, Connecticut, where the North Church was organized in December.

In October, 1816, it was decided to establish a Foreign Mission School in Cornwall, Litchfield County, Connecticut, for the instruction of heathen youth like Obookiah; and as the person desired for the office of principal was then engaged elsewhere, Mr. Dwight was employed in his place from May, 1817, to May, 1818.

Later in 1818 he was called to the pastorate of the Congregational Church in Richmond, Massachusetts, in the immediate vicinity of his birthplace, on a salary of $600, and he was ordained and installed there on January 13, 1819, Dr. Beecher preaching the sermon.

He married, on April 24, 1821, Mary, daughter of Henry and Lois (Chidsey) Sherrill, of Richmond.

From 1832 until his death he was one of the Trustees of Williams College.

In April, 1837, on account of poor health, he was obliged to resign his pastoral charge, and he then removed to Stockbridge, where his wife died of a malarial fever on October 11, 1838, at the age of 37. In these last years he preached with some regularity at Housatonic village, in the northern part of Great Barrington, where a Congregational church was organized shortly after his death He died in Stockbridge, on February 25, 1841, in his 52d year.

His children were four daughters and three sons The second daughter married Jared Reid (Yale 1846), and the youngest daughter married the Rev Dr. Henry M. Field (Williams Coll. 1838). The youngest son was graduated at Williams in 1850 The eldest son died in infancy, and the eldest daughter in early womanhood

Mr. Dwight was a man of tender and refined feelings, and a solemn and earnest preacher.

He published:

1 Memoirs of Henry Obookiah, a native of Owhyhee, and a member of the Foreign Mission School; who died at Cornwall, Conn, Feb. 17, 1818, aged 26 years. New-Haven, 1818 18°, pp 109 + pl [Y C.

Anonymous Numerous editions appeared (including one by the American Tract Society in 1832, revised by the author), and the work had a powerful effect in leading the way to mission work in Hawaii

2 A History of the Town of Richmond In A History of the County of Berkshire, Massachusetts .. —By Gentlemen in the County... Pittsfield, 1829 12°, pp. 320–35

AUTHORITIES

Durfee, Williams Biogr. Annals, 75. *B. W Dwight,* Dwight Genealogy, ii, 751, 754-55. *R.H W Dwight,* in Berkshire Courier, Jan 31, 1907, and Springfield Republican, Jan 23, 1910

THEODORE EAMES, son of Lieutenant Samuel and Abigail (Frye) Eames, was born in Haverhill, Massachusetts, on July 28, 1785, and spent the first two years of his course in Harvard College. At graduation he delivered an Oration on the Desire of Distinction.

After graduation he studied law in Salem with Leverett Saltonstall (Harvard 1802), and began practice there in 1812.

About 1820 he became the Master of the Latin School in Salem, and went thence in 1831 to Brooklyn, New York, as the senior principal of a new English and classical school for boys. About 1840 he was made a Judge of the Municipal Court in Brooklyn, and held that position until his death. He was also an elder in the First Presbyterian Church

He died in Brooklyn on February 5, 1847, in his 42d year.

He was a man of great energy and strict integrity, and a stern but faithful instructor

He married on July 25, 1811, Abigail, only daughter of Samuel and Abigail (Crowninshield) Very, of Salem, who survived him.

He published:

1. An Address delivered at the opening of Eames and Putnam's English and Classical Hall, Brooklyn, Long Island, March 24th, 1831 New York, 1831. 8°, pp. 32
[*A. C. A. B. Publ. Harv M H. S. Y. C.*

2 An Introductory Lecture, delivered before the Brooklyn Lyceum, November 7, 1833 Brooklyn, 1833. 8°, pp 32
[*B. Ath B. Publ Harv N. Y. H. S. Y C*

AUTHORITIES.

Chase, Hist of Haverhill, 630 *Cooke,* Driver Family, 328 Haverhill Vital Records, i, 101. Hist. Collections of the Essex Institute, ii, 36.

HOWLAND FISH, son of Peter Fish, of Amenia, Duchess County, New York, was born in North East in that County on December 8, 1786. His mother was Elsie, daughter of Samuel and Esther (Brownell) Howland, of Dartmouth, Massachusetts, and Duchess County, who were Quakers. He was prepared for College by the Rev. John Barnett (Yale 1780), of Amenia.

After graduation he studied law with Philip Parker, of Hudson, in Columbia County, and pursued his profession with success in Montgomery County, residing in that part of Charleston, which was set off in 1823 as the town of Glen.

He represented the county in two sessions of the Legislature (in 1820–21 and 1827), and served as a delegate to the Constitutional Convention of 1821 He held the office of District Attorney from 1843 to 1846.

He retired from practice at the age of 70, and died at his residence in the village of Fultonville, in Glen, honored and respected by all, on June 21, 1862, in his 76th year.

Four sons survived him.

AUTHORITIES.

Frothingham Fisk, MS Letter, May, 1865

JOSIAH WILLARD GIBBS, third son of Henry Gibbs (Harvard 1766), of Salem, Massachusetts, and grandson of Henry Gibbs (Harvard 1726) and Katharine (Willard) Gibbs, of Salem, was born in that ancient town on April 30, 1790 His mother was Mercy, fourth daughter of Benjamin and Rebekah (Minot) Prescott, of Salem His father died in January, 1794; and as two sisters

(Mrs. Roger Sherman, and Mrs. Henry Daggett) and a brother of his mother were settled in New Haven, it was natural that he should be sent to Yale. A brother was graduated here in 1814. He won distinction in College as a scholar, and delivered an Oration at graduation on a characteristic subject, The Love of Truth.

From College he returned to Salem, and was engaged there in teaching school. His appointment as Tutor, in September, 1811, brought him back to New Haven, and he discharged the duties of that office for four years His time was partly given to theological studies, and he received a license to preach from the New Haven West Association on September 27, 1814, but rarely availed himself of it.

On leaving the tutorship he went to Andover, where Professor Moses Stuart (Yale 1799) was in the first flush of his enthusiasm for Hebrew study He devoted himself mainly to linguistic research, while pursuing theology under Professor Stuart's direction. Meantime, he not only became proficient in Hebrew, but was impressed with the importance of introducing the methods and results of German scholarship into America.

He assisted Professor Stuart materially in the preparation of his edition of Gesenius's Hebrew Grammar in 1821, and meantime was preparing his own edition of the Hebrew Lexicon of Gesenius, which appeared in January, 1824 In 1819 he published a catalogue of the Seminary Library; and in September, 1824, he was induced to return to New Haven as Lecturer in Biblical Literature, with pupils from among the resident graduates and the students in the Divinity School. At the same time he undertook the duties of College Librarian.

Two years later he was promoted from this lectureship to the rank of Professor of Sacred Literature in the Divinity School.

In the meantime he was occupied with the preparation of an abridgement of his Lexicon, which appeared in

1828, and reached a second edition in 1832 In 1833 a new and improved edition of the original prompted him to undertake an English version, with additions from the larger work of the same author. He had slowly printed about one-third of the proposed work, prepared with characteristic thoroughness and accuracy, when a translation by Dr. Edward Robinson appeared, in 1836, and Mr. Gibbs's labor and large expenditure of money (for Hebrew and other Oriental type) became of no avail.

Keenly disappointed, he then turned from the work of Hebrew lexicography, to which he had devoted so many years, and fixed his main interest on general linguistics and the new science of comparative philology, in which he became a pioneer for America.

In 1843 he resigned the office of Librarian

In 1853 the honorary degree of Doctor of Laws was conferred on him by Princeton College, in special recognition of his attainments in philology.

He died in New Haven on March 25, 1861, aged nearly 71 years. A commemorative discourse by his pastor, Professor Fisher, was afterwards published

He married, on September 30, 1830, Mary Anna, daughter of Dr. John VanCleve (Princeton Coll. 1797), and Louisa Anna (Houston) VanCleve, of Princeton, New Jersey, who died in New Haven, after a lingering illness of nearly three years, on February 8, 1855, in her 50th year A sister of hers married Professor Ebenezer A. Johnson (Yale 1833).

Their children were four daughters, of whom two died in early womanhood, and a son. The third daughter married Addison VanName (Yale 1858), a classmate of her brother, who bore his father's name and added to it new lustre, as an investigator in mathematical physics

Professor Gibbs deserves remembrance as the most thoroughly equipped scholar of his College generation. His cautious habit of mind, however, led him to expend on minute investigations the powers which might have been applied to broader constructive reasoning. He was a great lover of accurate knowledge, and had a remarkable power of felicitous statement.

A characteristic instance of his method and thoroughness was furnished in 1839, when the Amistad captives were brought to New Haven, and he undertook the difficult task of establishing communication with them and of compiling vocabularies of the various African dialects which were the native tongues of the different members of the group. His unwearied patience and skill were rewarded with complete success

A portrait, painted by F. B. Carpenter in 1856, is owned by the Divinity School, and has been reproduced in Kingsley's *Yale College,* and in President Dwight's *Memories of Yale Life and Men.*

He published·

1. Catalogue of the Library belonging to the Theological Institution in Andover Andover, 1819 8°, pp. 161.
Without the compiler's name

2. A Hebrew and English Lexicon of the Old Testament, including the Biblical Chaldee, from the German works of Prof. W. Gesenius. Andover, 1824. 8°, pp. viii, 715 [*U. T. S Y. C.*

The same London, 1827 8°, pp. viii, 656. [*Y. C.*

3 A Manual Hebrew and English Lexicon, including the Biblical Chaldee. Designed particularly for beginners. Andover, 1828. 8°, pp. iv, 211 [*B. Publ Harv.*

The same. Second edition, revised and enlarged. New-Haven, 1832. 8°, pp. iv, 236.
[*A A S B. Ath B Publ Br. Mus. Columbia Univ. Harv Y C*

4. Selections from the Holy Scriptures; intended as Sabbath Exercises for Children.—Part I—Devotional Extracts from the Book of Psalms: accompanied with short notes and questions New Haven, 1830 12°, pp. viii, 88 [*M. H. S. Y. C*
Part II, consisting of moral extracts, was never published.

5. Philological Studies with English illustrations. New Haven, 1857. 12°, pp vii, 244.
[*A C. A. B Ath Columbia Univ Harv. Y. C*

6 A Latin Analyst on modern philological principles New Haven, 1858. 12°, pp. viii, 150.
[*Br. Mus. Harv U. S. Y. C.*

7 Formation of Teutonic Words in the English Language New Haven, 1860. 12°, pp viii, 139 [*Harv Y. C.*

He also contributed extensively to periodicals, the following examples may be specified·

American Journal of Science and Arts, vol. 24, pp. 87–96 (April, 1833)· On the Orthography of Hebrew words in the Roman character

Volume 33, pp 324–28 (January, 1838), and vol. 41, pp 28–31 (July, 1841)· Contributions to English Lexicography

Volume 34, pp 337–47 (July, 1838)· Table of Greek Correlatives, with explanations.

Volume 37, pp 112–15 (July, 1839): Greek Conjugations.

Volume 38, pp 41–48 (January, 1840): Gissi or Kissi, Vai or Vey, and Mendi Vocabularies

Volume 39, pp 255–62 (October, 1840): Characteristics of the Language of Ghagh or Accra

Volume 41, pp 32–39 (July, 1841)· Origin of the Names of Beasts, Birds, and Insects

Volume 45, pp 96–102 (July, 1843). on the Adverbial Genitive Case in English; pp. 284–92 (October, 1843)· Greek Verbal Roots in English.

Second Series, vol 6, pp 206–09 (September, 1848): English Prefixes derived from the Greek

Quarterly Christian Spectator, vol 6, pp. 156–59 (March, 1834) On the Biblical Use of the word Son.

Volume 9, pp 109–134, 415–34 (March and September, 1837): Historical and Critical Views of Cases in the Indo-European Languages

American Biblical Repository, 2d Series, vol. 2, pp 166–74 (July, 1839): Natural Significancy of Articulate Sounds; pp 480–85 (October, 1839): Biblical Criticisms and Remarks

Second Series, vol 11, pp 441–46: Notes on the Septuagint Version of Psalms i, ii.

Third series, vol 2, pp. 360–63 (April, 1846): The Formations of Compound Words.

Bibliotheca Sacra, vol 9, pp. 220–22 (January, 1852): Notice of Brewer's Patmos and the Seven Churches; pp 226–27: Notice of Fergusson's Palaces of Nineveh and Persepolis

Volume 11, pp. 836–39 (October, 1854): Notice of Curtius on Comparative Philology

Volume 13, pp 665–67 (July, 1856): Correspondence on the use of Dii and Deus, etc

Volume 14, pp 425–27 (April, 1857): Correspondence on Hebrew Parallelism, Vocalic Harmony, and Mammon.

Volume 16, pp 302–09 (April, 1859): Philological Studies, on the Latin Negation, and on Interrogative Words in the Indo-European Languages

American Quarterly Register, vol 15, pp 170–75 (November, 1842): Analysis of the English Interrogatives; Disguised verbal roots in English.

New Englander, vol 1, pp 140–41 (January, 1843): Resemblance of certain Languages to the Latin; pp. 434–39 (July, 1843): On Vowel Changes in the English Language

Volume 10, pp. 102–08 (February, 1852): Messianic Prophecies; pp 300–08 (May, 1852). Catholic Complaints against the Early Protestant Versions of the Scriptures, pp 433–37 (August, 1852): The Jewish Kabbala, pp 472–79, Scientific Miscellany: On the Particle But

Volume 11, pp. 320–24 (May, 1853), Scientific Miscellany: On Guna and Vriddhi

Volume 15, pp. 242–49 (May, 1857): The Use of Testament for Covenant; pp 666–74 (November, 1857): Critical Miscellanies.

Volume 16, pp 691–95 (August, 1858): The Ante-Mosaic Origin of the Sabbath, and Septuple times in the Pentateuch.

Volume 17, pp 489–528 (May, 1859). Common Version and Biblical Revision

Volume 18, pp. 226–29 (February, 1860): Hints on Lexicography, pp 429–40 (May, 1860). Common Schools and the English Language

Journal of the American Oriental Society, vol 1, pp 360–73 (1849). On the Mandingo and the Susu Dialects.

Volume 2, pp 125–34 (1851). Characteristics of the Peshito Syriac Version of the New Testament

Volume 3, pp 235–40 (1853). The Jews at Khaifung-fu in China; pp 469–72: Remarks on Grout's Essay on the Phonology and Orthography of the Zulu and kindred Dialects, pp 502–03. Melek Tâus of the Yezidis

Volume 4, pp 444–45 (1854). The so-called Nestorian Monument of Singan-fu.

Volume 5, p 194: Vestiges of Buddhism in Micronesia.

David N. Lord's *Theological and Literary Journal*, vol 3, pp. 446–48 (1851). The Advent

Volume 4, pp 82–91 (1851) Philological Contributions

Volume 9, pp 167–68 (1856): Proverbial Phrases in the New Testament.

American Journal of Education, vol. 2, pp 198–202, and vol 3, pp 101–24 (1856–57): Philological Contributions

American Journal of Education and College Review, vol. 2, pp. 53–58 (1856): List of two hundred Latin verbal roots found in the English Language.

Massachusetts Teacher, vol 12, pp 332–33 (1859): What is expressed in language

He published the following translation:

An Essay on the Historical sense of the New Testament—By G C Storr. Boston, 1817 12°, pp. iv, 92.

He contributed largely to two editions (1850 and 1855) of Professor W. C. Fowler's *English Grammar*.

He furnished the Rev Dr. Sprague in 1854 with a brief memoir of the Rev Samuel Willard (Harvard 1659), which is printed in the *Annals of the American Pulpit*, vol 1, pp 164–67.

AUTHORITIES

Bond, Hist of Watertown, 236. *Dwight*, Memories of Yale Life and Men, 265–77 *Fisher*, Discourse commemorative of Professor Gibbs *Gibbs*, Memoirs of Gibbs Family, 40–43 *Kingsley*, Yale College, II, 37–40, 494. Prescott Memorial, 68, 95, 135. Semi-Centennial Anniversary of the Divinity School, 18, 80, 82–86. Willard Memorial, 403.

ALFRED HEYLIGER, son of John and Elizabeth (Solomons) Heyliger, was born on July 19, 1788, on the island of Saint Croix, in the Danish West Indies. When he was about ten years old, his father, a native of Denmark, removed to New Haven; he afterwards returned to Saint Croix, and died there in 1811.

The son was prepared for College by the Rev. Frederick William Hotchkiss (Yale 1778), of Saybrook.

He became a dry-goods merchant in New Haven, being in partnership successively with John H. Jacocks and Justin Redfield.

In his later years he lived in seclusion. He died very suddenly, while calling at a friend's house, on Sunday evening, July 5, 1863, at the age of 75. He was never married.

AUTHORITIES

New Haven Daily Register, July 6, 1863.

Samuel Johnson Hitchcock, the eldest of twelve children of Benjamin and Mary (Johnson) Hitchcock, of Bethlehem, then part of Woodbury, Connecticut, and grandson of Benjamin and Elizabeth (Averett) Hitchcock, of Woodbury, was born in Bethlehem on February 4, 1786 His father being in straitened circumstances, this promising son, after having taught school for some winters, was gratuitously prepared for the Sophomore Class, by his pastor, the Rev. Azel Backus (Yale 1787). He was graduated with the highest honors, delivering with the Valedictory an Oration on the Wisdom of aiming at High Attainments.

On leaving College he taught for two years in the Fairfield Academy, and then entered on the office of Tutor at Yale, in the meantime also studying law under the direction of Seth P Staples (Yale 1797). At Commencement in 1812 he gave a Master's Oration on Newspapers

He resigned his office at Commencement in 1815, and was then admitted to the bar, and entered on practice in this city, where he soon attained distinction.

In 1820 he became associated with Mr. Staples as a teacher in his private Law School, which in 1824 was first recognized as a part of the College. To this School for the rest of his life he devoted much of his time and energy, with great success.

Although he preferred to avoid public office, he served as Judge of the New Haven County Court from 1838 to 1842, as Mayor of the City for three years from June, 1839, and as Chief Judge of the City Court from 1842 to 1844.

The honorary degree of Doctor of Laws was conferred on him by Yale in 1842.

He took an active interest in internal improvements, and was a member of the first Board of Directors of the Hartford and New Haven Railroad Company, and its President from 1837 to 1840.

He was also concerned in securing the first surveys for a railroad from New Haven to New York, and spent the winter before his death in Albany, endeavoring to procure from the Legislature the necessary franchises.

He died in New Haven on August 31, 1845, in his 60th year.

Judge Hitchcock was distinguished in his profession for accurate legal knowledge and great power of application; of studious and methodical habits, and sound, discriminating judgment, he was probably more eminent as a teacher than as an advocate. He served as a Deacon in the Center Church from 1833 until his death

His portrait, painted by Jared B. Flagg, about 1840, belongs to the University

He was married by the Rev. Aaron Dutton, on May 18, 1818, to Laura, daughter of Simeon and Parnel (Fowler) Coan, of Guilford, who died of consumption on October 3, 1832, in her 35th year.

He next married, on December 25, 1834, in Fredericksburg, Virginia, Narcissa, daughter of Walter and Elizabeth Burr (Sturges) Perry, of Southport, Connecticut, and widow of Joseph Whittemore, of Fredericksburg, who died in Fairfield in July, 1831. She died while visiting in Southport on November 3, 1854, in her 59th year.

By his first marriage he had two sons and three daughters, of whom all but one daughter survived him. The youngest daughter married Judge Thomas D. Sherwood (Yale 1846).

By his second marriage he had one son, who was for a time a member of the Class of 1861 in Yale.

AUTHORITIES

Hitchcock Family, 69, 81–82 New Haven City Year Book, 1864, 85–86 *Perry*, Old Burying Ground of Fairfield, 207 Religious Intelligencer, xvii, 319.

William Hungerford, the second child of Robert and Olive Hungerford, of East Haddam (Hadlyme Parish), Connecticut, and grandson of Robert and Grace (Holmes) Hungerford, was born on November 22, 1786. His mother was the youngest child of Lieutenant Joseph and Rebecca (Selden) Ely. His father was a farmer, and the family had to make great sacrifices to send him to Yale

He was prepared for College by his pastor, the Rev. Joseph Vaill (Dartmouth Coll 1778).

For six months after graduation he taught in a high school in Westchester Parish, in the town of Colchester, and then entered on the study of law with Judge Matthew Griswold (Yale 1780) and his brother, Lieutenant-Governor Roger Griswold (Yale 1780), in Lyme.

He was admitted to the bar in 1812, and opened an office in his father's house. Seven years later he removed to East Haddam Landing, where he acquired as extensive a practice as any lawyer in that region.

In 1829 he removed to Hartford, where he formed in 1832 a partnership with William R. Cone (Yale 1830), which continued until the end. He retired from active practice in 1860, and after a few months of confinement to the house died in Hartford on January 15, 1873, in his 87th year. He was buried in Hadlyme He was never married.

While at East Haddam his income was extremely small, but he devoted himself earnestly to study, and became with the foundation thus laid a profoundly learned lawyer. He had a mind of comprehensive grasp and wonderful industry, and was beyond question the peer of any advocate of his time in Connecticut.

His pre-eminence was acknowledged by the honorary degree of Doctor of Laws conferred on him by this College in 1856.

He was the last surviving member of the Constitutional Convention in 1818. In politics he was successively a Federalist, a Whig, and a Republican.

He represented East Haddam in the General Assembly in October, 1818, May, 1819, 1820, 1824, 1825, and 1828; and Hartford in 1834 and 1836. Beyond this he consistently declined to accept public office

His portrait is reproduced in the *History of Hartford County*.

AUTHORITIES

Conn Reports, xxxix, 605-16 Ely Ancestry, 121 *Trumbull,* Hist. of Hartford County, i, 139

Philo Judson, the younger son of Philo and Emm (Minor) Judson, of Woodbury, Connecticut, and grandson of Elijah and Sarah (Hollister) Judson, of Woodbury, was probably born in January, 1784 (In his later years he was wont to say that he was born in January, 1782; but this is doubtful.) His father died in November, 1788.

He studied theology after graduation for about two years with the Rev. Dr Charles Backus (Yale 1769), of

Somers, and was ordained and installed on September 11, or 26, 1811, as pastor of the Congregational Church, in Ashford, in Windham County, where he enjoyed a successful ministry until his dismission at his own request, on account of impaired health, on March 27, 1833. There had been two hundred and fifty-eight accessions to the church in this period.

On April 11, 1833, he was called to the Congregational Church in Hanover Parish in Lisbon, and now in Sprague, on a salary of $500. He was installed there on June 6, but was dismissed in July, 1834

In December, 1834, he was installed over the small Congregational Church in the village of Willimantic in Windham, where he continued until March 21, 1839.

He then served as stated supply of the Congregational Church in North Stonington from the later part of 1839 to the close of 1844; and in 1846–47, for a little over a year, performed a similar service in Middle Haddam, a parish in Chatham.

When the Rev. Dr. Calvin Chapin (Yale 1788), of Rocky Hill, retired from the ministry in November, 1847, Mr. Judson was employed as a supply, and his labors were rewarded by an awakening of religious interest, but during this experience he was prostrated by a severe attack of bleeding at the lungs. For some years longer, until about 1855, he was able to preach as opportunity offered. Later he was engaged to some extent as a book agent; and his closing days were spent in retirement on his farm.

He died on March 12, 1874, in the Hartford Hospital, and was buried in Wethersfield

He married soon after his ordination, Currence, youngest daughter of David and Sarah (Minor) Curtiss, of Woodbury, who was baptized on October 5, 1783

The *History of Wethersfield* states that his wife died on December 20, 1857, aet. 66

He was married on March 15, 1866, by the Rev. William W Turner (Yale 1819) to Mrs. Aulenia Barnard, of Hartford, who survived him.

He left no children.

AUTHORITIES.

Congregational Quarterly, i, 267–68 *Cothren*, Hist. of Woodbury, i, 445, 536, 597; iii, 171, 173. *Dutton*, Hist. Discourse at Ashford, 20. 125th Anniversary of Hanover Church, 33–34 *Stiles*, Hist of Wethersfield, i, 856, 881, ii, 462

JOHN LANGDON, a son of the Rev. Timothy Langdon (Yale 1781) and Lucy (Trumbull) Langdon, of Danbury, Connecticut, and brother of Timothy Langdon (Yale 1806), was born in Danbury on February 12, 1790. His mother died in 1794, and his father in 1801. He united with the College Church in March, 1809 At graduation he delivered the Salutatory Oration.

After graduation he taught in Hartford. He served as Tutor in the College for four years from the fall of 1811, and during this time studied theology, and was licensed to preach on September 28, 1813, by the Hartford North Consociation.

In January, 1816, he was unanimously called to the Congregational Church in Bethlehem, and having reluctantly (on account of infirm health) accepted the call, he was ordained and installed there on June 16, the sermon being preached by the Rev. Dr. Nathan Perkins, of West Hartford

He married on March 5, 1817, Elizabeth, second daughter of James and Elizabeth (Collins) Pierpont, of the adjoining parish of Litchfield South Farms, now Morris, and sister of the Rev. John Pierpont (Yale 1804). She died on September 21, 1823, in her 32d year; and he next married, on December 9, 1824, her youngest sister Abby.

After a long period of ill health he was dismissed at his own request in 1825, having admitted eighty-three members to the Church

He remained in Bethlehem, and died there on February 28, 1830, aged 40 years.

By his first wife he had three sons and one daughter, the eldest son being a graduate of the Yale Medical School in 1841.

By his second wife he had two sons, of whom the younger died in infancy, and one daughter.

His widow married on February 10, 1834, Samuel Church, of Bethlehem, whom she survived, dying on November 4, 1859, at the age of 62, and having been for many years bereft of her reason

Mr. Langdon was characterized by love of study, great decision, and pious devotion to his work under many infirmities.

AUTHORITIES.

Cothren, Hist of Woodbury, i, 256, 526. Dwight Genealogy, ii, 1060. *Farnam,* Descendants of John Whitman, 628–30 Litchfield County Consociations' Centennial Anniversary, 117–18. *T. Robbins,* Diary, i, 566, ii, 157 *Sprague,* Annals of the Amer. Pulpit, i, 410 *Trowbridge,* Hist Sermon in Bethlehem, 1890, 14 *Walworth,* Hyde Genealogy, i, 300–01. *Woodruff,* Litchfield Geneal. Register, 177

Gurdon William Lathrop was the only child of Dr. William Lathrop, and a grandson of Captain Elisha and Hannah (Hough) Lathrop, of Bozrah, Connecticut, and Lebanon, New Hampshire. His mother was Lydia, daughter of Benjamin and Ann (Waterman) Harris, of Norwich. About the time of his birth, his parents removed from Lebanon to Washington, in the central part of Duchess County, New York At graduation he delivered a Dissertation on Luxury.

After graduation he studied law, and finally settled in New York City, where from about 1818 to 1823 he shared the office of Aaron Burr. His talents gave promise of considerable success at the bar, but his unfortunate connection with Burr hampered and discredited him

He appears to have left New York about 1825, but is said to have fallen a victim to the cholera in the summer of 1832.

He was never married.

AUTHORITIES

Huntington, Lathrop Family Memoir, 176 *Walworth,* Hyde Genealogy, i, 127; ii, 1153

JONATHAN LEE, the second son and child of Deacon Milo Lee, a farmer of Salisbury, Connecticut, and grandson of the Rev Jonathan Lee (Yale 1742), the first minister in Salisbury, was born on July 19, 1786. His mother was Ruth, daughter of Hezekiah and Sarah (Northrop) Camp, of Salisbury. He was prepared for College by the Rev. Ammi R. Robbins (Yale 1760), of Norfolk, and spent the first half of the course with the Class of 1808; but being hampered by poor health he was obliged to lose an entire year. He united with the College Church on profession of his faith in July, 1808.

During the three years after graduation he took the regular course of study in the Andover Theological Seminary, and in November, 1814, he was invited to preach in the Congregational Church in Otis, Berkshire County, Massachusetts, as a candidate for settlement; with the result that he was ordained and installed there on June 28, 1815.

On November 5, 1817, he married Harriet Dewey, third daughter of the Hon Colonel Joshua and Salome (Noble) Danforth, of Pittsfield, who died on November 14, 1826, aged nearly 31 years.

He married secondly, on December 20, 1827, Mary, eldest daughter of Colonel Adonijah Strong, of Salisbury, and sister of the Rev. William L. Strong (Yale 1802) and the Rev Henry P Strong (Yale 1807).

He was dismissed at his own request from the church in Otis on July 10, 1831; and went the next year to a brief term of service as pastor of a Congregational Church in Tecumseh, in the southeastern part of Michigan Territory.

On July 4, 1834, he was installed over the Congregational Church in Weybridge, near Middlebury, Vermont, where he remained until May 25, 1837 His salary here was $275, with a parsonage; and his dismission was mainly due to his disapproval of the "protracted meetings" then common

In January, 1838, he returned to his native town, where he resided thenceforth, partially occupied in teaching

His wife died on December 24, 1863, in her 77th year; and his own death followed, in Salisbury, on September 13, 1866, in his 81st year

His children, by his first marriage, were a daughter, who married the Rev William J. Smith (Auburn Theol. Sem. 1842), and a son (Williams Coll. 1841).

Mr Lee was a fine classical scholar, and a man of lovely character.

He published:

1. Guilt and Punishments increased by abused privileges. Sermon [from Luke xii, 47] at Otis, November 2, 1822. Stockbridge, 1823. 8°.

2. The truths of the Bible harmonious, and inseparably united — A Sermon [from Matt xix, 6], preached at Otis, Mass September 16th, 1827. Pittsfield, 1827. 8°, pp. 20 [*U. T. S. Y C*

3 A History of the Town of Otis. In A History of the County of Berkshire, Massachusetts .. —By Gentlemen in the County Pittsfield, 1829 12°, pp. 311–19

4 The Labors of a Pastor defeated and his hopes disappointed. An Address designed to be presented to a Mutual Council called for the Dismission of a Pastor from his Charge Middlebury, 1837. 8°, pp 23 [*A C. A B. Ath. Harv U. T S. Y C*

At the dismission of the author from the Church in Weybridge, he was prepared to read this Address, but was dissuaded from doing so.

5. An account of the Rev Asahel Nettleton's College life, and, Account of the revival in Salisbury in 1815. In Tyler's *Memoir of Nettleton* Hartford, 1844. 12°, pp. 32–38, 82–85

He was the author of several occasional poems, such as·

A hymn, composed for the Centennial Celebration of the Congregational Church in Salisbury, November, 1844 (pp. 60–61, Reid's *Historical Address*)

A poem for the Centennial Celebration, Litchfield County, August, 1851 (pp 198–99)

AUTHORITIES.

Boltwood, Noble Genealogy, 114 Danforth Genealogy, 141 *Dwight,* Strong Genealogy, ii, 976, 978, 1042, 1054. *Lee,* John Lee and Descendants, 2d ed, 414, 424–25 *Rev Dr. A Reid,* MS Letter, January, 1867. *T. Robbins,* Diary, i, 476

EDWARD BLAKE LINING, son of Major Charles Lining, of Charleston, South Carolina, an officer of the Revolution, was born on March 12, 1790. His mother was Polly, eldest daughter of Edward Blake, and widow of Thomas Rose.

He studied law after graduation, and was admitted to the Charleston bar in 1813. He practiced his profession for a few years; but in the meantime he married Henrietta, daughter of John Perkins, of Hillsboro plantation, in St. Andrew's Parish, on the Ashley River, opposite Charleston, and about 1822 removed thither.

He died in Charleston on August 15, 1849, in his 60th year

His wife survived him with one daughter and four sons.

He was a member and officer of the Society of the Cincinnati.

AUTHORITIES

Miss I. DeSaussure, MS Letter, October, 1911

Benjamin Clark Meigs, the second son of Dr. Phineas Meigs, of Bethlehem, formerly a parish in Woodbury, Connecticut, and grandson of Dr. John and Rebecca (Clark) Meigs, of Bethlehem, was born on August 9, 1789. His mother was Sarah, youngest child of Captain Isaac and Sibyl (Russell) Tomlinson, of Woodbury. He was prepared for College by his pastor, the Rev. Dr. Azel Backus (Yale 1787). His father died in August, 1805, and his mother soon married the Rev. John Griswold (Dartmouth Coll. 1789), of Pawlet, Vermont. He joined the College Choir late in Senior year. At graduation he delivered a Dissertation on Foreign Immigration.

Soon after graduation he took charge of a select school in Bedford, Westchester County, New York, where he continued until the spring of 1811, at the same time beginning his studies in theology. He then entered the Junior Class in the Andover Theological Seminary.

In September, 1813, he offered himself to the American Board of Commissioners for Foreign Missions for appointment as a missionary.

On his graduation from Andover, in the fall of 1813, he visited his mother in Vermont, and spent the ensuing winter in preaching in Rupert, about six miles from Pawlet In the spring he went to Connecticut, and preached for some time in Litchfield South Farms (now Morris) and in his native town In the autumn of 1814 he supplied the pulpit in Fitchburg, Massachusetts, but refused to consider a call.

On June 21, 1815, he was ordained, with five other missionary candidates, at Newburyport; and on August 14 he was married at Bethlehem to Sarah Maria, only daughter of Richard and Joanna (Prindle) Peet, and sister of Dr Harvey P Peet (Yale 1822) On October 23 they sailed from Newburyport for Ceylon, where they arrived on March 22, 1816. On October 2 he reached Jaffna, where the mission was to be located.

His long period of faithful and useful service was broken by a brief visit to this country in 1840–41, and in October, 1857, he retired from the field to spend his last days among his children and friends in this country, and, so far as strength permitted, to labor here for the cause in which his life had been given. His health was, however, seriously affected, and he spent the winter of 1861–62 in Kingston, Jamaica, without material benefit. He died in New York City on May 12, 1862, in his 73d year, and is buried beside his mother, in Oxford, Connecticut.

His wife died at her residence in New York on December 23, 1863, in her 77th year

Of their eleven children, three died in infancy; of the others, five daughters and three sons, one son was graduated at the New York University in 1850

His portrait is given in the *Meigs Genealogy*.

AUTHORITIES

Cothren, Hist. of Woodbury, ii, 1444, 1516 [*Loomis*], Memoirs of Missionaries at Andover, 77–80 Meigs Family, 43, 65, 239–40 Missionary Herald, lviii, 205–06. *Orcutt*, Tomlinsons in America, 41 Prindle Genealogy, 169–70

Alfred Mitchell, the youngest of the six sons of the Hon. Stephen Mix Mitchell (Yale 1763), of Wethersfield, Connecticut, who were graduated at Yale, was born in Wethersfield on May 22, and baptized on December 26, 1790 He was prepared for College in Wethersfield,—probably by Frederick Butler (Yale 1785). He united with the College Church at the close of Junior year.

On graduation he began the study of theology with the Rev. Dr. Ebenezer Porter (Dartmouth Coll 1792), of Washington, Connecticut, and when Dr. Porter removed to a professorship in the Andover Theological Seminary, in March, 1812, he went also and finished the year with the Senior Class.

He then preached for a short time to a congregation in Bridgewater, Massachusetts; and after the death of the Rev. Asahel Hooker (Yale 1789), pastor of the Second Congregational Church at Chelsea, on the Landing, in Norwich, Connecticut, in April, 1813, he preached in that parish for about six months, and then received a unanimous call to the pastorate

Having accepted this call, he was ordained and installed on October 27, 1814, the ordination sermon being preached by Professor Porter His prosperous pastorate was terminated by his death, in Norwich, after a painful illness of eight weeks, on December 19, 1831, at the age of 41. A commemorative discourse by the Rev. Charles Hyde, of Norwich, was afterwards published; and also a Sermon preached in Wethersfield by the Rev. Dr. Caleb J Tenney.

He married, on January 16, 1815, Lucretia Mumford, second daughter of Nathaniel Shaw and Elizabeth (Mumford) Woodbridge, of what is now Salem, Connecticut, who died on March 29, 1839, in her 45th year

Their children were four daughters and five sons. Two daughters and a son died in infancy. The eldest son was a member of the Class of 1838 in Amherst College, but withdrew on account of pulmonary disease which proved fatal in 1839. The second son was graduated at Yale in 1841, and won distinction as an accomplished writer.

The youngest son was a member of the Class of 1854 at Yale, but left on account of his health, and received an honorary degree in 1879.

Mr. Mitchell was a man of reticent manners and dignified bearing; of uncommon delicacy and refinement of feeling; of remarkable independence of character, distinct literary gifts, and single-hearted devotion to his calling His miniature is copied in Miss Perkins' *Chronicles of a Connecticut Farm.*

He published:

1. A Sermon [from I Tim i, 15], preached in the Congregational Church, in Chelsea, December 25th, 1823. Norwich, 1824 8°, pp 16. [*U. T. S.*

2 Sermon on the death of Mrs Sarah Lanman. 1829

3 Sermons, delivered in the Second Congregational Church in Norwich; on the second Sabbath in July, 1829 [from Haggai ii, 9], and on the evening of March 4, 1830 [from I Thess iii, 8] Norwich, 1830. 8°, pp 32.

[*A C. A B. Publ Br Mus M H S. U. T. S. Y. C.*

The first sermon was preached on a re-occupation of the house of worship, after extensive enlargement; and the second in commemoration of the addition of seventy-eight persons to membership

---

AUTHORITIES

Caulkins, Hist of Norwich, 554 Congregational Quarterly, iii, 334 Evangelical Magazine, i, 34-38. *Mitchell,* Woodbridge Record, 157-59. *Perkins,* Chronicles of a Conn Farm, 161-67 Religious Intelligencer, xvi, 495 *Salisbury,* Family-Histories and Genealogies, i, 181-84. *Sprague,* Annals of the Amer. Pulpit, ii, 601-05. *Stiles,* Hist of Wethersfield, ii, 507.

Asahel Nettleton, the eldest son of Samuel and Anne (Kelsey) Nettleton, of North Killingworth parish, now the town of Killingworth, Connecticut, and grandson of Josiah and Sarah (Davis) Nettleton, was born in Killingworth on April 21, 1783. His father, who was a farmer in moderate circumstances, died in August, 1802; and the son, who had become a Christian and aspired to preach the gospel to the heathen, was prepared for College by his pastor, the Rev. Josiah B. Andrews (Yale 1797).

On graduation he filled for a year the office of College Butler, devoting what leisure he could command to the study of theology. For the succeeding year he went to the adjoining town of Milford, and continued his studies under the Rev. Bezaleel Pinneo (Dartmouth Coll. 1791). On May 28, 1811, he received a license to preach from the Western Association of New Haven County.

He was intending to go as a foreign missionary, when the way should open, and therefore from the first refused to consider any offers for settlement, but devoted himself wholly to the work of an evangelist.

He began his labors in Eastern Connecticut, and after a few months spent among churches there which had long been destitute of pastors, he found continuous employment of a similar nature for the next ten years in his native State and in neighboring portions of New York and Massachusetts. Remarkable success attended his efforts, and he did not spare himself for the cause

He received ordination as an evangelist from the South Consociation of Litchfield County at Harwinton, on April 9, 1817, at the same time with the ordination of Elias Cornelius (Yale 1813) as a missionary. His preaching was distinctly aimed at the promotion of revivals of religion, and was accordingly mainly extemporaneous, in a high degree Calvinistic, and always pointed and searching As he never married, and had few expenses, he expected no compensation for his services and accumulated no property. In zeal and devotion he is worthy to be compared with Edwards and Whitefield.

At length his constitution was exhausted by strenuous labor, so that when in October, 1822, he contracted typhus fever, he was completely prostrated. For the next two years he was rarely able to preach, and he never regained his former strength.

He resumed gradually his former course of life, and in the fall of 1827 went South for the benefit of his health, and spent the next three winters mainly in Virginia

In the spring of 1831 he took a voyage to England, for his health, and returned in August, 1832.

In the fall of 1833 a new Theological Seminary was established in East Windsor, Connecticut, and he sympathized strongly with the purposes of the founders. He was invited to fill the professorship of Pastoral Duty, and though he declined the appointment he took up his residence in East Windsor and consented to deliver occasional lectures.

For the next ten years, while East Windsor was his home, he spent several winters at the South and preached as strength allowed in different places in New England.

In 1839 the honorary degree of Doctor of Divinity was conferred on him, without his previous knowledge, by Hampden-Sidney College in Virginia, and Jefferson College in Pennsylvania; he had already by earnest remonstrance some years before prevented its being given him by a New-England College.

In the summer of 1841 he began to be afflicted with urinary calculi, and was thenceforth subject to extreme suffering. The operation of lithotomy was resorted to in February, and again in December, 1843, but his strength failed gradually until his death in East Windsor, on May 16, 1844, at the age of 61.

A Memoir of his Life and Character by his attached friend, the Rev. Dr. Bennet Tyler (Yale 1804), was published the same year. What seems a copy of his portrait is prefixed to the volume, and is reproduced in volume 3 of the *New Englander*

He published:

1 Obituary. Rev. Philander Parmele
In the *Religious Intelligencer,* vol. 7, pp. 780–83. (May, 1823)

2 Village Hymns for Social Worship. Selected and original. Designed as a Supplement to the Psalms and Hymns of Dr. Watts. Hartford, 1824. 12°, pp. viii, 480 [*Br Mus*
Several editions

3. Letter to the Rev. Mr Aikin, of Utica, January 13, 1827
1828

4 Remarks, on a recent Sermon by the Rev. Mr Finney. In a Letter addressed to the Rev Dr Spring, of New York. (Dated Durham, N. Y, May 4, 1827.) 8°, pp 8. [*A C A.*
A severe criticism of Mr. Finney's arguments.

After his death appeared:

Remains of the late Rev. Asahel Nettleton, D.D., consisting of sermons, outlines and plans of sermons, brief observations on texts of Scripture, and miscellaneous remarks. Compiled and prepared for the press, by Bennet Tyler, D.D. Hartford, 1845. 12°, pp 408 [*B Publ. U T. S. Y. C.*

Contains thirty-seven sermons, besides other matter.

The *Memoir* by Dr. Tyler contains large extracts from Dr. Nettleton's Journal and correspondence,—parts of which had been published elsewhere, but not by himself, as, for instance:

Extracts from a letter, dated Union College, Schenectady, April 28th, 1820, to a friend in Connecticut, on the revival in Saratoga County In the *Religious Intelligencer,* vol. 4, pp 822–23 (May, 1820).

Letter to Dr. Lyman Beecher on Revivals,—written in May, 1822. In the *Spirit of the Pilgrims,* vol. 2, pp. 112–15 (February, 1829).

An extract from a letter to Dr Beecher, with the title, Temperance and Revivals, was published as a tract by the American Tract Society, Boston. 12°, pp. 8.

AUTHORITIES

Christian Review, x, 210–38 Loomis Female Genealogy, i, 79 *Miller,* Hist Discourse at Killingworth, 33–36. New Englander, iii, 79–89 *Sprague,* Annals of the Amer. Pulpit, ii, 542–54. *Tyler,* Memoir of Nettleton.

Charles Goodrich Olmsted, youngest son of Colonel David Olmstead, of Ridgefield, Connecticut, and grandson of Deacon Nathan and Millicent (Goodrich) Olmstead, of Ridgefield, was born on August 4, 1787. His mother was Abigail, fourth daughter of the Rev. Jonathan Ingersoll (Yale 1736), of Ridgefield.

In his boyhood the family removed to Manlius, Onondaga County, New York, and he was prepared for College by the Rev. Robert Porter (Yale 1795), at Hamilton Oneida Academy in Clinton.

After graduation he studied law in Onondaga, and settled for the practice of his profession in Franklin, Tennessee, where he married a widow with children.

The remainder of his life was spent in that region, and for the last eight or ten years he resided in the family of his wife's son-in-law, General Humphrey Marshall (U. S. Mil. Acad. 1832), of Kentucky.

He died in Spring Port, Henry County, a short distance northeast of Louisville, Kentucky, in September, 1865, at the age of 78 He left no children.

He never attained eminence as a practicing lawyer, but was remarkable for a spirit of philosophical investigation. During the Civil War he was consistently loyal, having previously avowed frankly his abolition sentiments.

JOHN STILL WINTHROP PARKIN was born in New London, Connecticut, on March 25, 1792 His father, Richard William Parkin, a native of Malton, in the North Riding of Yorkshire, England, emigrated to this country as a young man, and married Mary, daughter of John Still Winthrop (Yale 1737), of New London He died in comparative youth, leaving a family of six children, and this son was educated by his uncle, Francis Bayard Winthrop, who was also the father of one of his classmates. He began his preparation for College in the Episcopal Academy at Cheshire, and completed it under the Rev Frederick W Hotchkiss (Yale 1778), of Saybrook.

He studied medicine in New York, and as he expected to practice in the South, he also studied pharmacy, so as to be able to compound his own prescriptions.

He settled in Selma, Alabama, and while there, besides practicing his profession, kept a general store.

He married in Selma, in 1818, Mary Ann, daughter of Judge Samuel Hitchcock (Harvard 1777), of Vergennes, Vermont; her mother was Lucy Caroline, second daughter of General Ethan Allen, and one of her brothers, General Ethan Allen Hitchcock (U S. Mil. Acad. 1817), was a distinguished soldier

She died in Selma on September 16, 1823, leaving an only child, who was the father of William Parkin (Yale 1874).

He returned to New York City in 1824, and there resumed practice. On June 12, 1834, he was married by the Rev Dr. John Frederick Schroeder (Princeton 1819) to Mrs Sarah Elizabeth Parsons, daughter of the late Ralph Thurman, of Troy, by whom he had seven children, four of whom are still living

In 1839 or 1840 he retired from practice, at his wife's solicitation, on the ground of the wearing nature of his occupation, and its insufficient returns. He had been especially overworked during an epidemic of the yellow fever, his experience of which at the South had made his services much in demand.

For some years he resided in Newark, New Jersey, but later returned to New York, and died there on November 2, 1866, in his 75th year.

AUTHORITIES

Wm Parkin, MS Letter, March, 1911.

PHILANDER PARMELE, second son of Josiah Parmele, Junior, of the North parish in Killingworth, Connecticut, and grandson of Josiah and Mercy (Hull) Parmele, was born in Killingworth on August 31, 1783, and united with the church there in 1801 His mother was Mary, daughter of Jeremiah and Mattaniah (Ward) Buell, of Killingworth.

He began the study of divinity immediately after graduation, and was licensed to preach by the New Haven East Association of Ministers on September 25, 1810.

He was ordained and installed as pastor of the Presbyterian church in Victor, a new town just set off from Bloomfield, in Ontario County, Western New York, on May 5, 1812; but in consequence of embarrassments connected with the progress of the war of 1812 he was dismissed from that charge on December 28, 1814

On November 8, 1815, he was installed as pastor of the Congregational Church in Bolton, Connecticut, where he labored earnestly and faithfully for seven years.

His classmate and fellow-townsman, Nettleton, by whose means he had been introduced to the Bolton Church, was taken ill at his house in October, 1822, with typhus fever, and both Mr Parmele and his wife contracted the disease. After a severe illness of ten days he expired on December 27, in his 40th year.

He married a Miss Wright, of Killingworth, who survived him

He published:

A brief account of a Revival of Religion in Bolton, Conn, in 1819

In the *Religious Intelligencer*, vol. 5, pp 362-65 (November, 1820)

AUTHORITIES

Miller, Hist. Discourse at Killingworth, 33 Religious Intelligencer, vii, 780-83. *Sprague*, Annals of the Amer Pulpit, ii, 546 *Tyler*, Memoir of Nettleton, 2d ed, 18, 70, 85, 149-50 Ward Family Genealogy, 87 *Welles*, Buell Family, 127

LEMUEL PURNELL was born in Snow Hill, Worcester County, Maryland, in 1789 His preparation for College was completed in New Haven under Jeremiah Evarts (Yale 1802).

After graduation he studied law with the Hon James B. Robbins, and was admitted to the bar of his native county in 1812. He pursued the practice of his profession with zeal and success to the time of his death, at Snow Hill, in the latter part of 1818, in his 30th year. He was never married.

John [Parker] Rice, the only son of Solomon Rice. of Princeton, Massachusetts, and grandson of Gershom and Lydia (Barrett) Rice, of Marlborough, was born in Princeton on September 24, 1786. His mother was Mary, elder daughter of John and Dinah (Beaman) Binney, of New Ipswich, New Hampshire. His father died in September, 1794, and in April, 1799, his mother married Deacon Ebenezer Parker, of Princeton; out of respect to this connection he assumed a middle name, by act of the State Legislature in December, 1816. His half-brother, Aurelius D. Parker, was graduated here in 1826.

He was prepared for College by his pastor, the Rev. James Murdock (Yale 1797), and by Ebenezer Adams (Dartmouth Coll. 1791) at the Leicester Academy.

After graduation he began the study of law, but soon engaged in teaching in Salem.

Here he was married, on November 18, 1816, to Sarah (or Sally), daughter of George and Mary (Derby) Crowninshield, and at that time gave up the work of teaching and settled in Philadelphia

In the summer of 1818 he removed to Boston, where the greater part of his married life was spent. Here he became much interested in various benevolent and public enterprises, such, in particular, as the opening of the Boston and Worcester Railroad, and the introduction of water into Boston. He was also ardently interested in the education of the young.

He was for a few years in active business, as a dealer in men's furnishing goods He resided for part of the time in Dedham; and a few years after the death of his wife, in Boston, on February 5, 1847, in her 63d year, he fixed his residence there permanently

Finally, he gave up all his business connections, and in 1856 returned to his family estate in Princeton, where he continued in honored retirement until his death on September 20, 1875, at the age of 89

His only child, a daughter, survived him. He will be long remembered as a high type of a true and courteous Christian gentleman.

AUTHORITIES.

Binney Genealogy, 72 *Mrs C B Ward,* Rice Family, 104, 181 *Sherman,* MS. Letter, May, 1876

HUGH ROBINSON, son of John and Gertrude Robinson, of Albany, New York, was born in 1792, and entered College at the opening of the Junior year. The family name appears also to have been written Robison

After graduation he returned to Albany, where he studied law with John B Henry. In the War of 1812 he saw some service as a militiaman. He was admitted to practice in 1816, but pursued the profession for only a short time

About 1840 he removed to Schenectady, where he died on June 12, 1855, aged 63 years.

He was never married

AUTHORITIES

Munsell, Annals of Albany, vii, 329

HEZEKIAH BOOTH SANFORD, the second of six children of Hezekiah Sanford, and grandson of Hezekiah and Hannah (Hawley) Sanford, of Redding, Connecticut, was born in Redding on December 9, 1785. His mother was Betsey Booth, probably daughter of Stephen Booth, of Derby A brother was graduated in 1812 Their father became known as a local Methodist exhorter, and removed to Putnam County, New York, after 1812

He took his second degree in 1817.

His name is first starred as deceased in the Triennial Catalogue issued in 1829.

AUTHORITIES.

Thomas Sanford Family, i, 198.

Benjamin French Shelton was a son of Benjamin Shelton, of Huntington, Connecticut, and grandson of Daniel and Mary (French) Shelton, of Stratford. His mother was Rebecca, daughter of Nathan and Mabel (Wheeler) Peirce He was prepared for College by the Rev Dr. David Ely (Yale 1769), of Huntington

He studied law after graduation, and settled in practice in Stamford

He married Sylvia, the youngest child (born November, 1794) of Dr. Bennett and Sarah (Beers) Perry, of Newtown, and about 1816 removed thither, where he died on November 21, 1826

His widow long survived him. Their children were two sons and two daughters.

AUTHORITIES

Cothren, Hist of Woodbury, i, 667–68 Shelton Reunion, 62

Moses Simons entered College from Jacksonboro, Colleton District, South Carolina, about twenty-five miles west of Charleston At his entrance he used Aaron as a middle name, but later discarded it.

He was probably a son of Moses Simons, a Jewish immigrant to South Carolina, who died in 1808, and who was perhaps a son of Isaac Simons, of the Duke's Place Synagogue in London.

He studied law, and practiced in New York City from 1816 to 1821.

He then went to London, where he died in 1822.

Charles Smith was born in Redding, Connecticut, in 1789 or 1790, and entered College at the opening of the Sophomore year

He was admitted to deacon's orders in the Protestant Episcopal Church by Bishop Hobart of New York (the

Connecticut diocese being then without a Bishop) on April 27, 1817, and to priest's orders by the same authority on March 17, 1818.

Early in 1818 he became rector of St. Matthew's Church in Wilton and St. Stephen's in Ridgefield, his residence being in Wilton, to which two-thirds of his time was to be given

He left this post in 1824, and in 1826 was sent by the Society for the advancement of Christianity in Pennsylvania to Meadville, where he became the rector of the newly organized Christ Church, with the care of other outlying parishes in the vicinity. Under his leadership a house of worship was erected in Meadville in 1827–28, which was the first built in the diocese west of the Allegheny River.

The strain upon his health led him to resign these duties in April, 1829, and to return to Connecticut, where he was able for about four years from the early part of 1830 to serve as Rector of St. Paul's Church, in Southport village in Fairfield.

He then went to Oxford, in New Haven County, where he was Rector of St. Peter's Church and Christ Church (united) until his death, in Milford, on October 13, 1836, at the age of 47.

His wife, Mrs. Lydia Augusta Smith, survived him

AUTHORITIES.

Bates, Our County, 282 Conn Episc. Convention Journal, 1866, 176 *Cornwall*, Hist Discourse at Fairfield, 46

EBENEZER SMITH, the second son of Ebenezer and Dorothy (Child) Smith, of (West) Woodstock, Connecticut, and grandson of Ebenezer and Margaret (Bowen) Smith, of Woodstock, was born in Woodstock on December 30, 1787, and baptized on March 9, 1788.

He was prepared for the Sophomore Class by Fanning Tracy (Yale 1796).

After graduation he was engaged in teaching in an academy in New Jersey, and later continued there, interested in manufacturing and other business

From New Jersey he went to Hartsville, in Warwick Township, Bucks County, Pennsylvania, where he opened a classical boarding-school for boys. He was also licensed as a minister, and preached occasionally.

He died in Hartsville, on January 1, 1830, at the age of 42.

AUTHORITIES

L B Barbour, MS. Letter, Dec, 1911 *J. McClellan,* MS Letter, July, 1847.

SOPHOS STAPLES, a son of the Rev. John Staples (Princeton Coll 1765) and of Susanna (Perkins) Staples, of Westminster Society in Canterbury, Connecticut, was born in Canterbury on December 12, 1789. Two brothers were graduates here, in 1797 and 1808 respectively. His preparation for Yale was completed under Henry Davis (Yale 1796), in New Haven.

After practicing law in New Haven for some years, he removed in the summer of 1817 to Hancock County, Georgia, settling in Sparta, where he built up an extensive practice and was much respected as a citizen.

He died in Sparta, on July 22, 1826, in his 37th year He was never married

AUTHORITIES

Perkins Family, pt 3, 38. Conn Journal, August 15, 1826

ELISHA BEEBE STRONG, second son of Elisha Strong, of Windsor, Connecticut, and grandson of John Warham and Azubah (Griswold) Strong, of Windsor, was born on November 29, 1788. His mother was Mary, daughter of David and Mary (Dibble) Beebe, of Salisbury An elder sister married Heman Norton (Yale 1806). He was prepared for College by Nathan Johnson (Yale 1802) in Windsor.

After graduation he began the study of law in the Litchfield Law School; but subsequently, on making a trip to Niagara Falls he was so pleased with the Western country that he decided to settle in Canandaigua, and there entered the law-office of Nathaniel W Howell (Princeton 1788) and John Greig as a student

He was admitted to practice in 1812, and entered into partnership with William H. Adams

On June 24, 1813, he married Dolly Goodwin, second daughter of Captain James Hooker, of Windsor, and sister of James Hooker (Yale 1810)

In 1816 he purchased, in company with Elisha Beach (a brother-in-law of Heman Norton), one thousand acres of land about twenty-five miles northwest of Canandaigua, in the suburbs of the present city of Rochester, and removed to that place.

In 1820 he was a member of the State Assembly from Ontario County; and on the organization of Monroe County in March, 1821, he was appointed presiding Judge of the County Court, which position he held for two years. In 1824 he was a Presidential elector

His wife died in Rochester on February 15, 1850, in her 63d year. Her children were five sons and three daughters,—of whom four sons and one daughter survived both parents.

Having met with many reverses, and several of his children having settled in the West, he removed in 1861 to Detroit Soon after his removal he married Ellen O'Keefe, of Detroit; she was a Roman Catholic, and he embraced that faith in September, 1866

He died in Detroit on October 14, 1867, aged nearly 79 years. His second wife survived him

---

AUTHORITIES

Dwight, Strong Family, i, 97, 110–11 Hooker Descendants, 78, 169–70. *Kelsey,* Pioneers of Rochester, 38–39 *Stiles,* Hist. of Windsor, 2d ed, ii, 745–46 *Turner,* Hist of Phelps and Gorham's Purchase, 607–09.

HENRY MATSON WAITE, the eldest of ten children of Remick Wait, of Lyme, Connecticut, and nephew of Ezra Wait (Yale 1782), was born in Lyme on February 9, 1787. His mother was Susannah, eldest daughter of Nathaniel and Dinah (Newton) Matson, of Lyme, and an aunt of Governor William A Buckingham. He was prepared for admission to the Sophomore Class by John Adams (Yale 1795), at Bacon Academy, Colchester. At graduation he delivered an Oration on Patriotism

He taught for a while in Fairfield County, and began the study of law with Joseph Wood (Yale 1801), in Stamford; but soon became an assistant in Bacon Academy, until he resumed his legal studies at Blackhall, in Lyme, under the instruction of Matthew and Roger Griswold (Yale 1780). In December, 1812, he was admitted to the bar, and began practice in Middletown, but soon transferred his office to his native town, where he thenceforth resided.

On January 23, 1816, he married Maria, fourth daughter of Colonel Richard Ely and Desire (Colt) Selden, of Hadlyme Parish, on the northern border of Lyme, and sister of Richard E Selden (Yale 1818).

In 1815, 1825, and 1826, he was a representative of Lyme in the General Assembly, and in 1830 and 1831 a member of the State Senate He was affiliated successively with the Federalists, the National Republicans, and the Whigs

As a practicing lawyer he had gained the confidence and respect of the community; and when at the close of 1834 Chief Justice Daggett of the Supreme Court retired, he was elected an Associate Judge. In October, 1854, by an almost unanimous vote of the General Assembly he was elected Chief Justice, and held that post until he reached the constitutional limit of age in February, 1857.

The honorary degree of Doctor of Laws was conferred on him by this College in 1855

Soon after he left the bench his bodily health became broken, but his intellectual powers were undimmed.

Judge Waite and his wife celebrated their golden wedding in January, 1866; but Mrs Waite's death occurred in 1867, and Judge Waite died in Lyme on December 14, 1869, in his 83d year.

He had seven sons, of whom two died in infancy, and one daughter. Three sons were graduates of Yale, in 1837, 1840, and 1853, respectively. The eldest son became Chief Justice of the Supreme Court of the United States

An engraved portrait of Judge Waite is given in volume 24 of the *New-England Historical and Genealogical Register.*

When elected to the bench, Judge Waite's retiring disposition and mildness of temper caused some doubts whether the choice was justified; but he proved fully competent for the position, and his integrity, fair-mindedness, and firmness led to his possessing as large a share of the respect and esteem of the bar as had been given to any of his predecessors.

AUTHORITIES.

Chapman, Buckingham Family, 182 Conn Reports, xxxv, 597–99. Ely Ancestry, 159, 179, 295 N E Hist. and Geneal. Register, xxiv, 101–05.

Samuel Dexter Ward, the eldest son of the Hon. Artemas Ward (Harvard 1783), Chief Justice of the Court of Common Pleas in Boston, and grandson of Brigadier-General Artemas Ward (Harvard 1748) and Sarah (Trowbridge) Ward, was born in Weston, Massachusetts, on October 24, 1789, and baptized the next day by his pastor, the Rev. Samuel Kendal (Harvard 1782). His mother was Catharine Maria, daughter of the Hon Samuel Dexter, an eminent Boston merchant, and sister of the distinguished lawyer, Samuel Dexter

(Harvard 1781). One of his sisters married his classmate Barrell, and the other married the Rev. Dr. Alvan Lamson (Harvard 1814). One brother was graduated at Harvard in 1816. Henry D. A. Ward (Yale 1819) was a first cousin. He spent three years of his College course at Harvard. His father's residence at this time was in Charlestown.

He became a lawyer in Boston, and was a member of the Common Council during the first years of the City charter; but disapproval of political methods led him to refuse further suggestions of office.

He died in Boston, from pneumonia, on May 28, 1871, in his 82d year.

He was never married

AUTHORITIES

A H Ward, Hist of Shrewsbury, 463. *C. T. Ward*, MS. Letters, July, 1871. Weston Births, Deaths and Marriages, 508.

GAYLORD WELLES, the elder son of Deacon James and Abigail Wells, of Newington Parish in Wethersfield, Connecticut, and grandson of William and Mary (Hunn) Wells, of Newington, was born on April 15, and baptized on May 8, 1788. His mother was Abigail Gaylord, of Bristol. His preparation for College was completed under the Rev. Joab Brace (Yale 1804) At graduation he delivered an Oration on Superstition.

He studied medicine and surgery with Solomon Everest, M D (honorary, Yale 1816), of Canton, and on June 16, 1814, married Electa, daughter of James Brace, of Harwinton.

In 1815 he began practice in Hebron; but soon removed to Harwinton, where Mrs. Welles died on March 8, 1836, from consumption, at the age of 45.

The honorary degree of Doctor of Medicine was conferred on him by Yale in 1827.

In 1842 he removed to Hillsdale, Columbia County, New York, where he continued to practice until 1855, when at the request of his daughters he retired from regular professional service and removed to their residence, which was then in West Hartford, and subsequently in Bristol, Connecticut

His second wife, Diana W S Welles, died on July 17, 1856, in her 64th year, and is buried in Wethersfield.

Early in January, 1869, he was disabled by paralysis, from which he partially recovered. He retained, however, the full possession of his mental powers, and up to the day preceding his death was attending the sick He died in Bristol, from a sudden attack of apoplexy, on September 24, 1870, in his 83d year.

Besides his professional usefulness, he was well known as a firm supporter of the temperance and anti-slavery causes, and of the work of the American Peace Society in its earlier and more active years

He served as a Representative of Harwinton in the State Legislature in 1833, and as Town Clerk in 1834.

Of eight children by the first wife, five survived him.

His name was spelt *Wells* until his last years.

AUTHORITIES

Stiles, Hist of Wethersfield, ii, 779 *Tillotson,* Wethersfield Inscriptions, 190 *Miss M J Welles,* MS Letter, September, 1870 *R. Welles,* Annals of Newington, 98.

William Henry Winthrop, son of Francis Bayard Winthrop, of New London, Connecticut, and New York City, and grandson of John Still Winthrop (Yale 1737), of New London, was born in New York in October, 1792. His mother was Phebe, daughter of John Taylor, of New York. Two of his half-brothers were graduated here in 1804 His preparation for College was completed under Henry Davis (Yale 1796), in New Haven He was probably the youngest member of his Class

Shortly after graduation he married his first cousin, Margaret A Parkin, of New London, the sister of a classmate, and removed thither, where the rest of his life was spent.

He followed no profession, but occupied himself with the care of his estate, especially of Fisher's Island, which had been in the possession of his family since 1640 He also inherited in 1826 from an uncle valuable lands in Huron, Ohio, which he soon disposed of.

He died in New London on September 3, 1860, in his 68th year. His widow died in New London on February 27, 1863, aged 64 years.

He had three sons and two daughters, besides several children who died in infancy.

AUTHORITIES

W. C Crump, MS Letter, July, 1870 Firelands Pioneer, iv, 66 N London County Hist Society's Papers, i, pt 4, 91

Alexander Wolcott, the younger son of Alexander Wolcott (Yale 1778), of Windsor, Connecticut, by his first wife, Frances Burbank, was born in Windsor on February 14, 1790 His father removed to Middletown in 1801, and he was prepared for College by John Adams (Yale 1795) in Bacon Academy, Colchester.

After graduation he pursued the study of medicine with Dr Nathan Smith in Hanover, New Hampshire In March, 1812, he enlisted in the army of the United States as Surgeon's Mate, and in April, 1816, was promoted to the rank of Post Surgeon.

He resigned from the army in April, 1817, and then settled in the practice of his profession in Vincennes, Indiana; but very soon (certainly by September, 1818) he was appointed the government's Indian Agent at Detroit, whence he was transferred towards the end of 1819 to a similar post in Chicago, with an annual salary of thirteen hundred dollars.

At this early date the settlement consisted of only four or five families, clustered around Fort Dearborn. One family, which had settled there as early as 1804, was that of John and Eleanor (Lytle, McKillip) Kinzie, whose eldest daughter, Ellen Marion, the first white child born in Chicago, Dr. Wolcott married on July 20, 1823. As there was then no one in Chicago legally authorized to perform a marriage, a Justice of the Peace who was on his way from Green Bay, Wisconsin, to his home in Peoria, was called on for the ceremony. Dr. Wolcott received a commission as Justice of the Peace in September, 1825.

He continued in office until his death, in Chicago, on October 23, 1830, in his 41st year. He left no children.

His widow married in Detroit, on May 26, 1836, the Hon George C. Bates, and died in that city on August 1, 1860, in her 56th year.

AUTHORITIES

Fergus Historical Series, vii, 15, 23, 51, xvi, 26, 85 *Heitman*, Hist. Register of U S Army, i, 1053 *Hurlbut*, Chicago Antiquities, 38–39, 188–90, 201, 280, 410, 477, 490. *Kinzie*, Wau-Bun, New ed, 83–84. *Stiles*, Hist of Windsor, ii, 816 Wolcott Memorial, 211.

SIMEON WOODRUFF was born in Litchfield South Farms, now Morris, Connecticut, on July 26, 1782, a son of Samuel and Anne (Nettleton) Woodruff, from Milford. He was prepared for College by James Morris (Yale 1775) in his native parish. He was probably the oldest in his Class at graduation.

He entered at once the Andover Theological Seminary, and remained there for the course of three years.

He was ordained as an evangelist in Washington, Connecticut, on April 21, 1813, and went immediately to the Western Reserve of Ohio, under a commission from the Missionary Society of Connecticut. He preached during a part of the summer in Tallmadge, Summit

County, and in May, 1814, was installed over the Congregational Church in that town. He was also for a time the principal of the Academy in Tallmadge. As early as 1820 it was evident that he had become obnoxious to a majority of the Society, though the members of the Church stood by him Things came to such a pass that in May, 1822, the town voted to raise no money for the support of the ministry; and Mr. Woodruff finally retired in September, 1823.

After a brief interval, during which he supplied the church in Bath in the same county, he removed to Strongsville, in Cuyahoga County, where he was installed as the first minister of the Congregational Church on January 12, 1825, and remained until early in 1834.

He next went to Worthington, near Columbus, and for three or four years supplied vacant churches there or in that vicinity.

In 1838 he was commissioned as a home missionary to Bainbridge, in the southwestern corner of Michigan, and he died there on August 28, 1839, in his 58th year.

He married, in October, 1817, Mary (or Polly), eldest daughter of William and Ruth (Deming) Granger, who had emigrated in 1815 from Sandisfield, Massachusetts, to Deerfield, Portage County, Ohio; she was ten years his junior, and survived him with several children

---

AUTHORITIES

Granger Genealogy, 133 *Johnson,* Hist of Cuyahoga County, 525. Proceedings on 50th Anniversary of Settlement of Tallmadge, 17–18, 102 *Whittlesey,* Sketch of Tallmadge, 18–19.

Annals, 1809-10

At Commencement in 1810, the Senior Fellow, the Rev. Dr. Josiah Whitney (Yale 1752), of Brooklyn, resigned his office, and the Rev. Amos Bassett (Yale 1784), of Hebron, was elected in his stead.

At the same time the resignations of four Tutors, David Austin Sherman (Yale 1802), Sereno Edwards Dwight (Yale 1803), Thomas Hopkins Gallaudet (Yale 1805), and Henry Strong (Yale 1806), were accepted, and the following were elected to the office:—Mills Day (Yale 1803), Nathaniel William Taylor, Araetius Bevil Hull, and William Avery Whelpley (Yale 1807), and Matthew Rice Dutton and Jonathan Knight (Yale 1808).

At this Commencement Professor Elizur Goodrich also resigned his office as Professor of Law; the place was left unfilled.

A Committee was appointed to go to the General Assembly of the State, in conjunction with a Committee of the State Medical Society, to apply for a charter for a Medical School.

Sketches, Class of 1810

*Nathanael Adams	*1837
*Ethan Allen Andrews, A.M 1823, LL.D. 1847, in Univ. Carol. Bor. Lingg. Prof.	*1858
*Edvardus Avery, Reip. Ohion. Cur. Supr. Jurid.	*1866
*Hezekias Herveius Baldwin	*1826
*Jonathan Barnes	*1861
*Isaacus Stockton Keith Bennett	*1822
**Asa Blair*	*1823
**Chauncaeus Booth,* A M. 1814	*1851
*Dyar Throop Brainard, M.D. 1826	*1863
*Josephus Bulkley, A.M.	*1851
*Sylvester Bulkley, M.D. Dartm. 1813	*1857
*Royal Bullard, A.M	*1846
*Samuel Griswold Chaffee, A M. 1818	*1864
*Christophorus Champlin	*1811
*Alphaeus Dimmick	*1865
*Guilielmus Wolcott Ellsworth, LL.D. Univ. Nov. Ebor 1838, in Coll. Trin Jurispr. Prof., e Congr., Reip. Conn. Gubern et Cur. Supr. Jurid., Socius ex officio	*1868
*Henricus Leavitt Ellsworth, A M.	*1858
*Elias Hubbard Ely, A.M.	*1874
**Eleazarus Thompson Fitch,* A.M. 1817, S T.D. Univ. Penns 1829, S T. Prof.	*1871
**Chauncaeus Allen Goodrich,* A.M. S.T.D. Brun. 1835, Tutor, Rhet. etiam Cur. Past. Prof.	*1860
*Radulphus Granger	*1843
*Paulus Chaplin Grimball, 1828, A M. 1828	*1863
*Fredericus Grimke, Reip. Ohion Cur Supr. Jurid.	*1863
*Fredericus Gunn	*1852

*Abrahamus Bruyn Hasbrouck, A.M. 1819, LL.D. Columb. 1840 et Conc. 1841, e Congr., Coll. Rutg. Praeses *1879
*Augustus Lucas Hillhouse, A.M. *1859
*Georgius Hinckley, A.M 1818 *1818
*Josias Holbrook, A M. *1854
*Jacobus Hooker *1858
*Johannes Hooker, A M 1816 *1857
*Johannes Howard *1849
*Ebenezer Kellogg, A.M. 1814 et Guilielm. 1815, in Coll. Guilielm Lingg. Graec. et Lat Prof. *1846
*Daniel Kissam *1857
*Simon Larned *1810
**Ammi Linsley* *1873
*Thomas Lyman *1832
*Daniel Ferguson McNeil, A M 1814
*Nathanael Mather *1837
*Samuel Finley Breese Morse, A.M. 1816, LL.D. 1846, in Univ. Nov. Ebor. Picturae et Sculpt. Prof *1872
*Lott Newell, A M *1864
*Edvardus Nicoll *1820
**Birdseye Glover Noble,* A.M. *1848
*David Hillhouse Raymond *1820
*Ashurus Robbins *1846
*Daniel Robert *1878
*Josephus Pynchon Rossiter, A M. *1826
*Lutherus Spaulding, A M. 1822 *1825
**Herveius Talcott,* A.M. 1817 *1865
*Asahel Thomson, M.D. 1859 *1866
*Walker Todd *1840
**Josephus Treat,* A.M. *1841
*Samuel Turney *1823
*Radulphus Wells *1837
*Othniel Williams *1832

NATHANIEL ADAMS, son of Nathaniel and Salome (Hyde) Adams, of Green's Farms Parish, Westport, then part of Fairfield, Connecticut, was born in Westport on September 24, and baptized on December 6, 1789.

His life was mainly spent in teaching in Connecticut, though he also studied law, and practiced for a time in Milford.

He died in Green's Farms on April 7, 1837, aged 47 years.

He married Jerusha Bull, of Milford, who died in March, 1835, aged 37 years.

AUTHORITIES

Miss D R Adams, MS Letter, September, 1911.

ETHAN ALLEN ANDREWS, the younger son of Levi Andrus or Andrews, a successful farmer of New Britain, then part of Berlin, Connecticut, and grandson of Joseph and Sarah (Wells) Andrews, of Wethersfield, was born on April 7, and baptized on May 20, 1787. His mother was Chloe, fourth daughter of Captain Robert and Abigail (Burnham) Wells, of Newington Parish in Wethersfield. His preparation for College was completed under the Rev. Noah Porter (Yale 1803), of Farmington. At graduation he delivered the Valedictory Oration.

He at once entered on the study of law with Samuel Cowles, of Farmington, and married on December 19, 1810, Lucy, daughter of Colonel Isaac and Lucina (Hooker) Cowles, of Farmington, and sister of Samuel H Cowles (Yale 1821).

He began the practice of law in New Britain in 1812, but during the war with England he was appointed aid to General Levi Lusk, of the State militia, and spent some months on duty in New London.

He re-opened his law-office in New Britain in January, 1814, but not being fully occupied in his profession he opened a school in his house where he prepared young men for College. He also served as one of the Representatives of Berlin in the General Assembly of the State in October, 1815, May, 1816, and May, 1817. He united with the Congregational Church in New Britain in August, 1821

In 1822, on the recommendation of his classmate, Professor Goodrich, he was appointed Professor of (Ancient) Languages in the University of North Carolina, at Chapel Hill, where he remained for six years

He then, in order to be near his aged parents, returned to New Haven to teach Latin in the "Gymnasium," a boys' boarding-school, conducted by Sereno E. Dwight (Yale 1803) and his brother Henry (Yale 1815); but a year later, finding his resources inadequate to the support of his family, he retired from this enterprise, and established the "New Haven Young Ladies' Institute," which had a remarkably successful, if brief career

In the spring of 1833 he removed to Boston as successor to Professor Jacob Abbott (Bowdoin Coll 1820) in the conduct of the Mount Vernon Female Seminary.

While at Chapel Hill he had formed the plan of preparing a new Latin grammar; and while teaching in the New Haven Gymnasium in conjunction with Solomon Stoddard (Yale 1820), the idea had been further prosecuted, and the result of their joint study appeared in 1836 in a *Latin Grammar,* which proved so excellent a text-book that it held undisputed place as the best Latin grammar in the language for many years.

The success of this venture determined the future occupation of Professor Andrews. . He gave up his school in 1839 and returned to the paternal homestead in New Britain, to give his time more exclusively to the continuation of a series of Latin text-books, already begun. From 1840 to 1843 he spent mainly in New

Haven, perfecting his books and teaching a small select school for young ladies; and he was still much in New Haven for the next five years.

In 1848 the honorary degree of Doctor of Laws was conferred on him by Yale.

His judgment and ability were highly esteemed by his fellow-townsmen; and when, in 1850, New Britain was made a separate town, against the wish of its inhabitants, he was unanimously chosen as their representative in the next legislature. In that capacity he served as Chairman of the Committee on Education, and was largely instrumental in securing the location of the Normal School in New Britain. He was also Judge of Probate for the Berlin District for two years, and took an active interest in all public matters, especially those bearing on education. Late in 1857 a thoroughly revised edition of his *Grammar* appeared, and he then began a revision of his *Dictionary*.

He died in New Britain, after an illness of twelve days, on March 24, 1858, in his 71st year His wife survived him.

Their children were four sons and six daughters. One daughter married Archelaus Wilson (Yale 1844); and two married successively Professor Edward Dromgoole Sims (Univ. N. C. 1824). The eldest son entered Yale in the Class of 1833, but died at the end of the Freshman year The third son was graduated from Yale College in 1841, and the fourth from the Yale Law School in 1851.

Professor Andrews was highly esteemed in his private character, as a Christian, a self-denying benefactor of the poor, a man of taste and refinement, and a most generous and warm-hearted friend An appreciative Eulogy, delivered at New Britain in May, 1858, by the Rev. Dr. Hubbard Winslow (Yale 1825), was afterwards printed An engraving from his portrait is given in Camp's *History of New Britain.*

He published·

1 Remarks on the present state of agricultural science, and the general means of improving the art of husbandry in the County of Hartford: read before the Hartford County Agricultural Society, at their annual meeting, February, A.D. 1819 Hartford, 1819. 8°, pp 24.

[*B Ath. C H S N. Y. H. S. Y. C.*

The address occupies pp. 1–16.

2. Plan of Education to be pursued in the Mount Vernon Female Seminary. [Boston, 1835.] 12°, pp. 7.

[*B. Publ Y C.*

The same [Revised edition] [Boston, 1836] 12°, pp. 4. Appended to a recommendation of the Seminary by others

3. Slavery and the Domestic Slave-Trade in the United States In a series of letters addressed to the executive committee of the American Union for the relief and improvement of the colored race. Boston, 1836 12°, pp. 201.

[*A A S A C. A B. Ath B. Publ. Harv U. T. S. Y C.*

Notes of a trip to Maryland and Virginia in July, 1835. The Union was a short-lived orthodox rival of the American Anti-Slavery Society

4 A Grammar of the Latin Language, for the use of Schools and Colleges. By E A. Andrews and S. Stoddard Boston, 1836. 12°, pp. xii, 323 [*N. Y Publ U. S Y. C*

In numerous editions

Also, Questions upon Andrews and Stoddard's Latin Grammar. Boston, 1836. 12°, pp. 52

5. Latin Exercises; adapted to Andrews and Stoddard's Latin Grammar. Boston, 1837. 12°, pp 308

[*B Publ. N Y. Publ Y C*

Also, A Key to Latin Exercises .. Boston, 1838. 12°, pp 111

[*U. S.*

6 The First Part of Jacobs and Doring's Latin Reader adapted to Andrews and Stoddard's Latin Grammar, and to Andrews' First Latin Book Boston, 1837 12°, pp. 266

7. First Lessons in Latin, or an Introduction to Andrews and Stoddard's Latin Grammar. Boston, 1837 12°, pp 208. [*U. S*

8 Sallust's History of the War against Jugurtha, and of the Conspiracy of Catiline: with a Dictionary and Notes. New Haven, 1841 12°, pp 309. [*U. S. Y. C.*

9. Lhomond's Viri Romæ; adapted to Andrews and Stoddard's Latin Grammar. With Notes, and a Copious Dictionary. Boston, 1842. 12°, pp. 276

10. C. Julius Cæsar's Commentaries on the Gallic War; with a Dictionary and Notes. Boston, 1844 12°, pp 373 + map.

11. Selections from the Metamorphoses and Heroides of Ovid. With notes, grammatical references, and exercises in scanning. Boston, 1844. 12°

12. A First Latin Book; or progressive lessons in Reading and Writing Latin Boston, 1846 12°, pp 334 [*B. Ath B Publ Harv*

13 A Synopsis of Latin Grammar; comprising the Latin Paradigms, and the Principal Rules of Latin Etymology and Syntax Boston, 1851. 12°, pp 40. [*B. Publ. Harv*

14. A copious and critical Latin-English Lexicon, founded on the larger Latin-German Lexicon of Dr. William Freund .. New York, 1851 Large 8°, pp. xxv, 1663 [*N. Y Publ U S*
In many editions.

15 A Manual of Latin Grammar, for the use of schools Intended especially as a first grammar; and to be used preparatory to the study of the more copious and complete Grammar of Andrews and Stoddard Boston, 1859 12°, pp. 250 [*U. S.*

All the volumes of this series of text-books passed through many editions

He edited the following:

16 The Religious Magazine and Family Miscellany New Series. Boston, 1837–38 2 volumes 8° [*B Ath B Publ*
The first series of this monthly periodical, ending in December, 1836, was edited by Gorham D and Jacob Abbott, whom Mr Andrews had assisted for some months before he took the editorship.

17. Leisure Hours: a choice collection of Readings in Prose New illustrated edition Boston, 1844 12°, pp. 340 + 5 pl [*B. Publ*

Containing tales and essays from English publications.

AUTHORITIES.

Andrews, New Britain Memorial, 173, 256, 279–80. *Battle,* Hist. of Univ of N C, i, 287, 319, 417–18. *Camp,* Hist. of N Britain, 235, 465–67 Geneal Hist. of Conn, ii, 912–13 Hooker Descendants, 158. Life of W. L Garrison, i, 473–74. N Y Observer, April 15, 1858 Puritan Recorder, April 29, 1858 *Trumbull,* Hist of Hartford County, ii, 310. Tuttle Family, 129

EDWARD AVERY, the youngest son of the Rev. John Avery (Yale 1777) and Anne (Hazard) Avery, of Stamford, Connecticut, was born in Stamford on February 20 (or 21), 1790 His father died in 1791, and his mother returned to her former residence in Green's Farms, now Westport, then part of Fairfield A nephew was graduated here in 1840

After graduation he studied law, and was admitted to the Connecticut bar. In 1816 he visited England, and in 1817 settled in Wooster, Ohio, where he resided until his death

From 1819 to 1825 he served as Prosecuting Attorney of Wayne County, and from 1824 to 1827 he was a member of the State Senate. In 1847 he was elected a Judge of the Supreme Court of Ohio for a term of four years, after which he returned to the practice of his profession.

He died in Wooster on June 27, 1866, in his 77th year.

He married in November or December, 1823, Jane, daughter of John Galbraith, of Steubenville, Jefferson County, who died soon, leaving one daughter.

Judge Avery was esteemed as an enlightened and patriotic citizen, an accomplished, honorable man, and a consistent member of the Presbyterian Church.

AUTHORITIES.

Douglass, Hist. of Wayne County, O, 353 *Huntington,* Stamford Registration, 7. *Sweet,* Averys of Groton, 73, 132–33

HEZEKIAH HERVEY BALDWIN, the second son of Hezekiah Baldwin, of Woodbridge, Connecticut, and grandson of Sylvanus and Mary (French) Baldwin, of Woodbridge, was born on February 17, 1790 His mother was Elizabeth, second daughter of Stephen and Elizabeth (Carrington) Hine, of Woodbridge He was prepared for College by the Rev. Amasa Porter (Yale 1793), of Derby.

In May, 1813, he married Polly, daughter of Nathan Clark, of Woodbridge, and about the same time established himself in New York City, in the business of manufacturing sulphuric acid and other chemicals. A younger brother (Marcus Baldwin) had shown some aptness in chemical research and analysis and with the encouragement of Dr. Isaac Goodsell, of Woodbridge, he went to Paris about 1812 for study and while there surreptitiously obtained a knowledge of the French methods of manufacture.

With this brother Hezekiah (or Harvey, as he was more frequently called) entered into partnership in New York; but the close of the war with England broke up a profitable business, and after that he was not very successful.

About 1824 he returned to Woodbridge, and after a long period of feebleness died there on January 13, 1826, aged nearly 36 years.

His wife died there on January 8, 1828. Their two children, a son and a daughter, survived them.

AUTHORITIES.

Baldwin Genealogy, i, 118, 151 *Marvin*, MS Letter, March, 1867. Hine Genealogy, 46 *Rev. S P*

Jonathan Barnes, the eldest child of Jonathan Barnes (Yale 1784), of Tolland, Connecticut, was born in Tolland on November 21, 1789, and was prepared for College by Saul Alvord (Yale 1800), of Bolton, a neighboring town, where his mother had been brought up.

He began the study of law after graduation with his father, and in 1811 removed to Middletown, where he completed his preparatory studies with Chauncey Whittelsey (Yale 1800).

He was admitted to the bar in 1813, and from that time practiced his profession in Middletown with unusual industry and success He shunned public office, but was held in the highest esteem as a counsellor and a citizen, for his great legal acquirements and his conscientious and upright character He was thus for many years the acknowledged head of the bar of Middlesex County.

He married on April 29, 1819, Maria Ward, daughter of Dr. Ebenezer and Maria (Ward) Tracy, of Middletown, and sister of the wife of his former preceptor, Mr. Whittelsey

He had long suffered from a disease of the heart, and he died in Middletown after several weeks of great weakness, on December 24, 1861, in his 73d year

His widow died on April 30, 1873.

Their children were four daughters and two sons, all of whom grew up and married. The eldest daughter married the Rev. Elisha C Jones (Yale 1831)

Mr Barnes was an occasional contributor, without his name, to local periodicals; and in particular furnished in 1838 a series of sketches on "Lessons from History" to *The Constitution*, a weekly newspaper published in Middletown.

AUTHORITIES.

Conn Reports, xxix, 614–15. *Field*, Centennial Address at Middletown, 207 *Timlow*, Hist of Southington, xix, xxi

---

Isaac Stockton Keith Bennett, son of Thomas and Anna (Warnock) Bennett, of Charleston, South Carolina, and a brother of Joseph Bennett (Yale 1807), was born in Charleston in 1790. He was named for the Rev. Dr. Keith (Princeton 1755), the pastor of the Congregational (Circular) Church in Charleston.

After his early training in private schools at home, he completed his preparation for College in New Haven under Jeremiah Evarts (Yale 1802) His reputation in his undergraduate days was that of a socially popular but rather gay young man.

He studied law after graduation, and was admitted to the Charleston bar in 1813; but eventually went into business with his father as an architect and builder.

He married, on April 21, 1814, Catharine Elizabeth Faber, by whom he had six children.

He died in Charleston on September 5, 1822, aged 32 years.

AUTHORITIES

Miss S J Bennett, MS. Letter, April, 1911.

ASA BLAIR, the second son of Captain Asa and Mehitable (Carnahan) Blair, of Blandford, Massachusetts, and grandson of Deacon Robert and Hannah (Thompson) Blair, of Western (now Warren) and Blandford, was born on May 12, 1784. He did not enter Yale until the Senior year

After graduation he studied theology with the Rev. Ebenezer Porter (Dartmouth Coll. 1791), of Washington, Connecticut, and was licensed to preach in 1811 by the Litchfield South Association of Ministers.

On May 26, 1813, he was ordained and installed as pastor of the Congregational Church in Kent, in the immediate vicinity of Washington, where he exercised a useful ministry for about nine years He received one hundred and seventy members to the church

Failing health led him on the approach of winter in 1822 to seek a Southern climate; and he died, on January 13, 1823, in Georgetown, South Carolina, in his 39th year, from typhus fever, after nineteen days' illness

He married Myra Ann, daughter of Dr. John Raymond, of Kent, who survived him with one son.

Mr. Blair was a studious and devoted pastor, and won universal love and respect.

AUTHORITIES.

Atwater, Hist. of Kent, 52. Centennial of Litchfield County Consociations, 118–19 *Gibbs,* Hist Address at Blandford, 58 *Leavitt,* Blair Family, 61, 76. Religious Intelligencer, vii, 576, 636–37.

CHAUNCEY BOOTH, the third son of Colonel Caleb Booth, of East Windsor, Connecticut, and grandson of Caleb and Hannah (Allen) Booth, of East Windsor, was born on March 15, 1783. His mother was Anne, youngest daughter of Captain Jonathan and Hannah (Watson, Bissell) Bartlett, of East Windsor He united with the College Church at the end of his Sophomore year. At graduation he was the oldest member of the class.

He studied theology for three years in the Andover Seminary, and spent some time in 1814–15 in home missionary work in Bridgewater, New Hampshire.

On September 20, 1815, he was ordained and installed as pastor of the feeble Congregational Church in (South) Coventry, Tolland County, Connecticut; where he was instrumental in building up the church and in uniting the people.

He married, on November 16, 1815, Laura, daughter of Peter and Sylvia Farnam, of Salisbury.

After a highly successful ministry, in the course of which two hundred and ninety-two persons, mostly the fruits of five seasons of revival, were added to the church, he was obliged by ill health to take a dismission on March 20, 1844 He preached but little after his dismission, and sank gradually under a complication of diseases

His residence continued in Coventry, where he died on May 24, 1851, in his 69th year A commemorative discourse by the pastor of his old church, the Rev. Charles Hyde, was afterwards published

His widow died in Ellington, in the same county, on September 6, 1875, aged 83 years

They had seven sons and three daughters. Two sons became physicians. The eldest daughter married Timothy Dimock, M D. (Yale Medical School 1823).

Mr. Booth was a grave, dignified, prudent, and sincere clergyman, who enjoyed in an unusually high degree the confidence and esteem of his people.

AUTHORITIES

Dimock, Coventry Records, 11-12, 130, 174, 268. *Hyde,* Sermon at Mr Booth's Funeral *Stiles,* Hist of Windsor, 2d ed, ii, 112-13.

DYAR THROOP BRAINARD, the second son of Judge Jeremiah G. Brainard (Yale 1779), of New London, Connecticut, was born in New London on June 10, 1790, and was named for General Dyar Throop (Yale 1759), with whom his father had studied law.

After graduation he studied medicine with Dr. James Lee and Dr Archibald Mercer, of New London, and was admitted in 1813 to practice in his native city.

In 1814, during the war with England, he served as Surgeon of the Third Brigade of the State militia.

In the winter of 1819-20 he continued his studies by attending a course of medical lectures in New York.

The rest of his life was devoted to his profession, except for repeated calls upon him for public service. Thus, he was long a director of the New London Bank, and served the city as an alderman and as Judge of the City Court (1847)

The honorary degree of M.D. was conferred on him by Yale in 1826.

He died in New London, in the house in which he was born, on February 6, 1863, in his 73d year, being the last male representative of one of the old families of the city.

He was never married, but made a home for the daughters of his brother (Yale 1802), who died in 1844.

In addition to his skill as a physician, he was well known as a botanist and chemist, and highly respected and esteemed for his genial temperament and upright character.

He published:

The Annual Address to the Candidates for Degrees and Licenses, in the Medical Institution of Yale College, January 21, 1840 New Haven, 1840. 8°, pp 16. [*Surg. Gen'l's Office. Y C.*

AUTHORITIES

Brainard, Brainerd-Brainard Genealogy, pt 1, 62 *Field,* Brainerd Genealogy, 20.

JOSEPH BULKLEY, the fourth son of Captain Joseph Bulkley, a merchant of Rocky Hill, then part of Wethersfield, Connecticut, and grandson of Peter and Abigail (Curtis) Bulkley, of Rocky Hill, was born on October 28, 1789, and baptized on February 21, 1790. His mother was Martha, eldest child of Captain Moses and Martha (Robbins) Williams, of Rocky Hill. He was prepared for College by his pastor, the Rev. Dr. Calvin Chapin (Yale 1788)

He studied law, and practiced in New York City from 1815 until his death. For some years he was fairly successful, but later he incurred losses through the failure of his eldest brother, in business in New York, and lost his courage.

He died in Rocky Hill on March 21, 1851, in his 62d year. He was never married.

AUTHORITIES

Chapman, Bulkeley Family, 104 *Stiles,* Hist of Wethersfield, ii, 157 *Tillotson,* Wethersfield Inscriptions, 214

SYLVESTER BULKLEY, the second son of Captain Hosea Bulkley, of Rocky Hill, then part of Wethersfield, Connecticut, and grandson of Gershom and Thankful (Belding) Bulkley, of Rocky Hill, was born on June 1, and baptized July 22, 1787. His mother was Abigail Griswold, of Wethersfield He was a second cousin of his classmate, last mentioned, and they were prepared for College together.

During the winter after graduation he taught school in Wethersfield, in the meantime pursuing the study of medicine under the instruction of Daniel Fuller, M.D. (honorary Yale 1831), of Rocky Hill He then attended lectures in the medical department of Dartmouth College, and received the degree of Doctor of Medicine there in 1813.

He began practice in Haddam, where he remained five years, and then disposed of his business to Dr. Ebenezer Munger, and removed to the adjoining parish of Chester. He very soon returned to Higganum, a village in the northern part of Haddam, in association with Dr. Munger, and almost immediately after, a more favorable offer presenting itself, he settled in Upper Middletown, now Cromwell, where he was in successful practice for about twelve years (1821–33).

He then spent some months in advanced medical study in New York, and on his return established himself in Berlin; but in 1848, Rocky Hill being destitute of a resident practitioner, he returned to his native place and continued in active service until within a few days of his death

He died in Rocky Hill on February 1, 1857, in his 70th year.

He first married Mary, the youngest child of Captain Stephen and Ann (Lord) Johnson, of Lyme, who died in Cromwell on March 2, 1824, aged 36 years.

On May 1, 1825, he married Nancy, eldest daughter of William and Elizabeth (Lewis) Bradford, of Rocky Hill, who died in Rocky Hill on October 21, 1872, at the age of 86.

His children, by his first wife, were two sons (of whom one died young) and one daughter.

AUTHORITIES

Chapman, Bulkeley Family, 106, 127-29. Conn Med Society's Proceedings, 1857, 61-63 Hist. of Middlesex County, 1884, 27 *Salisbury,* Family-Histories and Genealogies, ii, 349 *Stiles,* Hist. of Wethersfield, i, 939-40, ii, 158, 161. *Tillotson,* Wethersfield Inscriptions, 214, 217

ROYAL BULLARD, the second son of the Rev. John Bullard (Harvard 1776), of Pepperell, Massachusetts, and grandson of Henry and Jemima (Pond) Bullard, of Medway, was born on May 15, 1786. His mother was Elizabeth, eldest child of the Rev. Amos Adams (Harvard 1752), and Elizabeth (Prentice) Adams, of Roxbury. He was prepared for College at the Groton academy and entered Yale at the opening of the Senior year. A brother was graduated at Harvard in 1819.

On leaving College he went to Camden, South Carolina, where he entered the office of Judge Abram Blanding as a student of law. He was in 1814 admitted to the bar, and soon gained a desirable reputation for ability as a lawyer He served as Mayor of Camden for two years, 1820–22.

On October 25, 1820, he married Esther Lewis, daughter of James Syng Murray, of Camden, a native of Elkton, Maryland, and his wife, Sarah Barry (Willett) Murray. She was an aunt of Dean James O. Murray, of Princeton College.

On becoming a Christian, about 1833, he judged it his duty to exchange the legal for the clerical profession, and he was led to connect himself with the Methodist denomination.

He was induced to remove from Camden to northern Illinois, settling in the township of Newark, near the Fox River, about fifty miles west of Chicago Here as a local preacher of the Methodist Episcopal Church, he performed a large amount of missionary labor, built a schoolhouse with his own hands, and there during the winter taught such as chose to avail themselves of instruction gratuitously given. He also engaged in agricultural pursuits, for which he had a natural aptitude and fondness, and did much to advance the community by his general intelligence and enterprise.

When Kendall County was organized in 1841, he was appointed a Justice of the Peace.

He died on his farm ("Milbrook") near Newark, on December 13, 1846, in his 61st year.

AUTHORITIES

Adams, Geneal Hist of Henry and John Adams, 31 *Butler,* Hist of Groton, 470 *Professor J O Murray,* MS Letter, July, 1861

Samuel Griswold Chaffee, the younger son of Dr. Hezekiah Chaffee, Junior, of Windsor, Connecticut, was born in Windsor on May 15, 1791, and baptized on January 15, 1792. Like his brother of the preceding Class, he was prepared for College by Nathan Johnson (Yale 1802).

On his graduation he settled in Hartford, where he established himself as a merchant, and continued in the same career until a short time before his death.

He married in Bloomfield, then part of Windsor, on April 13, 1815, Rebecca, daughter of Nathan Phelps, of Bloomfield, who died on November 18, 1818.

He was married, secondly, in Hartford, on October 20, 1824, by the Rev. Dr. Joel Hawes, to Julia, daughter of Daniel Lombard, of Springfield, Massachusetts, who died in Hartford on December 20, 1863, aged 70.

His first wife left a son and a daughter; his second wife had four daughters, of whom two died in infancy, and one son

He died in Hartford on July 10, 1864, in his 74th year.

AUTHORITIES

Chaffee Genealogy, 205, 365 *O. B. Stiles,* Hist of Windsor, ii, 143. *Loomis,* MS Letter, August, 1865.

CHRISTOPHER CHAMPLIN of Newport, Rhode Island, entered College at the opening of the Senior year He was born in 1794, the only son of the Honorable Christopher Grant Champlin (Harvard 1786), and grandson of Christopher and Margaret (Grant) Champlin, of Newport, and his mother was Martha Redwood, daughter of Benjamin and Mehetabel (Redwood) Ellery, of Newport. He was the youngest member of the class at graduation.

He died in Nassau, New Providence, in the Bahamas, about four months after graduation, perhaps in the latter part of January, 1811; and his father was so affected by the loss that he resigned his seat in the Senate of the United States and never re-entered public life.

AUTHORITIES.

Columbian Centinel, February 27, 1811 *Mason,* Annals of Trinity Church, Newport, i, 298

ALPHEUS DIMMICK was born in Mansfield, Connecticut, on March 22, 1787, and entered at the opening of Sophomore year, having been prepared by the Rev Dr Moses C. Welch (Yale 1772), of Mansfield His father was Deacon Oliver Dimock, of Mansfield

On graduation he went to the village of Bloomingburg, in Mamakating township, Sullivan County, New York, and while studying law in the office of Charles Baker supported himself by serving as Principal of the Academy. In 1814 he was admitted to the bar, and he continued in practice in Bloomingburg until his retirement some eight or ten years before his death.

He was Presiding Judge of the County Court from 1826 to 1830, and again from 1847 to 1850 In 1828 he represented Sullivan County in the State Assembly. From 1836 to 1847 he was District Attorney.

Judge Dimmick died in Bloomingburg in January 16, 1865, in his 78th year

He was a man of remarkable simplicity of character and unworldliness, which with his unswerving honesty and truthfulness and high sense of justice, gained for him the confidence and friendship of all who knew him, so that he was appealed to as a friendly counsellor and arbitrator throughout his entire neighborhood. His invariable advice to disputants was, not to invoke the aid of the law until all other methods of settling differences had been tried.

He married Maria Franklin Carr, of Maryland, whose parents were Virginians; they had eight children.

Two grandsons were graduated at Yale, in 1878 and 1881, respectively.

AUTHORITIES

Hon. J Benjamin Dimmick, MS Letter, April, 1911 *John C Dimmick,* MS Letter, May, 1865. *Quinlan,* Hist of Sullivan County, 438-39.

Henry Leavitt Ellsworth, one of twin sons of Chief-Justice Oliver Ellsworth (Princeton 1766), of Windsor, Connecticut, was born in Windsor on November 10, 1791 Besides the twin brother who was his classmate, two other brothers received Yale degrees, in 1799 and 1801, respectively. He was prepared for College by Nathan Johnson (Yale 1802) in Windsor; and became a Christian in the Spring of his Sophomore year.

After graduation he studied law at the Litchfield Law School.

He was married, by President Dwight, on June 22, 1813, to Nancy, the only daughter of the Hon Elizur Goodrich (Yale 1779), of New Haven, and sister of his classmate, and settled in Windsor, engaging in the practice of his profession and in agriculture

A few years later he removed to Hartford, and while residing there he did much for the prosperity of the city in the way of improvement of real estate.

In the meantime he was appointed in 1832 by President Jackson as Commissioner to superintend the settlement of the Indian tribes transplanted to the south and west of Arkansas; and while thus employed he made extensive tours in that region. On one such tour over the prairies of Eastern Oklahoma, in the fall of 1832, he was accompanied by Washington Irving, who has preserved his impressions in print, while the Yale Library has also an elaborate manuscript memoir by Mr. Ellsworth concerning the same journey.

In April, 1835, as a Jacksonian Democrat, he was elected Mayor of Hartford; but resigned the office in the following month on his appointment by Jackson as United States Commissioner of Patents. During his administration he developed the business of that office in a remarkable manner, and presented to Congress a series of reports which rendered the department one of the most useful and popular in connection with the Government

These reports not only gave a calendar of mechanical inventions, but also, in conformity with his personal tastes and interests, dealt in a large way with the agricultural condition of the country and with inventions and discoveries calculated for the benefit of land-owners He also first led the way to obtaining valuable seeds from other countries and circulating them by means of the post-office His conduct of the department was marked by sound judgment, keen insight into character, uncommon dexterity in the despatch of business, great physical endurance, and enthusiasm in the advancement of the useful arts and in the development of the country's resources.

In May, 1845, he resigned his position and established his residence in Lafayette, Indiana, as an agent for the purchase and settlement of the public lands. He there became one of the largest land-owners in the West.

His wife died, in consequence of a fractured leg, in Lafayette on January 14, 1847, at the age of 54 A discourse occasioned by her death, by her pastor, the Rev. Joseph G. Wilson, was afterwards published.

He next married, on October 18, 1852, Marietta Mariana, daughter of Daniel and Lucretia (Benton) Bartlett, of North Guilford, Connecticut, who died on April 17, 1856, in her 58th year.

He married, thirdly, Catharine, eldest daughter of the Rev Dr. David Smith (Yale 1795), of Durham, and a first cousin of his first wife; and in April, 1858, on account of ill-health, he returned to Connecticut, and established his residence at Fair Haven, in the suburbs of New Haven He died there, from the effects of a paralytic stroke ten days before, on December 27, 1858, in his 68th year.

His widow died in Durham, on November 16, 1869, aged 70 years

His children, by his first marriage, were two sons and a daughter. The elder son was graduated at Yale in 1834. The daughter married Roswell C. Smith (Brown Univ 1852)

By Mr. Ellsworth's will his residuary estate, in Western lands, the proceeds of which now amount to about $96,000, was bequeathed to Yale, and is used for the assistance of students preparing for the ministry.

He published:

1 Sketches of an Address delivered before the Hartford County Agricultural Society, on the twenty-fourth of March, 1818. Hartford, 1818 8°, pp 23.

[*Br. Mus. C. H. S N Y H S. Y C*

The Address, which is on practical matters, occupies pp. 1–14

2 Report of the Commissioners of Indian Affairs, West, dated Fort Gibson, February 10, 1834. In House Report No. 474, 23d Congress, 1st Session, May, 1834, pp 78–103 + map

3 Reports of the Commissioner of Patents, for the years 1835 to 1844, inclusive Washington, 1836–45. 8°.

The Report of 1843 was reprinted by the New York Tribune, as one of the *Tribune Publications*

4 Report to the Secretary of State, and transmitted to the Select Committee on the Patent Laws. [Washington, 1836] 8°, pp. 10 [*Y C.*
On desirable changes in the laws governing the Patent Office An Act, passed July 4, 1836, was based on these recommendations.

5 Information to persons having Business to transact at the Patent Office [Washington] 8°, pp. 16. [*Y. C.*
Anonymous.

6. A Letter on the Cultivation of the Prairies, dated January 1, 1837. Appended to
Illinois in 1837 Philadelphia, 1837 8°, pp 130-33.
[*Br Mus Harv Y. C.*

7. A Digest of Patents, issued by the United States, from 1790 to January, 1839· published by Act of Congress, under the Superintendence of the Commissioner of Patents . . Washington, 1840-41. 8°, pp 672 [*B. Ath Br Mus Y. C*
Also, revised editions

8 An Appeal to the Friends of the Colonization Society, being the substance of a statement of facts, presented at a public meeting, held in the First Presbyterian Church, Sabbath evening, May 8, 1842. [Washington, 1842] 8°, pp. 14
[*A. C A B Ath B. Publ. Br Mus Y C*
With cover-title, Appeal to the friends of African Colonization.

9 Letter to the Commissioner of Patents, with Experiments in Feeding, dated December 15, 1847. In the Appendix to Annual Report of the Commissioner of Patents, for the year 1847. Washington, 1848. 8°, pp 534-39

AUTHORITIES

J Q Adams, Diary, xii, 188. *Case,* Goodrich Family, 128. *Crosby,* Annual Obituary Notices, 1858, 103-04 *Fowler,* Chauncey Memorials, 162 Hist Mag, iii, 94-95 *Irving,* Crayon Miscellany, ch 1 N-Y. Observer, January 13, 1859 *Stiles,* Hist of Windsor, 2d ed, ii, 219, 225 *Trumbull,* Hist of Hartford County, i, 128, 385, 661-62

WILLIAM WOLCOTT ELLSWORTH, twin brother of the preceding graduate, was born in Windsor, Connecticut, on November 10, 1791, and was prepared for College with his brother.

After graduation he began his legal studies in the Litchfield Law School, and continued them in Hartford, in the office of Thomas Scott Williams (Yale 1794), who married his youngest sister in January, 1812

He was admitted to the bar in 1813, and on September 14 of that year married Emily, eldest daughter of Noah Webster (Yale 1778), then of Amherst, Massachusetts.

He established a successful practice in Hartford, and was taken into partnership with his brother-in-law, Judge Williams, then the foremost lawyer in the city, in 1817, when the latter was elected to Congress. In 1827 he accepted an appointment as Professor of Law in Trinity College, which he held until his death.

In 1829 he was elected to Congress as a Whig, and he was twice re-elected, but resigned at the close of the First Session of the 23d Congress, in June, 1834, to return to the practice of his profession. He had been during the whole of this period a member of the Judiciary Committee, and in that capacity had taken an active part in preparing and reporting measures to carry into effect President Jackson's proclamation against nullification. He prepared and reported for that Committee the copyright law which for many years governed our practice He was also a member of the important Committee appointed to investigate the United States Bank at Philadelphia.

In the Spring of 1838 he was persuaded, much against his own wishes, to be the candidate of the Whig party for the Governorship of the State; he was successful at the polls for that and the three following years (1838–42), and twice during that period declined an election to the United States Senate, from unwillingness to be further drawn away from his profession.

In 1838 he received the honorary degree of Doctor of Laws from the University of New York

In 1847 he was elected by the Legislature a Judge of the Supreme Court of the State; and he retained that office until his term expired by limitation, on his reaching the age of seventy, in 1861.

His wife died in August 23, 1861, in her 71st year.

His last years were spent in retirement, and his death occurred in Hartford, after three months' gradual decline, on January 15, 1868, in his 77th year.

A good copy of his portrait is given in Norton's *Governors of Connecticut.*

His interest in religious and charitable enterprises was conspicuous through his life He served as Deacon in the First Congregational Church in Hartford from 1821 to his death The sermon delivered at his funeral, by his pastor, the Rev. Dr. George H Gould, was afterwards published

His children were two sons and four daughters The elder son was graduated at Yale College in 1836. The eldest daughter married the Rev. Dr. Abner Jackson (Trinity Coll 1837).

He published.

1. Speech, delivered in the House of Representatives, on the Bill for the removal of the Indians, May 17, 1830. In the volume of Speeches on that Bill, edited by Jeremiah Evarts, Boston, 1830. 12°, pp 133-46

2 Speech, in the case of Samuel Houston, charged with a contempt and breach of the privileges of the House, by assaulting the Hon. William Stanbery, a member from the State of Ohio, for words used in debate Delivered in the House of Representatives, May 8, 1832. Washington, 1832. 8°, p. 14. [*Y. C*

A defence, in reply to Mr Polk, of the right of Congressmen to debate freely

3 Argument in Defence of Miss Prudence Crandall, in Report of the Trial of Miss Crandall. Before the County Court for Windham County, August Term 1833, on an information charging her with teaching colored persons not inhabitants of this State. Brooklyn, 1833 8°, pp. 7-14. [*Y C*

4. Speech, on the question of the Removal of the Deposites. Delivered in the House of Representatives, March 27, 1834 Washington, 1834. 8°, pp. 15
[*A. C A. B Publ. Columbia Univ. Y. C*

5 Speech from His Excellency, the Governor of Connecticut, to the Legislature of the State, May, 1838 New Haven, 1838 8°, pp. 14 [*U T. S Y C.*

6 The same, for May, 1839. Hartford, 1839. 8°, pp 16.
[*Y C*

7. The same, for May, 1840 New Haven, 1840 8°, pp. 16.
[*Y. C*

8. The same, for May, 1841. New Haven, 1841. 8°, pp 16.
[*B. Ath Y C*

9. Speech, on the Tract Society and Slavery, in a pamphlet of Speeches, delivered in the Center Church, Hartford, Conn, at the Anniversary of the Hartford Branch of the American Tract Society. Hartford, 1859. 8°, pp 21-26

AUTHORITIES

Conn. Reports, xxxiv, 581-85. *Norton,* Governors of Conn, 181-86. *Stiles,* Hist. of Windsor, 2d ed, ii, 223-25 *Trumbull,* Hist. of Hartford County, ii, 529-30

ELIAS HUBBARD ELY, the youngest of nine children of Elihu Ely, of Old Lyme, Connecticut, and a nephew of the Rev. Richard Ely (Yale 1754), was born in Old Lyme on June 26, 1790. His mother was Anne, second daughter of Joseph and Rebecca (Selden) Ely.

After graduation he studied law in New York City with George W. Strong (Yale 1803), and was admitted to the bar in 1814. He immediately entered on practice there, and was continuously and successfully employed until his retirement and removal from the city in 1864.

His death occurred in Portland, Maine, on February 8, 1874, in his 84th year

He married, on November 5, 1832, Eliza, eldest child of Henry and Prudence (Brainerd) Nichols, of Lyme and East Haddam, Connecticut. She died in 1860, aged 49 years

Their children were two sons and two daughters

AUTHORITIES

Brainerd-Brainard Geneal, pt. 6, Brainerd Geneal, 232. 85 Ely Ancestry, 107, 197 *Field,*

Eleazar Thompson Fitch, the youngest child of Captain Nathaniel Fitch, of New Haven, and grandson of Deacon Eleazar and Lavinia (Wales) Fitch, of Windham, was born on January 1, and baptized on February 27, 1791 His father died in October, 1798 His mother was Mary, a daughter of Lieutenant Abraham and Mary (Alling) Thompson, of New Haven. He was prepared for College by Henry Davis (Yale 1796). His scholarship in College was distinguished, and at graduation he delivered an Oration on Ancient and Modern Poetry. He had united with the College Church at the beginning of his Junior year

After graduation he was the principal of an academy, until he succeeded his classmate Goodrich, for a few months in 1812, as Rector of the Hopkins Grammar School in New Haven.

In the fall of 1812 he entered the Andover Theological Seminary, where he completed the full course of three years, and remained, pursuing advanced studies, assisting the Professor of Homiletics in instruction, assisting Jeremiah Evarts in editing the *Panoplist,* and preaching, until recalled to New Haven by his election, in July, 1817, to the office of Professor of Divinity in the College, which had been vacated by the death of President Dwight

His ordination and installation took place on November 5, the sermon delivered by the Rev. Dr. John Elliott

(Yale 1786), a member of the Corporation, being afterwards published

Like his predecessor, he found it his duty to instruct a number of resident graduates in theology; and this led him to urge on the authorities, in April, 1822, the appointment of an additional theological instructor, which resulted in the organization of the Yale Divinity School. With this School he was actively connected for nearly forty years: with the title of Acting Professor of Sacred Literature for two years (1822–24), or until the appointment of Professor Josiah W Gibbs (Yale 1809); and with that of Lecturer on Homiletics from 1824 to 1861. As the Livingston Professor of Divinity his main duty was the supply of the College pulpit, though he was also responsible for instruction in Natural Theology and the Evidences of Christianity. Pastoral duty was uncongenial to him, because of constitutional shyness; but this deficiency was supplied by his classmate Professor Goodrich and by others of the Faculty. In the difficult post of College preacher he maintained himself with credit.

In July, 1852, his growing infirmities induced him to resign his office as Professor, while retaining his appointment as Lecturer in the Divinity School for nine years longer.

He died in New Haven on January 31, 1871, at the age of 80.

He was married on November 12, 1817, by the Rev Samuel Merwin, to Elizabeth Lucia, the only child of Joseph Lucius Wooster (Yale 1781), of New Haven, who died on August 30, 1821, in her 27th year.

He next married, on September 5, 1822, Susan Augusta, the seventh of eight daughters of Joel and Eleanor (Stong) Root, of New Haven, who died, after four years of continued suffering, on October 2, 1846, in her 47th year.

He was next married by the Rev. Dr. Withington (Yale 1814), on January 6, 1848, to Mary Coffin, daughter of

Micajah Lunt, of Newburyport, Massachusetts, who died in Newburyport on March 21, 1893, in her 91st year.

His children, by his first wife, were one daughter, who died in infancy, and one son (Yale 1840).

Professor Fitch received the honorary degree of Doctor of Divinity from the University of Pennsylvania in 1828.

His portrait, owned by the Divinity School, is a copy of one painted in 1855.

Dr. Fitch presented an unusual combination of high qualities. As has been truthfully said of him, he was a theologian, a metaphysician, a preacher, a poet, and a musician; he also possessed rare mechanical skill, and was a lover of nature in an unusual degree. Probably in the extent and variety of his faculties, he was the most remarkable of the remarkable group of men then connected with the College; but a certain nervous sensibility interfered constantly with the free use of his powers, and limited both his productiveness and his continued power of work The earlier years of his occupancy of the College pulpit were his best years, but his retirement at the age of 61 came none too soon for his fame.

He published:

1. The Minister presenting his people to Christ· a Sermon [from Col. i, 28]; preached at the Ordination of the Rev. Joel H. Linsley, as pastor over the Second Congregational Church and Society in Hartford, Conn, Feb 25, 1824. New-Haven, 1825 8°, pp 40 [*Harv. Y. C.*

This sermon was also delivered at the ordination of the Rev Seth Bliss (who married a sister of Dr. Fitch's second wife), in June, 1825, and at the ordination of the Rev. William C Fowler (Yale 1816), on August 31, 1825; and copies were printed with a corresponding change of title-page

2 A Sermon [from Job vii, 1]· preached at the Funeral of the Rev John Elliott, D.D New-Haven, 1825. 8°, pp. 19 [*A C A. Harv U. T. S. Y. C*

Dr Elliott died in December, 1824.

3. Two Discourses [from Rom v, 13] on the Nature of Sin; delivered before the Students of Yale College, July 30th, 1826. New-Haven, 1826. 8°, pp. 46.
[*B. Publ Harv U. T S Y. C*

The same [Second edition, revised] New-Haven, 1842. 8°, pp 48 [*U. T S Y. C.*

4 An Inquiry into the Nature of Sin· in which the views advanced in "Two Discourses on the Nature of Sin," are pursued; and vindicated from objections, stated in the Christian Advocate. New-Haven, 1827. 8°, pp. 95
[*A C. A Harv U T. S Y C*

5 Sermons: The Repentance of Peter, Mark xiv, 72, and, The Duty of Reproof, Eph v, 11 In the *National Preacher,* vol 2, pp. 49–64 (September, 1827)

6 National prosperity perpetuated A Discourse [from Ps cxv, 15] delivered in the chapel of Yale College; on the day of the Annual Thanksgiving November 29, 1827 New-Haven, 1828 8°, pp. 34. [*A C A B Ath B. Publ Harv. Y C*

7 Review of Erskine on the Gospel. In the *Quarterly Christian Spectator,* vol. 1, pp 289–306 (June, 1829)

8. Liberal Christians, helpers to the truth:—a Sermon [from III John, 8]: delivered in the Centre Church, New-Haven, on the Anniversary of the Female Education Society of New-Haven, July 1, 1829. New-Haven, 1829. 8°, pp. 28. [*A. C A. Y. C.*

9 Review of Tyler's Lectures on Future Punishment In the *Quarterly Christian Spectator,* vol. 1, pp. 598–624 (December, 1829).

10 Review of Fisk on Predestination and Election In the *Quarterly Christian Spectator,* vol. 3, pp. 597–640 (December, 1831).

11. Divine Permission of Sin. In the *Quarterly Christian Spectator,* vol. 4, pp. 614–60 (December, 1832); also published separately with title, A vindication of the divine purpose in relation to the existence of sin New Haven, 1832 8°, pp. 48.

12. An Address, delivered in the Centre Church, New Haven, Dec. 4th, 1833, at the Funeral of Martha Day In the *Literary Remains* of Martha Day New Haven, 1834 12°, pp 55–70.

13 A Translation and Exposition of Romans ix, 22–24. In the *Quarterly Christian Spectator*, vol 7, pp 382–92 (September, 1835).

14 An Account of the Meeting of the Class which graduated at Yale College in 1810, held at New Haven, Aug 18, 1840. New Haven, 1840. 8°, pp 14 [Y. C

15 [Review of The Works of] Nathanael Emmons, D.D In the *New Englander*, vol 1, pp 110–21 (January, 1843).

16 On Perfect Intonation and the Euharmonic Organ. In the *New Englander*, vol 12, pp 278–92 (May, 1850).

17. The true Doctrine of Divine Inspiration In the *Bibliotheca Sacra*, vol. 12, pp 217–63 (April, 1855).

18. Sermon The mode of preaching the Gospel that is adapted to success, Acts xiv, 1. In the *National Preacher*, vol 37, pp. 169–85 (July, 1863)

19 A Statement submitted to the Prudential Committee, by the Professor of Divinity in Yale College Dated April 23, 1822. In W C Fowler, Origin of the Theological School of Yale College, 1869. 8°, pp 17–26.

After his death the following were published by his son:

20 Sermons, practical and descriptive, preached in the pulpit of Yale College. New Haven, 1871 8°, pp. viii, 365.
[U. T. S. Y. C.

Containing twenty-three sermons, composed from 1816 to 1847.

21. Music as a Fine Art Its history—its productions—the elements of its beauty. A Lecture In the *New Englander*, volume 31, pp 689–725 (October, 1872)

He was one of the committee of the General Association of Connecticut which prepared and published the following:

Psalms and Hymns, for Christian Use and Worship New-Haven, 1845 12°, pp. 720.

He furnished the Rev Dr Sprague in 1852 with his recollections of the Rev Dr. John Elliott (Yale 1786), which are printed in the *Annals of the American Pulpit*, vol. 2, pp 322–23.

AUTHORITIES.

B W Dwight, Strong Family, i, 82 *T Dwight,* Memories of Yale Life and Men, 76–86 *Kingsley,* Yale College, ii, 41–46 *Mitchell,* Reveries of a Bachelor, new ed (1883), 231–32. New Englander, xxx, 215–30, 739–44 N. Y Geneal and Biogr Record, xlii, 43 Semi-Centennial Anniversary of the Yale Divinity School, 18, 73–79

CHAUNCEY ALLEN GOODRICH, the younger son of the Hon Elizur Goodrich (Yale 1779), of New Haven, was born in New Haven on October 23, 1790. His preparation for College was completed under Henry Davis (Yale 1796). He united with the College Church at the end of the Sophomore year At graduation he delivered an Oration on the Influence of Novelty.

For the greater part of the two years next after graduation he served as Rector of the Hopkins Grammar School in New Haven From the fall of 1812 to September, 1814, he was a tutor in the College, at the same time studying theology with President Dwight.

On September 27, 1814, he was licensed to preach by the New Haven West Association of Ministers, and he subsequently preached with acceptance in various places He spent several months during the winter of 1815–16 in graduate study in Andover, Massachusetts, and in the following spring received calls, almost simultaneously, from three of the churches which he had supplied,—the Park Street Church in Boston, and the Congregational Churches in Salisbury and Middletown, Connecticut. He accepted the last named, and was ordained and installed there on July 24, 1816.

On October ·1, 1816, he was married to Julia Frances (originally, Frances Juliana), second daughter of Noah Webster (Yale 1778), then of Amherst, Massachusetts.

His health, however, proved unequal to the demands of the pastorate, and just at the time when his plans were therefore broken up, he was invited (in September, 1817) to fill a new professorship at Yale, that of Rhetoric

He was accordingly dismissed from the pastorate in December, 1817, and although for some years hampered by infirm health, he devoted himself with zeal and energy to the duties of instruction

He also took a very active interest in the establishment of the Theological Department in 1822, and one result of this interest was his purchasing in 1828 the *Monthly Christian Spectator,* which had been published in New Haven since 1819, and editing it as a Quarterly from 1829 to 1836, for the exposition and defence of what now began to be called the "New Haven theology"

The honorary degree of Doctor of Divinity was conferred on him by Brown University in 1835.

His concern for the Theological Department led him to propose in 1838 the addition of another professor to the corps of instruction, and to provide from his own resources a part of the funds necessary for the foundation of a chair of the Pastoral Charge. When the first nominee of the Corporation declined to accept an election Professor Goodrich was himself elected (in August, 1839), and transferred his services from the College to the Seminary for the remainder of his life He retained, however, to the last an unofficial relation to the religious life of the College, which was of the utmost value He not only supplemented in general the pastoral labors of his classmate, Professor Fitch, but he established and conducted for all these years a weekly meeting for the students, which was, it is not too much to say, the most distinctly vital religious influence of the place

An outside labor which absorbed much of his time devolved upon him after the death of his father-in-law, Dr. Webster, in 1843. Professor Goodrich had already superintended an abridgment of Dr Webster's *Dictionary,* and he was responsible, as the representative of the family, for the revision of 1847 and later enlargements.

His life was shadowed by ill health, but he continued at his post until the end He died in New Haven, after a week's illness, terminating in a paralytic shock, on February 25, 1860, in his 70th year. A commemorative discourse by President Woolsey was afterwards published.

His widow died in New Haven on August 17, 1869, at the age of 76

Their children were two sons (Yale 1837 and 1843) and two daughters. The elder daughter married the Rev. George E. Hill (Yale 1846), and the younger married Henry K. W. Welch (Yale 1842)

A portrait painted in 1830 is owned by the College, and one painted in 1856 or 1857 is in the Divinity School. The Yale Library has also a marble bust, which is less satisfactory.

Professor Goodrich was an enthusiastic and effective teacher, an active and energetic College officer, and a fervent promoter of all social reforms.

He published:

1 Elements of Greek Grammar, taken chiefly from the Grammar of C. F. Hachenberg. . . New-Haven, 1814. 12°, pp viii, 318 [*Harv. Y. C.*

Prepared while he was tutor, at President Dwight's suggestion; five hundred copies were purchased by the Yale Corporation in September, 1814 Several editions.

2 A Letter to the Rev. Harry Croswell, A M, on the subject of two publications, entitled "A Serious Call," and "A Sober Appeal." New-Haven, 1819. 12°, pp 12 [*U. T S Y. C.*

Professor Goodrich's *Letter* is an anonymous reply to Mr. Croswell's "Appeal," which was occasioned by the "Serious Call" of the Rev Bennet Tyler (Yale 1804)

3 Lessons in Greek Parsing; or, outlines of the Greek Grammar, divided into short portions, and illustrated by appropriate exercises in parsing. New-Haven, 1831 12°, pp. iv, 138

Prepared originally for the use of one of his sons, and issued in many editions.

4. Lessons in Latin Parsing; containing the outlines of Latin Grammar, divided into short portions, and exemplified by appropriate exercises in parsing. New-Haven, 1832 12°, pp viii, 197. [*U S.*

Also in several editions.

5 Narrative of Revivals of Religion in Yale College from its commencement to the present time. In the *American Quarterly Register,* vol. 10, pp. 289–310 (February, 1838)

6. Revivals of religion. Chapter 8 in Book 5 of Robert Baird's Religion in the United States of America. Glasgow, 1844 8°, pp 442–84.

7. Can I conscientiously vote for Henry Clay? New Haven, 1844. 8°, pp. 4 [*Y. C*

An anonymous defence of a Christian's support of Clay.

8 What does Dr. Bushnell mean? From the New York Evangelist. Hartford, 1849. 8°, pp. 28. [*Y. C.*

An anonymous hostile criticism of Dr. Horace Bushnell's *God in Christ*

9 Select British Eloquence, embracing the best Speeches entire, of the most eminent Orators of Great Britain for the last two Centuries; with sketches of their lives, an estimate of their genius, and notes, critical and explanatory. New York, 1852. Large 8°, pp vii, 947 [*B. Publ Harv. Y. C.*

Based on his College lectures

10 [Review of volumes 1, 2, of] Sprague's Annals of the American Pulpit In the *New Englander,* vol 15, pp 169–84 (May, 1857) He had himself contributed to vol 1 (pp 506–13) an article on his grandfather.

11. A Letter to the Secretaries of the American Tract Society, written in behalf of the Rev. Jeremiah Day, D.D, LL D., Eleazar T. Fitch, D D, and others New Haven, 1858 8°, pp 16. [*A. C. A U. T. S Y C.*

On the policy of the Society in regard to publishing on the subject of slavery.

Long after his death was printed:

12 The Excursion. [New Haven.] 12°, pp 10. [*Y. C*

A poetical *jeu d'esprit,* in commemoration of the excursion given by the Messrs Joseph E. Sheffield and Henry Farnam, on the completion of the Chicago and Rock Island Railroad in 1854

' During his editorship of the *Quarterly Christian Spectator,* Dr Goodrich made many contributions to its pages, the following may be mentioned —

Vol 1, pp. 200–04 (March, 1829), Letters from a Traveller on the Continent of Europe [being his own observations in France, during a tour for health in 1826]; pp. 343–84 (June, 1829), Review of Taylor and Harvey on Human Depravity [in conjunction with Rev Noah Porter]; pp. 674–92 (December, 1829), Review of Dana's Poem before the Porter Rhetorical Society in Andover; and Review of Wilson's edition of Wilberforce's Practical View.

Vol. 2, pp. 61–70 (March, 1830), Review of Wilson's Lectures on the evidences of Christianity; pp 380–84 (June, 1830), Brief Notice of Dr. Tyler's Vindication, pp. 608–21 (December, 1830), Letter from a Traveler on the Continent of Europe; pp. 720–50, Review of High Church and Arminian Principles

Vol. 3, pp 75–85 (March, 1831), Review of Robbins' Ancient and Modern History; pp 162–68, Remarks on Protestant [=Moses Stuart] and the Biblical Repertory, respecting the doctrine of Imputation; pp 495–97 (September, 1831), Review of the Child's Book on the Soul.

His work upon Webster's *Dictionary* was largely original, though nominally only editorial In 1829 he edited an abridgment of Dr Webster's work, which had been prepared by Joseph E Worcester (Yale 1811). In 1847 he revised and enlarged the original dictionary, and prefixed an admirable Memoir of the author In 1859 he added an exhaustive treatise on the Principles of Pronunciation

AUTHORITIES

Beardsley, Hist of Episcopal Church in Conn, ii, 213–14 *Case,* Goodrich Family, 128, 219–21 *B. W. Dwight,* Strong Family, ii, 1289 *T Dwight,* Memories of Yale Life and Men, 86–89 *Hazen,* Hist Discourse at Middletown, 10 Hist. Magazine, iv, 126. *Kingsley,* Yale College, ii, 47–50. Semi-Centennial Anniversary of the Yale Divinity School, 19, 87–90 *Woolsey,* Discourse commemorative of Professor Goodrich

RALPH GRANGER, the eldest child of the Hon Gideon Granger (Yale 1787), of Suffield, Connecticut, was born in Suffield on November 22, 1790. From 1801 to 1814 his father was Postmaster-General of the United States. He was prepared for College by his father's classmate, the Rev. Ebenezer Gay, of Suffield.

He studied law in Washington, and was admitted to the bar in the District of Columbia, Maryland, and Virginia. In 1816 he settled in practice in Fairport, on Lake Erie, in Northern Ohio.

He married, on April 16, 1821, Catharine, eldest daughter of Judge William Peter VanNess (Columbia Coll. 1797) and Mary (Bay) VanNess, of New York City, who was ten years his junior. They had no children He was engaged successfully in practice until 1825, at which date he became a cripple.

He was a member of the Ohio State Senate during two sessions, from 1835 to 1837

He died in Cleveland, on December 7, 1843, aged 53 years.

AUTHORITIES

Granger Genealogy, 181-82

PAUL CHAPLIN GRIMBALL, son of Paul Grimball, of St. Helena Island, near Beaufort, South Carolina, and grandson of Joshua Grimball, was born on that island on March 17, 1788. His mother was Sarah, daughter of William and Martha (Fripp) Chaplin, of St. Helena Island.

His father removed in his childhood to Sunbury, Georgia, leaving him with relatives in Charleston.

His preparation for College was completed in New Haven, under Leonard Cowles (Yale 1805). He did not receive his degree with his Class at graduation, because his College bills were not fully settled; but he was admitted to a degree in 1828

He settled as a planter in his native State, residing for part of the time in Charleston, and partly in St. Johns Colleton, in the same District, on the Stono River, about six miles southwest of the city

He married on June 7, 1814, Widow Elizabeth (Jenkins) Huntscome, who died before him.

He was at one time a member of the State Senate.

At the outbreak of the rebellion he was residing on John's Island, and in May, 1862, fell under suspicion as being unfriendly to the Southern cause, so that he was driven from his home, and took refuge with a daughter in Sumter County, where he died on October 3, 1863, in his 76th year. He was buried at the Concord Presbyterian Church in Sumter County.

His children were three sons and two daughters

FREDERICK GRIMKE, the fourth son of Judge John Foucheraud Grimke, of Charleston, South Carolina, and brother of Thomas Smith Grimké (Yale 1807), was born in Charleston on September 1, 1791. His preparation for College was completed under Alfred Hennen (Yale 1806), in New Haven.

Having studied law after graduation, he settled in practice in Columbus, Ohio, and in January, 1830, was elected Presiding Judge of the Court of Common Pleas for Franklin County, for three years. (He had already filled a vacancy in the same office for a single year, in 1819–20.) At the close of his term of office, he removed to Chillicothe In January, 1836, he was elected by the Legislature to the bench of the Supreme Court for a term of seven years This position he resigned in March, 1842, in order to devote his time to philosophical studies

In his later years he was entirely withdrawn from society. He died in Chillicothe, after an illness of several weeks, on March 8, 1863, in his 72d year.

He was never married.

His memory was endeared to his friends by the recollection of his unassuming manners, his kindness of heart, and purity of life

He published:

1. Essay on the Ancients and Moderns [New Haven, 1831.] 12°, pp. 14 [*A. A S. B. Publ M H S*

This is paged as a continuation of his brother's Reflections on the Character and Objects of all Science and Literature (cf. above, p 114).

2. Considerations upon the Nature and Tendency of Free Institutions. Cincinnati, 1848 8°, pp viii, 544
[*A A S B Ath Br Mus Harv. M H S. U. S.*

The same Second edition New-York and Cincinnati, 1856. 8°, pp. viii, 670. [*U S. Y. C*

In accordance with a provision in his will, after his death was published.—

3. The Works of Frederick Grimke Columbus, 1871 2 vols in 1. 8°, pp v, 733; 261 [*Columbia Univ Harv. Y C.*

Vol. 1 contains No 2, above, with later revisions, vol 2, Letters, Reflections on the present crisis, Essays, and Apothems

AUTHORITIES

Biogr Encyclopedia of Ohio, 547 Magazine, iv, 50
Hist Magazine, vii, 136 S C. Hist

FREDERICK GUNN, son of Epenetus Gunn, of New Milford, Connecticut, and grandson of Abner and Mary (Buckingham) Gunn, of New Milford, was born on September 1, 1787. His mother was Sarah Botsford, eldest child of Enos and Sarah (Botsford) Camp, of New Milford. He was prepared for College by the Rev Dr. David Ely (Yale 1769), of Huntington.

He studied law with the Hon. David S. Boardman (Yale 1793), of New Milford, from January, 1811, to August, 1812, and after a few months' additional study in the Litchfield Law School he was admitted to the bar, but never offered himself as a candidate for practice

He was the owner of considerable real estate in New Milford, and turned his attention to farming, but early fell into intemperate habits, which grew on him to such an extent that he lost both property and character After many years of degradation, he reformed entirely (about 1840), and for the rest of his life led an exemplary career. His wife, who had been separated from him, returned to him, he became a professor of religion, and in 1843, to mark the general recognition of his course, he was sent to the State Legislature as one of the Representatives of the town.

He died in New Milford on November 21, 1852, in his 66th year

AUTHORITIES

Hon D S Boardman, MS Letter, January, 1853

ABRAHAM BRUYN HASBROUCK, son of Judge Jonathan Hasbrouck, of Kingston, Ulster County, New York, of French Huguenot descent, and grandson of Colonel Abraham and Catharine (Bruyn) Hasbrouck, of Kingston, was born on November 29, 1791 His mother was Catharine, second daughter of Colonel Cornelius C and Maria Catherina (Roel or Ruhl) Wynkoop, of New York City. He was prepared for College in Kingston by Thomas Adams (Yale 1800).

After graduation he began his law-studies in the Litchfield Law School, and continued them in the office of Elisha Williams, of Hudson. In 1814 he began practice in Kingston, and in 1817 he formed a partnership with Charles H. Ruggles, which continued until the appointment of Mr. Ruggles to the bench in 1831. This firm enjoyed a wide reputation for ability and integrity, and a large amount of the practice of the County was transacted through their office In the fall of 1833 Mr Hasbrouck took into partnership Marius Schoonmaker (Yale 1830), whose preparatory studies had been pursued with him. This connection continued until 1840

Meantime he had served with credit for one term (1825–27) in Congress, as a Whig representative from Ulster and Sullivan Counties; and had been the President of the Ulster County Bank since its establishment in 1831.

But neither professional nor political life was thoroughly congenial; and an opportunity more suited to his tastes was opened to him in the offer of the Presidency of Rutgers College, at New Brunswick, New Jersey, in 1840. He was inducted into office in September of that year, and during the ten years which followed did much to strengthen and upbuild that institution His scholarly attainments, his high religious character, his interest in young men, and the dignity and courtesy of his manner combined to secure the substantial success of his administration The honorary degree of Doctor of Laws was conferred on him by Columbia College in 1840 and by Union College in 1841. One useful service of his presidency was the delivery of a course of lectures on Constitutional and International Law.

He resigned his office in July, 1850, and after about five years' residence in New York City removed to his native town, where he passed the rest of his life in dignified retirement.

When the Ulster Historical Society was formed in 1859, he was elected its President.

He died at the old family residence in Kingston, after a few days' illness, on February 23, 1879, in his 88th year, having outlived all his classmates

He married on September 12, 1819, Julia Frances Ludlum, who died on June 4, 1869, in her 74th year. An Address delivered at her funeral by the Rev A. Blauvelt was afterwards printed.

Two sons and four daughters survived him, one daughter being the wife of Judge Joseph F. Barnard (Yale 1841), another the wife of General George H. Sharpe (Rutgers Coll. 1847), and another the wife of the Rev. Dr. John Lillie (Univ. of Edinburgh 1833).

As a lawyer Mr. Hasbrouck held high rank. He was a diligent student, a pleasing and impressive speaker, and had a character for manliness and probity which won universal confidence. As a member of Congress he maintained his reputation for intelligence, efficiency, and high-bred courtesy. In the presidency of Rutgers College he fulfilled amply the expectations of his friends, and retained through life the honor and affection of his pupils In his native county, he was trusted and influential in his earlier years, and honored as few others have been in his later life. He was connected with the Reformed Dutch Church, and died as he had lived, in Christian faith

His only publications were:

1. Inaugural Address. In Addresses delivered at his Inauguration, as President of Rutgers College, New Brunswick, N J Sept. 15, 1840. New York, 1840 8°, pp. 11–39 [*B. Publ. Y C.*

2. Address, delivered before the Ulster Historical Society October 17th, 1859. In the *Collections* of the Society. Vol. I. Kingston, 1860. 8°, pp xxv–xxxix [*Y C*

AUTHORITIES

Rutgers College Centennial Celebration, 62–63 *Schoonmaker,* Hist of Kingston, 449 *Sylvester,* Hist of Ulster County, 1, 103–05 Wynkoop Genealogy, 2d ed, 67

AUGUSTUS LUCAS HILLHOUSE, the younger son of the Hon. James Hillhouse (Yale 1773), of New Haven, was born in New Haven on December 9, 1791. He was prepared for College by Henry Davis (Yale 1796), and at first entered the Class of 1807. His elder brother was graduated in 1808.

He was distinguished as a student for scholarship and poetical genius, and seemed to be entering on life with the fairest hopes.

After graduation he became a victim of severe chronic dyspepsia, and fell into a state of physical and mental depression. He was elected to a tutorship in College in 1812, and would have succeeded to the office in 1814, had he not declined. In the hope that change of scene and of climate and the excitement of foreign travel might benefit him, his father consented to his going abroad, in 1816.

He landed at Bordeaux, traveled through the south of France, tarried a short time in Geneva, and by early fall was settled in Paris, in or near which was his home for the rest of his life

In his first years there he interested himself actively in efforts for the diffusion of evangelical influences among the French people. A little later, he gave considerable time to the translation of a new work on the forest trees of North America, and in that connection tried to promote the cultivation of the olive in the Southern part of the United States.

About 1823 he set about the composition of a philosophical work, to be entitled "A Demonstration of the Natural Method in Politics, or, the Political Experience of the United States, applied to Europe," which occupied him for the rest of his life. He withdrew from society, and postponed his return to his family home until his great work should be completed.

In July, 1853, he made an arrangement by which his unimproved real estate in New Haven was transferred to Yale College, in return for an annuity of $1,200, the property was held for many years, but ultimately realized much more than the amount paid to Mr Hillhouse

In his lonely life he found his chief pleasure in beneficence to the poor; and when he died on March 14, 1859, in his 68th year, he was sincerely mourned by the peasants of the little village of Eragny, where the event occurred, on the left bank of the Oise, about fifteen miles northwest of Paris

He was never married. His body was brought to America for burial, in accordance with his own expressed wish.

He left behind him a large collection of manuscripts, but not in condition to be printed.

He printed:

1. Description of the European Olive Tree [Paris, 1818.] Large 8°, pp 43 + pl [*B. Publ. Harv. Y. C.*

This article was written for the *North American Sylva*, by F. A Michaux, and appears in Mr. Hillhouse's translation of that work, volume 2, pp 156–204.

Another edition is —

An Essay on the History and Cultivation of the European Olive Tree. Paris, 1820 8°, pp. 54 + pl. [*B. Publ. M. H S.*

2. A Hymn. In the *Christian Spectator*, vol 4, pp 195–96 New Haven, April, 1822. 8°.

Seven stanzas, of four lines, signed with initials only See the biographical article on the author, by the Rev. Dr Bacon, in the New Englander.

3 The Natural Method in Politics, being the abstract of an unpublished work. Paris, 1826.

Said to have been privately printed, in a very small edition

He was also the author of the following anonymous translation from the French —

4. The North American Sylva, or a description of the forest trees, of the United States, Canada and Nova Scotia. Considered particularly with respect to their use in the Arts and their introduction into Commerce, to which is added a description of the most useful of the European forest trees .. By F Andrew Michaux. Philadelphia and Paris, 1817–19 3 vols 8°

[*Harv. Philad. Libr. Co. U S*

About the same date he translated and adapted from the English into French, numerous tracts by Hannah More.

AUTHORITIES.

Dwight Family, ii, 1092 Hist Magazine, iii, 192. New Englander, xviii, 557–72 N Y Geneal and Biogr. Record, iv, 146 *Walworth*, Hyde Family, ii, 929

George Hinckley, the elder son of Judge Samuel Hinckley (Yale 1781), of Northampton, Massachusetts, was born in Northampton on August 22, 1790, and was prepared for College by Jonathan H. Lyman (Yale 1802), of Hatfield, who afterwards married his sister.

He studied law after graduation, and entered on practice with flattering prospects in his native town, but died early, on September 22, 1818, aged 28 years He was never married.

AUTHORITIES

Bridgman, Northampton Epitaphs, 79 *Clark,* Northampton Antiquities, 312 *Dwight,* Strong Family, ii, 1202

JOSIAH HOLBROOK, son of Colonel and Deacon Daniel and Anne (Hitchcock) Holbrook, of Derby, Connecticut, and grandson of Daniel and Elizabeth (Riggs) Holbrook, of Derby, was born in the summer of 1788. His father was a substantial farmer, and he was prepared for College by the Rev. Amasa Porter (Yale 1793), of Derby.

Immediately after graduation he opened a select school in Derby, and in the following winter he conceived a plan for an Agricultural School for Boys, using a portion of his father's farm as the exercise-ground for his pupils. His parents dying suddenly in April, 1813, he took the whole farm, and thus found the opportunity of expanding his general plan

Probably in the fall of 1814, he married Lucy, second daughter of his pastor, the Rev Zephaniah Swift (Dartmouth Coll 1792), and Sarah (Packard) Swift, who died on August 5, 1818, after a long and distressing illness, in her 23d year, leaving two sons

An unpleasant picture of Mr. Holbrook at this period is given in the *Autobiography* of the Rev Charles Nichols, who lived in his family from 1813 to 1817.

In these years he attended Professor Silliman's lectures at Yale on chemistry, mineralogy, and geology.

He passed some years in this manner on his farm, but was meantime developing in his mind the idea of an agricultural institution (after the example of Fellenberg), where manual labor should be combined with education, and the pupils should be instructed by practice in such particulars as land-surveying, road-making, the analysis of soils, and all departments of farm-labor.

Finally, in the spring of 1824, such a Seminary was opened in Derby, under the direction of Mr. Holbrook and the Rev. Truman Coe (honorary M A. Yale 1825), with the design of qualifying the pupils for practical farm-life and for teaching

The Seminary was given up in the fall of 1825, owing to lack of capital for its development; but a useful beginning had been made

Mr. Holbrook then turned his attention to the field of popular scientific lecturing; and after a year's experience in Connecticut and Massachusetts, he began in August, 1826, the establishment of town Lyceums, with Boston as his base of operations.

About 1826 he also began the manufacture of cheap school-apparatus, for illustrating the various sciences

He was the leading spirit in calling the Convention at Boston in May, 1830, which resulted in the organization of the American Institute of Instruction

In 1830 he began another branch of activity, in editing a series of *Scientific Tracts,* designed for the popularization of knowledge.

In 1831 he was appointed corresponding secretary of the School Agents' Society, an organization for providing traveling agents in behalf of schools and lyceums.

In June, 1832, having transferred the *Scientific Tracts* to other hands, he began the publication of a weekly paper, called *The Family Lyceum,* which survived, however, for only a single year.

He left Boston about 1834, and for a few years was chiefly occupied with a fairly successful effort to establish the lyceum system in Pennsylvania While thus engaged he conceived the plan of a Universal Lyceum, to include national lyceums all over the world

He had for some time had in contemplation the idea of a series of Lyceum villages, to be scattered over the country, as centres of the Lyceum enterprise, where teachers might be trained; and in 1837 he founded such a village at Berea, in Middleburg Township, Cuyahoga County, Ohio, about twelve miles southwest of Cleveland, where a flourishing settlement was soon established A second village was also projected at Westchester, New York. But the enterprise at Berea came into financial difficulties, leaving Mr. Holbrook under a load of debt, which crippled all his subsequent efforts He maintained a manufactory for globes in Berea until 1852.

New York City was his next place of residence, where he was serving in 1842 as central agent for a plan of School Exchanges, which was part of his original scheme of Lyceums This involved the collection of museums of natural and other objects in the schools, which should be made the basis of lectures, and should be exchanged for collections from other schools.

In the spring of 1849 he went to Washington for a brief visit, but found such encouragement for the promotion of the objects in which he was interested, that he remained there permanently.

In May, 1854, he went to Lynchburg, Virginia, in pursuance of his plan of interesting such communities in his method of education, and while collecting mineral specimens, alone, on Saturday morning, June 17, fell (as is supposed) from a high rocky bluff, above the Blackwater creek, and was drowned His body was found on the 19th, and was interred at Lynchburg, the same day.

He left two sons. Zephaniah Swift Holbrook (honorary M.A. Yale 1887) was a grandson.

Mr. Holbrook's main interest was the establishment of popular associations for the diffusion of scientific knowledge connected with the useful arts. In this he was extensively useful, as also in the more distinctive object of naturalizing the Lyceum in New England.

An engraving from his portrait is given in volume 8 of the *American Journal of Education.*

Among his many small publications were:

1. Five hundred questions, selected from a full course of illustrations and experiments upon Chemistry, applied to the useful arts, given at the Agricultural Seminary at Derby, (Conn) with a short statement of the course of instruction pursued at that institution New Haven, 1825.

Anonymous

2. Associations of Adults for mutual education In the *American Journal of Education,* vol 1, pp 594–97 (October, 1826)

3 American Lyceum of Science and the Arts for the diffusion of useful and practical knowledge. Worcester, 1827 4°, pp. 7.
[*A. A S*

4. American Lyceum, or Society for the improvement of schools, and diffusion of useful knowledge. Boston, 1829 8°, pp. 16.
[*U S. Y. C.*

The same. [Revised edition.] Boston, 1829. 12°, pp 24.
[*U S. Y. C.*

Anonymous.

5. Easy Lessons in Geometry, intended for Infant and Primary Schools; but useful in Academics, Lyceums and Families Boston, 1829. 12°, pp. 36.

6. Schools, Lyceums, and Lyceum Seminary Boston, 1829 12°, pp. 12 [*A C. A. Br Mus Y C*

7. Scientific Tracts, designed for instruction and entertainment, and adapted to Schools, Lyceums, and Families Conducted by Josiah Holbrook, and others. Boston, 1830–32 2 vols. 12°.
[*B. Publ U. S.*

A semi-monthly publication, consisting of familiar treatises on the physical and natural sciences, with their practical applications, and on various subjects of common life. Continued under another editor.

8. Apparatus for Schools, Academies and Lyceums. Devised and collected by J. Holbrook and for sale.. Boston. 12°, pp. 18.
[*B Publ.*

9. The Family Lyceum.—Designed for Instruction and Entertainment, and adapted to Families, Schools and Lyceums. Boston, July 28, 1832—August 10, 1833. folio. [*B. Publ.*

Only one volume of this weekly newspaper was issued

10 First Lessons in Geometry, for the use of Families, Schools, and Lyceums. Boston, 1833 12°, pp. 52 [*Harv. U. S.*

11 First Lessons in Geology, for the use of Families, Schools, and Lyceums. Boston, 1833 sq 16°, pp 64. [*M H. S U S.*

12 A familiar treatise on the Fine Arts, Painting, Sculpture, and Music Boston, 1833 sq 16°, pp 277. [*U. S.*

13 County Museums In *Niles' Weekly Register*, vol. 46, pp 418–19 (Aug 16, 1834).

Signed, "A Farmer"

14 Lyceum Seminaries. In the same, pp 445–47 (Aug. 30, 1834).

15 Education Conventions. Five articles in *Niles' Weekly Register*, vol 47, pp 24, 39, 56, 70, 87 (Sept–Oct 1834), signed, "An Observer"; the second has a sub-title, School Moneys, the third, Circuit Schools; the fourth, Itinerating Libraries; the fifth, County Lyceums

16. First Quarterly Report of the Universal Lyceum 12°, pp. 24 [*Y. C.*

17. Letter to the Executive Committee of the Trustees of the Public School Society of New York, proposing a plan of instruction in the elements of Natural Science, as a part of Public School instruction, dated 1845 In the Appendix to the 40th Annual Report of the Trustees. New York, 1846. 8°, pp 17–19

18. Geological Cabinet, an introduction and aid to books New-York, 1848. 12°, pp 16 [*U. S.*

The same [Revised edition.] Washington, 1853 24°, pp. 32 [*A A S.*

With cover-title, Geology. Agriculture, Wealth, Morals

19 Agricultural Geology. Baltimore [1851] 16°, pp. 36. [*A. A. S U. S.*

He published many other small books and newspaper articles, in furtherance of his favorite ideas

AUTHORITIES

Barnard's Amer Journal of Education, II, 320-22; VIII, 229-48; XIV, 558 *C. Johnson,* Hist. of Cuyahoga County, 475 Library Journal, XXVI, 261-64. *C. Nichols,* Autobiography, 114-72 *Orcutt,* Hist. of Derby, 211-12, 557-60, 730, 768

JAMES HOOKER, the second son of Captain James Hooker, a merchant, of Windsor, Connecticut, by his third wife, Mary Chaffee, and nephew of the Rev Nathaniel Hooker (Yale 1755), was born in Windsor on July 12, 1792. His classmate Chaffee was his first cousin. He was prepared for College in Windsor by Nathan Johnson (Yale 1802). One sister married Elisha B. Strong (Yale 1809), and another married the Rev. Dr. Andrew Yates (Yale 1794).

After graduation he studied law in the Litchfield Law School, and later in Poughkeepsie, New York, where he was admitted to the bar in 1813 and settled in practice He was regarded as one of the safest and most conservative of counsellors.

He married in Poughkeepsie, on January 24, 1816, Helen Sarah, youngest daughter of the late John Reade and Catharine (Livingston) Reade, of Poughkeepsie and New York City

From 1828 to 1840 he held the office of Surrogate of Duchess County. He was a Presidential Elector in 1836, and one of the Canal Commissioners of the State in 1842. He was a Vestryman of Christ Church from 1817 until his death.

He died in Poughkeepsie on September 3, 1858, in his 67th year. His widow died on January 30, 1879

Their children were two daughters, of whom only the elder married

---

AUTHORITIES.

Chaffee Genealogy, 204 Hooker Descendants, 78, 170-71 *Reynolds,* Records of Christ Church, Poughkeepsie, 141 *Stiles,* Hist of Windsor, 2d ed, II, 400-01.

JOHN HOOKER, the eldest child of the Hon. John Hooker (Yale 1782), of Springfield, Massachusetts, and of Sarah (Dwight) Hooker, was born in Springfield on December 15, 1791. His preparation for College was completed under Henry Sherman (Yale 1803).

After graduation he studied law with the Hon George Bliss (Yale 1784), in Springfield, and was admitted to the bar in 1813. He practiced his profession in his native city for about a year, and then removed to Pittsfield, where, however, he continued in practice for only three years, and then returned to Springfield.

He died in Springfield on May 13, 1857, in his 66th year.

He was never married.

AUTHORITIES.

Dwight Family, ii, 845 Hooker Descendants, 121

JOHN HOWARD, the eldest son of the Rev. Dr. Bezaleel Howard (Harvard 1781), of Springfield, Massachusetts, and grandson of Nathan and Jane (Howard) Howard, of Bridgewater, Massachusetts, was born in Springfield in 1791 His mother was Prudence, third daughter of Sheriff and Deacon Ezekiel and Prudence (Stoddard) Williams, of Wethersfield, Connecticut A brother died while a member of Harvard College, Class of 1818. John W. Salter (Yale 1818) was a first cousin.

He studied law and on being admitted to the bar in 1813 settled in practice in Springfield, but was early drawn into business life. In 1823 he entered the service of the Springfield Bank as cashier, and in 1836 was transferred from this office to the presidency of the Bank, which he held until 1849

He was a member of the Governor's Council in 1837–38.

He died in Springfield on October 23, or 24, 1849, aged 58 years

He married, on December 18, 1818, Mary Stoddard, elder daughter of Colonel Thomas and Hannah (Worthington) Dwight, of Springfield, and sister of John Worthington Dwight (Yale 1812) She died in Springfield on July 20, 1836, aged 54½ years.

Their children were four daughters, three of whom married

Mr. Howard was of dignified personal appearance, and universally respected as an upright, active, and influential citizen.

AUTHORITIES

Chapin, Old Springfield, 228-30 Dwight Family, ii, 829-30 *McLean*, Descendants of Ezekiel Williams, 64-65 *Mitchell*, Hist. of Bridgewater, 199. *Sprague*, Annals of the Amer Pulpit, viii, 183 *Stiles*, Hist of Wethersfield, ii, 817. Tuttle Family, 354.

EBENEZER KELLOGG, the eldest child of Ebenezer Kellogg, a farmer of Vernon, then known as North Bolton, Connecticut, and grandson of the Rev. Ebenezer Kellogg (Yale 1757), of that parish, was born in Vernon on October 25, 1789. His mother was Abigail, sixth daughter of Nathaniel and Sarah (Pitkin) Olmsted, of East Hartford. Professor Denison Olmsted (Yale 1813) was his first cousin. He was prepared for admission to the Sophomore Class by the Rev. Ephraim T. Woodruff (Yale 1797), of the adjoining parish of North Coventry. His scholarship was distinguished, and he pronounced the Salutatory Oration at graduation.

On leaving College he spent two years as the teacher of an academy in New London, and then completed the three-years' course in the Andover Theological Seminary

While in Andover he was licensed to preach, but in the autumn of 1815 he accepted an appointment as Professor of Languages in Williams College, at Williamstown, Massachusetts, and abandoned the design of entering the ministry

In the fall of 1817, while on a visit in Vernon, he was suddenly attacked with bleeding at the lungs, and in consequence passed the next winter at the South. He then resumed his College duties, but his constitution never recovered from this seizure and he was only able to continue at his post by the utmost carefulness

On June 2, 1826, he married Susan, youngest child of the Hon. Joshua Coit (Harvard 1776) and Ann Boradill (Hallam) Coit, of New London.

In the fall of 1844, in view of his infirm health, he resigned his professorship, but continued his residence in Williamstown. He died there on October 2, 1846, at the age of 57. A commemorative Sermon by President Mark Hopkins was afterwards published.

His widow returned to New London, but died suddenly, while visiting in Williamstown, on April 8, 1847, aged 49 years Their only child died at birth.

Professor Kellogg was extremely conscientious as a disciplinarian, and not generally popular with his pupils; but those who knew him recognized his unusual integrity and purity of motive, his refined taste, his kindness of heart, and thorough devotion to Williams College.

He printed:

1 A History of the Town of Williamstown In A History of the County of Berkshire .. By Gentlemen in the County Pittsfield, 1829. 12°, pp. 397-416.

2 Memoirs of William A. Porter, A.M, with Selections from his writings—Not Published. 1832 12°, pp. 115.

[*A. C. A. Br Mus*

Mr Porter (Williams Coll 1818) was at the time of his death, in 1830, Professor of Rhetoric and Moral Philosophy at Williams. The Memoir occupies pp. 1-48

AUTHORITIES

Bolton and Vernon Vital Records, 103. *Chapman*, Coit Family, 60, 114 *Durfee*, Biogr Annals of Williams College, 142-43 Kelloggs in the New World, 1, 330 *Perry*, Williamstown and Williams College, 422-26

DANIEL KISSAM, son of Daniel Kissam, of North Hempstead, Long Island, and grandson of Daniel and Peggy (Tredwell) Kissam, was born at Manhasset in North Hempstead, on September 27, 1790. His mother was Phebe, daughter of Philip Smith Platt His preparation for College was completed under Henry Davis (Yale 1796), in New Haven

He spent his life on a farm in Manhasset, and died there on May 25, 1857, in his 67th year

He was elected to a judgeship of Queens County in 1840, but declined to serve.

He married Peggy Tredwell, who died on October 22, 1840. By her he had three daughters, and a son, who was for a time a member of the Class of 1836 at Yale.

He next married, on March 22, 1847, Hannah Tredwell, a sister of his first wife, who died on May 26, 1858.

AUTHORITIES

Daniel T. Kissam, MS. Letter, July, 1857 Kissam Family, 27, 45-46 Platt Lineage, 49

SIMON LARNED, the eldest child of Thaddeus Larned, of Thompson, Windham County, Connecticut, and grandson of Deacon Simon and Rebekah (Merrils) Larned, of Thompson, was born on November 25, 1787. His mother was Abigail, daughter of the Rev. Noadiah Russell (Yale 1750), of Thompson. He was prepared for College at the Woodstock Academy.

He was a young man of promise, but died in Thompson on September 21, 1810, in his 23d year, nine days after receiving his degree.

AUTHORITIES.

Learned Genealogy, 2d ed, 109

AMMI LINSLEY, the sixth in a family of nine children of Rufus and Abigail Linsley, of North Branford, then part of Branford, Connecticut, was born on March 12, 1789. He was prepared for College by the Rev David Smith (Yale 1795), of Durham

In 1810 he began the study of theology with the Rev Bezaleel Pinneo (Dartmouth Coll. 1791), of Milford, and a year later transferred himself to the care of the Rev Ebenezer Porter (Dartmouth 1792), of Washington. When Dr. Porter removed to a professorship at Andover a few months later, he went to reside with the Rev Bennet Tyler (Yale 1804), of South Britain, and studied under his direction until October, 1812, when he was licensed to preach by the Litchfield South Association of Ministers

After being employed in various localities in New York and Connecticut, he was ordained and installed on July 19, 1815, as pastor of the Congregational Church in East Hartland, in Hartford County

He was married, on August 23, 1815, to Abigail Minor, of Milford.

He remained in East Hartland until compelled by poor health and inadequate support to resign his pastorate in 1835

In the winter of 1836–37 he preached in Wolcott; and for about two years thereafter in the neighboring town of Prospect.

Still preaching occasionally, and teaching, he resided in North Haven from 1839 until 1855, when he removed to New Haven. In 1857 he retired to North Branford, but in 1859 was again in North Haven, which remained his home until his death there, on December 21, 1873, in his 85th year.

His wife died in North Haven on February 20, 1868.

Their children were two sons, both of whom were graduated at Yale in 1843, and two daughters

THOMAS LYMAN, the eldest son of Chief-Justice Daniel Lyman (Yale 1776), of Newport, Rhode Island, was born in Newport on December 25, 1791, and was prepared for College at home in the school of Mr. John Frazer.

After graduation he studied law with his brother-in-law, Benjamin Hazard (Brown Univ. 1792), of Newport, and afterwards became a merchant in New York City (for a short time) and in Philadelphia

He died in Philadelphia on November 4, 1832, aged nearly 41 years He was never married.

AUTHORITIES

Coleman, Lyman Genealogy, 208

DANIEL FERGUSON MCNEIL entered College from Camden, South Carolina, at the opening of the Sophomore year.

He took his Master's degree in 1814

He was reported as deceased at the Class Meeting held in August, 1840.

NATHANIEL MATHER, son of Colonel Oliver Mather, of Windsor, Connecticut, was born in Windsor on September 22, 1788. A brother was graduated here in 1799.

He studied law after graduation in the Litchfield Law School, and in 1814 removed to Ohio.

On May 16, 1820, he married Sarah Jones Mills, of Hartford, and in 1821 returned to Windsor, to remain for the rest of his life.

He died in Windsor on April 23, 1837, in his 49th year.

His widow removed to Columbus, Ohio, and died on April 6, 1865, in her 68th year.

Their children were two daughters and two sons (of whom the elder died in infancy).

AUTHORITIES

Mather Family, 1890, 145, 204 *Stiles*, Hist of Windsor, 2d ed, ii, 486–87

SAMUEL FINLEY BREESE MORSE, the eldest of the three surviving sons of the Rev. Dr Jedediah Morse (Yale 1783), of Charlestown, Massachusetts, was born in Charlestown on April 27, 1791. He was prepared for College in Phillips Academy, Andover, under Mark Newman (Dartmouth Coll. 1793), and entered Yale in the fall of 1805. Domestic reasons, however, induced his father to call him home during Freshman year, and he joined the Class of 1810 in September 1807. From childhood he had a passion for taking likenesses, and in College, though entirely without instruction, he employed his leisure time in painting, and supported himself in part by making rude portraits of his classmates on ivory.

He returned home at graduation with the fixed purpose of becoming a painter; and at once began to study under the direction of Washington Allston, who was then settled in Boston, and was the chief American artist of that day. An interesting portrait of his father painted by young Morse at this time, is in the Yale collection. In July, 1811, Allston returned to England, and Morse went with him for further study He gained admission to the Royal Academy as a student, and had the benefit of the criticism of both Allston and Benjamin West. He returned to America in October, 1815

He opened a studio in Boston, but as patrons were slow in appearing, he was constrained after a year to go out in search of employment. He spent the following winter in portrait-painting in New Hampshire and Vermont. In January, 1818, he went to Charleston, South Carolina, for a similar purpose; and returned to Boston in May, after a successful season

While in Concord, New Hampshire, in the winter of 1816–17, he had become engaged; and on September 29, 1818, he was married in that city, by the Rev. Dr. Asa McFarland, to Lucretia Pickering, the elder daughter of Charles and Hannah (Pickering) Walker.

He soon returned to Charleston, where he continued until the spring of 1820. By that time his father had removed to New Haven, where the son also made his home for the time being. He was, however, mainly occupied in the practice of his profession in various localities; and in the fall of 1823 for the first time he opened a studio in New York

In 1825, while in Washington, painting a portrait of General Lafayette for the corporation of the city of New York, his wife died suddenly in New Haven, on February 7, at the age of 25, from heart-disease, leaving one daughter and two sons.

He continued to pursue his profession in New York, and in January, 1826, he was the leading spirit in organizing the National Academy of Design, of which he was the first President, retaining office for sixteen years.

He remained in lucrative practice as a portrait-painter in New York until November, 1829, when he sailed for Europe to prosecute his studies in Italy and France.

On his return from Havre in October, 1832, recent discoveries in electro-magnetism were the subject of discussion on ship-board; and Mr. Morse, who had always been interested in such studies, conceived the idea of transmitting intelligence almost instantaneously by electricity, and began to devise the necessary apparatus.

The importance of his invention pressed upon him urgently during the next two or three years, while he pursued his profession with diminished zeal. In the fall of 1835 he was appointed Professor of the Literature of the Arts of Design in the University of the City of New York, and before the close of that year he had a telegraphic instrument in actual operation in his rooms in the University buildings. Two years more were spent in further experiment and inquiry and in elaboration of his imperfect system, and having applied for a patent in Washington in April, 1838, he went abroad in May for the purpose of obtaining patents in England and France.

He returned in April, 1839, having been successful in the latter country only. Another year elapsed before a patent was secured (June 20, 1840) in the United States; and then followed a long period of delay, caused by Professor Morse's pecuniary inability to construct an experimental line. Finally, in March, 1843, a Congressional appropriation of thirty thousand dollars for a trial of the telegraph was secured; and on the completion of a trial-line, between Washington and Baltimore, the first message was dispatched (by a daughter of his classmate, H. L Ellsworth) on May 24, 1844. He had also before this time laid the telegraph successfully under water, and had foretold of the use of ocean cables.

The new invention made its way slowly, amid many discouragements, including rival claims and lawsuits; but finally an extension of his patent was granted in April, 1846, and a competency assured him. In 1847 he established his children in a home on the east bank of the Hudson, near Poughkeepsie; and August 9, 1848, he was married in Utica, by the Rev. Dr. Pierre A. Proal, to Sarah Elizabeth, daughter of the late Lieutenant Samuel B Griswold, of the United States army, and of his wife Catharine Walker (Breese) Griswold, Mrs. Griswold being Professor Morse's first cousin.

His remaining years were chiefly spent in his country home, and in New York City, with intervals of long residence in Europe In these years he was the recipient of many honors, both from his countrymen and from foreign governments, and witnessed the world-wide progress of his inventions.

After a brief final illness he died in New York City on April 2, 1872, having nearly completed his 81st year

Yale conferred on him the degree of LL.D. in 1846, and in succeeding years many decorations were bestowed on him by foreign governments

In 1871 a bronze statue of Professor Morse, of heroic size, was erected in the Central Park in New York City.

His Life by the Rev. Dr Samuel Irenæus Prime (Williams Coll 1829) was published in 1875, and contains two engraved portraits A Memorial volume was also issued by order of Congress in 1875, including an account of the ceremonies of respect held in Washington and elsewhere. Two daughters and five sons survived him. The youngest son was graduated at Yale in 1878, and follows his father's profession as an artist; this instance of 68 years' difference in graduation between father and son is apparently unparalleled in our annals.

Professor Morse was a liberal benefactor of Yale In 1868 he presented to the Art School the painting of Jeremiah, by Washington Allston, at the cost of $7,000; he also contributed $10,000 to the fund for the erection of Edwards Hall for the Divinity School.

He published:

1 Key to Morse's Picture of the House of Representatives New-Haven, 1823. 8°, pp 4 + pl.

[*B Ath B. Publ M. H S. Y C.*

2 Academies of Arts—A Discourse, delivered on Thursday, May 3, 1827, in the Chapel of Columbia College, before the National Academy of Design, on its First Anniversary. New-York, 1827. 8°, pp 60

[*A. A S B. Ath. B Publ Columbia Univ. Harv U T S. Y. C*

3. The Serenade In *The Talisman,* an annual, for 1828. New-York, 1827. 12°, pp 116–18 + pl

A poetical composition, anonymous; with engraving from a design by the author.

4 Fine Arts.—A Reply to Article x, No. lviii, in the North American Review, entitled "Academies of Arts," etc.—Originally published in the Journal of Commerce. New-York, 1828. 8°, pp. 45.

[*A A S. B Ath. B. Publ Columbia Univ Harv M H S. U T S Y. C*

Mr Morse's Reply occupies pp 1–27. The article in the *Review* was written by Franklin Dexter (Harvard 1812), and especially criticized the assumption of the name "National" by a local Academy

5. A Biographical Sketch of Lucretia Maria Davidson Prefixed to her Amir Khan, and other Poems. New York, 1829. 12°, pp v–xxvi. [*Columbia Univ. Y. C*

6. Descriptive Catalogue of the Pictures, thirty-seven in number, from the most celebrated masters, copied into the Gallery of the Louvre—Painted in Paris, in 1831–32. New-York, 1833 8°, pp 8. [*Y C.*

A description of a large picture, by Morse, giving a view of the Gallery of the Louvre, in which are introduced some of the choicest pictures in the collection.

7 Examination of Col Trumbull's Address, in opposition to the projected Union of the American Academy of Fine Arts and the National Academy of Design New-York, 1833. 8°, pp. 20 [*A. A. S Columbia Univ.*

Colonel Trumbull's Address is reprinted, in pp 17–20

8 Foreign Conspiracy against the Liberties of the United States· the numbers of Brutus, originally published in the New-York Observer. Revised and corrected with notes, by the Author New-York, 1835 12°, pp 188

[*B. Publ. Columbia Univ. U S Y C*

Anonymous. In twelve numbers of the *Observer*, August-November, 1834. Also, later editions, slightly enlarged, the seventh in 1852

9 Imminent Dangers to the Free Institutions of the United States through Foreign Immigration, and the present state of the Naturalization Laws. A Series of Numbers, originally published in the New York Journal of Commerce By an American.—Revised and corrected, with additions. New-York, 1835. 8°, pp 32 [*B. Publ. N Y H S U S.*

A later edition New York, 1854. 8°, pp 32.

[*A. A S Harv U S*

10 The Twilight Bow. In *The American Journal of Science and Arts*, vol. 38, pp. 389–90 (April, 1840).

On a common meteorological phenomenon.

11. Our Liberties defended—The question discussed, is the Protestant or Papal System most favorable to civil and religious liberty? By a Protestant, under the signature of Obsta Principiis, and a Roman Catholic, under the signature of Catholicus. New York, 1841 12°, pp. 129. [*U T. S.*

Mr. Morse was the Protestant champion The articles originally appeared in the *Journal of Commerce* in December, 1836, and January, 1837.

12. Letter .. giving a brief history of the telegraph since 1838, dated December 6, 1842 In Report No 17, House of Representatives, 27th Congress, 3d Session, pp. 6–12.

13 Experiments made with one hundred pairs of Grove's Battery, passing through one hundred and sixty miles of insulated wire; in a letter to the Editors, dated New York, Sept. 4th, 1843 In *The American Journal of Science and Arts*, vol. 45, pp. 390–94, October, 1843.

14. A letter, relative to the magnetic telegraph, dated, Washington, December 12, 1844. In House Documents, No. 24, 28th Congress, 2d Session, 1844 8°, pp 18

15. Magnetic Telegraph Controversy —Lord Campbell and Professor Morse —Statement of the case of the refusal to grant a Patent for Morse's Telegraph in Great Britain in 1838, as Published in the Poughkeepsie American of December 16, 1848. 8°, pp 8 [*B. Publ. Y. C.*

16 The Memorial of S. F B Morse, Alfred Vail, and Amos Kendall, to the Senate and House of Representatives [1849] 8°, pp. 7 [*B Ath*

17 The Electro-Magnetic Telegraph —A Defence against the injurious deductions drawn from the Deposition of Prof. Joseph Henry (in the Several Telegraph Suits), with a critical review of said Deposition, and an examination of Prof. Henry's alleged discoveries, bearing upon the Electro-Magnetic Telegraph. [Paris] [1857?] 8°, pp. vii, 111. [*B. Publ Y. C.*

A reprint of an article in the *Telegraph Companion* magazine for January, 1855

18 Mémoire présenté aux Gouvernements Européens [Paris, 1857] 8°, pp. 10.

19 The present attempt to dissolve the American Union, a British Aristocratic Plot By B. New York, 1862 8°, pp. 42

[*A C A. B. Publ. Br. Mus Harv U. S. Y. C*

The main part of this pamphlet had appeared in articles in the New-York *Journal of Commerce*

20 Papers from the Society for the Diffusion of Political Knowledge No. 1.—The Constitution. Addresses of Prof. Morse [and others], at the organization New York, February, 1863 8°, pp 16.

The same No 4—The Letter of a Republican, Edward N Crosby, Esq, of Poughkeepsie, to Prof S F. B. Morse, Feb 25, 1863, and Prof. Morse's Reply, March 2d, 1863 New York, 8°, pp 12

The same No 12—An Argument on the Ethical Position of Slavery in the Social System, and its Relation to the Politics of the day. By S F. B. Morse New York, August, 1863 8°, pp. 20 [*Y. C.*

21. Modern Telegraphy.—Some Errors of dates of events and of statement in the History of Telegraphy exposed and rectified [Paris, 1867.] 8°, pp 50 + 38 [*B. Publ. U. T. S Y. C*

22. Paris Universal Exposition, 1867 Reports of the United States Commissioners—Examination of the Telegraphic Apparatus and the Processes in Telegraphy. Washington, 1869 8°, pp. 166. [*Y C*

He edited

23 The proscribed German Student being a Sketch of some interesting incidents in the life and melancholy death of the late Lewis Clausing To which is added, a Treatise on the Jesuits the posthumous work of Lewis Clausing. New-York, 1836 12°, pp 244. [*Br Mus. Harv. U. T. S. Y. C*

Pages 7–58 are occupied with Professor Morse's Sketch.

24. Confessions of a French Catholic Priest. To which are added, Warnings to the People of the United States. By the same Author. New York, 1837. 12°, pp. xiv, 255 [*Harv U. S*

AUTHORITIES

G Allen, Reminiscences, 50 *Ammidown,* Hist Collections, i, 380–90. *Cummings,* Hist. Annals of the National Academy, 37–66, 95–108, 116, 144, 170, 300–02 *Drake,* Mansions of Middlesex, 19–21 *Prime,* Life of Morse *Trowbridge,* S. F B Morse. Wentworth Geneal, ii, 307–08

LOTT NEWELL, the younger son of Captain Samuel Newell (Yale 1781), of Bristol, Connecticut, was born in Bristol in 1788. His parents died in 1798.

His residence was in Bristol until his death, and he was occupied chiefly with money-lending and other financial transactions of a wide variety and of very doubtful repute. For a time he also maintained an office in Hartford.

He was an active worker for the success of the Democratic party, and on January 1, 1813, he secured from President Madison the appointment of postmaster of Bristol. The general lack of confidence in his integrity led to a formal and emphatic remonstrance being passed in town-meeting, in November, 1819, with the result that his appointment was revoked, on February 3, 1820.

His business transactions gradually became of an increasingly doubtful character, and he was repeatedly arrested on civil process on charges of fraud, and spent much of his time on the jail limits in Hartford. One of his favorite ventures was the issue of bank bills with his signature as an officer of a bogus institution, which were sent to distant places to be disposed of for what they would bring.

He died from exposure to the cold, due to his miserly neglect of sufficient clothing, in New York City, on March 30, 1864, at the age of 76. His valuables were missing, and he was probably the victim of a robbery. There was long delay in his identification, and he was not buried in Bristol until April 14.

He married on November 26, 1817, Naomi, youngest daughter of Abel Lewis, a substantial farmer of Bristol, who died on January 7, 1854, at the age of 67.

They had two children: a son, who died in infancy, and a daughter, who died unmarried at the age of 21.

AUTHORITIES

Hall, Newell Genealogy, 32 *Hon Peck,* MS Letter, July, 1864. *E Peck,* MS Letters, 1911 *J T*

EDWARD NICOLL's birthplace and parentage are unknown. New Haven was given as his residence while in College, but no family of that name was then living here.

He is reported to have died, a pauper, in Cincinnati, on September 2, 1820, in his 30th year.

BIRDSEYE GLOVER NOBLE, the eldest child of Sylvanus Noble, of New Milford, Connecticut, and grandson of Thomas and Mary (Curtis) Noble, of New Milford, was born on April 26, 1791. His mother was Elizabeth, daughter of John and Betsey (Curtis) Glover, of Newtown His preparation for College was partly supervised by Asa Chapman (Yale 1792), of Newtown.

After graduation he studied for the ministry of the Episcopal Church, and was ordained deacon by Bishop Jarvis, of Connecticut, on June 2, 1812. He married on January 17, 1813, Charlotte, daughter of John and Amy (Northrop) Sanford, of Newtown. He was invited in April, 1814, to officiate in Christ Church, Middletown, and while thus engaged was advanced to the priesthood by Bishop Griswold of the Eastern Diocese on May 5, 1815. On April 17, 1816, he succeeded to the rectorship of this church, and retained this office until his resignation in September, 1828

On March 8, 1829, he was called to St. John's Church, in Elizabeth, New Jersey. He accepted the call, some three weeks later, and remained there until October 15, 1833. His salary was $500 and the use of the rectory.

He then carried on a private school in Bridgeport, Connecticut, for two or three years, and in 1836 settled on a farm in East Bridgeport, mainly demitting the ministry. His wife died on May 11, 1843, in her 52d year

In 1845 he became assistant rector of the Church of the Holy Trinity, in Brooklyn, New York, the rector being the Rev William B. Lewis (Yale 1831), a cousin of the late Mrs Noble During the summer of 1848 he returned to Connecticut in feeble health, and died at the house of his eldest son, in Bridgeport, on November 16, 1848, in his 58th year.

His children were four sons (the youngest of whom died in infancy) and a daughter. The eldest son was graduated at Yale in 1832. The daughter married the Rev. Charles H. Force (N. Y Univ. 1846).

Mr. Noble served once as delegate to the General Convention of the Church, and filled repeatedly the office of Secretary of the Diocesan Convention In 1826–27 he acted as editor of the last half of volume 5 of the *Churchman's Magazine.*

AUTHORITIES

Boltwood, Noble Genealogy, 58, 88–89 *Clark,* Hist. of St. John's Church, Elizabeth Town, 173. *Field,* Centennial Address at Middletown, 176. *Hatfield,* Hist. of Elizabeth, 680 *Orcutt,* Hist. of New Milford, 744, Hist of Stratford, II, 851–53, 856 *Sprague,* Annals of the Amer Pulpit, v, 154.

DAVID HILLHOUSE RAYMOND, the fifth son of Daniel Fitch Raymond, of Montville, Connecticut, and grandson of Dr. Christopher and Eleanor (Fitch) Raymond, of Montville, was born on January 26, 1789. His mother was Rachel, second daughter of Judge William Hillhouse, of Montville, and sister of the Hon. James Hillhouse (Yale 1773) and William Hillhouse (Yale 1777). A brother was graduated here in 1818, and a sister married Calvin Colton (Yale 1812).

He became a lawyer, and settled in Paoli, in the southern part of Indiana Territory, before the admission of Indiana to statehood, in December, 1816

He married his fourth cousin, Miriam, second daughter of Timothy and Mary (Baldwin) Leonard, of Lansingburg, New York, and sister of Dr. Frederick B. Leonard (Yale 1824).

He was commissioned as presiding Judge of the First Circuit of the Territory on February 24, 1816.

His wife died on September 18, 1818, at the age of 27, in Canton, Ohio, while returning from a visit to her mother.

He died in the early part of the year 1820, in St. Francisville, Louisiana, in his 32d year.

His only child, a daughter, died unmarried

AUTHORITIES

Baker, Hist. of Montville, 585 Baldwin Genealogy, II, 539 Indiana Territory Executive Journal, 240 *Walworth*, Hyde Genealogy, I, 347; II, 937.

ASHER ROBBINS, the youngest of ten children of Captain Wait and Hannah (Robbins) Robbins, of Rocky Hill, then Stepney Society, in Wethersfield, Connecticut, and a brother of Levi Robbins (Yale 1796), was born in Stepney on March 28, and baptized on May 20, 1787 He was prepared for College by his pastor, the Rev. Calvin Chapin (Yale 1788).

He studied law after graduation, with Judge Sylvester Gilbert, of Hebron, and Judge Asher Miller (Yale 1778), of Middletown

In 1814 he began the practice of his profession in his native town, acquiring especially the enviable reputation of persuading his clients to settle their cases without going to law He represented the town in the General Assembly in 1820 and 1821.

As he grew older, and his children were maturing, he fancied, though probably without sufficient reason, that he ought to make more money for the sake of his family. In 1830, accordingly, he built a hemp-mill and rope-walk in Wethersfield, and in 1832 with others organized the Griswoldville manufacturing company for the manufacture of edge-tools.

For managing such enterprises successfully he was altogether unfitted, and the result was disastrous to his private fortune, and moreover broke his heart.

In 1834 he sold the rope works and removed to Hartford. The manufacturing company also failed, but before this time "Squire Robbins," as he was popularly known, had again removed to New York City, where he died on February 3, 1846, in his 59th year He was buried in Rocky Hill

He married, on October 23, 1815, Martha (or Patty) Griswold, who died on July 1, 1817, aged 24 years. He next married, on January 14, 1819, Eliza, second daughter of the Rev. Dr. Calvin Chapin, of Rocky Hill, who died on September 29, 1875, in her 79th year.

The only child of his first marriage died in infancy. By his second marriage he had three daughters The youngest daughter married the Rev. George A. Bryan (Yale 1843). Arthur R. Kimball (Yale 1877) is a son of the second daughter.

AUTHORITIES

A R Kimball, MS Letter, May, 1911. *Stiles,* Hist. of Wethersfield, i, 651; ii, 205, 558, 562 *Tillotson,* Wethersfield Inscriptions, 220 *Trumbull,* Hist. of Hartford County, i, 128; ii, 486

Daniel Robert, the eldest son of Dr Daniel Robert, of Huguenot descent, of the village of Mastic, in Brookhaven, Long Island, was born in Mastic on October 2, 1792. His mother was Mary, daughter of Judge William and Ruth (Woodhull) Smith, of Mastic. A brother was graduated here in 1815 He was prepared for College by the Rev. Herman Daggett (Brown Univ. 1788), of Brookhaven.

He studied law in the Litchfield Law School, and was admitted to the bar of New York City in 1815. For upwards of twenty years he practiced his profession in New York, and maintained a creditable position. In 1819 he was appointed by Governor DeWitt Clinton Judge Advocate of the First Brigade of Artillery in the

State militia, and that office he retained for several years.

He married on June 27, 1827, Jane, younger daughter of John and Susan (Martense) Cowenhoven, of New Utrecht, a suburb of Brooklyn, a lady of considerable wealth She was born on February 1, 1805.

In 1836, partly on account of financial reverses, and partly for the sake of the health of his children, he retired to a farm in New Utrecht, where he remained uninterruptedly in the seclusion of his family for the rest of his life.

He died in New Utrecht, on August 21, 1878, in his 86th year, after an illness of three weeks, his death being principally caused by a gradual decay of the vital powers, his mind being clear to the last.

His wife survived him, with their children, three sons and two daughters.

AUTHORITIES

N Y. Geneal and Biogr Record, viii, 65 *Dr J C Robert,* MS Letter, March, 1879 *Thompson,* Hist of L I, 2d ed, ii, 447

Joseph Pynchon Rossiter was born in Guilford, Connecticut, on September 12, 1789, being the eldest son of Sheriff Nathaniel Rossiter (Yale 1785), and grandson of Joseph Pynchon (Yale 1757) He was prepared for College by Henry Davis (Yale 1796), his father's residence being then in New Haven.

After graduation he studied law, and practiced his profession for a short time in Salina, Onondaga County, New York

He was also distinguished as a portrait-painter

He was drowned while bathing, in Lake St. Clair, at Detroit, on June 10, 1826, in his 37th year.

On January 19, 1818, while a resident of Adams, Massachusetts, he was married by the Rev Dr Simon Hosack, at Johnstown, New York, to Cornelia, daughter of Beekman and Catharine (Marsh) Livingston, of Herkimer County, and niece of the Rev. Dr. John H. Livingston (Yale 1762). She next married Mr. Purdy, of Watertown, Jefferson County.

AUTHORITIES.

Holgate, Amer Genealogy, 180

Luther Spalding, the younger son of Ebenezer Spalding, of Brooklyn, Connecticut, and grandson of Ebenezer and Mary (Fassett) Spalding, of that part of Canterbury which is now Brooklyn, was born on October 24, 1789 His mother was Molly, daughter of Solomon and Polly (Bacon) Paine, of Canterbury. He was a nephew of Asa Spalding (Yale 1778), and first cousin of Rufus P. Spalding (Yale 1817).

He studied medicine at the University of Pennsylvania, and in 1813, during the war with Great Britain, was employed in the hospital in New London.

Later he settled in the practice of his profession in New Braintree, Worcester County, Massachusetts, and on November 11, 1816, was married to Maria, daughter of Luther and Sibyl (Dyer) Paine, of Canterbury. His eldest child was born in New Braintree in November, 1818; but before the birth of his next child he had returned to his native place. After a short sojourn there, he removed in 1822 or 1823 to Windsor, and thence to Stow, in the Western Reserve of Ohio, where he died on August 16, 1825, in his 36th year. His widow died in 1845.

Their children were three sons and one daughter.

AUTHORITIES

Spalding Memorial, 94, 167.

Hervey Talcott, the fifth son of Deacon Joseph Talcott, of (North) Coventry, Connecticut, and grandson of Captain Joseph and Eunice (Lyman) Talcott, of Coventry, was born on January 6, 1791. His mother was Rebecca, daughter of William and Esther (Carpenter) Porter, of Coventry Eleazer P. Talcott (Yale 1832) was a nephew. He was prepared for the Junior Class in College by his pastor, the Rev. Ephraim T. Woodruff (Yale 1797), and had united with the church at home before coming to Yale.

After a year spent in teaching in Newcastle, Maine, he entered the Andover Theological Seminary, where he completed the regular course of three years During the next two years he preached in various localities, partly under the direction of the Connecticut Domestic Missionary Society, of which he was the earliest missionary.

On October 23, 1816, he was ordained and installed as pastor of the First Congregational Church in Portland, then part of Chatham, Connecticut, where he remained, greatly useful and honored, until his death. He was relieved from active duty by the settlement of a colleague in April, 1861; and he died in Portland, after six days' illness, from typhoid pneumonia, on December 19, 1865, aged nearly 75 years. The sermon delivered at his funeral by his colleague, the Rev. Andrew C Denison (Yale 1847), was afterwards published.

Mr. Talcott had a symmetrical, well-balanced mind, and was eminently successful and beloved in his work.

He married on August 26, 1817, Cynthia, only daughter of Ebenezer and Cynthia (Barber) Osborne, of East Windsor, who died in Waterbury on April 23, 1869, aged 69 years. His children were four daughters, of whom three survived him. The second daughter married the Rev. Aaron C. Beach (Yale 1835), and the third married Dr. Gershom C. H. Gilbert (Yale 1841).

AUTHORITIES

Stiles, Hist. of Windsor, 2d ed., II, 543 Talcott Pedigree, 176, 179–80

ASAHEL THOMSON, son of Jonathan and Eunice (Fitch) Thomson, of Farmington, Connecticut, was born in Farmington on April 16, 1790, and was prepared for College by the Rev Noah Porter (Yale 1803).

After graduation he taught for two years in the Academy conducted in Ellsworth Society, in Sharon, by the Rev Daniel Parker (Yale 1798), and for a third year in the Academy in East Windsor. In the fall of 1813 he became a private tutor in the family of Lawrence Lewis, a nephew of General Washington, in Woodlawn, Virginia.

In the spring of 1815 he began the study of medicine with Dr. Eli Todd (Yale 1787), of Farmington, and he attended the medical lectures of that and the succeeding winter in the Yale Medical School. In the spring of 1817 he began the practice of his profession in his native town, and continued it until his death.

He was a member of the State Legislature in 1850 and 1858. In 1859 he received the honorary degree of M D. from Yale.

He died in Farmington, from inflammation of the prostate, on May 2, 1866, aged 76 years.

He was never married. He bequeathed to the Yale Library several manuscript volumes of notes of the lectures which he attended, in the College and the Medical School.

AUTHORITIES

Julius Gay, MS. Letter, May, 1866

WALKER TODD, a son of Captain Eli Todd, of New Milford, Connecticut, and grandson of Dr Jonah Todd, of New Milford, was born in New Milford about 1787. His mother was Mercy, eldest child of John and Mercy (Warner) Merwin, of New Milford A half-brother was graduated here in 1829. He was prepared for College by the Rev. Dr David Ely (Yale 1769), of Huntington.

After graduation he studied law and settled in practice in 1812 in Carmel, New York. He was appointed District Attorney for Putnam County in June, 1818, and retained that office until February, 1821 He was also County Surrogate from March, 1819, to February, 1821.

He was a member of the State Senate during four sessions, from January, 1828, to April, 1831. From 1832 to 1840 he was one of the Board of Inspectors of Sing Sing prison; and from January, 1833, to January, 1840, he was again County Surrogate. In 1836 he was a Democratic candidate for Congress, but was defeated.

He died at Mount Pleasant, in Westchester County, near the end of August, 1840, at the age of 54, and was buried in Carmel.

He married Sarah Ann Smith, and had a large family of children four sons survived him.

AUTHORITIES

Pelletreau, Hist. of Putnam County, 228 Tuttle Family, 21.

JOSEPH TREAT, the ninth in a family of ten children of Gideon Treat, of that part of New Milford, Connecticut, which is now Bridgewater, and grandson of Joseph and Clemence (Buckingham) Treat, of New Milford, was born on December 10, 1783. His mother was Lucretia, third daughter of Gideon and Esther (Allen) Washburn, of Derby.

He studied theology after graduation with the Rev. Ebenezer Porter, of Washington, and was licensed to preach by the Litchfield South Association of Ministers on October 15, 1811.

On May 25, 1814, he was ordained by the Litchfield South Consociation, in session at Woodbury, as an evangelist, and for the next two years labored as a missionary in Pennsylvania and New York

In June, 1816, he went on a missionary tour to the Western Reserve of Ohio; and on September 24, 1817, he was installed as pastor of the Presbyterian Church in Sharon, now Windham, in Portage County, with the understanding that he should be at liberty to labor for half of his time in the destitute and scattered settlements in the vicinity.

He married, on September 20, 1820, Julia, daughter of Jabez and Mary (Robbins) Burrill, of Sheffield, in Lorain County, who had come to Ohio in 1816.

He gave up his pastoral charge in 1827, but continued to reside in Windham, and to supply two feeble churches in the vicinity. Though of delicate constitution, he was incessant in his devotion to his work, and greatly beloved in the community. He was concerned in the movement for the founding of Western Reserve College, and served on the Board of Trustees from 1835 until his death.

He died in Windham on May 9, 1841, in his 58th year. His widow next married the Rev. Luther Humphrey (Middlebury Coll. 1813), and died in 1882 in her 87th year.

Their children were two sons and four daughters. The elder son was graduated at Western Reserve College in 1842. The younger son's College course was interrupted by ill health. The eldest daughter married the Rev. William F. Millikan (Western Reserve Coll. 1846). The youngest daughter was graduated at Oberlin College in 1857.

AUTHORITIES

Orcutt, Hist. of New Milford, 631–32, 781. Treat Family, 252, 314–15.

Samuel Turney entered the Junior Class from Fairfield, Connecticut, in the fall of 1808, his preparation having been completed under Matthew R. Dutton (Yale 1808).

He died in 1823, aged about 36 years.

RALPH WELLS came to College from Hartford, Connecticut, entering at the opening of the Sophomore year.

After graduation he studied law in the Litchfield Law School, and was admitted to the Litchfield County bar in 1813, when he began practice in Hartford. In 1815 he removed to New York City, where he was for a few years engaged in the dry-goods business, but from about 1820 was a broker. Late in life he returned to Hartford, and died there on November 17, 1837, at the age of 48. His estate was insolvent

---

OTHNIEL WILLIAMS, son of David and Mindwell (Sage) Williams, of Kensington Society, in Berlin, Connecticut, and grandson of David and Mehetabel Williams, was born in January, 1787. His father removed to Whitestown, Oneida County, New York, in his childhood, and he was sent to the Hamilton Oneida Academy at Clinton, in the same county. In the fall of 1807, when his instructor, Seth Norton (Yale 1804), returned to Yale as tutor, he accompanied him, and was admitted to the Sophomore Class.

During the year after his graduation he remained in New Haven as College Butler. He then began the study of law with Judge Jonas Platt, of Whitestown, and during the year 1812–13 taught school in Bath, in Steuben County.

He was married in Killingworth, now Clinton, Connecticut, on November 4, 1813, to Mary (or Polly), eldest daughter of Deacon George Eliot, and sister of the Rev. Dr. John Elliott (Yale 1786)

Their eldest child was born in Killingworth, in November, 1814, and he removed shortly after to Waterville, in the township of Sangerfield, Oneida County, New York, where he opened a law-office in 1815

In 1820 he removed to Clinton in the same county, where the rest of his life was spent. In May, 1827, he was elected a member of the corporation of Hamilton College, in Clinton, and from August, 1828, to his death he served as their Treasurer At that period the prospects of the College were gloomy, and its finances embarrassed, and he became deeply interested and actively engaged in the efforts to promote its interests He was also prominent as a lawyer, was the librarian of the village Library, and an influential and honored citizen.

He died suddenly, after a brief illness, from typhus fever in Clinton, on December 7, 1832, in his 46th year. He was at that time the nominee of the Democratic party for the State Assembly, and died on the eve of the election He had recently moved into a large new house, which was not entirely completed, and which, surrounded by large grounds, is one of the landmarks of Clinton, and still occupied by his descendants.

His widow died in Clinton on October 9, 1858, in her 84th year.

Their children were one son and one daughter. The latter died unmarried. The son was graduated at Hamilton College in 1831, and succeeded his father in the office of Treasurer.

AUTHORITIES

Descendants of John Eliot, 2d ed, 77. *Mrs A G Hopkins,* MS Letters, May, 1911

Annals, 1810-11

At the opening of this college year Messrs Mills Day (Yale 1803), Araetius B. Hull (Yale 1807), and Matthew R. Dutton and Jonathan Knight (Yale 1808) entered on office as Tutors. The last named withdrew at the close of the year, as did also Tutor Edward Hooker (Yale 1805).

At Commencement, 1811, new Tutors were chosen, as follows:—Samuel Johnson Hitchcock, John Langdon, and Josiah Willard Gibbs, all of the Class of 1809.

To the great satisfaction of all the friends of the College, Colonel George Gibbs, of Newport, offered in 1810 to deposit here his rich and extensive cabinet of minerals.

Sketches, Class of 1811

*Georgius Baldwin *1826
*Rogerus Sherman Baldwin, A.M., LL.D. 1845 et Trin. 1844, Reip. Conn Gubern., Socius ex off, Rerumpubl. Foed. Sen. *1863
*Solomon Baldwin, A.M. *1816
*Milo Lyman Bennett, LL.D. Dartm. 1851, Reip. Viridim Cur. Supr. Jurid. *1868
*Abiel Kent Botsford *1844
**Ely Burchard* *1866
*Moses Chapin, A.M *1865
*Jacobus Clarke Cooke *1827
*Guilielmus Danielson, A.M. 1816, Tutor *1819
*Guilielmus Deming *1865
*Jonathan Eastman, A.M. *1830
**Radulphus Emerson,* A.M. 1816, S.T.D. 1830, Tutor, in Acad. Theol. Andov. Hist. Eccl. Prof. *1863
*Henricus Collins Flagg *1863
*Jonathan Foote *1846
*Alexander Forbus, A.M. *1856
**Guilielmus Ripley Gould,* A.M. Ohion. 1825 *1867
*Franciscus Granger, 1831, et A.M. 1831, e Congr., Rerumpubl. Foed Rei Vered. Curat. Summus *1868
*Ezra Haskell *1858
*Guilielmus Franklin Hodges, A.M 1821 *1837
*Henricus Guilielmus Huntington, 1814, A.M. 1814 *1854
**Leverett Israel Foote Huntington,* A.M. Neo-Caes. 1815 et Conc. 1815 *1820
*Solomon Lathrop, A.M. *1862
*Juda Lord, A M 1820 *1839
*Edvardus Carrington Mayo *1852

**David Meaubec Mitchell* *1869
*Levinus Monson, A.M 1818, Reip. Nov. Ebor. Cur. Supr. Jurid. *1859
*Sidneius Edwards Morse, A.M. *1871
**Samuel Nichols,* A M. Columb 1818, S.T.D Guil. 1880 *1880
*Samuel Bird Northrop, A.M. *1826
**Isaacus Parsons,* A.M 1816 *1868
*Edvardus Perot, A M 1861 *1866
*Samuel Shethar Phelps, A M. Mediob., Reip. Viridim. Cur Supr. Jurid., Rerump. Foed Sen. *1855
*Ephraimus Pease Prudden *1836
*Nathan Sherman Read, A.M. *1821
**Henricus Robinson,* A M 1817 et Bowd. 1817 *1878
*Edvardus Selden *1823
**David Marsh Smith,* A M. 1826 *1880
*Josephus Spencer *1823
**Samuel Spring,* 1821, et A M. 1821, S.T.D. Columb 1858 *1877
*Nathan Stark *1858
**Julius Steele* *1849
*Byam Kerby Stevens, A M. *1870
*Sela Brewster Strong, A M , e Congr., Reip. Nov. Ebor. Cur. Supr Jurid. *1872
*Fredericus Augustus Tallmadge, e Congr. *1869
*Johannes Thomas, 1814, A.M. 1814 *1866
**Josephus Vaill,* A.M , S T.D Amh 1851 *1869
*Elisaeus Dana Whittlesey, A.M. *1823
*Guilielmus Channing Woodbridge, A.M. *1845
*Josephus Emerson Worcester, A.M. et Harv. 1820, LL.D. Brun. 1847 et Dartm. 1856 *1865

GEORGE BALDWIN was a son of Samuel Wilkinson Baldwin, of Winchester, Connecticut, and grandson of David and Hannah (Canfield) Baldwin, of Litchfield His mother was Sabra Catlin, of Litchfield. The family had removed to Whitestown, Oneida County, New York, before he entered College in 1809.

After graduation he returned to Oneida County, where he followed the law. He settled in the village of Oneida Castle, in the township of Vernon. He was the first postmaster of the village, and active in his profession

He is believed to have died there in 1826.

AUTHORITIES

Baldwin Genealogy, ii, 538. *Boyd,* Oneida County, pt. 1, 570
Hist of Winchester, 236 *Wager,*

Roger Sherman Baldwin, the younger son of the Hon. Simeon Baldwin (Yale 1781), of New Haven, by his first wife, Rebecca, daughter of the Hon Roger Sherman, was born in New Haven on January 4, 1793. He was prepared for College at the Hopkins Grammar School under his cousin, Henry Sherman (Yale 1803). He delivered at graduation an Oration on the Genius of a Free Government.

After graduation he studied for a time in his father's office, and in 1812 entered the Litchfield Law School.

He was admitted to the New Haven bar in 1814, and, his father being now on the bench, began practice alone in this city.

On October 25, 1820, he was married to Emily, the youngest daughter of the Hon. Enoch Perkins, of Hartford, a classmate of his father's.

He early made good progress in his profession, and began to accumulate a library, which was notable for its strength in titles on the philosophy of law and on general legal topics It was characteristic of his special tastes that his eldest son was named for the recently deceased Chief-Justice of England, Lord Ellenborough.

He served as a member of the Common Council of the city in 1826, and as Alderman in 1828. In 1837 and 1838 he was elected to the State Senate, as a Whig

His hereditary antislavery sentiments had early been shown, and in 1839–40 the defense of the slaves who had revolted on the schooner "Amistad," and who were prosecuted for murder and piracy, gave occasion for the conspicuous exercise of his powers and established his reputation on a permanent basis.

In 1841 and 1842 he represented New Haven in the General Assembly In 1843 he was the unsuccessful candidate of his party for the governorship He was elected Governor in 1844, and again in 1845, and a number of important measures which he recommended to the Legislature during his term of office were favorably acted on.

In 1844 Trinity College conferred on him the honorary degree of Doctor of Laws, and Yale conferred the same degree in 1845

On the death of Senator Jabez W Huntington (Yale 1806) in November, 1847, he was appointed by Governor Clark Bissell (Yale 1806) to fill the vacancy in the United States Senate, and he was subsequently elected by the Legislature to serve for the remainder of the term (until March, 1851) His re-election for a second term was made impossible by the opposition of the Free Soil party, who held the balance of power in the General Assembly; and by his refusal, on principle, to pledge himself in advance to a definite course of action.

In 1860 he was a Presidential Elector and voted for Abraham Lincoln

His last public service was rendered in February, 1861, when he was sent by Connecticut as one of her delegation to the National Peace Convention at Washington He was placed upon the principal committee of that body,—that on resolutions, and he prepared the minority report of that Committee (signed by Massachusetts, Connecticut, New York, and Virginia), which recommended an application to Congress by the States for the calling of a convention for proposing amendments to the Federal Constitution.

On the expiration of his senatorial term he had resumed his professional practice; and it proved during his later years more lucrative than that of any other lawyer in the State. In a sketch of him prepared soon after his death a competent critic pronounced him the ablest lawyer that Connecticut had ever produced.

His health had always been good, but he died in New Haven, after a brief illness, on February 19, 1863, having recently entered on his 71st year. The address delivered at his funeral, by his pastor, the Rev. Dr. Samuel W. S. Dutton (Yale 1833), was afterwards published. An admirable sketch of his life and character by his youngest son is included in Lewis's *Great American Lawyers*

A portrait painted after his death is owned by the University. An engraving from a likeness taken in middle life is given in the *American Review* for October, 1849

Mrs Baldwin died in New Haven on July 29, 1874, in her 79th year.

Their children were six sons and three daughters. Two sons and a daughter died in infancy or early childhood. The remaining sons were graduated at Yale in 1842, 1847, 1853, and 1861, respectively. The eldest daughter married Professor William Dwight Whitney (Williams Coll 1845), of Yale, and the second married the Hon Dwight Foster (Yale 1848).

He published:

1 Considerations suggested by the establishment of a Second College in Connecticut Hartford, 1824 8°, pp. 36. [*Y. C.*

Anonymous, but supposed to have been written by Mr Baldwin. Replied to, also anonymously, by the Rev. Nathaniel S Wheaton (Yale 1814) Trinity College was chartered in 1823, after an acrimonious struggle, and this review of the situation was meant to be a dispassionate statement of the sentiment in Yale circles

2 An Examination of the "Remarks" on Considerations suggested by the establishment of a Second College in Connecticut Hartford, 1825 8°, pp 26. [*Y C*

An anonymous rejoinder to Mr. Wheaton

3 Argument, before the Supreme Court of the United States, in the case of the United States, Appellants, vs. Cinque, and others, Africans of the Amistad New York, 1841. 8°, pp 32.
[*A. A S B Publ Br. Mus. Harv. M. H. S. Y. C.*

4. Speech of His Excellency Roger S Baldwin, Governor of Connecticut, to the Legislature of the State, May, 1844 New Haven, 1844 8°, pp 23
[*B. Ath. Br Mus. M. H. S Y C.*

5. Speech .. to the Legislature of the State, May, 1845 Hartford, 1845 8°, pp 20 [*B Ath Br. Mus M H. S. Y. C.*

6 Message of the Governor, returning the Resolution on the petition of John J. Howe and others vs The Washington Bridge Co. with his objections Hartford, 1845. (House Doc. No. 14.) 8°, pp. 8

7. Speech on the bill to establish a Territorial Government in Oregon, delivered in the Senate of the United States, June 5, 1848 Washington, 1848 8°, pp 8 [*A A S Harv. Y. C.*

8 Speech on the territorial compromise bill. Delivered in the Senate of the United States, July 25, 1848 Washington, 1848 8°, pp 8 [*N Y. Publ*

9. Speech, at a Whig Meeting held at the Exchange Hall, in the City of New Haven, on the 8th of September, 1848. 8°, pp 8
[*Y. C.*

A speech in the Presidential campaign of 1848, in favor of General Taylor.

10 Speech in favor of the Admission of California into the Union, and on the Territorial bills, and the bill in relation to fugitive slaves, in connection with Mr. Bell's Compromise resolutions. Delivered in Senate of the United States, March 27 and April 3, 1850 Washington, 1850 8°, pp 20
[*A A S B Ath B Publ Harv. Y. C.*

11 Texas' Claim to New Mexico.—Speech in the Senate of the United States, Thursday, July 25, 1850, on the claim of Texas to New Mexico [Washington, 1850] 8°, pp. 8. [*B. Publ Y C*

12. Remarks on Mr Mason's Speech in the Senate of the United States, September 26, 1850 [Washington, 1850] 8°, pp 4

A defence of the part taken by Connecticut in the Revolution, and in the creation of her School Fund.

13. Opinion as to the liability of the New York and New Haven Railroad Co. for the Frauds of Robert Schuyler in issuing false certificates of stock. New York, 1856. 8°, pp 21.
[*N. H Col. Hist. Soc.*

14. Argument in the case of Pike vs. Potter, Rhode Island District, Circuit Court of the United States, Aug. 26, 1859: shorthand report. New Haven, 1857 [*sic*]. 8°, pp. 32.

AUTHORITIES

J. Q Adams, Diary, x, 359-60, 429-30 Baldwin Genealogy, i, 278, 285-86. Conn Reports, xxx, 609-13 *Dutton,* Address at Gov Baldwin's Funeral. Dwight Genealogy, ii, 1108. *Lewis,* Great American Lawyers, iii, 493-527. N H. Colony Hist. Society's Papers, iv, 339, 356-57, 363 N. Y Geneal. and Biogr. Record, xlii, 43 Perkins Family, pt 3, 40, 79-80. Prescott Memorial, 121-23, 172-74

SOLOMON BALDWIN, the youngest son of Thaddeus and Sarah Baldwin, of that part of New Milford, Connecticut, which is now included in Brookfield, and grandson of Caleb and Ann (Tibbals) Baldwin, of Newtown, was born on August 31, 1783.

While a student he was much interested in geology, and while exploring in the vicinity he discovered in the eastern part of Milford a vein of beautiful serpentine marble

After graduation he undertook the management of a company formed to prepare this marble for the market, but the enterprise was not a financial success.

He died in Brookfield on October 2, 1816, in his 34th year. This was the first death in the Class.

His wife, Betsey, survived him, with an infant daughter.

AUTHORITIES

Baldwin Genealogy, i, 344. *Lambert,* Hist of N. H. Colony

MILO LYMAN BENNETT, son of Captain Edmund Bennett, a blacksmith of Sharon, Connecticut, and a native of Columbia, formerly part of Lebanon, was born in Sharon on May 28, 1789. His mother was Mary, daughter of Charles Gillet, also a blacksmith of Sharon, and a native of Colchester, who was killed in Canada during the Revolution, and of his wife, Jerusha (Jewett) Gillet.

He was prepared for the Sophomore Class in Williams College by his pastor, the Rev David L Perry (Williams 1798), but after a very short stay there entered Yale.

After graduation he studied law, in part with Barzillai Slosson (Yale 1791) and Cyrus Swan, both of Sharon, and in part in the Litchfield Law School; and was admitted to the bar of Litchfield County in September, 1813

He then began practice in Bennington, Vermont, removing a year later to Manchester, some twenty miles northwards In 1821 and 1822, and again in 1833, he was State's Attorney for Bennington County, and from 1824 to 1828 he held the office of Judge of Probate

About 1836 he became largely interested in the development of some lumber lands in Maine, and removed thither to take charge of the business; the speculation proved, however, a disastrous failure, and in 1838 he returned to Vermont and settled in Burlington, where he resided for the rest of his life.

A few months after his return he was elected as an Associate Justice of the Supreme Court of the State, taking the place vacated by his classmate, Phelps. He held this office until 1849, and again from 1852 until October, 1859,—being in the interval Judge of the Circuit Court in 1850–51

The honorary degree of Doctor of Laws was conferred on him by Dartmouth College in 1851

In 1860 he was appointed on a commission to revise and compile the Statutes of the State, and this occupied him for two years.

After some three months of failing health, being left alone by his wife's death, he broke up his home and went to Taunton, Massachusetts, the residence of one of his sons, where he died on July 7, 1868, in his 80th year

Judge Bennett was a thoroughly read and able lawyer, a respected and influential citizen, a man of unblemished integrity, and an earnest Christian.

He served as a member of the Board of Trustees of Williams College from 1826 to 1837

One of his sons was graduated at the University of Vermont in 1843.

AUTHORITIES

Durfee, Biogr Annals of Williams College, 71. *Hemenway,* Vt. Gazetteer, 1, 471–72 Orcutt, Hist. of New Milford, 647 *Sedgwick,* Hist of Sharon, 2d ed, 112

ABIEL KENT BOTSFORD was born in Newtown, Connecticut, about 1791, and was prepared for College by Judge Asa Chapman (Yale 1792).

He studied law after graduation and began practice in Newtown, removing his office thence to Huntington about 1816.

About 1819 he is said to have given up the law, and to have removed to one of the Western States, where he was engaged in business.

He died about 1844.

ELY BURCHARD, the eldest child of Jonathan Birchard, of West Springfield, Massachusetts, and grandson of John and Anna (Barker) Burchard, of Norwich, Connecticut, was born in West Springfield on April 24, 1788. His mother was Beulah, third daughter of Nathan and Silence (Morgan) Ely, of West Springfield In 1798 his parents removed to Marshall, Oneida County, New York, and he was prepared for College at Hamilton Oneida Academy, in Clinton

After graduation he took charge for a time of the Academy in Onondaga. He then pursued theological studies under private direction, and was licensed to preach in 1817 by the Oneida Presbytery

In January, 1818, he began to supply the Presbyterian church in Augusta, Oneida County, and he was ordained and installed as their pastor on February 4, 1819, and labored there with acceptance and success. Fifty-eight persons were added to the church during his ministry

On April 4, 1821, he married Harriet, only child of General Henry and Margaret (Simmons) McNiel, of Paris Hill, Oneida County.

He was dismissed from the Augusta church on October 15, 1822, and for the most of the rest of his life was occupied in teaching in Paris and other places in that vicinity with preeminent success.

His wife died in Clinton, on May 30, 1845, aged 48 years; and he next married, on May 21, 1847, Sarah VanEpps, who also died before him

By his first marriage he had one son and three daughters

He died, after a brief illness, of pneumonia, in Clinton, at the residence of his son, on February 4, 1866, in his 78th year

He was remarkable for probity and promptness, industry and temperance, and retained his physical vigor unimpaired to the last.

Soon after leaving College he changed the spelling of his name from Birchard to Burchard, to conform to an early use.

AUTHORITIES

Descendants of N Ely, 67, 166. *P Jones,* Annals of Oneida County, 105

MOSES CHAPIN, the eldest son of Moses Augustus Chapin, a farmer, of West Springfield, Massachusetts, and grandson of Moses and Elizabeth (Dwight) Chapin, of Somers, Connecticut, was born in West Springfield on

May 2, 1791 His mother was Lucinda, second daughter of Seth and Mary (Dickinson) Graves, of Hatfield.

A brother was graduated here in 1817, and another at Amherst College in 1826. He was prepared for College by his pastor, the Rev. Dr. Joseph Lathrop (Yale 1754), and spent the first two years of his course at Williams College.

In 1812 he began the study of law with Augustine G Monroe, of Leesburg, Virginia, where he was at the time engaged in teaching. A year later he entered the Litchfield Law School, but after a few months went to Albany, New York, to continue his legal studies. When the Albany Academy was founded, in September, 1815, he consented to serve as Tutor for one year

He was licensed to practice in Albany in August, 1816, and in October settled in Rochester, then a village of six hundred inhabitants.

In September, 1818, he married Esther Maria, the third daughter of Dr. Levi and Mehitabel (Hand) Ward, of Rochester, who died on October 9, 1823, in her 25th year.

He united, on profession of faith, with the Presbyterian church in Rochester, in March, 1823, and held office as Ruling Elder in that church from July, 1824, until his death.

After service as a Justice of the Peace for two years, he was appointed the first Judge of Monroe County, and filled that office with ability and uprightness from February, 1826, to February, 1831, after which he devoted himself exclusively to the practice of his profession.

On October 31, 1826, he was married to Lucy Terry, eldest child of General William and Mary (Terry) Barton, of Hartford, Connecticut, and widow of Simeon Terry Kibbe (Yale 1815), of Canandaigua, who died in January, 1825.

After a long life of conspicuously faithful and conscientious service at the bar, in the church, and in private life, he suffered from a paralytic stroke early in 1864, and after a lingering illness died in Rochester, on October 8, 1865, in his 75th year. The discourse delivered at his funeral by the Rev Dr. Albert G. Hall was afterwards published

His wife survived him.

By his first wife he had two daughters, and a son (who died in infancy). The elder daughter married the Rev Dr. Eli Smith (Yale 1821), and the second daughter married the Rev. Darwin Chichester (Union Coll 1840). By his second marriage he had two sons and a daughter. The elder son was graduated at Yale in 1847, and the daughter married the Rev. Corydon W Higgins (Williams Coll 1849)

AUTHORITIES

Chapin Geneal, 46, 96–97 Dwight Genealogy, 1, 289–90, 349–51 *Hall,* Memorial of M Chapin. Hist of Monroe County, 1877, 138 *Kelsey,* Pioneers of Rochester, 80–82 *Munsell,* Annals of Albany, 1, 200. Terry Families, 78. Ward Family Genealogy, 141, 224.

JAMES CLARKE COOKE, son of Daniel B. Cooke (Yale 1788), of Danbury, Connecticut, was born about 1792, and was prepared for College by the Rev. Ammi R. Robbins (Yale 1760), of Norfolk.

He settled as a lawyer in Montgomery, Orange County, New York, where he died on February 20, 1827, aged 35 years.

His small estate (less than $800 in personal property) was administered by his brother, no wife or child surviving him.

WILLIAM DANIELSON, a son of General and Deacon James Danielson, of (West) Killingly, now Danielson, Connecticut, and a nephew of Samuel Danielson (Yale 1764), was born on January 20, 1790, and was prepared for College in the Plainfield Academy. His mother was Sarah Lord, of Abington Society in Pomfret.

He returned to Yale as Tutor in the fall of 1814, and held that office for three years.

He died in Killingly in July, 1819, in his 30th year. He was never married.

AUTHORITIES

C T Preston, MS Letters, December, 1911.

WILLIAM DEMING, the youngest son of Captain Julius Deming, of Litchfield, Connecticut, and grandson of David and Mehitable (Champion) Deming, of Lyme, was born in Litchfield on March 1, 1792 His mother was Dorothy, second daughter of Colonel Henry and Deborah (Brainard) Champion, of Westchester Society in Colchester, and first cousin of her husband. His eldest brother died while a Sophomore at Yale, in the Class of 1801. He was prepared for College, partly by the Rev. Joseph E. Camp (Yale 1787), of Northfield Society in Litchfield, and partly by James Morris (Yale 1775), at Litchfield South Farms, now Morris.

In 1816, in company with his two brothers he engaged in mercantile business in New York City, under the firm name of F & C Deming & Co. After about five years of successful experience the firm was dissolved, and he returned to Litchfield. His father being a wealthy man, for those days, he had abundant leisure to follow the sports of hunting and fishing, in which he was extraordinarily expert He also devoted much time to religious and political reading, being (as the result of his early training) an ultra-Calvinist in theology, and a believer in Calhoun's doctrine of state rights.

On April 29, 1830, he was married by the Rev Nathaniel S. Wheaton to Charlotte Tryon, daughter of Amos and Clarissa (Tryon) Bull, of Hartford For about a year after that date he resided in Hartford; but then returned to Litchfield, where the rest of his life was spent.

He died in Litchfield on May 2, 1865, in his 74th year. His widow died in Litchfield on June 16, 1886, at the age of 79.

Their children were three daughters and four sons The youngest son was graduated at Yale in 1872

AUTHORITIES

Deming Genealogy, 122, 223-24. Geneal Hist of Connecticut, ii, 938 *Payne*, Litchfield Inscriptions, 73. *Russell*, Hist of Christ Church, Hartford, ii, 247. *Trowbridge*, Champion Genealogy, 288, 303-04

JONATHAN EASTMAN, the third son of John Eastman, of Amherst, Massachusetts, and grandson of Joseph and Sarah (Ingraham) Eastman, of Amherst, was born on March 21, 1790. His mother was Hephzibah, daughter of John Keyes.

A brother was graduated at Yale in 1821, and another at Amherst College in 1835; and a sister married Henry Clary (Yale 1818) He was prepared for Williams College by the Rev. Dr. Joseph Lyman (Yale 1767), of Hatfield, and spent the first three years of his course there.

He studied law after graduation, and entered into practice in his native town.

In 1827 he removed to New York City, and was in practice there until his death, in that city, on September 7, 1830, in his 41st year.

He was never married.

AUTHORITIES

Judd, Hist. of Hadley, revised ed, pt. 2, 49 *Rix*, Eastman Genealogy, i, 189

RALPH EMERSON, the third son of Deacon and Captain Daniel Emerson, a leading citizen of Hollis, New Hampshire, and grandson of the Rev Daniel Emerson (Harvard

1739) and Hannah (Emerson) Emerson, was born in Hollis on August 18, 1787. Through his grandmother he was a second cousin of Ralph Waldo Emerson. His mother was Anna, daughter of Joseph and Elizabeth (Underwood) Fletcher, of Hollis Willis Hall (Yale 1824) and Daniel E. Hall (Yale 1834) were his nephews. He was prepared for College by Dr. Benjamin Burge (Harvard 1805), of Hollis At graduation he delivered the Valedictory Oration, on Energy of Character. He united with the church in his native place in the winter vacation of his Freshman year.

He spent the three years after graduation in the Andover Theological Seminary, and was then for two years a tutor at Yale.

In the spring of 1815 he began to preach in Norfolk, Connecticut, and on May 22 he was unanimously called to the pastorate of the Congregational church there, with a salary of seven hundred dollars. His engagements at College, however, prevented his acceptance at this time; but the church waited for him, and he was finally ordained and installed there on June 13, 1816, in the midst of a remarkable religious revival

On November 26, 1817, he was married to Eliza, daughter of Martin and Mary (Burrall) Rockwell, of the adjoining town of Colebrook, and sister of the Rev Charles Rockwell (Yale 1824).

Mr. Emerson's pastorate in Norfolk was remarkably happy and successful; and he enjoyed the full confidence and affection of a united people

In the early summer of 1828 he was invited to the presidency of Western Reserve College, in Hudson, Ohio; but in deference to the strong opposition of his parish, he dismissed the invitation

In September, 1829, however, he was called to the professorship of Ecclesiastical History in the Andover Theological Seminary, and he felt it his duty to accept the call, although his people remonstrated strongly. He was dismissed on November 24. During his pastorate he had admitted to the church 257 members. His duties at Andover included also those of a Lecturer on Pastoral Theology; and after 1842 he served as acting President of the Faculty

The honorary degree of Doctor of Divinity was conferred on him by Yale in 1830.

He was a diligent and thorough student, well equipped for his work, but very modest in its performance. Throughout his career he was eminent for discretion and cool judgment, as well as for kindness of heart and honesty of purpose

In April, 1854, he resigned his professorship, and for the next five years resided in Newburyport, supplying for part of the time the pulpit of the Fourth church.

In 1859 he removed to Rockford, Illinois, to be near his children. The only public work which he undertook after that date was the repetition, by request, of his lectures on the history of Christian doctrine to the students of the Chicago Theological Seminary.

After the gradual failure of his health for several months, he died in Rockford on May 26, 1863, in his 76th year, and was buried in Beloit, Wisconsin, the home of his second son. The discourse delivered at his funeral by his son-in-law, Dr. Haven, was published

His widow died in Rockford on December 11, 1875, in her 79th year.

Their children were six sons and three daughters. The eldest son was graduated at Western Reserve College in 1839, and three others at Yale, in 1841, 1844, and 1848, respectively The eldest daughter married Professor Joseph Haven (Amherst Coll 1835); the second married the Rev Simon J Humphrey (Bowdoin Coll 1848), and the youngest married the Rev William B. Brown (Oberlin Coll. 1841).

An engraving from his portrait is given in the *History of Hollis*, and is copied in Crissey's *History of Norfolk*

He published:

1. A Sermon [from Hebr xiii, 17], preached at Norfolk, Connecticut, May 16, 1816, the first Sabbath after his Ordination Hartford, 1817 8°, pp. 31.
[*A. C. A C H. S U. T S. Y C*

2. Faith, the guide and support of the believer.—A Sermon [from Hebr xi, 1]; delivered at Norfolk, September 30, 1829, at the Funeral of Mrs. Elizabeth Robbins, relict of Rev. Ammi R. Robbins Hartford, 1829. 8°, pp. 27 [*Y. C.*

3 A Farewell Discourse [from Joshua xxiv, 14] to his people, delivered at Norfolk, Conn, November 29, 1829 Hartford, 1829. 8°, pp. 23 [*A. C. A. C. H. S. Y. C*

4. Life of Rev. Joseph Emerson .. Boston, 1834 12°, pp. 454.
[*A C. A B Publ Harv U T. S. Y. C.*
A life of the author's brother.

5. Call and Qualifications for the Christian Ministry [Boston, American Tract Society, 1835.] 12°, pp 20 [*Y C.*

6 A Sermon [from Job vii, 16], delivered at Hollis, N H, at the Funeral of Rev Eli Smith, on Friday, May 14, 1847 Andover, 1847. 8°, pp. 20 [*A. C. A*

Of his contributions to periodicals, the following may be mentioned:

In the *American Journal of Science and Arts.* On the Divining Rod, with reference to the use made of it in exploring for Springs of water, vol 3, pp. 102–04 (February, 1821).

In the *National Preacher:* Sermon from Ps li, 4, on the Chief evil of sin, vol. 3, pp. 57–63 (September, 1828).

In the *Quarterly Christian Spectator* Review of Pitkin's Political and Civil History of the United States, vol. 1, pp 78–100, March, 1829, Review of Adam Clarke's Discourse, pp. 553–85, December, 1829.

On the Catechetical School, or Theological Seminary, at Alexandria in Egypt, vol. 4, pp. 1–61, 189–240, 617–62, January–October, 1834

In the *Biblical Repository:* Review of Coleman's Antiquities of the Christian Church, vol 6, 2d series, pp 212–27, July, 1841.

In the *Bibliotheca Sacra* The Early History of Monasticism,—from the original sources, vol 1, pp. 309–31, 464–525, 632–69, May–

Nov., 1844, Review of Chase's edition of the Apostolical Constitutions, vol. 5, pp 296–311, May, 1848; Review of Palfrey's History of New England, vol 18, pp. 178–206, January, 1861

He published the following translations from the German —

An historical presentation of Augustinism and Pelagianism from the original sources, by G. F. Wiggers —With notes and additions Andover, 1840 8°, pp. 383

In the *Biblical Repository* The Nature and Moral Influence of Heathenism, especially among the Greeks and Romans, viewed in the light of Christianity. By Augustus Tholuck, vol 2, pp 80–123, 246–90, 441–98, January–July, 1832; and republished in a volume of the *Biblical Cabinet,* Edinburgh, 1832; On the Origin and Commencement of the Reformation, from Planck's Protestant Theology, vols 9, pp. 332–58, 10, 104–41, 253–97, April–October, 1837.

In the *Bibliotheca Sacra* · Correspondence between Professor Voigt and the Bishop of Rochelle, vol 4, pp 540–52

He contributed to Sprague's *Annals of the American Pulpit* brief notices of the Rev. Dr Ebenezer Porter (Dartmouth Coll 1792) and the Rev. Salmon Giddings (Williams Coll 1811), in vols 2, pp 357–58, and 4, 509

AUTHORITIES

Bailey, Hist Sketches of Andover, 571–72 *Boyd,* Hist of Winchester, 369 *Crissey,* Hist of Norfolk, 150–51, 157, 163, 169–77 Emerson Family 149, 220–21 *Haven,* Discourse at Dr Emerson's Funeral N. Y. Observer, June 18, 1863 Norfolk Centennial, 1876, 12–16 *T Robbins,* Diary, i, 628–29, 644, 671, 703, 723; ii, 154, 158. Rockwell Family, 64, 169–70 *Worcester,* Hist of Hollis, 300

HENRY COLLINS FLAGG, the elder son of Dr Henry Collins Flagg, Surgeon-General of the Revolutionary army in the South, and grandson of Ebenezer and Mary (Ward) Flagg, of Newport, Rhode Island, was born in the parish of St. Thomas, a few miles north of Charleston, South Carolina, on January 5, 1792. His father died when he was nine years old. His mother was Rachel, daughter of John and Elizabeth (Vanderhorst) Moore, and widow of Captain William Allston, of Charleston Washington

Allston, the noted painter, was his half-brother. He was prepared for College by Robert Rogers (Brown Univ. 1775) in Newport.

Before the close of Senior year, on March 20, 1811, he married Martha, daughter of the late William Joseph Whiting (Yale 1780), of New Haven, although by so doing he ran the risk of losing his degree

After graduation he studied law in New Haven, with Seth P. Staples (Yale 1797), and then returned to Charleston, where he was admitted to the bar in May, 1814. A short experience, however, proved that the climate was unsuited to the health of his wife and children, and he fixed his residence accordingly in New Haven, where he was admitted to practice in June, 1815.

Early in 1817, being actively interested in politics as a Democrat, he retired from his profession to edit the *Connecticut Herald,* a weekly paper in New Haven which he had purchased. While thus engaged he reported for his paper, in an especially extended and graphic form, the proceedings of the State Constitutional Convention of 1818 He withdrew from the newspaper in September, 1819, and resumed practice. He was also Clerk of the County Court from 1821 to 1823.

About 1824 he returned to South Carolina, where he practiced law until 1833, when he again took up his residence in New Haven, for the education of his children He had courageously opposed nullification in 1832.

He continued in the practice of law until 1842 In June, 1834, he was elected Mayor of the city, and he retained that office for five years In 1835 he was also a member of the State Senate.

He was at one time nominated as Minister of the United States to Portugal, but failed of confirmation by the Senate.

His residence continued in New Haven until his death, in this city, on March 8, 1863, in his 72d year. He was buried with Masonic honors

Mayor Flagg was a graceful and eloquent public speaker, with a powerful voice and fluent utterance, and a ready and effective writer. His attachment to his native State was strong, but secondary to his devotion to the Union.

His widow died in New York City on July 22, 1875, aged 83½ years. Their children were five sons and two daughters, all of whom lived to mature years. The eldest son rose to the rank of Commander in the United States Navy. Three sons were distinguished as artists. Two sons entered the Episcopal ministry The younger daughter married Albert Mathews (Yale 1842), and was also the grandmother of Cornelius Vanderbilt (Yale 1895), Alfred G. Vanderbilt (Yale 1899), and Reginald C. Vanderbilt (Yale 1902)

He published·

1 An Oration delivered before the Harmony Society, in New-Haven, on the Fortieth Anniversary of American Independence. New-Haven, 1816 8°, pp 14 [*Y. C.*

2. An Oration on the Republican Celebration of the 44th Anniversary of American Independence New-Haven, 1820 8°, pp. 20 [*B Ath Harv*

3 Essays from the Counter of Jeremy Broadcloth, shop-keeper, Chapel-street, New-Haven

A series of witty, satirical articles, made up from his contributions to the *Connecticut Herald,* and reprinted in *Miscellanies selected from the Public Journals,* Boston, 1822, 12°, pp. 63–98 [*Y. C.*

AUTHORITIES

Connecticut Herald, July 29, 1817. Flagg Family Records, 122–23 New Haven City Year Book, 1864, 83–84

Jonathan Foote, the youngest son of Jonathan Foote, of Lee, Berkshire County, Massachusetts, and grandson of Jonathan and Sarah (Fenner) Foote, of Saybrook and Colchester, Connecticut, was born in Lee on February 11,

1788. His mother was Deliverance, daughter of Sylvanus Gibbs, of Sandwich, Massachusetts.

He settled on a farm in Windham, Portage County, Ohio, where he married Huldah, daughter of Edward Lyman.

He died in Windham on January 25, 1846, aged nearly 58 years.

AUTHORITIES

Goodwin, Foote Family, 104. Lee vol 1 (1907), 110 Vital Records, 43. Foote Family,

---

ALEXANDER FORBUS entered the Class in 1809 from Poughkeepsie, New York. He was born on February 23, 1790, the son of John Forbus, and was prepared for College at the Duchess County Academy in Poughkeepsie by the Rev. Cornelius Brower (Columbia Coll. 1792).

He studied law after graduation, and in 1814 began practice in Poughkeepsie, where he had a prominent and highly respectable career.

In 1834 he was elected President of the Board of Trustees of the village of Poughkeepsie By preference he avoided public appearance as a jury lawyer, but was in the first rank as a business attorney and counsellor. He was also actively interested in the promotion of public enterprises.

He died in Poughkeepsie on June 19, 1856, in his 67th year.

He was never married.

AUTHORITIES

Miss H. W Reynolds, MS Letter, January, 1912

WILLIAM RIPLEY GOULD, the youngest son of Lieutenant David Gould, of Sharon, Litchfield County, Connecticut, and grandson of Job and Sarah (Prindle) Gould, of Sharon, was born on May 27, 1789 His mother was

Mary, youngest daughter of Captain James and Faith (Ripley) Brewster, of Scotland Parish, in Windham, and Sharon. His eldest brother was graduated at Williams College in 1797. He was prepared for College by the Rev. Daniel Parker (Yale 1798), of Ellsworth Society, in Sharon, and spent the first two years of the course at Williams

After graduation he entered the Andover Theological Seminary, where he finished the course in September, 1814, and on the 14th of the next month he was ordained by the Hartford North Consociation at Enfield as an evangelist, to labor in Ohio for a year, under the direction of the Connecticut Missionary Society.

Before the year had passed, he was invited to settle permanently in Gallipolis, on the southern border of the State That neighborhood had been colonized by French Catholics, who were then without a priest; and the result was, that Mr Gould became the founder of Protestant worship over a wide region. He was installed in Gallipolis on May 30, 1816

After a ministry (in connection with the Presbyterian Church) of over eleven years, he returned to Connecticut, and was installed on February 28, 1827, as pastor of the Congregational church in Torrington, in his native county

He was dismissed from this charge on February 12, 1832, and on September 25 was installed over the Congregational church in Barkhamsted, in the same county

Leaving Barkhamsted early in 1838, he was recalled in 1839 to the church which he had organized in Gallipolis, where he spent the next seven years in further pastoral service

In 1846 he left Ohio, and after that held no charge, but resided mainly with his son-in-law, the Rev. Dr. Matthew K. Meigs (Union Coll. 1836), the founder of the Hill School for Boys, in Pottstown, Pennsylvania.

He died in Pottstown, after a long illness, on July 2, 1867, in his 79th year.

He was married, on September 18, 1815, by the Rev. Ira Hart (Yale 1797), to Eunice, eldest child of Oliver and Rebecca (Swan) York, of Stonington, Connecticut.

AUTHORITIES

Orcutt, Hist of Torrington, 39 Gould Family, 351. Brewster Genealogy, 1, 189. *Wheeler,* Hist of Stonington, 702, First Church of Stonington, 273 Barkhamsted Centennial, 56, 136 N. Y. Observer, July 11, 1867.

Francis Granger, the second son of the Hon. Gideon Granger (Yale 1787), was born in Suffield, Connecticut, on December 1, 1792. From 1801 to 1814 his father held the office of Postmaster-General of the United States, and the family residence was in Washington. In College he was indolent and mischievous, but quick-minded and promising.

In 1814 his father removed to Central New York

In the meantime Francis Granger had studied law, and he began practice in Canandaigua, New York, where his family had finally settled

He soon manifested, however, a marked preference for political life, and in 1825 he was chosen as a representative from Ontario County in the State Assembly. He was re-elected in 1826, and in 1828 received the nomination of the Anti-Masonic party for Governor, as well as the nomination for Lieutenant-Governor on the Adams ticket. He accepted the latter offer, but was defeated by the adherents of Van Buren. In 1829 he went back to the Assembly, and in 1830 was the candidate of the Anti-Masons for the governorship, but was defeated by a small Democratic majority. In 1831 he was for a fourth time returned to the Assembly; and in 1832 he was again supported for the Governorship by the Anti-Masons and the National Republicans, but was more decidedly defeated by the Jackson party.

When the Whig party was organized in 1834 he became one of its recognized leaders, but was defeated on the nomination for the governorship by William H. Seward Later in the same year he was nominated and elected to Congress, and he continued in that office for seven years.

In 1836 he was the candidate of the Anti-Masons and of the Whig ticket put forward by Massachusetts for the Vice Presidency No choice having been made, the election was thrown into the Senate, which voted for Colonel Richard M. Johnson.

He resigned his place in Congress on March 3, 1841, in view of his nomination to the position of Postmaster-General in President Harrison's cabinet. He was confirmed by the Senate on March 6, after some hesitation on account of his anti-slavery views; and remained at his post until the rupture of the cabinet in September, 1841, caused by President Tyler's peculiarly vacillating course.

On his return home he was re-elected to Congress, to fill a vacancy, and took his seat in December, but at the expiration of his term (in March, 1843) retired definitely to private life.

He had not only declined a re-nomination for Congress, but also the offer of a foreign mission; and henceforth only rarely consented to appear on public occasions. On one such occasion, in 1850, his "silver-gray" hair helped to give a name to a party which originated at a convention of which he was the chairman

In February, 1861, he consented to go to Washington, by appointment of Governor Morgan, as a member of the Peace Convention

His health began to fail seriously in 1863, and he died in Canandaigua on August 28, 1868, in his 76th year.

A copy of his portrait is given in the *Granger Genealogy*.

He married on May 20, 1817, Cornelia Rutsen, daughter of Jeremiah and Sybilla Adeline (Kane) Van Rensselaer, of Utica, who died in 1823

Their children were one daughter, who was twice married, her second husband being the Hon. Robert C Winthrop (Harvard 1828), and one son (Yale 1843), who died the week after his father.

Mr. Granger was remarkably prepossessing in appearance, with manners both dignified and popular, and a singularly happy temperament He was a fluent and easy speaker, of quick wit, abundant tact, and intellectual cleverness

---

AUTHORITIES

J Q Adams, Diary, viii, 326; ix, 114, 170–71; x, 434; xi, 16, 32 *G Allen*, Reminiscences, 50–51 Granger Genealogy, 182, 301–05 *Hammond*, Polit. Hist. of N Y., ii, 284–86, 334–37, 417, 424 *Holgate*, Amer Genealogy, 44 *Hone*, Diary, ii, 90–91 *W H Seward*, Autobiography, 70–71, 156, 171–72, 344–45, 349, 363–64, 366, 373, 516

Ezra Haskell was born in New Gloucester, about twenty miles north of Portland, Maine, on March 12, 1781 He was brought up as a farmer, but prepared himself for College, and earned enough money to meet his expenses He had joined the church in Hallowell in March, 1803 In 1808 he joined the Sophomore Class in Bowdoin College, and in 1809 the Junior Class in Yale. He was the oldest of his classmates at graduation.

He spent most of his life as a teacher, making at the same time a special study of theology

From 1818 to 1828 he was teaching in Boston, where he was connected with the Park Street and Essex Street Congregational churches. He was also specially active in the work of the Howard Benevolent Society, devoting himself to visiting in the prison and teaching there on Sundays.

In 1840 he settled in Dover, New Hampshire, where he died on March 27, 1858, aged 77 years

His wife, Mrs. Emily Haskell, was still living at his removal to Dover.

A son was graduated at Yale in 1849, but died just after he had entered on the profession of the ministry. Two other sons also became ministers

AUTHORITIES

Dover Hist Collections, 1, 232 Puritan Recorder, April 15, 1858

WILLIAM FRANKLIN HODGES, the third son of Dr. Elkanah Hodges, of Woodstock and Torrington, Connecticut, and grandson of George and Susannah Hodges, of Norton, Massachusetts, and Woodstock, was born in Torrington, on August 24, 1789. His mother was Rebecca, third daughter of Deacon John and Sarah (Foster) Whiting, of Torrington His father died in March, 1797, and he was prepared for College by the Rev Ammi R Robbins (Yale 1760), of Norfolk.

He studied law after graduation, and settled in practice in Mobile, Alabama, where he died, unmarried, on October 10, 1837, in his 49th year.

AUTHORITIES

Hodges Family, 150 *Orcutt,* Hist. of Torrington, 160–61, 717.

HENRY WILLIAM HUNTINGTON, the eldest child of the Hon Hezekiah Huntington, a distinguished lawyer of Suffield, Connecticut, and grandson of John and Mehetabel (Steele) Huntington, of Tolland, was born in Suffield on August 16, 1789. His mother was Susannah, daughter of Elihu and Susannah (Lyman) Kent, of Suffield A brother was graduated here in 1818. He was prepared for College by his pastor, the Rev Ebenezer Gay (Yale 1787). During the first three years of his College life he wrote his name William Henry Huntington

He studied law after graduation, and in 1816 was admitted to the bar in Hartford, but practiced there for only a few months.

He settled in Trinity, Catahoula Parish, Louisiana, about twenty-five miles west of Natchez, where he became a planter.

He died in Trinity on October 12, 1854, in his 66th year.

He married, on April 24, 1817, Helen, daughter of the late William Dunbar, of Natchez, by whom he had six daughters and four sons.

AUTHORITIES

Huntington Family Memoir, 239, 317

LEVERETT ISRAEL FOOTE HUNTINGTON, the younger son of the Rev. David Huntington (Dartmouth Coll. 1773), of Marlborough, Connecticut, and grandson of John and Mehitabel (Metcalf) Huntington, of Lebanon, was born in Marlborough on December 28, 1787 His mother was Elizabeth, eldest daughter of Israel and Elizabeth (Kimberly) Foote, of Colchester.

His father removed in 1797 from Marlborough to Middletown, and thence in 1803 to Hamburg Society in North Lyme. He was prepared for College in New York City, in the school conducted by Enoch Ely (Yale 1792), a native of North Lyme.

When Princeton Theological Seminary was opened for instruction in August, 1812, Mr Huntington was one of the first students. He completed the course there in 1815

On October 16, 1815, he was married to Phebe, second daughter of Joseph and Phebe (Sterling) Marvin, of North Lyme, and on the 6th of the following December he was ordained and installed by the Presbytery of New Brunswick as pastor of the First Presbyterian Church in New Brunswick, New Jersey, where he remained, laboring unweariedly in his profession, until his death there on May 11, 1820, in his 33d year.

He was distinguished for his equable and serene temper, his frankness and candor, and the warmth and permanency of his attachments. He was a diligent pastor and a zealous and fervent preacher

His children were a daughter and a son (Jefferson Coll, Pa., 1836).

Mrs Huntington next married, in October, 1839, the Rev. Urban Palmer, of Ohio, who died in 1847, and whom she long survived

AUTHORITIES

Christian Herald, vii, 192 *Goodwin*, Foote Family, 80 Huntington Family Memoir, 190, 279 Marvin Family, 99 *Salisbury*, Family Histories and Genealogies, iii, 169 *Walworth*, Hyde Genealogy, ii, 803

Solomon Lathrop, the elder son of Dr Seth Lathrop, of West Springfield, Massachusetts, and grandson of the Rev. Dr. Joseph Lathrop (Yale 1754), of West Springfield, was born on May 11, 1790. His mother was Anne, youngest daughter of Captain Abiel and Abigail (Fenton) Abbot, of Hampton, Connecticut. His only sister married the Rev. Elisha D Andrews (Yale 1803).

He was prepared for College by his grandfather, and spent the first two years of his course at Williams College.

After graduation he studied law with his uncle, Samuel Lathrop (Yale 1792), and settled on the family estate in West Springfield, in practice with his uncle

On March 31, 1820, he was married to Sophia, daughter of Willard and Catharine (Smith) Pomeroy, of Newfane, Windham County, Vermont.

In 1836 he removed to Michigan, settling in Oakwood, Oakland County, about forty miles northwest of Detroit. Subsequently he bought a large farm in Armada, Macomb County, but returned to Oakwood, where he died, on December 11, 1862, in his 73d year.

His wife died in Oakwood on November 15, 1853

Their children were four sons and three daughters, all of whom lived to maturity, besides two daughters who died early. The two eldest sons became physicians

Mr. Lathrop was active in organizing a Congregational church in Oakwood, of which he was for many years the senior Deacon

AUTHORITIES

Abbot Genealogical Register, 54
Dwight Genealogy, ii, 774, 776-77.
Huntington, Lathrop Family Memoir, 184, 261-62.

Judah Lord came to College from Lyme, Connecticut, having been prepared by the Rev. Joseph Vaill (Dartmouth Coll. 1778), of Hadlyme Parish, in East Haddam and Lyme.

He died in the West Indies in 1839, aged about 47 years, while engaged with a mining company in Porto Rico.

Edward Carrington Mayo was born in 1789, the only son of John Mayo, Jr., of Richmond, Virginia, a member of the Council of State in 1798, and the builder and owner of Mayo's Bridge, across the James River, which was for many years the only means of transportation between the North and South, and grandson of John and Mary (Tabb) Mayo. His mother was Abigail, daughter of the Hon John and Sarah (Dagworthy) De Hart, of Elizabethtown, New Jersey. A sister married General Winfield Scott.

He entered Yale at the opening of Junior year

After graduation he studied law, and was at first inclined to enter political life, but was deterred by the growing pressure of business and family cares. He married on March 10, 1829, Adeline, daughter of Joseph Marx, a wealthy cotton merchant of Richmond, and Richea (Myers) Marx, and granddaughter of Dr. Jacob Marx, physician to the Elector of Hanover, Germany

He died in Richmond on June 5, 1852, at the age of 63 Mrs. Mayo died in Richmond on January 18, 1879, in her 71st year. A son was graduated at Yale in 1852, and two grandsons (Howard and Edward C. Mayo Richards) at the Sheffield Scientific School in 1900 and 1909, respectively

Mr. Mayo was a man of unblemished character, and strong mentally and physically in proportion to the six feet and two inches of his height. He was cultivated and accomplished, a great reader, a celebrated chess player, and distinguished by his genial manners and dignified bearing He was eminently kind-hearted and hospitable in private life, and a devoted member of the Episcopal church.

AUTHORITIES

Mrs Harriet M Richards, MS Letter, December, 1911

DAVID MEAUBEC MITCHELL, the second son of Dr Ammi Ruhamah Mitchell, of North Yarmouth, now Yarmouth, Maine, and grandson of Judge David Mitchell, of North Yarmouth, was born in North Yarmouth on May 9, 1788 His mother was Phebe, youngest daughter of Captain William and Mehitable (Gray) Cutter, of Portsmouth, New Hampshire He received his middle name in memory of his father's indebtedness to an eminent French surgeon, Dr Meaubec, who had befriended him in his student days in Paris. He joined the church at his home shortly before coming to Yale.

He was prepared for College by Daniel Haskel (Yale 1802) in the Lincoln Academy, at Newcastle, Maine, and his scholarship was such as to entitle him to the Salutatory Oration at graduation.

He then spent three years in the Andover Theological Seminary, although greatly hindered by weak eyes. After graduating there he labored for a year or more in the service of the Maine Missionary Society, and then accepted an earnest and repeated invitation from the church and town of Waldoboro to settle with them in the ministry. The precarious condition of his health rendered it a grave question whether ordination was expedient; but a council proceeded to install him, on June 19, 1816, and for twenty-six years he labored there indefatigably.

At the time of his settlement Waldoboro was a frontier station, and the parish had an area of eight by sixteen miles, the church numbered not more than twenty members, and they had no meeting-house But a commodious house of worship was soon provided, in which ordinarily a large congregation gathered; and more than two hundred additions were made to the church under his leadership To the close of his pastorate he retained the unabated respect and implicit confidence of his people.

He married on August 26, 1816, Rebecca, daughter of P. Elwell, of Waldoboro, and after her death married, secondly, on March 14, 1821, Melinda, sixth daughter of General and Deacon John and Sarah (Wheeler) Crosby, of Hampden, Maine, and sister of the Rev. Daniel Crosby (Yale 1823).

His children were four sons and five daughters.

After the loss of several children by consumption, and with other losses threatening, he felt obliged to take a dismission, on June 14, 1842, for a drier climate.

He then spent three years in Andover, Massachusetts. From May, 1845, to November, 1852, he preached as stated supply at Cape Elizabeth, Maine, serving also during that period with much acceptance as City Missionary in Portland. In 1852, he undertook a similar work for the city mission connected with the Eliot Congregational church in Roxbury, Massachusetts, where he labored until January, 1861, preaching once every Sunday until February, 1859.

From Roxbury he went to reside with a son-in-law, the Rev Elnathan E Strong (Dartmouth Coll 1852), in South Natick until 1865, and then in Waltham, where he died on November 27, 1869, aged 81½ years. The Address given at his funeral, by the Rev. Dr. Augustus C Thompson, was afterwards published.

His eldest son was graduated at Bowdoin College in 1837, and died while in the Princeton Theological Seminary; another son was graduated at Bowdoin in 1849, and entered the ministry Two daughters and one son survived him.

He prepared a history of the church in Waldoboro, which is preserved in manuscript in its archives.

From 1816 to 1825, and again from 1827 to 1838, he was a member of the Board of Trustees of the Bangor Theological Seminary

AUTHORITIES

Congregational Quarterly, xv, 311 Cutter Family, 175-76 Maine General Conference Minutes, 1870, 30-31. *A. C Thompson,* Address at Mr. Mitchell's Funeral

---

LEVINUS MONSON, the eldest child of Joshua Munson, a farmer of Hamden, Connecticut, and grandson of Captain Jabez and Eunice (Atwater) Munson, of Hamden, was born on May 5, 1791. His mother was Sarah, daughter of Jonathan Booth, of Hamden. In his infancy the family removed to Canaan, in Litchfield County, whence he entered College in 1809

After graduation he studied law with the Hon Samuel Sherwood, of Delhi, Delaware County, New York. In 1815 he was admitted to the bar, and settled in the village of Hobart, in Stamford township, in the same county, where he resided until his death, excepting a short period (about 1845) in Newburgh

He married on March 23, 1836, Mary Parish, of Roxbury, in Delaware County.

In January, 1850, he was appointed a Justice of the Supreme Court of the State, to fill a vacancy, for the term ending in June, 1855.

He died in Hobart on September 23, 1859, in his 69th year

His widow died at the house of a son-in-law in New York City on May 3, 1883.

Their children were four daughters, of whom the second married Jonathan Sturges Ely (Yale 1845).

Judge Monson was a devoted member of the Episcopal church. As a judge he was upright, candid, and impartial

AUTHORITIES

Munson Record, ii, 959, 966.

SIDNEY EDWARD MORSE, the second son of the Rev. Dr Jedidiah Morse (Yale 1783), was born in Charlestown, Massachusetts, on February 7, 1794 In 1805, when only eleven and a half years old, he was admitted to Yale, and his name was enrolled in the Freshman Class, but he withdrew at once, and spent some of the time before his actual entrance, in Phillips Academy, Andover, under the tuition of Mark Newman (Dartmouth Coll. 1793) He was at graduation the youngest member of his Class.

He took up, on leaving College, the study of law in the Litchfield Law School, and meantime was led into journalism A series of striking articles which he contributed in 1812–13 to the *Columbian Centinel,* the leading Boston Federalist paper, attracted the attention of some of his father's friends, and led to his being invited to become the first editor of the *Boston Recorder,* which was founded in January, 1816, and which has been said to be the oldest religious newspaper in the world

His connection with the *Recorder* was, however, terminated in a little over a year, and he subsequently spent over two years, in 1817–20, in the Andover Theological Seminary.

In 1817 he was also associated with his elder brother, Samuel F B. Morse (Yale 1810), in patenting a flexible piston-pump, which was their joint invention

In 1823, in connection with his younger brother, Richard C. Morse (Yale 1812), he founded in New York City the *New York Observer,* of which he continued to be the senior editor and proprietor, until his retirement to private life in 1858

In 1839 he invented a method of printing maps in color on the common printing-press, which he called cerography, and used in his own publications, but never patented.

The last years of his life were devoted to experiments with a new bathometer for the rapid measurement of the depths of the sea, without the use of a line

He died of paralysis, at his residence in New York City, on December 23, 1871, in his 78th year.

He was married, on April 1, 1841, to Catharine, eldest child of the Rev Dr Gilbert Robert Livingston (Union Coll. 1805), of Philadelphia, who survived him, with one son and one daughter

His cast of mind was preeminently mathematical and statistical, and he enjoyed the pursuit of calculations which exercised these faculties. Of a particularly even temperament, his purity and integrity of character were always strikingly manifest.

He published:

1 The New States, or a comparison of the wealth, strength, and population of the Northern and Southern States; also their respective powers in Congress; with a view to expose the injustice of erecting new States at the South.—By Massachusetts Boston, 1813 8°, pp 36 [*B. Ath. Y C*

A reprint of twelve articles in the *Columbian Centinel,* 1812–13

2. Remarks on the controversy between Doctor Morse and Miss Adams, together with some notice of the Review of Dr, Morse's Appeal Boston, 1814 8°, pp. 33
[*B. Ath. B. Publ. M. H S. Y C*

The same Second edition, with additions. Boston, 1814 8°, pp 35 [*B. Publ Y C.*

Anonymous.

3 A new system of Modern Geography, or a view of the present state of the World With an Appendix, containing statistical tables of the population, commerce, revenue, expenditure, debt, and various institutions of the United States; and general views of Europe and the World. Accompanied with an Atlas New Haven, 1822. 8°, pp 676. Atlas, 8°, 20 maps
[*B. Ath. B. Publ. Br. Mus. Harv U. S. Y. C.*

4 An Atlas of the United States. New-Haven, 1823. 4°, pp. 24. [*B Ath.*

5 A geographical view of Greece, and an Historical Sketch of the recent Revolution in that country. Accompanied with a Map. [New Haven, 1825.] 12°, pp. 24 + map.
[*B Ath B. Publ. Br. Mus. M. H. S. U. S. Y. C.*

6 North American Atlas. New-York, 1842. Fol. 36 maps.
[*B. Ath. B Publ.*

7. The Cerographic Atlas of the United States. New York, 1842–45. Fol. 42 maps. [*B. Publ.*
In conjunction with his elder brother. A supplement to the *New-York Observer.*

8 A System of Geography, for the use of Schools. Illustrated with . . maps, and woodcut engravings. New-York, 1844. 4°, pp. 72 + maps and plates. [*B. Publ.*
Several editions.

9. Letter on American Slavery. Addressed to the Editor of the "Edinburgh Witness," 8th July, 1846. By an American. From the Edinburgh Edition, Revised and Corrected by the Author New-York, 1847 8°, pp 8.
[*A. C A B. Ath. B. Publ. Y. C.*
Signed, S E M

10. The Bible and Slavery From the New York Observer, October 4, 1855. 8°, pp. 8 [*B. Publ. M H. S.*

11. The Madness of the Hour. [From the New York Observer of the 12th June, 1856] 8°, pp. 4. [*Y. C.*
In denunciation of an anti-slavery speech by the Hon. William M. Evarts.

26

12. Premium Questions on Slavery, each admitting of a yes or no answer; addressed to the editors of the New York Independent and New York Evangelist New York, 1860. 8°, pp 30.
[*A. C. A. B. Ath. B. Publ. Br Mus Harv M H. S. Y. C.*

13 A geographical, statistical and ethical view of the American Slaveholders' Rebellion Illustrated with a cerographic map. New York, 1863 8°, pp. 19 + map
[*B. Ath B Publ Br Mus Y C.*

14. Memorabilia in the life of Jedidiah Morse, D.D .. Boston, 1867 12°, pp 24 + pl
[*A. C. A. B Publ. M. H. S U S. Y C*

From a volume published in commemoration of the founding of a Sunday-school in Charlestown, in 1816, of which Mr. Morse was one of the first teachers

AUTHORITIES

G. Livingston Morse, MS Letter, June, 1872 *Prime,* Life of S F. B. Morse, 9–11

SAMUEL NICHOLS, the son of Ephraim and Miriam (Bradley) Nichols, natives of Greenfield Hill, in Fairfield, Connecticut, was born in Greenfield Hill, on November 14, 1787. He received his preparation for College from the Rev. Horace Holley (Yale 1803), of Greenfield Hill, and at the Academy in Easton, and entered the Sophomore Class in the summer of 1809.

After graduation he studied for the ministry of the Protestant Episcopal Church, under the direction of the Rev. Timothy Clowes (Columbia Coll. 1808), of Albany, and was subsequently appointed by the wardens and vestry of Trinity church, New York, assistant in the academy in Fairfield, Herkimer County, where he remained for four years.

In the meantime he was married, on March 27, 1816, to Susan N., daughter of George James Warner, a wealthy merchant of New York City, and on June 1, 1817, he was ordained deacon by Bishop Hobart in New York City.

After a brief interval of residence in Connecticut, he was called in 1819 to the rectorship of St. Matthew's church, in Bedford, Westchester County, New York, and on March 10, 1820, was advanced to the priesthood by Bishop Hobart.

He retained this rectorship, with earnest devotion to the interests of his people, until obliged by failing health to resign in 1838.

He then retired to the place of his birth, where the rest of his life was spent, amid the universal esteem of the community.

His wife died on March 22, 1872, in her 74th year.

His own death occurred in Greenfield Hill, on July 17, 1880, in his 93d year, when he was the oldest living presbyter of the American Episcopal church, and the last survivor of his Class. The addresses made at his funeral were printed, in connection with those in commemoration of the Rev. Dr. Edward Livingston Wells, who took part in those services and died three weeks later.

The honorary degree of Doctor of Divinity had been conferred on Mr. Nichols by Williams College just before his death.

His seven sons and two daughters survived him,—the two eldest sons having graduated at Yale in 1835 and 1841, respectively.

After his death was published from his manuscripts:

Sermons. Edited by Rev. Sylvester Clarke. New York, 1882. 8°, pp. 396 + pl. [*Y. C.*

Containing 28 sermons, with a portrait of the author.

AUTHORITIES.

In Memoriam, Rev. Dr. Nichols.

Samuel Bird Northrop, son of Dr. Joel Northrop (Yale 1776), of New Haven, was born in New Haven in 1785, and was named for his maternal grandfather, the

Rev. Samuel Bird, of New Haven, who died in 1784. He was prepared for College at the Hopkins Grammar School, under Henry Sherman (Yale 1803).

In April, 1813, he received a commission in the United States Army as Captain of the 37th regiment of infantry, and was discharged from the service in June, 1815.

He married Ann Viola, daughter of James Wyatt, in Charleston, South Carolina, and resided there until the latter part of his life; but died in Waterbury, Connecticut, of dropsy in the chest, on October 12, 1826, aged 41 years. He is buried in New Haven.

His wife survived him, without children.

AUTHORITIES.

Anderson, Hist. of Waterbury, i, Appendix, 160 *Heitman,* Hist. Register of U S. Army, i, 751. New Haven Colony Hist Society's Papers, i, 117-18.

Isaac Parsons, the youngest child but one of Isaac Parsons, a farmer of Southampton, Massachusetts, and a nephew of the Rev. Elijah Parsons (Yale 1768), of East Haddam, Connecticut, was born in Southampton on August 28, 1790. His mother was Mindwell Kingsley, a native of Northampton. His preparation for College was completed under the Rev. Moses Hallock (Yale 1788), of Plainfield, and he entered Williams College in 1806. At the end of Sophomore year he took a dismission, and after a winter of private study he joined the Sophomore Class here at the beginning of the last term.

After graduation he held for a year the position of principal of the Hopkins Grammar School in Hartford, and then entered the Andover Theological Seminary, where he finished the course in 1815. He remained there until the next spring as a resident licentiate; and then, after having preached for two months during the illness of the pastor in Northampton, he was earnestly solicited by his uncle to appear before his people in East Haddam as a candidate.

The result was that he was called to be a colleague of his uncle, and was ordained and installed in that relation on October 23, 1816.

On January 21, 1819, he was married by President Dwight to Sarah Budd, the second daughter of Underhill and Mary (Halsted) Lyon, of Rye, New York, whose widowed mother had removed to New Haven in 1811 for the education of her children.

The senior pastor of the East Haddam church died in January, 1827; and Mr. Parsons continued in full service until April 23, 1856, when he retired by mutual consent. His residence remained in East Haddam, and he performed occasional ministerial labor in the vicinity as opportunity offered, as long as his strength allowed. He died in East Haddam on August 22, 1868, at the age of 78. The sermon preached at his funeral by his classmate, the Rev. Dr. Vaill, was afterwards published.

His widow died suddenly in Charlton, Massachusetts, at the house of her elder surviving daughter, after two or three years of enfeeblement from partial paralysis, on January 14, 1873, in her 83d year.

Of their children, four grew to maturity. The only son was graduated at Yale in 1848.

Mr. Parsons's career as a minister was dignified and crowned with success. Eight seasons of special religious revival were enjoyed by his church, and he admitted 449 persons to membership. He was an able preacher, and in sympathy with the older school of theology. He was a Trustee of the Theological Institute at East Windsor from 1837 to 1853. During his early ministry he had a succession of pupils in his own house.

An engraving from his portrait is given in the *Congregational Quarterly* for October, 1870

He published:

1 A Sermon [from Isa. lv, 8–9], occasioned by the death of Mrs. Carile Mary Whitmore, wife of the Rev Zolva Whitmore, who died at North-Guilford; preached at East-Haddam, on the following Lord's Day, Sept 29th, 1822. .. Middletown, 1822 8°, pp 23 [*A C. A Harv. U S U. T. S. Y. C*

2. A Sermon [from Ps. xcvii, 2], preached at Middle-Haddam, on the 20th of January, 1825, at the funeral of the Rev. David Selden. Middletown, 1825. 8°, pp. 24.
[*A C. A. U. T S. Y. C*

3. Memoir of Susannah Elizabeth Bingham, of East Haddam, Conn American Sunday School Union, Philadelphia. [1836.] 18°, pp. 90

4. Memoir of Amelia S Chapman American Tract Society, New York [1837?] 12°, pp 36 [*U T S.*

5. A Thanksgiving Sermon [from Mark xii, 17], preached at East Haddam, Conn, November 30th, 1837 . Hartford, 1838 8°, pp 16. [*A. C A. C. H. S*

6 Memoir of the life and character of Rev Joseph Vaill, late pastor of the church in Hadlyme New York, 1839 12°, pp 236 + pl
[*A A S A C A B Publ. U. S. U. T. S Y C*

7 A Retrospect—Two Sermons [from Zech i, 5], preached on Lord's Day, October 24, 1841, on occasion of the close of the quarter of a century in his ministry.—With an Appendix Hartford, 1841 8°, pp 32
[*A A S. A C A. B. Publ Br Mus. U. T S. Y. C.*

8. The faithfulness of God to his people who honor him in the worship of his house—A Sermon [from Mal. iii, 10], preached on Lord's Day, January 4th, 1846. Hartford, 1846. 8°, pp. 16
[*A. C A. Y. C.*

He also contributed largely to periodical literature. Thus, in the first year of his ministry he prepared for the *Panoplist* a series of papers on theological topics, which received a premium for the best prose composition contributed to that volume.

Two articles of his appeared in volume 5 (1838) of the *Literary and Theological Review:*

Thoughts on the Foundation and extent of Moral Obligation, pp. 206-13; and, Thoughts on the Nature and extent of Man's Dependence, pp. 514-23

He was one of the editors of the *Evangelical Magazine* in 1832

Among other periodicals to which he contributed were, *The Youth's Guardian, The Pilgrim, The Religious Intelligencer, The Connecticut Observer, The Watchman,* and *The New England Puritan.*

AUTHORITIES.

Baird, Hist. of Rye, 425 Congregational Quarterly, xii, 477-83; xv, 441-42 *Vaill,* Sermon at Mr. Parsons's Funeral.

EDWARD PEROT, the third son of John Perot, of Philadelphia, and grandson of James and Frances (Mallory) Perot, of Bermuda, was born in Philadelphia on November 9, 1789 His father's family had emigrated from France to New Rochelle, New York, after the revocation of the Edict of Nantes. His mother was Mary, only child of Andrew Tybout, of Philadelphia, by his first marriage A brother was graduated here in 1816. His preparation for College was completed in New Haven under Jeremiah Evarts (Yale 1802).

He spent his life in retirement, as a gentleman of leisure, in his native city, and died there on October 3, 1866, in his 77th year.

He was never married

AUTHORITIES.

Moon, Morris Family of Philadelphia, ii, 678.

SAMUEL SHETHAR PHELPS, the youngest child of Captain John Phelps, a wealthy farmer of Litchfield, Connecticut, and a soldier of the Revolution, and grandson of Captain Edward and Hannah (Marsh) Phelps, of Litchfield, was born on May 13, 1793. His mother was Sally, eldest daughter of Samuel and Sarah (Jones) Shethar, of Litchfield.

He was prepared for College by the Rev Ammi R Robbins (Yale 1760), of Norfolk, and was a brilliant scholar

After graduation he began the study of law in the Litchfield Law School, but in the spring of 1812 removed to Middlebury, Vermont, to prosecute his studies in the office of Horatio Seymour (Yale 1797). His course was soon interrupted by his being drafted into the United States Army, where after serving in the ranks for a brief period, he was commissioned, in August, 1812, as Paymaster, and held that office until his discharge in June, 1815.

Being now admitted to the Vermont bar, he began practice in Middlebury, where he thenceforth resided.

On November 21, 1821, he married Frances Shurtleff; and after her death he next married, on October 23, 1825, Electa, daughter of Judge James Satterlee, of Lyons, Wayne County, New York.

His first experience of public life was as a member of the Council of Censors in 1827.

In 1831 he was chosen to the Legislative Council, and later in the same year he was elected to the bench of the Supreme Court of the State, which office he held until 1838, when he was chosen to the Senate of the United States as a Democrat.

He remained in the Senate for two terms (1839–51), and in January, 1853, was appointed by Governor Erastus Fairbanks to fill an unexpired term (January–March, 1853) In the following December, the legislature having failed to make an appointment, Judge Phelps went to Washington to claim the seat, but the Senate decided against him.

At the close of his service in the Senate in 1851 he resumed practice, but after several years of suffering from a complication of diseases he died suddenly in Middlebury on March 25, 1855, in his 62d year.

By his first marriage he had three sons, and by his second marriage six sons and two daughters The eldest son was graduated at Middlebury College in 1840, and became Professor of Law in Yale College, and Minister of the United States to Great Britain.

As a lawyer Judge Phelps was a cogent and powerful reasoner and an eloquent advocate, as a judge discriminating and comprehensive in his views, as a legislator cautious and conservative His talents were sound and practical, and his grasp of a subject calm and thorough. He was equalled in eloquence by few of his generation as a lawyer and debater, but habits of over-indulgence in the use of liquor impaired to some extent the public confidence.

An engraved portrait is given in the *American Whig Review* for 1850, and a copy of another in the *Green Bag*, volume 6, page 79.

He published:

1. Address of the Vermont Council of Censors Middlebury, 1827.

2. Substance of the Speech of S S. Phelps on the Subject of the Tariff. Delivered in the Senate of the United States, February 16 and 19, 1844 Washington, 1844. 8°, pp 35
[*A. A. S B. Publ. Br. Mus M H S N Y. Publ*

3 Appeal to the People of Vermont, in vindication of himself, against the charges made against him, upon the occasion of his Re-Election to the Senate of the United States, in relation to his course as a Senator Middlebury, 1845 8°, pp 43. [*Br. Mus*
This called out a Reply by Governor William Slade

4 Rejoinder to Mr Slade's "Reply." Washington [1846.] 8°, pp 40 [*Br. Mus U. S.*

5. Speech on the War and the Public Finances, delivered in the Senate of the United States, January 27th, 1848 [Washington, 1848] 8°, pp 15. [*A A. S. Br. Mus Harv. Y. C.*

6 Remarks on the Oregon Bill, and also on the Compromise Bill. delivered in the Senate of the United States, June 29, and July 24, 1848 [Washington, 1848] 8°, pp. 32. [*Br. Mus.*

7. Speech on the subject of Slavery, etc.—In Senate, January 23, 1850. [Washington, 1850] 8°, pp 16.
[*A. A S Br. Mus Harv. M H. S. Y. C.*

AUTHORITIES

G Allen, Reminiscences, 51. Amer Whig Review, xii, 93-98 *Hemenway*, Vt Hist Gazetteer, i, 59-61 Phelps Family, i, 393, 691-93 Shethar Family, 37, 40-42 *Stiles*, Hist of Windsor, ii, 578, 584. *Swift*, Hist of Middlebury, 291-93 *Wilson*, Rise and Fall of the Slave Power, ii, 38, 219, 272 *Woodruff*, Litchfield Geneal Register, 178.

EPHRAIM PEASE PRUDDEN, the eldest child and only son of the Rev. Nehemiah Prudden (Yale 1775), of Enfield, Connecticut, was born in Enfield in 1788, and was named for his maternal grandfather. His preparation for College was completed in the New Haven Hopkins Grammar School, under Henry Sherman (Yale 1803).

He spent his life as a merchant in his native town, where he was much respected as a useful citizen, and where he died, of typhus fever, after three weeks' illness, on July 26, 1836, aged 48 years

He represented the town in the General Assembly in 1825, 1826, 1828, 1829, and 1831 to 1834

His widow, Laura Porter, died in Enfield on March 24, 1840, aged 44 years. Their children were two sons and two daughters The only child to marry was one daughter who married the Rev. Dr. George S. F. Savage (Yale 1844).

AUTHORITIES

Allen, Hist of Enfield, iii, 2289, 2294, 2375-76 Conn Courant, Aug 1, 1836 Prudden Genealogy, 82

NATHAN SHERMAN READ, the younger son of Daniel and Jerusha (Sherman) Read, of New Haven, and grandson of Daniel and Mary (White) Read, of Rehoboth or Attleborough, Massachusetts, was born in New Haven on

January 31, 1792 His father was a well-known composer of sacred music. His mother was a native of Huntington, Connecticut. He was prepared for College by Henry Sherman (Yale 1803) in the Hopkins Grammar School.

For about a year after graduation he served as College Butler, and as bookkeeper in his father's store; and then entered on the study of theology in Plainfield, under the direction of the Rev. Dr. Joel Benedict After ten weeks in Plainfield, he removed about the middle of July to East Hartford, where he continued his studies under the care of the Rev. Andrew Yates (Yale 1794).

He was licensed to preach on September 28, 1813, by the New Haven West Association of Ministers; but his license was revoked by that body in September, 1814, on evidence of imprudent conduct and over-indulgence in liquor.

He had already married, in April, 1814, Hannah, daughter of Captain Marcus Merriman, of New Haven.

He then engaged in teaching, and after abandoning his hope of inducing the Association to restore his license, on evidence of repentance and an upright life, he took a dismission in April, 1817, from the College church to the Episcopal church in New Haven.

He taught successively in Newbern, North Carolina, in the Washington (District of Columbia) Academy (1818), and in Shepherdstown, (West) Virginia

After years of declining health he returned to New Haven.

In the first week of August, 1821, he embarked on the Sloop Eliza Nicoll on a voyage from New Haven to Boston for his health; but he died suddenly on the vessel in a fit, on August 7, at the age of 29½ years. His body was buried in Edgartown on Martha's Vineyard.

His widow survived him, without children, two daughters and a son having died in infancy She next married, on December 18, 1831, Sidney Wells, of Cambridge, New York.

His portrait is owned by the New Haven Colony Historical Society

He published:

An Astronomical Dictionary, compiled from Hutton's Mathematical and Philosophical Dictionary, To which is prefixed an Introduction, containing a brief history of Astronomy, and a familiar illustration of its elementary principles New-Haven, 1817. 12°, pp xxiv, 13-208. [*N Y. Publ. Y. C.*

AUTHORITIES

Edgartown Vital Records, 258-59. Religious Intelligencer, vi, 207 N H. W. Association, MS Records

---

HENRY ROBINSON, the elder son of Deacon and Colonel Samuel Robinson, a farmer of Guilford, Connecticut, and grandson of Samuel and Elizabeth (Bishop) Robinson, of Guilford, was born on December 20, 1788. His mother was Content, daughter of Captain James and Amy (Spelman) Robinson, of Durham. A brother was graduated here in 1817. He was prepared for College by his pastor, the Rev. Aaron Dutton (Yale 1803).

For two years after leaving College he taught in an Academy in Wethersfield, and then entered the Andover Theological Seminary, where he finished the course in 1816. The next year was spent as a Tutor in Bowdoin College, at Brunswick, Maine.

His first settlement in the ministry was in Litchfield South Farms, now Morris, Connecticut, where he was ordained and installed as pastor of the Congregational church on April 30, 1823

On June 11, 1823, he was married to Wealthy Frances, third daughter of the late William Brown (Yale 1784), of Hartford.

On account of poor health he was dismissed from the church in Morris on October 27, 1829; but he recovered so as to be installed over the church in Suffield on June 1,

1831, as colleague pastor with the Rev. Ebenezer Gay (Yale 1787). Here his wife died on March 24, 1833, in her 33d year; and he was again married, on April 8, 1835, to Mary Cushing, the elder daughter of Mr. Gay, and the widow of Spencer Judd, of Springfield, Massachusetts, who died in October, 1832.

The senior pastor died on January 1, 1837, and Mr. Robinson took a dismission on the 29th of the following April

On November 20, 1838, he was installed as colleague pastor with the Rev. Elisha Atkins (Yale 1773) over the Congregational Church in North Killingly, now the First Church in (East) Putnam. Mr. Atkins died in June, 1839, and Mr. Robinson was dismissed on April 1, 1845

His last pastorate, and one in which he was—as in his earlier pastorates—most highly esteemed, was in Plainfield, where he was settled from April 14, 1847, to April 10, 1856.

He then retired to his native village, where he died, of pneumonia, on September 14, 1878, in his 90th year.

His widow died in Guilford on April 18, 1885, aged nearly 84 years.

By his first marriage he had a son, who was lost at sea, and three daughters, the eldest of whom died in infancy By his second marriage he had two daughters, of whom the younger died in infancy, and a son (Yale 1863).

His portrait is copied in his son's *Guilford Portraits*.

AUTHORITIES

Congregational Quarterly, ii, 293 *Dwight*, Strong Family, i, 274. N. E Hist. and Geneal Register, xxxiii, 54; lxv, 138 *Robinson*, Guilford Portraits, 224–26

EDWARD SELDEN, JUNIOR, the only son of 'Squire Edward Selden (Yale 1783), of Haddam, Connecticut, was born in Haddam in 1790. His father removed to

Windsor shortly before he entered College, and he was prepared for admission by the Rev. Jesse Townsend (Yale 1790), of Durham, New York, whose wife was his mother's sister.

Soon after graduation he went into business in Pittsburgh, Pennsylvania, in partnership with his kinsman, John Brainard (Yale 1808).

He died in Pittsburgh on December 25, 1823, aged 33 years.

AUTHORITIES.

May Family, 89

DAVID MARSH SMITH, the only child of David and Betsey (Marsh) Smith, was born in New Marlborough, Berkshire County, Massachusetts, on August 11, 1789. His mother died at his birth, and his father, under a new religious impulse, came to Yale in 1792, and was graduated in 1795. He was ordained and installed as pastor in Durham, Connecticut, in 1799, and there prepared his son for College.

Immediately upon graduation he entered the Andover Theological Seminary, where he completed the course in 1814.

He was married on August 29, 1815, to Clarissa, daughter of Judge Robert Parker, of Litchfield and Londonderry, New Hampshire.

In October, 1815, he was sent by the Missionary Society of Connecticut to labor for four months in Western New York

In 1816 he established himself at Lewiston, in Niagara County, where he was ordained and installed by the Presbytery of Niagara, on September 17, 1817, over a Presbyterian church, with which he remained until July 1, 1828.

He next supplied the church at Little Falls, Herkimer County, for about a year; and from 1830 to 1835 was in charge of the Presbyterian Church and of the Academy in Stockbridge, Madison County

He was then for four years principal of a seminary in Stockport, Columbia County, and for part of the time acting pastor of a church at Newman's Mills.

From 1839 to 1842 he served as corresponding secretary and general agent of the State Society for the improvement of popular education by the establishment of normal schools

He subsequently supplied weak churches in different parts of the State, especially in Lewis County, until his removal in 1860 to Princeton, New Jersey, where the rest of his long life was spent.

He died in Princeton on July 15, 1880, in his 91st year, of bilious fever

Mrs. Smith died in Princeton on September 24, 1863, in her 75th year.

His three sons and one of his three daughters survived him.

AUTHORITIES

Amer. Ancestry, iv, 209 Fowler, Hist. of Western N. Y, 509
Hist. of Durham, 75, 128 *Hotchkin,*

Joseph Spencer, son of the Hon. Isaac Spencer, of Millington Parish, in East Haddam, Treasurer of the State of Connecticut, and of Lucretia (Colt) Spencer, was born in East Haddam on December 29, 1789. A brother was graduated here in 1805. He was prepared for the Sophomore Class in College by John Adams (Yale 1795) in Bacon Academy, Colchester.

After graduation he studied law, and settled in practice in Rochester, New York.

He married on September 24, 1818, Phebe, second daughter of Calvin and Phebe (Ely) Selden, of Lyme, Connecticut.

In 1822 he was elected to the State Senate, and in January, 1823, he took his seat in that body, but died in Albany on May 2, after a severe illness of sixteen days, in his 34th year. He was buried in Albany.

He left one daughter.

His widow married on April 21, 1831, Lieutenant (later General) Amos Beebe Eaton (U. S. Mil. Acad. 1826), and became the mother of Professor Daniel C. Eaton (Yale 1857).

Mrs. Eaton died in Washington, District of Columbia, on May 8, 1868, aged 72 years.

AUTHORITIES

Munsell, Annals of Albany, vii, 121 *Salisbury,* Family Histories and Genealogies, iii, 53 *Walworth,* Hyde Genealogy, i, 584

Samuel Spring, the fourth son and sixth child of the Rev Dr. Samuel Spring (Princeton Coll. 1771) and Hannah (Hopkins) Spring, of Newburyport, Massachusetts, was born in Newburyport on March 9, 1792. A brother was graduated here in 1805. He was prepared for College under Dr. Benjamin Abbot (Harvard 1788), at Phillips Academy, Exeter, New Hampshire, and spent his Freshman year with the Class of 1809. At the end of Junior year he was sent away for a College prank, and was not admitted to his degree until 1821.

On leaving College he had at first begun the study of law, but very soon engaged in trade in his native town. During the war of 1812 while in command of a merchant vessel he was captured by the British. After the war he removed to Boston, and while in business there (from September, 1815, to the fall of 1817, in partnership with David Hale) was married, on November 27, 1816, to Lydia Maria, daughter of Winthrop B and Dorothy Norton, of South Berwick, Maine

Some three years later he resolved to prepare for the ministry, and entered the Andover Seminary, where he was graduated in 1821

In the fall of that year he was called to the pastorate of the First (Congregational) Church in Abington, Massachusetts, with a salary of $600, and he was ordained and installed there on January 2, 1822.

He was dismissed on December 6, 1826, to accept a call from the North (now Park) Congregational Church in Hartford, Connecticut, which he served as pastor from March, 1827, to January, 1833 He then retired, against the unanimous desire of his church, and accepted the pastorate of the church in East Hartford, with which he remained until his resignation on account of failing health in December, 1860.

His residence continued in East Hartford, but from 1863 to 1869 he officiated as chaplain for the Retreat for the Insane in Hartford. He was specially gifted in prayer, a model preacher, and greatly beloved and esteemed in all relations. His theological sympathies were with the East Windsor School. The honorary degree of Doctor of Divinity was conferred on him by Columbia College in 1858.

On the evening of November 24, 1877, he fell from his doorstep and fractured his hip, from which cause his death followed on December 13, in his 86th year.

His widow died in East Hartford, on September 19, 1881, aged 89 years.

Their children were six daughters and three sons, of whom two daughters and two sons survived him. One daughter married the Rev. James B R Walker (Brown Univ. 1841), and another married the Rev. John Edgar (Yale 1855).

He published:

1. The only safe expedient.—A Discourse [from I Tim. v, 22] delivered before the Hartford Temperance Society. Hartford, 1832 8°, pp. 31. [*Y. C.*

2 Memorial of the Rev Royal Robbins, late pastor of the church in Kensington, Ct. Compiled by S Spring. Hartford, 1862 8°, pp 57. [Y C

AUTHORITIES

Bond, Hist of Watertown, 447 *A Hobart,* Hist of Abington, 59 Trumbull, Hist of Hartford County, i, 389-90, 431, ii, 93, 101

NATHAN STARK was born in Windham County, Connecticut, in 1788, and was prepared for College by John Adams (Yale 1795) in Bacon Academy, Colchester. His residence was in Lyme at the time of his admission

After graduation he studied law, and began practice in Minisink, Orange County, New York.

He continued at the bar for about ten years, but then relinquished the profession for the more congenial one of teaching.

This he made his business for life, and followed it successfully until obliged by age and infirmity to lay it down.

He died in that part of Brooklyn which was formerly Williamsburg, New York, on June 18, 1858, in his 71st year

He married, in November, 1821, Mary, eldest child of Colonel Noah and Mary (Loomis) Porter, of North Coventry, Connecticut, who died in Williamsburg on January 25, 1841, aged 46 years

They had one son (Princeton Coll 1843) and one daughter, who married the Rev. William Bailey (Rutgers Coll. 1842)

Mr Stark was gifted with a strong mind, and could express himself in a clear, logical, and concise manner; but he was very diffident and retiring, and therefore not widely known. At the time of his death he was an Elder in the First Presbyterian Church of Williamsburg, and was much respected for his ability and his Christian character.

AUTHORITIES.

Andrews, Descendants of John Porter, i, 435 *G. W Edwards*, MS Letter, July, 1858. Loomis Female Genealogy, ii, 789

JULIUS STEELE, the youngest son of Elisha and Susannah (Strong) Steele, of Bethlehem, Connecticut, and a brother of Nathaniel Steele (Yale 1788), was born in Bethlehem on December 29, 1786, and was prepared for College by his pastor, the Rev. Dr. Azel Backus (Yale 1787).

In November after his graduation he united with the College Church on profession of his faith, and he then entered the Andover Theological Seminary, where he completed the course in 1814.

In 1815 he went to East Bloomfield, Ontario County, New York, where other members of his family had already settled, and began preaching in the Congregational Church in that village. He was ordained and installed as the pastor on March 13, 1816, and on October 1, 1818, he was married to Harriet, daughter of George and Hannah (Porter) Belden, of Windsor, Connecticut. In 1822 the church in East Bloomfield adopted the Presbyterian form of organization.

He was dismissed from his pastorate on January 21, 1829, and for the next two years preached in Warsaw, Wyoming County Then followed a residence of about seven years in West Bloomfield, during which he supplied the First Presbyterian Church in that village.

His health then requiring a change of climate, he removed in August, 1838, to White Pigeon, in southern Michigan, where he labored in the ministry for two years. In 1840 he removed to Constantine, in the immediate vicinity, where he died, of malignant pleurisy, on February 20, 1849, in his 63d year.

His widow died on July 2, 1865, aged 66 years

His children were five sons and four daughters The second son was graduated here in 1846.

AUTHORITIES

Durrie, Steele Family, 19, 34, 142
Dwight, Strong Family, ii, 1429, 1434
Hotchkin, Hist of Western N. Y, 563, 567 *Sprague*, Annals of the Amer. Pulpit, iii, 513.

BYAM KERBY STEVENS, a son of General Ebenezer and Lucretia (Ledyard, Sands) Stevens, of New York, was born in that city on April 20, 1792. Three of his brothers were graduated here, in 1805, 1807, and 1813, respectively. He was prepared for College by Rinaldo Burleigh (Yale 1803), at the Plainfield (Connecticut) Academy.

He passed a quiet and uneventful life as a merchant in New York, beloved and respected by all who knew him

He died in Astoria, Long Island, on February 15, 1870, in his 78th year.

He was married, on April 6, 1830, by the Rev Dr. Jonathan M. Wainwright, to Frances, only daughter of the Hon. Albert and Hannah (Nicholson) Gallatin, of New York City, who died on November 25, 1877, at the age of 74.

Seven children survived their father, of whom two were graduates of Yale, in 1854 and 1858, respectively.

AUTHORITIES

N Y Geneal and Biogr Record, vii, 13

SELAH BREWSTER STRONG, the eldest in a family of ten children of Judge Thomas Shepard Strong, of Mount Misery, now called Belleterre, a heavily wooded promontory in the northeastern part of the township of Brookhaven, Suffolk County, Long Island, near the present village of Port Jefferson, and a nephew of George Washington Strong (Yale 1803), was born on May 1, 1792. His mother was Hannah, daughter of Joseph and Rebecca (Mills) Brewster, of the village of Setauket in the same township, west of Port Jefferson. He was prepared for

College by Frederick Scofield (Yale 1801) in Stamford, Connecticut.

He studied law in New York City in his uncle's office, and was admitted to practice in November, 1814. He then began business there by himself, but after six years, just as he was beginning to earn a satisfactory income, he found that his health was breaking down from too close confinement.

He accordingly retired to his father's house, and gradually developed a good country practice

In March, 1821, he was commissioned by Governor DeWitt Clinton as District Attorney for Suffolk County, and served in that capacity (with only an interruption of nine months in 1830) until his election to Congress in the fall of 1842.

On August 14, 1823, he was married in Islip, Long Island, to Cornelia, daughter of Dr. Richard and Prudence (Carll) Udall. After his marriage he built a house for himself on St. George's Manor, near the village of Setauket.

In January, 1828, he was appointed by Governor Clinton as Commissioner to perform the duties of a Judge of the Supreme Court in Suffolk County. His father was First Judge of the Court, but he and all his associates were farmers, not lawyers; so that the District Attorney became practically the legal magistrate of the county, and guided for twenty years the administration of the law with remarkable strength and skill.

He served in Congress as a Democrat for the session of 1843-45

In March, 1844, he was again appointed (by Governor Bouck) as Supreme Court Commissioner for Suffolk County; and in March, 1846, by Governor Wright as Circuit Judge. In 1847, under the new State constitution, he was chosen a Judge of the Supreme Court of the Second District, drawing the short (or two years') term, which had the effect of taking him to the Court of Appeals. On the next vacancy he was again chosen (in 1851) for the full term, and served until January, 1860, being again, in 1857, a member of the Court of Appeals, and universally recognized as an able and honest Judge On his retirement from office, by request of his professional brethren, his portrait was painted, to be hung in the court-room in Brooklyn.

His last public service was as a member of the State Constitutional Convention of 1867.

He died at his country seat, St George's Manor, Setauket, on November 29, 1872, in his 81st year

His wife died on May 9, 1882, in her 77th year.

Their children were four daughters and six sons. One daughter and two sons died in infancy. The eldest son was graduated at Yale in 1855, two others here in 1864, and the youngest at Williams College in 1865.

An engraving from his portrait is given in the *Strong Family* and in volume 4 of the *New York Genealogical and Biographical Record*

AUTHORITIES

Dwight, Strong Family, i, 623–24 N Y Geneal and Biogr Record, iv, 49–53 Portrait and Biogr Record of Suffolk County, 426

FREDERICK AUGUSTUS TALLMADGE, third son of Colonel Benjamin Tallmadge (Yale 1773), of Litchfield, Connecticut, was born in Litchfield on August 29, 1792, and was prepared for College by the Rev. Ammi R. Robbins (Yale 1760), of Norfolk.

After graduation he studied law in the Litchfield Law School, and then settled in New York City He had already been an officer in the Connecticut militia, and in New York he served as Captain of a cavalry company upon Long Island, for the defence of the city during the war

He entered early into political life, and was closely identified for over half a century with the prosperity and public improvements of the city.

He served as Alderman in 1834, and while a member of the Common Council in the fall of 1836 was elected to the State Senate, in which he served for four sessions (1837–40), acting in the latter part of the time as President *pro tempore* of the body.

In 1841 he was appointed Recorder of the City of New York by the Governor and Senate, and served for five years

He was a member of Congress from the Fifth District in New York City for the session of 1847–49; and under the new State Constitution was elected Recorder of the City in the fall of 1848, serving to 1851.

In 1857 he was appointed General Superintendent of the newly-organized Metropolitan Police, and served for two years.

In 1862 he was elected Clerk of the Court of Appeals, and he retired from public life at the expiration of his term in November, 1865

As a politician he was ready, energetic, and fearless; as a Judge, dignified, courteous, and impartial.

He married Eliza, daughter of the Hon. Judson Canfield (Yale 1782), of Sharon, Connecticut, who survived him, with five children.

He died while on a visit to a daughter in Litchfield, on September 17, 1869, in his 78th year.

In 1858 he published his father's *Memoirs,* to which he added a brief supplementary sketch (pp. 69–70).

AUTHORITIES.

Kilbourne, Litchfield Biography, 313–14 *Woodruff,* Litchfield Geneal Register, 219

John Thomas, son of John Thomas, of that part of Woodbridge which is now Bethany, Connecticut, was born in Woodbridge on January 27, 1792, and was prepared for College by the Rev Dr. David Ely (Yale 1769), of Huntington. He did not complete the college course, but was admitted to a degree in 1814.

After leaving Yale he studied law in New Haven, and practiced here for several years. He married on December 3, 1815, Caroline, daughter of Elias and Jerusha (Fitch) Beers of New Haven.

In 1824 he removed to Cortlandville, in Cortland County, New York, where he attained prominence in his profession.

He was a member of the State Assembly in 1837, and became earnestly identified with the abolition party, and a frequent contributor to some of their publications. He is said to have been editorially connected with a paper in this interest, which was published in Syracuse.

In 1860 he removed to the residence of his only surviving child, a son, in Galesburg, Illinois.

He died in Galesburg on March 5, 1866, in his 75th year.

His widow died on March 20, 1867.

JOSEPH VAILL, the seventh of eight children of the Rev. Joseph Vaill (Dartmouth Coll 1778), of Hadlyme, Connecticut, and a brother of William F. Vaill (Yale 1806), was born in Hadlyme on July 28, 1790, and was prepared for College by his father

For the first six months after graduation he acted as principal of Morris Academy in Litchfield South Farms, and for the next six months taught in Salisbury in the same county. Meantime he began to study theology, and pursued the study during a second year with his father and brother.

He was licensed to preach by the Middlesex Association of Ministers on June 1, 1813, and began to supply pulpits as he had opportunity.

In the fall of 1813 he had before him calls from the churches in North Lyme and in Wintonbury Parish, now Bloomfield, Connecticut, and in Brimfield, Massachusetts

On consultation with his friends he decided to accept the last-named (unanimous) call, and before returning thither for ordination he was married, on December 7, to Anne, only daughter of Ambrose and Mabel Kirtland, of his native parish.

He was ordained and installed in Brimfield on February 2, 1814, the sermon preached by his father being afterwards published. His salary was $550, and he was obliged to till a farm to meet his expenses. There were then less than seventy professors of religion in the town.

His wife died in Brimfield on February 6, 1829, in her 36th year. The sermon preached at her funeral by the Rev Alfred Ely, of Monson, was afterwards published.

He next married, on January 7, 1830, Mrs. Nancy (Pope) Howe, of Ware, widow of Amos Howe, of Brookfield, who died in November, 1828.

His ministry in Brimfield was highly successful, but various reasons, and especially the spread of Perfectionism in the town, induced him in 1834 to listen favorably to a unanimous call from Portland, Maine, where he was installed as pastor of the Second Church, then the largest in that city, in succession to the Rev. Dr. Bennet Tyler (Yale 1804), on October 15, 1834. He had been dismissed from Brimfield on September 16.

He found, however, that the climate of Portland affected his health and spirits unfavorably; and when his old church in Brimfield found themselves without a pastor in the summer of 1837, and heard of his condition, they invited him to return, on a salary of $600. The Perfectionist excitement having subsided, he accepted the call, and was dismissed from Portland on October 15, and re-installed in Brimfield on November 1

Since 1821 he had been a Trustee of Amherst College, and he had repeatedly been called on to assist in the work of collecting funds. His success had been such that in the autumn of 1841, when it seemed necessary to appoint an agent who should devote his entire time to this business, "to his great grief and surprise" Mr. Vaill was unanimously selected for this office. He declined, but the Trustees insisted; and under the pressure of a sense of duty he resigned his pastorate in October, and gave himself wholly for nearly four years to saving the College from financial ruin, by raising for its use over one hundred thousand dollars.

Early in 1845 he had begun to supply the Congregational Church in Somers, Connecticut, and when his task for Amherst College was accomplished he was installed in Somers as pastor, on August 6, 1845. He declined in 1849 a suggestion that he should allow his name to be presented for election as a Fellow of Yale. The honorary degree of Doctor of Divinity was conferred on him by Amherst in 1851

In 1854, at the age of 64, he thought it advisable to retire from Somers to a smaller and less scattered parish, and therefore accepted a call to the Second Congregational Church in Palmer, an adjoining town to his old residence in Brimfield, where he was installed on December 6, and remained in active service until his final retirement on February 12, 1868.

In 1868 he was elected to the Massachusetts House of Representatives, and during his period of service died in Palmer, after five days' severe illness, from heart disease, on February 22, 1869, in his 79th year. The discourse preached at his funeral by President Stearns, of Amherst, was afterwards printed. He was buried in Brimfield

His widow died on February 3, 1871

Of his eight children by his first marriage, five sons and one daughter survived him. One son and one daughter died in infancy Two sons entered the ministry

An engraved portrait of Dr. Vaill is given in the *Congregational Quarterly* for 1870, and in the *History of Brimfield.*

He was a direct and practical preacher, with marked executive power and much native shrewdness.

Besides his labors in behalf of Amherst College, he was for nearly forty years a Trustee of Monson Academy, and while in Portland was a Trustee of the Bangor Theological Seminary (1835–38).

He published:

1. A Sermon [from Phil. iv, 17] delivered before the Hampshire Missionary Society, at their Annual meeting, Northampton, August 21, 1823. Northampton, 1823 8°, pp 24
[*A C A B Publ U. T. S Y C.*

2 An Address at the laying of the Corner-Stone of the Meeting House in the East Society in Ware, June 21, 1826. Being pp. 41–48, appended to the Sermon at the Ordination of the Rev. Parsons Cooke in Ware, by John Woodbridge, D D Amherst, 1826 8°.
[*A C A. B. Publ. Br. Mus Harv U. T. S Y C*

3. An Address delivered at the laying of the Corner-Stone of the Evangelical Congregational Church in Bolton, July 9, 1828 .. Lancaster, 1828 8°, pp. 15. [*A. C. A Y. C.*

4. An Historical Sermon [from Zech. i, 5] delivered at Brimfield, January 7, 1821, on the occasion of a New Year. Springfield, 1829 8°, pp. 27. [*Y. C*

The publication having been "inadvertently delayed," the sermon was now revised and the important historical information extended.

5 A Sermon [from Isa lvii, 1–27], delivered at Somers, on the Sabbath, April 1, 1849, at the Funeral of Mrs. Chloe Billings, wife of Deacon Solomon Billings. Springfield, 1849. 8°, pp. 22.
[*U. T S*

6. A Sermon preached at Palmer, May 20, 1859, on the occasion of the Funeral of Deacon Benjamin Converse

7 A Sermon [from Hebr. xi, 4] delivered at Palmer, February 21, 1861, at the Funeral of William C. Child. Springfield, 1861. 8°, pp. 18 + pl [*Harv. Y. C*

8 Address, delivered before the Eastern Hampden Agricultural Society at Palmer, October 15, 1863

9 A Memorial Sermon [from Deut xxxii, 7], in two parts, preached at Brimfield, February 7th, 1864, commemorative of his

settlement in that place, fifty years ago, and affectionately Dedicated to his Former Charge. Springfield, 1864. 8°, pp. 42.

[*A. C. A B Ath B. Publ M. H. S. Y C.*

An admirable model of such composition

10 Theological Education in Connecticut, seventy years ago; as connected with Dr. Charles Backus's divinity school In *The Congregational Quarterly*, vol 6, pp. 137–42, April, 1864.

11 Rev William Fowler Vaill. In *The Congregational Quarterly*, vol 7, pp. 422–24, July–October, 1865

12 A Sermon [from Acts xiii, 36] delivered at the Funeral of Rev. Alfred Ely, D D , . in Monson, Mass., July 9, 1866. Northampton, 1866 8°, pp 20 [*A C A U. T. S.*

13. A Sermon [from Acts xi, 24] preached in East Haddam, Conn , at the funeral of the Rev. Isaac Parsons, . August 25, 1868 Springfield, 1868 8°, pp 26. [*A C A. B. Publ Y C.*

AUTHORITIES

Congregational Quarterly, xii, 1–18 *Hitchcock*, Reminiscences of Amherst College, 19, 122 *Hyde*, Hist of Brimfield, 3, 106–11, 464 *Parsons*, Memoir of Rev J Vaill, 57, 68–69, 160–66 Pratt Family, 275 *Temple*, Hist of Palmer, 243–44 *Tyler*, Hist. of Amherst College, 15, 63, 182, 264–65, 489–500

ELISHA DANA WHITTLESEY, the second son of Elisha Whittlesey (Yale 1779), of Danbury, Connecticut, was born in Danbury on February 16, 1792, and was prepared for College by Alanson Hamlin (Yale 1799), of Danbury. His father died in 1802.

After graduation he studied law, and began practice in Waterloo, Seneca County, New York.

He returned, however, to his mother's house in Danbury, and died there on September 23, 1823, in his 32d year.

The published history of the family describes him as a man of noble character.

AUTHORITIES.

Bartow Genealogy, 159 Whittlesey Genealogy, 82

William Channing Woodbridge, the only son of William Woodbridge (Yale 1780), was born in Medford, Massachusetts, where his father was then teaching, on December 18, 1794. In his infancy the family removed to Middletown, Connecticut; and their residence was in Newark, New Jersey, when he entered College, from his father's tuition, in June, 1808. He was the youngest member of his Class.

By the time of his graduation, Philadelphia was the family residence, and he spent a year there in advanced study. From July, 1812, to November, 1814, he had charge of Burlington Academy, New Jersey.

He then returned to New Haven, for a course of general graduate study, during which his religious life was quickened, so that he united with the College Church on profession of his faith in April, 1815.

In September, 1815, he began a course of theological study with President Dwight, and when this was interrupted by the President's death, he entered in July, 1817, the Princeton Seminary. But he was barely settled there when an invitation came to him to join the force of teachers in the American Asylum for the Deaf and Dumb, just opened in Hartford. His plan had been to become a foreign missionary; but after serious deliberation he decided that the position offered him was so truly missionary service that it was his duty to accept it, and he began his work in December. His preparation for the ministry was so far completed that he was licensed to preach by the Hartford North Association of Ministers on February 3, 1819.

His engrossing labors in the classroom, with the preparation for the press of geographical text-books on an original plan, and occasional service as a preacher, soon broke down his naturally feeble constitution, so that in October, 1820, he was obliged to give up his post and sail for Southern Europe.

He returned in July, 1821, and was mainly occupied for the next three years in the publication of his geographies. His health not allowing him to teach or to preach, he went abroad again in the fall of 1824, and remained for five years. During this time he was partly engaged in studying educational systems in Switzerland and Germany, and partly in collecting material for the improvement of his geographical works and in preparing new editions. He returned in the fall of 1829, but was still so hampered by ill health that he was long prevented from undertaking new responsibilities.

In 1831 he purchased the *American Journal of Education* in Boston, and proceeded to develop the magazine as editor, under a new title, with no sparing of pains or expense. He settled in Boston in the fall of 1831, and was married, on November 27, 1832, to Lucy Ann, daughter of Benjamin Tyler and Rebecca (Blackley) Reed, of Marblehead, who had been a teacher in Miss Catharine Beecher's school in Hartford. One of her sisters married the Rev Ornan Eastman (Yale 1821).

The responsibility for the monthly *Annals of Education* was a heavy one, and in October, 1836, his failing health compelled him to go again to Europe His wife's health was equally precarious, and she died in Frankfort, Germany, on May 31, 1840, in her 38th year

He returned in October, 1841, and spent the next three winters, with steadily declining health, in Santa Cruz, West Indies After his final return he sank rapidly, and died in Boston, on November 9, 1845, in his 49th year.

His children, a son (Yale 1855) and a daughter, survived him.

Mr Woodbridge was an efficient pioneer in the educational awakening in Massachusetts after 1830, and an important agent in the improvement of common-schools, according to the methods of Pestalozzi and Fellenberg

A portrait is given in Barnard's *Educational Biography*.

He published

1. Rudiments of Geography, on a new plan, designed to assist the memory by Comparison and Classification· with numerous engravings . Accompanied with an Atlas, exhibiting the prevailing religious forms of government, degrees of civilization, and the comparative size of Towns, Rivers, and Mountains Hartford, 1821 12°, and Atlas 8°, 9 maps.

Numerous editions See, also, below, No 11.

2 Universal Geography, ancient and modern, on the principles of Comparison and Classification. Modern Geography by W C. Woodbridge .. Ancient Geography by Emma Willard Hartford, 1824 12°, pp. xxx, 336; 88, and Atlas, 4°. [*Harv. U S*

The same. 2d edition, with title, A System of Universal Geography . Hartford, 1827. 12°; and Atlas.

Also, later editions.

3 The Fellenberg Institution at Hofwyl In the *Quarterly Christian Spectator,* vol 1, pp 625–31, December, 1829.

Anonymous

4 Persecutions in Switzerland. In the *Quarterly Christian Spectator,* vol 2, pp 99–118, March, 1830.

5. On the System of Instruction in the Fellenberg Establishment at Hofwyl And, Review on Religious Liberty in Switzerland In the *Quarterly Christian Spectator,* vol 2, pp 358–79, June, 1830.

6. A Lecture on Vocal Music as a branch of common education Delivered in the Representatives' Hall, Boston, August 24, 1830, before the American Institute of Instruction Boston, 1831. 8°, pp 25 [*U S.*

Also in the volume of Lectures before the Institute, pp. 231–55.

7 Preparatory Lessons for beginners: or, First Steps to Geography. [1831.] 12°, pp. 36. [*U S*

8 Communication on the Size and Ventilation of School-Rooms In the Lectures before the American Institute of Instruction, 1831. Boston, 1832 8°, pp 261–71.

9 Report of the Committee on the Propriety of Studying the Bible in the Institutions of a Christian country, presented to the Literary Convention at New York, October, 1831. Boston, 1832 8°, pp. 24 [*Y C*

10 Lecture on the best method of Teaching Geography. In Lectures before the American Institute of Instruction, August, 1833 Boston, 1834 8°, pp 207–40

11. Modern School Geography, on the plan of Comparison and Classification, with an Atlas, exhibiting on a new plan, the Physical and Political characteristics of countries, and the comparative size of Countries, Towns, Rivers and Mountains. Hartford, 1844. 12°, pp. 352; Atlas, 4° 18 maps + 6 pp.
[*B Ath. B. Publ. Harv. U. S. Y. C.*

A new edition of No 1

Much of his writing appears in the following monthly periodical, edited by him

American Annals of Education and Instruction .. Boston, 1831–36 6 vols., 8°. [*U. S. Y. C.*

His name also appears on volume 7, as Foreign Editor.

A specially valuable series of articles by Mr Woodbridge is· Sketches of the Fellenberg Institution at Hofwyl, in a Series of Letters to a Friend in volumes 1 and 2

In connection with the above, he also conducted for two years, 1831–33, a weekly paper, called the *Juvenile Rambler*

AUTHORITIES.

Barnard's Amer Journal of Education, v, 51–64. *S G Goodrich,* Recollections of a Lifetime, ii, 112 *Mitchell,* Woodbridge Record, 90, 136 *J W. Reed,* Reed Family, 44. *T Robbins,* Diary, i, 771.

JOSEPH EMERSON WORCESTER, the second son of Jesse Worcester, of Bedford, New Hampshire, and grandson of Captain Noah and Lydia (Taylor) Worcester, of Hollis, was born in Bedford on August 24, 1784 His mother was Sarah, daughter of Josiah Parker, of Hollis. In 1794 his parents returned to their native town of Hollis. A younger brother was graduated at Yale in 1828, and others at Harvard in 1823, 1830, and 1831, respectively.

After working on the farm until he was twenty-one, he determined to obtain a collegiate education; and with characteristic perseverance he prepared himself for the

Sophomore Class at Yale, in part at the Academy in Salisbury, and in part at Phillips Academy, Andover.

After graduation he taught a private school in Salem, Massachusetts, for five years, and then spent two years in Andover, for the preparation of his early geographical works.

In 1819 he removed to Cambridge, where he spent the rest of his long and useful life.

After issuing a succession of text-books in geography and history, he entered a new field of labor with the preparation, in 1827, of an edition of Johnson's *Dictionary*, combined with Walker's Pronunciation.

In 1830 appeared the first of his own dictionaries, and in November, 1831, he sailed on a tour of eight months in Europe, for health, recreation, and the enlargement of his resources for the works which he had in hand

On his return he assumed the literary editorship of the *American Almanac*, a work requiring great industry, wide correspondence, and careful research and verification, which he conducted for eleven years with his accustomed fidelity.

He was married, on June 29, 1841, to Amy Elizabeth, daughter of the late Rev. Professor Joseph McKean (Harvard 1794) and Amy (Swasey) McKean, of Cambridge.

Meantime he had continued the preparation of additional lexicographical works of great value; and though handicapped by a partial loss of sight (since 1846), due to overwork, he was able to persevere and to issue finally his quarto *Dictionary of the English Language* in 1860, at the age of 76

The honorary degree of Doctor of Laws was conferred on him by Brown University in 1847 and by Dartmouth College in 1856.

He died in Cambridge, after a brief illness, on October 27, 1865, in his 82d year. The monument erected to his memory in Mount Auburn describes him as "geographer, historian, lexicographer, a man of Christian uprightness and beneficence" He bequeathed to the Library of Harvard University the works used by him in making his *Dictionary*

His wife survived him. They had no children.

His engraved portrait appears in the *History of Hollis*, in the *Proceedings* of the Massachusetts Historical Society for June, 1880, and in the *Granite Monthly* for April, 1880

Some of his early geographical and historical works have had a wide circulation, but his reputation rests chiefly on his lexicographical labors. In these he displayed sound judgment and good taste, combined with patient industry and conscientious solicitude for accuracy. In regard to orthography and pronunciation he took great pains to ascertain the best usage.

He published:

1. A Geographical Dictionary, or Universal Gazetteer; ancient and modern Andover, 1817 2 vols, 8°, unpaged
[*A. A. S. B Ath. B Publ. Harv U S Y C.*

The same Second edition. Boston, 1823. 2 vols, 8°, pp viii, 972, iv, 960. [*B Publ. Br. Mus. U. S. Y. C.*

2 A Gazetteer of the United States abstracted from the Universal Gazetteer, with enlargement of the principal articles. Andover, 1818 8°, unpaged.
[*A A S. B. Ath. B Publ. Br. Mus Harv M H. S. U S Y C.*

3 Elements of Geography, ancient and modern; with an Atlas. Boston, 1819 12°, pp 322. [*B. Ath Harv. U S.*

The same. Second edition Boston, 1822. 12°, pp. xii, 324 + 2 pl. and Atlas, 4°, 12 maps [*B Publ Y. C.*
Many later editions

4 Epitome of Modern Geography Boston, 1820 12°.
[*B Ath.*

5. Sketches of the Earth and its Inhabitants: with one hundred engravings Boston, 1823. 2 vols, 12°, pp viii, 372, iv, 350; and plates. [*B Ath B. Publ. Br Mus. M H. S. U S. Y C.*

6. Elements of History, ancient and modern: with Historical Charts. Boston, 1826. 12°, pp. xii, 324. And Atlas. Folio. [*Y. C.*

Several editions

7. Illustrations of the Historical Atlas, with Questions. Boston, 1826. 12°, pp. 24. [*B. Publ.*

8. An Epitome of Geography, with an Atlas. Boston, 1826. 12°, pp. vi, 165; and Atlas. [*U. S.*
Several editions.

9. An Epitome of History, with Historical and Chronological Charts. Cambridge, 1827. 12°, pp. viii, 130, and Atlas. 4°. [*B. Publ. U. S.*
An abstract of No. 6. Several editions.

10. Outlines of Scripture Geography, with an Atlas. Boston, 1828. 12°, pp. 44; and Atlas, 12°, 6 maps. [*Harv.*
Several editions.

11 A Comprehensive Pronouncing and Explanatory Dictionary of the English Language, with pronouncing vocabularies of classical and Scripture proper names Boston, 1830 12°, pp xx, 400. [*Harv. N. Y. Publ.*

The same. Second Edition, Boston, 1831 12°. [*B Ath*

To an edition published in 1835 a Vocabulary of Modern Geographical Names was added.

The same. Revised and Enlarged, and made substantially an abridgement of the author's "Universal and Critical Dictionary." Boston, 1847. 12°, pp 491. [*Y. C.*
Several later editions.

12. Remarks on Longevity and the Expectation of Life in the United States, relating more particularly to the State of New Hampshire, with some Comparative Views in relation to Foreign Countries. In *Memoirs* of the American Academy of Arts and Sciences, New Series, vol. 1, pp. 1–44. Cambridge, 1833. 4°.
Prepared in 1825, after his election to the Academy.

13. An Elementary Dictionary of the English Language Boston, 1835 12°.
Many editions.

14 Elements of Ancient Classical and Scripture Geography: with an Atlas Boston, 1839. 12°, pp. v, 74, and Atlas, 4°.
[B. Publ.

15. A Pronouncing and Explanatory Dictionary of the English Language. Boston, 1842. 12°. [B Publ
Many editions.

16. A Universal and Critical Dictionary of the English Language: to which are added Walker's Key to the Pronunciation of Classical and Scripture Proper Names, much enlarged and improved, and a Pronouncing Vocabulary of Modern Geographical Names. Boston, 1846. 8°, pp. lxxvi, 956.
[B Ath. Harv. M. H. S. Y. C
The prospectus of this edition was issued in August, 1844.
Many later editions

17. A Primary Pronouncing Dictionary of the English Language; with Vocabularies of Classical, Scripture and Modern Geographical Names. Boston, 1850. 16°, pp 352. [U. S
Many later editions.

18 A Gross Literary Fraud Exposed, relating to the publication of Worcester's Dictionary in London Boston, 1853. 8°, pp. 24 [A. A. S Br. Mus Harv. M. H. S U S.

The same; together with Three Appendixes; including the Answer of S Converse to an Attack on him by Messrs G & C. Merriam. Boston, 1854. 8°, pp 34 + 11.
[B Publ. Br. Mus. M. H. S. Y C.
This pamphlet was due to a misunderstanding, as the publication referred to was the work of an English publisher, who issued an edition of Mr. Worcester's Dictionary of 1846, with a misleading title-page and back-label, implying that the work was compiled by Worcester from Webster's materials; this pamphlet charges that the fraud was due to Webster's publishers

19. A Pronouncing Spelling-book of the English Language Philadelphia [1857.] 12°, pp. 180. [B. Publ
Several editions.

20. A Dictionary of the English Language. Philadelphia, 1860 4°, pp. 1786.
[B. Ath. B. Publ Harv. M. H. S. U S Y C.

21. A Comprehensive Spelling book of the English Language, Boston, 1864. 12°, pp. 156.

He also edited the following.

Johnson's English Dictionary, as improved by Todd, and abridged by Chalmers, with Walker's Pronouncing Dictionary combined .. Boston, 1828. 8°, pp. 1156

An American Dictionary .. by Noah Webster. Abridged from the quarto edition of the author. New York, 1830. 8°, pp. xxiv, 1011. [*Y C.*

The American Almanac and Repository of Useful Knowledge, for the years 1831–42. Boston, 1830–41. 12 vols., 12°. [*Y. C*

AUTHORITIES.

Granite Monthly, iii, 245–52 Historical Magazine, 2d series, ii, 169–70. Mass Hist. Society's Proceedings, viii, 467–68; xviii, 169–73 *J F Worcester,* Worcester Family, 31, 57–58. *S. T. Worcester,* Hist. of Hollis, 297–300, 392

Annals, 1811-12

In the prospect of the early establishment of a Medical Department, the Corporation at a Special Meeting in April, 1812, offered to Dr. Mason F. Cogswell (Yale 1780), of Hartford, the appointment of Professor of Surgery and Anatomy, and to Dr. Jonathan Knight (Yale 1808) that of Assistant Professor in the same subjects.

At the same meeting a committee was named to represent to the General Assembly the need of another dormitory; but no result followed from this application.

The Rev. Dr James Dana, of New Haven, for fourteen years a Fellow of the Corporation, died in August, 1812; and at the ensuing Commencement, the Rev. John Elliott (Yale 1786), of East Guilford, was elected as his successor. At the same Commencement the Rev. Noah Benedict, of Woodbury, resigned his seat in the Corporation, and the vacant place was offered to the Rev Dr. Azel Backus (Yale 1787), of Bethlehem; but he was simultaneously elected to the presidency of Hamilton College, which office he accepted.

Tutor Mills Day (Yale 1803) died at the house of his brother, Professor Day, in June, 1812, and Chauncey A Goodrich (Yale 1810) was elected at Commencement to fill the vacant tutorship. A tutor's salary was then $380, with board in the Commons

Sketches, Class of 1812

**Carolus C. Austin* *1849
**Elihu Whittelsey Baldwin,* A.M., S.T.D. Hanov. 1837, Coll. Wabas. Praeses *1840
*Elija Baldwin, A.M. *1819
*Hezekias Selleck Beach
*Alexander Bliss *1827
*Georgius Bliss *1873
*Guilielmus Whiting Boardman, A.M. Trin. 1845, LL.D Trin. 1863, Soc. ex off., e Congr. *1871
**Solyman Brown,* A.M. 1817 *1876
*Guilielmus Platt Buffett *1874
**Calvinus Colton,* 1813, A.M. 1832, LL.D. Hobart. 1852, in Coll. Trin. Oecon. Polit. Prof. *1857
*Platt Hiramus Crosby
**Johannes Crukshanks,* A.M. *1818
*Johannes Davis, A.M. 1822, LL.D. Harv. 1834, e Congr., Reip. Mass. Gubern., Rerumpubl. Foed. Sen. *1854
*Benjamin Day *1872
*Edvardus Delafield, M.D. Coll. Med. et Chir. N. Ebor. 1816 et in eod. Obstetr. Prof. et ejusd. Praes. *1875
*Theodorus Dexter *1849
*Nathanael Dike *1867
*Thomas Dunlap, A.M. *1864
*Johannes Worthington Dwight *1836
*Samuel Lynson Edwards, A.M. 1834 *1877
*Robertus Gibson *1829
**Carolus Augustus Goodrich* *1862

*Nathan Guilford *1854
*Edvardus Holden *1827
*Stephanus Farrar Jones
*Dennis Kimberly *1862
*Ezra L'Hommedieu *1819
*Richardus Harrison Long, 1813
*Samuel Coit Morgan *1876
*Richardus Cary Morse, A.M. et Mediob. 1825 *1868
*Carolus Nichols *1865
*Josephus Noble *1822
*Daniel Noyes *1852
**Georgius Payson,* A.M. 1819 *1823
*Nathanael Shaw Perkins, A.M., M.D. 1829 *1870
*Thomas Shaw Perkins, A.M. *1844
*David Prentice, A.M. et Columb. 1833, LL.D. Conc 1839, in Coll. Hobart. Lingg. et Litt. Graec. et Lat. Prof. *1857
*Isaacus Trimble Preston, A.M., Reip. Ludov. Cur. Supr. Jurid. *1852
*Guilielmus Rumsey, A.M, M D Univ. Penns 1817 *1871
*Ahaz Sanford *1813
*Abrahamus Curtis Sheldon *1834
*Georgius Smith *1827
**Ward Stafford,* A.M. *1851
*Augustus Russell Street *1866
*Theodorus Strong, A M. Hamilt., LL D. Rutg. 1835, in Coll. Hamilt. et Coll. Rutg. Math. et Phil Nat. Prof., Acad Nat. Soc. *1869
*Johannes Wagner, A.M., M.D. 1818, in Coll Med. Carol Austr. Chirurg. Prof. *1841
*Andreas Ferdinandus Warner, A.M. *1825
*Julius Wilcoxson *1852
*Johannes Witter, A.M., Tutor *1858
*Caleb Smith Woodhull, A M. 1822 *1866

CHARLES [C.] AUSTIN, the youngest of eight children of Elijah Austin, a merchant of New Haven, who died suddenly of yellow fever in 1794, and grandson of Elias and Eunice Austin, of Durham, was born in New Haven on July 30, 1793 A younger brother of Elijah Austin was Moses Austin, the Texan pioneer. His mother was Esther, eldest daughter of John and Mary (Richardson) Phelps, of Stafford, and sister of Timothy Phelps (Yale 1780). She next married in 1798 Peleg Sanford, another New Haven merchant, who died in 1802; and thirdly Elisha Lewis, also of New Haven. Peleg Phelps Sanford (Yale 1820) was a son of her second marriage.

His father's estate was insolvent, and he was prepared for College by his brother-in-law, the Rev Horace Holley (Yale 1803), and entered during the Junior year. After leaving College he assumed a middle name.

The family were communicants in the Episcopal Church, and he was prepared for holy orders under the direction of Bishop Kemp of Maryland, who ordained him as deacon on June 13, 1819.

He had while studying theology been employed as tutor in the family of the Hon Alexander C Hanson, of Elk Ridge, Baltimore County, Maryland, and had acted as lay-reader in Christ Church, Elk Ridge.

On his ordination he took charge of St. Matthew's Church, Prince George's County, and Rock Creek Church, District of Columbia; but on December 1, 1820, he was elected to the rectorship of St Thomas's Church, Owings Mills, Baltimore County, with the duty of officiating on alternate Sundays at St John's Church, Worthington Valley. In this position he spent the rest of his life.

It was at first arranged that he should receive a salary of $670, but the amount paid dwindled so seriously (after about 1834 to only a little over $100), that he was compelled to resort for support to keeping a school in his house, which was well patronized

He was married, on November 21, 1821, to Ann, daughter of Thomas Buckler, of Baltimore, by whom he had three daughters and two sons.

He died at his rectory, after a brief illness, on February 9, 1849, in his 56th year. His second daughter died the next day, in her 20th year, and they were buried in one grave

Mr. Austin was a man of great activity and energy, and prompt to respond to every call of duty. He maintained a high character for frankness, integrity, and independence.

He printed one sermon, delivered on September 12, 1823, in St. Thomas's Church, before a detachment of the Eleventh Brigade, Maryland Militia.

AUTHORITIES.

Rev E. Allen, The Garrison Church, 80-87 Phelps Family, 1, 303, 529-30 *Rev Hobart Smith,* MS Letter, June, 1911.

Elihu Whittelsey Baldwin, the fourth child and eldest son of Deacon Jonathan Baldwin, of Durham, Greene County, New York, and grandson of Abiel and Mehitabel (Johnson) Baldwin, of Durham, Connecticut, was born on December 25, 1789 His mother was Submit, youngest child of Deacon Christopher and Patience Lord, of Saybrook, Connecticut, and niece of the Rev. Nathan Strong (Yale 1742). He was prepared for college by his pastor, the Rev. Jesse Townsend (Yale 1790), and entered Yale in the fall of 1807 In May of the Freshman year he united with the College Church on profession of faith.

He left College at the opening of the Sophomore year in order to earn money, and spent nearly a year in Bethlehem, Connecticut, as an assistant in the school of the Rev. Azel Backus (Yale 1787), and during the next winter had charge of the Academy in Fairfield,—returning to the next lower class in College in June, 1810

For the two years next after graduation he again had charge of the Fairfield Academy, and he then spent three years in the Andover Theological Seminary.

On May 1, 1817, he was licensed to preach by the Presbytery of Newburyport, and with the expectation of spending some time in missionary labor in western New York and Ohio, he was ordained as an evangelist on September 10, at Londonderry, New Hampshire, by the Presbytery of Londonderry.

While visiting in New York city, on his way to his destination, he was persuaded to accept an appointment as City Missionary, and for three years from October, 1817, labored without stint in that arduous field.

On May 12, 1819, he was married to Julia Cook, only daughter of Elias A. and Elizabeth (Cook) Baldwin, of Newark, New Jersey, and sister of the Rev. Joseph B. Baldwin (Yale 1827)

His labors in a populous portion of the city resulted in the formation of a church, in March, 1818, with the title of the Seventh Presbyterian Church, over which he was installed pastor on December 25, 1820

He retained this position, amid many trials and discouragements, and many tokens of success, for upwards of fourteen years, declining meanwhile various offers of other fields

In addition to his pastoral duties he undertook much labor in connection with the New York Evangelical Missionary Society of Young Men, by which he was in part supported, and of which he became the Corresponding Secretary in 1821.

In November, 1834, he was approached by an agent for Wabash College, an institution founded two years before at Crawfordsville, Indiana, for the supply of educated ministers for that State, with the offer of the presidency.

The claims of such a service appealed to him strongly, and in February, 1835, he signified his acceptance of the appointment He left his people on the first of May; and devoted several months to securing funds for the College, before entering on his duties, early in November. He was duly inaugurated at Commencement, in July, 1836.

In February, 1838, he received an urgent call to the pastorate of the Manhattan Presbyterian Church in New York City, but he declined from a sense of duty to the College He declined a similar invitation, later in the same year, from the Second Presbyterian Church in Indianapolis

In July, 1839, he received the honorary degree of Doctor of Divinity from Hanover College, Indiana, an institution under the control of the Old School branch of the Presbyterian Church, to which President Baldwin did not belong.

After the College Commencement in July, 1840, he made a tedious journey into the Northern part of the State, and in September he was seized with the local bilious fever of which he died, in Crawfordsville, after a month's painful illness, on October 15, in his 51st year.

His widow died in Indianapolis, on December 12, 1850, in her 51st year.

Their children were four sons and four daughters, of whom three sons and a daughter died in early life The surviving son was graduated at Wabash College in 1846

Dr. Baldwin impressed all beholders as a remarkably gentle, guileless, and godly man, a simple, practical preacher, of uniform equanimity and indefatigable industry.

His portrait is given in the *Memoir* by Dr Hatfield.

He published:

1. Fashionable Amusements. [A Tract] New York (American Tract Society); 12°, pp. 12 [*Y. C*
Written in 1815.

2 The Final Judgment A Sermon, from Hebr. ix, 29. In *The National Preacher*, vol 2, pp. 107–11, December, 1827

3 Considerations for the American Patriot. A Sermon [from Ps ii, 11] delivered on occasion of the Annual Thanksgiving, December 12, 1827. New-York, 1828. 8°, pp 24.

[*A. C. A. N. Y. H. S. U. T. S. Y. C*

4 The Five Apprentices. (Procrastination; or the history of Edward Crawford.) Philadelphia, 1828 12°. [*Br. Mus*

Written for the American Sunday School Union.

5. Extracts from a charge delivered at the Ordination of five Home Missionaries, in Newburyport, Massachusetts, on October 25, 1828, are given in the *Home Missionary,* vol. 1, pp. 111-13 (November, 1828).

6. The young Freethinker reclaimed. Philadelphia, 1830 12°.

Written for the American Sunday School Union.

7. An extract from a private letter, of December, 1832, on the voluntary church efforts of American Christians, is printed in the *Congregational Magazine* of London, vol. 16, pp. 495-97, August, 1833.

8 An Address delivered in Crawfordsville, Indiana, July 13th, 1836. On occasion of his Inauguration as President of Wabash College Cincinnati, 1836. 8°, pp 33

[*B. Publ. Harv. Y C.*

On liberal education

9. A Sermon [from Ps. cxxvi, 3] preached at the Dedication of the Presbyterian Church in Madison-Street, New-York, 27th August, 1837. New-York, 1837. 8°, pp. 20. [*U. T S. Y. C.*

The Madison-street church was a colony from that of which Dr Baldwin had been pastor.

Copious extracts from his diary, parts of his Addresses to the graduating classes of Wabash College, and other compositions, are given in his *Memoir* by the Rev. Edwin F Hatfield (New-York, 1843. 12°, pp vi, 404 + pl).

AUTHORITIES

Baldwin Genealogy, ii, 518, 527, 557-58. *Hatfield,* Memoir of E. W Baldwin. N Y Observer, Oct 31, 1840. *Sprague,* Annals of the Amer Pulpit, iv, 572-81 Wabash College Semi-Centennial, 24-27

ELIJAH BALDWIN, the younger son of Joshua and Abigail Baldwin, of Milford, Connecticut, and grandson of Joshua and Elizabeth Baldwin, of Milford, was born in 1789, and was prepared for College by his pastor, the Rev. Bezaleel Pinneo He was a second cousin of the father of his classmate, just noticed

He studied theology after graduation, and was licensed to preach. His health had for some time been feeble, and he died after a brief illness, on June 6, 1819, at the age of 30, at the house of the Rev. Zephaniah Swift, of Derby.

His father's will, dated in 1817, states that he has advanced nine hundred dollars for the education of this son.

AUTHORITIES

Baldwin Genealogy, ii, 501

HEZEKIAH SELLECK BEACH, son of Hezekiah Beach, of Huntington, Connecticut, was baptized on May 2, 1790, and was prepared for College by his pastor, the Rev. Dr. David Ely

After graduation he went South, and for a few years his relatives received occasional letters from him; but these finally ceased, and no particulars of his later history are known.

The only fixed date which has been recovered is that he was in Wilmington, North Carolina, in the summer of 1817. An uncertain rumor places him later in New Orleans.

AUTHORITIES.

J. Tomlinson, MS Letter, January, 1865

ALEXANDER BLISS, JUNIOR, the second son of Alexander Bliss, of Springfield, Massachusetts, by his second wife, Abigail, daughter of Thomas and Abigail Williams, of

Roxbury, was born in Springfield on August 16, 1792. Edmund Bliss (Yale 1806) was a half-brother.

After graduation he studied law, and settled in Boston, where he was taken into partnership by Daniel Webster.

He married on June 6, 1825, Elizabeth, the youngest child and only daughter of the Hon. William and Rebecca (Morton) Davis, of Plymouth.

He was regarded as a brilliant lawyer, but died early, while on a visit in Plymouth, on July 15, 1827, in his 35th year.

His children were two sons, who were graduated at Harvard University in 1846 and 1847, respectively.

Mrs. Bliss next married, on August 16, 1838, the Hon George Bancroft (Harvard 1817), by whom she had one daughter. She died in Washington on March 15, 1886, in her 83d year An interesting volume of her Letters from London, while Mr Bancroft was United States Minister, has been published.

AUTHORITIES

Bliss Genealogy, 88, 159-60. *Bridgman,* Northampton Epitaphs, 111

George Bliss, the only son of the Hon. George Bliss (Yale 1784), of Springfield, Massachusetts, was born in Springfield on November 16, 1793. His grandfather, Moses Bliss (Yale 1755), was a half-brother of the father of Alexander Bliss, just noticed

Upon graduation he entered his father's law-office as a pupil, and during the war with England served as an aid to General Jacob Bliss, of Springfield, for a few months, thus acquiring the title of Colonel On being admitted to the bar, in September, 1815, he established himself in the neighboring town of Monson, where he remained for seven years.

He then returned to Springfield and entered into partnership with the Hon. Jonathan Dwight (Harvard 1793), whose eldest daughter, Mary, he married on April 20, 1825. She was a niece of Charles Shepherd (Yale 1798).

In 1827 he entered public life as a member of the State House of Representatives, and was re-elected for the next two years, as also in 1831–33, and 1839. He was also a member of the State Senate in 1835, and served as President of that body. He was elected to the Governor's Council in 1848–49, and was a Presidential Elector in 1852. In 1853 he was again chosen to the Lower House of the General Court, and was made Speaker

Among many public enterprises which claimed his attention, the chief was his bringing the Western Railroad, between Worcester and Albany, to successful completion. He was the General Agent of the road from 1836 to 1842, and its President from 1843 to 1846. He was one of the earliest promoters of the Hartford and Springfield Railroad.

On retiring from the Western Railroad presidency he visited Europe, and after his return became interested in other similar enterprises at the west, in conducting which he gained an enviable reputation. Thus, he was the President of the Michigan Southern and Northern Indiana Railroad from 1849 to 1852, and from 1858 to 1860; and President of the Chicago & Mississippi Railroad in 1853–54. In May, 1860, he withdrew from all active business

He was a warm friend of local improvements and of public charities in his native place To the City Library he gave the land on which its building stands (valued at $20,000), besides $10,000 in cash.

His wife died on April 12, 1869, in her 69th year; and his own death followed, in Springfield, on April 19, 1873, in his 80th year.

Besides a daughter who died in infancy, he left one daughter, the wife of George Walker (Dartmouth Coll. 1842), and one son (Harvard 1851), a distinguished lawyer of New York

His portrait is copied in Chapin's *Old Springfield.*

He published:

1. An Address to the Members of the Bar of the counties of Hampshire, Franklin and Hampden at their Annual Meeting at Northampton, September, 1826 Springfield, 1827 8°, pp. 85.

[*A. A. S. B Ath. B. Publ Br. Mus. Harv. M. H. S. U. S Y. C*

Giving a history of the Bar of Old Hampshire County.

2. An Address delivered at the Opening of the Town-Hall in Springfield, March 24, 1828. Containing Sketches of the early History of that Town, and those in its vicinity. Springfield, 1828. 8°, pp 68.

[*A. A S. B. Ath. B. Publ. Br. Mus. Harv. M. H. S. U S. Y. C.*

Re-published in the *Chapin Genealogy,* 1862, pp 257–328.

3 A Letter to the Majority of the Joint Committee of the Legislature, on the Affairs of the Western Rail Road, with some additional testimony proposed. By the President of the Corporation. Boston, 1843. 8°, pp. 26 [*Y C.*

4. Historical Memoir of the Springfield Cemetery, read to the Proprietors at their meeting, May 23, 1857. By G Bliss, their President. .. Springfield, 1857. 8°, pp 23.

[*A. A. S B. Publ. Harv M. H S U S. Y. C.*

The Memoir occupies pages 3–8

5. Letter to the Stockholders of the Michigan Southern & Northern Indiana Railroad Company. New York, 1860. 8°, pp. 13. [*Harv. N. Y. Publ.*

6. Historical Memoir of the Western Railroad. Springfield, 1863. 8°, pp. 191

[*B. Ath. B. Publ. Harv. M H. S. U. S. Y. C.*

AUTHORITIES.

Bates, Hist. Address, Springfield, 64. Bliss Genealogy, 157, 295 *Chapin,* Old Springfield, 59–62. Dwight Family, ii, 882–83.

William Whiting Boardman, the eldest child of the Hon. Elijah Boardman, a wealthy merchant of New Milford, Connecticut, afterwards United States Senator, and nephew of the Hon David Sherman Boardman (Yale 1793), was born in New Milford on October 10, 1794. His mother was Mary Ann, daughter of Dr. William and Ann (Mason) Whiting, of Great Barrington, Massachusetts. His youngest brother was graduated at Union College in 1818. He was prepared for Yale at Bacon Academy, in Colchester, under John Adams (Yale 1795). He was the youngest member of his class at graduation.

The College year 1812–13 he spent at Cambridge, Massachusetts, as a resident graduate, and he then read law under the direction of his uncle in New Milford and at the Litchfield Law School

When admitted to the bar he began practice in his native town, but in 1819 opened an office in New Haven

For the five following years he was clerk of the State Senate, and the death of his father in August, 1823, threw on him a great deal of private business. Besides filling minor city offices, from 1825 to 1829 he served as Judge of Probate for the New Haven District, and in 1830, 1831, and 1832, he was a member of the State Senate In 1836 and three succeeding years he was elected to the State House of Representatives, and served as Speaker in 1838 and 1839. In September, 1840, he was elected to Congress, to fill a vacancy, and in April, 1841, was re-elected and served for the ensuing term, ending in March, 1843, but declined a re-nomination. He was again a member of the State Legislature in 1845 (when he was also Speaker), 1849, and 1851.

Judge Boardman was also prominently engaged in many of the successful business corporations of the city, and had large influence in the councils of the Episcopal Church of the diocese. He was a Trustee of Trinity College from 1832 until his death, and was long a warden of Trinity Church, New Haven

On July 28, 1857, he was married to Lucy Hall, of Poland, Ohio, and he spent the following year in European travel.

The honorary degree of Doctor of Laws was conferred on him by Trinity College in 1863.

He died in New Haven on August 27, 1871, in his 77th year. His widow died here on March 29, 1906, in her 87th year. They had no children.

His large fortune was mainly distributed by his widow in works of public charity. A building, named Kirtland Hall, was given to the Sheffield Scientific School for instruction in mineralogy and allied subjects.

He published.

1. A Plan for Insurance against Fire, for the City of New Haven; prepared at the request of several of the citizens, and read at a public meeting, January 28, 1834. New Haven, 1834 8°, pp. 16. [*Harv* Y. C

A plan by which the city should undertake to insure all buildings within its limits, the expense being collected by taxation.

2 Remarks upon the speech of Hon. R. I. Ingersoll, on being conducted to the Chair, at the late Democratic Convention, held at Hartford. New Haven, 1839 8°, pp. 16 [*Y. C*

Anonymous

AUTHORITIES.

Boardman Genealogy, 333, 409–10 *Kilbourne,* Litchfield Biography, 319–20

Solyman Brown, a son of Nathaniel Brown, of Litchfield, Connecticut, was born in Litchfield on November 17, 1790. His mother was Thankful, fourth daughter of Nathaniel and Mary (Kilborn) Woodruff, of Litchfield, and a sister of Ezekiel Woodruff (Yale 1779). His father's circumstances prevented his thinking of a College education, but James Morris (Yale 1775), of Litchfield South Farms, became interested in him and received him gratuitously, as looking forward to the ministry, into his academy.

After graduation he studied theology, and was licensed to preach for four years by the Litchfield North Association of Ministers on September 30, 1813. For the most of the next three winters he taught in Kent, preaching also in Amenia, New York, and elsewhere in the vicinity. About the 1st of June, 1817, he was invited to preach in Ellsworth Society, in Sharon, for a year; but on applying to the Association in September for a renewal of his license he was refused, on the ground of constitutional levity, which had led him into various imprudences.

At this time he seems to have contemplated teaching as a permanent vocation, and in 1821 he removed to New York City, where he continued to be employed as a classical teacher until 1832.

After settling in New York he embraced the doctrines of Swedenborg, and was licensed as a preacher of the New Jerusalem Church. He served for some years, about 1841 to 1844, as Associate Minister of the Second Society of that Church in New York, with the Rev. Charles J. Doughty (Yale 1806).

In 1832 he studied dental surgery with Dr. Eleazer Parmly, of New York, and for many years followed that profession with enthusiasm.

Dr. Brown was married, on December 23, 1834, by the Rt. Rev. B. T. Onderdonk, to Elizabeth, daughter of Amos Butler, for many years editor and proprietor of the *New York Mercantile Advertiser*.

He removed his residence about 1845 to Brooklyn, and finally in 1874 went to Minnesota, where he made his home with a son-in-law, Judge C. D. Tuthill, in Dodge Centre, until his death, on February 13, 1876, in his 86th year. His mental faculties were clear and vigorous, up to his last brief illness.

His wife survived him with five daughters and a son, two sons having died in early manhood.

He published:

1. A Funeral Discourse [from Rev. xxii, 17], delivered in Ellsworth, Sharon, on the Death of Mrs. Julia Fuller, Wife of Mr. Ephraim Fuller .. : who died June 1st, 1817, aged 19 years. New-Haven, 1818. 12°, pp. 23. [*Y. C.*

Two poetical pieces are appended to the Discourse.

2. An Address to the People of Litchfield County. New-Haven, 1818. 12°, pp. 22. [*Y. C.*

Rehearsing his personal history with reference to his license to preach. Dated, December 26, 1817.

3. An Essay on American Poetry, with several Miscellaneous Pieces on a variety of subjects, sentimental, descriptive, moral, and patriotic. New-Haven, 1818 12°, pp. 191.

[*A C. A. B. Publ. Harv. N. Y. Publ. Y. C.*

Dedicated, January 1, 1818, to James Morris. The contents are entirely poetical; among the Miscellanies are some Lines on President Dwight.

4 Second Address to the People of Litchfield County. [1818] 12°, pp. 24 [*Br. Mus. Harv. Y. C.*

Dated at New Haven, February 10, 1818.

5. A comparative view of the systems of Pestalozzi and Lancaster; in an Address delivered before the Society of Teachers of the City of New York New York, 1825. 8°. [*Br. Mus.*

6 Sermons, illustrating the Method of Interpreting the Sacred Scriptures in their Spiritual Sense New-York, 1829. 8°, pp. 80. [*U. T. S.*

Containing five sermons.

7. Dentologia: a Poem on the diseases of the teeth, and their proper remedies.—With Notes .. by Eleazar Parmly, Dentist. New York, 1833. 8°, pp. 176. [*Surg. Gen'l's. Libr.*

The same. New-York, 1840. 8°, pp. 104.

Re-published, as a part of successive numbers of the American Journal of Dental Science, for 1840–41.

The same [Without the Notes.] New-York, 1840. 8°, pp. 46. [*Y. C.*

8 Dental Hygeia, a Poem, on the health and preservation of the teeth. New-York, 1838. 12°, pp. iv, 54. [*Y. C.*

9. Llewellen's Dog, a Ballad.—From the Young Ladies' Journal of Literature and Science, for December, 1840 New-York, 1840. 12°, pp. 12 [*A. A. S.*

10. Essay on the importance of regulating the teeth of children before the fourteenth year, or the period of life when the second set of teeth become perfectly developed. New York, 1841. 8°, pp 11. [*Surg. Gen'l's. Libr.*

11. Essay on the most direct methods by which a dental practitioner may succeed, without a possibility of a failure, in degrading both himself and his profession. New York, 1842. 8°, pp. 12.
[*Surg. Gen'l's. Libr.*

12. The Citizen and Strangers' Pictorial and Business Directory, for the City of New-York and its vicinity.—1853. New-York, sq. 12°, pp. 300. [*Br. Mus. N. Y. Publ. U. T. S.*
Issued on occasion of the World's Fair, and largely consisting of advertisements.

13. Union of Extremes: a Discourse [from Lev. xxv, 10] on Liberty and Slavery, as they stand related to the justice, prosperity, and perpetuity of the United Republic of North America. New-York. [1861?] 8°, pp. 24. [*A. C. A.*

He was also an editor of the following:

The American Journal of Dental Science .. New-York, 1839-43, vols. 1-4. 8°.

Semi-Annual Dental Expositor. New York, 1852-54. 8°.

AUTHORITIES.

Miss E. S. Brown, MS. Letter, June, 1876. Conn. Journal, Apr. 28, 1818. Kilbourn Family, 113.

William Platt Buffett, a son of Isaac and Hannah (Hedges) Buffett, of Smithtown, Long Island, and grandson of Joseph and Sarah (Smith) Buffett, of Smithtown, was born in Smithtown on April 1, 1793. He was prepared for College by his uncle, the Rev. Platt Buffett (Yale 1791), in Greenwich, Connecticut.

During the second year after graduation he attended the Litchfield Law School, and after two years' further study in an office in New York, he was admitted to practice in that city in 1817.

He then formed a partnership with his classmate, Ezra L'Hommedieu, and after his early death he returned, in 1820, to his native place, where he died on October 7, 1874, in his 82d year.

He was married on April 25, 1825, to Nancy, daughter of Jarvis Rogers, of Islip, who survived him, with five children.

Mr. Buffett was from early life a member of the Presbyterian Church, and for many years before his death a Ruling Elder.

He held numerous appointments in the line of professional advancement, and in 1851 was elected Judge of the Suffolk County Court and Surrogate.

AUTHORITIES.

W T Buffett, MS Letter, April, 1875

Calvin Colton, the third son of Major Luther Colton, of Longmeadow, Massachusetts, and grandson of Captain Simon and Abigail (Burt) Colton, of Longmeadow, was born on September 14, 1789. His mother was Thankful, youngest daughter of Richard and Naomi (Wright) Woolworth, of Longmeadow. Both parents died in his childhood. He was prepared for College by Levi Collins at the Monson Academy.

After graduation he entered the Andover Theological Seminary, completing the course in two instead of three years.

On September 17, 1817, he was ordained at Lewiston, New York, by the Presbytery of Niagara, for missionary service in that State, and spent two years in that work. On February 2, 1820, he was installed as pastor of a Presbyterian Church in Lenox, Genesee County, where he remained until February 11, 1824. He then removed to Batavia, in the same County, where he was installed over the Presbyterian Church on March 17, 1825, but was dismissed on account of the failure of his voice on September 30, 1826

In the following years he traveled widely in this country, and in August, 1831, went to England as correspondent of the *New-York Observer*. He had already contributed to that paper series of letters from the West and Southwest.

He remained there for four years, during which he wrote and published extensively, besides regularly contributing to the *Observer*.

He returned in the spring of 1835, and was admitted to deacon's orders in the Episcopal Church by Bishop Onderdonk, of New York, on April 24, 1836. He received priest's orders from the same hands on July 2, 1837, and officiated as Rector of the Church of the Messiah in New York City for one year, in 1837–38. But his infirm health still unfitted him for pulpit labor, and he soon resumed the work of a journalist.

His spirited pamphlets over the signature of Junius, in the campaign of 1840, had a considerable influence in securing the election of President Harrison, and from 1842 to 1844 he edited the *True Whig* in Washington.

Meantime certain of his publications (beginning with one in 1839, on *Abolition a sedition*) had attracted the notice of the Hon. Henry Clay, and an acquaintance was begun which resulted in Mr. Colton's going in 1844 to the Clay homestead in Ashland, Kentucky, where he was engaged for some two years in writing Mr. Clay's *Life*.

He had also become favorably known as an advocate of protection, and in recognition of his publication in 1848 of an elaborate work on political economy, advocating this system, a chair of instruction in that department was provided in Trinity College, at Hartford, for his acceptance, and he held that professorship from 1852 until his death. His duties, however, were only nominal, and his residence continued in New York City. His voice was restored in these last years, and he frequently preached, both in English and in French. His death occurred in Savannah, Georgia, on March 13, 1857, in his 68th year. He had gone to Savannah, in feeble health, at the beginning of February, and was buried at his birthplace.

A portrait is given in his *History of American Revivals,* and in the *International Monthly Magazine,* volume 4.

He was married, on February 16, 1820, to Abby North, youngest sister of David H. Raymond (Yale 1810), of Montville, Connecticut, who died in Batavia on February 1, 1826, in her 30th year. He left no children.

The honorary degree of Doctor of Laws was conferred on him by Hobart College in 1852.

He published:

1. History and Character of American Revivals of Religion. London, 1832. 12°, pp. xvi, 294. [*B. Ath B. Publ*

The same Second edition. London, 1832. 12°, pp. xvi, 294 + pl. [*B Publ. Br. Mus. Columbia Univ Y. C*

2 Manual for Emigrants to America. London, 1832 12°, pp. x, 203. [*B. Publ Br. Mus*

3. The Americans By an American in London. London, 1833 12°, pp. xii, 389.
[*B Ath B Publ Br Mus N Y. Publ. U. S. Y. C.*
A defence against the works of Captain Basil Hall and Mrs. Trollope

4 Tour of the American Lakes, and among the Indians of the North-West Territory, in 1830: disclosing the Character and Prospects of the Indian Race. London, 1833. 2 vols. 12°, pp xxxii, 316; vii, 387
[*A A S. B Ath. B Publ. Br. Mus Columbia Univ Harv. U. S. Y. C.*

5 The American Cottager, or, Conscience and the Lord's Supper. London, 1833.
A religious narrative.

6. Church and State in America. Inscribed to the Bishop of London. London, 1834. 8°, pp. iv, 64.
[*Br. Mus. N. Y. Publ. Y. C*
Includes a tribute to President Dwight.

7 Church and State in America—Part II. Review of the Bishop of London's Reply. London, 1834. 8°, pp. 20
[*Br. Mus N. Y. Publ. Y. C.*

Bishop Blomfield's Reply is contained in a note to the latter of two sermons which he had just published, on The Uses of a Standing Ministry and an Established Church.

8. Four Years in Great Britain. 1831–1835. New-York, 1835. 2 vols. 12°, pp. 312; 315. [*A. A. S. B. Ath. Y. C.*

The same. New and improved edition. New-York, 1836. 12°, pp. 359. [*Br. Mus. N. Y. Publ. U. S.*

Based on his letters to the *New-York Observer.*

9. Thoughts on the Religious State of the Country; with reasons for preferring Episcopacy. New-York, 1836. 12°, pp. 208. [*A. C. A. B. Ath. B. Publ. Harv. U. T. S. Y. C.*

Reprinted in London.

10. Protestant Jesuitism. By a Protestant. New-York, 1836. 12°, pp. 295. [*B. Publ. N. Y. Publ. U. T. S. Y. C.*

An anonymous criticism, of the methods of many of the benevolent and religious societies, and also preeminently of the Temperance reformation.

11. A Voice from America to England, by an American Gentleman. New York, 1837.

The same. London, 1839. 8°, pp. xii, 321. [*B. Publ. U. S.*

12. Abolition a Sedition.—By a Northern Man. Philadelphia, 1839. 12°, pp. vii, 187.

[*A. C. A. B. Ath. Columbia Univ. Harv. M. H. S. U. S. Y. C.*

Anonymous.

13. Colonization and Abolition contrasted. Philadelphia. [1839.] 8°, pp. 16.

[*A. C. A. B. Publ. C. H. S. Columbia Univ. U. S. Y. C.*

14. Reply to Webster. A Letter to Daniel Webster, .. in Reply to his Legal Opinion to Baring, Brothers & Co. upon the Illegality and Unconstitutionality of State Bonds, and Loans of State Credit. By Junius. New York, 1840. 8°, pp. ii, 79.

[*B. Ath. Br. Mus. Harv. M. H. S. U. S.*

15. The Crisis of the Country. By Junius. [1840.] 8°, pp. 16. [*B. Ath. Br. Mus. Harv. U. S. Y. C.*

Several editions.

16 Sequel to The Crisis of the Country. By Junius. [New York, 1840] 8°, pp 8 [*B. Ath. Br. Mus*

17. American Jacobinism By Junius .. [New York, 1840.] 8°, pp 8 [*B. Ath. Br. Mus*

18. One Presidential Term By Junius .. [New York, 1840] 8°, pp 12 [*Br. Mus N Y Publ*

19. The Right of Petition By Junius. [New York, 1840] 8°, pp. 16. [*B. Ath B. Publ*

20. The Junius Tracts New York, 1843-44. 10 numbers. 8°, each of 16 pp.

[*B. Publ Br. Mus. Columbia Univ. Harv. U. S. Y. C.*

No I, The Test, or Parties tried by their Acts; II, The Currency; III, The Tariff; IV, Life of Henry Clay; V, Political Abolition; VI, Democracy; VII, Labor and Capital; VIII, The Public Lands; IX, Annexation of Texas; X, The Tariff Triumphant.

21. The Life and Times of Henry Clay. New York, 1846. 2 vols. 8°, pp. 504 + pl.; 504 + pl.

[*A A. S Br. Mus Columbia Univ Harv. N. Y. Publ U. S. U. T. S. Y. C.*

22. The Rights of Labor. New York, 1846. 8°, pp. 96.

[*B Ath. B. Publ. Br. Mus. Columbia Univ. Harv*

23 Public Economy for the United States. New York, 1848. 8°, pp. 536. [*B Ath Br. Mus. U. S*

The same Second edition New York, 1849. 8°, pp. 536.

[*M. H. S. N. Y Publ U. S. Y C*

A protectionist work.

24. A Lecture on the Railroad to the Pacific. Delivered, August 12, 1850, at the Smithsonian Institute, Washington, at the request of numerous members of both Houses of Congress. New York, 1850. 8°, pp. 16.

[*Br. Mus Columbia Univ. N. Y. Publ U. T. S. Y C*

25. The Genius and Mission of the Protestant Episcopal Church in the United States. New York, 1853 12°, pp. 306

[*A. C. A B. Publ Br Mus Harv M H S Y. C.*

Also, republished in London

26. The Last Seven Years of the Life of Henry Clay. New York, 1853. 8°, pp. 504 + pl.
[*B. Ath. Br. Mus. Columbia Univ. U. S. Y. C.*

Towards the end of his life he was occupied in editing the following:
The Private Correspondence of Henry Clay. New York, 1855. pp. 642.

The Works of Henry Clay. New York, 1856–57. 6 vols. 8°. Volumes 1–3 contain Nos. 21 and 26, above.

AUTHORITIES.

Amer. Church Review, x, 309–10. *Baker,* Hist. of Montville, 585. *Crosby,* Annual Obit. Notices, 1857, 96–97. *Hotchkin,* Hist. of Western N. Y., 547–48. International Monthly Magazine, iv, 1–3. Longmeadow Centennial, Appendix, 39.

PLATT HIRAM CROSBY was born in Amenia, Duchess County, New York, in 1792, and was probably a son of Dr. Cyrenius (or Cyrenus) and Sally (Sutherland) Crosby. He was prepared for College by the Rev. Azel Backus (Yale 1787), of Bethlehem. His father is said to have been an apothecary in Poughkeepsie in 1819.

After graduation he studied law in the Litchfield Law School, and by or before 1817 he was established in his profession in New York City.

His name appears in the New York Directory of June, 1819, but no later.

He is said to have emigrated to South America in destitute circumstances, and to have died there about 1827.

He published the following translation from the Spanish:

Letters on the United Provinces of South America, addressed to the Hon. Henry Clay, Speaker of the House of Representatives of the U. States, by Don Vicente Pazos. New-York, 1819. 8°, pp. 260 + map. [*Y. C.*

JOHN CRUKSHANKS was born in Charleston, South Carolina, in 1793 or 1794, and entered College in 1809 At graduation he delivered an Oration on Literary Enterprise

He at once entered the Princeton Theological Seminary, and remained there between two and three years.

He then returned to South Carolina, and was ordained by the Presbytery of Harmony on May 8, 1816, and installed over the church in the parish of John's Island and Wadmalaw, some ten or twelve miles west of Charleston.

Here he remained until his death, which took place in Princeton, New Jersey, on August 27, 1818, at the age of 25 He left home in May, for a voyage to the North for the benefit of his health; but pulmonary consumption had so far weakened him that he sank gradually after his arrival in Princeton He was unmarried.

AUTHORITIES.

N. Y. Spectator, Sept. 4, 1818

JOHN DAVIS, the youngest son of Deacon Isaac Davis, of Northboro, Worcester County, Massachusetts, and grandson of Simon and Hannah (Gates) Davis, of Rutland, was born in Northboro on January 13, 1787. His mother was Anna, daughter of Dr. Samuel and Anna (Gott) Brigham, of Marlboro, and step-daughter of Captain Stephen Maynard, of Westboro. He was prepared for College in part at the Leicester Academy, under Simeon Colton (Yale 1806).

After graduation he studied law with the Hon. Francis Blake (Harvard 1789), of Worcester, and on his admission to the bar in December, 1815, he established himself in Spencer, in his native county; but found the opportunities there so narrow that he removed five months later to Worcester, where he soon attained high professional eminence.

He married, late in March, 1822, Eliza, daughter of the Rev. Dr. Aaron Bancroft (Harvard 1778) and Lucretia (Chandler) Bancroft, of Worcester

In 1823 he formed a partnership with the Hon. Levi Lincoln (Harvard 1802), who was, however, appointed a Justice of the Supreme Court of the State in February, 1824, on Mr. Lincoln's retirement from the bar, Mr Davis became the acknowledged head of the profession in Worcester County. Later he was associated in partnership with Charles Allen (1824-31), and with Emory Washburn (1831-34).

In the fall of 1824 he was chosen as a Representative in Congress, and he held that office until January, 1834, when he entered on the duties of the Governorship of Massachusetts, to which he was elected by the Legislature, no choice having been made by the people. While still in that office he was elected in January, 1835, to the United States Senate; but in January, 1841, two months before the expiration of his term, he resigned to resume the position of Governor, which he held for two years longer.

He then retired to private life until March, 1845, when he was elected to the Legislature to fill the unexpired term of the late Hon Isaac C. Bates (Yale 1802) in the United States Senate At the expiration of the succeeding term, in March, 1853, he retired definitely, after over twenty-five years of strenuous and eminently successful public service.

His Congressional career was distinguished for his championship of the protective policy, and for his services as Chairman of the Senate's Committee on Commerce. His personal influence was unusually strong, and his fidelity to duty, his discretion, firmness, and spotless integrity gave him an enviable preeminence. The familiar cognomen of "Honest John Davis" was richly deserved. In public life his simplicity and aversion to display were marked characteristics. In the words of Senator Hoar, "Mr. Davis was a man of great practical wisdom, infrequent speech, compact, clear, and convincing in statement and reasoning."

Although Mr Davis was not remarkably gifted as a debater, his sound, practical judgment, his rare political sagacity, and acquaintance with the wants of the people, made him a safer and better legislator than most of those with whom he was specially brought into comparison In character he was a good specimen of the New England puritan, plain and simple in manners, of absolute integrity both in public and private life, prudent, modest, and self-reliant.

His senatorial career was overshadowed by the eloquence and ambition of his brilliant colleague, Daniel Webster; but he was second to none in enlightened and patriotic statesmanship. He showed his sturdy independence in such acts as his vote against the war with Mexico, and his opposition to the Compromises of 1850 and the Fugitive slave bill; an impromptu reply of his to Mr. Buchanan in 1840 was an effective agency in the overthrow of Van Buren's administration.

In 1844 he was the most promising candidate of the Whigs for the nomination to the Vice-Presidency, but his opposition to slavery made him ineligible; Mr Clay, however, was proposing, in case of his own election, to make Mr Davis his Secretary of the Treasury.

He died suddenly, at his home in Worcester, on April 19, 1854, in his 68th year. A sermon on his death by his pastor, the Rev Dr. Alonzo Hill, was afterwards published.

His widow died in Worcester, on January 24, 1872, at the age of 81.

His children were five sons, all of whom survived him. The eldest son (Harvard 1840) won distinction as a diplomatist; the third son (Williams Coll 1845) was a general in the civil war, the fourth (Harvard 1849) was a President of the University of California; and the youngest (Harvard 1854) is an authority on history, especially of finance.

A portrait is owned by the University.

The honorary degree of LL.D. was conferred on him by Harvard in 1834.

He was greatly interested in the American Antiquarian Society, which has its home in Worcester, and filled the office of President at the time of his death. His valuable manuscript correspondence has been deposited in the Library of that Society, which also owns a discriminating sketch of Mr. Davis's character, in manuscript, by the Hon. Charles Hudson.

He published:

1. An Oration, pronounced at Worcester, (Mass.) on the Fortieth Anniversary of American Independence. Worcester, 1816. 8°, pp. 23.

[*A A S B. Ath. B Publ. Br. Mus Harv. M. H S. U. S.*

At a celebration by the Federal Republicans.

2. An Account of the proposed Canal from Worcester to Providence. .. with some remarks upon Inland Navigation .. Worcester, 1822. 8°, pp. 18. [*A. A. S. B. Publ.*

Anonymous

3 An Address delivered at the Dedication of the Town Hall, in Worcester, (Mass) on the second day of May, 1825. Worcester. 8°, pp. 36.

[*A A. S B. Publ Br Mus. Harv. U. S. Y. C.*

4. Duties on Woolens.—Speech in the House of Representatives, on the Bill for protecting the woolen manufacturers. [Washington, 1827.] 8°, pp. 8. [*B. Publ Harv M. H. S.*

5. Speech on the Tariff Bill—Delivered in the House of Representatives, March 12, 1828. Washington, 1828 8°, pp. 38. [*B Publ. Br Mus.*

Another edition Washington, 1828. 12°, pp. 36 [*N. Y. Publ.*

6 Speech on the Bill for the more effectual collection of Impost Duties. Delivered in Committee of the Whole on the state of the

Union—House of Representatives, May 4, 1830. Washington, 1830 8°, pp. 28

[*A. A. S. B. Ath. B. Publ. Harv. M. H. S. Y. C.*

7. Speech, delivered in the House of Representatives of the United States, in Committee of the Whole, on the Tariff Bill of 1832—From the National Intelligencer. Boston, 1833 8°, pp 24.

[*A. A. S.*

8. Addresses to the Two Branches of the Legislature, January, 1834, 1835, 1841, 1842 Boston. 8°. [*B. Publ.*

9. Obituary Notice of Christopher C. Baldwin, late Librarian of the Society In Transactions and Collections of the American Antiquarian Society, vol. 2, pp. 557–64. Worcester, 1836. 8°.

10. Speech upon the Bill reported by the Committee of Finance, and commonly called the Sub-Treasury Bill—Delivered in the Senate of the United States on the 28th of February and 1st of March, 1838. Washington, 1838. 8°, pp. 27.

[*A. A. S. B. Ath. Br. Mus. M. H. S*

11. Eleventh Anniversary Address. Delivered before the Officers, Members and Friends of the American Institute, in Chatham-street Chapel, Oct 18, 1838.

In the *Journal* of the Institute. Vol. 4, pp 1–29, and separately.

12. Government Expenditures—Remarks in the Senate, December 21, 1838, in relation to the wasteful expenditures of the Federal Government under the last and present administrations [Washington, 1838.] 8°, pp. 8

[*A. A. S. B. Ath. Br. Mus Harv. M H. S.*

13. Speech on the Sub-Treasury Bill. Delivered in the Senate of the United States, January 23, 1840. Washington, 1840. 8°, pp. 16. [*B. Ath. Br. Mus. M. H. S. Y. C.*

The same with new title. Sub-Treasury Bill—Reply to Mr. Buchanan, of Pennsylvania, on the reduction of wages and of the value of property. Delivered in the Senate of the United States, January 23, 1840. Washington, 1840. 8°, pp. 16

[*B Ath. B. Publ. M. H. S. Y. C.*

14. Reply to the charge of misrepresenting Mr. Buchanan's argument in favor of the Hard-Money System, and the consequent reduction of wages—Delivered in the Senate of the United States, March 6, 1840. Washington, 1840. 8°, pp. 8.

[*B. Publ. Br. Mus Harv. M. H. S. Y. C*

15 Address to the American Antiquarian Society, at the Annual Meeting, in Worcester, October 23d, 1843 In the *Proceedings* of the Society, Oct., 1843, pp. 3–10.

16 Speech upon the Bill "to reduce duties and for other purposes," in which the modern doctrines of free trade in their application to the United States are examined.—Delivered in the United States Senate on the 16th and 17th of July, 1846. Washington, 1846 8°, pp 31 [*A A. S. B Ath. Harv Y C.*

17. Sketch of the Life of John Quincy Adams. Prefixed to his Poems of Religion and Society, New York, 1848 12°, pp. 7–11.

18 Speech on the Compromise Bill, delivered in the Senate of the United States, June 28th and 29th, 1850. Washington, 1850. 8°, pp. 16 [*A. A S B. Publ. Harv.*

19. Speech in the Senate of the United States, January 28, 1851, on the Compromise Question . [Washington] 8°, pp. 7. [*B Ath Harv Y C.*

20 Report of the Council of the American Antiquarian Society, April 30, 1851. In the *Proceedings* of the Society, 1851–52, pp. 4–12.

AUTHORITIES

J Q Adams, Diary, ix, 64–66, 75, 206, 263 *G Allen,* Reminiscences, 54–55. Amer Antiquarian Society's Proceedings, April, 1854, 4–8, 11–27, 43–44; Oct, 1893, 15–24, 334–335 *C C Baldwin,* Diary, 24, 32, 38, 143, 186, 235, 242, 244, 264–66, 344–45, 352. *Hon Horace Davis,* Ancestry of John Davis *Estabrook,* Northboro Davises, 8, 44–45, 50, 56, 79–81. *Lincoln,* Hist of Worcester, 207–08 N. England Magazine, xxv, 542–43 *Polk,* Diary, ii, 75–77

BENJAMIN DAY, the fourth son of Heman Day, of West Springfield, Massachusetts, and nephew of Benjamin Day (Yale 1768), was born in West Springfield on November 9, 1790. His mother was Lois, eldest child of Colonel Benjamin and Esther (Backus) Ely, of West Springfield.

After graduation he studied for the profession of the law, and was admitted to the bar in 1815, but engaged in practice for only a short time.

He was married, on December 3, 1820, to Frances, second daughter of James Scutt and Mary (Sanford) Dwight, of Springfield.

He became the cashier of the Springfield Bank, and so continued until 1823. In 1824 he removed to Geneva, New York, and for three years held the position of cashier in a bank in that city.

He then returned to Springfield, and became the head of the firm of Day, Brewer & Dwight, of which his wife's eldest brother was a member. His brother-in-law died in 1831, and he was afterwards engaged in the dry-goods business in the firm of Day & Willard. In 1833–34 he was agent of the Chicopee Manufacturing Company, at Chicopee Falls, and in 1834 was a member of the State Legislature. Subsequently he was from 1835 to about 1843 a broker in New York City.

From 1849 to 1856 he was President of the Springfield Bank, and from March, 1859, to June, 1869, Treasurer of the Holyoke Water Power Company.

He then retired from active business, and died in Springfield on May 13, 1872, in his 82d year.

His widow died on December 23, 1872, in her 77th year.

Their children were three daughters and a son. Two daughters only survived their parents, the elder being the wife of the Rev. Dr. Thomas H. Skinner (Univ. N. Y. 1840).

AUTHORITIES

Chapin, Old Springfield, 159–60 Day Genealogy, 2d ed., 24, 39. Dwight Family. ii, 868–69 Nathaniel Ely's Descendants, 56, 121.

EDWARD DELAFIELD, the fifth son of John and Ann (Hallett) Delafield, and a brother of Major Joseph Delafield (Yale 1808), was born in New York City on May 17, 1794, and was prepared for College in Union Hall Academy, in Jamaica, Long Island, under Lewis E. A. Eigenbrodt (Univ. of Giessen 1793).

On graduation he entered the office of Dr. Samuel Borrowe, of New York, and pursued the course of study in the College of Physicians and Surgeons, where he received his diploma as Doctor of Medicine in 1816.

He had served as Assistant House Physician for a year in the New York Hospital, before going in the summer of 1816 to Europe, where he continued his studies for about a year, chiefly in London, where he was a pupil of Dr. Abernethy and Sir Astley Cooper.

On his return he began practice in the City of New York. He early conceived the idea of an institution for the exclusive treatment of diseases of the eye; and in connection with his special friend and associate, Dr. John Kearny Rodgers (Princeton Coll. 1811), he opened rooms in August, 1820, for such treatment, from which beginning grew the New York Eye Infirmary, organized in 1821, of which Dr. Delafield continued to be an Attending Surgeon until 1850, and after that Consulting Surgeon until 1870, when he was elected Vice President.

Soon after the founding of the Infirmary, he became a partner of Dr. Borrowe, and was thus early introduced into a large and lucrative practice. In 1825 he was made Professor of Obstetrics and of the diseases of women and children in the College of Physicians and Surgeons, and in 1834 an attending physician to the New York Hospital. He filled the professorship with signal ability until 1838, when his increasing private practice obliged him reluctantly to withdraw both from this and from his position at the hospital

In 1842 he was able to carry out a project which he had long entertained by founding the New York Society for the relief of Widows and Orphans of Medical Men, of which he was the President (until 1850), and to the management of whose affairs he devoted much time.

In 1858 he was elected President of the College of Physicians and Surgeons, a position which he held until his death. He thus became officially one of the Board of

Governors of the Roosevelt Hospital, and as chairman of the Building Committee gave himself unsparingly to the details of that work and the organization of the institution.

After an illness of about eighteen months, he died in New York, of pneumonia, on February 13, 1875, in his 81st year. By a strange coincidence the three surviving sons of John Delafield died on three successive days, February 12, 13, and 14, aged 84, 80, and 82 years, respectively, and one funeral service was held for the three.

Dr. Delafield married on October 12, 1821, Elinor Elizabeth Langdon, second daughter of Thomas and Elizabeth (Langdon) Elwyn, of Portsmouth, New Hampshire, who died on April 23, 1834, aged 35 years.

He married, secondly, on January 31, 1839, Julia, daughter of Colonel Nicoll and Phebe (Gelston) Floyd, of Mastic, Long Island, and a sister of Augustus Floyd (Yale 1814), who died in Darien, Connecticut, on August 18, 1879, in her 72d year.

A son by the second marriage was graduated here in 1860, and has followed with distinction his father's profession.

Dr. Delafield was of stately manner, but a great favorite with his students; as a teacher he was clear, methodical, and emphatic in his views, and terse, distinct, and elegant in his mode of expression. As a private practitioner he achieved a high reputation; great medical sagacity and extensive experience, combined with unusual devoted and kindly interest, brought him the affection as well as gratitude of his patients.

He published:

1. An Inaugural Dissertation on Pulmonary Consumption New-York, 1816. 8°, pp. 68.

[*Columbia Univ. N. Y H S. Surg. Gen'l's Office. U. S. Y. C*

2 Introductory Address to the Students in Medicine of the College of Physicians and Surgeons of the University of the State

of New-York. Delivered Nov. 7, 1837. New-York, 1837. 8°, pp. 44. [*B Publ. Surg. Gen'l's Office. U. S.*

3. Biographical Sketch of J. Kearny Rodgers, M.D. Read before the New York Academy of Medicine on Wednesday, October 6th, 1852, and Published under its Authority. New York, 1852. 8°, pp. 28.
[*A A S. B. Ath B Publ Harv. Surg Gen'l's Office. U S Y C*

4. An Address at the Dedication of the new building of the New York Eye Infirmary, April 25, 1856. New York, 1856. 8°, pp 47. [*Surg. Gen'l's Office.*

He also edited, with notes and additions, the following.

A Synopsis of the Diseases of the Eye, and their treatment.— By Benjamin Travers, F. R. S.— First American from the third London edition New-York, 1825. 8°, pp xxi, 474

AUTHORITIES

Med and Surg Reporter, xv, 509-12 N Y Geneal and Biogr Record, vi, 111-12 *Thompson*, Hist of L I, 2d ed, ii, 436 Wentworth Genealogy, i, 337 *Weston*, Memorial Sermon

---

THEODORE DEXTER, son of William Dexter, of Mansfield, Connecticut, and grandson of Jonathan and Sarah (Rice) Dexter, was born in 1791. His mother was Lurania, daughter of Uriah and Irene (Case) Hanks, of Mansfield. His father settled in Hartford about 1795, and was engaged in the manufacture of combs. The son was prepared for College by his pastor, the Rev. Abel Flint (Yale 1785). At the time of his entrance he gave his Christian name as Theodorus.

After graduation he studied medicine in Hartford with Dr. Mason F Cogswell (Yale 1780), and in August, 1814, entered the United States service as Hospital Surgeon, and was stationed at Charlestown, Massachusetts.

He retired from the service in June, 1815, and settled in Boston for the practice of his profession.

About the middle of June, 1817, he married Sarah H. Fowle, of Boston.

He was admitted to membership in the Massachusetts Medical Society in 1818.

He continued in Boston until his death, which occurred in Queechy Village, Windsor County, Vermont, while on a tour for the benefit of his health, on September 7, 1849, at the age of 58. His body was taken to Boston for burial.

One son and three daughters survived him.

NATHANIEL DIKE, son of Deacon John Dike, of Beverly, Massachusetts, was born in Beverly on January 15, 1792. His mother was Abigail, daughter of Thomas and Anna (Rea) Stephens, of Beverly. He was prepared for College at Phillips Academy, Andover, then under the charge of Mark Newman (Dartmouth Coll. 1793).

He settled in Steubenville, Ohio, as a lawyer, and merchant, and was a member of the State House of Representatives in 1842.

He is believed to have died in Steubenville in 1867, in his 76th year

---

AUTHORITIES

Beverly Vital Records, I, 102

THOMAS DUNLAP was born in Philadelphia, probably in 1792.

He entered the Senior class in 1811, with his second cousin, William Rumsey.

He studied law, and was admitted to the bar in Philadelphia on September 4, 1816.

During the most of his life he was engaged in professional practice in his native city

When Nicholas Biddle resigned the presidency of the United States Bank of Pennsylvania, in March, 1839, Mr.

Dunlap was chosen to succeed him; and he held the office until the Bank failed in 1841, when he resumed his profession.

He died in Philadelphia on July 11, 1864, in his 72d year. By his wife, Ann W. Dunlap, he had several children.

JOHN WORTHINGTON DWIGHT, the only son of Colonel Thomas Dwight (Harvard 1778), of Springfield, Massachusetts, and grandson of Colonel Josiah Dwight (Yale 1736), was born in Springfield on October 31, 1793. His mother was Hannah, daughter of Colonel John Worthington (Yale 1740), of Springfield. His preparation for College was completed under Araetius B. Hull (Yale 1807).

His father died when he was about 25, leaving him an ample estate He followed no profession, and never married He was a man of pleasing social qualities, and a generous nature.

He died in Springfield on February 12, 1836, in his 43d year.

AUTHORITIES.

Chapin, Old Springfield, 171 Dwight Family, ii, 829

SAMUEL LYNSON EDWARDS, the second son of Samuel Edwards, of that part of Stratford, Connecticut, which was afterwards Trumbull, and grandson of David and Mehitabel (Treadwell) Edwards, was born on February 14, 1789. His mother was Jane, daughter of Daniel and Mehitabel (Shelton) Shelton, of Huntington. He was prepared for College by his pastor, the Rev Daniel C. Banks (Yale 1804). David Shelton Edwards (Yale 1814) was a first cousin.

After graduation he went to Manlius, in Onondaga County, New York, and pursued law studies in the office of Messrs. Nathan P. Randall and James O. Wattles

In October, 1815, he was admitted to practice as an attorney, and shortly after took the place of Mr. Wattles as a partner of Mr. Randall for several years.

He was a member of the State Assembly for two sessions, from January, 1823, to November, 1824, and in April, 1831, was appointed Presiding Judge for two years of the County Court of Common Pleas. In 1832 he was elected as a Democrat to the State Senate, and served for two terms, of four years each. For half of this period he was the chairman of the Judiciary Committee.

On leaving the Senate he retired from public office, and thenceforth devoted himself to his professional practice, until a short time before his death. He was rewarded with a full share of the success which attends on careful preparation and persevering industry. He also held other responsible positions in the community, and was active and faithful in the discharge of all his duties. He served as a vestryman in the Episcopal Church in Manlius, until laid aside by the infirmities of age.

He died in Manlius, having survived all his classmates, on April 7, 1877, in his 89th year.

He was married, on May 12, 1819, to Harriet Bristol, of Clinton, Oneida County, who died in 1832. He next married Julia Gorham, of Stratford, Connecticut, who died in 1864.

His children, by his first marriage, were a daughter, who survived him, and a son (Yale 1850), who died early.

AUTHORITIES.

J Appleton, MS. Letter, May, 1877 *Bruce*, Onondaga's Centennial, 1, 231, 280, 331, 346-47. Shelton Reunion, 64-65 Ward Family Genealogy, 170

Robert Gibson entered College from Charleston, South Carolina, in 1809, at the age of 17.

He studied theology after graduation, and was licensed to preach by the Presbytery of New Brunswick, New

Jersey In 1818 the General Assembly appointed him to do missionary work for four months in Mississippi.

He died in Princeton, New Jersey, after a lingering illness, on March 15, 1829, aged 37 years.

CHARLES AUGUSTUS GOODRICH, the eldest son of the Rev. Samuel Goodrich (Yale 1783), of Ridgefield, Connecticut, was born in Ridgefield on August 19, 1790, and was prepared for College mainly by Alanson Hamlin (Yale 1799), of Danbury. He entered Yale in 1807, and in that year became a Christian and united with the College Church, but on account of ill health he soon withdrew, and in 1808 joined the next Freshman Class. In the spring of his Junior year his father removed to Berlin. At graduation he delivered an Oration on the Glory of the Missionary Character.

After graduation he was for a short time a tutor in the family of General Stephen Van Rensselaer (Harvard 1782) in Albany, and then studied theology in East Hartford with the Rev. Dr. Andrew Yates (Yale 1794).

After his licensure as a preacher he was employed in a distant part of New York State, until invited to preach to the First (Congregational) Church in Worcester, Massachusetts, where he was offered a settlement, with a salary of $900, on July 15, 1816 The Rev Dr. Samuel Austin, a classmate of his father, had left this pastorate in 1815, but had not been formally dismissed, since a suit was pending in his name in the courts for the recovery of certain lands to the parish, which might be prejudiced by his withdrawal. Mr. Goodrich, therefore, was invited to become colleague-pastor, with the succession to the sole pastorate, whenever Dr. Austin should be dismissed. The call was unanimous from the Church, and nearly unanimous (64 to 2) from the Society. When Mr. Goodrich learned of some opposition, he requested that another vote be taken; and on August 26 the Society again called him (88 to 2).

He accepted the call, and was ordained and installed on October 9,—the sermon preached by his father being afterwards published

The opposition to the call of Mr. Goodrich (originating with the wealthiest member of the Society) grew stronger after his settlement, and was much increased by the agitation which culminated in the dismission of the senior pastor in December, 1818. Objections of a personal nature to Mr. Goodrich, and others to the discipline of the church, led to long and acrimonious controversy, which was only terminated by his asking on October 13, 1820, a dismission, which was voted by a council on November 14.

Mr. Goodrich had been married, on June 24, 1818, to Sarah, daughter of the Rev. Dr. Benoni Upson (Yale 1776), of Berlin, Connecticut.

On retiring from the pulpit he fixed his residence in Kensington Parish, in Berlin, where he conducted for some time a boys' school He was also largely occupied in the preparing of popular text-books and other literature, partly in connection with his brother, Samuel G. Goodrich ("Peter Parley").

After his father's death, in 1835, he removed to the family residence in the central part of Berlin. In 1838 he was a member of the State Senate. In 1847 he settled in Hartford, where he died on January 4, 1862, in his 72d year.

His children were four daughters and three sons. The second daughter married the Rev. William W. Woodworth (Yale 1838).

He published among other works:

1. An Address, delivered June 26, 1817, before the Female Reading and Charitable Society, of the First Parish in Worcester, Mass Worcester, 1817 8°, pp. 20

[*A. A. S. B Publ Br Mus N. Y Publ. Y. C.*

2 History of the United States of America, on a plan adapted to the capacity of youth .. Hartford, 1822. 12°, pp. vi, 344 [*M H. S.*

The first in time of the numerous popular school histories of the United States

The same, in a somewhat expanded form Hartford, 1823. 12°, pp. iii, 379 + 12 pl. [*A A. S. A C. A. U. S.*

Many later editions,—a thoroughly revised one in 1834, and another enlarged one (from the 100th edition) in 1847.

3. An Outline of Biblical History; with Notes and Observations; adapted to the minds of youth. Hartford, 1825

4. An Address delivered before the Hartford County Agricultural Society, October 12th, 1826. Hartford, 1826. 8°, pp. 20. [*A. A S. Br. Mus N. Y. Publ Y. C.*

He was for several years the President of this Society.

5 Outlines of Modern Geography, on a New Plan Brattleborough, 1827. 12°, pp 252 + plates. [*B Publ.*

Later editions, with Atlas

6. Outlines of Ecclesiastical History, on a new plan; designed for Academies and Schools. . Hartford, 1829 12°, pp iv, 13–124. [*A. C. A. N. Y. Publ*

7. A Pictorial and Descriptive View of All Religions .. Hartford, 1829. 8°.

Several editions, with various titles. Based on Picart's *Religious Ceremonies and Customs.*

8 Lives of the Signers to the Declaration of Independence. New-York, 1829. 12°, pp. 460 + 7 plates [*A. A S. A C A. Br Mus Columbia Univ Harv U. S*

Many editions.

9 Stories on the History of Connecticut; designed for the Instruction and Amusement of Young Persons .. Hartford, 1829. 12°, pp. 203. [*A. A S Br. Mus. U. S*

The same, with title: A History of Connecticut, Designed for Schools. Hartford, 1833. 12°, pp. 173. [*Br. Mus N. Y. Publ.*

10. A New Family Encyclopædia; or, compendium of Universal Knowledge. ..

The same. Second improved edition. Philadelphia, 1831. 12°. [*Br Mus* .

Also, later editions.

11. The child's Book on the Creation. 1832.

12. Incidents in the Life of President Dwight. New Haven, 1833. 18°.
Anonymous.

13. The Influence of Mothers on the character, welfare and destiny of individuals, families and communities, illustrated in a series of anecdotes: with a preliminary essay . Boston, 1835 12°, pp. 193. [*B. Publ U S.*

14. The Ecclesiastical Class Book, or History of the Church. Hartford, 1835. 16°, pp. 236. [*B. Publ.*

15. The Universal Traveller· designed to introduce readers at home to an acquaintance with the arts, customs, and manners of the principal modern nations on the globe. .. Hartford, 1837 12°, pp. 504 + plates. [*A. C. A.*

16. The heavenly mansions.—A Sermon [from John xiv, 1-3], delivered in the First Congregational Church in Berlin, Dec. 20, at the Funeral of Mrs. Martha Robbins, who died Dec. 15, 1837 Hartford, 1838. 8°, pp. 22. [*A. C. A. N. Y. Publ. Y. C.*
Mrs. Robbins was the wife of the Rev. Royal Robbins (Yale 1806).

17. The Family Sabbath-Day Miscellany; comprising over three hundred Religious Tales and Anecdotes, original and select, with occasional reflections, adapted to the use of families, on the Lord's Day. Hartford, 1841. 12°, pp. 540. [*Y. C.*

18. The Bible History of Prayer, with practical reflections. Hartford, 1847. 12°, pp. 384. [*A. A. S. B. Publ.*
Many editions.

19. The Family Tourist.—A Visit to the principal Cities of the Western Continent: embracing an account of their situation, origin, plan, extent, their inhabitants, manners, customs, and amusements, .. etc. Hartford, 1848. 8°, pp. 640.
[*B. Publ Columbia Univ. Y. C.*

Also, later editions Such is

The Land we live in, or, Travels, Sketches and Adventures in North and South America. . Cincinnati. 1857. 8°, pp 879 + plates. [*U. S.*

20. Great Events in the History of North and South America, from the alleged Discovery of the Continent, by the Northmen, .. to the Present Time, with biographical sketches .. Hartford, 1851. 8°, pp 914 + 2 pl. [*B Publ. Harv Y C*

21. Sin Universal· reasons for preaching that doctrine, set forth in a Discourse [from Rom. iii, 12], originally delivered to the First Congregational Church and Society in Worcester, Mass. In *Smalley's* Worcester Pulpit, 1851, pp 179–98.

22 The Pocket Bible The Precious Gift of a Dying Man. Edinburgh. [1855.] 16°. [*Br. Mus*

23. A Geography of the Chief Places mentioned in the Bible, and the principal events connected with them. Adapted to parental, Sabbath-School and Bible-class instruction. New York, 1856. 12°, pp 195. [*B. Publ N. Y. Publ*

He also issued several volumes as editor, as·

Fox's Book of Martyrs, Middletown, 1832, and later editions.

AUTHORITIES

Case, Goodrich Family, 129, 221 *Fowler,* Chauncey Memorials, 167–68 *S G Goodrich,* Recollections of a Lifetime, i, 151; ii, 112 *Lincoln,* Hist. of Worcester, 161–62 Origin and Progress of the Difficulties in the 1st Church in Worcester 75th Anniversary of the Central Church, Worcester, 78–89 *Smalley,* Worcester Pulpit, 173–98 *Stiles,* Hist of Wethersfield, ii, 386 *Trumbull,* Hist of Hartford County, ii, 26–27

NATHAN GUILFORD, the eldest son of Dr. Jonas Guilford, of Spencer, Worcester County, Massachusetts, and grandson of John and Susanna (Whitney) Gilford, of Spencer, was born in Spencer on July 19, 1786 His mother was Lydia, daughter of John and Bulah Hobbs, of the adjoining town of Brookfield.

He was prepared for College in Leicester Academy, under Simeon Colton (Yale 1806). His father died at the end of his Freshman year, leaving an insolvent estate, and a dependent family.

For a few months after graduation he conducted a classical school in Worcester He then determined to follow the law, and entered at once on the study of his profession, with his classmate Davis, in the office of the Hon. Francis Blake, of Worcester.

In the autumn of 1814 he proceeded to Kentucky, arriving in Lexington in November.

For the next year and a half he was partly engaged in teaching, and was living in Alexandria, when he formed a law-partnership, in May, 1816, with Amos Kendall (Dartmouth Coll 1811), afterwards President Jackson's postmaster-general They settled in Georgetown, but the partnership lasted only until October, when Mr. Kendall was obliged to withdraw by newspaper and other engrossing business.

Mr. Guilford then removed to Cincinnati, where he passed the examination for admission to the bar in December, 1816, and began practice. He was for a short time in partnership with James W. Gazlay, afterwards a Member of Congress, as also later with Bellamy Storer, a future Judge of the Supreme Court.

But his interests were largely extra-professional, and in particular he devoted his best powers for the rest of his life to the advocacy and promotion of a liberal system of common schools for his adopted state

He early formed a partnership with his brother George, under the firm-name of N. & G Guilford, for the bookselling and publishing business, to advance his object; and when, under the first general school-law for Ohio, commissioners were appointed, in May, 1822, to devise and report a common-school system, he was one of that body. He refused, however, to coöperate with the committee, deeming their plan inadequate, and instead he presented a Memorial to the Assembly, advocating general taxation for school purposes.

In 1824 he was elected to the State Senate on this platform, and as chairman of the Senate committee on schools he succeeded in carrying, in February, 1825, the first Ohio School Law.

He then devoted himself to the promotion of legislation for the development of free public schools in Cincinnati, and succeeded in obtaining the first statute for that purpose in February, 1829. The earliest meetings of the Board of Trustees (later called the Board of Education) were held in his house, and he served on the Board until his resignation in July, 1832.

In consequence of these labors he mainly withdrew from the practice of the law, and in connection with his occupation as a publisher (which he maintained until about 1840) gave much attention to the improvement of text-books. He was also interested in the Cincinnati Type Foundry, and later in the Ohio Type Foundry. In 1843 he established the Cincinnati *Daily Atlas,* a Whig Journal, of which he was the chief editor and proprietor until 1847.

On the creation of the office of Superintendent of the City Schools, he was chosen by popular vote to that position, and served from April, 1850, until June, 1852, with an annual salary of $500. He lost his office, owing to the expression of unpopular opinions, in connection with an agitation of the question of the reading of the Bible in the schools.

In the spring of 1854 he was elected a City Magistrate, and held this office at the time of his death, at his home, on December 18, 1854, in his 69th year.

An engraving from his portrait is given in Foote's *Schools of Cincinnati,* and in Shotwell's similar work

Mr. Guilford was a man of great kindness of heart, and marked simplicity of manners. He was extremely fond of children, and had a special gift for entertaining and interesting them. He had also a marked fondness for nature. One of the District Schools of Cincinnati bears his name

He married in Cincinnati, on August 29, 1819, Eliza Wheeler, daughter of Oliver and Nancy (Mumford) Farnsworth, of Woodstock, Vermont, who had emigrated to the west, and aroused his interest while stricken with fever on her passage down the Ohio river.

They had three daughters and two sons One son, bearing his father's name, served in the Civil War and was subsequently successful in railroad administration

He published:

1. Ode for the Fourth of July, 1814. [Worcester, 1814.] 1 page. 4°. [*M. H. S.*

Four stanzas, to the tune of *Hail Columbia*

2. An Oration delivered at Alexandria, Kentucky, on July 4, 1816.

3. A Letter on free education. 1822.

4 A Memorial to the General Assembly. 1823

5. An Arithmetic, of wide circulation

6. In the Western Souvenir, a Christmas and New Year's Gift for 1829, Edited by James Hall, and published at Cincinnati by N and G Guilford, are the following articles, contributed by him:

Traditions of the Mammoth, pp 19–32;
Ohio [poem], p. 36;
Ode to music, pp. 104–05.

He edited for seven years an Educational Almanac, under the pseudonym of Solomon Thrifty, during the early part of his campaign for free education.

He also edited:

The Western Spelling Book; being an improvement on the American Spelling Book, by Noah Webster—Designed for the use of Common Schools. Cincinnati, 1831. 12°, pp. 144. [*N. Y Publ*

AUTHORITIES.

Amer. Journal of Education, viii, 289–94. Cincinnati Gazette, Dec 20, 1854. *Draper,* Hist of Spencer, 143–44, 203. Farnsworth Memorial, 313. *Greve,* Centennial Hist. of Cincinnati, 617 T M *Hinkle,* MS Letter, July, 1911 A *Kendall,* Autobiography, 132–33, 169, 175, 181–82 *Nelson,* Hist. of Cincinnati (1894), 104–06. *Shotwell,* Hist. of Cincinnati Schools, 12, 38, 40–41, 60, 482 Spencer Vital Records, 44. *Venable,* Beginnings of literary culture in the Ohio Valley, 419, 424.

Edward Holden, the oldest child of Edward Holden, a merchant of Boston and Dorchester, Massachusetts, and grandson of Samuel and Hannah (Kilbon) Holden, of Dorchester, was born in Dorchester late in 1791. His mother was Anne, daughter of Samuel and Anne (Robinson) Payson, of Dorchester. He entered Yale in 1809 Professor Edward S. Holden, the distinguished astronomer, is a nephew

He studied law, and settled in 1814 in Kentucky, where he followed his profession.

He married in 1820 Eliza F. Williams, who died in 1821, aged 24 years, leaving no issue.

He next married in 1825 Sarah McClenahan, by whom he had one son, born in 1826, in Falmouth, Kentucky.

He died on March 5, 1827, in his 36th year.

AUTHORITIES

Hist. of Dorchester, 1859, 545. Letter, Dec. 1911 *Professor Edward S Holden*, MS.

Stephen Farrar Jones, the eldest son of Peter Jones, and grandson of Jonas and Abigail (Hartwell) Jones, of New Ipswich, New Hampshire, was born in 1786. His mother was Eunice, the eldest daughter of the Rev. Stephen Farrar (Harvard 1755), of New Ipswich, and Eunice (Brown) Farrar. His father settled in or near Augusta, Maine, but died early; and his mother returned to her father's house The son was sent to Phillips Academy, Exeter, and entered the Junior Class at Yale in January, 1811.

After graduation he went as a teacher to South Carolina, at first to Charleston, and thence to Beaufort, where he soon died,—probably within two or three years after leaving New Haven.

AUTHORITIES.

Adams, Life of Jared Sparks, i, 44-46, 54

Bond, Hist of Watertown, 728

Hon T. Farrar, MS Letter, Febr., 1865

DENNIS KIMBERLY, the eleventh in a family of twelve children of Captain Silas Kimberly, of the village of West Haven, Connecticut, and a brother of Lester Kimberly (Yale 1807), was born in West Haven on October 23, 1790. His father died in 1803, and he was prepared for Yale by James Morris (Yale 1775), of Litchfield South Farms.

During his Senior year he undertook some reading, as an amateur student of law, with Ralph I. Ingersoll (Yale 1808), who had just opened his office; and immediately after graduation he set about his preparation in earnest, in part with George Bliss (Yale 1784), of Springfield, Massachusetts, the father of a classmate, and in part with Roger Minott Sherman (Yale 1792), of Fairfield.

He was admitted to the bar in March, 1814, and immediately began practice in New Haven, where he soon acquired a solid reputation, which he maintained unimpaired until the day of his death.

In early life he gave much time to military affairs, reaching finally the rank of Major General of the militia, which he held from 1826 to 1829

He served as an alderman of the city from 1825 to 1830, and was Mayor for one year, 1831–32. He was again elected Mayor in 1833, but declined the office.

He was a member of the General Assembly of the State for seven years (1825–29, 1832, 1835), and in 1827 Clerk of the House.

In May, 1838, he was elected by the Whigs in the Legislature to the United States Senate; but, after several months' deliberation, he decided not to accept the office, probably on account of his somewhat straitened circumstances at the time. He also at one time declined a nomination for Governor of the State, when his election was regarded as certain

In 1845 he was appointed State's Attorney for New Haven County, and discharged this duty until his resignation in 1848.

General Kimberly also devoted much attention to public improvements. In his early years he rendered important service in regard to the extension of the Farmington Canal, and at a later period he was a valued counsel of the New York and New Haven Railroad, of which he was also for a few years a Director

In July, 1852, on account of impaired health, he retired mainly from practice, and spent the next two years, until May, 1854, in a tour of Europe, from which he returned in somewhat improved condition, though still far from well

He died at the Tontine Hotel in New Haven on December 15, 1862, in his 73d year A commemorative discourse by his pastor, the Rev Dr. Elisha L. Cleaveland, was afterwards printed. He was never married

General Kimberly was lamented by the community as a man of distinguished attainments, high honor, and unblemished integrity.

AUTHORITIES

Cleaveland, Address at Gen. Kimberly's Funeral Conn Reports, xxx, 605–07 New Haven City Year Book, 1864, 78–80.

EZRA L'HOMMEDIEU, a son of Samuel L'Hommedieu, of Sag Harbor, Long Island, and grandson of Sylvester and Elizabeth L'Hommedieu, of Southold, was born in 1790. His mother was Sarah, daughter of Charles White, and granddaughter of the Rev. Ebenezer White (Harvard 1692), of Bridgehampton A sister married the Rev. John D. Gardiner (Yale 1804).

He studied law after graduation, and began practice in New York City, in partnership with his classmate, Buffett;

but was overtaken by death on December 7, 1819, at the age of 29

RICHARD HARRISON LONG was the eldest son of Colonel Nicholas Long, of Washington, Wilkes County, Georgia, and entered Yale in 1809. He did not receive his degree until 1813

After graduation he studied law at the Litchfield Law School, and entered on the practice of his profession in his native county, which he subsequently represented in the State Legislature.

He married Nancy, eldest daughter of Dr Gilbert and Elizabeth (Gilbert) Hay, of Washington.

After some years he removed to Florida, where his wife soon died after years of suffering, from cancer.

The date of his death has not been recovered

AUTHORITIES

Gilmer, Georgians, 218, 230

SAMUEL COIT MORGAN, the younger son of Captain Elisha Morgan, of Newent Society, in Lisbon, Connecticut, and grandson of Captain Daniel and Elizabeth (Gates) Morgan, of that part of Preston which is now Griswold, was born on August 12, 1789. His mother was Olive, youngest child of Colonel Samuel and Sarah (Spalding) Coit, of Preston. He was prepared for College by John Adams (Yale 1795), at Bacon Academy, in Colchester

After graduation he studied law with Thomas Day (Yale 1797), of Hartford, and with the Hon. Timothy Pitkin (Yale 1785), of Farmington, and in 1816 began practice in Jewett City, in Griswold; but, being elected in 1842 President of the Quinebaug Bank, in Norwich, he removed thither in 1843, and devoted himself to that business, relinquishing in great degree the practice of his profession

In 1860 he retired from office, and he died in Norwich on September 11, 1876, aged 87 years

He was a sound and accurate lawyer, and faithful in the discharge of all duties. He represented Griswold in the General Assembly in 1825, 1830, and 1834.

His portrait is given in the *Morgan Genealogy*

He married, late in September, 1816, Maria Belinda, the eldest child and only daughter of the Rev. Edward Porter (Yale 1786), of Farmington, who died on November 11, 1848, in her 54th year He was next married, on November 26, 1849, to Frances Augusta, younger daughter of General Moses Cleaveland (Yale 1777), of Canterbury, who died on February 18, 1860, in her 63d year. He married, thirdly, on June 12, 1861, Mary C., daughter of Dr. John C. Tibbits, of Jewett City

He had no children, and by his will made liberal bequests to various literary institutions and objects of benevolence

---

AUTHORITIES

Chapman, Coit Family, 68, 141 Morgan Genealogy, 76, 138 *Trowbridge,* Champion Genealogy, 292

RICHARD CARY MORSE, the youngest son of the Rev. Dr. Jedidiah Morse (Yale 1783), of Charlestown, Massachusetts, was born in Charlestown on June 18, 1795, and was prepared for College under Mark Newman in Phillips Academy, Andover. At graduation he delivered an Oration on the Policy of establishing a National University He was the youngest member of his Class.

After graduating he continued in New Haven for a year as President Dwight's amanuensis, and in 1817 completed the three years' course at the Andover Theological Seminary

He was licensed to preach in October, 1817, and during the ensuing winter supplied the pulpit of the Presbyterian Church on John's Island, South Carolina

In the following years he preached occasionally, and assisted his father, who removed to New Haven in 1820, in the issue of a new edition (1821) of his *Universal Gazetteer,* and of an extract of the same (1823), called *The Traveller's Guide, or Pocket Gazetteer of the United States*

On January 1, 1823, he engaged with his elder brother (Yale 1811) in founding the *New-York Observer,* the oldest religious newspaper in that State, of which he remained an associate editor and proprietor until 1858. He was gifted with fine literary taste, and a great aptness for acquiring languages. His contributions to the *Observer* included numerous translations from the French and German.

He continued to reside in New York City until 1863, when he removed to New Haven.

In May, 1868, he left home for a foreign tour, and he died in Kissingen, Bavaria, on the 22d of the following September, in his 74th year.

He was married, in Claverack, New York, on September 30, 1828, by the Rev. Richard Sluyter, to Sarah Louisa, daughter of Charlotte and the late William H. Davis, of Catskill, and granddaughter of the Rev. John Gabriel Gebhard, of Claverack. After more than a year of feeble health, her husband took her abroad in July, 1851, but she died in Paris on October 17, 1851, at the age of 43. He was next married, in New York, on August 12, 1856, by the Rev. Dr. Stephen H. Tyng, to Harriet Hinckley, fourth daughter of the late Colonel Daniel and Susanna (Hinckley) Messinger, of Boston, who survived him.

His children, by his first marriage, were five sons and five daughters. The four sons who survived him were graduates of Yale in 1856, 1862, 1867, and 1868, respectively. His daughters all survived him The eldest married Samuel Colgate, the distinguished benefactor of Colgate University, and her six sons were graduated here. Another daughter married the Rev. Dr. J. Aspinwall Hodge (Univ. of Pa. 1851).

AUTHORITIES.

Gebhard, The Parsonage between two Manors, 309–15 Messinger Genealogy, 14 *Prime,* Life of S F B Morse, 9

CHARLES NICHOLS was born in Newtown, Connecticut, of Episcopalian parents, in 1790, and was prepared for College by the Rev. Dr. Tillotson Bronson (Yale 1786), at the Cheshire Academy. He is said to have been a scion of the family of Sir Richard Nicolls, the first English Governor of New York.

He became about 1817 a merchant in New York City, and was there married by Bishop Hobart to a daughter of Major Benjamin Romaine

Under President Tyler he received the appointment of United States Consul at Amsterdam, and he was continued in office by President Polk.

He died at his residence in Brooklyn on June 2, 1865, aged 75 years.

JOSEPH NOBLE was the youngest son of Alexander Noble, of Abbeville, South Carolina, and grandson of John Noble, of Donegal County, Ireland, and Augusta County, Virginia, and of Mary (Calhoun) Noble. His mother was Catharine, daughter of Ezekiel and Jane (Ewing) Calhoun, and first cousin of her husband, as well as of the Hon. John C Calhoun (Yale 1804) He entered College at the opening of the Sophomore year

He studied law after graduation, and was admitted to the bar at Columbia in 1816.

He then emigrated to Alabama Territory, where he practiced his profession, and where he died, unmarried, on October 17, 1822, aged about 30 years

---

AUTHORITIES

Boltwood, Noble Genealogy, 738.

DANIEL NOYES, the eldest child of Lieutenant Ephraim Noyes, of Abington, Massachusetts, and grandson of Captain Daniel and Mary [or Mercy] (Burrill) Noyes, was born in Abington on December 31, 1791. His mother was Sarah, second daughter of Samuel and Mary (Perkins) Dike, of North Bridgewater He was prepared for College by the Rev David Gurney (Harvard 1785), of Middleboro

For a few years after graduation he followed the calling of a teacher, and in 1814 he was Principal of the Bradford (Massachusetts) Academy

In 1816 he settled in Boston as a druggist (firm of Maynard & Noyes), and married on November 16, 1820, Eleanor Clark.

He was well known as a prominent Congregational layman, and after the formation in 1825 of the Hanover (later called the Bowdoin Street) Church, he transferred thither his membership from the Union Church, and was at once elected senior Deacon. Throughout Dr Lyman Beecher's ministry in that church, Deacon Noyes was the person on whom he most relied for counsel and aid.

In 1849 he removed to Andover, where in 1850 he was chosen a Trustee and Treasurer of Phillips Academy and the Theological Seminary. He spent his closing years in that relation, dying in Andover on April 8, 1852, in his 61st year.

His children were five daughters and two sons. The youngest daughter and the younger son died in infancy The elder son was graduated at Yale in 1847, and the third daughter married Professor Charles A. Aiken (Dartmouth Coll. 1846).

AUTHORITIES.

Congregational Quarterly, xiv, 271–72 *Hobart*, Hist of Abington, 424. *Kingman*, Hist of North Bridgewater, 582–83 Noyes Genealogy, i, 79, 103–04.

George Payson, the eldest child of Deacon John Howe Payson, of Pomfret, Connecticut, and his first wife, Cynthia Willison, and grandson of John and Thankful (Howe) Payson, of Pomfret, was born in Pomfret on July 12, and baptized on July 19, 1789

A sister married the Rev Orin Fowler (Yale 1815), and two half-brothers were graduated here, in 1819 and 1828, respectively Edward Payson (Harvard 1803), the eminent minister of Portland, was a first cousin He was prepared for College by John Adams (Yale 1795)

He spent the three years succeeding graduation in the Andover Theological Seminary, and on July 3, 1816, he was ordained and installed as pastor of the Congregational Church in Arundel, now Kennebunkport, Maine.

He married on June 1, 1819, Lois W. Lord, of Kennebunkport

He was an eloquent and effective preacher and pastor, and although reserved in manner was generally admired. Continued feeble health led him to take a dismission on July 19, 1820.

He then spent a winter at the South, and was sufficiently improved after his return to take charge of an Academy in Limerick, and later of a Seminary for young ladies in Portland; but his health proved unequal to this exertion, and he finally returned to Kennebunkport, where his death occurred on October 22, 1823, in his 35th year

His widow subsequently married Nathaniel Dana, of Boston

AUTHORITIES.

Bradbury, Hist. of Kennebunkport, 192, 194-95 Maine General Conference Minutes, 1866, 22, 1876, 25 York County Conference Semi-Centennial, 7, 113

Nathaniel Shaw Perkins, the eldest of six children of the Hon. Elias Perkins (Yale 1786), of New London, Connecticut, was born in New London on February 11,

1792. He was mainly prepared for College by John Adams (Yale 1795) in Bacon Academy, Colchester.

Afer graduation he began the study of medicine with Dr. Elisha North, of New London, and completed it at the University of Pennsylvania.

In 1815 he began practice in his native city, with the assistance of the best social advantages, large wealth, and extensive family influence. His tact and skill were well seconded by his courteous and genial manner and his earnest professional zeal.

He married in May, 1818, Ellen, daughter of Benjamin and Mary (Coit) Richards, of New London.

In 1819 he united with the First Congregational Church of New London, and after a life of great usefulness and acceptableness as a physician, much beloved and trusted, he died in New London, in the house in which he was born, after four days' illness from pneumonia, on May 25, 1870, in his 79th year.

The honorary degree of Doctor of Medicine was conferred on him by Yale in 1829.

His wife survived him, with six of her fourteen children. One son fell in the civil war, and another was graduated at Yale in 1842.

AUTHORITIES.

Conn. Medical Society's Proceedings, 1871, pp. 478–81 *Mitchell,* Woodbridge Record, 107 *Morse,* Richards Family, 101

THOMAS SHAW PERKINS, the next younger brother of the last-named graduate, was born in New London on August 10, 1793, and was prepared for College with his brother.

He studied for the legal profession, and married on January 4, 1818, Caroline, youngest daughter of Timothy and Mary (Baldwin) Leonard, of Lansingburg, New York, and sister of Dr. Frederick B. Leonard (Yale 1824). They soon sailed for Europe, but his wife died on May 5 (or 8), on the passage from New York to Bordeaux He next married, on February 23, 1820, her fourth cousin, Mary Ann, or Marian, daughter of the Hon. Roger Griswold (Yale 1780), of Lyme

They settled in the adjoining town of Waterford, but later removed to New London, where he followed his profession He was appointed by Governor Ellsworth (Yale 1810) as the Commissioner of Common Schools for New London County for the year 1839

He died while on a voyage for his health from Valparaiso to Hamburg, on October 14, 1844, in his 52d year.

His wife survived him for many years. Their children were four daughters and seven sons

AUTHORITIES.

Mitchell, Woodbridge Record, 107. *Perkins,* Chronicles of a Conn. Farm, 155, 165–66, 168 *Salisbury,* Family-Histories and Genealogies, ii, 110–11. *Walworth,* Hyde Genealogy, i, 347, ii, 890–91

DAVID PRENTICE, the eldest child of Sherman and Susan (Richards) Prentice, of Bethlehem, Connecticut, and a first cousin of the Rev. Charles Prentice (Yale 1802), was born in Bethlehem on September 7, 1787. He was prepared for College by his pastor, the Rev. Azel Backus (Yale 1787).

After graduation he studied law in Oxford, Chenango County, New York, with Henry Van Der Lyn (Union Coll. 1802), and was admitted to practice in 1816 He was, however, better adapted by character and tastes to a studious life than to the struggles of the bar, and in 1820 he took charge of the flourishing academy in Oxford

After discharging the duties of this post with fidelity for four years, he was elected Principal of the Academy in Utica, and entered on his new office early in 1825. Here he remained for twelve years, and became distinguished for his thorough work with his pupils.

In the fall of 1836 he was elected to the professorship of the Greek and Latin languages and literatures in Geneva (now Hobart) College, in Geneva, Ontario County.

He assumed his new duties in January, 1837, and fulfilled them with characteristic assiduity until the summer of 1847, when he resigned his chair, owing to the withdrawal of the State grant to the College, under the new Constitution.

He then returned to Utica, and opened a private classical school, which he conducted successfully for about five years He then, on account of failing health, went back to the more favorable climate of Geneva, where he was also able to be under the care of a son-in-law who was a practitioner of medicine.

He also opened a classical school in Geneva, which he conducted with the aid of an assistant until 1855. After an illness of severe suffering, he died in Geneva on August 14, 1857, at the age of 70. He was a devout member of the Episcopal Church, and his old friend, Bishop DeLancey (Yale 1817) officiated at his funeral.

He married Cordelia Willis, a lady of remarkable personal beauty, by whom he had three daughters.

AUTHORITIES

Binney, Prentice Genealogy, 292, i, 673 *Crosby,* Annual Obit Notices, 313-14. *Cothren,* Hist of Woodbury, i, 285-86.

Isaac Trimble Preston, a grandson of Colonel William and Susannah (Smith) Preston, of Montgomery County, Virginia, and a first cousin of the Hon. William Ballard Preston, President Taylor's Secretary of the Navy, was born in Rockbridge County, Virginia, in 1793. Before entering Yale, from Abingdon, Washington County, Virginia, at the opening of the Sophomore year, he had been a student in Greenville College, Tennessee.

His scholarship was such that he was awarded the Valedictory Oration at graduation.

He spent the winter of 1812–13 in the Litchfield Law School, but in March, 1813, he accepted a Captain's commission in the 35th Infantry regiment of the United States, with which he remained until June, 1815

He then resumed his studies, under the direction of William Wirt, in Norfolk, Virginia, and soon after his admission to the bar he settled in New Orleans, Louisiana, where he practiced his profession with success.

He was from March, 1850, a Judge of the Supreme Court of the State.

He spent the Fourth of July, 1852, out of the city, and on his return to New Orleans from Biloxi, Mississippi, on the morning of the 5th, on board the steamboat *St James,* he with several other passengers was killed on Lake Pontchartrain by the explosion of the boilers

AUTHORITIES.

Amer Almanac, 1853, 343–44. *Heitman,* Hist Register of U S. Army, i, 806

William Rumsey was born in Kent County, on the Eastern Shore of Maryland, in 1792, and entered the Senior Class from Wilmington, Delaware, at the same time with his second cousin, Thomas Dunlap, in 1811

He began the study of medicine after graduation, but it was interrupted by a period of service in the army during the war with Great Britain, in which he was stationed at Camp Dupont in Delaware.

He received the degree of Doctor of Medicine from the University of Pennsylvania in 1817, and entered on the practice of his profession in Philadelphia.

In 1829 he married his cousin, Anna Rumsey Dunlap, of Philadelphia, a sister of his classmate.

She died in 1835, leaving a daughter, who died three years later

He continued in practice until April, 1869, when he removed to the house of a sister, near Wilmington, where he died of old age, on April 23, 1871, in his 79th year. Although a native of a slave-holding State, his attachment to the Union was warm and decided during the civil war.

AHAZ SANFORD, the third child of Hezekiah and Betsey (Booth) Sanford, of Redding, Connecticut, and a brother of Hezekiah Booth Sanford (Yale 1809), was born in Redding on January 19, 1789 He entered College in 1807, having been prepared by the Rev Dr David Ely (Yale 1769), of Huntington. He left the Class of 1811 early in Junior year, and joined the next Class a year later.

He died in 1813, in his 25th year, being the first of the Class to die.

AUTHORITIES

Thomas Sanford Family, i, 198.

ABRAHAM CURTIS SHELDON was born in Rupert, Bennington County, Vermont, on March 26, 1788, and was prepared for College by his pastor, the Rev. William Jackson (Dartmouth Coll 1790), of the adjoining town of Dorset. He spent the first two years of the course in Middlebury College.

He was intending to enter the ministry; but having lost the sight of one eye, he found that close application to study affected the other eye so seriously that he was obliged to give up his chosen object.

He opened a select school in Albany, New York, but continued it for only a single year Subsequently he went into mercantile business there in company with a Mr. Phipps from Connecticut

They failed, and Mr Sheldon then returned to Rupert, where he spent several years with a brother, working on a farm

He married a widow, Mrs Miranda Colby, and purchased a farm in Portage, on the Genesee River, in western New York, where he occupied himself in farming, until he was killed by the fall of a tree, on January 21, 1834, in his 46th year.

AUTHORITIES.

Aaron Sheldon, MS Letter, June, 1866.

GEORGE SMITH, the youngest of five sons of Dr. Phineas and Abigail (Lay) Smith, of Sharon, Connecticut, was born in Sharon in October, 1793, and was baptized on April 13, 1794. His eldest brother was graduated here in 1797 Both parents died in his infancy. He was prepared for College by the Rev Daniel Parker (Yale 1798), of Ellsworth Society in Sharon

He studied law after graduation, and for a few years after his admission to the bar he practiced his profession in Watertown, Jefferson County, New York

On the failure of his health he removed to Texas, where he lived for some time the life of a hunter, hoping by open-air exercise to regain strength.

He was in intimate relations with Colonel Stephen F. Austin, the Texan pioneer, and assisted him in framing a code of laws for the proposed colony, and in founding (in 1823) the town of San Felipe de Austin, on the western bank of the Brazos river, in the present county of Austin, where he died on January 16, 1827, in his 34th year.

He was never married

AUTHORITIES

Van Alstyne, Sharon Births, etc., 116 *Mrs L W Whitcomb*, MS Letter, Jan, 1867.

WARD STAFFORD, the youngest of eleven children of John Safford, of Harvard, Massachusetts, and Washington, New Hampshire, was born in Washington on April

6, 1788, and was named for a brother of his father. His mother was Mehitabel, eldest child of Simeon and Martha (Hall) Farnsworth, of Harvard. In September, 1807, though with scanty pecuniary resources, he began his preparation for College in Phillips Academy, at Andover, and after some supplementary instruction by Mills Day (Yale 1803) in New Haven, he entered the Freshman Class at Yale. He united with the College Church in September, 1811, on profession of his faith. At graduation he delivered the Salutatory Oration. After leaving College he changed his family name from Safford to what he believed the earlier form.

After some hesitation on account of feeble health, he determined to study for the ministry under President Dwight's direction, and during a part of the time (in 1813) he served as Rector of the Hopkins Grammar School.

He received a license to preach from the New Haven Western Association of Ministers on September 26, 1815, and in the following December he went to New York City, intending to embark for Charleston, South Carolina, for the benefit of his health; but finding in New York a large opening for work among the destitute he tarried there.

In June, 1816, he engaged in the service of the Female Missionary Society for the poor of New York, and in the following winter he completed the first missionary canvass of that city.

For the furtherance of his work he was ordained as an evangelist by the Consociation of the Western District of New Haven County, at Middlebury, on October 1, 1817.

A considerable part of his attention was early directed to the moral improvement of seamen, and in connection with his exertions the Marine Bible Society, of which he was the Corresponding Secretary, was formed in March, 1817, and a Society for Promoting the Gospel among Seamen was organized in May, 1818. In November he was engaged to give his entire services to the work of a pastor and preacher for seamen.

On March 23, 1819, he was married by the Rev. Dr. Edward D. Griffin (Yale 1790) to Hannah, daughter of General Thomas Ward, of Newark, New Jersey

He had begun regular services for seamen as early as December, 1816, and through his exertions a house of worship, called The Mariners' Church, was opened in June, 1820, which he served as pastor until November, when he accepted an agency of the American Bible Society, with the purpose of extending its work in the Atlantic States from New Jersey to South Carolina.

Early in 1822 he returned to New York, and in April, chiefly through his labors, a mission church, called the Bowery Presbyterian Church, was organized, over which he was regularly installed on October 30, 1823. He remained with them about four years longer, and in 1828 removed to Newark

In 1830 he accepted a call to the Presbyterian Church in Youngstown, Trumbull County, Ohio, where his wife died on December 13, 1836.

In the spring of 1837, on account of failing health, he resigned his charge, and after a brief employment as agent for the Western Reserve College he spent the ensuing winter in supplying the Congregational Church in West Stockbridge, Massachusetts. In the spring of 1838 he became the Principal of a School for Young Ladies in Pittsfield, but a year later removed to Hudson, New York, where he was similarly occupied until the fall of 1841.

On October 1, 1841, he was married by the Rev. Edward L. Parker to Mary Lettisse, only daughter of Deacon Samuel Burnham (Dartmouth Coll. 1795) and Mary (Dalton) Burnham, of Derry, New Hampshire.

Soon after this he removed to Brooklyn, where he continued to be employed as a teacher until the spring of 1844, when he returned again to Newark.

His wife died in Brooklyn on September 29, 1843, at the age of 35. The sermon delivered at her funeral by the Rev. Dr Samuel H. Cox was published

In the spring of 1845 he became a resident of Bloomfield, New Jersey, where he spent his remaining years in farming. As the climate affected him unfavorably, he decided to remove to California, but the fatigue and anxiety attending the proposed removal proved too severe for his frail health, and after two weeks' suffering from fever, he died in Bloomfield on March 26, 1851, at the age of 63.

By his first marriage he had four sons and four daughters, of whom three sons and one daughter survived. The only child of his second marriage died in infancy.

He published:

1 New Missionary Field—A Report to the Female Missionary Society for the Poor of the City of New-York and its vicinity, at their quarterly prayer meeting, March, 1817. New-York, 1817 8°. [*A. A. S. B. Ath M. H. S.*

The same. Second Edition New-York, 1817. 8°, pp. 55. [*Br. Mus Y. C.*

An epoch-making report in the history of city missions.

2 An Address to Merchants, Shipmasters, and others of the City of New York

An appeal which led to the building of the Mariners' Church in 1819–20.

3 He was also the author of the Annual Reports of the Marine Bible Society of New-York, issued in 1817 and 1818.

AUTHORITIES

Burnham Family, 221–23 *Carter*, N Hampshire Native Ministry, 793 Farnsworth Memorial, 346 *Greenleaf*, Hist. of N. Y Churches, 154–55, 302–03

AUGUSTUS RUSSELL STREET, the only son of Titus Street, a wealthy merchant of New Haven, and grandson of Samuel and Sarah (Atwater) Street, of Wallingford, Connecticut, was born on November 5, 1791, and was baptized on June 3, 1792 His mother was Amaryllis, daughter of Major Reuben and Mary (Russell) Atwater, of Cheshire, and a second cousin of her husband. A sister married the Hon. William W. Hoppin (Yale 1828). He was prepared for College by the Rev. David Smith (Yale 1795), of Durham

From early life his health was delicate, and although he studied law after graduation with Judge Charles Chauncey, of New Haven, he never practiced. Nor did he engage in any business, except for a term of years as a silent partner in the bookselling and publishing firm of Hezekiah Howe & Co., of New Haven.

He was married on October 16, 1815, to Caroline Mary, elder daughter of William Leffingwell (Yale 1786), of New Haven, a lady of remarkable vivacity and strength of mind

He resided in New Haven, indulging his cultivated tastes and exercising a wide and discriminating benevolence. From 1843 to 1848 he and his wife resided abroad, devoting much attention to the modern languages and to the study of art.

In 1855 he began a series of gifts to the College with the partial endowment of a professorship of Modern Languages, which was completed in 1863. In 1864 he undertook the erection of a building for the use of a School of the Fine Arts. Before this building was completed he died, in New Haven, on June 12, 1866, in his 75th year. His will provided for the completion of the unfinished building and for the partial endowment of the School, and also for the endowment of a professorship in the Divinity School Mrs Street died in New Haven on August 24, 1877, in her 88th year, and by her will supplemented her husband's bequests by the endowment of two professorships in the Art School. Their children, seven daughters, all died before them. Of these the eldest only was married,—to Rear Admiral Andrew Hull Foote, who left two sons.

Mr. Street's character commanded the highest respect, and his gifts to the College were based on a deliberate and far-seeing grasp of principles The amount of his and Mrs. Street's benefactions to Yale was upwards of four hundred thousand dollars.

Mr Street's portrait, painted soon after his death by Nathaniel Jocelyn, is owned by the College.

AUTHORITIES

Atwater Family, 155 Leffingwell Genealogy, 47, 84-86. Ward Family Record, 81, 114-16. N Y. Geneal. and Biogr. Record, xlii, 43 Street Genealogy, 147, 234. Yale Courant, June 27, 1866.

THEODORE STRONG, the second son and child of the Rev. Joseph Strong (Yale 1784), was born at his maternal grandfather's house in South Hadley, Hampshire County, Massachusetts, on July 26, 1790. A few weeks later his father was settled over the church in Heath, in what is now Franklin County. He was adopted by his uncle, Colonel Benjamin Ruggles Woodbridge, of South Hadley, and was prepared for College by the Rev. Ezra Witter (Yale 1793), of Wilbraham

He distinguished himself at Yale in mathematics as well as in other studies; and manifested his proclivities by delivering at graduation an Oration on the Folly and Inconsistency of Theories and Hypotheses, illustrated in comparison of the Philosophy of Des Cartes and Newton So that when in the fall of 1812 President Dwight was asked to recommend a recent graduate for the office of tutor of mathematics in Hamilton College, at Clinton, New York, he named Mr Strong, who accepted the position, and after filling it for four years was promoted to the professorship of mathematics and natural philosophy in the same institution.

He was married on September 23, 1818, to Lucy, daughter of Captain John and Huldah (Warren) Dix, of Boston.

His increasing reputation as a scholar and teacher was such that in 1825-26 he was called to Rutgers College, Columbia College, and the University of Pennsylvania.

These invitations were all for various reasons declined; but when, in December, 1827, a second call came to the Professorship of Mathematics and Natural Philosophy in Rutgers College, he concluded to accept it, and removed with his family to New Brunswick.

He received the honorary degree of Doctor of Laws from Rutgers College in 1835

As age grew on, his teaching was less popular, and in 1859 the Trustees of the College deemed it advisable to appoint an associate professor in his department, who relieved him to a large extent from active class-room duty. In 1861 he was made Professor *emeritus*, and in 1863 he retired from the College altogether. He died in New Brunswick on February 1, 1869, in his 79th year. A *Memorial* was printed after his death, containing the addresses delivered at his funeral and other tributes. A very satisfactory *Memoir*, by Judge Joseph P. Bradley (Rutgers 1836), was prepared for the National Academy. He was an earnest patriot and a thorough Christian gentleman

His wife survived him, with two of their five daughters and their elder son (Rutgers 1847); the younger son (Rutgers 1857) died in service in the civil war.

An engraved portrait is given in the *Strong Family Genealogy*

He was a member of various learned societies, such as the American Academy of Arts and Sciences and the American Philosophical Society, and one of the original members (in 1863) of the National Academy of Sciences

He published separately.

1. A Treatise on Elementary and Higher Algebra New York, 1859 8°, pp ix, 551. [*Harv. U. S.*

A work remarkable for its originality and depth.

After his death appeared.

2. A Treatise on the Differential and Integral Calculus. New York, 1869 12°, pp. viii, 617 [*Y. C*

Composed in 1867.

He also contributed many fugitive articles to various periodicals. Among them may be specified.

Nine papers in *The Scientific Journal,* Amboy, 1818–19;

Twenty-nine papers in *The American Journal of Science and Arts,* New Haven, 1819–45,

Numerous brief articles in *The Mathematical Diary,* New York, 1825–32;

Twenty-two brief papers in *The Mathematical Miscellany,* New York, 1836–39;

Seven brief papers in *The Cambridge Miscellany,* 1842–43,

A brief paper in the *Proceedings* of the American Philosophical Society, Philadelphia, 1843;

Two papers in *The Mathematical Monthly,* Cambridge, 1860–61.

AUTHORITIES

Biogr Memoirs of National Acad of Sciences, ii, 1-28. *Dwight,* Strong Family, i, 361-64 N Y. Geneal and Biogr Record, ii, 136

JOHN WAGNER was born in Charleston, South Carolina, on July 7, 1791, the fourth child of George and Ann Wagner.

His preparation for College was completed under the Rev. Dr. David Ely (Yale 1769), of Huntington, Connecticut

After graduation he began the study of medicine in New York City under the direction of Dr. Dwight Post, then Professor in Columbia College.

Before he had completed his studies Dr. Post was obliged by the state of his health to go abroad for a prolonged absence, and Mr. Wagner embraced the opportunity to visit London, where he attended three courses of lectures (1815–17) on surgery and anatomy by the distinguished surgeon, Astley P. Cooper, at Guy's Hospital and the Royal College of Surgeons.

On his return to America in 1818 he had the distinction of an honorary degree of M.D. from Yale. He married on July 7, 1818, Lydia M. Brett, of Fishkill, New York, and began practice in New York City, but after a year or two returned to Charleston, where he had a brilliant career as a surgeon, from his advanced knowledge, his dexterity as an operator, and his kindness and gentleness

In the winter of 1826 he began a course of dissections and demonstrations in practical anatomy, which met with great success. In 1829 he was appointed Professor of Pathological and Surgical Anatomy in the Medical College of South Carolina, and in 1832 after a closely contested election he was transferred to the chair of Surgery in the same institution, which he held until his death, in Charleston, on May 22, 1841, in his 50th year.

His widow died in Matteawan, New York, on August 24, 1860.

AUTHORITIES

Amer Journal of the Med Sciences, new series, ii, 526-27 Miss I DeSaussure, MS Letter, Dec, 1911.

ANDREW FERDINANDO WARNER, son of Selden Warner, of Hadlyme Society in Lyme, Connecticut, and grandson of Jonathan and Elizabeth (Selden) Warner, of Hadlyme, was born in December, 1791 His mother was Dorothy Selden, a second cousin of her husband A brother was graduated here in 1817. He was prepared for College by his pastor, the Rev Joseph Vaill (Dartmouth Coll. 1778).

After graduation he studied medicine with Dr. Thomas Miner (Yale 1796), of Lyme, and in the Yale Medical School, and began practice in Westchester Parish, in Colchester. Shortly after he removed to the North Parish (Chester) in Saybrook, and finally in 1820 to Haddam, where he labored with great acceptance until his death there, after five days' illness from dysentery and fever, on June 23, 1825, in his 34th year A sermon on that occasion by his pastor, the Rev. John Marsh (Yale 1804), was afterwards published.

Dr. Warner became a Christian believer during a revival in Hadlyme in 1815, and lived a consistent life.

He married in Westchester on November 4, 1817, Lucintha, youngest sister of the Rev. Jonathan Cone (Yale

1808). She next married, on March 16, 1826, Ira Hutchinson, M.D. (Yale 1825), who had succeeded to Dr. Warner's practice; and died in Haddam on October 1, 1848, in her 53d year

Dr. Warner's children were two sons and a daughter (who died in infancy). The sons never married.

AUTHORITIES.

Cone Family, 170, 184–85 Conn. Med Society's Proceedings, 1892, 565 N E Hist.-Geneal Society's Memorial Biographies, iii, 74–75

JULIUS WILCOXSON was born in Huntington, Connecticut, in 1791. He was prepared for College by the Rev. Dr. David Ely (Yale 1769), of Huntington, but gave New Haven as his residence during the first three years of his College course

He studied law after graduation, and began practice in Kinderhook, Columbia County, New York, in 1816. From March, 1821, to October, 1832, he served as District Attorney for Columbia County. In 1835 he was a Representative in the State Legislature; and in the same year he was appointed an associate Judge of the Court of Common Pleas for Columbia County. He retained this office until May, 1846, and then filled for one year the position of Presiding Judge of the same Court.

He is believed to have died in Kinderhook in 1852, at the age of 61; but there is no record of the settlement of his estate in Columbia County

---

JOHN WITTER, the eldest son and second child of Jonah Witter, of Brooklyn, then part of Pomfret, Connecticut, and grandson of Nathan and Keziah (Branch) Witter, of Brooklyn, was born in Brooklyn on April 28, 1785 His mother was Eunice Cady, of Brooklyn. The Rev. Thomas Williams (Yale 1800) was a first cousin, and Professor John H Hewitt (Yale 1859) is a nephew. In the year of his birth his parents removed to Preston, and after having taught for a few terms he was prepared for College by John Adams (Yale 1795) in Bacon Academy, Colchester.

For the three years next after graduation he taught in the Hopkins Grammar School in Hartford. He then returned to Yale as Tutor, declining the offer of a post in the Academy where he was educated In March, 1816, he united with the College Church on profession of his faith.

In the fall of 1817, he returned to Bacon Academy, and on April 30, 1819, he was married to Eliza Loomis, eldest child of Asa and Sophia (Loomis) Bulkeley, of Colchester

After a few years he became principal of the Academy in Plainfield; and after retiring from that position his residence continued in the town, where he was occupied with the cultivation of his farm and occasional teaching until his death on December 30, 1858, in his 74th year

He maintained a good reputation as a scholar and as an instructor, and was esteemed for his high character He was for years a deacon in the Congregational Church in Plainfield.

After the death of his first wife, he married Olive Smith, of Plainfield

By his first marriage he had three daughters and two sons. One son and one daughter died in infancy.

AUTHORITIES

Allen, Allen and Witter Genealogy, 221 *Chapman,* Bulkeley Family, 140. *Professor J H Hewitt,* MS. Letters, Dec, 1911 Loomis Female Genealogy, ii, 728-29.

CALEB SMITH WOODHULL, fourth son of Merritt Smith Woodhull, of the village of Miller's Place, in Brookhaven, on the northern coast of Long Island, and grandson of Judge John and Elizabeth (Smith) Woodhull, of Miller's Place, was born on February 26, 1792. His mother was Mary, daughter of Samuel Davis. The Rev. Selah Strong Woodhull (Yale 1802) was a first cousin He was prepared for College by the Rev Herman Daggett (Brown Univ. 1788), of the neighboring village of Middle Island, and by Frederick Scofield (Yale 1801) in Stamford, Connecticut.

For some months after graduation he taught school, and in 1814 he began the study of law in New York with George W. Strong (Yale 1803), but his course was interrupted in the fall of 1814 by a brief term of service in the army.

He was admitted to the bar in 1816, and on February 19, 1818, was married by the Rev. Alexander McClelland (Union Coll. 1809) to Lavina, or Lavinia, daughter of George Nostrand, of New York, who died on the 15th of the following December, after a brief illness, in her 25th year

On December 30, 1830, he was married by the Rev. Dr. Gerardus A Kuypers to Harriet, daughter of Abraham Fardon, of New York.

In the spring of 1836 he was chosen a member of the Common Council (Assistant Alderman) of the City of New York, and remained in office for eight years, being an Alderman from 1839, and for the final year President of the Board and during the Mayor's absence Acting Mayor In 1843 he was a candidate of the friends of Henry Clay for the office of Presidential Elector.

In the year 1850 he was the Mayor of the city.

Soon after this he retired to the homestead in Miller's Place, where he afterwards resided.

His wife died while visiting in New York on April 25, 1865, at the age of 66, and he died at Miller's Place on July 16, 1866, in his 75th year.

By his second marriage he had two sons and one daughter. One son died before him.

AUTHORITIES

N Y. Geneal. and Biogr Record, iii, 13, 16 *Thompson*, Hist. of L. I., 2d ed., ii, 400, 402. Woodhull Genealogy, 87, 131, 324-25

Annals, 1812-13

At a meeting held before Commencement, the Rev. Peter Starr (Yale 1764), of Warren, was elected to the seat in the Corporation which had been declined by the Rev. Dr. Azel Backus.

At this meeting the Medical Institution was organized by the appointment of five Professors,—Æneas Munson, Nathan Smith, Benjamin Silliman, Eli Ives, and Jonathan Knight.

Sketches, Class of 1813

**Georgius Allen* *1883
*Nathanael Allen, M D Coll. Med. et Chirurg. Nov. Ebor. 1817 *1822
*Aaron Arms, A.M. 1818 *1849
*Russell Atwater *1823
**Johannes Avery,* A.M. 1817, S. T. D. Univ. Carol. Bor. 1833 *1837
*Fredericus Fanning Backus, M.D. 1816 *1858
*Georgius Edmundus Badger, 1825, A.M. 1825, LL D. 1848 et Univ. Car. Bor. 1834, Reip. Car. Bor. Cur. Super. Jurid, Rerump Foed Sen. et Rerum Marit. Secr. *1866
*Anderson Bagley *1813
**Zedekias Smith Barstow,* A.M. et Hamilt., S. T. D. Dartm. 1849 *1873
*Dudleius Pettibone Bestor *1813
*Jacobus Beebee Brinsmade *1856
*Moses Bristol, M.D. 1816 *1869
**Ebenezer Brown,* A.M. Harv. 1822 *1872
**Norris Bull,* A.M. 1818, S. T. D. Conc. 1846 *1847
*Stephanus Mitchell Chester *1862
*Guilielmus Cone *1819
*Sherman Converse *1873
**Elias Cornelius,* A.M , 1818, S. T. D. Dartm. 1829 *1832
*Johannes Crane *1860
*Jacobus Cuthbert, A.M. *1838
*Henricus Daggett *1837
**Thomas Fredericus Davies,* A M. *1865
*Nicoll Havens Dering, A.M., M.D. Med. et Chir. Nov Ebor 1817 *1867

*Thomas Pollock Devereux, A.M. 1817 et Univ Car. Bor. 1818 *1869

*Abramus Dixon *1875

*David Bates Douglass, A.M. et Neo-Caes. 1819 et Conc. 1825, LL.D. 1841 et Hobart. 1841, in Rerump. Foed. Acad. Milit. Mach. Bellic. Scient Prof., in Coll. Ken Log. et Rhet. Prof. et ejusd. Praes. *1849

**Guilielmus Theodorus Dwight,* A.M., S.T.D. Bowd. 1846, Tutor *1865

**Ludovicus Dwight* *1854

**Ambrosius Eggleston* *1865

*Georgius Augustus Elliot *1870

**Guilielmus Ely* *1850

**Joy Hamlet Fairchild,* A M 1817 *1859

**Benjamin Fenn* *1869

*Alexander Metcalf Fisher, A.M , Tutor, Math. et Philos Nat Prof *1822

*Johannes Douglass Fowler, A M. *1817

**Thomas Downes Frost* *1819

*Josephus Winborn Hand *1844

*Carolus Hawley, A M 1817, Reip Conn Vice-Gubern , Soc ex off. *1866

*Minor Hotchkiss, A.M. *1825

*Richardus Hubbard *1839

**David Lathrop Hunn,* A M. 1817 *1888

*Lemuel Ingalls *1819

*Jacobus Derham Johnson, A.M *1860

*Elias Kent Kane, 1825, A M 1825, Reip. Ill Secr., Rerumpubl Foed Sen *1835

*Guilielmus Kimball *1822

**Augustus Baldwin Longstreet,* A M Univ. Georg. 1823, LL.D. 1841, Reip Georg. Cur. Super. Jurid , Coll Emor. et Univ. Mississ. et Coll Car. Austr. Praeses *1870

*Stephanus Mack *1857

*Hiramus Foot Mather *1868

*Gideon Johannes Mills *1825
**Elisaeus Mitchell,* A.M., S.T.D. Univ. Alab 1838, Tutor, in Univ. Carol. Bor. Math et Philos. Nat. etiam Chem et Mineral et Geol. Prof. *1857
*Fredericus Morgan, A M., M D 1817, Tutor *1877
*Jacobus Morris *1826
*Milo Linus North, M.D. 1834 *1856
*Denison Olmsted, A.M , LL.D Univ Nov. Ebor. 1845, Tutor, in Univ Carol. Bor Chem. Prof , Math., Philos. Nat., Astron. Prof. *1859
*Russell Parish *1855
**Silas Parker,* 1816
*Carolus Perkins *1856
**Reuben Sherwood,* A.M. 1817, S.T.D. Hobart. 1840 *1856
**Johannes Singletary,* 1814 *1845
*Rogerus Sherman Skinner, A.M *1838
*Josias Spalding *1852
*Johannes Austin Stevens *1874
*Georgius Sumner, A.M., M D Univ. Penns. 1817, in Coll Trin. Botan. Prof , Soc. Med. Conn. Praeses *1855
*Henricus Wythe Tabb, A.M. 1826 *1863
*Jeremias VanRensselaer, A.M , M.D. Acad Med. Viridim. 1823 *1871
*Johannes Guilielmus Weed, A.M. 1821, M.D. Nov. Ebor. Reg 1847 *1875
**Samuel Weed,* A.M. *1820
*Jonathan Ashley Welch *1859
*Guilielmus Caecilius Woolsey, A.M 1817 *1840
*Johannes Mumford Woolsey, A.M. 1820 *1870

GEORGE ALLEN, a son of the Hon Joseph Allen, of Worcester, Massachusetts, clerk of the county courts, was born in Worcester on February 1, 1792 His father was a Representative in Congress during this son's College course, and was the son of James Allen, a tailor, of Boston, and of his wife Mary, only sister of the patriot, Samuel Adams. He was thrice married, and his second wife, the mother of his son George, was Dorothy, elder daughter of Lemuel and Dorothy (Roberts) Kingsbury, of that part of Coventry which is now Andover, Connecticut, her parents died in her infancy, and she was brought up by an uncle in Enfield.

Another son, the Hon. Charles Allen, was for a time a member of the Class of 1815 at Yale, and received an honorary degree here in 1836.

George Allen was prepared for College at Leicester Academy (of which his father was one of the founders), under the tuition of the Rev. Zephaniah Swift Moore (Dartmouth Coll. 1793) and Luther Wilson (Williams Coll. 1807)

After graduation he began the study of theology with the Rev. Andrew Yates (Yale 1794), of East Hartford, Connecticut, who removed to Union College in the summer of 1814 Later he pursued his studies under the Rev. Thomas Robbins (Yale 1796), of East Windsor, and was married, on July 13, 1815, to his first cousin, Elizabeth, only daughter of Elisha and Elizabeth (Kingsbury) Pitkin, of Hudson, New York, and granddaughter of Elisha Pitkin (Yale 1753), her father died in 1802, and her mother was now the wife of Colonel Amos Alden, of Enfield.

In 1816 he was engaged for some months in teaching in Albany, and he then resumed his theological studies with Dr. Yates, in Schenectady.

He was licensed to preach by the Hartford North Association on February 4, 1818, and spent the next few years as a missionary in Central and Western New York. In 1819 he was supplying the recently organized Presbyterian Church in Waterloo, Seneca County, and during the next two years he was in charge of the Presbyterian

Church in Aurora, Cayuga County, where he accepted a call to settle, but was unable to satisfy the doctrinal demands of the Presbytery which undertook to ordain him

In August, 1823, he was called to be a colleague with the Rev Dr. Joseph Sumner (Yale 1759), pastor of the Congregational Church in Shrewsbury, the adjoining parish to his native town, where he was ordained and installed on November 19, 1823.

Dr. Sumner died in December, 1824, and Mr. Allen remained sole pastor until his dismission at his own request on June 18, 1840, after severe domestic afflictions, and with threatened blindness He had also been subjected to uncomfortable trials in his parish

He then returned to Worcester, where his wife died on March 14, 1843, in her 56th year.

In 1840 he accepted the position of Chaplain at the State Lunatic Hospital in Worcester, and he officiated in that capacity, with some intervals of rest, until he arrived at the age of eighty in February, 1872

The remainder of his life was spent in retirement, under the burden of an almost total loss of sight

In January, 1882, he fractured a thigh by a fall, but after a few months' confinement, he was again able to take his accustomed exercise. He died in Worcester, after a brief and painless illness, on March 31, 1883, in his 92d year.

His children, two sons and two daughters, all died before him. The eldest child was graduated at Yale in 1838. His last years were cared for by a devoted niece.

Mr Allen was a man of marked individuality, active mind, and strong will. He was thorough and exact in scholarship, and gifted with unusual powers of expression His style was clear, concise, and pungent.

He was extremely liberal in his theology for one who was classed as an Orthodox believer.

From early life he took a deep interest in moral and political reforms, and in particular his opposition to slavery was intense and forcible. He aided actively in the formation of the Free Soil party.

His photograph, taken in extreme old age, is given in his *Reminiscences*.

He published

1. The Moral Providence of God.—A Sermon [from Ps. lxxiii, 24] delivered in Shrewsbury, January 4, 1829 Worcester, 1829. 8°, pp 19

[*A. A. S A. C. A. B. Publ. Br. Mus M H. S Y C.*

A New-Year's sermon.

2. An Address to the Freemen of Massachusetts.—By a Freeman. Worcester, 1832. 8°, pp. 16.

[*A. A. S A C A. B Publ. Harv.*

In reply to a Masonic Declaration

3 A Freeman on Freemasonry [1832] 8°, pp 8.

[*B. Publ. Y C.*

Anonymous.

4. Thoughts on "The Excitement" in Reply to a Letter to Hon. Edward Everett. . . Worcester, 1833. 8°, pp. 44.

[*A A. S. B Publ Br Mus. C H S. Harv Y C*

Six anonymous letters, from the standpoint of an Anti-Mason.

5 Report of a Declaration of Sentiments on Slavery, December 5, 1837. Worcester, 1838 8°, pp. 12.

[*A. A S A C. A B Publ Br Mus Harv U. S Y. C.*

Two editions.

6. Speech delivered, at the Convention of ministers of Worcester county, at Worcester, on the 16th of January, 1838, in favor of the adoption of the Report on Slavery, presented by Rev Mr. Peabody. [Boston.] 1838 8°, pp 46.

[*A. A. S. A. C. A. B. Ath. B. Publ. Br. Mus. C. H. S Harv. M. H. S. Y. C.*

With reference to No. 5 Also published with the title:

Speech on ministers leaving a moral kingdom to bear testimony against sin; liberty in danger, from the pollution of its principles; the Constitution a shield for slavery; and the Union better than freedom and righteousness

7. Report of the School Committee of the Town of Shrewsbury, offered in Town Meeting, April 1, 1839 Worcester, 1839 8°, pp. 16.

Mr. Allen was the chairman of the Committee.

8 The Complaint of Mexico, and Conspiracy against Liberty. Boston, 1843. 8°, pp 32. [*U. S.*

The same. [With Appendix, containing Letter of Daniel Webster to Waddy Thompson.] Boston, 1843. 8°, pp. 44.
[*A A. S. U. S. Y. C.*

Anonymous. Written in the summer of 1842, against the annexation of Texas.

9. An Appeal to the People of Massachusetts, on the Texas Question. Boston, 1844. 8°, pp. 20 [*A. A. S. Harv.*

The same [Second edition.] Boston, 1844. 8°, pp 20
[*A A S Harv U. S. Y C.*

Anonymous; signed A Massachusetts Freeman.

10 Resistance to Slavery every Man's Duty—A report on American Slavery, read to the Worcester Central Association, March 2, 1847. Boston, 1847. 8°, pp. 40.
[*A. C. A B. Ath B Publ. Harv. M. H. S. U. S. Y. C.*

11. A Review of the Reverend Aaron Pickett's "Reply" and "Defence." By Vindex Boston, 1848. 8°, pp. 57.
[*A C. A Br Mus. M. H. S. U. T. S.*

An anonymous criticism of the proceedings in regard to the excommunication of certain members of the South Congregational Church in Reading, Massachusetts; an enlarged edition of a communication in the ***Boston Reporter*** of February 10, 1848.

12 Remarks on the Attack of the "Family Ægis" upon Judge Allen. [Worcester, 1848.] 8°, pp. 8

Anonymous. Signed ***Plus Ultra.***

13. The Andover Fuss or, Dr. Woods versus Dr. Dana, on the Imputation of Heresy, against Professor Park, respecting the Doctrine of Original Sin. Boston, 1853. 8°, pp. 31.
[*A C. A B Ath B Publ. Harv. U T. S. Y. C.*

An anonymous demonstration of Professor Woods's inconsistency.

14. An Address to the Electors of the Ninth Congressional District of Massachusetts [Worcester, 1860.] 8°, pp 14.
[*A A. S. B Publ M. H S Y. C*

An anonymous electioneering attack on the Hon. Eli Thayer, signed Heart of the Commonwealth

15. Historical Remarks concerning the Mechanic Street Burial Ground, in the City of Worcester, offered to the Joint Committee of the Legislature of Massachusetts, March 14, 1878.—First published in Numbers in the *Bay State Ledger,* July and August, 1846 Worcester, 1878 8°, pp. 17.
[*A A. S A C A B Publ M H. S. U S. Y. C.*

After his death appeared his

16. Reminiscences. With a Biographical Sketch and Notes by Franklin P. Rice Worcester, 1883 8°, pp. 127 + pl.
[*A A. S. A C. A Harv. U. S. Y. C.*

17. Samuel Jennison [Worcester, 1897.] Sq. 16°, pp 25.
[*A. A. S.*

From a newspaper, 1860.

AUTHORITIES.

G Allen, Reminiscences Kingsbury Family, 274. Leicester Academy Centenary, 47. *Lincoln,* Hist. of Worcester, 228, 331–32 Pitkin Family, 57, 113 *T Robbins,* Diary, 1, 626, 731. *Ward,* Hist of Shrewsbury, 182–83, 221 Worcester Society of Antiquity's Proceedings, 1883, 14–22, 119–20

NATHANIEL ALLEN, the seventh child and fifth son of Thomas Allen, of New London, Connecticut, and grandson of Thomas and Elizabeth (Christophers) Allen, of New London, was born in New London on June 23, 1791. His mother was Amelia, daughter of Pardon and Elizabeth (Harris) Taber, of New London. The family removed in 1793 to Fisher's Island, at the end of Long Island Sound, southeast from New London. They adhered to the Episcopal Church, and this son was prepared for College by the Rev. Dr. Tillotson Bronson (Yale 1786), at the Cheshire Academy.

He studied medicine at the College of Physicians and Surgeons in New York City, where he received the degree of M.D. in 1817

He settled in Alabama, where he was highly respected. He died there on August 5, 1822, in his 32d year

He married in Claiborne, Monroe County, Alabama, Martha Helen Foster, who survived him and next married Edward L. Smith.

She died on May 15, 1857.

AUTHORITIES

Jolley Allen, Narrative, ed Mrs Stoddard, 47

Aaron Arms, the fourth son of Aaron Arms, of Deerfield, Massachusetts, and grandson of Daniel and Mary (Stebbins) Arms, of Deerfield, was born on March 20, 1789 His mother was Lucy, only daughter of Christopher and Lucy (Munn) Tyler, of Deerfield. He was prepared for College at the Deerfield Academy by Hosea Hildreth (Harvard 1805)

For the first two years after graduation he taught successfully the Academy in his native town, and then he studied law. He was admitted to practice in 1817, and spent his life in Deerfield, where he died on April 11, 1849, aged 60 years

He married in 1821 Sophia, daughter of Jonas and Susanna (Willard) Holland, of Belchertown, who died on March 28, 1822

He next married, on June 27, 1826, Eliza, eldest daughter of Hutchins and Betsy (Grout) Hapgood, of Petersham, who died on September 24, 1835, aged 39 years.

By his second marriage he had one son and two daughters. The elder daughter married the Rev. Dr. Heman Lincoln Wayland (Brown Univ. 1849), a great-grandson, Wayland Wells Williams, was graduated at Yale in 1910.

AUTHORITIES

Doolittle, Sketch of Congregational Church, Belchertown, 162 Hapgood Family, 199 Petersham Vital Records, 28, 104. *Sheldon*, Hist of Deerfield, II, pt 1, 848, 853, 855; pt. 2, 35, 40-41

Russell Atwater, the third son of the Hon. Russell and Clarissa (Chapman) Atwater, of Blandford, Massachusetts, and a grandson of Major Reuben and Mary (Russell) Atwater, of Cheshire, Connecticut, was born in Blandford on January 8, 1795 He was a first cousin of Augustus Russell Street (Yale 1812), and was prepared for College at the Cheshire Academy by the Rev. Dr. Tillotson Bronson (Yale 1786).

His father removed about 1805 to a tract of new land in St. Lawrence County, New York, where a town, named Russell in his honor, was formed in 1807.

He attended the Litchfield Law School after graduation, but died of consumption on December 22, 1823, at the age of 29.

AUTHORITIES

Atwater Family, 155 *Davis*, Hist of Wallingford, 633

John Avery, the eldest child of Deacon John Avery, of Conway, Massachusetts, and grandson of William and Bethiah (Metcalf) Avery, of Dedham, was born in Conway on January 19, 1786. His mother was Mary, or Molly, third daughter of Jacob and Elizabeth (Read) Cushman, of Attleborough. Professor John Avery (Amherst Coll. 1861), of Bowdoin College, was a nephew. He was prepared for College by his first cousin, the Rev. William Fisher (Williams Coll 1805), of what is now Darien, Connecticut, and spent two years at Williams before entering Yale as a Junior. His roommate there was William Cullen Bryant, who planned to accompany him to Yale, and was only prevented by pecuniary inability to complete a College course.

On graduation he went to Edenton, North Carolina, as a teacher.

Though brought up as a Congregationalist, he studied in Edenton for the Episcopal ministry, and received

Deacon's orders from Bishop Kemp, of Maryland, on October 22, 1817.

He then took charge of St. Paul's Church, in Edenton, of which he was rector for eighteen years. On November 11, 1818, he was advanced to the priesthood.

He was married in Edenton, on November 14, 1827, to Ann, only daughter of Ebenezer Paine, a native of Pomfret, Connecticut, who had settled in Edenton, and his wife, Sarah (DeCroe) Paine.

He served also as Principal of the Edenton Academy, and in consideration of his scholarly attainments the honorary degree of Doctor of Divinity was conferred on him by the University of North Carolina in 1833.

In December, 1835, he removed to Alabama, whither many of his friends in North Carolina had already gone. Here he became the Rector of a small country parish, called St. John's in the Prairies, in Greene County, which was composed of a few wealthy planters with their families.

He also officiated in Greensboro, in what is now Hale County, about seven miles distant, and being convinced that a school for girls would advance the interests of the Church there, he bought property near Greensboro in 1836, and arranged to establish such a school

He was a man of learning, an experienced teacher, with a lovely Christian character, and without doubt if his life had been spared, such a school would have been a success.

In the new diocese of Alabama he took at once a prominent part, and was chosen President of the Convention of February, 1836.

He died suddenly on board a steamboat in which he was returning home from Mobile, on January 17, 1837, at the age of 51.

A monument, erected by his parishioners at Edenton, commemorates his piety, learning, and exemplary life A tablet to his memory was also placed in St Paul's Church, Edenton, and a memorial chair in the chancel of St Paul's

Church, Greensboro. A beautiful little memorial chapel was also built by his family on the site of St. John's in the Prairies, and after the adjacent plantations were entirely broken up by the civil war, this was removed to a village near by.

His widow took up the work of establishing the school which he had planned, and remained in Greensboro until her death, on March 28, 1878.

Dr. Avery left two sons, and two daughters (who are still living), the younger is the wife of the Rev. Dr. Richard H Cobbs, Rector of St. Paul's Church in Greensboro.

AUTHORITIES

Battle, Hist of Univ of N C, i, 354. *Carter and Holmes,* Avery Genealogy, 76 *Rev Dr R H Cobbs,* MS Letter, August, 1911 Cushman Genealogy, 160. *Godwin,* Life of Bryant, i, 34-35, 90-92 Paine Family Records, i, 112; ii, 152. *Sprague,* Annals of Amer Pulpit, v, 754.

FREDERICK FANNING BACKUS, son of the Rev Dr Azel Backus (Yale 1787), of Bethlehem, Connecticut, was born on June 15, 1794, and was prepared for College by his father. During his Senior year his father became the first President of Hamilton College, in Clinton, New York.

He studied medicine in New Haven under the special instruction of Dr. Eli Ives (Yale 1799), and received the degree of M.D. from the Medical School in 1816 In June of that year he began practice in the new settlement of Rochester, New York, where he continued in an extensive and lucrative career until his death.

In 1818 he married Rebecca Anne, daughter of Colonel William and Anne (Hughes) Fitzhugh, who had emigrated from Hagerstown, Maryland, to Geneseo, in Livingston County; one of her sisters subsequently married Gerrit Smith (Hamilton Coll. 1818), whose first wife was Dr. Backus's only sister, and another married James G. Birney (Princeton Coll. 1810).

He took an active interest in politics as a whig, and was a member of the State Senate during four sessions (1844-47). He was also a delegate to the State Constitutional Convention of 1846.

While in the Senate he was conspicuous for his intelligent and earnest advocacy of liberal aid to asylums and hospitals; and two able reports from his pen on the education of idiots gave the first impulse to the movement in this country in behalf of those unfortunates. From its establishment in 1846 to the time of his death he was the medical attendant and President of the Board of Managers of the Western House of Refuge in Rochester.

He died in Rochester after two years' enfeeblement from paralysis, on November 4, 1858, in his 65th year.

One daughter and four sons survived him, together with his wife.

An obituary notice emphasizes his sound sense, his pleasant wit and humor, his acknowledged skill as a physician, his uncompromising hostility to every form of quackery, his undoubted sincerity as a Christian, his advocacy of the cause of the unfortunate, his sterling integrity, and rare political fidelity.

AUTHORITIES.

Crosby, Annual Obit. Notices, ii, 16 Historical Magazine, ii, 367–68 N Y State Medical Society's Transactions, 1860, 176–80. *Peck,* Hist of Rochester, 335–36 *Turner,* Hist of Phelps and Gorham Purchase, 365 Va. Hist. Magazine, viii, 316

George Edmund Badger, the eldest child and only son of Thomas Badger, an artist and lawyer of Windham, Connecticut, and Newbern, North Carolina, and grandson of Edmund and Lucretia (Abbe) Badger, of Windham, was born in Newbern on April 17, 1795. His mother was Lydia, daughter of Colonel Richard Cogdell, of Newbern, a Revolutionary leader Samuel Badger (Yale 1805) was an uncle. His father died of yellow fever in 1799

At the end of his Sophomore year his father's eldest brother, who had hitherto met his College bills, withdrew his support, so that he was obliged to return home. His degree was granted him and he was enrolled with his class, in 1825, on the petition of several of his classmates.

He studied law with his cousin, the Hon. John Stanly, of Newbern, and was granted a license to practice in the County Courts in the summer of 1814, and in the Superior Courts in 1815 In 1814 he took the field with the State Militia, for the defence of the coast, serving as aide-de-camp to General Calvin Jones, with the rank of Major.

In 1816, the year of his majority, he was sent to the Legislature, and through the friendship then formed with the Speaker of the House, the Hon. Thomas Ruffin, who was at this session elected a Judge, he was induced to remove to Hillsborough, the county seat of Orange County, and take Judge Ruffin's practice.

While residing there he was married on December 24, 1818, to Rebecca, only daughter of James Turner, of Warren County, formerly Governor and United States Senator, and sister of Thomas Turner (Yale 1815), after which he removed to Warrenton, the home of the Turner family, and thence a little later to Louisburg, in Franklin County

In 1820, in consequence of his high professional standing, he was elected by the Legislature a Judge of the Superior Court, and he retained this office until his resignation in the spring of 1825 As a Judge his ability and impartiality were universally admitted, though he was not popular, and was sometimes thought to err from quick temper and over-confidence. His resignation was prompted by the superior attractions of a lucrative practice.

On his retirement he removed to Raleigh, where he resided until his death.

In 1826 he and his classmate Devereux were appointed Reporters of the Superior Court of the State, but Mr. Badger soon resigned the office.

In 1840 he was a prominent advocate of the election of General Harrison to the Presidency, and in March, 1841, he entered reluctantly his Cabinet as Secretary of the Navy. After Harrison's death he remained in Tyler's Cabinet until September, when he resigned on account of Tyler's breach with the whig party.

In 1846 he was elected to fill a vacancy in the United States Senate, and continued in that body for another full term, from 1849 to 1855.

In 1851 he was nominated by President Fillmore for the bench of the Supreme Court, but the Senate refused to confirm the nomination.

Mr. Badger had voted for the Compromise of 1850, and in 1854 for the repeal of the Missouri Compromise; and in 1860 he accepted the nomination for Presidential elector on the Bell and Everett ticket, with the distinct hope of preventing the plans of the secessionists.

He disbelieved in the constitutional right of secession; and in February, 1861, when the proposition to hold a State Convention for the purpose of considering the subject of secession was submitted to the people, he consented to leave private life and ran as a Union candidate, to serve if the Convention should be called; but the people rejected the proposition.

Three months later, when a Convention was called, he served as a Representative of Wake County He spoke ably in defence of the Union, until the ordinance of secession was passed, after which he felt obliged to go with his State. His sons served in the Confederate army, but he was stricken with paralysis in January, 1863, which partially obscured his faculties and withdrew him from public view.

He died in Raleigh on May 11, 1866, in his 72d year.

His wife dying in June, 1824, and leaving no issue, he married Mary, daughter of Colonel William and Sarah (Hawkins) Polk, of Raleigh, and a sister of Bishop and General Leonidas Polk, by whom he had two children; she also died early, and he married, thirdly, about 1835, Mrs. Delia B. Williams, daughter of Sherwood Haywood, who survived him, with several children by his last two marriages

A portrait is given in Peele's *Lives of distinguished North Carolinians.*

Mr Badger excelled as an advocate in dialectic skill and argument He had remarkable colloquial powers and social attractiveness. His morals were inflexibly pure, and he was a devout and earnest member of the Episcopal Church, and for many years a vestryman of Christ Church, Raleigh

He served as a Trustee of the University of North Carolina from 1818 to 1844

He published:

1. An Argument in defence of the University of North Carolina 1826

2 Address delivered before the Philanthropic and Dialectic Societies, at Chapel Hill, N. C, June 26, 1833 Richmond, 1833. 8°, pp. 21 [*A A S B Ath B Publ. M. H S.*

3 Speech on the Ten Regiment Bill.—Delivered in the Senate of the United States, January 18, 1848 [Washington, 1848.] 8°, pp 16 [*Harv. U S Y C.*

4 An Examination of the Doctrines Declared and Powers Claimed by the Right Reverend Bishop Ives. By a Layman of the Protestant Episcopal Church in North Carolina. 1849.

5 Speech on the Slavery Question.—In Senate, March 18 and 19, 1850 [Washington, 1850] 8°, pp 18
[*A A. S Harv M H. S. U S Y C.*

Reprinted, in part, in Peele's *Distinguished North Carolinians*

6. Speech on the Territorial Question, and against Secession, Disunion, and forcible Resistance on account of the Wilmot Proviso—and for the Union and the Constitution, and for constitutional remedies in the Union.—In the Senate of the United States, August 2, 1850 [Washington, 1850.] 8°, pp. 8.
[*A. A. S. Harv. M H. S.*

7. American Steam Navigation.—Speech for the Collins Steamers.—In the Senate of the United States, May 6, 1852 Washington, 1852. 8°, pp. 13.
[*A. A. S. Harv. M. H. S. U. S.*

8 Speech in the United States Senate, February 16, 1854, on the Nebraska Bill. Washington, 1854 8°, pp. 14. [*M. H. S*

9. Speech delivered in the Senate of the United States, May 11, 1854, on the President's Veto-Message. Washington, 1854 8°, pp. 16. [*Harv. M. H. S*

10 Proposed Ordinance of Secession, 1861.
In Peele's *Distinguished North Carolinians*, pp. 210–12.

11 Letters to the Hon. Alfred Ely, 1862.
In Wheeler's *Reminiscences of North Carolina*, 18.

AUTHORITIES

Battle, Hist of Univ. of N C, i, 295, 353, 356, 394–96, 823 *W. A Graham*, Discourse in memory of G E Badger Land We Love, i, 282–86, 335–38. *Peele*, Lives of distinguished North Carolinians, i, 181–228 *Polk*, Diary, iii, 43–44, 50–51. *Weaver*, Ancient Windham, 62. *Wheeler*, Reminiscences of N C, 17–19, 142–43

ANDERSON BAGLEY came to College from Raleigh, North Carolina. His preparation was completed in New Haven under Jeremiah Evarts (Yale 1802).

He was physically feeble, and his exertions in meeting his College work overtaxed his powers. He died of consumption in the vicinity of New York, in the month after graduation, aged about 23 years.

AUTHORITIES

G Allen, Reminiscences, 52.

ZEDEKIAH SMITH BARSTOW, the youngest child of Deacon John Barstow, of Westminster Society, in the western part of the town of Canterbury, Connecticut, and grandson of John and Elizabeth (Newcomb) Barstow, of Canterbury, was born on October 4, 1790 His mother was Susannah Smith, of Westminster A brother was graduated at Brown University in 1807. He entered College after a very brief preparation, conducted by his pastor, the Rev. Erastus Learned, and was obliged to support himself in part by teaching.

He remained in New Haven after graduation, studying theology under President Dwight and teaching for part of the time in the Hopkins Grammar School.

He was licensed to preach by the New Haven West Association of Ministers on May 30, 1815, and about the end of that year went to New York City to become an assistant in the High School conducted by Dr. John Griscom But he had hardly begun his work there, when he was offered and accepted a tutorship in Hamilton College, at Clinton, New York.

The President of the College, Dr. Azel Backus (Yale 1787), died in December, 1816; and until his resignation at the ensuing Commencement Mr. Barstow supplied the College pulpit on Sunday mornings, in addition to his work as Tutor.

He then returned to New Haven, and was occupied in preaching in that vicinity, until he was called to supply the vacant pulpit of the Congregational Church in Keene, New Hampshire, in February, 1818

He was ordained and installed as pastor of this church on July 1, 1818, and on August 19 was married by the Rev. Elisha Rockwood (Dartmouth Coll. 1802) to Elizabeth Fay, eldest daughter of Elihu and Elizabeth (Whitney) Blake, of Westborough, Massachusetts, niece of Eli Whitney (Yale 1792), and sister of Eli Whitney Blake (Yale 1816). They had known each other since the time of her attendance at the school of the Rev. Claudius Herrick (Yale 1798) in New Haven.

In Keene he completed fifty years of pastoral service, on an annual salary of $700, resigning on July 1, 1868, but continuing to preach for destitute parishes in the vicinity for four years longer. A Golden Remembrance of the fiftieth wedding anniversary of Dr. and Mrs Barstow in 1868 was printed by their children.

His wife died in Keene, after a lingering illness, on September 15, 1869, in her 78th year; and his death followed on March 1, 1873, in his 83d year The Discourse preached at his funeral by Professor Henry E. Parker (Dartmouth 1841), of Dartmouth College, a native of Keene, was published, with other memorials.

Their children were four sons and a daughter. Two sons died in infancy, and the daughter in early childhood The sons who survived their parents were graduates of Dartmouth College in 1842 and 1846, respectively

He received the honorary degree of Doctor of Divinity from Dartmouth College in 1849; and served as a Trustee of that College from 1834 to 1871, never missing attendance on a single meeting of the Board during that time. He was also for a long series of years a laborious member of the School Committee of Keene, and the projector of the Keene Academy, which went into operation in 1837, and of which he was Trustee and Secretary until his death.

His influence was felt throughout the State as of one foremost and ardent in all moral, educational and religious enterprises. In 1867 and 1868 he was sent as a Representative of the State Legislature, serving also as Chaplain.

The respect and affection of his own people he retained undiminished to the end During his ministry 782 persons were added to the church

He published.

1. Remarks on the "Preliminary History" of Two Discourses by the Rev. Aaron Bancroft, D.D. Bellows Falls, 1821. 8°, pp. 24

[*A. A. S. A C. A B. Publ C H S Harv. M. H. S. U. T S Y C*

With reference to two sermons preached by Dr. Bancroft, a Unitarian, in Mr Barstow's pulpit.

2. The Ministers of Christ should not miss their aim —A Sermon [from I Cor ix, 26] preached at Acworth, N H, October

14, 1829, at the installation of Rev. Moses G. Grosvenor, as Pastor of the Congregational Church. Boston, 1829. 8°, pp. 28.
[*A. A. S. A. C. A. Harv. Y. C.*

3. A Sermon [from Acts xx, 24] preached at Dunbarton, N. H., July 8, 1830, at the installation of Rev. John M. Putnam, as pastor of the Congregational Church in that place. .. Concord, 1830. 8°, pp. 32. [*A. C. A. B. Publ. Y. C.*

The sermon occupies pp. 1-20.

4. The Ministers of Christ should not be afraid.—A Sermon [from Matth. xxv, 25] preached at the Installation of Rev. Salmon Bennet as Colleague Pastor .... of the First Congregational Church, in Boscawen, N. H. Concord, 1833. 8°, pp. 24.
[*A. C. A. Br. Mus. U. T. S.*

5. Sketch of the Rev. Dr. Walter Harris. In Sprague's *Annals of the American Pulpit,* volume 2, pp. 277-80, 1856.

6. Preaching Christ Jesus the Lord: a Sermon [from II Cor. iv, 5], delivered Nov. 5, 1857, at the Ordination of the Rev. Charles Greenwood, as pastor of the First Church in Westmoreland. .. Keene, 1858. 8°, pp. 16. [*A. C. A. Harv.*

The sermon occupies pp. 3-8.

7. Obituary notice of the Rev. Roger C. Hatch (Yale 1815). In the *Congregational Quarterly,* volume xi, pp. 69-71 (January, 1869).

8. Rest for the Righteous.—A Sermon [from Hebr. iv, 9] preached in the Second Congregational Church, Keene, N. H., April 12, 1871, at the funeral of Rev. A. W. Burnham, D.D. Boston, 1871. 8°, pp. 20.
[*A. C. A. M. H. S. N. Y. Publ. Y. C.*

After his death was published by his children:

9. "Remember the days of old."—A Semi-Centennial Discourse [from Deut. xxxii, 7] preached in the First Congregational Church, Keene, New Hampshire, July 1, 1868, at the close of his Fifty Years' Pastorate. New York, 1873. 8°, pp. 28.
[*A. C. A. M. H. S. U. S. Y. C.*

In the Appendix to the Sermon delivered at his funeral some of his early Reminiscences are printed.

AUTHORITIES.

Barry, Hist. of Hanover, Mass., 222, 233. Congregational Quarterly, xii, 58. *Hale,* Annals of Keene, 110-13. *Lawrence,* New Hampshire Churches, 279. N. E. Hist. and Gen. Register, xxviii, 94-95. Westborough Vital Records, 20, 120.

Dudley Pettibone Bestor, the eldest child of Dr. John Bestor, of Simsbury, Connecticut, was born in Simsbury on June 15, 1792, and was prepared for College by his pastor, the Rev. Samuel Stebbins (Dartmouth Coll. 1775). His father was a native of Rehoboth, Massachusetts, and received the honorary degree of M.D at Yale in 1816. His mother was Rosetta, daughter of Dudley and Mary (Lattemore) Pettibone, of Simsbury.

At his graduation on September 1, he delivered an Oration on Theoretical Improvements, and also took part in a Colloquy written by himself on a Liberal Education.

He was ill at the time, and the day after his return home was more violently seized with dysentery, from which he never recovered. After a painful illness he died at his father's house, in assured Christian faith, on November 2, in his 22d year.

AUTHORITIES.

Conn Courant, Nov 10, 1813 Simsbury Records, 268.

James Beebee Brinsmade, son of Daniel Brinsmade, of that part of Stratford which is now Trumbull, Connecticut, and grandson of Abraham and Mary (Wheeler) Brinsmade, of Trumbull, was baptized on March 29, 1785. His mother was Mary, second daughter of the Rev. James Beebe, of Trumbull, and his two grandfathers were both graduates of the Class of 1745. He was prepared for admission to the Sophomore Class by his pastor, the Rev. Daniel C. Banks (Yale 1804).

For some years after graduation he was the principal of an academy in Easton, Pennsylvania

In 1820 he entered on a mercantile life in New York City.

The last twenty-five years of his life were mainly devoted to works of benevolence, particularly as an officer of the Public School Society, the American Sunday School Union, and the American Tract Society.

About 1851 he removed his residence to Brooklyn, where he died on March 16, 1856, aged 71 years.

He married Phebe Smith, a native of New York City, who died in 1844.

A son was graduated at Yale in 1845, and two grandsons, in 1888 and 1895 (Sheffield Scientific School), respectively.

AUTHORITIES.

Orcutt, Hist. of Stratford, ii, 1164.

MOSES BRISTOL, son of Eli Bristol, a farmer of Oneida County, New York, and a native of Oxford, Connecticut, and Sarah (Peck) Bristol, was born in Clinton on October 21, 1790, and entered at the opening of Sophomore year from Paris, a few miles from Clinton. He had been trained in the Hamilton Oneida Academy in Clinton, under Seth Norton (Yale 1804). He united with the College Church on profession of his faith in March of the Senior year.

In the year of his graduation he engaged in teaching in a classical school in Clinton, but soon returned to the Yale Medical School, and received his diploma here in the spring of 1816.

He then began practice with Dr. Hastings in his native village, but soon removed to Manlius, in Onondaga County; and thence in 1822 to Buffalo, where he practiced successfully until compelled to retire by failing health in 1849. As a physician he was noted for kindness of heart and genial sympathy, as well as professional skill.

He was the President of the Erie County Medical Society in 1833 and 1838; and served as Clerk of the County Courts from November 1846, to November, 1849.

Later, he was for some years an Associate Justice of the Erie County Court.

From 1824 he was a Ruling Elder in the First Presbyterian Church of Buffalo. He was eminently a good man, and highly respected.

He was stricken with paralysis on November 5, 1869, and died on the next day in his 80th year.

He married, on October 17, 1817, Cornelia, only child of Dr. Sewall and Ruth Strong (Norton) Hopkins, of Clinton, by whom he had three children, all of whom died early. She died on August 1, 1823, in her 26th year.

He next married, on October 26, 1824, Emily, eldest daughter of Asa and Hannah Woodruff, of Clinton, who died on December 30, 1885, in her 89th year.

By her he had five sons, of whom the two youngest died in infancy, and two daughters, who also died young. The eldest son is a Presbyterian clergyman.

AUTHORITIES.

Buffalo Med. and Surg. Journal, ix, 150. *Dwight,* Strong Family, i, 297. *F. J. Shepard,* MS. Letters, Dec., 1911. *H. P. Smith,* Hist. of Buffalo, ii, 421. *Wager,* Hist. of Oneida County, pt. 1, 272.

Ebenezer Brown, son of Bartholomew and Lucy (Dunn) Brown, of Brimfield, Hampden County, Massachusetts, and grandson of Jonathan and Abigail (Russell) Brown, of Brimfield, was born on July 14, 1788, and was prepared for Yale by Levi Collins (Yale 1802) in the Monson Academy. He was admitted to the College Church on profession of his faith in June of his Senior year.

He studied Theology after graduation in New Haven, and his first settlement as pastor was in the First or North Parish of Wilbraham, in his native county, where he was ordained and installed, notwithstanding formidable opposition to his call (on December 16, 1818), over the Congregational Church on March 3, 1819. This charge he resigned after a turbulent pastorate, in which he had administered discipline with a firm hand, in July, 1827, to accept a call from the Congregational Church in Prescott, in Hampshire County, where he was installed on October 17.

An extensive revival of religion was experienced during his ministry there. He was dismissed on March 25, 1835, to accept a call from the Second Congregational Church in (North) Hadley, in the same county, of which he was the first settled pastor, from April 8, 1835, to the spring of 1838, when he went to Northern Illinois, under a commission from the American Home Missionary Society; he was not, however, formally dismissed from North Hadley, until a council met for the installation of his successor in September, 1841.

Meantime he was stationed at Byron, on Rock River, in Ogle County. In November, 1843, he assisted in forming a Congregational Church in Roscoe, Winnebago County, just south of the Wisconsin line; of which he assumed the pastoral care two months later. He was known there as strictly conservative in his theology. About 1850 he retired from his pastorate and took up farming. Subsequently he served as stated supply for a short time to a Presbyterian Church, which was started in Roscoe, having transferred his ecclesiastical relations to the Old School Presbyterians.

He retained his residence in Roscoe until his death, preaching in different churches in Winnebago and Boone Counties. After a few years of retirement, he died in Roscoe on February 13, 1872, aged 83½ years.

He married Sabra, daughter of Captain Hezekiah and Sarah (Trumbull) Wells, of East Windsor, Connecticut, who died on July 23, 1881, aged 93 years. Three children died in infancy, and one son is still living.

AUTHORITIES

Amer. Quart. Register, x, 262, 382, 384, 393–94, 405. Hist. of Winnebago County, 1877, 450. *Holland,* Hist. of Western Mass., ii, 159, 224, 268. *Judd,* Hist. of Hadley, 2d ed., 435. *Mrs. Laura Short,* MS Letter, Dec., 1911. *Stebbins,* Wilbraham Centennial, 143. *Prof. H. M. Whitney,* MS. Letter, May, 1880.

Norris Bull, son of John and Martha (Rogers) Bull, of Harwinton, Litchfield County, Connecticut, was born in Harwinton on October 24, 1790. His father was a farmer, who had served in the Revolution. He was prepared for College by his pastor, the Rev. Joshua Williams (Yale 1780).

On graduation he became the principal of a school in Lansingburg, New York, where he was highly successful. While there he became a Christian, and united with the Presbyterian Church. He then formed the purpose of entering the ministry, and accordingly resigned his charge, and in the fall of 1816 entered the Theological Seminary at Princeton.

In 1818 he secured a license to preach from the Presbytery of Columbia, in session at Catskill, New York; and then accepted a commission from the New York Young Men's Missionary Society to labor in the western part of the State. After a brief engagement in Norwich, in Chenango County, he served for about two years as stated supply of the Presbyterian Church in Warsaw, Wyoming County, whence he was called in 1821 to the Presbyterian Church in Geneseo, Livingston County, where he was ordained and installed as pastor on June 19, 1822.

After some years, during which the church enjoyed great prosperity, Mr. Bull became involved in a painful controversy with a member of the church who had embraced Unitarianism. This so impaired his usefulness that he gladly resigned his charge, on July 3, 1832, to accept one from the Presbyterian Church in Wyoming, about twelve miles to the westwards.

In Wyoming he held also, after the first year, the office of Principal of a very flourishing Academy; but he took a dismission on February 11, 1836, to accept an invitation to Clarkson, in Monroe County, where also he was to be the head of a public school, as well as the pastor of the Presbyterian Church.

He was installed in the pastorate on June 27, 1837, and his experience and reputation as a teacher rendered the school very popular; but at the end of six years he retired from the latter duty, to devote himself entirely to the work of the ministry

In 1846 he received the honorary degree of Doctor of Divinity from Union College.

In the earlier part of the year 1846 he resigned his ministerial charge, owing to some peculiar circumstances in his congregation

In the ensuing fall he accepted an invitation to supply the vacant Presbyterian Church in Lewiston, Niagara County, in which service he continued until his sudden death, from inflammation of the stomach, in Lewiston, on December 7, 1847, in his 58th year. A funeral sermon by the Rev Dr. John C. Lord, of Buffalo, was afterwards published.

He married, on June 9, 1819, Mary Ann Henry, of Saugatuck village, in the present township of Westport, Connecticut, who survived him.

They had four children, one of whom was graduated at Union College in 1842, and died in 1844

Dr. Bull's only acknowledged publication was an Address delivered before the Kappa Phi Society of Wilson Collegiate Institute, at its first Anniversary, 1846.

He was especially efficient as a counsellor and as a master of debate in ecclesiastical assemblies In theology he was a decided Calvinist.

AUTHORITIES.

Hotchkin, Hist of Western N. Y, 494, 554, 556, 573 *C R Johnson,* Hist of Congregational Church in Norwich, 18, 47. *Sprague,* Annals of the Amer Pulpit, iv, 615–22

STEPHEN MITCHELL CHESTER, the eldest son of Stephen Chester (Yale 1780), of Wethersfield, Connecticut, was born in Wethersfield on October 18, 1793, and was prepared for College by the Rev. Azel Backus (Yale 1787), of Bethlehem.

Soon after graduation he went to North Carolina, where he was engaged in mercantile pursuits for about nine years.

For many years later he was in the carpet business with his cousins, W. W. & T. L. Chester, in New York City. He was an officer in several insurance companies there, and an elder in the Madison Square Presbyterian Church.

He was distinguished for fine literary taste, and he cultivated assiduously his natural appreciation and enjoyment of music and painting, devoting himself to the improvement of the choirs of the churches with which he was connected, and collecting a gallery of valuable pictures by old masters.

The last five years of his life were spent in his native town, under the infirmities consequent upon paralysis, but usefully to the last. He died suddenly in Wethersfield on April 14, 1862, in his 69th year. He was never married.

He was beloved and respected in private life, and uniformly sustained the character of a sincere and consistent Christian.

AUTHORITIES.

Rev. W. S. Colton, MS. Letter, May, 1862. N. E. Hist. and Geneal. Register, xxii, 342. N. Y. Observer, May 1, 1862. *Stiles*, Hist. of Wethersfield, ii, 217. *Tillotson*, Wethersfield Inscriptions, 39.

William Cone, the youngest son of Israel Cone, of East Haddam, Connecticut, a Revolutionary soldier, and grandson of Deacon Nathaniel and Mary (Graves) Cone, of East Haddam, was born on September 24, 1794, and was prepared for College by the Rev. Joseph Vaill (Dartmouth Coll. 1778), of Hadlyme Society.

In 1817 he accepted an offer to teach in Phillips Academy, Andover, Massachusetts, at the same time studying in the Theological Seminary.

At the end of a year he was so ill from consumption, that he was obliged to return to his father's house, where he died, unmarried, on March 5, 1819, in his 25th year.

AUTHORITIES.

Cone Family, 168.

Sherman Converse, the youngest son of Chester Converse, of Thompson, Windham County, Connecticut, and grandson of Lieutenant Jacob and Anna (White) Converse, of Thompson, was born in Thompson on April 17, 1790. His mother was Esther, daughter of Hezekiah Green, of Thompson. About 1800 his family removed to Monson, Massachusetts, and he was prepared for College by Levi Collins (Yale 1802) in the Monson Academy.

At graduation he was appointed College Butler, and after retiring from that office in 1815, he remained in New Haven and soon established himself in an extensive printing, publishing and bookselling business.

He was from 1817 to 1826 the editor and publisher of the weekly *Connecticut Journal;* and among the more prominent enterprises with which he was connected as publisher may be mentioned the *American Journal of Science and Arts* from 1820 to 1826, the *Christian Spectator* from 1821 to 1825, Swift's *Digest of Connecticut Laws,* 1822-23, and the first edition of Webster's *Dictionary,* 1828. The last-named was an undertaking of formidable magnitude. He also did a part of the official printing for the College, from 1819 to 1825.

He published in 1822 a pamphlet of 183 pages, giving a report of his trial before the Superior and Supreme Courts in 1820 for a libel upon Joshua Stow, whom he had described in his newspaper as an infidel.

In 1820 he was married to Ann, elder daughter of Deacon Samuel Perkins (Yale 1785), of Windham, who died in New Haven, after a painful illness, on May 17,

1821, at the age of 27. He was next married, on June 28, 1824, to Eliza Bruen, daughter of the Rev. Dr. Samuel Nott (Yale 1780), of Franklin.

He entered into the book and publishing business in New York City, in 1826, and was actively engaged there in business of various kinds

From 1838 to 1844 he resided in Quebec, and then returned to New York for a few years

His wife died in New York City on January 19, 1845, in her 47th year.

About the year 1850 he was crippled by a severe attack of rheumatism, which made him an invalid for the rest of his days. Besides his sufferings from disease, he was sorely tried by grave financial embarrassments; but he bore all his troubles with Christian patience.

In the spring of 1863 he removed to the house of his son in Boston Highlands, Massachusetts, and for the next ten years never left his room. He died there, after a brief final illness, on December 10, 1873, in his 84th year He was buried in New Haven, by the side of his wives.

His only child by his first wife died in infancy. The only child by his second wife was graduated here in 1850, and became an Episcopal clergyman.

An engraving from a likeness of Mr. Converse is given in the *Converse Family.*

He published:

1. Thoughts on the administration of God's Moral Government over our fallen world. By a Plain Man New-Haven [printed, Cambridge], 1860 pp. 143 [*Y. C.*

2 In 1854 was published, as an Appendix (11 pp.) to a pamphlet by Joseph E Worcester (Yale 1811) entitled *A Gross Literary Fraud Exposed,* a letter in which he gave details relating to his experience as the publisher of Webster's dictionaries.

AUTHORITIES

Converse Family, i, 106, 230-32 Perkins Family, pt 3, 42, 84
Huntington Family Memoir, 180

Elias Cornelius, the only son of Dr. Elias Cornelius, a Revolutionary surgeon, and his wife, Sarah Cornelius, of Somers (formerly Stephentown), Westchester County, New York, and grandson of Jonathan and Mary (Baldwin) Cornelius, of Long Island, was born on July 30, 1794. His preparation for the Sophomore Class at Yale was completed in the Academy in the neighboring town of North Salem, under the Rev. Herman Daggett (Brown Univ. 1788) and Daniel Banks (Yale 1809). In College he was especially interested in the pursuit of natural history. He became a Christian in the spring of his Senior year.

He remained in New Haven for two years after graduation for the study of theology with President Dwight; and then spent another year in Litchfield with the Rev. Dr. Lyman Beecher (Yale 1797). He was licensed to preach on June 4, 1816, by the Litchfield South Association of Ministers, and during the rest of that year was employed in soliciting funds in New England and New York for the use of the American Board of Commissioners for Foreign Missions in establishing schools in India.

He was so successful in this agency that he was appointed, in December, 1816, to raise funds for establishing schools for the education of the children of American Indians in the Southwest.

After beginning this work he decided to make a tour to the Cherokee country, and in preparation he was ordained, in Harwinton, Connecticut, on April 9, 1817, by the Litchfield South Consociation,—at the same time with the ordination of Asahel Nettleton (Yale 1809) as an evangelist. The sermon on this occasion was preached by the Rev. Dr. Beecher. In this connection he was commissioned by the Missionary Society of Connecticut to spend six months in labor in New Orleans.

He then proceeded on his tour to the Cherokee and Creek settlements in Northern Georgia, and thence to Natchez and New Orleans.

He spent the first three months of the year 1818 in active missionary labors in the latter city, and reached Boston on his return in August

On September 28 he was married, in Andover, to Mary Ann, elder daughter of the late Rev Asahel Hooker (Yale 1789), of Goshen, Connecticut, whose widow was now the wife of Samuel Farrar, of Andover

With Andover as his residence, he engaged for a few months in further solicitations for the American Board, and in theological study.

On July 21, 1819, he was installed as colleague to the Rev. Samuel Worcester (Dartmouth Coll. 1795), pastor of the Tabernacle Church in Salem. Dr. Worcester's time was largely devoted to his duties as Corresponding Secretary of the American Board, and after a period of feeble health his death followed in June, 1821.

The duties of sole pastor then devolved on Mr. Cornelius, but his proved fitness for public charitable labors led to his being invited in the early part of 1824 to take the position of Secretary of the American Education Society, an agency for the support of indigent young men preparing for the ministry.

He declined this offer, but was again elected two years later. He again declined, but in August, 1826, a third appeal induced him to submit the question to his church; and on the advice of a council he was finally dismissed on September 29.

He then removed to Andover, and entered on his duties as Secretary.

In this field of labor he continued until January, 1832. In the meantime he had declined an election to the chair of Divinity in Dartmouth College. The honorary degree of Doctor of Divinity was conferred on him by Dartmouth in 1829, but he declined on principle to use it.

In the fall of 1829 the headquarters of the Education Society were removed from Andover to Boston, and he changed his residence accordingly.

In June, 1831, he removed to New York City, where, while retaining his former duties, he undertook the secretaryship of the Presbyterian Education Society, a cognate institution.

In October, 1831, he was elected to succeed Jeremiah Evarts (Yale 1802) as Corresponding Secretary of the American Board. After very serious deliberation, he accepted the office in December, and arrived in Boston in January, 1832, to arrange for beginning his work.

He started on his return journey on February 4, but was taken seriously ill with brain fever at the house of the Rev. Dr. Joel Hawes in Hartford, and died there, after great suffering, on February 12, in his 38th year. The sermon preached at his funeral by Dr. Hawes was afterwards published. He was buried in Hartford.

His widow died in Newton Centre, Massachusetts, on October 17, 1880, in her 85th year. Their children were four sons and two daughters. The younger daughter married the Rev. George B. Little (Bowdoin Coll. 1843).

An engraving from a painting of Mr. Cornelius is given in his *Memoir.*

He was a direct and forcible preacher, an energetic and effective man of business, and a devoted Christian.

He published:

1. On the Geology, Mineralogy, Scenery, and Curiosities of Parts of Virginia, Tennessee, and the Alabama and Mississippi Territories, &c., with Miscellaneous Remarks, in a letter to the Editor.

In the *American Journal of Science and Arts,* vol. 1, pp. 214–26, 317–31 (May, 1819). Also, reprinted in Sir Richard Phillips's *New Voyages and Travels,* London, 1820, vol. 3.

2. Account of a singular position of a Granite Rock.

In the same, vol. 2, pp. 200–01 (November, 1820).

3. God's ways not as our ways.—A Sermon [from Isa. lv, 9], occasioned by the death of the Rev. Samuel Worcester, D.D. .. Salem, 1821. 8°, pp. 56.

[*A. C. A. B. Ath. B. Publ. Br. Mus. M. H. S. N. Y. Publ. U. T. S. Y. C.*

4. The little Osage Captive, an authentic Narrative. . . York [Canada], 1821. 12°, pp. 182. [*Br. Mus.*

Several reprints. The work is designed for children.

5. A Sermon [from Ex. xiv, 15], delivered in the Tabernacle Church, Salem, Mass., Sept. 25, 1823, at the Ordination of the Rev. Edmund Frost, as a Missionary to the Heathen. . . Boston, 1823. 8°, pp. 32.

[*A. A. S. A. C. A. B. Publ. Br. Mus. M. H. S. N. Y. Publ. U. T. S. Y. C.*

6. The Moral and Religious Improvement of the Poor.—A Sermon [from Levit. xxv, 35] delivered on the evening of October 20, 1824, in the Tabernacle Church, Salem. Salem, 1824. 8°, pp. 24. [*A. C. A. B. Publ. Br. Mus. N. Y. Publ. U. T. S.*

7. A Review of the Rev. Mr. Colman's Sermon, delivered at the opening of the Independent Congregational Church, in Barton Square, Salem. Boston, 1825. 8°, pp. 36.

[*A. A. S. B. Publ. Harv. N. Y. Publ. U. T. S. Y. C.*

The same. Second Edition. Containing a reply to Mr. Colman's Notes. Boston, 1825. 8°, pp. 64.

[*A. A. S. B. Ath. B. Publ. Harv. N. Y. Publ. Y. C.*

An anonymous criticism, bearing on the Unitarian controversy.

8. A Sermon [from Eph. ii, 18] on the Doctrine of the Trinity. Andover, 1826. 8°, pp. 43.

[*A. A. S. A. C. A. B. Publ. Br. Mus. N. Y. Publ. U. T. S. Y. C.*

The same. Second Edition. Salem, 1826. 8°, pp. 44.

[*A. A. S. B. Ath. B. Publ. Br. Mus. Harv. U. T. S. Y. C.*

He edited the *Quarterly Journal and Register* of the American Education Society for three years, 1827–30.

Copious extracts from his letters and journals are given in his *Memoir* by Professor Edwards.

AUTHORITIES.

A. B. C. F. M. Memorial Volume, 178, 213–216. Amer. Quart. Register, iv, 249–64; v, 1–18. Eclectic Magazine, lviii, 260–61. *Edwards,* Memoir of Cornelius. Hooker Descendants, 215. Quarterly Christian Spectator, vi, 308–31. Religious Intelligencer, xvi, 607, 672, 694–96, 821–23. *Sprague,* Annals of the Amer. Pulpit, ii, 633–43.

JOHN CRANE, the youngest of nine children of Henry Crane, a well-to-do farmer of Durham, Connecticut, and grandson of Henry and Mercy (Francis) Crane, of Durham, was born on July 21, 1791. His mother was Jerusha, daughter of Joel and Rhoda (Camp) Parmalee, of Durham In his infancy the family removed to Whitestown, Oneida County, New York He was prepared for College by Seth Norton (Yale 1804) at Hamilton Oneida Academy, at Clinton, and entered soon after the opening of the Sophomore year

After graduation he studied law with the Hon. Thomas R. Gold (Yale 1786), of Whitesboro

In 1817 he was admitted to practice and emigrated to Chautauqua County, in the southwest corner of the State, where he settled in the village of Fredonia, in the township of Pomfret

He was at first in partnership with the Hon. Daniel G Garnsey, and afterwards with the Hon. James Mullett.

About the year 1822 he was appointed an Associate Judge of the County Court, which office he held for about two years. He did much to promote the cause of education in Fredonia, especially in connection with the Academy, of which he was one of the founders and liberal benefactors. He was a pillar of the Presbyterian Church in the village.

After some two years of declining health, he died in Fredonia, from a stroke of apoplexy, on May 20, 1860, in his 69th year.

He married on November 19, 1829, at Fredonia, Priscilla Jones Eddy, a native of Hoosick Falls, in Rensselaer County, who died in Fredonia on December 28, 1878, in her 70th year.

His children were five sons and two daughters, all of whom survived him

---

AUTHORITIES.

Crane Genealogy, i, 84, 103–04 *Dr. E. T Foote,* MS Letter, June, 1860

JAMES CUTHBERT, the eldest son of John Alexander and Mary Caroline Dupré (Heyward) Cuthbert, of South Carolina, and grandson of James Cuthbert, an emigrant from Inverness, Scotland, was born in 1794. A brother was graduated in 1816.

He entered as a Sophomore from Charleston, his preparation having been completed in New Haven under Henry Sherman (Yale 1803).

He studied medicine, but never practiced, becoming instead a large land owner and planter, residing chiefly in Charleston. He married his first cousin, Anne Miles Heyward, and had a large family of children, most of whom reached maturity.

He held the rank of Lieutenant Colonel in the militia, and was distinguished for his benevolence and liberality in civil and religious life.

He died at his summer home near Brailsfordville (near Beaufort) on August 16, 1838, at the age of 44. His wife long survived him.

AUTHORITIES.

Miss I. DeSaussure, MS. Letter, Dec., 1911.

HENRY DAGGETT, the second son of Henry Daggett (Yale 1775), of New Haven, was born in 1794. He was prepared for College at the Hopkins Grammar School by Elizur Goodrich (Williams Coll. 1806).

He went South after graduation, and for years was in business in Mobile, Alabama. While filling the position of Assistant Cashier of the Bank of Mobile, he died there on December 24, 1837, at the age of 43.

He was probably never married.

AUTHORITIES.

Columbian Register, Jan. 6, 1838. Doggett-Daggett Family, 147.

Thomas Frederick Davies was born in Redding, Connecticut, on August 24, 1793 His father, Dr Thomas Davies, a half-brother of the Rev. Thomas Davies (Yale 1758), and a native of what is now Washington, began practice as a physician in the North Society of New Fairfield, now Sherman, but removed to Redding early in 1793.

He was prepared for College by the Rev. Dr. David Ely (Yale 1769), of Huntington.

After his graduation he remained in New Haven for two years, engaged in teaching and in pursuing theological studies under President Dwight.

He was licensed to preach by the Fairfield East Association of Ministers on May 29, 1816, and the next month began preaching in the Huntington pulpit, vacant by the recent death of Dr. Ely.

He was ordained and installed there as pastor of the Congregational Church on March 5, 1817, having already, on February 24, been married to Julia, elder daughter of Deacon Lemuel and Mary (Heron) Sanford, of Redding.

His heavy labors in his own parish and in vacant adjoining parishes brought on a hemorrhage of the lungs, which suspended his work in February, 1818, and compelled his dismission in the following July.

Though unable to continue pastoral labor, he was not wholly incapacitated; and in response to a suggestion from the Rev. Nathaniel W. Taylor (Yale 1807), he removed, later in 1818, to New Haven, and undertook the editorship of the (monthly) *Christian Spectator,* which was begun in January, 1819. After three years of this occupation, and a further similar connection (from October, 1822) with the *Religious Intelligencer* of New Haven, he again broke down with what seemed like consumptive symptoms, and he returned to Redding late in 1826, with slight prospects of recovery. But after two years of open-air life and exercise, he was able in 1828 to resume preaching, and in May, 1829, he began to supply the Congregational Society in Green's Farms in the present township of Westport, of which he was installed pastor on October 29.

Ill health again compelled his resignation in August, 1839; and as a son was about to enter College he then removed to New Haven, where he remained for about ten years.

When the *New Englander* magazine began publication in 1843, he was invited to become the editor, but declined the offer, on account of his health.

The last years of his life were divided between his native town, New Haven, and the home of his daughter in Westport.

He died in Westport, after an illness of about ten days, on February 16, 1865, in his 72d year.

His wife died on June 8, 1858, in her 61st year; a second wife, Elizabeth Merriman, daughter of Joseph H. and Betsey (Merriman) Jocelin, or Josselyn, of New Haven, died in New Haven on January 28, 1881, aged 69 years.

His children were two daughters and two sons.

One son was graduated here in 1843, and the other, who became the Episcopal Bishop of Michigan, in 1853. The elder daughter married Ebenezer B. Adams (Yale 1835).

Mr. Davies was a man of genial and polished manners, and of superior intellect and culture, but was always hampered by infirm health.

He published:

A Sermon [from Ps. lxxvii, 5] delivered March 29, 1839; and published by request of the Congregational Society in Green's Farms. New Haven, 1839. 8°, pp. 31.

[*Br. Mus. C. H. S. M. H. S. Y. C.*

On the two hundredth anniversary of the settlement of Fairfield.

He contributed to the Rev. Dr. Sprague's *Annals of the American Pulpit* sketches of the Rev. Nathan Birdseye (Yale 1736), the Rev. Dr. Hezekiah Ripley (Yale 1763), and the Rev. Dr. David Ely (Yale 1769), in volumes 1, pp. 439-40, 647-50, and 2, 4-7.

His contributions to the *Christian Spectator* have not been identified A letter from him in relation to that work is given in Dr. Lyman Beecher's *Autobiography*, vol. 1, pp 380–83

He assisted Professor Olmsted in preparing the account of their Class Meeting in 1843, and it included a poem by himself.

AUTHORITIES.

Hurd, Hist. of Fairfield County, 821 N. Y Observer, April 6, 1865. Thomas Sanford Family, 1, 291, 316

Nicoll Havens Dering, son of General Sylvester Dering, of Shelter Island, New York, and grandson of Thomas and Mary (Sylvester) Dering, of Shelter Island, was born on January 1, 1794 His mother was Esther Sarah, daughter of Nicoll Havens (Yale 1753), of Shelter Island He was prepared for College at Bacon Academy, in Colchester, Connecticut.

Soon after graduation he began the study of medicine in New York City with Dr John C Osborn, and in 1817 he received the degree of M D. from the College of Physicians and Surgeons.

From this date until 1843 he was engaged in the practice of his profession in New York

In 1818 he was appointed Health Commissioner by Governor DeWitt Clinton, a responsible position for so young a man, especially from the prevalence of yellow fever during the summer of 1819 He held the office for two years. From 1820 until 1843 he was one of the Trustees of the College of Physicians and Surgeons, and Registrar from 1826 to 1843.

He married on June 6, 1826, his first cousin, Frances, second daughter of the Hon. Henry Huntington (Dartmouth Coll. 1783) and Catharine M. (Havens) Huntington, of Rome, New York, who died on February 2, 1841, in her 42d year.

His health, impaired by the exhausting labors of a long practice, caused him to remove to Rome in May, 1843; and on October 1, 1844, he married Sarah Huggins, eldest daughter of Benjamin and Sarah (Weeks) Strong, of New York City, and niece of George W. Strong (Yale 1803).

From Rome he removed, in 1847, to Utica, where he resided thenceforth, though debarred from practice by infirm vision. He died in Utica, after an illness of nearly five months caused by prostration of the nervous system and impaired digestion, on December 19, 1867, aged nearly 74 years.

His widow died on February 21, 1889, aged 93.

By his first marriage he had no children. By his second marriage he had six daughters and one son; four daughters and the son survived him.

Dr. Dering was a deacon in the Brick Church, New York, from 1832 to 1843; and after his removal to Utica he held the office of Elder in the First Presbyterian Church in that city.

His tastes were largely antiquarian and genealogical, but his always imperfect vision made it difficult for him to indulge them to a great extent. He was also until the last particularly interested in whatever concerned education.

He was associated with Dr. John Watts in the following publication, addressed to the State Legislature:

Memorial of the Trustees of the College of Physicians and Surgeons of New York, in reply to the "Memorial of the Professors of Rutgers' Medical Faculty." New York, 1830. 8°, pp. 24.
[*U. S. Surg. General's Library.*

AUTHORITIES.

Amer. Ancestry, iv, 51. *Dwight,* Strong Family, 1, 625-26. Huntington Family Memoir, 194. *Mallmann,* Hist. of Shelter Island, 177-78, 244. N. Y. State Medical Society's Transactions, 1868, 307-10. *Wood,* Sketch of L. I., 197.

THOMAS POLLOCK DEVEREUX, the elder son of John Devereux, an emigrant from Wexford, Ireland, to Newbern, North Carolina, was born in Newbern in 1793. His mother was Frances, daughter of Thomas and Eunice (Edwards) Pollock, of Newbern,—Eunice Edwards being the youngest daughter of Jonathan Edwards (Yale 1720). A sister married Bishop and General Leonidas Polk, and a brother was graduated here in 1815. In his boyhood the family made their principal residence in Stratford, Connecticut, the home of Mrs Devereux's relatives, for the education of the children

After graduation he studied law in the Litchfield Law School, but for some years did not seek for practice, as a competent fortune made it unnecessary. Later, some business reverses changed the course of his life, and he resolved to devote himself to his profession. He held for some years the office of United States District Attorney for the District of North Carolina, being appointed as a staunch Federalist

In 1826 he was appointed reporter of the Supreme Court of the State, and so continued for thirteen years, during which he published four volumes of Law Reports and two of Equity Reports

In middle life by the death of an uncle he received the care of a large estate, and lived thenceforth on his plantation of Connemara, on the Roanoke river, in Halifax County, near the northern border of the State. He served also as the presiding Justice of the County Court.

He died at Connemara on March 7, 1869, in his 76th year.

Colonel Devereux first married on October 7, 1815, Catharine Anne, eldest daughter of Robert Charles Johnson (Yale 1783), of Stratford, Connecticut, who died at White Sulphur Springs, Virginia, on July 17, 1836, aged 40 years, by her he had nine daughters and three sons.

After her death he married Ann Mary, daughter of Robert Maitland, of New York City, who died in Petersburg, Virginia, on February 16, 1881, aged 83 years. Their only child was a daughter.

He was survived by seven daughters and his eldest son (Yale 1840).

He was a Trustee of the University of North Carolina from 1820 to 1827.

AUTHORITIES.

Battle, Hist. of Univ. of N. C., i, 258, 351, 549, 823. Geneal. Hist. of Conn., i, 206. N. Y. Geneal. and Biogr. Record, xii, 22. N. C. Hist. and Geneal. Register, iii, 157. Tuttle Family, 425–26.

Abram Dixon, a brother of David Raymond Dixon (Yale 1807), was born in Manchester, Vermont, in July, 1787. His family removed to Sherburne, Chenango County, New York, in 1794 or 1795, and he was prepared for admission to the Junior Class by Seth Norton, in the Hamilton Oneida Academy, at Clinton.

After graduation he studied law with Judge Isaac Foot, of Hamilton, in Madison County, and on August 29, 1817, was married to Caroline, eldest daughter of Reuel and Lucy (Barnes) Pelton, of Kirkland township, in which Clinton is situated.

Immediately after his marriage he settled in Westfield Village, in Chautauqua County, where he pursued his profession until enfeebled by age, and was highly respected as an honest lawyer.

Mrs. Dixon died on September 10, 1837, in her 40th year, and he was next married, about 1840, to Mrs. Eliza Williams Higgings, daughter of General Elijah and Mary (Adams) Holt, of Cherry Valley, who died on March 10, 1858.

He was a member of the State Senate during four sessions, 1840-43.

He died in Westfield on April 19, 1875, in his 88th year, after a very brief illness, from pneumonia.

By his first wife he had two daughters and a son; and by his second marriage a daughter and a son.

AUTHORITIES.

Durrie, Holt Family, 105. Pelton Genealogy, 390. *Young*, Hist. of Chautauqua County, 597.

David Bates Douglass, the youngest son of Deacon Nathaniel Douglas, of Newark, New Jersey, and grandson of David and Esther (Reed) Douglas, of Hanover Neck, was born in Pompton, on March 21, 1790. His mother was Sarah, daughter of Captain David and Phebe (Tappan) Bates, of Whippany. He was prepared for the Sophomore Class by the Rev. Samuel Whelpley in Newark.

On October 1, 1813, he entered the army, and was commissioned as Second Lieutenant of Engineers, and ordered to West Point. He went to the front in the Niagara campaign of 1814, and was promoted to a First Lieutenancy, with a brevet appointment as Captain, for distinguished services during the siege of Fort Erie.

On January 1, 1815, he was appointed Assistant Professor of Natural Philosophy in the Military Academy at West Point, and on December 12 of the same year he was married to Ann Eliza, daughter of Andrew Ellicott, Professor of Mathematics at West Point, and Sarah (Brown) Ellicott.

In 1817 he was ordered to make a reconnoissance with a view to fortifying the eastern entrance of Long Island Sound. In March, 1819, he was promoted to the rank of Captain; and in the same year was appointed the astronomical surveyor for the United States to the joint commission for the survey of the Niagara river and the islands of Lake Erie.

In 1820 he accompanied, as engineer and astronomer, an expedition under General Cass for the exploration of the country bordering on Lake Superior and the head waters of the Mississippi.

On the death of his father-in-law in August, 1820, he was appointed his successor as Professor of Mathematics at West Point, and in May, 1823, he was transferred to the professorship of engineering.

During his vacations for some years he found employment in various engineering works, and he was repeatedly urged to take other important positions. Thus, he was invited by Governor Clinton to take charge of the Western section of the Erie Canal, was offered the place of chief engineer of the State of Georgia, and the superintendence of the system of internal improvements in Pennsylvania. He was retained as consulting engineer in certain important enterprises in New York and Pennsylvania; and finally in March, 1831, he resigned from the army and settled in Brooklyn.

In 1828 he had made an examination for the line of the Morris and Essex Canal, and he now took charge of that work, and introduced an important improvement in the use of inclined planes over long slopes, in place of locks.

In 1832 Major Douglass was appointed Professor of Natural Philosophy in the New York University, but finding that regular duties interfered with his outside engagements he relinquished his chair in 1833, and accepted instead the appointment of Professor of Civil Engineering and Architecture, with the understanding that no duties would be required of him except such as he chose to perform. In fact, he lectured only during a single year, 1836-37, but he also performed the service of designing the new Collegiate building of the University, in Washington Square.

In 1833 he surveyed a route for a railroad from Brooklyn to Jamaica, and in the same year began preliminary surveys for supplying New York City with pure water, and in 1834-36 as the first chief engineer of the Croton water-works projected the outlines of that great work.

In 1838-39 he planned and laid out the Greenwood Cemetery, in Brooklyn, and he continued in charge of its development until March, 1841

In the meantime, on the solicitation of his former friend and pastor, the Rt. Rev. Charles P. McIlvaine, he accepted in September, 1840, an election to the presidency of Kenyon College, at Gambier, Ohio, where he began his duties in March, 1841; he also took the duties of Professor of Intellectual and Moral Philosophy, Logic, and Rhetoric. The College was in a precarious condition, and did not grow as Bishop McIlvaine had hoped under his friend's administration; and in February, 1844, the President was summarily dismissed from office

He then resumed his professional labors, and among other works laid out the Albany Rural cemetery in 1845-46, and the Protestant cemetery in Quebec in 1848, and designed the supporting wall for Brooklyn Heights and the supplying of that city with water.

In August, 1848, he was elected Professor of Mathematics and Natural Philosophy in Geneva, now Hobart College, at Geneva, New York. A fall in Quebec had, however, injured him permanently, and he died in Geneva, after a brief illness, from the effects of a paralytic stroke, on October 21, 1849, in his 60th year

A discourse occasioned by his death, by the Rev. President Hale, which emphasizes his deeply religious spirit, was afterwards published

At the request of the Trustees of Greenwood cemetery his remains were removed thither for burial.

An engraving from his portrait is given in Stuart's *American Engineers, Van Nostrand's Engineering Magazine,* and the *Douglas Genealogy.*

His widow died in Batavia, New York, on July 1, 1873, at the age of 81

Their children were four daughters and four sons, all of whom survived their parents. The two eldest sons were graduated at Kenyon College in 1837 and 1838, respectively, the third at Trinity College in 1846, and the fourth at West Point in 1852. The first and third sons became clergymen.

The honorary degree of Doctor of Laws was conferred on him in 1841 by Yale College and also by Hobart College.

He published:

1. Report on the Coal and Iron Formation of Frostburg and the Upper Potomac, in the States of Maryland and Virginia. [1838.] 8°, pp. 29. [*B. Publ. Y. C.*

2. Statement of Facts and Circumstances connected with the Removal of the Author from the Presidency of Kenyon College.—Printed for private circulation.—1844. 8°, pp. 37.
[*B. Publ. Br. Mus. Harv. M. H. S. U. S. Y. C.*

The same. Second Edition. New York, 1844. 8°, pp. 30.
[*B. Publ. Br. Mus. Y. C.*

3. Further Statement of Facts and Circumstances connected with the Removal of the Author from the Presidency of Kenyon College, in answer to "The Reply of Trustees," etc. Albany, 1845. 8°, pp. 71. [*B. Publ. Br. Mus. Harv. M. H. S. Y. C.*

AUTHORITIES.

Douglas Genealogy, 429, 432. *Stuart,* Lives of Civil and Military Engineers of America, 199–221. Van Nostrand's Engineering Magazine, xxxvii, 1–6.

Louis Dwight, the youngest of three sons of Henry W. Dwight, and a brother of the Rev. Edwin W. Dwight (Yale 1809), was born in Stockbridge, Massachusetts, on March 25, 1793. His father died in 1804, and he was prepared for College by the Rev. Dr. Azel Backus (Yale 1787), of Bethlehem, Connecticut. He became a Christian while living with Dr. Backus.

In his Senior year, at the close of a chemical lecture, he inhaled some "exhilarating gas," which induced a severe hemorrhage of the lungs, that in the end changed his plans for life.

On account of his health he deferred the beginning of theological studies until 1816, when he entered the Andover Seminary, and on his graduation in 1819 he decided, on account of his weak lungs, to accept an agency of the American Tract Society.

For the furtherance of his work he was ordained to the ministry, in Salem, on November 27, 1822.

In the spring of 1823 he accepted a pressing call from the American Education Society to become their agent, and on May 20, 1824, he was married in Boston to Louisa H., second daughter of Nathaniel and Hannah (Parker) Willis, and sister of N. P. Willis (Yale 1827).

While connected with the Education Society he originated the observance of an annual day of fasting and prayer for Colleges.

His father-in-law was the editor and proprietor of the weekly *Boston Recorder*, and Mr. Dwight undertook, in addition to his other duties, to assist Deacon Willis in his editorial work; but after a few months he was so disabled that an entire rest became necessary. After long horseback journeys, which took him as far south as Carolina, and in which he occupied himself in the distribution of Bibles, especially in jails and State prisons, he returned to Boston in May, 1825, with health much restored.

On his journey he had been appalled at the conditions in the prisons which he had visited, and his report brought into action a sentiment on this subject which had for some years been gathering head, with the result that the Prison Discipline Society was formed in Boston in June, 1825, and he was appointed its Secretary and principal Agent, resigning his other duties to give his entire time to this object.

For the rest of his life he devoted himself to indefatigable labors for this Society, carrying out great reforms in the prisons of the country, and being also instrumental in the establishment of Lunatic Asylums and Juvenile Reform Schools by several States. His personal religious life was peculiarly humble and cheerful; for many years he preached regularly to the insane poor in the Asylum in South Boston.

His wife died in Boston on April 6, 1849, in her 42d year.

In June, 1853, he was stricken with paralysis, from which he partially recovered; but after a year of feebleness an attack of congestion of the brain caused his death, in Boston, on July 12, 1854, in his 62d year. He was buried in Mount Auburn cemetery.

His children were two daughters and a son; the elder daughter married the Rev. Dr. William T. Eustis (Yale 1841).

The first twenty-nine Reports of the Prison Discipline Society (1826-54) are mainly from his pen; and he published in 1831 (Boston, 12°) an abridged edition of James Baldwin Brown's *Memoir of John Howard.*

AUTHORITIES.

Dwight Family, ii, 752, 757–60. *Rev. W. T. Eustis*, MS. Letter, July, 1854. *Jenks*, Memoir of L. Dwight. *Sprague*, Annals of Amer. Pulpit, ii, 669–74.

William Theodore Dwight, the seventh of eight sons of the Rev. Dr. Timothy Dwight (Yale 1769), was born at Greenfield Hill, in Fairfield, Connecticut, on June 15, 1795, ten days before his father's election as President of Yale College. He was prepared for College by Matthew R. Dutton (Yale 1808), in Fairfield, and was admitted in 1807; but although his entrance was delayed for two years, he was still the youngest member of his Class. At graduation he delivered a poem, entitled *The Campaign.*

He won the Berkeley Scholarship, but soon after leaving College, owing to inflammation of the eyes, he was obliged to suspend for a time his studies; but he spent some time as a clerk in the Eagle Bank of New Haven, and was enrolled as a graduate student in the College. From 1815 to his father's death, in January, 1817, he aided him as his amanuensis. When he received his Master's degree in September, 1816, he delivered a poem, entitled *The Wanderer*. In the fall of 1817 he entered on a College tutorship, which he filled with success for two years.

In the fall of 1819 he entered the office of Charles Chauncey (Yale 1792), of Philadelphia, as a law-student, and he was admitted to the bar in November, 1821. He at once engaged in practice in that city, and had attained an enviable position, when in the spring of 1831 he became personally interested in religion, with the result that in the ensuing summer he decided to prepare for the ministry. He was licensed to preach by the Third Presbytery of New York on October 6, and on the 12th was married to Elizabeth Loockerman, daughter of Thomas and Elizabeth (Loockerman) Bradford, of Philadelphia.

He soon after received a call from a new congregation in New York City, followed by proposals from other societies. After preaching in Boston he visited Portland, and met with such evident success there that early in May, 1832, he accepted a unanimous call to the pastorate of the Third Congregational Church.

He was ordained and installed there on July 6, and a laborious and happy service of thirty-two years followed.

The honorary degree of Doctor of Divinity was given him by Bowdoin College in 1846. He was a member of the Board of Overseers of that College from 1839 to 1860. He was also one of the Board of Visitors of the Andover Theological Seminary from 1856 to 1865. He was active and efficient in the organized work of the denomination within and without the State, and reaped a well-deserved reputation for practical wisdom, as well as the highest respect for his Christian character. He declined all offers to other fields of labor, including the suggestion at different times of the chair of didactic theology in the seminaries at Bangor, East Windsor, and Chicago.

Mrs. Dwight died in Portland, suddenly, on October 2, 1863, at the age of 53.

In consequence of this affliction and of his own infirm health, he resigned his pastoral charge on May 1, 1864. He then removed to the home of his married daughter in Andover, Massachusetts, where he died, after a suffering illness, on October 22, 1865, in his 71st year.

A sermon occasioned by his death was preached in Philadelphia by the Rev. Dr. Henry A. Boardman (Yale 1828), which was afterwards published. A sketch of his life and ministry by his son-in-law, Dr. Smyth, appeared in the *Congregational Quarterly*, and was republished with additions.

His children were three sons, the youngest of whom died in infancy, and two daughters. His sons were graduated at Yale, in 1852 and 1859 respectively. The elder daughter married the Rev. Dr. Egbert C. Smyth (Bowdoin Coll. 1848).

An engraved portrait of Dr. Dwight is given in the *Congregational Quarterly*, volume 11, and in the *Dwight Family*.

He published:

1. An Oration before the Washington Benevolent Society of Pennsylvania, delivered in the Hall of the Musical Fund Society, on the 22d of February, 1827. Philadelphia, 1827. 8°, pp. 34.
[*A. C. A. B. Ath. M. H. S. N. Y. H. S. U. S U. T. S. Y. C.*

The subject is, the character of the American Revolution, and its influence upon mankind.

2. Review, on the character of Oliver Cromwell. In the *Christian Spectator*, vol. 1, pp. 385–425 (Sept., 1829).

3. Review of Judge Story's Inaugural Address. In the *Christian Spectator*, vol. 2, pp. 43–61 (March, 1830).

On the Common Law and Written Codes.

4. Religion, the only preservative of national freedom.—A Discourse [from II Cor. iii, 17]: delivered in the Third Congrega-

tional Church of Portland, on the day of the Annual Thanksgiving: December 1, 1836. Portland, 1836 8°, pp. 16
[*A. C. A. Harv Y. C*

5 The Church, the Pillar and Ground of the Truth.—A Sermon [from I Tim. iii, 15], delivered in Brunswick, June 26, 1839, before the Maine Missionary Society, at its thirty-second anniversary Portland, 1839 8°, pp. 48.
[*A. C A Br. Mus Harv M H S. U. T. S. Y. C.*
The sermon occupies pp 5–24

6 A Sermon at the Organization of the Bethel Church, Portland. In the *Christian Mirror*, October 15, 1840.

7 "A Great Man Fallen."—A Discourse [from II Sam iii, 38], on the death of President Harrison: delivered in the Third Congregational Church of Portland, on Sabbath morning, April 18, and on Thursday evening, April 22, 1841—the day of the Annual Fast. Portland, 1841. 8°, pp. 19
[*A C A. B. Publ M H. S U. T. S. Y. C.*

8 A Discourse [from Gen ix, 6] on the rightfulness and expediency of Capital Punishments. Portland, 1843 8°, pp. 34.
[*A C A B Ath B Publ Br Mus Harv M H. S. U. S U T S Y C.*

9 Repudiation In the *New Englander*, vol 1, pp 534–45 (Oct., 1843)

10 An Address delivered before the Association of Alumni of Yale College, August 14, 1844 New Haven, 1844 8°, pp 36
[*A C. A B. Publ Br. Mus M. H. S. U. T. S Y C*
A comparison of the English, German, and American systems of university or collegiate training

11 The Adaptation of the Truth to promote the Salvation of Men —A Discourse [from James i, 18 and John xvii, 17], delivered at the Installation of Rev Oren Sikes, over the Trinitarian Congregational Church and Society, in Bedford, Mass, June 3, 1846. Boston, 1846 8°, pp 23.
[*A C. A B Publ. Br Mus U. T. S.*

12 An Address, delivered before the Phi Beta Kappa Society, Alpha of Maine, in Bowdoin College, Brunswick, September 6, 1849 Portland, 1849 8°, pp. 23. [*A C A. U T. S Y. C.*
The subject is, the immensity of the field of knowledge, and the influence of such a conviction on the student.

13. In 1851 he edited a volume of Select Discourses of his brother Sereno (Yale 1803), to which he prefixed a Memoir of his life (pp. vii, lxviii).

14. Characteristics of New England Theology.—A Discourse [from Eccl. xii, 9–11], delivered at the first public anniversary of the Congregational Board of Publication, at the Tremont Temple, Boston. Boston, 1855. 8°, pp. 34.
[*A. A. S. A. C. A. B. Publ. M. H. S. U. T. S. Y. C.*

15. The Pulpit, in its relation to Politics.—A Discourse [from Mark xii, 17], delivered in the Third Congregational Church, Portland, November 20, 1856, and January 18, 1857. Portland, 1857. 8°, pp. 27. [*A. C. A. B. Publ. U. T. S. Y. C.*

16. A Discourse [from Deut. xxix, 29] on Spiritualism, delivered in the Third Parish Church, Portland, April 26, 1857. Portland, 1857. 8°, pp. 28. [*A. A. S. A. C. A. Y. C.*

17. The Work; and the Workmen.—A Discourse [from Luke xxiv, 47] in behalf of the American Home Missionary Society, preached in the City of New York, May 8, 1859. New York, 1859. 8°, pp. 31.
[*A. A. S. A. C. A. B. Publ. Br. Mus. M. H. S. U. T. S. Y. C.*

18. Address delivered at the forty-fifth Anniversary of the American Tract Society, in the Tremont Temple, Boston, Wednesday Evening, May 25, 1859. 12°, pp. 20. [*A. C. A. U. T. S.*

19. The nationality of a people, its vital element.—An Oration, delivered in the New City Hall, before the City Government, and Citizens, of Portland, July 4, 1861. Portland, 1861. 8°, pp. 32.
[*A. C. A. Harv. Y. C.*

AUTHORITIES.

Congregational Quarterly, xi, 181–202. Dwight Family, i, 171, 205–09.

AMBROSE EGGLESTON, the second son of Nicholas and Mary (Stewart) Eggleston, of Northeast, Duchess County, New York, and grandson of Samuel and Abigail Eggleston, of what is now Portland, Connecticut, was born in Northeast on May 16, 1793, and was prepared for College by the Rev. Daniel Parker (Yale 1798), in Ellsworth Society, in Sharon, Connecticut.

After graduation he taught for one year in an Academy in Whitecreek, Washington County, New York, and for a part of the following year taught a family school in the old Livingston homestead at Clermont In the fall of 1815 he began the study of law in Poughkeepsie, and on being admitted to practice in 1818, settled in Unadilla, Otsego County. On August 18, 1819, he was married to Elizabeth (or Betsey) B, daughter of Judge George Harper, of Windsor, Broome County

While a student of law he had become a Christian; and a sense of duty now impelled him to become a minister.

In 1821 he entered the Theological Seminary just opened at Auburn, and in September, 1822, he was licensed to preach by the Susquehanna Presbytery. After supplying the pulpit in Palmyra, Wayne County, for about a year, he went to Coventry, Chenango County, in 1824, where he was ordained and installed by the Chenango Presbytery in May, 1825, as pastor of the First Presbyterian Church He continued there until 1831, and was next engaged as supply of the Congregational Church in Egremont, Berkshire County, Massachusetts, for two years.

In December, 1835, he was called to the pastorate of the Reformed Protestant Dutch Church in Fallsburg, Sullivan County, New York, where he was installed on June 14, 1836. He resigned his office there on April 24, 1838, and returned to his wife's early home in Windsor, where he remained without a pastoral charge until the spring of 1842. He then removed to Fulton, Oswego County, and preached to two small churches for two years; after which, on account of throat-disease, by his physician's advice he almost entirely ceased public speaking. From about 1846 most of his time was spent with a son in Coldwater, in Southern Michigan In these later years he was a member of Coldwater Presbytery. He spent much labor on a history of the Eggleston family, which he nearly completed for the press.

Injuries received upon a railroad in 1862 increased his infirmity, and he died in Coldwater, after a little over a week's illness, from paralysis, on January 23, 1865, in his 72d year. He was buried in Binghamton, New York.

His wife survived him. Their children were three sons and a daughter.

AUTHORITIES.

Hotchkin, Hist. of Western N. Y., 300. Presbyterian Historical Almanac, viii, 214–15. *Quinlan,* Hist. of Sullivan County, 270–71. *Stiles,* Hist. of Windsor, 2d ed., ii, 203, 205.

George Augustus Elliot, the youngest of three sons of William Elliot, a farmer of Guilford, Connecticut, and a grandson of Nathaniel and Beulah (Parmelee) Eliot, of Guilford, was born in Guilford on June 7, 1792. His mother was Ruth, sister of Nathaniel Rossiter (Yale 1785). He was prepared for College by William Todd (Yale 1806), in Guilford.

On graduation he began the study of law with Seth P. Staples (Yale 1797), of New Haven, and on his admission to the bar in the fall of 1815 he left home with the intention of settling in Cincinnati. But when he reached northwestern Pennsylvania, about the first of November, he decided to remain there, and settled in Erie, where he followed his profession successfully until 1855, when he retired from active business in somewhat impaired health. He then devoted his leisure to the oversight of his farm, in which he took great pride.

He died in Erie on July 23, 1870, from paralysis, in his 79th year.

He married on November 12, 1818, Sarah M., eldest daughter of Robert Brown, of Erie, who died on May 20,

1874, in her 75th year. Of their two sons, only one survived their parents.

AUTHORITIES

Eliot Genealogy, 2d ed., 116, 155. *J Eliot,* MS. Letter, June, 1871.

WILLIAM ELY, the eldest child of Dr. Richard Ely (Yale 1785), was born in (North) Killingworth, Connecticut, on June 27, 1792. In 1804 his father settled in Chester, then part of Saybrook. He was prepared for College by John Adams (Yale 1795) at Bacon Academy in Colchester. He became a Christian while in College.

During the first year after graduation he taught acceptably in the Academy in Wethersfield. He then entered the Andover Theological Seminary, was licensed to preach by the Middlesex Association of Ministers on June 3, 1817, and left the Seminary in the following September.

On March 11, 1818, he was ordained and installed as pastor of the Congregational Church in Vernon, Tolland County, where he had been supplying the pulpit since leaving Andover; and on May 5, 1820, he was married to Harriet, daughter of Spencer Whiting, of Hartford, and sister of Dr. Spencer Whiting, Jr. (Yale 1824).

He was dismissed from the church in Vernon on February 21, 1822, and after an interval, during which he supplied for some months the church in West Hartland, he was installed in August, 1825, as pastor of the Second Congregational Church in (North) Mansfield, about ten miles east of Vernon, on a salary of $400

His efficient ministry in this parish was interrupted by a mental affection, which at times disqualified him for his duties. He was dismissed at his own request in May, 1841, and he removed to the adjoining parish of North Coventry.

Thence he went to Easthampton, Massachusetts, where his wife died in 1846, at the age of 46

His residence continued in Easthampton, but his death occurred in the Insane Hospital in Worcester on November 20, 1850, in his 58th year. He was buried in Easthampton.

His children were three daughters and three sons.

Mr. Ely was a man of very small stature, and afflicted with lameness. His theological sympathies were with the East Windsor Seminary. After his retirement from the pastorate he continued to preach as he had opportunity, and also instructed private pupils.

AUTHORITIES.

Calhoun, Rev. W. Ely. *Dwight,* Strong Family, ii, 1127. Ely Ancestry, 185, 308–09. *T. Robbins,* Diary, i, 735; ii, 123, 161.

JOY HAMLET FAIRCHILD, the youngest of sixteen children of Lewis Fairchild, of Guilford, Connecticut, and of eight by his second wife, the widow Mehetabel Parmelee, of Chester, in Saybrook, by birth Waterhouse, was born in Guilford on April 24, 1790. His father died in his infancy.

He was prepared for College by his pastor, Aaron Dutton (Yale 1803).

At graduation he went to Monson, Massachusetts, as Preceptor of the Academy, at the same time studying theology with the Rev. Alfred Ely (Princeton Coll. 1804), in whose family he resided.

He was licensed to preach by the Hampden Association of Ministers in October, 1814, and remained in Monson until May, 1816, when he was called to the Congregational Church in East Hartford, Connecticut.

Having accepted this call, he was ordained and installed on June 26.

He was married about the same date, and his wife, Mrs. Cynthia Fairchild, a native of Chester, died in East Hartford on February 22, 1824, in her 35th year. The sermon preached at her funeral by his nearest ministerial neighbor, the Rev. Thomas Robbins (Yale 1796), of East Windsor, was afterwards published.

He was again married, to Mary, daughter of William Bradford, in Philadelphia, in July, 1825

He was dismissed from East Hartford at his own request on August 28, 1827. During his ministry the church had enjoyed two seasons of revival, and upwards of two hundred members had been added to their numbers.

In the following October he was called to the Evangelical Congregational Church, afterwards called the Phillips Church, of 37 members, in South Boston, Massachusetts, where he was installed on November 22

His ministry there came to an abrupt conclusion by his resignation on May 15, 1842, due to charges of improper conduct, privately made against him by the deacons of the church.

He was dismissed in good standing by a council on June 2. Three hundred and fifty-six members had been added to the church during his ministry.

After an interval of rest and of occasional supplies elsewhere, he began in March, 1843, to supply the pulpit of the First Congregational Church in Exeter, New Hampshire, where he was regularly installed on September 20.

In April, 1844, the charges hitherto kept private were made public; and in May a board of referees investigated them and unanimously reported their unshaken confidence in Mr. Fairchild's innocence.

In June, 1844, however, a new charge was publicly made, of adultery with a servant maid in 1841, and a council was summoned by Mr. Fairchild for advice. A majority of this council voted, in July, against his innocence, and in favor of his deposition from the ministry. His request, previously made, for a dismissal from his pastorate, accordingly took effect. Earlier in the same month he was indicted by the grand-jury for trial in Boston.

The trial came on in March, 1845, and Mr. Fairchild was acquitted. His friends in South Boston organized a new church, called the Payson Church, in July, 1845, of which he was installed pastor on November 19.

Failing health obliged him to resign this office shortly before his death, which took place in South Boston, on February 21, 1859, in his 69th year.

His engraved portrait is given in his published autobiography.

He published:

1. The essential doctrines of the Gospel.—A Sermon [from John xviii, 38]. Boston, 1829. 8°, pp. 40.
[*A. A. S. B. Ath. B. Publ. Br. Mus. C. H. S. Y. C.*

The same. Second Edition. Boston, 1830. 12°, pp. 36.
[*B. Publ. Y. C.*

A statement of the current orthodox belief.

2. Objections to the Deity of Christ considered.—A Sermon [from Matth. xxii, 42]. Boston, 1831. 12°, pp. 36.
[*A. C. A. B. Publ. Y. C.*

3. The Gospel Defended against Infidels.—A Sermon [from Phil. i, 17] preached in Holliston, Mass., October 31, 1832, at the installation of the Rev. Elijah Demond. Boston, 1833. 8°, pp. 31.
[*A. C. A. Br. Mus. Y. C.*

4. In *The South-Boston Unitarian Ordination,* Boston, 1841, 8°, is a Report by him and others of a sermon preached by Theodore Parker at the ordination of C. C. Shackford, protesting against its sentiments (pp. 3-4), and his letters to the Rev. Samuel K. Lothrop (pp. 17-25, 43-52) on the same subject.

5. Iniquity unfolded!—An account of the Treatment of Mr. Fairchild by the Deacons in South Boston, and others. Exeter, 1844. 8°, pp. 84. [*A. C. A. B. Ath. Br. Mus. Harv. Y. C.*

Several editions.

6. Correspondence between Rev. Nehemiah Adams and Rev. J. H. Fairchild, with Notes and Comments by a Committee of the Payson Church. Boston, 1846. 8°, pp. 48.
[*A. C. A. B. Ath. B. Publ. Br. Mus. Harv. Y. C.*

With reference to alleged persecution by Mr. Adams of Mr. Fairchild in his troubles.

7. The new doctrine of clerical privilege—An Address delivered in Tremont Temple, on the 26th and 27th of January, 1852. Boston, 1852. 12°, pp. 60
[*A C. A B Ath. B. Publ Br. Mus. Harv. M H S. U S U. T S. Y C*

A further defence of himself, against Mr. Adams and others.

8. Remarkable Incidents in the Life of Rev. J H Fairchild Boston, 1855 12° [*A. A. S. B. Publ. U S*

The same. Second Edition Boston, 1855 12°. [*B. Publ Br. Mus*

The same Third Edition. Boston, 1856 12°. [*Br. Mus.*

The same Fourth Edition. Boston, 1857. 12°, pp xi, 464 + pl [*Y. C.*

9 Farewell Address [from II Tim 1, 16] to the Payson Church, South Boston, delivered November 22, 1857 Boston, 1858 16°, pp 63 + plate.
[*A A. S A C. A B. Ath. B. Publ. M. H. S. Y. C*

AUTHORITIES

Congregational Quarterly, i, 314. *Fairchild,* Autobiography *Lawrence,* New Hampshire Churches, 49-50. Monson Academy Jubilee, 18, 89. *T. Robbins,* Diary, i, 668, 672, 957, 1013, ii, 62, 65, 374

BENJAMIN FENN, a son of Benjamin Fenn, of (North) Milford, now Orange, Connecticut, and grandson of Lieutenant Benjamin and Sarah (Treat) Fenn, of Milford, was born on October 29, 1792. His mother was Comfort, son of Jonathan and Comfort (Baldwin) Fowler, of Milford He was prepared for College by his pastor, Erastus Scranton (Yale 1802)

After graduation he studied divinity with the Rev Bezaleel Pinneo (Dartmouth Coll. 1791), of Milford, and was licensed to preach by the Western Association of New Haven County on May 28, 1816.

After a period of labor in Western Connecticut, he went to Ohio in 1818, and was ordained and installed by the Presbytery of Portage over the church in Nelson, Portage

County, on June 16, 1819. On August 3, 1820, he was married to Anna, daughter of Stephen Gunn, of Milford.

In April, 1835, he was dismissed from Nelson, to accept a call from the Presbyterian Church in Gustavus, Trumbull County, about twenty miles distant, where he was installed on June 16. He retired from this office in 1842, but remained in Gustavus until his installation on June 16, 1847, in Hartford, in the same county, about ten miles to the southeast; and after fourteen years' service, he resumed on June 14, 1861, his former charge in Nelson.

In October, 1867, at the age of 75, he was dismissed at his own request.

He died at his son's residence in Hartford, from hematuria and cancerous enlargement of the prostate gland, on June 25, 1869, in his 77th year. He was buried in Tallmadge, Summit County, beside his parents, who emigrated thither.

His wife survived him. Their children were one daughter and three sons. The eldest son was graduated in 1854 at Western Reserve College (of which the father was a trustee from 1826 to 1855), and the youngest at Williams College in 1859.

AUTHORITIES.

B. Fenn, Jr., MS. Letter, July, 1869. *C. Nichols*, Autobiography, 145-47.

ALEXANDER METCALF FISHER, the eldest child of Deacon Caleb and Sally Fisher, of Franklin, Massachusetts, and grandson of Hezekiah and Abigail (Daniels) Fisher, of North Franklin, was born on July 22, 1794. His mother was a woman of uncommon mathematical talent. She was the second daughter of Solomon and Mary (Burr) Cushing, of Hingham. One of his sisters married Dr. John W. Tenney (Brown Univ. 1823). He was prepared for College in Leicester Academy by Luther

Wilson (Williams Coll. 1807). He was of small and very slender physique, but of remarkable mental quickness.

At his graduation he delivered the Salutatory Oration.

He then spent a year in study under the direction of his pastor, the Rev. Dr. Nathanael Emmons (Yale 1767), and began a second year of study in mental and moral science and theology in the Andover Seminary, but in the course of the year returned to his father's farm on account of ill health.

At Commencement in 1815 he was elected a tutor in the College, and notwithstanding the apprehensions of his friends he entered on the office in the fall. Attention to his favorite studies seemed to invigorate his health, and in July, 1817, when Professor Day was elected President, he was made Adjunct Professor of Mathematics and Natural Philosophy. He was promoted to the full professorship in 1819.

In the spring of 1822 he determined to visit Europe, for the benefit of his health, and to acquire the French language, and even more with the design of improving himself in his profession by observing the condition of foreign institutions; and on April 1 he sailed from New York for Liverpool in the packet *Albion* for eight months' absence. On the 22d of that month the vessel was driven in a storm upon the rocks near Kinsale, on the southern Irish coast, and he, with all the other cabin passengers but one, was lost. He had not completed his 28th year.

In so brief a life there was little opportunity for great achievement; but Professor Fisher's friends and colleagues have left on record unstinted praise of his character and promise. His mental endowments were unquestionably superior, and his attainments in various departments of knowledge unusual. In the judgment of his classmate Olmsted, writing after an interval of years, "His greatness as a mathematician was the fruit of no peculiar bias or genius for that particular field of knowledge, but it resulted naturally from the application of a mind of remarkable strength and acuteness to a subject of the greatest difficulty."

He was engaged to be married to Catharine Esther, the eldest daughter of the Rev. Dr. Lyman Beecher (Yale 1797), who remained single through her life.

A portrait of Professor Fisher, painted after his death by S. F. B. Morse (Yale 1810), is owned by the College; as also a bust by Hezekiah Augur, presented by his classmates.

An *Eulogy* on Professor Fisher was delivered in the College in June, 1822, by Professor Kingsley, and was afterwards published; and some *Reminiscences* by his classmate, Professor Olmsted, appeared in the *New Englander* in 1843.

He published:

1. In the *American Monthly Magazine and Critical Review*, vols. 1, 2, New-York, 1817–18, various mathematical questions, and solutions, over the signature of X.

2. Essay on Musical Temperament. In the *American Journal of Science and Arts*, vol. 1, pp. 9–35, 176–99 (1818).

Professor Fisher was very fond of music, and this was his most elaborate publication.

3. Review of Dr. Brown's Essay on the existence of a Supreme Creator. In the *Christian Spectator*, vol. 1, pp. 414–21, 586–88 *bis* (Aug. & Nov., 1819).

4. The literary gentleman's visit to his country uncle and family. In the *Microscope*, vol. 2, pp. 25–30, 33–39 (June, 1820).

5. A newly discovered fragment of an aerial voyage by Captain Lemuel Gulliver.

In the same, vol. 2, pp. 177–91 (Sept., 1820). Showing an unusual power of fancy.

6. On the Orbit of the Comet of 1819. In *Memoirs* of the American Academy of Arts and Sciences, vol. 4, pp. 309–16, Cambridge, 1821.

7. Remarks on Dr. Enfield's Institutes of Natural Philosophy. In the *American Journal of Science and Arts,* vol. 3, pp. 125–57 (1821).

Giving the author's conception of what a college text-book should be.

8. On some recent improvements in the construction of the Printing Press.

In the same, pp. 311–25.

9. On Maxima and Minima of Functions of two variable quantities.

In the same, vol. 5, pp. 82–93 (1822).

Remarkable for the neatness and brevity of the solutions of the problems.

After his death appeared:

10. In Leybourn's *Mathematical Repository,* vol. 5, London, 1830, various solutions, over the signature, Nov-Anglus, to Mathematical Questions proposed some years before.

AUTHORITIES.

Amer. Journal of Science and Arts, v, 367–76. *L. Beecher,* Autobiography, i, 478–80. *Blake,* Hist. of Franklin, 152–54, 245. Christian Spectator, iv, 389–92, 432–37. *W. C. Fowler,* Essays, 141–50. *W. L. Kingsley,* Yale College, i, 229–31. New Englander, i, 457–69. *Olmsted,* Life of E. P. Mason, 232–34. *Park,* Memoir of Emmons, 234–36.

John Douglass Fowler, the eldest son of Deacon Solomon Fowler, of Northford Parish, in the present town of North Branford, Connecticut, was born on February 6, 1789. His mother was Olive, elder daughter of Colonel William and Hannah (Mansfield) Douglas, of New Haven and Northford, and niece of Benjamin Douglas (Yale 1760). A sister married the Rev. Epaphras Chapman (Yale 1816). He was prepared for College by Sylvester Selden (Williams Coll. 1807).

He studied law after graduation, and opened an office in New Haven. Exposure in the winter of 1816–17 brought on consumption, which obliged him to retire from business, and he died at his father's house in Northford, in Christian faith, on August 25, 1817, in his 29th year. He was unmarried.

AUTHORITIES.

Conn. Journal, Sept. 2, 1817. Douglas Genealogy, 207.

THOMAS DOWNES FROST, a son of the Rev. Thomas Frost (B.A. Gonville and Caius Coll. Cambridge 1780), of Norfolk, England, and Charleston, South Carolina, was born in Charleston on February 24, 1794. His mother was Elizabeth, daughter of Richard Downes, a Charleston merchant. His father died in July, 1804. His preparation for College was completed in New Haven under Jeremiah Evarts (Yale 1802).

After graduation he pursued the study of theology under the direction of Bishop Dehon in Charleston, and at the same time instructed a few pupils, to earn money, until his health obliged him to desist.

He received Deacon's orders in the Episcopal Church at the hands of Bishop Dehon on February 21, 1815, and on March 12 was elected Assistant Minister of St. Philip's Church in Charleston,—the Rector being the Rev. Dr. Christopher E. Gadsden (Yale 1804),—at the same time also resuming his school.

In October, 1817, he was obliged by frequent hemorrhages from the lungs to visit Cuba; and he returned much improved in May, 1818.

On June 16 he was married to Anne, third daughter of the Hon. John F. Grimké, of Charleston,—two of her brothers being graduates of Yale, in 1807 and 1810, respectively. He spent the ensuing summer in the hill country, and after his return was able to preach several times; but a violent recurrence of hemorrhages, early in 1819, led him to embark for Havana on April 4. He was there taken into the country, and died suddenly on May

16, in his 26th year. He was buried in the churchyard of Laguira.

His wife died on December 30, 1882, in her 88th year. They had one daughter, who grew up and married.

AUTHORITIES.

Dalcho, Episc. Church in S. C., 209, 221, 232-36, 605-06. S. C. Hist. and Geneal. Magazine, iv, 50, 69. *Sprague,* Annals of Amer. Pulpit, v, 427.

JOSEPH WINBORN HAND, son of Janna Hand, of (East) Guilford, now Madison, Connecticut, and grandson of Captain Joseph and Lucy (Meigs) Hand, was born in 1792. His mother was Joanna, daughter of Colonel Return Jonathan and Joanna (Winborn) Meigs, of Middletown, and a second cousin of her husband. His father died in August, 1794, and he was prepared for College by his pastor, the Rev. John Elliott (Yale 1786).

After graduation he studied law in the office of Elias B. Caldwell (Princeton Coll. 1796), of Washington, District of Columbia, where he was admitted to the bar. His uncle, Return J. Meigs (Yale 1785), was Postmaster-General of the United States from 1814 to 1823, and Mr. Hand was connected with the Post Office department from 1815 to 1836,—for a considerable portion of the time as Solicitor.

From 1836 until his death he was Chief Clerk in the Patent Office.

He died suddenly in Washington on May 25, 1844, aged 52 years.

He married Catharine Worthington, second daughter of Reuben Rose and Catharine (Chauncey) Fowler, of Madison, and sister of Professor William C. Fowler (Yale 1816).

Their children were six daughters and two sons. The elder son was graduated at Yale in 1850.

He was an Elder in the Presbyterian Church in Washington.

AUTHORITIES.

Fowler, Chauncey Memorials, 194-95.

CHARLES HAWLEY, the only son of Captain Cyrus Hawley, of that part of Huntington which is now Monroe, Connecticut, and grandson of Milton and Hepsey (De-Forest) Hawley, of Monroe, was born on June 15, 1792. His mother was Mary, daughter of Elijah and Jane (Moss) Curtiss. His father died in October, 1798, and his mother soon married Hall Beardsley, of Huntington. He was prepared for College by the Rev. Dr. David Ely (Yale 1769), of Huntington. As an undergraduate he was somewhat distinguished for wit and humor, and a dialogue which he wrote for a College exhibition gained for him a high reputation.

He studied law partly with the Hon. Asa Chapman (Yale 1792), of Newtown, and partly in the Litchfield Law School. In 1816 he opened an office in Stamford; but, meeting with some discouragements, he soon after made plans to settle in East Haddam, which were fortunately abandoned. He then returned to Stamford, where he continued in active practice until his death.

On January 28, 1821, he was married by the Rev. Jonathan Judd to Mary Stiles, eldest daughter of David and Martha (Coggeshall) Holly, of Stamford.

He was a Representative in the Legislature in 1821, 1823, 1824, and 1826 to 1829; and a State Senator in 1830. In 1828 he was a Presidential Elector, and from May, 1838, to May, 1842, Lieutenant Governor of the State.

He died suddenly in Stamford on January 23, 1866, in his 74th year, leaving a large estate.

His wife died in Stamford on August 26, 1875, in her 79th year. His children were six daughters and two sons, all of whom survived him, except the eldest daughter, who died in 1865.

As a lawyer Mr. Hawley stood in the first rank. His mind was quick, acute, and logical, and his industry almost without parallel. He had the advantage of a commanding personal presence, and his private character was stainless.

AUTHORITIES.

Conn. Reports, xxxii, 598–600. Hawley Genealogy, 28, 465. *Huntington,* Hist. of Stamford, 373–76; Stamford Registration, 40, 45.

MINOR HOTCHKISS, the youngest son of Silas Hotchkiss, of New Haven, and a grandson of Joshua and Mary (Punderson) Hotchkiss, of New Haven, was born on June 3, 1791. His mother was Esther, eldest child of Captain John and Lydia (Ives) Gilbert, of New Haven. He was prepared for College by Dr. James Gilbert (Yale 1800).

After graduation he studied law in the Litchfield Law School and in New Haven, and was admitted to the bar late in 1815. He immediately settled in Middletown, where his brief career was full of promise.

He was a member of the State House of Representatives in 1824, and was again elected in 1825, but died in Middletown, in Christian faith, after a long and distressing illness, on October 21, 1825, in his 35th year.

He married Clarissa, daughter of Eli and Eunice Hotchkiss, of New Haven, who married again after his death. Four infant sons are buried by his side in New Haven. The only child who survived him was a daughter, who lived to marry.

AUTHORITIES.

Chapman, Trowbridge Family, 46–47. Conn. Journal, Oct. 25, 1825. *Field,* Centennial Address at Middletown, 207–08, 213. Tuttle Family, 653.

Richard Hubbard, son of Colonel Nehemiah Hubbard, of Middletown, Connecticut, and grandson of Nehemiah and Sarah (Sill) Hubbard, of Middletown, was born on March 27, 1792. His mother was Lucy, youngest daughter of Major Jehosaphat and Sarah (Stow) Starr, of Middletown. He was prepared for College by John Adams (Yale 1795), in Bacon Academy, Colchester. In June, 1813, he united with the College Church on profession of faith.

He settled in his native city, and married on September 7, 1814, Mary (or Polly), the eldest child of the Rev. Salmon Cone (Yale 1789), of Colchester.

He followed no profession, but filled various business positions, like the presidency of the Middlesex Mutual Assurance Society. In 1838 he was elected Mayor of the city, and he died while in office, on September 1, 1839, in his 48th year.

Of his children, two daughters and two sons, only the younger son survived infancy. Mrs. Hubbard died at his house, in Ashtabula, Ohio, in 1870, aged 77 years.

AUTHORITIES.

Cone Family, 280, 287–88. *Field,* Centennial Address at Middletown, 221. Hubbard Hist. and Genealogy, 344. Loomis Female Genealogy, i, 524. Starr Family, 227. *Walworth,* Hyde Family, ii, 836.

David Lathrop Hunn, the eldest child of Ephraim Hunn, of Hadlyme, Connecticut, and Colerain, Massachusetts, was born in Colerain on November 5, 1789. His mother was Submit (or Mitty), youngest daughter of Thatcher and Submit (Loomis) Lathrop, of East Windsor, Connecticut. His father (who lived to the age of 96) settled in Longmeadow, Massachusetts, in 1800, and the son was prepared for College by Levi Collins (Yale 1802) at the Monson Academy. In August, 1813, he united with the College Church on profession of faith.

After graduation he spent three years in Andover Theological Seminary, and was licensed to preach by the Hampden Association of Ministers in June, 1816.

After preaching for a time in Greenfield, and in Vernon, Connecticut (where he was called to settle in July, 1817), he was ordained and installed on February 25, 1818, as pastor of the Congregational Church in Sandwich, where he remained until his dismission twelve years later.

From November, 1830, to March, 1832, he supplied the Church in Vernon, Connecticut, and from July, 1832, to May, 1835, the Church at Wapping, in South Windsor.

His next engagement was for two years in Somerset, Niagara County, New York, followed by a like period with the Second Congregational Church in (North) Hadley, Massachusetts.

From 1841, when he was installed in Lenox, Madison County, he remained permanently in New York State, and in connection with the Presbyterian denomination. In 1844 he resigned his charge at Lenox, and removed to Rochester, where a son was living. He continued there, often preaching in neighboring pulpits, until 1858, when he went to Buffalo, and thence to Angelica in 1863, and back to Rochester in 1872.

In 1881 he returned to Buffalo, where he lived with his youngest daughter until his death. From 1881 he was the oldest living graduate of the College. His mental powers continued vigorous to the last, though his sight had nearly failed and his hearing was impaired.

He died in Buffalo on January 29, 1888, in his 99th year.

He married Eunice Sexton, of Wilbraham, Massachusetts, who died about 1873. Of his eight children, five sons and two daughters survived him.

AUTHORITIES.

Huntington, Lathrop Family Memoir, 127. Longmeadow Centennial, 140, 146; Appendix, 70.

Lemuel Ingalls, the youngest son of Judge Lemuel and Dorothy (Sumner) Ingalls, of Abington Society, in Pomfret, Connecticut, and grandson of Captain Zebediah and Esther (Goodell) Ingalls, of Pomfret, was born on September 22, 1793, and was prepared for College by Rinaldo Burleigh (Yale 1803) at the Plainfield Academy.

After graduation he studied law, and settled in Mobile, Alabama, with flattering prospects; but died there of yellow fever, unmarried, on September 21, 1819, at the age of 26.

AUTHORITIES.

Conn. Journal, Oct. 26, 1819. Ingalls Genealogy, 122.

James Derham Johnson, son of Richard and Martha (Rayner) Johnson, was born in Hanover Township, Morris County, New Jersey, on March 30, 1788. His parents were farmers, and members of the First Presbyterian Church in Morristown.

His eldest sister was the wife of James Stevenson, a Scotchman, who conducted a classical school, called Erasmus Hall, near Brooklyn, New York; while assisting his brother-in-law in instruction he began there his preparation for the Sophomore Class, and completed it in New Haven under Jeremiah Evarts (Yale 1802). He joined the College Church on profession of faith in April, 1813.

The most of his life was spent in teaching. For the first few months after graduation he taught in private families in New Jersey, and in May, 1814, he began a seven years' service as principal of the Morris Academy in Morristown.

In December, 1821, he took charge of an academy in Oxford, North Carolina, from which he removed in October, 1833, to Norfolk, Virginia, where he taught a select classical school with much reputation and success until 1849, when some constitutional infirmities induced him to seek more active employment.

He accordingly spent a year in traveling as the soliciting agent for the Seamen's Home Society in Norfolk, and then opened a school for young ladies in New York; but after a single quarter he returned to Norfolk and established there a select high school, which he continued until 1855.

He then returned to Morristown, and settled in the family homestead with two sisters, unmarried like himself. He conducted a select high school for young ladies for about two years, or until his health failed.

He died in Morristown on August 3, 1860, in his 73d year, leaving the memory of a strictly honest and sincerely religious man.

AUTHORITIES.

Dr. L. Condict, MS. Letter, July, 1861.

Elias Kent Kane, son of Elias Kane, a merchant of New York City, and grandson of Colonel John and Sybil (Kent) Kane, was born in New York City on June 7, 1796. His grandfather was an emigrant from Ireland, and his grandmother a daughter of the Rev. Elisha Kent (Yale 1729). John K. Kane (Yale 1814) was a first cousin. He left College during Senior year, but in 1825 received a degree and was enrolled with his Class. He was the youngest on the list.

He studied law in New York, and in 1815 settled in Nashville, Tennessee, but very soon removed to Kaskaskia, on the Mississippi, in the southern part of Illinois Territory.

He took a leading place in the political life of the Territory, and was a member of the Convention which formed the State Constitution in 1818. At the first state election, he was elected Secretary of State. He was also an early member of the Legislature, and in 1824 was elected to the United States Senate as a Jacksonian Democrat. He was re-elected in 1830, and served until his death.

In the fall of 1835 he suffered at his home from an attack of bilious fever, and was only partially recovered when he made the journey to Washington for the opening of Congress on December 7. The exposure and exhaustion caused his death, at his father's house in Washington, on December 12, in his 40th year.

A daughter married William Henry Bissell, who was the Governor of Illinois from 1856 to 1860.

He published:

1. Speech upon the arrangement of the Colonial Trade with Great Britain; delivered in the Senate of the United States, on the 8th April, 1832. Washington, 1832. 8°, pp. 23. [*Columbia Univ.*

2. Speech on the Motion of Mr. Poindexter that the Protest of the President of the United States against the Resolutions of censure passed by the Senate, be not received. [Washington, 1834.] 8°, pp. 8. [*Y. C.*

AUTHORITIES.

J. Q. Adams, Diary, viii, 10. Oneida Hist. Society's Transactions, 1881–84, 90. *Reynolds*, Pioneer Hist. of Illinois, 410.

William Kimball, the youngest child of Deacon Stephen Kimball, of Hanover, New Hampshire, and grandson of Stephen and Hannah (Perley) Kimball, of Bradford, Massachusetts, was born in Hanover on January 4, 1789. His mother was Betty Wilson, of Exeter. His father died in March, 1807, and a brother was graduated at Dartmouth College the same year.

He entered Dartmouth in 1808, but took a dismission from the Sophomore Class in October, 1809, and entered the Sophomore Class at Yale the next summer.

He spent the three years after graduation in the Andover Theological Seminary, but was never ordained.

He went South, and died near Natchez, Mississippi, in the year 1822, in his 34th year. Administration on his estate was granted to one of his brothers on September 26, 1822.

AUTHORITIES.

Morrison and Sharples, Kimball Family, i, 162 Religious Intelligencer, vii, 640

AUGUSTUS BALDWIN LONGSTREET, son of William Longstreet, of Augusta, Georgia, a skillful inventor, who claimed to have anticipated Robert Fulton, and grandson of Stoffel and Abigail (Wooley) Longstreet, of Monmouth County, New Jersey, was born in Augusta on September 22, 1790. His mother was Hannah, daughter of James and Deliverance (Coward) FitzRandolph. His preparation for the Junior Class at Yale was completed under the Rev. Dr. Moses Waddel, of Columbia County, Georgia.

The first year after graduation he spent in the Litchfield Law School, and after another year of study in Georgia, he was admitted to the bar in Richmond County in 1815, and began practice in Augusta, but removed to Greensboro, in Greene County, in the winter of 1816–17.

On March 3, 1817, he was married to Frances Eliza Parke, of Greensboro

In 1821 he represented Greene County in the Legislature, and in November, 1822, he became Judge of the Ocmulgee circuit, but declined a re-election after one term of three years.

In the fall of 1824 he was nominated for Congress; but before the election a change in his religious views led him to give up the contest.

In the fall of 1827 he returned to Augusta, and in addition to a flourishing practice, he took charge of the *Augusta Sentinel,* an advocate of nullification.

In the fall of 1838 he was licensed as a Methodist preacher, and in 1839 he was stationed in charge of a church in Augusta, where part of his time was spent in winding up his law business.

Later in the same year he was elected President of Emory College, an infant institution in Oxford, Newton County, and in February, 1840, he entered on the duties of his appointment.

His administration was happy and successful, until he resigned in 1848 in the anticipation of an election to the presidency of the University of Mississippi, in Oxford.

This expectation was disappointed; but after a few months of ministerial supply, he became the President of Centenary College, at Jackson, Louisiana. After four or five months' experience of this position he resigned it, in July, 1849; and was then elected to the position in the University of Mississippi which had been suggested to him the year before. He began his duties there in September, 1849, and continued in office with credit until his resignation in July, 1856, with the intention of devoting himself to agricultural pursuits.

In November, 1857, however, he was unanimously elected President of the University of South Carolina, at Columbia. He assumed the office in 1858, and remained there until the students volunteered as a body in the service of the Confederacy in 1861.

He then retired to Oxford, Mississippi, where his two daughters lived, and where his wife died on November 13, 1868, and his own death followed on September 9, 1870, at the age of 80.

His portrait is given in a sketch of his life by Bishop Fitzgerald, and in Donald G. Mitchell's *American Lands and Letters;* a very different one is given in the *Century Magazine* for 1901.

He had eight children, four of whom died in infancy; one daughter married the Hon. Lucius Q. C. Lamar (Emory Coll. 1845). General James Longstreet was a nephew.

The honorary degree of Doctor of Laws was conferred on him by this College in 1841.

He was an influential member of the General Conference of the Methodist Episcopal Church in New York in 1844, which led to the rupture of the denomination into the Northern and Southern churches, on account of slavery.

In 1857 he was elected an honorary member of the Board of Regents of the Smithsonian Institution.

In 1860, by appointment of President Buchanan, he went to London as a delegate to the International Statistical Congress

He published:

1. Georgia Scenes, Characters, Incidents, &c in the first half century of the Republic. By a Native Georgian Augusta, 1835 12°, pp. 235. [*Columbia Univ. Harv N. Y. Publ*

The same New-York, 1840. 12°, pp. 214 + plates [*A. A S B Ath B Publ*

A series of anonymous newspaper sketches of humble life in the South, full of genuine humor, an edition issued in 1867 purports to be revised, but it is doubtful if he had anything to do with it

Judge Longstreet wrote other similar sketches which are still uncollected. Such are the two following·

2. Patriotic Effusions, by Bob Short New York, 1819 24°, pp 47 [*B. Publ*

3. The Ghost of Baron Steuben; or, Fredonia in Arms' being a Description of that most bloody campaign, . a Georgia Training . 16°, pp 8 [*Watkinson Libr*

Signed, Timothy Crabshaw

4 Address delivered before the Faculty and Students of Emory College, Oxford, Ga.—At his Inauguration, 10th February, 1840 Augusta, 1840 12°, pp 22 [*Y C*

Reprinted in Bishop Fitzgerald's Sketch of the author, pp. 76–87

5 Letters on the Epistle of Paul to Philemon, or the connection of apostolical Christianity with Slavery Charleston, 1845. 8°, pp. 47. [*Y C*

Five letters addressed to the Rev. Drs Durbin, Bangs, Peck, and Elliott, of the Northern Methodists.

6. A Voice from the South: comprising Letters from Georgia to Massachusetts, and to the Southern States .. Baltimore, 1847. 8°, pp. 72. [*B. Ath. U. S. Y. C.*

Anonymous. In criticism of the attitude of the North on slavery.

7. Know Nothingism Unveiled. Letter addressed to Rev. William Winans, in reply to a communication published by him in the Natchez (Mississippi) Courier, and addressed to Judge Longstreet, on the subject of Know Nothingism. [Washington, 1855.] 8°, pp. 8. [*U. S.*

Reprinted in Bishop Fitzgerald's Sketch of the author, pp. 116-27. Judge Longstreet opposed the action of Southern Methodists in joining the Know-nothings.

8. Baccalaureate Address delivered at the University of South Carolina to the Graduating Class of 1859.

Reprinted in Bishop Fitzgerald's Sketch of the author, pp. 97-106.

9. Shall South Carolina Begin the War? 1861.

Reprinted by Bishop Fitzgerald, pp. 128-34.

10. Master William Mitten: or A youth of brilliant talents, who was ruined by bad luck. Macon, 1864. 8°, pp. 239. [*U. S.*

He is also said to have contributed largely to periodical literature, as to the *Methodist Quarterly Review*, the *Magnolia*, edited by W. G. Simms in 1842-43, the *Orion*, edited by W. C. Richards, the *Field and Fireside*, etc.

He furnished the Rev. Dr. William B. Sprague in 1849 with a sketch of the Rev. Dr. Moses Waddel, which is printed in the *Annals of the American Pulpit*, vol. 4, pp. 63-67.

He left unpublished:

A Revision and Correction of Canonized Errors of Biblical Interpretation.

AUTHORITIES.

Amer. Ancestry, v, 189. Century Magazine, xli, 48, 50. *Fitzgerald,* Judge Longstreet. In Memoriam Bishop Andrew, etc. *Mitchell,* Amer. Lands and Letters, ii, 26-28.

STEPHEN MACK, son of Stephen and Mary (Chambers) Mack, was born in Kinderhook, Columbia County, New York, on December 29, 1784, and entered College from New Marlborough, Berkshire County, Massachusetts, during the Sophomore year. He had been prepared by the Rev. Daniel Parker (Yale 1798), in Ellsworth, Connecticut At the time of his graduation his father was Chief Judge of the County Court of Broome County, New York He was the oldest member of the Class.

After graduation he studied law in Delhi, Delaware County, New York, with the Hon. Samuel Sherwood In 1814, on the death of his father, who was also conducting a printing business in Tioga County, he went to Owego, and about 1816 settled in Ithaca, in Tompkins County, where he had a long and successful career. He was a methodical, diligent, and learned lawyer, quiet and retiring in his habits

He was never married, and died in Ithaca from consumption, after a brief illness, at the house of the widow of a brother, on January 7, 1857, at the age of 72

AUTHORITIES.

Martin, Mack Genealogy, ii, 1585 *Selkreg*, Landmarks of Tompkins County, 68, 120

Hiram Foot Mather, the third son of Gibbons Mather, of Colchester, Connecticut, and grandson of Benjamin and Irene (Pearson) Mather, of Lyme, was born in Colchester on February 13, 1796. His mother was Hannah, daughter of Jeremiah and Ruhamah (Northam) Foot, of Colchester. He was prepared for College by John Adams (Yale 1795) in Bacon Academy, Colchester. His residence while in College was in Chatham He joined the College church on profession of faith in June, 1813

On graduation he entered the Andover Theological Seminary, but after nearly two years of study, he decided not to become a minister He then began the study of law, and in 1819 was admitted to practice in Elbridge, Onondaga County, New York.

On April 8, 1821, he was married to Sally Ann, younger daughter of Walter and Jerusha (Williams) Hyde, of Auburn, who died in Elbridge on November 4, 1824.

He was a member of the State Senate during four sessions, from 1829 to 1832. At that period the Senate constituted the Supreme Court of Errors, and from this circumstance he came to be generally known by the title of Judge.

On November 26, 1831, he married a first cousin of his former wife, Mary Parsons, second daughter of Joseph and Sarah (Hyde) Cole, of Auburn.

In October, 1844, Judge Mather removed to Niles, Michigan, and thence to Chicago in 1853.

His wife died of typhoid fever on December 29, 1855, in her 50th year; and he was next married on October 15, 1857, to Anna, daughter of William and Sarah (Talman) Smith, and widow of Henry Norton, of Chicago.

He continued in active practice until his last brief illness, being especially eminent as a Chancery lawyer. He was a Whig and Republican in politics. He was an Elder in the Presbyterian Church in the successive places of his residence. At the time of his death he was the President of the Association of Yale Alumni in Chicago.

He died in Chicago on July 12, 1868, in his 73d year. His wife survived him.

By his first marriage he had one son, who died in infancy, and a daughter, who had died before him. By his second marriage he had four sons and four daughters. The eldest son was graduated at Williams College in 1859.

AUTHORITIES.

Goodwin, Foote Genealogy, 114. *Phœnix,* Whitney Family, i, 758-59. Mather Genealogy, 1890, 171, 254-55. *Walworth,* Hyde Family, ii, 856-57.

Gideon John Mills, a son of the Rev. Samuel Mills (Yale 1776) and Sarah (Gilpin) Mills, of Chester, then a parish in Saybrook, Connecticut, was probably born in 1792. He was prepared for College by his father.

After graduation he studied law, and in 1817 settled in Utica, New York. In 1818 he entered into partnership with Richard R. Lansing (Union Coll. 1809), but about a year later he removed to Mobile, Alabama, where he fell a victim to the climate in 1825.

AUTHORITIES.

Bagg, Pioneers of Utica, 449.

Elisha Mitchell, the eldest son of Abner Mitchell, a farmer of Washington, Litchfield County, Connecticut, and grandson of Elnathan and Sarah (Tenney) Mitchell, of Washington, was born on August 19, 1793. His mother was Phoebe, fourth daughter of Nathan and Clarina (Griswold) Eliot, of Kent. A brother was graduated in 1820. He was prepared for College by the Rev. Azel Backus (Yale 1787), of Bethlehem.

On graduation he became a teacher in the Union Hall Academy of Dr. Lewis E. A. Eigenbrodt, in Jamaica, Long Island, but returned a year later to New Haven as a graduate student, whence he was called in the spring of 1815 to succeed his classmate Olmsted in the charge of the Union Academy in New London, Connecticut. In 1816 he entered on a tutorship in Yale, from which he was called in the fall of 1817, on the recommendation of the Rev. Sereno E. Dwight (Yale 1803), to the chair of Mathematics and Natural Philosophy in the University of North Carolina, at Chapel Hill.

He accepted this appointment, and went at once to the Andover Theological Seminary, where a brief period of study enabled him to secure licensure from the Western Association of New Haven County on December 30.

He arrived at Chapel Hill at the end of January, 1818, and began a career of illustrious service, which lasted for nearly forty years.

About the 1st of December, 1819, he was married in Lyme by the Rev. Abel McEwen to Maria S., daughter of Dr. Elisha and Hannah (Beach) North, of New London.

In August, 1821, he was ordained in Hillsborough, North Carolina, to the ministry by the Presbytery of Orange.

His classmate, Professor Olmsted, resigned the chair of Chemistry in 1825, and in 1826 Professor Mitchell was transferred from the chair of Mathematics and Natural Philosophy to a new one, of Chemistry, Mineralogy, and Geology, which he retained until his death. But this by no means exhausted his employments. He served the University during long periods as bursar, as preacher, as Acting President (1834–35), as amateur roadmaker and civil engineer, and as general business adviser. The chief outside duty which he undertook was that of State Geologist in 1826.

He received the honorary degree of Doctor of Divinity from the University of Alabama in 1838.

His long and diversified and very effective and devoted service of the University met with a tragic end.

He was accustomed to making frequent botanical and geological expeditions, and in particular was greatly interested in the exploration of the Black Mountains in the Western part of the State. His measurement of the highest peak, called in his honor (as its discoverer) Mount Mitchell, having been questioned, he set out in the summer of 1857 to verify his work; and while journeying alone over the mountain, on June 27, he slipped over a precipice forty feet high into a deep pool, where his body was found on July 8; after a temporary burial in Asheville, it was re-interred with impressive ceremonies on the summit of Mount Mitchell, the highest peak east of the Mississippi. He had nearly completed his 64th year.

His wife survived him. Their children were four daughters and three sons.

A memorial pamphlet was published in 1858, with an engraving of an excellent portrait, which has been reproduced elsewhere.

His name is perpetuated at the University by the Elisha Mitchell Scientific Society, formed in 1883.

He published:

1. Correspondence respecting two publications which appeared in the Raleigh Register in the month of December, 1824, between Bishop Ravenscroft and Professor Mitchell. Raleigh, 1825. 8°, pp. 30. [*Y. C.*

A discussion of the policy of encouraging Bible Societies.

2. Remarks on Bishop Ravenscroft's Answer to the Statements contained in Professor Mitchell's Printed Letter, of the 12th of February last. Raleigh, 1825. 8°, pp. 48. [*B. Ath. Y. C.*

3. Agricultural Speculations. [Written in 1822.] In Papers on agricultural subjects .. Published by order of the Board of Agriculture of North Carolina, Raleigh, 1825, pp. 49–58. 8°.

4. Report of the Geology of North Carolina, conducted under the direction of the Board of Agriculture.—Part III.—November, 1827. [Raleigh] sm. 4°, pp. 27.

Parts I and II were prepared by Professor Denison Olmsted (Yale 1813).

5. Arguments for Temperance; a Sermon [from I Tim. v, 23] addressed to the students of the University of North-Carolina, March 13th, 1831, and published by their request. Raleigh, 1831. 8°, pp. 29. [*Y. C.*

6. Elements of Geology, with an outline of the Geology of North Carolina: for the use of the Students of the University. 1842. 8°, pp. 141 + map. [*Harv. U. S. Y. C.*

Similar Manuals of Natural History and of Chemistry were printed.

7. Geological Report on North Carolina. In Papers on agricultural subjects, conducted under the direction of the Board of Agriculture, part 3, pp. 101–08. Raleigh, 1828. sm. 4°.

He contributed the following articles to the *American Journal of Science and Arts:*

On the Character and Origin of the Low Country of North Carolina: vol. 13, pp. 336–47 (January, 1828).

On the Geology of the Gold Region of North Carolina: vol. 16, pp. 1–19 (April, 1829).

On the Effect of Quantity of Matter in Modifying the Force of Chemical Attraction: same, pp. 234-42 (July, 1829).

On a Substitute for Welther's Tube of Safety, with Notices of other subjects: vol. 17, pp. 345-50 (January, 1830).

On the proximate causes of certain Winds and Storms: vol. 19, pp. 248-91 (January, 1831).

Analysis of the Protogæa of Leibnitz: vol. 20, pp. 56-64 (April, 1831).

On Storms and Meteorological Observations: same, pp. 361-72 (July, 1831).

After his death appeared:

Diary of a geological tour in 1827 and 1828, with Introduction and Notes by Dr. K. P. Battle. Chapel Hill, 1905. 8°, pp. 74.

Being the James Sprunt Historical Monograph of the University of North Carolina, No. 6.

AUTHORITIES.

Battle, Hist. of Univ. of N. C., i, *passim.* *Cothren,* Hist. of Woodbury, i, 641-42; ii, 1435-43. Eliot Descendants, 2d ed., 65-66. E. Mitchell Scientific Society's Journal, i, 9-18. Memoir of E. Mitchell, 1858. *Walworth,* Hyde Family, ii, 946.

Frederick Morgan, the eldest child of Dr. Elisha Morgan, of Groton, Connecticut, and grandson of Deacon Solomon and Mary (Walworth) Morgan, of Groton, was born on September 6, 1791. Solomon Morgan (Yale 1791) was a first cousin. His mother was Abigail, second daughter of John and Dorothy (Avery) Morgan, of Groton. Both his parents died in April, 1796. He was prepared for College in the Plainfield Academy by Rinaldo Burleigh (Yale 1803).

After four years' experience in teaching elsewhere, and the study of medicine with John O. Miner, M.D. (honorary Yale 1816), he became a tutor in College in the fall of 1816, and held office for two years. He also continued his medical studies, and received the degree of M.D. from the Medical School in 1819.

In January, 1820, he began practice in Colchester, where he married on May 20, 1823, Caroline, daughter of John R Watrous, M D. (honorary Yale 1818).

In April, 1824, he removed to Middle Haddam, and from there in April, 1826, to Middletown, and again in February, 1829, to Ellington; but in October, 1830, he returned to Colchester, where he remained until his death, and was engaged in practice as long as his health allowed He was confined to his house for the most of the last year of his life He was able, however, to attend public worship on Sunday, the 17th of June, 1877, and died during sleep on the next day, in his 86th year.

His wife survived him, with three sons and a daughter; four other children were deceased,—the eldest son having died in the civil war.

Dr. Morgan was a deacon in the First Congregational Church in Colchester from March, 1837, to his death.

He was long a trustee of Bacon Academy, and occasionally, until he was over eighty years old, he had temporary charge of the instruction.

In 1845 he represented Colchester in the General Assembly.

AUTHORITIES

Conn Med Society's Proceedings, 1878, 211-13 Morgan Family, 58, 111-12. *Willard,* Memorial of Dr Morgan

---

James Morris, son of Colonel Thomas Morris, of Charleston, South Carolina, was probably born in 1792 His mother was Mary, only daughter of General Christopher Gadsden, of Charleston, and he was thus a first cousin of Bishop Gadsden (Yale 1804) and his brothers His preparation for College was completed under Jeremiah Evarts (Yale 1802) in New Haven.

He returned to Charleston after graduation, and lived for some years (at least until 1819) in the city, where he was occupied as an accountant. Later he became a planter.

He died in 1826, aged about 34 years, leaving descendants.

AUTHORITIES.

Miss I. DeSaussure, MS. Letter, Dec., 1911.

MILO LINUS NORTH was born in Sharon, Connecticut, in 1789, and was prepared for College by the Rev. Daniel Parker (Yale 1798), of Ellsworth Society, Sharon. He entered from Canaan in Sophomore year.

After graduation he taught in the academy in East Windsor for two years, and was admitted to the Congregational Church in what is now South Windsor on profession of his faith in June, 1814.

He then studied medicine, and in April, 1817, settled in Sharon. In 1822 he removed to Ellington, and thence to Hartford in 1828. The honorary degree of M.D. was conferred on him by Yale in 1834.

In 1838 he again removed, on account of broken health, to Saratoga Springs, New York, where he not only found new strength from the use of the waters, but succeeded to the large practice of Dr. John H. Steel among the frequenters of the Springs.

He died in Spuyten Duyvel in Yonkers, New York, on February 22, 1856, at the residence of a son, in his 67th year.

His wife, Mrs. Julia North, was living when he removed to Hartford.

He published:

1. Saratoga Waters. Four articles in the *Boston Medical and Surgical Journal,* vol. 20, pp. 138–39, 149–51, 186–88, 208–09 (April–May, 1839).

2. Saratoga Waters, or the Invalid at Saratoga. New York, 1840. 12°, pp. 70. [*A. A. S. B. Publ. Harv.*

The same. Second edition, with the analyses of various mineral springs. New York, 1843. 12°, pp 72.
[*B Publ Harv. M H. S.*

The same Third edition, with title, Analysis of Saratoga waters, also, of Sharon, Avon, Virginia, and other mineral waters of the United States. With directions for invalids. New York, 1846 16°, pp. 72. [*M. H. S Surg Gen'l's Office*

Also, later editions.

AUTHORITIES.

T Robbins, Diary, 1, 591-92, 700 754, 835 *Sumner and Russell,* Physicians of Hartford, 39.
Stiles, Hist of Windsor, 2d ed, 1,

DENISON OLMSTED, the youngest child of Nathaniel Olmsted, a farmer in moderate circumstances, of East Hartford, Connecticut, and grandson of Nathaniel and Sarah (Pitkin) Olmsted, of East Hartford, was born on June 18, 1791. His mother was Eunice, third daughter of Denison and Lydia (Jones) Kingsbury, of Hebron, and her husband having died in June, 1792, she married in 1800 Ephraim Webster, of Farmington He was prepared for Yale by his pastor, the Rev. Noah Porter (Yale 1803). He took a high stand in College, and excelled in writing. At graduation he delivered a striking Oration on the Causes of Intellectual Greatness.

He then went to New London as the teacher of the Union School, a private institution for boys. While there he became interested in personal religion, and when he entered on a Yale tutorship in the fall of 1815, it was with the intention of entering the ministry that he also began the study of theology under President Dwight.

At Commencement in 1816 he delivered a Master's Oration, on the State of Education in Connecticut, in which he broached the project of a Seminary for schoolmasters (or Normal School), and he was looking forwards to establishing such an institution at the end of his tutorship; but in the fall of 1817 he was elected to the professorship of Chemistry in the University of North Carolina, with the opportunity of a year of preparation under Professor Silliman before entering on his duties. On the advice of friends he reluctantly abandoned his former plans, and accepted this offer, and towards the end of the year, about the first of June, 1818, he was married to Eliza, daughter of Captain Allyn, of New London.

Besides his University duties, Professor Olmsted was appointed in 1822 State geologist and mineralogist,—North Carolina being the earliest State to institute a survey of this nature, at his suggestion, made in 1821.

In September, 1825, Professor Olmsted was appointed to the chair of Mathematics and Natural Philosophy at Yale, vacant by reason of the death of Professor Matthew R. Dutton (Yale 1808). He resigned his position in Chapel Hill in December, 1825, and soon began his duties here. The new field of teaching to which he was thus introduced was not altogether congenial, and as soon as the College finances allowed he obtained a division of his chair, Mathematics being assigned to a new officer in August, 1836.

In the meantime he had supplied the lack of good text-books in Natural Philosophy by beginning the publication of books of his own composition, to which were subsequently added others in Astronomy. These text-books found a ready sale, and proved a considerable source of income.

For the last twenty years of his life his class-room teaching was of astronomy only, while he gave lecture-courses in natural philosophy, astronomy, and meteorology. In the last named subject he was a leading authority, from the time of his remarkable papers on the shower of shooting stars in November, 1833.

He was also conspicuous for his interest in the promotion of the lower grades of education.

His wife died on June 9, 1829, aged 34 years. Their children were five sons and two daughters. Four of the sons were graduates of Yale College, but all died early from consumption.

On August 24, 1831, he was married in New York City by the Rev Cyrus Mason to Julia, daughter of Charles and Rebecca (Nichols) Mason, of Rensselaer County, who was at the time a member of the family of her uncle, the officiating clergyman

He had been subject for years to rheumatic complaints, and he died in New Haven, after some months' suffering, from gout of the stomach, on May 13, 1859, in his 68th year. A commemorative discourse by President Woolsey was published. A portrait painted in 1833 is owned by the College; an engraving from a daguerreotype taken in later life is prefixed to President Woolsey's Discourse, and a still later likeness is reproduced in Kingsley's *Yale College*

The honorary degree of Doctor of Laws was conferred on him by the New York University in 1845.

His widow died in New Haven, after a long period of patient suffering, on February 16, 1884, in her 81st year. Her only child, a daughter, died unmarried in 1880.

Professor Olmsted was a courteous gentleman of the old school in his manners, and an earnest Christian. He was a teacher by nature

He published:

1 Thoughts on the Clerical Profession. In the *Religious Intelligencer,* vol. 1, pp. 604–07, 617–20, 636–39, 668–70 (New Haven, February–March, 1817).

2 Biographical Memoir of the Rev Timothy Dwight, S.T D., LL.D. In the *Connecticut Journal,* March 11, 1817, and reprinted (November, 1817) in the *Port Folio,* 4th series, vol 4, pp. 355–69.

3 Outlines of the Lectures on Chemistry, Mineralogy, and Geology, delivered at the University of North-Carolina.—For the use of the Students. Raleigh, 1819 8°, pp. 44. [*Y. C.*

4. Remarks on the Preparation of Mortar—Addressed to the Agricultural Society of North Carolina.—Read in Society and ordered to be printed, December 14, 1821

The same. Reprinted by order of the Board of Agriculture, June, 1825. In Papers on agricultural subjects. Raleigh, 1827. 8°, pp. 59–84. [*Y. C.*

5. Report on the Geology of North-Carolina, conducted under the direction of the Board of Agriculture.—Part I.—November, 1824. And Part II.—November, 1825.
In Papers on agricultural subjects. Raleigh, 1827. 8°, pp. 1–44, 85–142. [*Y. C.*

6. Review. The Christian Philosopher .. By T. Dick. In the *Christian Spectator,* new series, vol. 1, pp. 149–61 (March, 1827).

7. An Oration on the Progressive State of the Present Age. Delivered at New Haven, before the Connecticut Alpha of the Phi Beta Kappa, September 11, 1827. New Haven, 1827. 8°, pp. 24. [*B. Publ. Br. Mus. Harv. Y. C.*

8. Outlines of the Experimental Lectures in Natural Philosophy, delivered at Yale College.—For the use of the students. New-Haven, 1828. 12°, pp. 39. [*Y. C.*

9. Outlines of a Course of Lectures, on select subjects of Natural Philosophy and Astronomy, addressed to the Senior Class in Yale College.—For the use of the students. New Haven, 1829. 8°, pp. 24. [*Y. C.*
Many later editions.

10. Review of Sir Humphry Davy's Salmonia. In the *Quarterly Christian Spectator,* vol. 2, pp. 133–47 (March, 1830).

11. An Introduction to Natural Philosophy: designed as a Text Book, for the use of the students in Yale College. Compiled from various authorities. New Haven, 1831–32. 8°, pp. xv, 346; x. 352 + pl. [*U. S. Y. C.*
Also, several later editions.

12. A Compendium of Natural Philosophy: adapted to the use of the general reader, and of Schools and Academies. New Haven, 1833. 8°, pp. v, 336. [*B. Ath. B. Publ. Y. C.*

The same. Stereotype edition. New Haven, 1844. 12°, pp. 420. [*U. S.*

13. Facts respecting the Meteoric Phenomena of November 13th, 1834. In the *Journal* of the Franklin Institute, New Series, vol. 16, pp. 367–69.

14. Observations on the School System of Connecticut. In the *Lectures* delivered before the American Institute of Instruction, 1838. Boston, 1839. 8°, pp 95–110.

15. Observations on the Use of Anthracite Coal. In the *American Almanac*, for 1837 Boston [1836] 12°, pp 62–69

16. Outlines of Lectures on the Atmosphere and its phenomena Delivered before the Mercantile Library Association. New York, 1839. 8°, pp 12. [*Harv*

17. An Introduction to Astronomy; designed as a Text Book for the Students of Yale College 1839 8°, pp xvi, 284 + pl
[*B. Publ. Harv*

The same. 2d edition New York, 1841. 8°, pp. xvi, 284 + pl
[*U. S.*

Also, later editions.

18 A Compendium of Astronomy; containing the elements of the science, familiarly explained and illustrated . Adapted to the use of Schools and Academies, and of the General Reader New York, 1839. 12°, pp. vi, 284 + pl. [*B. Publ*

Also, later editions.

19. Letters on Astronomy, addressed to a lady; in which the elements of the science are familiarly explained in connexion with its literary history. Boston, 1840. 12°, pp 419 + pl
[*B. Publ. U. S. Y. C.*

Also, reprinted at Edinburgh, in 1853, with the title, The Mechanism of the Heavens . .

20. Second Annual Report of the Board of Commissioners of Common Schools in Connecticut . . . May, 1840 Hartford, 1840. 8°, pp 8 [*Y. C.*

21. Life and Writings of Ebenezer Porter Mason; interspersed with hints to parents and instructors on the teaching and education of a child of genius. New York, 1842 12°, pp 252.
[*B Ath. Br Mus. M. H S. Y. C.*

Mason (Yale 1839) was a favorite pupil of the author.

22. Memoir of John Treadwell, LL D, late Governor of Connecticut. Boston, 1843 8°, pp. 31 + pl. [*B. Publ Y. C*

First published in the *American Quarterly Register* for February, 1843

23. Meeting of the Class of 1813, on the 16th and 17th of August, 1843. [New Haven, 1843.] 8°, pp. 16. [*Y. C.*

Prepared with the assistance of the Rev. T. F. Davies.

24. Rudiments of Natural Philosophy and Astronomy: designed for the younger classes in academies, and for common schools. New York, 1844. 12°, pp. 288. [*B. Publ. U. S. Y. C.*

In many editions; on account of its clearness and compactness adopted as a text-book for the blind, an edition being printed in raised letters in 1845.

25. Lecture on the Beau Ideal of the Perfect Teacher. Boston, 1845. 12°, pp. 29. [*Harv.*

Also, In the *Lectures* delivered before the American Institute of Instruction, at Hartford, August, 1845. Boston, 1846. 12°, pp. 83–109.

26. Memoir of Eli Whitney, Esq. First published in the American Journal of Science, for 1832. New Haven, 1846. 8°, pp. 80 + pl. [*B. Ath. B. Publ. Harv. M. H. S. U. S. Y. C.*

27. Roger Sherman. In the *American Literary Magazine*, vol. 4, pp. 699–708 +pl. (June, 1849).

28. On the recent secular period of the Aurora Borealis. Washington, 1856. 4°, pp. 52.

In the *Smithsonian Contributions to Knowledge*, vol. 8.

29. Address, on occasion of the Fiftieth Anniversary of the Ordination of Noah Porter, D.D., as Pastor of the First Church, in Farmington, Conn., November 12th, 1856. With Dr. Porter's Half-Century Discourse, Farmington, 1856. 8°, pp. 44–48.

30. Address on the scientific life and labors of William C. Redfield, A.M., first President of the American Association for the Advancement of Science. Delivered before the Association at their Annual Meeting in Montreal, August 14, 1857. New Haven, 1857. 8°, pp. 28 + pl.
[*B. Publ. Harv. M. H. S. U. S. Y. C.*

He also contributed largely to periodicals, besides the few cases above mentioned. Among these may be cited,

American Journal of Science and Arts: Red Sand Stone formation of North-Carolina, vol. 2, pp. 175–76 (April, 1820).

Descriptive Catalogue of Rocks and Minerals collected in N. Carolina, and forwarded to the American Geological Society, vol. 5, pp. 257–64 (Sept, 1822).

Illuminating Gas from Cotton Seed, vol 8, pp. 294–99 (August, 1824), and vol 10, pp 363–65 (Febr., 1826).

On the Gold Mines of North Carolina, vol. 9, pp. 5–15 (1825).

On the present state of Chemical Science, vol 11, pp 349–58, vol. 12, pp 1–14.

Remarks on Dr. Hare's Essay on the question, Whether Heat can be ascribed to motion? Volume 12, 359–63 (June, 1827).

Meteorological Report for the year 1827, vol. 14, pp 176–82 (April, 1828).

The same for 1828, vol. 16, pp. 70–78 (April, 1829).

Review of the Scientific Labors and Character of Sir Humphrey Davy, vol 17, pp 217–48 (January, 1830)

Of the Phenomena and Causes of Hail Storms, vol. 18, pp. 1–11 (April, 1830)

Mode of adjusting lightning rods, vol 18, pp. 362–63 (July, 1830).

Reply to Dr. Christie on Hail Storms, vol 20, pp 373–76 (July, 1831).

Observations on the Meteors of November 13th, 1833, vol 25, pp 363–411, and vol 26, pp. 132–74 (Jan–April, 1834)

Zodiacal Light, vol. 27, pp 416–19 (January, 1835).

On the cause of the Meteors of November 13th, 1833, vol. 29, pp 376–83 (January, 1836).

Aurora Borealis of Nov 17, 1835, vol 29, pp. 388–91 (January, 1836).

Remarks on Shooting Stars, in reply to Rev. W A Clarke . . , vol 30, pp 370–76 (July, 1836).

On the Meteoric Shower of November, 1836, vol 31, pp. 386–95 (January, 1837)

Observations on the Aurora Borealis of January 25th, 1837, vol. 32, pp 176–81 (April, 1837).

On the Meteoric Shower of November, 1837, vol 33, pp. 379–93 (January, 1838).

Observations made at Yale College on the Eclipse of the Sun of September 18, 1838, vol 35, pp. 174–78 (October, 1838).

On the Meteoric Shower of November, 1838, vol. 35, pp. 368–70 (January, 1839)

Observations on the New Haven Tornado of July 31, 1839, vol. 37, pp 340–47 (October, 1839)

Meteors of November, vol 40, pp 202–03 (December, 1840)

New Experiments on the Solar Spectrum, vol. 48, pp. 137–40 (December, 1844).

Report of Observations on the Transit of Mercury, May 8th, 1845, vol. 49, pp. 142–49 (June, 1845).

Review of Sir J. Herschel's Astronomical Observations at the Cape of Good Hope, vol. 5, 2d series, pp. 86–100 (January, 1848).

Great Aurora Borealis of February 19th, 1852, vol. 13, 2d series, pp. 426–30 (May, 1852).

Eclipse of the Sun, May 26, 1854, vol. 18, 2d series, p. 142 (July, 1854).

New Englander:

Reminiscences of Alexander Metcalf Fisher . . , vol. 1, pp. 457–69 (October, 1843).

Thoughts on the Discovery of Le Verrier's Planet, vol. 5, pp. 126–36 (January, 1847).

Thoughts on the Revelations of the Microscope, vol. 5, pp. 231–46 (April, 1847).

Thoughts on the Riches of the Natural World, vol. 6, pp. 404–17 (July, 1848).

Thoughts on the sentiment that "The World was made for Man," vol. 7, pp. 17–46 (February, 1849).

John Pitkin Norton, vol. 10, pp. 613–31 (November, 1852).

Professor Stanley, vol. 11, pp. 325–28 (May, 1853).

[Review.] Silliman's Visit to Europe, vol. 12, pp. 24–32 (February, 1854).

The Plurality of Worlds, vol. 12, pp. 570–603 (November, 1854).

A Philosophical Survey of the Ocean, vol. 13, pp. 117–28 (February, 1855).

The Divine Love of Truth and Beauty exemplified in the Material Creation, vol. 16, pp. 770–89 (November, 1858).

Meteorology of Palestine, vol. 17, pp. 459–68 (May, 1859).

Proceedings of the American Association for the Advancement of Science:

Notes on some Points of Electrical Theory, 4th meeting, 1850, pp. 2–7; On some peculiar Properties of a Compound of Lard and Rosin, pp. 33–35.

Observations on the Zodiacal Light . . . ., 6th meeting, 1851, pp. 112–27 (also, in part, in *American Journal of Science and Arts*, vol. 12, 2d series, pp. 309–22).

Notes on the Wilmington Gunpowder Explosion, 9th meeting, 1855, pp. 136–40.

On the Electrical Hypothesis of the Aurora Borealis, 11th meeting, 1857, pp. 113–23.

American Journal of Education and College Review
On the Democratic Tendencies of Science, vol 1, pp 164-73 (January, 1856); The Gift of Teaching, pp 333-44 (April, 1856)

American Journal of Education:
Timothy Dwight as a Teacher, vol. 5, pp 567-85 (September, 1858).

In Sprague's *Annals of the American Pulpit* are two brief letters, on President Timothy Dwight (vol. 1, pp. 159-61) and President Joseph Caldwell (vol. 4, pp. 174-76).

AUTHORITIES.

Amer Journal of Education, v, 123-24, 367-72. Amer. Journal of Science, 2d series, xxviii, 109-18 *Battle,* Hist of the Univ. of N. C, i, 250, 252-53, 289, 299-300, 417 *Dwight,* Memories of Yale Life, 140-51. Kingsbury Family, 270 *Kingsley,* Yale College, i, 232-49 Loomis Female Genealogy, i, 32, 46 New Englander, xvii, 575-600.

RUSSELL PARISH was born in Branford, Connecticut, on October 27, 1789, the son of Jonathan and Polly (Russell) Parish. He was prepared for College by his pastor, the Rev. Timothy P Gillett (Williams Coll. 1804).

In November, 1813, he began to teach in the academy in Lowville, Lewis County, New York, and in 1814 undertook the study of law there in the office of Isaac W. Bostwick. He settled in Lowville in the practice of his profession, and was married there on January 24, 1832, to Jane Elizabeth, second daughter of Melanchthon Woolsey and Abigail (Buell) Welles, and granddaughter of the Rev. Dr. Noah Welles (Yale 1741)

He was a delegate to the State Constitutional Convention of 1846.

He died in Lowville on February 20, 1855, in his 66th year.

His children were two daughters.

A portrait is given in Hough's *History of Lewis County.*

AUTHORITIES.

Hough, Hist of Lewis County, 153 Lowville Academy Semi-Centennial, 80. N Y. Geneal and Biogr. Record, v, 143

SILAS PARKER entered College from St. John's, Newfoundland, and was probably born in 1793.

His course was interrupted in the Senior year and he was not admitted to a degree until 1816.

He is supposed to have returned to his native place, and to have become a clergyman; but his name is marked as deceased in the Triennial Catalogue of Graduates issued in 1820.

CHARLES PERKINS, son of Captain Andrew Perkins, a merchant of Norwich, Connecticut, and grandson of Dr. Joseph Perkins (Yale 1727), was born in Norwich on June 21, 1792. His mother was Betsey, third daughter of Eldad Taylor, of Westfield, Massachusetts. He was prepared for admission to the Sophomore Class by John Adams (Yale 1795) in the Bacon Academy, Colchester.

After graduation he studied law in the Litchfield Law School, and in 1817 began practice in Norwich. In 1826 he removed to Rochester, New York, where he remained for about two years, partly engaged in his profession and partly in land business.

For the rest of his life he resided in Litchfield, Connecticut, where he had married on April 20, 1817, Clarissa, sister of William Deming (Yale 1811), who died in Litchfield on August 6, 1837, in her 42d year.

While traveling abroad, he died suddenly in London on November 18, 1856, in his 65th year.

His children were four sons and four daughters, of whom two sons and three daughters died in infancy. The eldest daughter married Professor James M. Hoppin (Yale 1840).

AUTHORITIES.

Deming Genealogy, 122. Perkins Family, pt. 3, 31. *Trowbridge*, Champion Genealogy, 305.

Reuben Sherwood was born on Mill Hill in Fairfield, Connecticut, in 1789 or 1790, and entered College at the beginning of the Sophomore year.

He studied theology after graduation, and was ordained as deacon by the Rt. Rev. Alexander V. Griswold, of the Eastern Diocese, at Middletown on June 6, 1815. In the same year he took charge of St. Paul's Church, Norwalk, where on November 4, 1816, Bishop Hobart, of New York, admitted him to priest's orders, though he was not formally instituted to the rectorship of St. Paul's until December, 1819.

In addition to the work of the ministry, he conducted a successful academy for boys and girls.

He continued in Norwalk until April, 1830, when he was induced by Bishop Brownell to relinquish his post, in order to take charge of an academy established by churchmen in Hartford to serve as a feeder for Washington (now Trinity) College. At the end of one year, however, he gave up this task, and spent the next four years in missionary service in Ulster County, New York, with his residence in Ulster. Among other fruits of his labor was the founding of parishes in Saugerties and Esopus.

In 1835 he became rector of St. James's Church, in Hyde Park, Duchess County, where the rest of his life was usefully and happily spent.

The honorary degree of Doctor of Divinity was conferred on him by Hobart College in 1840.

He died in Hyde Park, on Whitsunday, May 11, 1856, in his 67th year.

He married, in April, 1819, Catharine, eldest daughter of Fitch and Hannah (Bell) Rogers, of New York City and Stamford, Connecticut, one of whose sisters had previously married John Still Winthrop (Yale 1804).

By her he had two daughters.

After her death, he married, late in life, Penelope, daughter of Champlain Harrison.

AUTHORITIES.

Beardsley, Hist. of the Episcopal Church in Conn., ii, 115, 135, 289. Church Review, ix, 301. New York Geneal. and Biogr. Record, xv, 157. *Selleck,* Norwalk, i, 95, 167, 170–71, 216; Centenary of St. Paul's Church, 15–17.

John Singletary was born in Washington, Beaufort County, North Carolina, on January 23, 1792. His degree was not voted him until 1814.

After graduation he studied law with Moses Mordecai, of Raleigh, and began practice in his native place.

He subsequently studied theology, and received deacon's orders in the Episcopal Church, on April 6, 1834, from Bishop Ives. He served for two or three years, while still in the diaconate, as a missionary in the vicinity of Tarboro, Edgecombe County. Later, he was rector of St. Peter's Church in Washington, and finally for a short time, perhaps about a year, rector of St. John's in the Wilderness, at Flatrock, in the Western part of the State, whither he had gone on account of failing health.

He died at the house of Mr. Baring, in Rock Spring, Orange County, on June 21, 1845, in his 54th year, and is buried near the church of which he was last rector.

He married Eliza Williams, of Pitt County, who left three sons, all of whom were officers in the Confederate army. One son was graduated at the University of North Carolina in 1858.

AUTHORITIES.

Rev. N. Harding, MS. Letter, September, 1911.

Roger Sherman Skinner, the eldest and only surviving child of Dr. John Skinner, of East Hartford, Connecticut, and grandson of John and Sarah (Kennedy) Skinner, of East Windsor, was born in East Hartford on January 19, 1795. His mother was Chloe, daughter of the Hon. Roger and Elizabeth (Hartwell) Sherman, of New Haven.

The family settled in New Haven about 1799, and the son was prepared for College by Elizur Goodrich, Junior (Williams Coll. 1806), at the Hopkins Grammar School.

On graduation he entered the Yale Medical School, but soon transferred himself to the Litchfield Law School, and in March, 1816, was admitted to the bar.

He settled in New Haven, and was married on September 27, 1817, to Mary Lockwood, daughter of Lockwood and Mehitable (Wheeler) DeForest, of New York.

He was for several years, about 1820, Clerk of the City and County Courts.

About 1828 he removed to New York City.

He died while temporarily in Peru, Lasalle County, Illinois, on December 6, 1838, in his 44th year.

His children were three sons and three daughters, all of whom survived him. The second daughter married the Rev. Samuel D. Marsh (Yale 1844), and is now the widow of the Rev. Professor Samuel Harris, of the Yale Divinity School, while the youngest daughter is the wife of President Timothy Dwight (Yale 1849).

His widow died at President Dwight's house in New Haven, on June 17, 1889, aged 92 years.

He published:

The New-York State Register, for the year of our Lord 1830 .. New-York, 1830. 12°, pp. 408. [*Br. Mus. U. S. Y. C.*

The same, for 1831. New York, 1831. 12°, pp. 284, 20, 74. [*Br. Mus. U. S. Y. C.*

A laborious compilation, of great accuracy and usefulness.

AUTHORITIES.

DeForests of Avesnes, 229. Dwight Family, ii, 1107–08. Loomis Female Genealogy, ii, 937.

Josiah Spalding, the second son of Reuben and Hannah (Peabody) Spalding, of Pomfret, Connecticut, and grandson of Josiah and Priscilla (Paine) Spalding, of Plainfield and Ashford, was born in Pomfret on February

24, 1793. A brother was graduated at Brown University in 1821. He was a nephew of the Rev. Solomon Spalding (Dartmouth Coll. 1785), whose name has been connected with the origin of the Book of Mormon. He was prepared for College by Rinaldo Burleigh (Yale 1803) in the Plainfield Academy. At his graduation he delivered the Valedictory Oration.

From 1814 to 1817 he served as a tutor in Hamilton College, Clinton, New York. He was elected to a tutorship at Yale in September, 1815, but declined the offer.

He then studied law, and in the winter of 1819-20 he settled in practice in St. Louis, Missouri, where he was for a short time in partnership with Abraham Beck, who died in 1821.

In March, 1822, when the *Missouri Republican* newspaper was begun in St. Louis, he undertook for a short time the editorship, in order to assist in the campaign against certain recent laws, which gave undue relief to debtors and authorized a paper currency of little value.

On April, 2, 1823, he married Mrs. Agnes P. Gay, a widow from the East, with two children, who had been for some time a teacher in St. Louis.

He continued industriously employed at the bar until his death, and rose to the very highest rank among the lawyers of the State. At one time he was in partnership with the Hon. Hamilton R. Gamble, afterwards Governor, and later in life with John R. Shepley.

After a considerable period of delicate health, he died in St. Louis on May 14, 1852, in his 60th year.

His wife survived him with a large family of children.

He had been the Senior Warden of Christ Church for many years.

AUTHORITIES.

Bay, Bench and Bar of Missouri, 104-08. *Billon,* Annals of St. Louis, 346. *Houck,* Hist. of Missouri, iii, 23, 65. *Scharf,* Hist. of St. Louis, ii, 1471-72. Spalding Memorial, 159, 293. *Stewart,* Bench and Bar of Missouri, 114, 117.

JOHN AUSTIN STEVENS, the youngest of the four sons of General Ebenezer Stevens who were graduated at Yale, was born in New York City on January 22, 1795. His brothers were in the Classes of 1805, 1807, and 1811, respectively. He was prepared for College by Rinaldo Burleigh (Yale 1803) in the academy in Plainfield, Connecticut.

In 1818 he became a partner in his father's business house in New York, and he was thenceforth associated with that firm (Ebenezer Stevens' Sons) in its long and honorable career in West Indian, French and Mediterranean trade. He was a member from 1820 and long Secretary of the Chamber of Commerce, and the first President of the Merchants' Exchange. He was the President of the Bank of Commerce from its organization in 1839 until 1866, when he voluntarily retired on account of the approaching infirmities of age.

At a critical moment in the history of the Civil War, as Chairman of a Committee of the banks of New York, Boston, and Philadelphia, he strongly advocated the loan of money ($150,000,000) to the United States Treasury, and by his prompt and bold action was largely instrumental in preserving the Government's credit.

He died in New York City on October 19, 1874, in his 80th year.

He married in 1824 Abby, daughter of the late Benjamin Wild, of Brunswick, Maine, and Boston.

A large family of children survived him. A son bearing his father's name was graduated at Harvard University in 1846, and became a well-known historical student and writer.

AUTHORITIES.

N. Y. Geneal. and Biogr. Record, vii, 13.

George Sumner, son of George and Mary (Tyler) Sumner, was born in Abington Society, in Pomfret, Connecticut, on December 13, 1794, and was prepared for College by Rinaldo Burleigh (Yale 1803) in the Plainfield Academy. He was distinguished at Yale for his mathematical ability, and was commonly regarded as the cleverest member of the Class.

Upon graduation he began medical studies under the direction of Dr. Thomas Hubbard, of Pomfret, subsequently a Professor in the Yale Medical School, and after two years with him, spent the two following years at the University of Pennsylvania, where he received the degree of M.D. in 1817.

He then established himself in Providence, Rhode Island, but was soon called home by the illness of his father, who after long confinement died in 1818.

On January 1, 1819, Dr. Sumner removed to Hartford, his home for the rest of his days.

On December 10, 1819, he was married to Elizabeth, daughter of Daniel and Catharine (Hutchinson) Putnam, of Brooklyn, Connecticut.

In the early years in Hartford, before much business had come to him, botanical pursuits were his recreation and partial employment,—one result of which was his appointment in 1824 as Professor of Botany in Washington, afterwards Trinity College, which he held until his death.

He gradually came to be regarded as one of the ablest and most capable physicians in the city, and acquired a large practice among the best families.

He was among the most active of the early advocates and supporters of the Retreat for the Insane in Hartford, and on the death of the first Superintendent, Dr. Eli Todd, in 1833, he was unanimously chosen to that office, but declined the appointment.

He was also active in his interest in the State Medical Society, and served as its President in 1849 and 1850. He was a vestryman of Christ Church from 1845.

After a gradual failure of his physical powers, in the fall of 1853 he gave up active labor, and his death followed, in Hartford, on February 20, 1855, in his 61st year.

His wife died of apoplexy on December 29, 1844, in her 51st year They had five children.

He published:

1 A Compendium of Physiological and Systematic Botany. Hartford, 1820 12°, pp xii, 300 + 8 pl
[*Br. Mus Harv U. S. Y. C*

2 Address on the early Physicians of Connecticut. In *Proceedings* at the forty-ninth annual Convention of the Connecticut Medical Society, May, 1851. Hartford, 1851. 8°, pp 25-64.
Of prime authority.

After his death appeared:

3. Reminiscences of Physicians in Hartford in 1820. With Sketches of the same in 1837, by G W. Russell, M.D Hartford, 1890. 8°, pp 3-28.
Prepared in 1848 for the Hartford Medical Society.

AUTHORITIES

Conn Med Society's Proceedings, 1855, 53-71 *Russell,* Hist of Christ Church, i, 112, 393, 458, ii, 163, 245, 301, 304 *Trumbull,* Hist of Hartford County, i, 143. *Sumner & Russell,* Sketches of Hartford Physicians, 4, 35-38

HENRY WYTHE TABB, the youngest child of Philip Tabb, of Richmond, and of Toddbury, Gloucester County, Virginia, and grandson of Edward and Lucy (Todd) Tabb, was born on January 12, 1791. His mother was Mary Mason Booth, daughter of Nathaniel and Elizabeth Wythe His preparation for College was completed under Jeremiah Evarts (Yale 1802) in New Haven

He spent the two winters after graduation in medical study in Philadelphia. In the spring of 1815 he sailed for England, and after a brief visit to the Continent, including an inspection of the field of Waterloo, he spent six months as a pupil in the London hospitals. For the following twelve months, until his graduation, he held the appointment of assistant to Henry Cline, Junior, the surgeon at St. Thomas's Hospital. He then visited other medical schools, in Edinburgh, Dublin, Paris, etc., and in the fall of 1817 returned to Virginia and settled in Richmond, where he practiced with some success until the fall of 1821.

He then married Hester VanBibber, who resided near his father's country place, and this induced him to remove to Auburn, Matthews County, on Chesapeake Bay, where he practiced his profession for many years, besides managing a plantation.

His wife died in February, 1822, and he next married, in July, 1828, Martha Tompkins, by whom he had four daughters and a son; the son and the third daughter died in infancy.

Mrs. Tabb died on September 17, 1842, and he was next married, in Brooklyn, New York, by the Rev. Dr. Francis Vinton, on October 6, 1846, to Ellen A. Foster of Philadelphia, by whom he had one son and three daughters.

He died in July, 1863, in his 73d year.

AUTHORITIES.

William and Mary College Quarterly, xiii, 170.

Jeremiah Van Rensselaer, son of John Jeremias and Catharine (Glen) Van Rensselaer, of Albany, and grandson of Jeremiah and Judith (Bayard) Van Rensselaer, was born at Fort Crailo, the old family mansion in Greenbush, Rensselaer County, New York, on August 4, 1793. He was prepared for College by the Rev. Dr. David Ely (Yale 1769), of Huntington, Connecticut.

He studied medicine for three years after graduation in New York with his uncle, Dr. Archibald Bruce (Columbia 1797), and then began practice in the city; but soon left to spend three years abroad, in Edinburgh, London, and Paris, in further study, returning in December, 1819. In July, 1819, he and a companion ascended Mont Blanc, being the first Americans to do so.

He then engaged successfully in practice in New York, but early in 1840 went to Europe again, for a three years' stay, on account of the health of one of his children.

In 1852 he retired from active pursuits, and removed to Fort Crailo, in Greenbush, where he occupied himself with the care of his estate. He was the Senior Warden of the Church of the Messiah up to his death.

In 1867 he again visited Europe, but returned in the fall of 1870 in feeble health, and died in New York, from pneumonia, on March 7, 1871, in his 78th year

He was twice married: first to Charlotte Foster, of Boston; and secondly to Anne Ferrand Waddington, of New York, who survived him for over twenty years.

He had six children; one son survived him.

He received the honorary degree of Doctor of Medicine from the Medical College in Castleton, Vermont, in 1823.

From Dr. Bruce he acquired a taste for the natural sciences, and he was for many years active in the work of the New York Lyceum of Natural History, and long its Corresponding Secretary.

He published:

1. An Essay on Salt, containing notices of its origin, formation, geological position and principal localities, embracing a particular description of the American Salines ..—Delivered as a Lecture before the New-York Lyceum of Natural History. New-York, 8°, pp 80.
[*A A S. B Publ. Columbia Univ Y. C*

2. Lectures on Geology; being outlines of the science, delivered in the New-York Athenæum, in the year 1825 New-York, 1825 8°, pp 358. [*A. A S. Br Mus Columbia Univ U.S Y C.*

He contributed the following articles to the *American Journal of Science and Arts:*

Account of a journey to the summit of Mount Blanc, vol. 2, pp. 1–11 (May, 1820).

On the Natural History of the Ocean, with two sea journals, vol. 5, pp. 128–40 (May, 1822).

On Lightning-Rods, vol. 9, pp. 331–36 (June, 1825).

Notice of a recent discovery of the fossil remains of the Mastodon, vol. 11, pp. 246–50 (October, 1826).

On the Fossil Remains of the Mastodon lately found in Ontario County, New-York, vol. 12, pp. 380–81 (June, 1827).

On Larvæ in the Human Body, vol. 13, pp. 229–34 (January, 1828).

On the Fossil Tooth of an Elephant, found near the shore of Lake Erie, and on the skeleton of a Mastodon, lately discovered on the Delaware and Hudson Canal, vol. 14, pp. 31–33 (March, 1828).

Temperature of the cities of Rome (Italy) and New York, vol. 42, pp. 120–22 (December, 1841).

AUTHORITIES.

Holgate, Amer. Genealogy, 44. Medical Record, vi, 71. *Van Rensselaer,* Annals of the Van Rensselaers, 194, 236–37.

John William Weed, son of Benjamin and Mary (Waterbury) Weed, of Middlesex Society, in Stamford, now Darien, Connecticut, was born on February 21, 1792, and was prepared for College by Frederick Scofield (Yale 1801), in his native parish. Previous to entering College he taught in a select school in New York City.

After graduation he studied medicine in New York, in the College of Physicians and Surgeons, being also an office-student of Dr. Alexander H. Stevens (Yale 1807).

To this succeeded nearly fifty years of professional practice in New York.

The last ten years of his life were spent in Metuchen, New Jersey, where he died, from pneumonia, after a brief illness, on January 7, 1875, in his 83d year.

For a long series of years he was a Ruling Elder in the Central Presbyterian Church of New York; and after removing to Metuchen he filled the same office in the First Presbyterian Church there with devoted zeal

He was married in New York, on September 5, 1825, by the Rev. Ithamar Pillsbury (Yale 1822) to Margarette Macomber, daughter of Elihu and Nancy (Atwater) Mix, of New Haven

She survived him, with two daughters and four sons.

AUTHORITIES.

Huntington, Stamford Registration, 131 *Rev G S. Plumley,* MS. Letter, May, 1875

SAMUEL WEED, son of Ananias and Sally (Brown) Weed, of (North) Stamford, Connecticut, and grandson of Benjamin and Sarah (Smith) Weed, of Stamford, was born on October 16, 1794. His family removed to North Salem, Westchester County, New York, and he was prepared for College in the Academy there

After graduation he began the study of theology with the Rev. Ebenezer Phillips, of East Hampton, Long Island, and after being licensed to preach he supplied the Presbyterian Church in Babylon, on the south shore of Long Island, for a year While there he received a call to settle in his native parish, in succession to the Rev. Amzi Lewis (Yale 1768), and decided to accept it

Being under appointment to the Presbyterian General Assembly, in Philadelphia, in May, 1820, he went thither, but was prostrated by illness, and died in Philadelphia, in June, in his 26th year.

AUTHORITIES.

Huntington, Hist of Stamford, 430–31, Stamford Registration, 132

JONATHAN ASHLEY WELCH, son of the Rev Dr Moses Cook Welch (Yale 1772) and Clarissa (Ashley) Welch, of the North parish in Mansfield, Connecticut, was born in Mansfield on February 4, and was baptized on March 25, 1792, with the name of his maternal grandfather. He was prepared for College principally by his father, and entered the Junior Class in the fall of 1811.

After graduation he spent a year as private tutor and student of law in the family of a son of the Hon. Gouverneur Morris, of Morrisania, New York. The second year of his legal study was spent in the office of Seth P. Staples (Yale 1797), of New Haven, while at the same time he continued to teach, and engaged in graduate study.

He was admitted to the bar in 1815, and began practice in Windham, in partnership with David Young. In 1818 he removed to Lebanon, in New London County, and early in 1819 he was married to Mary Devotion, youngest daughter of Dr. Joseph Baker, of Brooklyn, in Windham County.

In the latter part of the same year he removed to Brooklyn, where the rest of his life was spent; twice, however, he attempted to establish himself elsewhere in a larger sphere (once in New York City, and once in Fall River, Massachusetts), but in both cases the attractions of a rural home recalled him to Brooklyn.

He died in Brooklyn, after three days' illness from paralysis, on September 9, 1859, in his 68th year.

His wife died on November 3, 1845, and he next married, on February 15, 1847, Harriet E., widow of Judge John Fitch (Yale 1803), of Mansfield, who survived him.

His children, by his first wife, were six sons and two daughters. One son, a graduate of West Point in 1845, died before him; another son was graduated at Yale in 1853.

Mr. Welch was esteemed as an eloquent and learned lawyer, a man of strict integrity, and an earnest Christian.

AUTHORITIES.

Dimock, Mansfield Records, 295, 439. *Joseph A. Welch*, MS. Letter, July, 1860.

JOHN MUMFORD WOOLSEY, one of twin sons of William Walton Woolsey, a hardware merchant of New York City, and grandson of the Rev. Benjamin Woolsey (Yale 1744), was born in New York on January 10, 1796. His mother was Elizabeth, youngest sister of President Timothy Dwight (Yale 1769). His twin brother was a classmate, and his only other brother, President Woolsey, was graduated in 1820. The family removed to New Haven in 1805, and he was prepared for College by Matthew R. Dutton (Yale 1808) in the Fairfield Academy

His father returned to business in New York in 1815, and was joined by both his elder sons, who remained with him until his final retirement in 1827.

John Woolsey then settled in Cleveland, Ohio, where he was occupied as a land-agent and capitalist until 1852, when he retired from business and returned to New Haven, where he died after long feebleness on July 11, 1870, in his 75th year. He was buried in the ancestral Woolsey burial-ground in Dosoris, Long Island

He married on May 22, 1832, Jane, daughter of John Andrews, M D (honorary Yale 1827), and Abigail (Atwater) Andrews, of Wallingford, Connecticut, and sister of the Hon. John W. Andrews (Yale 1830).

Mrs Woolsey survived her husband with her children, four daughters and a son. The eldest daughter became well known as a writer, under the name of "Susan Coolidge." The second daughter married the Rev. Henry A. Yardley (Yale 1855), and the third married President Daniel C. Gilman (Yale 1852) Two grandsons are graduates of Yale, in 1898 and 1901, respectively

AUTHORITIES

Dwight Family, i, 250, 254

WILLIAM CECIL WOOLSEY, twin brother of the last named graduate, was born in New York on January 10, 1796, and was prepared for College with his brother

After graduation he began the study of medicine, but in 1815 went into business in New York with his father and brother.

He subsequently became an auctioneer in New York, and died there on November 14, 1840, in his 45th year. He was buried beside his parents in New Haven.

He was married on March 31, 1829, by the Rev. Dr. William W. Phillips, to Catharine Rebecca, youngest daughter of General Theodorus and Rebecca (Talmadge) Bailey, of New York, who died in New Haven on July 24, 1844, in her 41st year.

Their children, two daughters and two sons, all survived them. The elder son was graduated at the Yale Medical School in 1853.

Woolsey Carmalt (Yale 1883) is a grandson.

AUTHORITIES.

Dwight Family, i, 250, 254-55.

Annals, 1813-14

At Commencement in 1814 the Rev Elijah Parsons (Yale 1768), of East Haddam, was elected a Fellow of the Corporation, in the place of the Rev Achilles Mansfield (Yale 1770), of Killingworth, now Clinton, who had died two months before.

At the same time Matthew R Dutton (Yale 1808) and Chauncey A. Goodrich (Yale 1810) resigned their places as tutors, and were succeeded by Ralph Emerson and William Danielson, both of the Class of 1811.

The Medical Institution went into operation in November, 1813, with an entering class of thirty-three members The building now known as Sheffield Hall, at the head of College Street, was rented from the Hon James Hillhouse, who had just erected it, probably for a hotel. The General Assembly of the State in May, 1814, appropriated $20,000 to the Institution, from money received from the incorporators of a new bank to be located in Hartford, called the Phœnix Bank

Mindful of the experience of New Haven in the Revolution, and the danger of another British invasion, precautions were taken by the Corporation in 1814 for the safety of the College property

The class graduated from the College in September, 1814, numbered 82, being larger than any preceding class, and not surpassed in size until 1826.

Sketches, Class of 1814

---

*Isaacus Adriance	*1862
**Edvardus Allen*	*1846
*Thomas Pinckney Alston	*1861
**Anson Sethus Atwood*	*1866
*Johannes Mulliken Atwood, A.M. 1818	*1873
*Elisaeus Averill, A.M.	*1824
*Guilielmus Rufus Babbitt	*1817
*Georgius Belden	*1855
**Amzi Benedict*	*1856
**Archibaldus Burgess*	*1850
*Guilielmus Barron Calhoun, A.M., LL.D. Amh. 1858, e Congr., Reip. Mass. Secr.	*1865
*Carolus Guilielmus Capers, A.M., M.D. Carol. Austr.	*1835
*Henricus Dwight Chapin, A.M.	*1862
*Donaldus Chester, A.M.	*1838
*Richardus Petrus Christophers	*1829
**Theodorus Clapp*	*1866
*Nathanael Coles	*1843
*Jacobus Cooley	*1828
*Alexander Copland	*1841
*Jacobus Hamilton Couper, LL.D. Univ. Mercer. 1848	*1866
*Austinus Denny, A.M. 1822	*1830
**Johannes Dickson,* A.M., in Coll. Carolop. Lingg. etiam Philos. Mor. Prof.	*1847
*Samuel Henricus Dickson, A.M., M.D. Univ. Penns. 1819, LL.D. Univ. Nov. Ebor. 1853, in Coll. Med. Car. Austr. et in Univ. Nov. Ebor. et in Coll. Med. Jeff. Med. Inst. et Prax. Prof.	*1872

*Josephus Heatly Dulles *1876
*Alexis Daniel Durand *1843
*Theodorus Dwight, A.M. *1866
*David Shelton Edwards, M.D. 1817, A.M. 1863 *1874
*Augustus Floyd *1878
*Henricus Gibbs *1855
*Carolus Backus Goddard, A.M. *1864
*Horatius Goodrich, A.M. 1818 *1872
**Radulphus Wells Gridley, A.M* *1840
*Minor Hallock *1821
*Hugo Halsey *1858
*Asa Hammond *1843
*Lowman Hawes *1831
*Alfredus McKinne Hobby
*Georgius Hooker, M.D. 1817 *1884
*Carolus Hopkins *1816
**Johannes Benedict Hoyt* *1862
**Hezekias Hull,* A.M. 1818 *1823
*Jedidias Huntington *1870
*Johannes Jarvis Ingersoll, M.D. Coll. Med et Chir. Nov. Ebor. 1817 *1830
*Carolus Jesup, A.M. *1837
*Johannes Kintzing Kane, A.M., Reip. Penns. Reb. Judic. Praefect., Rerumpubl Foed Cur. in Jurisd Penns. Jurid. *1858
*Carolus Jacobus Lanman *1870
*Johannes Law, A.M., Reip. Indian. Cur. Super. Jurid., e Congr. *1873
**Josua Leavitt,* A.M., S.T.D. Wabas. 1854 *1873
*Lucius Wooster Leffingwell, A.M. 1825 *1875
*Daniel Lord, A.M. 1820, LL.D 1846 *1868
*Johannes Erskine Lovett, A.M. 1831 *1847
*Whitman Mead, A.M *1833
*Johannes Daggett Meers *1877
*Anson Moody, M.D. 1840 *1855
*Guilielmus Johnson Rysam Mulford *1865
*Guilielmus Woolsey Mumford *1848

*Ebenezer Munger, A.M. *1857
*Fredericus Augustus Norton *1846
*Jesse Oakley *1848
**David Longworth Ogden*, A.M. *1863
*Jacobus Potter *1862
*Samuel Punderson, M.D. 1834 *1870
*Fredericus Allyn Richards *1846
*Abrahamus Topping Rose, A.M. *1857
**Isaacus Wakelee Ruggles* *1857
*Samuel Bulkley Ruggles, LL.D. 1859 *1881
*Ebenezer Seeley *1866
*Edvardus Petrus Simons *1823
*Guilielmus Smith *1839
*Georgius Evans Spruill, A.M. *1845
*Jacobus Landon Stark *1868
*Hemanus Stebbins *1838
**Josephus Clay Stiles*, S.T.D. Univ. Transylvan. 1846, LL.D. Univ. Georg. 1860 *1875
*Guilielmus Lucius Storrs, A.M., LL.D. Res. Occ. 1846, e Congr., Reip. Conn. Cur. Supr. Jurid. Princ., in Univ. Wesl. Jurispr. Prof., Jurispr. Prof. *1861
*Josephus Platt Taylor, A.M. *1825
*Johannes Titsworth, M.D. 1818, A.M. 1820 *1873
*Cornelius Tuthill, A.M. *1825
*Georgius Augustus Wasson *1849
*Johannes Bliss Watson, A.M. 1825 *1843
**Nathanael Sheldon Wheaton*, A.M., S.T.D. 1833 et Univ. Colb. 1832, Coll. Trin. Praeses *1862
**Thomas Scudder Wickes* *1876
**Leonardus Withington*, A.M. 1821, S.T.D. Bowd. 1850 *1825

Isaac Adriance, son of John Adriance, of Harlem, now a part of New York City, and grandson of Isaac Adriance, of Duchess County, was born in Harlem on

February 13, 1794. His mother was Mary, the only surviving child of John S. and Maria (Bussing) Sickels, of Harlem He was prepared for College by the Rev Daniel Smith (Yale 1791), of Stamford, Connecticut

After graduation he studied law in the office of Richard Riker, Recorder of the city of New York, and on his admission to the bar in 1817 he settled in Geneva, Ontario County, but returned within a year to his native place and practiced in New York through his life.

On December 28, 1830, he was married by the Rev Cornelius C Vermeule to Margaret E. McGown, of Harlem, who survived him with three of their four children A son was graduated at Williams College in 1855

He died in New York on August 26, 1862, in his 69th year

Mr. Adriance was zealously devoted to his profession, and conspicuously influential in the reform of municipal law and administration The city of New York was indebted to his sagacity and skill, in particular, for devising a new method for the taxation of real estate. His character was an effective compound of Dutch courage and firmness and New England enterprise and activity.

He edited anonymously the following

Conveyances on record in the Register's Office by Dudley Selden, from the 1st January, 1825, to the 1st January, 1838 N Y, 1838 8°, pp 175 + map (4 sheets). [*Columbia Univ*

With reference to the title to Harlem Commons

AUTHORITIES

J Adriance, MS Letter, July, 1863 56, 298, 420, 729, 795
Riker, Hist of Harlem, 2d ed, 155-

EDWARD ALLEN, son of Gabriel Allen, of the parish of Green's Farms, in Fairfield, Connecticut, was baptized on August 18, 1793, and entered College in the fall of 1811.

He remained in New Haven in 1814-15 as a graduate student, and then devoted himself to the law, and after his admission to the bar settled in practice in 1819 in Vernon, Oneida County, New York

On becoming a Christian about 1834 or 5, he relinquished his profession and studied for the ministry. He was ordained as an evangelist in 1836 by the Oneida Presbytery, and served several churches in Paris and vicinity in that county for ten years.

His health having failed, he removed in 1846 with his family to Fulton, Rock County, in southern Wisconsin, hoping to be able to undertake the pastorate of a church there; but after having preached for one Sunday, he fell ill, and died there on October 5, in his 54th year.

AUTHORITIES.

Albert G Allen, MS Letter, Dec, 1850 *Rev. D L. Ogden,* MS Letter, Dec, 1847 *Peet,* Churches and Ministers in Wisconsin, 84–85

THOMAS PINCKNEY ALSTON, son of Colonel William Alston, one of the largest slaveholders of South Carolina, and grandson of Joseph and Charlotte (Rothmahlar) Allston, was born on his paternal estate on the peninsula between the Waccamaw River and the ocean, opposite Georgetown, on April 19, 1795 His mother was Mary, daughter of Jacob and Rebecca (Brewton) Motte He was prepared for College by John Pierpont (Yale 1804), while a private tutor in the family A brother entered Yale with him, but did not graduate until 1815 Their eldest brother was Governor of South Carolina from 1812 to 1814, and the husband of Theodosia, daughter of Aaron Burr A sister married Senator and Governor Robert Y. Hayne.

He studied law after graduation in Charleston, and was admitted to the bar in 1817, but returned to his native parish and devoted himself to the occupations of the planter

He was married on May 20, 1820, by the Rev Dr Frederick Dalcho, to Jane Ladson, daughter of John

Rutledge and Susan Elizabeth (Ladson) Smith, of Charleston, by whom he had one son. She died on May 4, 1823, aged 23 years, and he was married on June 25, 1825, by the Rt. Rev. Nathaniel Bowen, to her sister, Susan Elizabeth Smith, who survived him. By her he had four sons, one of whom was killed in the Confederate service, and six daughters, two of whom died in infancy. The eldest daughter married Dr. James J. Waring (Yale 1850).

At the end of the year 1858 Colonel Alston removed his residence to Charleston, where he died on April 29, 1861, aged 66 years.

AUTHORITIES.

Groves, Alston Family, 79, 83–85.

Anson Seth Atwood, the eldest son of Nathan Atwood, of Woodbury and Watertown, Connecticut, and grandson of Deacon Nathan and Rhoda (Warner) Atwood, of Woodbury, was born in Woodbury on August 1, and baptized on October 17, 1790. His mother was Susanna, eldest daughter of Seth and Eunice (Root) Minor, of Woodbury. He came to College from Watertown.

After graduation he studied divinity chiefly under the direction of the Rev. Dr. David Porter, of Catskill, New York. He also taught a select school in Ashford, Connecticut.

After spending some time in missionary labor in central New York and northern Vermont, he was ordained and installed as pastor of the First Congregational Church in (South) Mansfield, Connecticut, on September 1, 1819.

He was married, on November 9, 1819, to Sarah, only daughter of Joseph Palmer, M.D. (honorary Yale 1816), of Ashford.

He retained his pastorate for nearly forty-three years, or until dismissed at his own request on April 22, 1862, on account of a failure of health. He then removed to East Hartford, where he died on July 22, 1866, at the age of 76; his wife had died on the 17th of the preceding May, in her 74th year

One of their three children survived him

Mr. Atwood was a man of great dignity of character and bearing, and greatly respected as a pastor. During his ministry a number of revivals visited his church, and 421 persons were added to its membership.

AUTHORITIES.

Cothren, Hist. of Woodbury, i, 494; iii, 172. *Glidden,* Centennial Discourse at Mansfield, 36–37

John Mulliken Atwood, the eldest son of Moses Atwood, an extensive merchant of Haverhill, Massachusetts, and grandson of Joseph and Sarah (Chresdee) Atwood, of Bradford, now Haverhill, was born on August 4, 1795. His mother was Mary (or Molly), youngest daughter of Deacon Thomas and Hannah (Stickney) Tenney, of Bradford, now Groveland. His father died in May, 1808 One of his sisters was Harriet Newell, the well-known missionary, of the others, one married the Rev. John B. Warren (Brown Univ 1815), another married the Rev. James Bates (Dartmouth Coll. 1822), and a third married the Rev. Aaron Warner (Williams Coll. 1815) A brother was graduated here in 1821

He studied law for one year in Haverhill, but then decided on a mercantile life. After a year's clerkship in Boston, he established himself in 1816 in Philadelphia, in partnership with a relative; and the firms of Atwood & Co., and Atwood, White & Co., became honored names in that city and among Western merchants. He withdrew from business in 1864, and died suddenly while on a visit at the house of his daughter, in Hartford, Connecticut, on May 29, 1873, in his 78th year.

He married on December 23, 1819, Henrietta Maria, daughter of Dr. William and Mary (Langdon) Coffin, of Gloucester, Massachusetts, who died on January 22, 1852, in her 54th year. Their children were three daughters and two sons; Atwood Collins (Yale 1873) is a grandson.

Mr. Atwood gave much of his time to public interests, and his name was connected with many efforts for the advancement of religion, knowledge, and charity. He was one of the founders of the American Sunday School Union, and on its committee of publication for over forty years. He had a fine literary taste, wide knowledge, and the pen of a ready writer. He was one of the founders, and for fifteen years President of the Merchants' Fund, a charity for relieving decayed merchants. As a man he was greatly beloved.

AUTHORITIES.

Atwood Family, 1888, 27. Haverhill Vital Records, i, 15. Tenney Family, 80.

ELISHA AVERILL, the ninth of twelve children of Colonel Perry and Dorothy (Whittlesey) Averill, of New Preston Society, in Washington, Connecticut, and grandson of Samuel and Patience (Perry) Averill, of New Preston, was born on April 30, 1792. He was a first cousin of Elisha D. Whittlesey (Yale 1811), and was prepared for College by his pastor, the Rev. Samuel Whittelsey (Yale 1803).

He studied law after graduation, and entered on practice in New York in 1817; but died at his father's house, in New Preston, of pulmonary consumption, on June 7, 1824, in his 33d year. He was never married.

AUTHORITIES.

Cothren, Hist. of Woodbury, i, 487. Whittlesey Genealogy, 1898, 81.

WILLIAM RUFUS BABBITT entered College at the opening of the Sophomore year from Huntington, Connecticut. He was prepared for admission by the Rev Dr. David Ely (Yale 1769), of Huntington.

He studied law after graduation, and in the fall of 1816 settled in Salem, in Washington County, southern Indiana, where he had attained to cheering prospects of success. He died, however, in Salem, from typhus fever, on August 21, 1817, aged about 24 years. He was not married.

AUTHORITIES.

Columbian Register, Oct 11, 1817. Conn. Journal, Oct. 14, 1817.

GEORGE BELDEN entered College at the opening of the Sophomore year from Carmel, in what is now Putnam County, New York. He was prepared by Daniel H. Barnes (Union Coll 1809).

He became a banker and broker in New York City, where he died in the early part of 1855, aged about 60 years.

AMZI BENEDICT, the youngest son of Deacon Isaac Benedict, of New Canaan, Connecticut, and grandson of Deacon Nathaniel and Mary (Lockwood) Benedict, of Norwalk, was born in New Canaan on May 19, 1791. His mother was Jane, daughter of Samuel Raymond, of Norwalk. He was intending to be a physician; but on becoming a Christian at the age of 18, he turned his attention to College and the ministry.

The year after graduation he spent in teaching, and he then took the three years' course in the Andover Theological Seminary.

On September 24, 1818, he was ordained as a home missionary by the Presbytery of Londonderry in Newburyport, Massachusetts, and the next two years were spent in that service. For two or three years more he found temporary employment in teaching or preaching; thus, during the last months of 1823 he was supplying the pulpit in Salisbury, Connecticut.

Late in March, 1824, he began to supply the Congregational Church in Vernon, Connecticut, and was called to the pastorate on May 19. His installation followed on June 24, and on the 5th of the following October he was married to Martha S., daughter of General Solomon Cowles, of Farmington.

On February 10, 1830, he was dismissed from his charge at Vernon, and on October 19, 1831, he was installed over the Congregational Church in Pomfret. A deep and powerful revival was experienced during his short pastorate there, which was terminated on July 15, 1834. He had received seventy-seven members into the church.

On December 6, 1837, he was installed over a New School Presbyterian Church in Manlius Centre, Onondaga County, New York, and remained there for four years; during that time a powerful revival of religion was experienced among the youth of the place.

He was then occupied in teaching in Farmington and in New Haven, and in preaching as he found opportunity. Thus, he supplied the pulpit of the Second Congregational Church in Norwich, in 1845–46, during the protracted absence of the pastor, the Rev. Dr. Bond.

In the spring of 1855 he took charge of a small Independent Society in Yorktown, Westchester County, New York, where he labored with much satisfaction, until he received an injury from a railroad engine at Stamford, Connecticut, in consequence of which he died, three weeks later, at the house of his eldest daughter, in Brooklyn, New York, on November 17, 1856, aged 75½ years.

His wife survived him, with two daughters and two sons, another daughter having died in infancy. The eldest daughter married Professor Joseph C. Hutchison, M.D. (Univ. Penns. 1848).

He published:

1. A Biblical Trinity. By Theophilus. Hartford, 1850. 12°, pp. 8, xxxvii, 15–332. [*Y. C.*

An original and novel explanation of the Trinity.

2. Ministerial support. A Sermon from I Cor. ix, 13–14, Gal. vi, 6–7, Luke xxi, 1–4. In the *American National Preacher,* vol. 29, pp. 129–40 (June, 1855).

AUTHORITIES.

Benedict Genealogy, 75, 122–23. Congregational Quarterly, ii, 379. Congregational Year Book, 1857, 88–89. *Hunt,* Hist. of Pomfret, 17–18. The Independent, Nov. 27, 1856. 150th Anniversary of Pomfret Church, 34–35. *T. Robbins,* Diary, i, 969–70.

Archibald Burgess, the sixth child of Asa and Sarah (Miles) Burgess, of Westminster Society, in Canterbury, Connecticut, and grandson of Joseph and Mehitable (Shepherd) Burgess, of Canterbury, was born on February 4, 1790, and was prepared for the Sophomore Class by his pastor, the Rev. Erastus Learned. A brother was graduated in 1818.

He studied theology, and was licensed to preach by the Windham Association of Ministers on May 16, 1821.

He was called on November 4, 1822, to the pastorate of the Congregational Church in Hancock, New Hampshire, and accepted the call on November 16. His ordination and installation took place on December 25, and his strong and useful ministry continued for twenty-seven years.

On October 7, 1824, he was married to Maria Georgianna, daughter of Elihu Blake, of Westborough, Massachusetts, and a sister of the wife of the Rev. Zedekiah S. Barstow (Yale 1813), of Keene, about fifteen miles west of Hancock, who preached the sermon at his ordination.

She died on August 25, 1841, at the age of 40; and he next married on June 20, 1843, Elizabeth F., daughter of Luther and Elizabeth (Fay) Chamberlain, of Westborough.

The failure of his health obliged him to take a dismission, on December 18, 1849, and after a lingering illness he died from paralysis in Hancock on February 7, 1850, at the age of 60.

His widow died in Westborough in February, 1878, in her 73d year.

By his first marriage he had four daughters and five sons. One daughter and one son died in infancy. The youngest daughter married the Rev. John Thompson (Univ. Mich. 1865). By his second marriage he had two sons.

His portrait is given in the *History of Hancock*. He was in every way a strong man, of commanding presence, impressive manner in the pulpit, and scholarly tastes.

AUTHORITIES.

Burgess Genealogy, 64, 125. *Hayward*, Hist. of Hancock, 21, 35–36, 194–98, 410–13. *Lawrence*, N. Hampshire Churches, 179. Westborough Vital Records, 134.

William Barron Calhoun, the eldest child of Andrew Calhoun, a Scotch merchant of Boston, and of Martha (Chamberlain) Calhoun, was born in Boston on December 29, 1795. A brother was graduated at Williams College in 1829, and became a well-known missionary. The father was one of the founders of the Park Street Church. The son's patronymic was written Colhoun while he was in College. He was prepared for Yale by William Wells (Harvard 1796). In his Senior year he was one of the editors of the *Athenæum*, a short-lived students' periodical. After graduation he began to read law in Concord, New Hampshire, where his father was then living, and later continued his studies for three years with the Hon George Bliss (Yale 1784), in Springfield, Massachusetts, where he opened an office in 1822.

He was not, however, most successful as a practicing lawyer, but the sterling qualities of his character were soon appreciated, and from 1825 to 1835 he was a member of the State Legislature, and Speaker of the House in 1828, 1829, 1830, 1832, and 1833; in 1829 he received the unprecedented tribute of a unanimous election.

In 1834 he was elected to Congress as a Whig, and he remained in office from 1835 to 1843. But his vigor began to be impaired from the inroads of consumption, catarrh, and dyspepsia, and largely for this reason he declined further re-election.

In the meantime he was married, on May 11, 1837, to Margaret Howard, eldest daughter of Dr. Samuel and Jemima (Chapin, Lyman) Kingsbury, of Springfield.

He was a Presidential Elector for Henry Clay in 1844. In 1846 he was elected to the State Senate as an anti-war Whig, and he presided over that body for two years.

He was then Secretary of the Commonwealth from January, 1848 to 1851, and bank commissioner from 1853 to 1855.

In 1858 he received the honorary degree of Doctor of Laws from Amherst College, of which he was a Trustee from 1829 to his death.

In 1859 he was mayor of Springfield, and in 1861, for his last public service, was again a member of the State Legislature.

His later years were an almost constant struggle with disease, and were spent largely in retirement on his farm.

He died in Springfield on November 8, 1865, aged nearly 70 years.

His widow died on May 7, 1877, at the age of 66

His children, one daughter and two sons, all survived him.

His portrait is given in Chapin's *Old Springfield.*

He was the soul of uprightness in all public and private relations. In his last years he was much gratified by an election to the office of Deacon in the First Congregational Church.

He was much interested in the improvement of public education. He was the chairman of the convention in Boston at which the American Institute of Instruction was organized in 1830, and after serving that body as Vice President for three years, was its President from 1833 to 1849.

He published:

1. An Address delivered in Springfield, July 4, 1825, in Commemoration of American Independence. Springfield, 1825. 8°, pp. 26. [*M. H. S. Y. C.*

Adapted to a half-century celebration.

2. Abstract of a Lecture upon the "Duties of School Committees": delivered . . . August, 1832. In *S. R. Hall's* Lectures to School-masters, on Teaching. 4th edition. Boston, 1833. 12°.

3. Addresses at the Dedication of the new Cabinet and Observatory of Amherst College, June 28, 1848. By Hon. William B. Calhoun and others. Amherst, 1848. 8°, pp. 9–22. [*U. S.*

4. Recollections of the Rev. Dr. William B. O. Peabody, in Sprague's *Annals of the American Pulpit,* vol. 8, pp. 501–03.

He was also for many years a valued editorial contributor to the *Springfield Republican* newspaper.

AUTHORITIES.

Amer. Journal of Education, xv, 212. *Bates,* Address at Dedication of Court House, 68–69. Boston, Record Commissioners' Reports, xxiv, 343. *Chapin,* Old Springfield, 123–27. *Green,* Hist. of Springfield, 380–81, 393–96, 398, 425–26, 443, 458, 461, 463–64, 494. Kingsbury Family, 311, 400.

Charles William Capers, a scion of the Capers family of St. Helena Island, South Carolina, came to College from New York City. He was prepared at the

Hopkins Grammar School in New Haven by Elizur Goodrich, Junior (Williams Coll. 1806).

After graduation he studied medicine in New York and at the South Carolina Medical College, receiving from the latter the degree of M.D.

He settled on his family plantation, about five miles south of Beaufort, and was at one time a member of the State Senate.

He died on St. Helena Island on June 24, 1835, aged 41 years.

Henry Dwight Chapin, the only surviving child of Jason Chapin of Wilbraham, Massachusetts, and a first cousin of Judge Moses Chapin (Yale 1811), was born in Wilbraham in 1794. His mother was Rachel, eldest child of Ebenezer and Rachel (Wright) Holman, of East Windsor, Connecticut. His father died in December, 1800. He was prepared for College by his pastor, the Rev. Ezra Witter (Yale 1793).

After graduation he studied law, and settled for practice in Prince George's County, Maryland, going thence to Baltimore, where he resided for many years. About 1844 he removed to New York City. In 1849 he retired to a country residence in Flushing, Long Island, where he died on July 14, 1862, in his 69th year. He was never married.

AUTHORITIES.

Chapin Genealogy, 46. Dwight Family, i, 355.

Donald Chester, the second son of Stephen Chester (Yale 1780), of Wethersfield, Connecticut, was born in Wethersfield on July 25, 1795.

He became a merchant in Baltimore, and in the prosecution of his business made several voyages round Cape Horn.

He died in Baltimore on September 29, 1835, in his 41st year. He was never married.

AUTHORITIES.

N. E. Hist. and Geneal. Register, xxii, 342. *Stiles,* Hist. of Wethersfield, ii, 217. *Tillotson,* Wethersfield Inscriptions, 39.

RICHARD PETER CHRISTOPHERS, son of Peter Christophers, of New London, Connecticut, and grandson of John and Jerusha (Gardiner) Christophers, of New London, was born on January 7, 1793. His mother was Rebecca, daughter of Winthrop Saltonstall (Yale 1756), of New London. He was prepared for College by the Rev. Abel McEwen (Yale 1804).

He studied medicine after graduation, and in the fall of 1815 emigrated to the Western Reserve of Ohio, settling at first in Huron, in Erie County.

In the winter of 1817–18 he was in Perkins, Mahoning County, and was engaged in school-teaching, as well as in the practice of his profession.

He finally settled in 1824 or 1825 in New London, Huron County, where he was highly esteemed.

He died in New London, much lamented, in 1829, in his 37th year.

He was of diminutive stature and decrepit frame, but universally respected as an honest, Christian gentleman.

He married a Miss Chapman, after arriving in Ohio.

AUTHORITIES.

Fire Lands Pioneer, vi, 11–14; x, 26; New Series, xvii, 488. *Williams,* Hist. of the Fire Lands, 372.

THEODORE CLAPP, a son of Deacon Thaddeus and Achsah (Parsons) Clapp, of Easthampton, Massachusetts, and grandson of Captain Joseph and Hannah (Lyman) Clapp, of Easthampton, was born on March 29, 1792. A brother was graduated at Williams College in 1835; Sumner G. Clapp (Yale 1822) was a first cousin

In the fall of 1810 he entered the Sophomore Class of Williams College, and a year later transferred his relation to Yale, but on account of health was absent for the most of the ensuing year, and thus dropped into the next class.

He graduated with the expectation of studying law in Litchfield, but his plans finally changed from the effect of the mortal illness of his classmate Hopkins

During the winter after graduation he taught school in South Hadley, and in the fall of 1815 he began the study of theology in Schenectady, New York, where he spent a year,—for the first half-year under the direction of Professor Andrew Yates (Yale 1794), and for the second, under President Nott. He next spent about six weeks with the Rev. Evan Johns, M A. (honorary Yale 1809), of Canandaigua, for instruction in Hebrew; and then entered the Seminary at Andover.

At the close of his first year there he accepted the offer of a place as private tutor in Lexington, Kentucky, with the expectation of resuming his work in Andover.

On his way to Kentucky he was licensed to preach, in October, 1817, by the Hampshire Association of Congregational ministers.

After a year and a half of employment in Lexington, he went in May, 1819, to Louisville, where he occupied himself in teaching a small school, and in preaching as opportunity offered

He went thence at the close of 1821 to New Orleans, where he was engaged to preach for a few weeks in the pulpit of the First Presbyterian Church, which had been vacated by the death of the Rev. Sylvester Larned, a former classmate of his at Williams College. He began preaching there on February 24, 1822, and in March he was unanimously called to be their stated supply He accepted the call, in the spring came north, and was married in Louisville, on May 31, to Adeline Hawes, who was originally from Boston. On September 12 he was ordained in his native town by the Hampshire Association.

He then returned to New Orleans, and began his ministry. In October, 1823, he was received as a member of the Presbytery of Mississippi.

Notwithstanding his eloquence in the pulpit and his devotion to duty in times of epidemic, he soon fell under suspicion for lack of conformity to Presbyterian standards, and after a series of complaints of his orthodoxy, the Presbytery finally proceeded to his trial in 1832, and deposed him from the ministry in January, 1833.

A majority of his parishioners supported him in forming an Independent Unitarian Society, of which he should be pastor. A church building was provided for him by Judah Touro, a wealthy Jew, who when this was burned in 1851, provided another temporary house.

In November, 1846, he was stricken with a dangerous illness, and after his convalescence he went abroad, in April, 1847, for a long rest. A new church was built for him, and finished in 1855, but his health only allowed him to preach in it for a short time.

He resigned his pastorate in 1857, on account of illness, and spent the rest of his life mostly in retirement in Louisville, Kentucky, where he died on May 17, 1866, in his 75th year.

His wife survived him with two of their four sons. Two daughters died in infancy from cholera.

His portrait is given in the *Clapp Family Memorial.*

He published:

1. Slavery: a Sermon [from I Tim. vi, 1–5], delivered in the First Congregational Church in New Orleans, April 15, 1838. New Orleans, 1838. 8°, pp. 67.
[*B. Ath. B. Publ. Harv. U. S. Y. C.*

2. A Discourse [from I Cor. xv, 22] delivered in Philadelphia. July 18, 1854, at the Funeral of the late Henry D. Richardson, of New Orleans. Boston, 1854. 8°, pp. 18. [*Harv.*

3. A Discourse [from Luke xv, 7, 10], delivered in the First Congregational Church, New Orleans, La. [on Christian Sympathy Angelic]. Appended to *J B Ferguson*, Spirit Communion. Nashville, 1855. 8°, pp. 12. [*B. Publ.*

4 Autobiographical Sketches and Recollections, during a thirty-five years' residence in New Orleans. Boston, 1857 12°, pp viii, 419.

[*A A S B Publ Br. Mus Harv. M H S U S Y. C.*

Several editions.

The book cannot be relied on as an accurate or consecutive compilation.

5 Theological Views, comprising the Substance of Teachings during a ministry of thirty-five years in New Orleans. Boston, 1859 12°, pp. 355. [*B. Publ. Harv*

In part a reproduction of sermons published in the New Orleans Picayune from 1849.

The following volume, issued by himself, also contains large contributions from him.

6. A Report of the Trial of the Rev Theodore Clapp, before the Mississippi Presbytery, at their sessions in May and December 1832 New Orleans, 1833. 8°, pp. xiv, 374.

[*Br. Mus. U. S. Y. C*

AUTHORITIES

E Clapp, Clapp Memorial, 77, 86–87, 347–48. *T Clapp,* Autobiographical Sketches *Lyman,* Hist of East-hampton, 148. *Sparks,* Memories of Fifty Years, 451–59

NATHANIEL COLES, son of General Nathaniel Coles, of West Island, near Dosoris, in the town of Oyster Bay, Long Island, and grandson of Nathaniel and Hannah (Butler) Coles, of Dosoris, was probably born in 1794 His mother was Elizabeth, daughter of James and Free-love (Wilmot) Townsend, of Oyster Bay. A sister married John N. Lloyd (Yale 1802), and a first cousin, Oliver Coles, was graduated here in 1823. He was prepared for

College by Matthew R. Dutton (Yale 1808) in Fairfield, Connecticut.

After graduation he studied law, and was admitted to the bar, but instead of engaging in practice he devoted himself to the care of his father's extensive landed and milling interests.

He died in New York City in May, 1843, in his 49th year. He was never married.

AUTHORITIES.

Cole Genealogies, 98. Townsend Brothers' Memorial, 162.

JAMES COOLEY, the eldest child of Calvin Cooley, of Longmeadow, Massachusetts, and grandson of Stephen and Mary (Field) Cooley, of Longmeadow, was born on April 7, 1791. His mother was Eunice, youngest child of Hezekiah and Mary (Hitchcock) Warriner, of West Springfield. He was prepared for College by Levi Collins (Yale 1802) at the Monson Academy.

After graduation he studied law in Springfield for a year, and then removed to Urbana, Champaign County, Illinois, where he completed his studies, was admitted to the bar, and settled in practice. In November, 1826, he was sent by Henry Clay, then Secretary of State, to Peru as *Chargé d'affaires*.

He died in Lima, after four days' illness, on February 24, 1828, in his 37th year.

He married, in 1823, Jeannette, eldest daughter of Abraham and Deborah (Fowler) Chittenden, of Guilford, Connecticut.

They had no children.

Mrs. Cooley married, in Carthage, Illinois, in June, 1837, Jonathan Ely (Union Coll. 1821), of South Hadley, Massachusetts, who died in Cincinnati in June, 1847. She next married, in November, 1860, Robert Neil, of Columbus, Ohio, and she died in Urbana, Ohio, on July 12, 1899, in her 93d year.

AUTHORITIES

J. Q Adams, Diary, vii, 166, viii, 17 Chittenden Family, 146, 198. *Miss M. B Cooley,* MS Letters, 1911 Longmeadow Centennial, 308, liv Nathaniel Ely's Descendants, 102. National Intelligencer, May 29, 1828

ALEXANDER COPLAND entered the Sophomore Class in 1811 from Richmond, Virginia.

He studied medicine, and settled in practice in Muskingum County, Ohio, and is said to have died in Zanesville in that county on June 19, 1841, aged about 45 years.

He was married.

JAMES HAMILTON COUPER was born in Sunbury, Liberty County, Georgia, on March 5, 1794. His residence while in College was St. Simon's Island, about thirty miles south of Sunbury. At the age of nine he was sent to school in New Haven, and five years later was transferred to St. Mary's College, a Roman Catholic institution in Baltimore, whence he came to Yale at the opening of the Sophomore year.

He spent a year at home after graduation, and in 1815 went to Europe for study and travel On his return he settled on his plantation, near the mouth of the Altamaha River, in Glynn County, with his summer residence about fifteen miles distant on St. Simon's Island.

He was married early to a Miss Wylie, of that vicinity.

His plantations were models of good government; Sir Charles Lyell, in the account of his visit to the United States in 1846, describes them with high praise.

He labored, not without success, to improve the cultivation of cotton and rice. He engaged in the experiment of pressing oil from cotton seed, but abandoned it after a year's trial

He was one of the contractors for the construction of the Brunswick Canal, between the Altamaha and Turtle rivers, in 1838-39, and his scientific knowledge preserved large numbers of fossils then unearthed, which he presented to public institutions.

He was a man of varied culture, and his private library was one of the largest in the South. Christ Church, Savannah, which was built after his plans in 1838, is a monument of his taste and skill in architecture.

The honorary degree of Doctor of Laws was given him by Mercer University in 1848.

He preferred to keep aloof from public life, and on only two occasions did he consent to assume office. One of these was when, in consequence of an effort to defeat the collection of debts, the office of Sheriff of Glynn County had become difficult and dangerous, and he accepted and executed it. Again, during the excitement on Nullification, he helped as a delegate to the Georgia Convention, to defeat the plan of disunion. He was also opposed to the movement for secession, and during the Civil War lived in close seclusion, on the confines of Florida.

On the close of the war, he returned to his home, but failed gradually, and died at his temporary residence, Carteret's Point, Georgia, on July 3, 1866, in his 73d year.

His wife survived him, with two daughters and three sons. A son who was graduated here in 1849 died before his father. All his sons were in the Confederate service.

AUTHORITIES.

Lyell, Second Visit to U. S., i, 327–61.

Austin Denny, the second son of Daniel Denny, of Worcester, Massachusetts, and grandson of Colonel Samuel and Elizabeth (Henshaw) Denny, of Leicester, was born in Worcester on December 31, 1795. His mother was Nancy, daughter of Matthew and Mary (Taylor)

Watson, of Leicester. He was prepared for the Sophomore Class by Josiah Clark (Williams 1809).

An accident at an early age occasioned painful attacks of rheumatism, which finally brought him to a premature grave His malady deprived him of the use of his right arm, and made walking difficult. He began the study of law with the Hon. Nathaniel Paine (Harvard 1775), of Worcester, and in December, 1817, was admitted to the bar, and began practice in Harvard, Worcester County. In 1819 he returned to Worcester.

He was the editor of the *Massachusetts Spy* until September, 1823, when he established another weekly newspaper, the *Massachusetts Yeoman,* in the interest of the Anti-Masonic movement, of which he continued to be the proprietor and conductor until his death, in Worcester, on July 1, 1830, in his 35th year.

He married on May 22, 1823, Amelia, daughter of Elijah and Elizabeth Burbank, of Worcester, by whom he had three sons and a daughter.

The *History of Worcester* says of him:

> He was a well-read lawyer, industrious and faithful in the transaction of business, and a vigorous and able writer. 'Of his intellectual powers,' says one who knew him well, 'the distinguishing feature was clearness and strength of comprehension. His views were distinct, his knowledge exact, his reasonings just and candid, his expressions forcible and pertinent.'

AUTHORITIES

Denny Family, 101, 132–33 *Lincoln,* Hist of Worcester, 208–09, 278–79 *Wall,* Reminiscences of Worcester, 313–14

JOHN DICKSON, elder son of Samuel and Mary (Neilson) Dickson, of Charleston, South Carolina, was born in Charleston on November 4, 1795. Both parents were strict Presbyterians, of Scottish descent, and emigrated from Belfast, Ireland, before the Revolution. The father was a schoolmaster by profession, but his sons were prepared for the Sophomore Class at Yale by Dr. Mackay.

After graduation he engaged in teaching, in Columbia and Charleston, and also studied theology, partly in private, and for one year (1820–21) in the Andover Seminary

He then returned to his native State, and while teaching in Charleston was made Professor of Languages in the College of Charleston in 1823, but was transferred the next year to the chair of Moral Philosophy, which he held until 1827 or 8.

He had already married on October 18, 1821, Mary Augusta, only daughter of the Rev. Dr. Andrew Flinn (Univ. N. C 1799) and Martha Henrietta (Walker) Flinn, of Charleston.

He was ordained to the ministry in Charleston on March 20, 1825, by the Charleston Union Presbytery, but the state of his health prevented his accepting a pastorate.

He supplied many churches in Charleston,—especially the Third Presbyterian, the First Baptist, and the Mariners' Churches,—but finally, on account of the unsatisfactory condition of his health, from weakness of the lungs, he gave up both preaching and teaching, studied medicine with his brother, and retired in 1832 to the table land of western North Carolina, where he spent the rest of his life, mainly in the vicinity of Flatrock and Asheville, practicing medicine, and to some extent still engaged in the business of instruction. He founded in Asheville both a Male and a Female Seminary, and died there on September 28, 1847, in his 52d year.

After the death of his first wife he was married, on March 26, 1839, in Charleston, to Louisa, daughter of James and Louisa O'Hear.

By his first marriage he had one daughter and five sons; by his second marriage a son and a daughter. His eldest son was graduated at Yale in 1845.

His life was one of simple piety, austere integrity, and obedience to duty. He was a constant student, greatly beloved and long remembered by his pupils.

He published:

1. The Mocking Bird. In blank verse. In the *Microscope,* vol. 2, pp. 135–36, New Haven, August 11, 1820.

2. Notices of the Mineralogy and Geology of parts of South and North Carolina. In the *American Journal of Science and Arts,* vol. 3, pp. 1–5 (February, 1821).

3. The essentials of Religion, briefly considered in Ten Discourses. Charleston, 1827. 12°, pp. 207.

[*A. C. A. U. T. S. Y. C.*

Published in June, 1827, under the conviction that his pulpit (and all literary) labors were ended, from the condition of his health.

AUTHORITIES.

Miss Henrietta Dickson, MS. Letter, October, 1911. *Sprague,* Annals of the Amer. Pulpit, iv, 277.

Samuel Henry Dickson, the only brother of the preceding graduate, was born in Charleston on September 20, 1798, and entered Yale with his brother in 1811.

In December, 1814, he began the study of medicine with Dr. Philip G. Prioleau, of Charleston, in whose office he remained for over four years, though in the mean time attending two courses of lectures in the University of Pennsylvania, and receiving there the degree of M.D. in the spring of 1819. His practical experience dated from 1817, when, during the prevalence of yellow fever in Charleston, he took an active part in its mastery. The personal interest thus aroused led him to select Yellow Fever as the subject of his thesis in Philadelphia.

In July, 1819, he entered on the duties of his profession in Charleston, and was at once appointed assistant to Joseph Glover, M.D. (Univ. Penns. 1800), of the Yellow Fever Hospital,—of which, as well as of the Marine Hospital, circumstances gave him the entire charge, though only twenty-one years of age.

His practice grew rapidly, and, until he abandoned it, continued to be overwhelming, taxing seriously both time and health. His income grew large, and he found it necessary to call into association with him two younger physicians for several years His visiting-list of patients numbered at one time as many as eighty-three in a single day.

Soon after his medical graduation he had formed the purpose of founding a medical school in Charleston; and in 1822-23, when only twenty-four, he began a course of lectures on physiology and pathology to a class of about thirty city students. This led him, in conjunction with Drs. Ramsay and Frost, to the establishment in Charleston, in 1824, of a Medical College in which he became Professor of the Institutes and Practice of Medicine

In consequence of a controversy with the Medical Society, he resigned his chair in 1832, but with other physicians of distinction he founded in 1833 another institution—the Medical College of South Carolina—which became entirely successful. His position here was the same as in the former case, and he only relinquished it in 1847, when he accepted the chair of Practice in the Medical Department of the New York University, where he remained for three winters.

In 1850 he received an urgent invitation to return to his old chair and to his extensive practice in Charleston This he accepted, partly for reasons of health, and on his arrival he received an ovation at a public dinner from professional and other friends The honorary degree of Doctor of Laws was conferred on him by the New York University in 1853

On the death, in April, 1858, of Dr. John K. Mitchell, Professor of Practice in the Jefferson Medical College of Philadelphia, who had always been a warm personal friend, he was called to the vacant chair, and continued to lecture until within a month of his death; he was said never to have lectured with more spirit and earnestness or with more satisfaction to his auditors than during his last course, although hampered by continual ill-health. His health had always been poor. While at Yale an inflammation of the stomach left him with impaired digestion, and for many years from 1825 he suffered from phthisis and large hemorrhages from the lungs, from which he did not recover until after a European tour. As far back as 1837 began the obscure and painful abdominal trouble (a tumor over the aorta), from which he suffered, at times agonizingly, until his death, in Philadelphia, on March 31, 1872, in his 74th year.

In spite of all drawbacks Dr. Dickson was a man of wonderful industry. His reading was as varied as it was incessant, embracing not only every phase of medical literature, but all other kinds of books. He was also a voluminous and very ready writer. Besides the books which he published, he made numerous contributions to medical and literary journals, and delivered a large number of addresses. He was an active member of all the scientific, historical, and literary bodies in his native city, and of similar societies elsewhere. He had a wide acquaintance among the literary men of his time, and in particular may be mentioned his intimate friendship with William Cullen Bryant. His religious views were those of the Unitarians.

As a lecturer he was remarkably clear and eloquent; as an author, brilliant and refined; as a medical adviser, full of kindly sympathy and clear judgment. His friends also cherished him for his cheerfulness and geniality, his fortitude and conscientiousness, his frankness and courtesy. In addition to the professorships held by him, he was offered chairs in Lexington, Nashville, Richmond, and Augusta.

He was three times married: first, to Elizabeth Brownlee, daughter of Samuel and Ann (Thomas) Robertson, of Charleston, and sister of Dr. John B. Robertson (Yale 1829), who died in 1832; in 1834 to Jane Robertson

Robertson, a sister of his former wife, who died in 1842; and in 1845 to Marie Seabrook DuPré, also of Charleston, who died in 1873. Of his sons only two reached maturity; the elder died from fever while serving as a volunteer in the Palmetto regiment in the Mexican War, and the younger became a surgeon in the United States navy.

Dr. Dickson had also a large family of daughters; three of these are still living, one of whom has attained distinction as a writer. He made them friends and companions, sharing with them his knowledge and his vivid interest in the events and discoveries of the day.

The epitaph upon his tombstone, in Woodlawn Cemetery, Philadelphia, written by his warm friend, William Cullen Bryant, describes him as "An eminent teacher of the Medical Art; able, learned, and eloquent; of a spotless life and of frank and engaging manners, warmly sympathetic, nobly disinterested, and inflexibly just."

He published:

1. Introductory Lecture, delivered at the Commencement of the Second Session of the Medical College of South Carolina—November, 1825. Charleston, 1826. 8°, pp. 31. [*M. H. S.*

On medical education.

2. Address before the South-Carolina Society for the Promotion of Temperance, April 6th, 1830 .... Charleston, 1830. 8°, pp. 72. [*A. A. S. B. Publ. M. H. S. U. S. Y. C.*

The Address occupies pp. 1–30; the author was the first person south of Mason and Dixon's line to deliver a Temperance address and to establish a society which was to use no distilled liquors.

3. An Address delivered before the Horticultural Society of Charleston, at the Anniversary Meeting, July 11th, 1832. Charleston, 1832. 8°, pp. 18. [*M. H. S.*

4. Syllabus prepared for the use of the class, by S. Henry Dickson, M.D., Professor of the Institutes and Practice of Medicine in the Medical College of the State of South-Carolina. Charleston, 1834. 8°, pp. 179. [*Surg. Gen'l's. Office. Y. C.*

The same. Charleston, 1835. 8°, pp. 196.
[*Surg. Gen'l's. Office. Y. C.*

5. Introductory Lecture delivered at the opening of the Medical College of the State of So. Ca. November 12th, 1838. Charleston, 1838. 8°, pp. 26. [*Surg. Gen'l's. Office. Y. C.*

6. On Dengue: its history, pathology, and treatment. Philadelphia, 1838. 8°, pp. 23. [*Surg. Gen'l's. Office.*

Same. Philadelphia, 1839. 8°, pp. 23.
[*B. Publ. Surg. Gen'l's. Office. Y. C.*

7. Manual of Pathology and Practice, being the outline of the course of lectures delivered in the Medical College of the State of South Carolina. Charleston, 1839. 8°, pp. 204. [*U. S.*

The same. Charleston, 1842. 8°, pp. 240.
[*Surg. Gen'l's. Office. Y. C.*

The same. New York, 1850. 8°, pp. 251.
[*Surg. Gen'l's. Office. U. S.*

8. Address delivered at the opening of the new edifice of the Charleston Apprentices' Library Society on the evening of the 13th January, 1841. Charleston, 1841. 8°, pp. 37. [*U. S.*

9. Annual Report to the President and Board of Trustees of the Medical College of the State of South-Carolina. With the Valedictory Address to the Class. Charleston, 1841. 8°, pp. 12.
[*Surg. Gen'l's. Office. Y. C.*

10. An Oration delivered at New Haven, before the Phi Beta Kappa Society, August 17, 1842. New Haven, 1842. 8°, pp. 47.
[*B. Ath. B. Publ. Br. Mus. Columbia Univ. Harv. M. H. S. Y. C.*

On the question, whether knowledge leads to happiness. Dr. Dickson was not a member of the Society while a student, but was afterwards complimented with honorary membership.

11. Remarks on certain topics connected with the general subject of Slavery .. Charleston, 1845. 8°, pp. 35.
[*A. C. A. B. Publ. Harv. N. Y. Publ.*

Consisting of two articles: 1, Slavery in the French Colonies, from the *Southern Literary Messenger,* May, 1844; 2, Reply to letter of Dr. W. B. Carpenter, published (in part) in the *Christian Examiner,* October, 1844.

12. Essays on Pathology and Therapeutics. Charleston, 1845. 2 vols. 8°, pp. 588; 651. [*Surg. Gen'l's. Office.*

13. Introductory Lecture, read at the Commencement of the Course. Monday, November 9th, 1846. Charleston, 1846. 8°, pp. 35. [*B. Publ. Y. C.*

14. A Lecture introductory to the course on the Theory and Practice of Medicine, in the University of New York. New York, 1847. 8°, pp. 19.
[*B. Ath. B. Publ. M. H. S. Surg. Gen'l's. Office. Y. C.*

15. Hygiene; an Introductory Lecture, delivered at the New York University—Medical Department. New York, 1848. 8°, pp. 24. [*Surg. Gen'l's. Office.*

16. Lecture introductory to the course on the Institutes and Practice of Medicine in the Medical College of the State of South-Carolina. Charleston, 1850. 8°, pp. 24.
[*Surg. Gen'l's. Office. Y. C.*

17. Asylums for the Insane. Observations upon the importance of establishing public hospitals for the Insane of the middle and higher classes .. London, 1852. 12°, pp. 62.
[*Surg. Gen'l's. Office.*

18. Essays on Life, Sleep, Pain, etc. Philadelphia, 1852. 8°, pp. 301. [*B. Publ. Br. Mus. Surg. Gen'l's. Office.*

19. Medical Progress, a Lecture introductory to the course on the Institutes and Practice of Medicine. Charleston, 1854. 8°, pp. 23. [*Surg. Gen'l's. Office.*

20. Speech delivered (in substance) at the dinner of the New England Society of Charleston, S. C., on their Anniversary, Dec. 22, 1854. Charleston, 1855. 8°, pp. 15. [*Harv. Y. C.*

21. Elements of Medicine: a compendious view of Pathology and Therapeutics; or the History and Treatment of Diseases. Philadelphia, 1855. 8°, pp. 753.
[*Br. Mus. Surg. Gen'l's. Office. U. S. Y. C.*

The same. Second edition. Philadelphia, 1859. 8°, pp. 768.
[*Surg. Gen'l's. Office. Y. C.*

22. Address, delivered at the Inauguration of the Public School, Fourth of July, 1856. Charleston, 1856. 8°, pp. 24. [*Harv.*

23. Lecture introductory to the course of Institutes and Practice of Medicine in the Medical College of the State of South Carolina. Charleston, 1856. 8°, pp. 19. [*Surg. Gen'l's. Office.*

24. The late Prof. J. K. Mitchell, M.D. Inaugural Lecture to the course on the Practice of Medicine, in the Jefferson Medical College of Philadelphia, delivered October 12, 1858. . . . Philadelphia, 1858. 8°, pp. 40. [*Surg. Gen'l's. Office.*

25. Valedictory Address delivered before the Graduating Class of Jefferson Medical College of Philadelphia. Philadelphia, 1862. 8°, pp. 23. [*A. C. A. B. Ath. Surg. Gen'l's. Office.*

26. Introductory Address delivered before the Students of Jefferson Medical College, Philadelphia, October 12, 1863. Philadelphia, 1863. 8°, pp. 31. [*Harv. Surg. Gen'l's. Office. Y. C.*

27. Studies in Pathology and Therapeutics. New York, 1867. 12°, pp. 201.
[*B. Publ. Br. Mus. Surg. Gen'l's. Office. U. S. Y. C.*

28. Valedictory Address to the Graduates at the forty-fourth Annual Commencement of the Jefferson Medical College of Philadelphia. Philadelphia, 1869. 8°, pp. 17.
[*Surg. Gen'l's. Office. Y. C.*

29. Lecture introductory to the course of Jefferson Medical College for the session of 1870–71. Philadelphia, 1870. 8°, pp. 27.
[*Surg. Gen'l's. Office.*

He was also a large contributor to medical periodicals, but no attempt has been made to collect these titles; among such periodicals were, the *American Journal of the Medical Sciences,* and the *Richmond Medical Journal.*

AUTHORITIES.

S. H. Dickson, M.D., U. S. N., MS. Letter, October, 1911. Philadelphia Med. Times, ii, 278, 292–93.

JOSEPH HEATLY DULLES, son of Joseph Dulles, of Charleston, South Carolina, and grandson of William Dulles, a merchant, of Limerick, Ireland, was born in Charleston on February 7, 1795. His mother was Sophia, daughter of Captain Charles Heatly, of Charleston. A sister married the Hon. Langdon Cheves, of South Carolina.

The Rev. Dr. Jedidiah Morse (Yale 1783) spent the winter of 1809–10 in Charleston, and brought North in May, 1810, young Dulles and his friend James Potter, to have them prepared for admission to Yale in the fall.

On graduation he entered on a mercantile career in Philadelphia. Although he had in large measure the talents which lead to success in business, from the beginning he never forgot what is due from a liberally educated man to the promotion of public interests. He was one of the founders of the Academy of Natural Sciences and of the Mercantile Library, and one of the earliest and most efficient friends of the Franklin Institute. He was also one of the organizers and for over fifty years a manager of the American Sunday School Union.

In business enterprises he was equally active, and in his maturer years was especially concerned with the development of the coal and iron interests of Pennsylvania.

He died in Philadelphia on March 12, 1876, aged 81 years.

In 1819 he married Margaret, daughter of John Welsh, of Philadelphia, and sister of the Hon. John Welsh, minister to England. She survived him with four sons and four daughters. Three sons were graduated at Yale, in 1839, 1844, and 1853, respectively. A daughter married the Hon. Charles J. Stillé (Yale 1839).

He prepared in 1825 the earliest Primer issued by the Sunday School Union.

Alexis Daniel Durand, son of John P. Durand, a woollen manufacturer of Newark, New Jersey, was prepared for the Sophomore Class at Yale by William A. Whelpley (Yale 1807) in the Morristown Academy.

He studied law after graduation, and about 1830 went South, probably to New Orleans, and thence to Mobile, Alabama, where he died on September 11, 1843, aged about 49 years.

AUTHORITIES.

Samuel H. Congar, MS. Letter, January, 1868. *Robert A. Nicoll,* MS. Letter, June, 1882.

THEODORE DWIGHT, the elder surviving son of the Hon. Theodore Dwight, M.A. (honorary, Yale 1798), of Hartford, a younger brother of President Dwight, was born in Hartford on March 3, 1796. His mother was Abigail, or Abby, third daughter of Richard and Mary (Wright) Alsop, of Middletown, and sister of Richard Alsop, a Connecticut author of repute. He was prepared for College by John Langdon (Yale 1809). He united with the College Church on profession of his faith at the end of his Junior year.

Before graduation he had intended to study theology with his uncle, but was prevented by an attack of hemorrhage from the lungs. His father, after a brief sojourn in Albany, settled in New York City in 1817.

He spent a year abroad, for his health, in 1818–19, and went again in October, 1820, for a longer tour. On his return he prepared an account of his tour for the press, and thenceforth devoted himself mainly to writing.

He was married, on April 24, 1827, to Eleanor (or Ellen), daughter of Samuel Boyd, a lawyer of New York, and Eliza (Pierson) Boyd.

He removed in 1833 from New York City to Brooklyn, where he resided until his death, devoted to literary and philanthropic pursuits. He had the editorial charge of a succession of periodicals, and was a frequent contributor to many other magazines and newspapers.

He was prominent in various movements for the extension and improvement of public-school and Sunday-School education, both in New York and Brooklyn. As a director of the New York Public School Society, he is said to have been responsible for the introduction of vocal music into the schools.

In 1834, he was honored with an election as Corresponding Member of the Massachusetts Historical Society.

He traveled extensively in Europe, and devoted much attention to the acquisition of foreign languages, and became especially interested in the condition of the people in various Roman Catholic countries. He was a director of the American Protestant Association, of the Foreign Evangelical Society, and of the Christian Alliance, and the founder of the Philo-Italian Society. His linguistic powers, united with an ardent love of liberty, made him an efficient friend of various political exiles who found refuge in America.

He also interested himself, in 1854–58, in an organized effort to settle eastern Kansas with free-state immigrants.

In the last years of his life he was employed in the New York Custom House, and was much engaged in translating useful books into Spanish, with a view to their introduction into the Spanish-American States.

He died at his home in Brooklyn, on October 16, 1866, in his 71st year. On the day before he saw one of his daughters on board a train at Jersey City, and was severely injured by jumping from a car while in motion.

His widow died in Brooklyn, on April 15, 1870, in her 68th year.

Their children were six daughters and a son. The son and the eldest daughter died before their parents.

He published:

1. A Journal of a Tour in Italy, in the year 1821. With a description of Gibraltar . . . By an American. New-York, 1824. 8°, pp. 468 + 10 pl. [*U. S. Y. C.*

2. The Northern Traveller; containing the Routes to Niagara, Quebec, and the Springs .. New-York, 1825. 12°, pp. 214 + 17 pl. [*Harv. U. S. Y. C.*

Anonymous.

The same. 2d edition. New York, 1826. 12°, pp. iv, 386 + plates. [*B. Ath. U. S.*

Several editions, the 6th in 1841, with author's name.

3. Sketches of Scenery and Manners in the United States.—By the Author of the "Northern Traveller." New-York, 1829. 12°, pp. 188 + 8 pl. [*A. A. S. B. Ath. U. S. Y. C.*

4. A new Gazetteer of the United States of America . . . —By William Darby and Theodore Dwight, Jr. Hartford, 1833. 8°, pp. 630.

[*B. Ath. B. Publ. Br. Mus. Harv. M. H. S. N. Y. Publ. U. S. Y. C.*

The work was under preparation from April, 1830, to November, 1832; Mr. Dwight was responsible for New York, New Jersey, and New England.

The same. 2d edition. Hartford, 1834. 8°, pp. 608 + map. [*U. S.*

5. Lessons in Greek; a familiar Introduction to the Greek Language, as a living tongue. Springfield, 1833. 12°, pp. xi, 9–105. [*B. Publ. Br. Mus. Columbia Univ. U. S.*

6. The Father's Book; or suggestions for the government and instruction of Young Children, on principles appropriate to a Christian Country. Springfield, 1834. 12°, pp. 199.

[*B. Publ. Columbia Univ. N. Y. Publ. U. S. U. T. S. Y. C.*

The same. London, 1834. 12°, [*Br. Mus.*

The same. Second Edition. Springfield, 1835. 12°, pp. 212 + pl. [*A. A. S. A. C. A. Y. C.*

7. South America. In the *Literary and Theological Review*, vol. 1, pp. 378–400 (September, 1834).

8. Review of Cousin's Report on Education in Russia.
In the same, vol. 2, pp. 326–43 (June, 1835).

9. The School-Master's Friend, with the Committee-Man's Guide: containing suggestions on education, modes of teaching and governing .. : plans of school-houses, furniture, apparatus, practical hints, and anecdotes on different systems, etc. . . . New York, 1835. 12°, pp. 360 + plates. [*A. C. A. U. S.*

10. Lecture on the management of a Common School. Pages 203–32 in *Lectures* delivered before the American Institute of Instruction, 1835.

11. Dictionary of Roots and Derivations. New York, 1837.

12. The History of Connecticut, from the first settlement to the present time. New-York, 1840. 12°, pp. 450.
[*B. Publ. U. S. Y. C.*

In Harper & Brothers' Family Library.

13. Lecture on public libraries. New York, 1841. 8°.

14. Summer Tours; or, Notes of a Traveler through some of the Middle and Northern States. Second Edition. New York, 1847. 12°, pp. 252 + 5 plates.
[*B. Publ. Br. Mus. U. S. Y. C.*

The same, with title, Travels in America. Glasgow, 1848. 12°.
[*Br. Mus.*

15. Sketch of the Polynesian Language, drawn up from Hale's Ethnology and Philology.

And, Sketch of the Mpongwes and their Language, from information furnished by Rev. J. L. Wilson.

In *Transactions* of the American Ethnological Society, vol. 2, pp. 223–34, 283–98. New York, 1848. 8°.

16. The Roman Republic of 1849; with accounts of the Inquisition, and the Siege of Rome, and Biographical Sketches .. New York [1851]. 12°, pp. 240 + 5 pl.
[*B. Publ. Br. Mus. Harv. N. Y. Publ. U. S. U. T. S. Y. C.*

17. The Charms of Fancy: a Poem, in four cantos, with notes. By Richard Alsop. Edited from the original manuscripts, with a Biographical Sketch of the Author. New York, 1856. 12°, pp. 214. [*Br. Mus. N. Y. Publ. Y. C.*

Richard Alsop was an uncle of the editor.

18. The Kansas War; or, the Exploits of Chivalry in the Nineteenth Century. New York, 1859. 12°.

19. The Life of General Garibaldi, translated from his private papers; with the history of his splendid exploits in Rome, Lombardy, Sicily and Naples, to the present time. New York, 1861. 12°, pp. xvi, 449 + 2 pl. [*N. Y. Publ. Y. C.*

Among the separate works which he edited may be named:

20. The Journals of Madam Knight, and Rev. Mr. Buckingham. From the original manuscripts, written in 1704 and 1710. New York, 1825. 12°, pp. 129. [*U. S. Y. C.*

21. President Dwight's Decisions of Questions discussed by the Senior Class in Yale College, in 1813 and 1814.—From Stenographic Notes. New-York, 1833. 12°, pp. 348. [*Y. C.*

22. Memoir of the Physical and Political Geography of New Granada .. By T. C. de Mosquera .. Translated from the Spanish. New York, 1853. 8°, pp. 105. [*B. Publ. N. Y. Publ. U. S.*

As already stated, editorial work on periodicals absorbed much of his time. On first going to New York he was employed on his father's paper, *The New York Daily Advertiser.* Later, he had charge at different times of *The Protestant Vindicator, The Family Visitor, and Silk Culturist, The Christian Alliance and Family Visitor, The New York Presbyterian,* and *The Youth's Penny Paper.*

His most important editorial venture was the following:

Dwight's American [Penny] Magazine, and Family Newspaper: with illustrative and ornamental wood engravings, for the Diffusion of Useful Knowledge, and moral and religious principles. Sixteen large octavo pages weekly, 1845–52.

AUTHORITIES.

Dwight Family, i, 231–33. Mass. Hist. Society's Proceedings, 1st Series, ix, 359; xv, 386–88.

David Shelton Edwards, son of Hezekiah and Martha Edwards, of that part of Stratford which is now Trumbull, Connecticut, and a first cousin of Samuel L. Edwards (Yale 1812), was born on June 22, 1794.

He was prepared for College by his pastor, the Rev. Daniel C. Banks (Yale 1804).

On graduation he entered the Yale Medical School and after three years' study received the degree of M.D.

In July, 1818, he entered the United States Navy as Assistant Surgeon, and was promoted to the rank of Surgeon in May, 1825.

He remained in the service until his death.

In November, 1830, he was married in Brooklyn, New York, to Harriet Eliza, youngest daughter of the late William Henry, of New York.

At the opening of the war with Mexico, he was attached to the army and accompanied General Scott, as Medical Director of the 4th Division. His last sea cruise ended in October, 1859.

During the Civil War he was stationed at the naval rendezvous in New Bedford, Massachusetts.

In 1869 he was appointed President of the Naval Medical Board of Examination.

Soon after this date he was retired from active duty, and thenceforth he divided his time between Washington and his ancestral homestead on Chestnut Hill in Trumbull. He died in Trumbull on March 18, 1874, in his 80th year.

AUTHORITIES.

Orcutt, Hist. of Stratford, ii, 1196.

AUGUSTUS FLOYD, the second son of Colonel Nicoll and Phebe Floyd, of Mastic, in the town of Brookhaven, on the south shore of Long Island, and grandson of William Floyd, a signer of the Declaration of Independence, by his first wife, Hannah Jones, was born in Mastic on May 28, 1795. His mother was the only child of David and Phebe (Mitchell) Gelston, of Bridgehampton. A younger sister married Dr. Edward Delafield (Yale 1812). He was prepared for the Sophomore Class by the Rev. Dr. Aaron Woolworth (Yale 1784), of Bridgehampton.

He studied law after graduation, and was admitted in 1817 to the bar of New York City, where he continued until 1849. As he was in independent circumstances, and was afflicted with an almost total loss of hearing, he then retired to the village of Yaphank, in his native town, where he led a very secluded life. He was never married.

He died suddenly in Brookhaven on September 25, 1878, in his 84th year.

AUTHORITIES.

N. Y. Geneal. and Biogr. Record, ii, 138.

Henry Gibbs, the youngest child of Henry and Mercy (Prescott) Gibbs, and a brother of Professor Josiah W. Gibbs (Yale 1809), was born in Salem, Massachusetts, on September 20, 1793. He entered Yale at the opening of the Junior year, having been prepared by his brother.

After two years of graduate study in New Haven he settled in Philadelphia as a merchant, and there married, on September 20, 1827, Anna Evans.

His wife died on May 8, 1835, and their only child died in infancy.

He died in Philadelphia on May 25, 1855, in his 62d year, and was buried in his brother's family lot in New Haven.

AUTHORITIES.

Gibbs Family Memoir, 41. Prescott Memorial, 95.

Charles Backus Goddard, the eldest child of Calvin Goddard (Dartmouth Coll. 1786), of Plainfield, Connecticut, and grandson of Daniel and Mary (Willard) Goddard, of Shrewsbury, Massachusetts, was born in Plainfield on October 6, 1796. His mother was Alice Cogswell, younger daughter of the Rev. Dr. Levi Hart (Yale 1760), of that part of Preston which is now Griswold, Connecticut. The family removed in his infancy to Norwich, where his father became a Member of Congress and Judge. Two brothers were graduated here in 1820 and 1828, respectively, and a sister married Asa Child (Yale 1821). He was prepared for College by Charles Griswold (Yale 1808) at the Chelsea Grammar School in Norwich.

After studying law with his father, and with Judge Matthew Griswold (Yale 1780), of Lyme, he was admitted to the bar, and soon after went to Zanesville, Ohio, where he resided in the uninterrupted practice of his profession from 1817 until his death.

He was married by the Rev. David Young, on June 6, 1820, to Harriet Munro, daughter of Daniel and Sarah (Munro) Convers, of Zanesville.

His political advancement was at first retarded by the knowledge of his father's prominence in the Hartford Convention, which the West regarded as disloyal, but he was a member of the General Assembly of the State in the session of 1838-39; and for four sessions (1845–49) a member of the State Senate, and Speaker for one term. He also attained the rank of General in the militia.

He died in Zanesville on February 1, 1864, in his 68th year

Mrs. Goddard survived him, with seven of their children They had six sons and six daughters, of whom three sons and one daughter died in infancy

AUTHORITIES.

Converse Family, ii, 466–67 *Timlow,* Hist of Southington, cxviii

---

Horace Goodrich, the youngest child of Josiah and Abigail Goodrich, of Wethersfield, Connecticut, and grandson of Elisha and Rebecca (Seymour) Goodrich, of Berlin, was born in Wethersfield on August 3, 1795. His mother was the youngest daughter of Samuel and Mary (Wyatt) Wolcott, of Wethersfield, and the widow of Levi Wright, of Wethersfield. His parents removed in his infancy to Pittsfield, Massachusetts, and thence to South Hadley, from which place he entered College. He was prepared by his pastor, the Rev. Joel Hayes (Yale 1773).

On graduation he began the study of medicine under Dr. Josiah Goodhue, of Hadley.

In 1819 or 1820 he began practice in Ware, where he remained for about thirty-five years and gained in a high degree the respect and esteem of the community. For seven or eight years from 1829 his classmate Moody was in partnership with him. He was a sincere Christian, a kind neighbor, and a genial companion.

On November 29, 1828, he married Elizabeth, third daughter of Deacon William and Dorothy (Warner) Dickinson, of Hadley.

In 1855, finding his health hopelessly impaired by a laborious and extensive practice, he retired to a farm in East Windsor, Connecticut, where he spent the most of his remaining days, in great feebleness. He finally found a milder climate necessary, and removed to the house of his eldest daughter, in Vineland, New Jersey, where he died on August 21, 1872, at the age of 77.

His wife died before him. Of their children, four sons and four daughters, one son and three daughters survived him.

He represented Ware in the Legislature for one or two years.

AUTHORITIES.

Chase, Hist. of Ware, 241. Goodrich Family, 83, 140. *Mrs. Charles O. Thompson,* MS. Letter, June, 1880.

Ralph Wells Gridley, the second son of the Rev. Elijah Gridley (Yale 1788), pastor of the First Church in Mansfield, Connecticut, was born in Mansfield on April 5, 1793. In his infancy his father removed to the church in Granby, Massachusetts. He was prepared for College by John Adams (Yale 1795) in Bacon Academy, Colchester, Connecticut.

After graduation he began the study of theology with President Dwight, and was licensed to preach by the Brookfield Association on September 20, 1815. He remained for another year in New Haven as a graduate student, and on September 12, 1816, he was married to Eliza, only child of Samuel and Wealthy (Trowbridge) Barnes, of New Haven.

On October 9, 1816, he was ordained and installed as pastor of the Congregational Church in Williamstown, and he fulfilled a faithful and laborious ministry there for seventeen and a half years. He was a trustee of Williams College from 1827 to 1834.

He was a man of more than usual capacity, and retained the esteem of his people, but about 1832 he manifested his earnest sympathy with the "New Haven Theology" and also with the so-called "new measures" in dealing with revivals, by which means he incurred the strong disapproval of President Griffin (Yale 1790), of Williams College The result was that the College students were withdrawn from his congregation, to form a new church, and he was dismissed at his own request on April 27, 1834. Over six hundred persons had been received into the church during his pastorate.

Depressed in spirits, he then undertook home missionary work in Jacksonville, Illinois, but his health soon declined, and he died, while on a visit to his children in Ottawa, Illinois, on February 2, 1840, in his 47th year. His wife died, two weeks before him, on January 19, in her 43d year.

They had three sons and five daughters; two of the sons and three daughters died in infancy or early life.

AUTHORITIES

Amer Quarterly Register, vii, 34 *Chapman*, Trowbridge Family, 67, 87. *Durfee*, Biogr Annals of Williams College, 72-73 *Perry*, Hist of Williamstown, ii, 130-32

Minor Hallock entered at the opening of Sophomore year from Brookhaven, Long Island He was born about 1792, and was prepared by Charles H. Havens (Yale 1806), of Moriches, in the southern part of Brookhaven

He studied law, and settled in his native town, where he died, probably early in 1821, as letters of administration on his estate were issued to a brother-in-law, William L. Jones, on March 16, of that year.

Hugh Halsey, son of Dr. Stephen Halsey, Junior, of Bridgehampton, Long Island, and grandson of Dr. Stephen Halsey, Senior, of Bridgehampton, was born in 1794. His mother was the youngest daughter of Philip and Cleopatra (Herrick) Howell, of Bridgehampton. A brother, the Rev. Herman Halsey, was graduated at Williams College in 1811. He was prepared for admission to the Sophomore Class by his pastor, the Rev. Dr. Aaron Woolworth (Yale 1784).

After graduation he studied law with the Hon. Franklin Viele, of Waterford, and was admitted to the bar of Saratoga County, but about a year later he returned to his native town, where he had a very useful career.

In 1822 and 1824 he was a member of the State Assembly, and in 1854–55 of the State Senate. He was the Surrogate of Suffolk County from April, 1827, to January, 1840, and Chief Judge of the County Court from February, 1833, to June, 1847. In 1844 he was a (Democratic) Presidential Elector, and Surveyor-General of the State from February, 1845, to November, 1847.

After an illness of about two years, during which he suffered extremely, he died in Bridgehampton on May 29, 1858, in his 64th year.

His wife survived him. Their children were three sons and a daughter. Two sons died in the Civil War.

Judge Halsey was an eminently devoted Christian, and for many years a ruling elder in the Presbyterian Church.

AUTHORITIES.

Howell, Hist. of Southampton, 2d ed., 268.

ASA HAMMOND, the second son of Moses Hammond, a farmer of Charlton, Massachusetts, and grandson of Deacon Ebenezer and Esther (Stone) Hammond, of Charlton, was born on February 16, 1786. His mother was Dorothy, daughter of Captain Richard and Dorothy (Marcy) Dresser, of Charlton. He entered College at the opening of Junior year.

After graduation he studied law, and settled in practice in Claiborne, on the Alabama River, in southwestern Alabama.

He was married there, on December 21, 1823, to Sarah A. Wilson, by whom he had two daughters and three sons.

His wife died on June 4, 1835, and not wishing to bring up his family in a slave State, he took them in 1843 to Marietta, Ohio, where a brother was living, intending to settle later in Illinois. He then went back to Claiborne to settle his affairs, and died there, of yellow fever, on September 23, in his 58th year

AUTHORITIES

Charlton Vital Records, 50. *H.* 1866 Hammond Genealogies, ii, 32, *Hammond*, MS Letter, September, 44-45

LOWMAN HAWES, son of Isaac and Anna (Whitlock) Hawes, of Warren, Connecticut, was born in Warren on March 25, 1792, and was prepared for admission to the Sophomore Class by the Rev. Daniel Parker (Yale 1798), of Ellsworth Society in Sharon

He settled as a lawyer in Maysville, Kentucky, and died there in 1831 or 1832.

He left a widow, who died soon. A son was graduated at Centre College, Kentucky, in 1842, and became a Presbyterian minister

AUTHORITIES

Wilson, Presbyterian Historical Almanac, 1862, 93

ALFRED MCKINNE HOBBY, son of Alfred Hobby, a proprietor of a bookstore in Augusta, Georgia, by his second wife, Sarah McKinne, was born in Augusta, about 1795. He was prepared for admission at the opening of Sophomore year by Hezekiah G. Ufford (Yale 1806) in New York.

He married in Macon, about 1834, Eliza (Slade), widow of William J. Danelly, and afterwards left Augusta for Tallahassee, Florida, where he was cashier of the Union Bank, and later settled in Newport, Wakulla County. He died in St. Marks, Wakulla County, probably in 1848. His widow died in Texas in 1877, at the house of a son by her first marriage. Several sons settled in Texas.

AUTHORITIES.

Mrs. L. B. Danelly, MS. Letters, 1912. *Rt. Rev. E. G. Weed, D.D.,* MS. Letters, 1912.

GEORGE HOOKER, the second child, and last survivor in a family of ten children of Judge John Hooker (Yale 1782), of Springfield, Massachusetts, was born in Springfield on March 17, 1793, and was prepared for College by the Rev. Ezra Witter (Yale 1793), of Wilbraham.

On graduation he entered the Medical Department, where he received the degree of M.D. in 1817. He then practiced for one year in connection with Dr. Eli Ives (Yale 1799) in New Haven.

He then for about six years engaged in practice in Springfield, being married on January 20, 1819, to Rachel, daughter of Joseph Hunt and Abigail (Kingsley) Breck, of Northampton, and sister of the Rev. Joseph H. Breck (Yale 1818).

He then spent twelve years in Syracuse, New York, and after a brief interval of residence in Chicopee, Massachusetts, he finally settled in Longmeadow, where he continued until his death.

His wife died on January 6, 1879, in her 87th year, and he died in Longmeadow, after a very vigorous and intelligent old age, on March 14, 1884, and was buried on the day when he would have reached the age of 91 years.

His children were four daughters and four sons. Two daughters and one son died in infancy, and another son in early manhood.

Dr. Hooker was a pillar in the church, honored and beloved, wherever he lived, and his Christian hope grew brighter until the end. He kept up until the last his interest in current events, and was a diligent reader of the daily and religious papers.

AUTHORITIES.

Dwight Family, ii, 845-46.

CHARLES HOPKINS, the eldest child of Deacon Timothy Hopkins, of Hadley, Massachusetts, and grandson of Timothy and Dinah (Miller) Hopkins, of West Springfield, was born in Hadley on June 13, 1793. The Rev. Dr. Samuel Hopkins (Yale 1749) was his great-uncle. His mother was Rebecca, daughter of Eliakim and Mehitabel (Smith) Smith, of Hadley.

He was intending after graduation to enter on the study of law in the Litchfield Law School; but before he was able to carry out his plans, he was prostrated with consumption, from which he died at his father's house in Hadley on December 28, 1816, in his 24th year. His death was the first in his Class.

AUTHORITIES.

T. Clapp, Autobiographical Sketches, 23-25. *Judd,* Hist. of Hadley, 2d ed., Appendix, 72.

John Benedict Hoyt, the second son of Thaddeus Hoyt, a farmer and shoemaker of New Canaan, Connecticut, and of Walton, Delaware County, New York, and grandson of Matthew and Mary (Lockwood) Hoyt, of New Canaan, was born in Walton on January 31, 1794. His mother was Jemima, eldest child of Lieutenant Ezra and Mary (Benedict) Benedict, of New Canaan. He was prepared for the Sophomore class by the Rev. Archibald Bassett (Yale 1796), of Walton.

He spent the year after graduation in teaching in Duchess County, New York, and soon after began the study of theology with the Rev. Dr. Seth Williston (Dartmouth Coll. 1791), of Durham, in Greene County.

In 1818 he was licensed to preach by the Associated Presbytery at Durham, and in 1820 he was ordained by the Union (Congregational) Association at Greene, in Chenango County, and he served as stated supply of the church there until 1829. During these years he also supplied at various times other destitute churches in that region.

In June, 1825, he organized the Second Congregational (afterwards Presbyterian) Church in the neighboring town of Coventry, of which he took charge as stated supply in 1829, and on June 19, 1833, he was installed as its pastor.

He continued in this field through life, and acquired a position of great influence in the vicinity. He had marked success in his ministry, receiving into the churches under his care over seven hundred members.

He died in Coventry, after long illness, from a dropsical affection, on July 4, 1862, in his 69th year.

He married on January 18, 1821, Emeline Cornelia, daughter of the Rev. Stephen Fenn (Yale 1790) of Harpersfield, in Delaware County, who died on April 7, 1843, aged 40 years.

He next married, on October 8, 1843, Eliza Ann, youngest child of James and Elizabeth (Drake) Phillips, of Coventry, who died on July 27–28, 1875, aged 70 years.

By his first wife he had four sons and three daughters; and by his second wife one son (Yale 1864). Five children survived him.

He published:

1. A Pastor's Tribute to his People. Norwich, N. Y., 1851. 12°, pp. 288.

A volume of sermons.

2. Address at the Hoyt Family Gathering in Walton, New York, June 16, 1858.

AUTHORITIES.

Hotchkin, Hist. of Western N. Y., 301–02. *Rev. James P. Hoyt*, MS. Letter, July, 1862. Hoyt Family, 515. 585. *Wilson*, Presbyterian Hist. Almanac, 1863, 299.

Hezekiah Hull, son of Samuel and Mabel Hull, of New Haven, and grandson of Ebenezer and Lydia (Dunbar) Hull, of New Haven, was born in New Haven on August 20, 1796. He joined the United Church in New Haven in January, 1809. He was prepared for College by Elizur Goodrich (Williams Coll. 1806), at the Hopkins Grammar School.

For two years after graduation he taught an academy in Wallingford with much credit. He then spent three years in the Andover Theological Seminary.

On October 13, 1819, he was ordained at West Hartford as an evangelist by the North Consociation of Hartford County, having been appointed by the Connecticut Missionary Society as a missionary to Louisiana. He left home in November, and on reaching Cincinnati, was dissuaded from going further, on account of the lateness of the season, and in response to an urgent request he spent a year in Montgomery, about thirteen miles to the northeast, teaching an academy and preaching.

He resumed his journey in November, 1820, and after some months spent upon the way in missionary labor arrived at Alexandria, in central Louisiana, on the Red River, in January, 1821.

Here he was immediately employed as a preacher, and also as the principal of the academy, and continued to be busy with these duties until the summer of 1822.

He then returned to New England, and was married on October 13 by the Rev. Dr. Justin Edwards to Sarah Kneeland, daughter of John Lovejoy and Phebe (Abbot) Abbot, of Andover, and sister of the Rev. John L. Abbot (Harvard Coll. 1805).

In December they arrived in Alexandria, and he resumed his occupations with new ardor and devotedness. He enjoyed uninterrupted health until he succumbed to fever, when his death followed, after nine days' illness, on August 3, 1823, at the age of 27.

His wife married in July, 1825, his older brother, Sidney Hull, of New Haven, and died here on January 8, 1834, aged 36½ years. Sidney Hull next married (as the fourth of his five wives) her younger sister Martha.

His promise of usefulness was great, and his enjoyment of life keen, but he met his fate with manly resignation.

AUTHORITIES.

Abbot Genealogical Register, 26. Christian Spectator, vii, 556–60. Conn. Missionary Society's Narrative for 1820, 12.

Jedidiah Huntington, the eldest child of Deacon Jabez Huntington (Yale 1784), of Norwich, Connecticut, was born in Norwich on September 15, 1794, and was prepared for College by Charles Griswold (Yale 1808) at the Chelsea Grammar School in Norwich.

He spent his life in Norwich, engaged in business, except for some extended sea-voyages in early years. At the time of his death he was a vice-president and director of the Norwich Savings Society.

He died in Norwich, from paralysis, on December 6, 1870, in his 77th year.

He married, on July 2, 1834, Rebecca M Snow, who died after a brief illness, on September 3, 1838, aged 33 years.

He next married, on February 24, 1841, Happy, eldest daughter of Newcomb and Sally (Branch) Kinney, of Norwich, who died in 1867, aged 69 years.

By his first marriage he had two daughters, and a son who died in infancy. Only the elder daughter survived him.

AUTHORITIES

Huntington Family Memoir, 320, 360 *Perkins*, Old Houses of Norwich, 502

JOHN JARVIS INGERSOLL was born in Stanwich Society in Greenwich, Connecticut, in November, 1792, and was prepared for College by his pastor, the Rev Platt Buffett (Yale 1791). His father was Dr. John Ingersoll, and his mother was Hannah, daughter of Samuel and Martha (Seymour) Jarvis, of Stamford, and niece of the Rt Rev. Abraham Jarvis (Yale 1761).

On graduation he began the study of medicine at the College of Physicians and Surgeons in New York City, where he proceeded to the degree of M D. in 1817

He settled in the practice of his profession in Harlem, and on November 12, 1817, he was married by the Rev Dr William Phœbus to Gertrude A. Vark, of New York

He was a worthy man and successful practitioner, but died early, after a lingering illness, on November 11, 1830, at the age of 38, and was buried in the family vault in St Mark's Churchyard, New York.

His wife died in Poughkeepsie, New York, in 1886. He left four children, two of whom survived their mother

AUTHORITIES

A L Allen, MS Letter, December, 1886

CHARLES JESUP, the third son of Major Ebenezer Jesup, of the village of Saugatuck, now Westport, Connecticut, and grandson of Dr. Ebenezer Jesup (Yale 1760), was born in Saugatuck on March 10, and baptized on June 5, 1796. His mother was Sarah, daughter of Obadiah and Sarah (Adams) Wright, of Norwalk. A younger brother was graduated here in 1824.

He began the study of law after graduation, but was obliged to relinquish it on account of his health, for the benefit of which he went first to Charleston, and afterwards to Europe, returning much improved. Under the advice of friends he gave up his intention of entering a profession, and devoted himself to mercantile pursuits, in New York City and in his native place, residing in Westport until his sudden death there, from apoplexy, on July 5, 1837, in his 42d year.

He married on September 9, 1821, Abigail, or Abby, youngest daughter of the Hon. Samuel Burr Sherwood (Yale 1786), of Saugatuck. She removed to New York City in 1842, and died on February 17, 1872, at the age of 72. Their children were two daughters and six sons. The fourth son, Morris K. Jesup, M.A. (honorary Yale 1891), has been a distinguished benefactor of Yale.

Mr. Jesup's religious life was especially active. He took a great interest in the Sunday School, and was a large contributor to the various objects of Christian benevolence.

AUTHORITIES.

Jessup Genealogy, 133, 177–80.

JOHN KINTZING KANE, the eldest of three children of Elisha Kane, a merchant of Albany, New York, was born in Albany, on May 16, 1795. His mother was Alida, daughter of General Robert and Cornelia (Rutsen) Van Rensselaer, of Claverack Manor; he was thus a second cousin of Dr. Jeremiah Van Rensselaer (Yale 1813) He was also a first cousin of Kane of that Class. The family removed about 1801 to Philadelphia. He was prepared for College by Henry Sherman (Yale 1803) in New Haven.

Upon graduation he entered on the study of law in the office of the Hon Joseph Hopkinson (Univ. Pennsylvania 1786), of Philadelphia, and in April, 1817, he was admitted to the bar, and began practice.

He was an able, if not a brilliant lawyer, but became early interested in politics, and was sent to the Legislature as a Federalist in 1823; but in 1824 he became a Democrat, and was prominent thenceforth in the counsels of that party He was a strenuous supporter of Jackson in the Presidential campaign of 1828

In 1828 he was appointed City Solicitor by the City Councils, and he held that office for two years He was re-appointed in 1832, but resigned when he was made, under the Act of Congress of July, 1832, one of the commissioners under the convention of July 4, 1831, for the settlement of outstanding claims of France and the United States; this duty occupied him until 1836.

His close personal relations with Jackson led to his assisting the President in the composition of several important letters and state papers; in particular, the first printed attack on the United States Bank is said to have been written by him, and to have caused his proscription for a time in social circles in Philadelphia. He was credited with being the chief strategist of the Democrats in the political struggle in December, 1838, in Pennsylvania, known as the "Buckshot War."

In January, 1845, he was appointed Attorney General of Pennsylvania by Governor Shunk, but he resigned this post, when President Polk named him, in June, 1846, as Judge of the United States District Court for the Eastern District of Pennsylvania. This office he retained until his death, and his decisions commanded general respect, especially in admiralty and patent cases. He was also distinguished for his attainments in Roman and continental law. His action, however, in the case of Passmore Williamson, in 1856, when he committed an abolitionist to jail for contempt of court in not producing certain fugitive slaves, excited much feeling.

He married in 1819 Jane Duval, fourth daughter of Thomas and Elizabeth Coultas (Gray) Leiper, of Philadelphia, who survived him.

They had seven children, of whom three sons and a daughter survived him. The eldest son was graduated from the medical department of the University of Pennsylvania in 1842, and after an active career as surgeon in the United States navy became distinguished as an Arctic explorer. His premature death in February, 1857, was a severe shock to his father's health and spirits. Another son attained the rank of brigadier-general in the Civil War.

Judge Kane was prominent in connection with the Presbyterian Church. He was an active and useful member of various artistic and scientific societies, such as the Academy of Fine Arts, the Musical Fund Society, the Academy of Natural Sciences, and the Franklin Institute. He was the President of the American Philosophical Society from 1856 until his death.

He was an accomplished scholar in *belles lettres,* and distinguished for his courtly manners.

He died in Philadelphia, after a few days' illness, from typhoid pneumonia, on February 21, 1858, in his 63d year. The Address delivered at his funeral by his pastor, the Rev. Dr. Charles W. Shields (who afterwards married his daughter), was afterwards published. Judge Kane was the President of the Board of Trustees of the Second Presbyterian Church.

His portrait is reproduced in Simpson's *Eminent Philadelphians,* in the *Thomas Book,* and in the *Century Magazine,* volume 34.

He published (besides many judicial opinions):

1. A Discourse pronounced before the Law Academy of Philadelphia, on the 26th of October, 1831. Philadelphia, 1831. 8°, pp. 32. [*A. A. S. U. S.*

On the constitutional law of the United States. Judge Kane was the Vice-Provost of the Academy.

2. Notes on some of the Questions decided by the Board of Commissioners under the Convention with France, of 4th July, 1831. Philadelphia, 1836. 8°, pp. 108.

[*B. Publ. Harv. N. Y. Publ. Y. C.*

3. Address on the Patent Laws, delivered before the Franklin Institute, at the close of the annual exhibition, Philadelphia, October, 1849. Washington, 1849. 8°, pp. 16.

[*B. Ath. B. Publ. Br. Mus.*

Published in connection with an effort to modify the Patent Laws.

4. Obituary notice of the late Dr. Robert M. Patterson. In the *Proceedings* of the American Philosophical Society, vol. 6, pp. 60–65, December, 1854.

AUTHORITIES.

Amer. Philosoph. Society's Proceedings, vi, 289–90. Century Magazine, xxxiv, 488–89. *Crosby*, Annual Obit. Notices, 1858, 187–88. *Pelletreau*, Hist. of Putnam County, 481. *Polk*, Diary, i, 463–64. *Simpson*, Lives of Eminent Philadelphians, 613–18. Thomas Book, 377, 439.

CHARLES JAMES LANMAN, the eldest of twelve children of the Hon. James Lanman (Yale 1788), was born in Norwich, Connecticut, on June 5, 1795, and was prepared for College by a first cousin of his mother, Charles Griswold (Yale 1808), in the Chelsea Academy in Norwich.

He studied law with his great-uncles, Matthew and Roger Griswold (Yale 1780), of Lyme, as well as with his father, and was admitted to the bar early in 1817.

Soon after this he was invited by the Hon. Henry Clay to settle in Kentucky, but decided to seek his fortune in Michigan, with the encouragement of William Woodbridge, a native of Norwich, who had just been appointed Secretary of the Territory, and Governor Cass.

He joined Mr. Woodbridge in his law office in Detroit, and while riding the circuit he visited Frenchtown, now Monroe, on Lake Erie, where he settled permanently, and married on March 18, 1818, Marie Jeanne Guie (or Ghee), daughter of Antoine Guie, a lady of French origin and Canadian birth.

He held many positions of local and general trust and honor, such as Judge of Probate, Colonel of the militia, Attorney for the Territory, Postmaster, and Inspector of Customs. In 1823 President Monroe appointed him to the responsible office of Receiver of Public Monies for the District of Michigan, and he was continued in office by President Adams.

In 1835, owing to family considerations, he returned to Norwich, and in 1838 he was elected Mayor of the city. In the financial crisis of 1837, he lost the bulk of his property, which was all located in Michigan.

After leaving the mayoralty he became the President of the Norwich Water Power Company; and at the conclusion of that service he retired in the main from active life. In 1862, lured by early recollections, and by his intense love of the scenery and air of the ocean, he went to New London to reside, and died there on July 25, 1870, in his 76th year. He was buried in Norwich.

His wife survived him, with one of their two sons, and their seven daughters. The son was well known as an author. Mrs. Lanman died in East Orange, New Jersey, on February 5, 1879.

AUTHORITIES.

Amer. Ancestry, x, 45. Chandler Family, 2d ed., 559. *Talcott,* Genealogical Notes, 581. *Walworth,* Hyde Genealogy, ii, 892–93.

John Law, the eldest son of the Hon. Lyman Law (Yale 1791), was born in New London, Connecticut, on October 28, 1796, and was prepared for College by his pastor, the Rev. Abel McEwen (Yale 1804).

He studied law with his father, who was at that time a Federalist Member of Congress, and was admitted to the Connecticut bar in 1817. But the West proved more attractive, and he left in October, 1817, for Indiana, which had just been made a State. There he was admitted to practice in December, and settled in Vincennes.

Within two months he was appointed prosecuting attorney for the Circuit Court, and he rose rapidly into prominence at the bar. As early as 1824 he was a member of the State Legislature, and then again District Attorney from 1825 to 1828. In 1830 he was elected by the Legislature, Judge of the Seventh Judicial Circuit, an office which he held for one year (until March 30, 1831).

From 1838 to 1842 he was receiver at the land-office in Vincennes. In March, 1844, he was again elected Judge, and retained that position until his resignation in March, 1850. In 1851 he removed to Evansville, where he resided until his death. He had already made large purchases of land in the vicinity in conjunction with one of his brothers; and these investments proved so valuable that he was obliged to make his residence there, in order to look after the family interests He had been for more than a quarter of a century the central figure in all public enterprises in Vincennes, and his graceful presence and attractive oratory were greatly missed.

Though in early life a Whig, he had long been in sympathy with the Democratic party, and in 1855 he was appointed by President Pierce as Judge of the Court of Land Claims, for the adjudication of the claims of early settlers in Indiana and Illinois This duty occupied him for two years. He was elected to Congress for the two sessions extending from July, 1861, to March, 1865.

He died in Evansville on October 7, 1873, at the age of 77, and was buried in Vincennes

He was married, on November 24, 1822, to Sarah, daughter of Nathaniel Ewing, of Vincennes, and sister of George W. Ewing (Yale 1819).

He published:

1. Address delivered before the Vincennes Historical and Antiquarian Society, February 22, 1839. Louisville, 1839. 8°, pp. 48. [*Br. Mus. Harv. U. S. Y. C.*

2. The same, revised, with title: The Colonial History of Vincennes, under the French, British and American Governments, from its first settlement down to the territorial administration of General William Henry Harrison, being an Address [as above] .. , with additional Notes and illustrations. Vincennes, 1858. 8°, pp. viii, 157. [*A. A. S. B. Ath. Harv. U. S. Y. C.*

Dedicated to his friend, the Hon. Lewis Cass.

3. Early Jesuit Missionaries in the North-West.—A Lecture delivered before the Young Men's Catholic Literary Institute, Cincinnati, on Wednesday Evening, January 31st, 1855.

In the *Collections* of the State Historical Society of Wisconsin, vol. 3, pp. 87–124, 1857.

This was originally published in the *Catholic Telegraph*, a Cincinnati newspaper, in 1855, and a critique by Dr. John G. Shea and other related articles are here included. The whole is founded on an anonymous paper by Judge Law, entitled The Early Jesuit Missionaries of North America, published in the *Democratic Review*, vol. 14, pp. 518–27 (May, 1844).

4. Speech on the "Bill Emancipating Slaves of Rebels," and the "Bill Confiscating the Property of Rebels" .. In the House of Representatives, May 23d, 1862. Washington, 1862. 8°, pp. 8. [*A. A. S.*

Against the bills named.

5. Speech .. delivered in the House of Representatives, July 1, 1864. Washington, 1864. 8°, pp. 16.

AUTHORITIES.

Cauthorn, Hist. of Vincennes, 185, 212–13. Indiana Hist. Society's Publications, i, 201–13. Learned Genealogy, 2d ed., 219–20. Magazine of American Hist., xxv, 409–12. *O. H. Smith,* Early Indiana Trials, 361–62.

Joshua Leavitt, the eldest child of Roger and Chloe Leavitt, of Heath, Massachusetts, and grandson of the Rev. Jonathan Leavitt (Yale 1758), was born in Heath on September 8, 1794. His mother was a sister of Sylvester Maxwell (Yale 1797). He was prepared for the Sophomore Class by the Rev. Dr. Joseph Lyman (Yale 1767), of Hatfield.

He won a Berkeley Scholarship at graduation, and probably resided here for a time, studying and teaching.

Later he studied law at home, and was admitted to the bar in Northampton in 1819 He then practiced as an attorney in Putney, on the Connecticut river, in southern Vermont, for a short time, and was elected deacon in the local church; but under conviction of duty in 1823 he returned to New Haven, and there pursued theological studies with the first class in the newly organized Divinity School.

He was licensed to preach in August, 1824, and on February 23, 1825, was ordained and installed as pastor of the Congregational Church in Stratford, Connecticut.

In the course of his ministry he became ardently interested in the new temperance movement, and served for four months as an agent of the American Temperance Society. The qualities which he showed caused him to be thought of as peculiarly fitted for the office of permanent agent of the Seamen's Friend Society, in New York; and on receiving an appointment to that office he was dismissed from his pastorate on October 22, 1828, and began his new duties on November 1.

In this position he took charge of the organ of the Society, the *Sailor's Magazine;* and the rest of his life was primarily devoted to editorial labors.

In December, 1831, he resigned his agency, and became the editor and proprietor of the *New York Evangelist,* which had been founded the year before as an organ of liberal religious movements, and he so continued until the financial crisis of 1837 obliged him to dispose of the paper.

Meantime he had been a pioneer in the anti-slavery cause, and now he gladly welcomed the opportunity of devoting his whole time to this object, as the editor of the weekly *Emancipator*, from 1837 to 1847. He pursued, however, an independent course, and was often at variance with Garrison and his sympathizers. The place of publication, and the editor's residence, were removed from New York to Boston in 1842.

In 1848 he became office editor of the *Independent*, and held this position until he reached the age of seventy, when he relinquished the management, but continued to be employed in a place of less labor and responsibility until his death. His residence was in Brooklyn.

He died of an apoplectic stroke, while temporarily visiting at the residence of a son in New York, on January 16, 1873, in his 79th year.

He married, on November 1, 1820, Sarah, the youngest child of the Rev. Solomon Williams (Yale 1770), of Northampton, who survived him, dying in her 80th year.

One son was graduated at Yale in 1840.

The honorary degree of Doctor of Divinity was conferred on him by Wabash College in 1854.

Dr. Leavitt was active in many other reforms, besides Temperance and Slavery. He was a diligent advocate of Free Trade, and of cheap postage.

He published:

1. Easy Lessons in Reading. 1823.

The same. 2d edition. Keene, 1829. 16°, pp. 156 + pl. [*N. Y. Publ.*

See, also, No. 14.

2. Review on Missions to China. In the *Quarterly Christian Spectator*, vol. 2, pp. 299–321 (June, 1830).

3. Seamen's Devotional Assistant, and Mariners' Hymns; prepared under direction of the American Seamen's Friend Society. New-York, 1830. 16°, pp. 512 + pl. [*Y. C.*

4. The Living Epistle: a Sermon, from II Cor. iii, 2, in the *National Preacher*, vol. 5, pp. 106–12 (December, 1830).

5. The Christian Lyre; a Collection of Hymns and Tunes adapted for social worship, prayer meetings, and revivals of religion. New-York, 1830–31 12° 2 volumes. pp 216; 216.
[A C. A B Publ. Y C.

Originally published in 12 monthly parts.

6. Supplement to the Christian Lyre, containing more than one hundred Psalm Tunes, such as are most used in churches of all denominations. New-York, 1831. 16°, pp. ii, 106.
[A C. A. Harv. Y C.

7. Seamen's Friend Society; and, Review of Hawes' Tribute to the Memory of the Pilgrims. In the *Quarterly Christian Spectator,* vol 3, pp. 253–67, 358–93 (June, September, 1831)

8. Companion to the Christian Lyre. Comprising the Hymns of the Lyre, with additional Hymns. New-York, 1833. 16°, pp. 544. [B. Publ. Y C

9. Visions of heavenly glory—The substance of an Address, delivered in the Broadway Tabernacle, New-York, December 15, 1836, at the Funeral of Rev. John R. McDowall New-York, 1837 8°, pp. 24. [B. Ath.

10 Memorial, setting forth the importance of an equitable and adequate market for American Wheat, accompanied with statistical tables Albany, May 20, 1841 8°, pp 32 (N. Y State Assembly Document No 295.)

11. Memorial, praying that, in the revision of the tariff laws, the principle of discrimination may be inserted in favor of those countries in which American grain, flour, and salted meat are admitted duty free. Washington, 1842 8°, pp 160. (U. S. Senate Document No. 339, 27th Congress, 2d Session)

12 The Amistad Case—The Creole Case. In *Appendix* to A View of the Action of the Federal Government, in behalf of Slavery By William Jay. Utica, 1844. 12°, pp 94–112

13. The Great Duellist. [1844.] 8°, pp. 16 [M. H. S.
Against Henry Clay.

14 Leavitt's Reading Series. Boston, 1847. 4 parts. 12°.
[U S.

Part 1, Primer; 2, Easy Lessons in Reading. For the Younger Classes in common schools; 3, Reading Lessons, for the use of the Middle Classes in common schools; 4, Selections for Reading and Speaking for the Higher Classes in common schools.

15. Post-Office Reform; The British System of Postage; Our Post-Office. In the *New Englander*, vol. 6, pp. 111-20; 153-65; 393-404 (January-July, 1848).

16. Cheap Postage.—Remarks and Statistics on the subject of Cheap Postage and Postal Reform in Great Britain and the United States. Boston, 1848. 8°, pp. 72.
[*A. A. S. A. C. A. B. Publ. Br. Mus. Harv. M. H. S. N. Y. H. S. U. S. Y. C.*

The same. Reprinted with A brief statement of the Exertions of the Friends of Cheap Postage in the City of New York .. — By Barnabas Bates. New York, 1848. 8°, pp. 52.
[*B. Publ. Br. Mus. U. S. Y. C.*

17. The Finance of Cheap Postage. From Hunt's Merchants' Magazine, for October, 1849. New York, 1849. 8°, pp. 7.
[*B. Publ. Harv. M. H. S. U. S. Y. C.*

18. The Moral and Social Benefits of Cheap Postage. From Hunt's Merchants' Magazine for December, 1849. New York, 1849. 8°, pp. 12.
[*A. C. A. B. Publ. Br. Mus. Harv. Y. C.*

19. The Practical Working of Cheap Postage.—From Hunt's Merchants' Magazine for January, 1850. New York. 8°, pp. 12.
[*A. A. S. A. C. A. B. Publ. Br. Mus. Harv. U. S. Y. C.*

20. American Democracy. [A review of Benton's Thirty Years' View.]
In the *New Englander*, vol. 14, pp. 52-74, 385-409 (February and August, 1856).

21. The Monroe Doctrine. New-York, 1863. 8°, pp. 50.
[*A. A. S. B. Publ. Harv. U. S. Y. C.*
From the *New Englander*, vol. 22, pp. 729-77 (October, 1863).

22. Denmark, and its relations.—Read before the American Geographical and Statistical Society, March 3, 1864. New York, 1864. 8°, pp. 36. [*B. Publ. Br. Mus. Harv. Y. C.*

23 Poland
In the *New Englander,* vol 23, pp. 276–95 (April, 1864)

24. The Key of the Continent.
In the same volume, pp 517–39 (July, 1864).

25. An Essay on the best way of developing improved political and commercial relations between Great Britain and the United States of America. London, 1869. sm. 8°, pp. 44.
[*Br Mus Harv. U S Y C*
Cobden Club Prize Essay.

Much of the best of his work was done in connection with the periodicals of which he was successively editor,—the chief of which have been named above He also contributed largely to other periodicals, among which may be especially mentioned the *Liberator* and the *Massachusetts Abolitionist*

AUTHORITIES

Orcutt, Hist of Stratford, i, 413–14 *Packard,* Churches and Ministers of Franklin County, 236

LUCIUS WOOSTER LEFFINGWELL, the fourth son of William Leffingwell (Yale 1786), of New York City and New Haven, was born in New Haven on September 25, 1796. His father retired to New Haven in 1809 He was prepared for College by the Rev. Dr Azel Backus (Yale 1787), of Bethlehem.

He remained in New Haven for one year as a graduate student.

In 1817 he went to Ohio, and settled on a farm in Ellsworth, Mahoning County, where he resided until about 1850. He held the rank of Colonel in the militia.

He then removed to Cleveland, where he was engaged in business for some years.

His last years were spent in New Haven, where he died of paralysis on February 1, 1875, in his 79th year.

He married, on January 11, 1819, Olive Douglas, second daughter of Christopher and Olive (Perkins) Starr, of Norwich, Connecticut, who died of consumption in

Ellsworth on October 29, 1830, in her 35th year, after a long illness.

He next married, on February 7, 1832, Catharine Denny Scott, of Warren, Trumbull County, Ohio, who died on September 17, 1841.

He married, thirdly, on August 10, 1843, Emily Gaylord Ward, of Hadley, Massachusetts, who died on February 7, 1895.

By his first marriage he had four sons and a daughter; by his second marriage one son and two daughters; and by his third marriage one son. One son was graduated at Trinity College, and became a clergyman; the youngest son was graduated at Union College in 1865.

AUTHORITIES.

Starr Family, 48. Leffingwell Record, 81, 116–17.

Daniel Lord, the only child of Dr. Daniel Lord, and grandson of Captain Daniel and Elizabeth (Lord) Lord, of North Lyme, Connecticut, was born in Stonington on September 23, 1795. His mother was Phebe Crary, of Stonington. His parents removed to New York City in 1797. In his Senior year he was an editor of the short-lived magazine, called the *Athenæum,* published by his Class.

He delivered the Latin Salutatory oration at graduation.

His law studies, which were begun in the Litchfield Law School, were completed in the office of George Griffin (Yale 1797), in New York City, where he was admitted to the bar and began practice in 1817. His practice embraced every variety of law, real property, commercial law including revenue cases, and the law of shipping and insurance. He devoted himself exclusively to his profession, steadily refusing all public office. He stood beyond question in the front rank of the lawyers of his generation for ability, and was held in the highest esteem for his Christian character He was an Elder in the Brick Presbyterian Church from 1834 to his death.

He twice declined a seat on the bench (to fill vacancies), because of his deep distrust of the system of an elective judiciary, and consequent unwillingness to be in any way involved in it.

He died in New York on March 4, 1868, in his 73d year. Indistinct threatenings of paralysis several years before had led him to withdraw gradually from professional business.

He was married on May 16, 1818, to Susan, second daughter of Lockwood and Mehitable (Wheeler) De-Forest, of New York, and formerly of New Haven, for whom he had formed an attachment early in his College course. She died in 1879, at the age of 80

Their children were four sons (one of whom died in infancy) and two daughters One son was graduated at this College in 1854; and one daughter married Henry Day (Yale 1845).

A *Memorial* of Mr. Lord, published at New York in 1869, contains his photograph

Yale conferred on him the honorary degree of Doctor of Laws in 1846.

He published:

1. A Vindication of the Award, between Boorman, Johnston, & Co. and Jacob Little & Co, by one of the Referees New York, 1842 8°, pp 24. [*B. Ath Br Mus*

With reference to a contract made with bookers for the purchase of bank stock.

2 On the extra-professional Influence of the Pulpit and the Bar.—An Oration delivered at New Haven, before the Phi Beta Kappa Society, of Yale College, at their anniversary meeting, July 30, 1851. New-York, 1851. 8°, pp 20 [*B Ath B Publ. U. T S Y C*

3. Address, delivered on the Opening of the Rooms of the New York Young Men's Christian Association, September 20th, 1852 New-York, 1852 12°, pp 17 [*A. C. A*

4. Address at the Memorial Meeting in commemoration of the Fiftieth Anniversary of the Installation of the Rev. Dr. Gardiner Spring as Pastor of the Brick Church. In the *Brick Church Memorial,* New York, 1861. 8°, pp. 151–62.

5. The Effect of Secession upon the Commercial Relations between the North and South, and upon each Section. New York, 1861. 18°, pp. 72 + map.

[*B. Publ. Columbia Univ. Harv. N. Y. Publ. U. S.*

Two editions. Anonymous. A reprint from articles in the *New York Times,* with slight changes.

Numerous legal arguments by him were printed. Of these may be cited:

6. District Court of the United States, for the Southern Dist. of New-York.—The "Crenshaw" and Cargo.—On treating property of residents of the seceding States as subject to belligerent capture.—Argument. New-York, 1861. 8°, pp. 40.

[*B. Ath. Y. C.*

AUTHORITIES.

DeForests of Avesnes, 229. *Knapp,* Hist. of the Brick Church, 201, 517. *Salisbury,* Family Histories and Genealogies, i, 277–80.

John Erskine Lovett, the eldest son of John Lovett (Yale 1782), was born in Albany, New York, in 1794.

He was a contributor, in his Senior year, to the *Athenæum* published by his Class, and in particular was the author of an especially amusing article on the Miseries of College life (p. 13).

He studied law in Albany, and was admitted to practice there in July, 1816. In October, 1819, he was appointed City Attorney, and he served also for two subsequent terms, in 1825–26, and 1830-31.

He was elected by the Democrats as an Alderman of the City in 1833, and again in 1838.

From 1833 until his resignation, a few days before his death, he was Secretary of the Albany Insurance Company.

He died in Albany on August 19, 1847, in his 53d year. He was never married.

He is described as "a man of amiable and refined manners, accurate learning, strict integrity, and possessing a high sense of honor."

AUTHORITIES.

Munsell, Annals of Albany, vi, 117, x, 380–81

WHITMAN MEAD, the younger son of Whitman Mead, of Greenwich, Connecticut, and grandson of Captain Sylvanus and Sibyl (Wood) Mead, was born in Greenwich on August 5, 1792. His mother was Rachel, third daughter of Deliverance and Abigail (Howe) Mead, of Greenwich. His father died in January, 1795, and his mother married in June, 1798, Richard Mead, of Greenwich He was prepared for College by the Rev. Platt Buffett (Yale 1791), of Stanwich Society, in Greenwich.

He studied law after graduation, and settled in practice in the city of New York about 1819.

He married, on June 8, 1821, Grace, daughter of William and Elizabeth (Rhodes) Cornwell, of Brooklyn, and after about 1824 he appears to have given up his law office.

He died in Brooklyn on September 10, 1833, in his 42d year.

His widow died at the house of her son-in-law in New York City, on September 15, 1879, in her 77th year. Their children were two daughters, of whom the elder died in infancy.

AUTHORITIES

Cornell Genealogy, 228 Mead Family, 394

JOHN DAGGETT MEERS, son of Dr Solomon Meers, was born in Hartford, Connecticut, on February 28, 1794. His mother was Sally, eldest daughter of President Naphtali Daggett (Yale 1748), of New Haven.

In his infancy his parents removed to New Haven, and thence to St. Mary's, Georgia, where his mother died of yellow fever in October, 1808, not long after her husband. He then returned to New Haven, and his education was continued at the expense of his uncle, Henry Daggett, Junior (Yale 1775). He was prepared for College by the Rev. William Belden (Yale 1803) at Staples Academy, in Easton.

After graduation he taught for a short time in the Wallingford Academy, and studied medicine with Dr. Charles Shelton (Yale 1802), of Cheshire.

In July, 1818, he was licensed to practice by the Medical Association of Greene County, New York, and for a short time he practiced in New York City; whence, on the death in January, 1824, of Dr. Nimrod Hull, of Salem Bridge, a parish in Waterbury, now the town of Naugatuck, Connecticut, he removed to that place. Here he continued to practice (with the exception of about two years, 1845-47, spent in Blackwoodtown, Camden County, New Jersey) until enfeebled by age, a few years before his death.

He died in Naugatuck on May 19, 1877, in his 84th year.

He was married about 1822 to Mrs. Julia B. Wickes; and again in 1835 to Susan Bateman, who survived him.

By his first marriage he had three children, of whom one son only (a physician) survived him. He had nine children by his second marriage, of whom four survived him. A son was graduated at the Yale Medical School in 1874.

AUTHORITIES.

Conn. Med. Society's Proceedings, 1878, 208-09.

Anson Moody, the second son of Captain Daniel Moody, of Granby, formerly a part of South Hadley, Massachusetts, was born on February 25, 1792. His mother was Abigail, elder daughter of Deacon David and Elizabeth

(Smith) Nash, of South Hadley He was prepared for College by the Rev. Joel Hayes (Yale 1773), of South Hadley.

After teaching a young ladies' school in Hatfield for one term, he began the study of medicine in South Hadley, and continued it in 1815–16 in the Yale Medical School. Being licensed to practice in the spring of 1817, he settled in Palmer, Massachusetts, and on November 7 in the same year married Clarissa, daughter of Ebenezer Collins, of South Hadley.

About 1822 or 1823 he removed to Belchertown, in the same vicinity In 1829 he again removed, to Ware, in the same immediate neighborhood, where he formed a partnership with his classmate Goodrich

About 1837, at the urgent request of the inhabitants of North Haven, Connecticut, he removed to that village, where he had an eminently useful career, until 1848, when he settled in New Haven. Here he continued in the active pursuit of his profession until his death on February 11, 1855, at the age of 63.

He was a deacon in the Congregational Church in Belchertown for a few months before his removal, was again elected a deacon in 1838 in North Haven, and again (from January, 1850) in the College Street Church in New Haven. He was greatly respected for his piety, as well as for his professional judgment. The honorary degree of Doctor of Medicine was conferred on him by Yale in 1840.

His wife survived him, with their three sons, two of whom received the degree of M D. from Yale, in 1844 and 1852, respectively; another child died in infancy.

The address at his funeral by his pastor, the Rev. Edward Strong (Yale 1838), was published.

AUTHORITIES.

Conn Med Society's Proceedings, 1861, 125–28 *Doolittle,* Hist Sketch of Church in Belchertown, 190–91 Nash Family, 130 *Strong,* Address at Deacon Moody's Funeral. *Temple,* Hist. of Palmer, 522–23.

WILLIAM JOHNSON RYSAM MULFORD, son of Edward and Fanny (Rysam) Mulford, of the village of Sag Harbor, in East-Hampton, Long Island, and grandson of Ezekiel and Amy Mulford, was born on October 18, 1794, and was prepared for College by the Rev. Dr. Aaron Woolworth (Yale 1784), of Bridgehampton.

For several years he was successfully engaged in the shipping and whaling business in Sag Harbor. Later, owing to ill health and a naturally reserved disposition, he led a very quiet and retired life, until his death, which occurred in Sag Harbor on July 24, 1865, in his 71st year.

He married on August 21, 1827, Harriet Elmira, eldest daughter of Henry B. and Hannah S. (Sayre) Havens, of Sag Harbor. Their children were two daughters, who survived him, the only son having fallen a victim, in 1864, to prison life in Andersonville.

AUTHORITIES.

Hedges, Hist. of East-Hampton, 315-16. *Mallmann,* Shelter Island, 165, 168. *R. M. Stilwell,* MS. Letter, January, 1868.

WILLIAM WOOLSEY MUMFORD, the eldest of nine children of Colonel Thomas Mumford (Yale 1790), of Aurora and Cayuga, New York, was born in Aurora on November 13, 1795, and was prepared for College by the Rev. Dr. Azel Backus (Yale 1787), of Bethlehem, Connecticut.

He studied law after graduation and settled in Rochester in practice, being admitted to the bar in 1818. He was also largely engaged in real-estate investments with a good degree of success.

He died in Rochester on January 9, 1848, in his 54th year.

He married on October 14, 1827, Angelina S. Jenkins, of Hudson, who died on March 25, 1836, in her 29th year. Their children were two sons and four daughters. The elder son was graduated at Union College in 1849, and the younger at Hamilton College in 1851. Three of the daughters died in infancy.

AUTHORITIES

Amer Ancestry, v, 195 Mumford Memoirs, 180–81.

EBENEZER MUNGER, son of Ebenezer Munger, and grandson of Ebenezer and Ann (Lee) Munger, of Guilford, was born in East Guilford, now Madison, Connecticut, on July 22, 1794. His mother was Sarah, only daughter of Nathaniel and Rebecca (Eliot) Graves, of Guilford He was prepared for College by his pastor, the Rev Dr. John Elliott (Yale 1786).

After graduation he spent two years as a private tutor in New Rochelle, New York, and then devoted two years to the study of medicine in New York City. He began practice in Middle Haddam, where he married on December 31, 1818, Cynthia, elder daughter of the Rev. David Selden (Yale 1782).

About 1822 he removed to Bainbridge, Chenango County, New York, where he became for the first time an active Christian Thenceforth he was distinguished by earnest efforts to advance religion, and was especially efficient as he went about by the distribution of tracts and other religious publications.

In 1836 he removed to Homer in Cortland County for the sake of the excellent educational advantages afforded by the academy in that place He then relinquished practice, and devoted himself mainly for the rest of his life to agriculture

He died in Homer from typhoid fever on October 13, 1857, in his 64th year. His widow died on April 7, 1868, in her 78th year.

A son was graduated at Yale in 1851, and became an honored member of the Yale Corporation

AUTHORITIES

Rev T T. Munger, MS Letter, May, 1858.

Frederic Augustus Norton was born in Goshen, Litchfield County, Connecticut, in 1794.

He was prepared for College by the Rev. Dr. Azel Backus (Yale 1787), in Bethlehem.

He never engaged in any business, and resided mainly in New York City, though partly in Goshen. His mind was much impaired for some years before his death.

He died in New York on December 7, 1846, aged 52 years.

Jesse Oakley entered College from Poughkeepsie, New York, at the opening of the Sophomore year, having been prepared by Daniel H. Barnes (Union 1809), at the Poughkeepsie Academy. He was born on June 21, 1795, and was a son of Lieutenant Jesse and Jerusha Oakley, of Beekman, now Lagrange, Duchess County, and a brother of Judge Thomas J. Oakley (Yale 1801). His mother was the second daughter of George and Sarah (Smith) Peters, of Pleasant Valley, in the same county. The family removed to Poughkeepsie in 1802.

He entered on the practice of law in the city of New York in 1817, and was a prominent member of the Tammany Society. He was made clerk of the Superior Court about 1844, and retained that place until his death.

He took his own life, by shooting, on September 23, 1848, in his 54th year.

He was unmarried.

AUTHORITIES.

Peters Lineage, 97.

David Longworth Ogden, the youngest child of Jacob Ogden, of Hartford, Connecticut, and grandson of David and Catharine (Ogden) Ogden, of Newark, New Jersey, was born in Hartford on October 6, 1792. His middle name was that of his grandmother's second husband His mother was Jerusha, daughter of Captain Joseph and Anna (Dodd) Rockwell, of Colebrook. His father removed to Stratford in 1804, and to New Haven in 1809, and was the proprietor of a well-known Coffee House here. He was prepared for College by Elizur Goodrich (Williams Coll. 1806) in the Hopkins Grammar School His father was an Episcopalian, and his mother a Congregationalist. He united with the First Church in January, 1809

During the year after graduation he remained in New Haven as a graduate student. He then went to Andover and spent two years in the Theological Seminary there, after which he spent a third year in New Haven, under the instruction of Professor Fitch. He was licensed to preach by the New Haven West Association of Ministers on December 7, 1817.

After having declined several calls, he began in April, 1821, to supply the pulpit of the Congregational Church in Southington, and in August he was called to be their minister, on a salary of $600.

He accepted the call, and was ordained and installed as pastor on October 31.

He was married on January 14, 1824, to Sarah Amanda, eldest child of Daniel and Sarah (Plant) Judson, of Stratford, and sister of David P. Judson (Yale 1831) and William Judson (Yale 1834).

His pastorate was a fruitful and happy one, but he was hampered by the want of promptness in paying his inadequate salary, and annoyed by the evident dissatisfaction of a few persons. His sensitiveness led him to request a dismission in August, 1836, and although his people then proposed an increase of salary, the lack of unanimity in their action led him to persist in his request, and he was accordingly dismissed on September 13. During the time of his candidacy and his settled ministry he had admitted four hundred and eighty-one members to the church; there had been several revivals of special power.

He had already received a call, on July 13, to the Presbyterian Church in Whitesboro, Oneida County, New York, which he accepted in November, and he was installed pastor on December 28. The period of his service there was one of agitation, on the slavery question, on "new measures" in theology, and on the division of the Presbyterian Church; and his direct success in building up his parish was not so marked as it had been in Southington, although it was very considerable.

He was elected a Trustee of Hamilton College in 1841, and held the office until 1847.

He was dismissed at his own request on October 3, 1844, and after brief periods of employment elsewhere, he was installed on April 26, 1848, as pastor of the Union (Congregational) Church in Marlboro, Massachusetts. A small number in the church soon became disaffected, and in consequence he was dismissed by a mutual council held on July 23, 1850. He left Marlboro in December, and retired to New Haven. In 1853 he preached for several months in Colebrook, but declined a unanimous call on account of long existing differences in the parish. In later years he preached only occasionally.

He died in New Haven on October 31, 1863, at the age of 71, of typhoid fever, after an illness of four or five days.

His widow died in New Haven on June 24, 1890, in her 91st year.

His children were four daughters, of whom two died early, and a son (Yale 1861), who followed his father's profession.

Mr. Ogden was a man of great simplicity and unreserved frankness, a good scholar, and a zealous preacher.

He published:

1. On Slander; A loving epistle on Idleness; A society for criticism on preaching; Sleeping in church.

In the *Microscope*, volume 1, pp. 57–64; volume 2, pp. 6–8, 153–60, 165–68 (New Haven, April–August, 1820).

2 Public Worship: a Sermon [from Ps lxxxix, 7] delivered at the Dedication of the New Congregational Church in Cheshire, August 1, 1827. New Haven, 1827. 8°, pp 24
[*A A S A C A. C H S. U. T S. Y. C*

3. The Excellence of Liberality—A Sermon [from Prov xi, 24] delivered at Farmington, before the Auxiliary Foreign Mission Society, of Farmington and vicinity, Oct 22, 1828. New Haven, 1828. 8°, pp 20. [*A. C A B Publ C H S. Y. C.*

4 Two Discourses, the first [from Isa v, 20], on the Misapplication of Religious Names, and the second [from Neh ii, 10], on the Misrepresentation of Benevolent Actions; delivered in Berlin, Worthington Society, June 13, 1830. Hartford, 1830 8°, pp. 49.
[*A A S A C A. C H S. U. T. S. Y. C.*

The first discourse is mainly in criticism of so-called liberal Christianity; the second is a defence of missionary operations

5 Discourses on Baptism and Close Communion New Haven, 1834 12°, pp. 148. [*A A. S. A C A B Publ Y C*

Contains five sermons.

6 A Farewell Sermon [from II Cor. xiii, 11], delivered to the Congregational Church and Society in Southington, September 18, 1836 New Haven, 1836 8°, pp 16
[*A. A. S. A C. A. C. H S. Y. C.*

7. Review of a Pamphlet entitled "Reply of the Congregational Church in Whitesboro to a Question of the Oneida Presbytery." Utica, 1839. 8°, pp. 16. [*C. H S.*

Mr. Ogden was known as a friend of the Colonization Society, when he was called to the Presbyterian Church in Whitesboro, which had a strong anti-slavery element; nevertheless a portion of the church took dismissions and formed a Congregational Church.

8 The Liturgy of the Protestant Episcopal Church in America. In the *New Englander,* volume 1, pp 469-91 (October, 1843)

9 College Reminiscences

In the same, volume 5, pp 572-76 (October, 1847).

A notice of a book by the Rev John Mitchell (Yale 1821), and in particular of a chapter on college revivals

10. A Statement of Facts concerning the dissolution of the late pastoral connection in Marlboro', Mass. New Haven, 1851. 8°, pp. 16. [*Y. C.*

An account of his pastorate in Marlboro.

11. The Trials of Bishop Ives; Baptist Close Communion.

In the *New Englander*, volume 13, pp. 363–78, 562–83 (August and November, 1855).

12. In the *History of Southington*, 1875 (pp. 144–46), is printed an account of the revival in Southington in 1831, written soon after by Mr. Ogden.

AUTHORITIES.

Hudson, Hist. of Marlborough, 208. *Orcutt,* Hist. of Stratford, ii, 1231. *Salisbury,* Family-Histories and Genealogies, ii, 268–69. *Timlow,* Hist. of Southington, 11, 13–15, 133–46, cc. *Wheeler,* Ogden Family, 100, 174–75.

JAMES POTTER was born in Charleston, South Carolina, on August 23, 1792. His father was John Potter, a native of Ireland, who emigrated to Charleston after the close of the Revolution, became a successful merchant there, and married Miss Fuller, an aunt of the distinguished Baptist preacher of Baltimore, the Rev. Dr. Richard Fuller. A sister of James Potter married Commodore Robert F. Stockton. He came North in May, 1810, with his classmate Dulles.

As his temperament did not incline him either to a professional or to a mercantile life, his father gave him a large rice plantation on the Georgia side of the Savannah River. After extended travel in Europe he settled there, married Miss Grimes, of Georgia, and entered with every advantage on his chosen occupation.

He was an industrious and successful planter, and a considerate and kind master to his slaves. His plantation and rice mills were regarded as models of systematic and skilful management.

As his children grew up, he spent the greater part of his time in Princeton, New Jersey, for the sake of their education. His wealth enabled him to exercise large hospitality, and to respond generously to the calls of charity and religion He was devotedly attached to the Episcopal Church.

When the Civil War began he repaired to his home in Georgia, to throw all his influence in favor of measures for peace. His anxiety over the political situation preyed upon his health and spirits, and hastened his death, which occurred in Savannah, on January 25, 1862, in his 70th year.

Six children survived him.

SAMUEL PUNDERSON, youngest son of Samuel Punderson, of New Haven, and a first cousin of the Rev. Thomas Punderson (Yale 1804), was born in New Haven on January 22, 1791. His mother was Eunice, daughter of Matthew Gilbert, of Hamden. He was prepared for College by the Rev. Bennet Tyler (Yale 1804), of South Britain.

He studied medicine with Dr James Gilbert (Yale 1800), of New Haven, and began practice here in 1818.

On May 21, 1823, he was married to Caroline Swift, of Cornwall, daughter of Philo and Eunice Swift, and niece of Erastus Swift (Yale 1800), who died in New Haven on October 3, 1860, in her 63d year.

In 1863 Dr. Punderson retired from practice After the gradual failure of his health, he died of pneumonia, after a week's illness, in New Haven, on March 13, 1870, in his 80th year.

He had four children, of whom only one son survived him; two sons died in infancy, and a daughter in early womanhood.

The honorary degree of Doctor of Medicine was conferred on him by Yale in 1834. He was highly respected in his profession, and a consistent member of the United Church.

The only article from his pen in permanent form which I have seen is:

Memoir of Dr. James Gilbert.

In *Thacher's* American Medical Biography, Boston, 1828. 8°, volume 2, pp. 247-49.

AUTHORITIES.

Chapman, Trowbridge Family, 48.

Frederick Allyn Richards, the second son of Colonel William and Eunice (Wells) Richards, of New London, Connecticut, and grandson of Samuel and Anna (Hough) Richards, of New London, was born on March 11, 1794, and was prepared for College by his pastor, the Rev. Abel McEwen (Yale 1804).

He became insane, from severe mental application, about the time of his graduation, and after having continued in that state for thirty years, he died at the Retreat for the Insane in Hartford, of general paralysis, on February 14, 1846, in his 52d year.

He was never married.

AUTHORITIES.

Dr. J. S. Butler, MS. Letter, December, 1864. *Morse,* Richards Family, 97.

Abraham Topping Rose, son of Dr. Samuel Rose, of Bridgehampton, in the township of Southampton, Long Island, and grandson of Abraham Rose, was born in Bridgehampton in 1792. He was prepared for the Sophomore Class by his pastor, the Rev. Dr. Aaron Woolworth (Yale 1784).

He studied law after graduation, and on being admitted to the bar in 1818 settled in practice in his native village. He became a locally famous advocate, being an easy and eloquent orator, popular, genial, versatile, and brilliant.

He was one of the Judges of the Suffolk County Court, and Surrogate from 1846 to 1851, and again from 1856 until his resignation, a fortnight before his death. He was a Whig Presidential Elector in 1848

After an illness of several months, he died in Bridgehampton on April 28, 1857, aged 65 years.

He was received into the Presbyterian Church on profession of his faith a few days before his death.

By his wife, Eliza, he had six daughters, besides one son, of much promise, who died in early manhood

AUTHORITIES

Hon. H. P Hedges, MS. Letter, June, 1870 *Howell,* Hist of Southampton, 2d ed., 370

Isaac Wakelee Ruggles was born in Brookfield, Connecticut, on July 14, 1783, and was prepared for admission to College at the opening of the Junior year by his pastor, the Rev. Richard Williams (Yale 1802). He was the oldest member of the Class at graduation.

For five years after leaving College he was occupied in teaching Having meantime prepared himself for the ministry, he was ordained and installed by the Union (Congregational) Association of Ministers, in February, 1820, as pastor of a small church in South Bainbridge, Chenango County, New York. He remained there until 1824, when he accepted a commission from the Domestic Missionary Society of New York, with a salary of one hundred dollars, and proceeded to Michigan, where he spent the remainder of his life. For many years he was the only Congregational or Presbyterian minister in the vicinity of Monroe and Pontiac, where he successively lived.

Some years before his death he was obliged by failing health to give up his work, and he found his recreation in the cultivation of fruit.

He died in Owosso on May 28, 1857, in his 74th year.

SAMUEL BULKLEY RUGGLES, the eldest child of the Hon. Philo Ruggles, a lawyer, of New Milford, Connecticut, and Poughkeepsie, New York, and grandson of Lazarus and Hannah (Bostwick) Ruggles, of New Milford, was born in New Milford on April 11, 1799. His mother was Ellen, only daughter of Captain Joseph and Ellen (Hubbell) Bulkley, of Greenfield Hill in Fairfield. The family removed to Poughkeepsie, in 1804, and he was prepared for admission to the Sophomore Class at the age of 13½ years by Daniel H. Barnes (Union Coll. 1809) at the Poughkeepsie Academy. He was the youngest in the Class at graduation.

He studied law in his father's office, was admitted to the bar in 1820, and established himself in New York City.

Success attended him from the first; and outside his professional career he early became so interested in real estate operations and in great public improvements, that in 1831 he retired from active practice, to devote himself to these objects. From 1833 to 1838 he was largely engaged in the preliminary steps for securing the construction of the Erie railroad; and when in 1838 he was elected to the Assembly, he made in his capacity as Chairman of the Committee of Ways and Means, such a reputation by his report on the canal policy of the State that in February, 1839, he was appointed a Canal Commissioner. He served as president of the Board of Commissioners from 1840 to 1858, and his work in this position was most important. In politics he was an intimate associate of William H. Seward. He was also a commissioner of the Croton aqueduct from 1842, and active in his office. He became a recognized authority in matters affecting the commercial standing of the city, and after his retirement from the Canal Board he devoted himself especially to the careful study of questions of finance and statistics. He was one of the founders of the Bank of Commerce in

1839, and one of the most respected members of the Chamber of Commerce.

He served with distinction on several important public commissions, and was repeatedly sent abroad to represent this country in international conferences.

His investments in real estate in New York enabled him to lay out Gramercy Park in 1831 and present it to the surrounding property owners He also contributed liberally to the formation of Union Square, and was an original promoter of the Central Park.

He was a trustee of Columbia College from 1836 until his death, he was also the last survivor of the trustees of the Astor Library, named in the founder's will

He was prominent in the councils of the Episcopal Church.

The honorary degree of Doctor of Laws was conferred on him by Yale in 1859.

In June, 1881, he suffered from a stroke of paralysis, which caused his death on the 28th of August, at a hotel on Fire Island, in his 83d year.

He married on May 15, 1822, Mary Rosalie, youngest daughter of John and Eunice (Wells) Rathbone, of New York; a sister married Dr. Charles H. Wetmore (Yale 1804). She died three or four years before her husband.

They had two sons, one of whom died in early life, and a daughter, who married George T. Strong (Columbia Coll 1838).

A portrait is given in the *Tribute* to his memory issued by the New York Chamber of Commerce; and another in the *Green Bag*, volume 1, page 147.

An incomplete list of his publications follows:

1. Report upon the Finances and Internal Improvements of the State of New-York 1838

In the New-York Assembly Documents, also, reprinted, New York, 1838 8°, pp 2+65+6; Boston, 1839 8°, pp 65+6.

Signed by Mr Ruggles, as chairman of the Committee of Ways and Means An epoch-making Report in the Canal policy of the State.

2. Articles of Association of the Bank of Commerce, in New-York. . . . New-York, 1839. 8°, pp. 28. [*Y. C.*

The Articles occupy pp. 1–18; they were drawn by Mr. Ruggles.

3. Memorial of the Panama Rail-road Company. 1849. pp. 24.

4. Vindication in 1849, of the Canal Policy of the State of New York, in a letter to Citizens of Rochester. [New-York, 1849.] 8°, pp. 50.

[*A. A. S. B. Publ. Harv. N. Y. Publ. Y. C.*

5. Speech, in behalf of a National University.

In Speeches in behalf of the University of Albany. . Published by the Committee of the Young Men's Association of the City of Albany—March, 1852. Albany, 1852. 8°, pp. 3–19.

[*B. Publ. Br. Mus. N. Y. Publ. Y. C.*

6. Evening Post Extra. Is a Law Against Slavery in the Territories necessary? Some hints to the Delegates of the Rome Conventions. New York, 1852. 8°, pp. 8.

7. Defense of the Right and the Duty of the American Union to improve its Navigable Waters, in a Speech, at Constitution Hall, in the City of New York, October 8, 1852. New York, 1852. 8°, pp. 31.

[*A. A. S. B. Publ. Br. Mus. Columbia Univ. Harv.*

8. The Duty of Columbia College to the community, and its right to exclude Unitarians from its Professorships of Physical Science. Considered by one of its Trustees. New York, 1854. 8°, pp. 54.

[*B. Publ. Br. Mus. Harv. N. Y. Publ. U. S. Y. C.*

A protest against the defeat of the candidacy of Dr. Wolcott Gibbs; two replies were printed.

9. An Examination of the Law of Burial, in a Report to the Supreme Court of New-York, by S. B. Ruggles, Referee. In the matter of taking a portion of the Cemetery of the Brick Presbyterian Church, in widening Beekman-Street, in the City of New-York. New-York, 1856. 8°, pp. i, 59.

[*B. Publ. N. Y. Publ.*

The same, with title, Law of Burial. . Albany, 1858. 8°, pp. 44.

[*Harv. N. Y. Publ.*

10 American Commerce & American Union: their mutual dependence briefly examined in a Review of the Address delivered at the Merchants' Exchange, by the Hon. Mr. Banks, Speaker of the House of Representatives of the United States [New York, 1856.] 8°, pp 12. [*B. Publ. M H. S. N Y Publ. Y. C.*
Originally published in the *New York Commercial Advertiser.*

The same With the Reply and Rejoinder. New York, 1856 8°, pp 34 [*B Publ N. Y Publ*

11 Report of the Select Committee of Columbia College, on Prize Scholarships. 1857.

12 Memorial of the Canal Board & Canal Commissioners.—Improvement of the Lake Harbors 1858. pp 30

13. Report of the State of the Canals in 1858. 1859

14 Speech in the General Episcopal Convention, at Richmond, on the Proposed Court of Appeals, October 12, 1859 New York, 1859 8°, pp. 16 [*B Publ Harv. M. H. S. N. Y. Publ.*
Cover-title, Union in the Church and Nation.

The same Reprinted 1874 8°, pp 16 [*A. A. S. Harv. M H. S.*
The speech is in opposition to the proposed Court, which was voted down in 1859

15 Speech in the General Convention of the Protestant Episcopal Church of the United States, held at Richmond, Va., Oct. 21, 1859, on the Duty of the Laity. New York, 1860 8°, pp 20. [*Harv. N Y Publ.*

16. Writings and Speeches. Republished with supplementary notes New York, 1860. 8°.

17 The Justice of a State—Argument, before the Canal Board of the State of New York, in support of the claim of the Niagara Manufacturing Company, September 20, 1860. New York, 1860. 8°, pp. 32 [*B Publ Y C*

18. Memorial in behalf of the State of New York in respect to Adapting its Canals to the Defense of the Lakes. with the Message of the President of the United States, commending it to Congress.—Washington, June 13th, 1862 Washington City 4°, pp 15. [*N Y. Publ Y C*

19 Report of S B Ruggles, Commissioner appointed by the Governor of the State of New York, under the Concurrent Resolu-

tion of the Legislature, of April 22, 1862, in respect to the Enlargement of the Canals for national purposes. Albany, 1863. 8°, pp. 105. [*Br. Mus. N. Y. Publ. U. S. Y. C.*

20. Reports of S. B. Ruggles, delegate to the International Statistical Congress, at Berlin, on the Resources of the United States, and on a Uniform System of Weights and Measures. .. Albany, 1864. 8°, pp. 131.
[*B. Ath. B. Publ. Br. Mus. Harv. Y. C.*
Editions were also published in New York and in Washington.

21. Union Square and the Sanitary Commission. Address, at Union Square, on the Opening of the Metropolitan Fair, April 8th, 1864. New York, 1864. 8°, pp. 15.
[*A. A. S. B. Ath. B. Publ. Harv.*
Including a history of Union Square.

22. The Past and the Present.—Semi-Centennial Address to the Alumni of Yale College, and Graduates of 1814, at their annual meeting, July 27, 1864. .. New York, 1864. 8°, pp. 47.
[*B. Ath. B. Publ. Br. Mus. Harv. M. H. S. U. S. Y. C.*

23. The English Heptarchy and the American Union. [New York, 1864.] 8°, pp. 8. [*B. Ath. Harv.*
Remarks made at a complimentary dinner to Professor Goldwin Smith, November 12, 1864.

24. The Railways and Telegraphs of the Nineteenth Century, considered in an Address, delivered at the Banquet given by the Chamber of Commerce of the State of New-York to Cyrus W. Field, November 15th, 1866. New-York, 1866. 8°, pp. 11.
[*B. Publ. Harv.*

25. Freedom of Ocean Telegraphs. Speech in Chamber of Commerce. New-York, December 6, 1866. New-York, 1866. 8°, pp. 7. [*Harv.*

26. International Coinage. Report to the Department of State by S. B. Ruggles, delegate from the United States in the International Monetary Conference at Paris, 1867. [Washington, 1867.] 8°, pp. 20. [*Harv. U. S.*

27. Uniformity of Gold Coinage. Speech, at the Public Banquet to the Chinese Embassy, New York, June 22, 1868. [New York, 1868.] 8°, pp. 8. [*B. Ath. B. Publ.*

28. Shall the President and Vice President of the United States be separately and directly elected by the People? Is it safe to elect

Gen Blair? Speech, at Delhi, N. Y, August 29, 1868—From the Delaware Express, Delhi, September 2, 1868. 4°, pp. 2
[*A. A S. B. Publ. Harv.*

29. Paris Universal Exposition, 1867. Reports of the United States Commissioners—Report on Cereals—[Part 1.] The quantities of different cereals produced in different countries compared Washington, 1869. 8°, pp 14 [*B. Publ. Harv. U S Y. C*

30. Internationality and International Congresses. Report to the Department of State by S. B Ruggles, Delegate of the United States to the International Statistical Congress at the Hague, in 1869, with the accompanying documents, including the Report to the Congress on the Comparative Population and Cereal Product of Europe and the United States Washington, 1869. 8°, pp. 76.
[*M. H S N Y Publ*

31. International Coinage Supplemental Report to the Department of State, by S B. Ruggles, United States' delegate to the International Monetary Conference at Paris, 1867. New York, 1870. 8°, pp 40 [*Harv. N. Y Publ. U. S.*

32. Report of the Committee of the Chamber of Commerce of the State of New-York, on Pacific Ocean Telegraphs, in connection with the Commerce of the World. Presented to the Chamber, March 2, 1871. New-York, 1871. 8°, pp 23 [*A A S.*

33. Tabular Statements, from 1840 to 1870, of the Agricultural Products of the States and Territories of the United States of America, Classified by their Proximity to the Oceans and other Navigable Waters, Natural and Artificial New York, 1874. 8°, pp 37. [*B. Publ. Br Mus. Harv. N. Y. Publ. U. S.*

34 The Relations of American Agriculture to the American Union and the Commerce and Population of the World. examined in Official Reports and other writings of S. B. Ruggles With Tabular Statements from 1840 to 1870. New-York, 1874. 8°, pp. 111+37. [*N Y Publ.*

Containing an extract from No. 1 (above), No 7, No. 32, No. 33, and a communication to the Department of State, June, 1869, on International and Intercolonial Relations of American Agriculture

35 The Rise and Growth of the Metropolis New York, 1875. 8°, pp. 16 + map [*N Y. Publ. U. S*

Also, with the following title: Letters on rapid transit in New York. [New York, 1877.] 8°, pp. 16 + pl. [*Columbia Univ.*

From the Minutes and Proceedings of the Board of Commissioners of Rapid Transit, New York.

36. "The Dollar of our Fathers." Movement of silver.—Speech before the Convention of the American Bankers' Association, held in the City of New-York, September 13, 1877.—Published for the information of the Chamber, with supplementary historical notes. New-York, 1877. 8°, pp. 16.
[*A. A. S. Columbia Univ. N. Y. Publ.*

37. The Vital Necessity of a Preliminary International Monetary Conference for Establishing the Relative Legal Values of Gold & Silver Coin.—Letter in behalf of the New-York Chamber of Commerce, to the Director of the Mint of the United States, November 25th, 1876. New-York, 1877. 8°, pp. 10.
[*A. A. S. B. Ath. Columbia Univ. N. Y. Publ.*

39. The Fiscal Importance of the Export of Animal Food from the United States. New York, 1879. 8°, pp. 13. [*N. Y. Publ.*

40. United States of America. Consolidated Table, exhibiting by decades and geographical divisions the agricultural progress of the nation, in cheapening the food of America and Europe. Supplementary to "The Relations of American Agriculture to the American Union....," examined... Printed for the use of the Chamber of Commerce of the State of New-York. New-York, 1880. 8°, pp. 31, xix + map. [*U. S.*

The same. 2d edition, with additional notes. New-York, 1880. 8°, pp. 31, xix + map. [*N. Y. Publ. U. S.*

AUTHORITIES.

Cooley, Rathbone Genealogy, 356. *Dwight,* Strong Family, i, 639. *Hone,* Diary, i, 298, 301. N. Y. Chamber of Commerce, Tribute to his memory. *Orcutt,* Hist. of New Milford, 606. *W. H. Seward,* Autobiography, i, 341–43, 359, 394, 439–40; ii, 94–95, 128. *Talcott,* N. Y. and N. E. Families, 647.

Ebenezer Seeley, son of Ebenezer Seeley, of Wilton, then a parish in Norwalk, Connecticut, was born in Wilton on April 9, 1793. His mother was a Miss Coley. He entered the Sophomore Class from the adjoining town of Weston, having been prepared by William Belden (Yale 1803), at Staples Academy in that part of Weston which is now Easton.

After graduation he began the study of law in New Haven with Seth P. Staples (Yale 1797), and during the year 1815-16 was the rector of the Hopkins Grammar School He then continued his legal studies with the Hon. Roger Minott Sherman (Yale 1792), in Fairfield, and began practice there, but about 1820 removed to Bridgeport.

In 1825, he returned to New Haven, and in June, 1832, was elected Mayor of the city for one year, and in 1834 was sent to the State Senate.

In 1837 he removed to New York, where he continued in practice until towards the time of his death, which occurred at his son's house in Sing Sing, on January 23, 1866, in his 74th year.

Mr. Seeley had a marked dislike of political distinction, and preferred to devote himself strictly to his profession. An able and learned lawyer, he also maintained through life an unusual familiarity with classical authors.

He first married Elizabeth, eldest daughter of John Titus, of Flushing, Long Island, who died in Bridgeport, on January 18, 1823, at the age of 39.

He married secondly Alice, daughter of John I. Glover, of New York, who died there on July 1, 1844.

His children were two sons by his first marriage, only one of whom (non-graduate Yale 1836) survived him.

AUTHORITIES

New Haven City Year Book, 1864. *J T. Seeley,* MS Letter, 1866

EDWARD PETER SIMONS, a son of Maurice Simons, of Georgetown, South Carolina, was born at Rice Hope, on September 15, 1794. His mother was Elizabeth, daughter of Peter Simons, and first cousin of her husband The family was of Huguenot descent. A nephew was graduated at Yale in 1847.

His parents both died in his infancy, and he was left without any near relatives to advise or control him. His preparation for College was completed under John Waldo in Georgetown.

After graduation he studied law for a year in Charleston with a relative, Colonel Keating Lewis Simons, and then attended lectures in the Litchfield Law School.

He was admitted to the Charleston bar in 1817, and soon acquired a reputation for eloquence and legal knowledge, so that when his preceptor, Colonel Simons, died in the latter part of 1819 he inherited the most of his large and profitable business.

His popularity was such that, at the first vacancy, he was elected a representative in the State Legislature, and was regularly returned until his death. He was also a member of the City Council from 1821. No young man in the community had brighter prospects.

He fell in a duel in Charleston on October 7, 1823, aged 29 years.

His wife and two children survived him.

AUTHORITIES.

O'Neall, Bench and Bar of S. C., ii, 488–500, 603.

William Smith was born in Springfield, Massachusetts, in 1793 or 1794, and was prepared for College by Rinaldo Burleigh (Yale 1803), in the Plainfield (Connecticut) Academy.

He studied law after graduation, and settled in St. Charles, Missouri, where he was a member of the Convention which formed the State government in 1821, as also in 1818 of the Territorial Legislature.

He removed in 1827 to Galena, Illinois, where he was recognized as an excellent lawyer, of fine talents, but of intemperate habits.

He died in Galena on May 26, 1839, aged about 56 years.

AUTHORITIES

Hist of Jo Daviess County. 1878, 497

GEORGE EVANS SPRUILL, son of Benjamin Spruill, of Tarboro, Edgecombe County, North Carolina, of Scotch descent, a member of the General Assembly of the State in 1776-84, and of Ann (Hines, Evans) Spruill, was born in 1793. His scholarship was so distinguished that he gave the Valedictory Oration at graduation He was also one of the Board of Editors of the *Athenæum* published by the Class, and author of the introductory Prospectus.

He studied law, and in 1818 married Maria Louisa, daughter of Thomas Blount and Rebecca (Norfleet) Hill. He then settled in the practice of his profession in Greenwood, Halifax County, but in 1821 removed to Warrenton, in Warren County, where he built up a successful business and was widely known as an honest lawyer and a model citizen. He held the office of State's Attorney, and was a member of the Legislature, but in general shrank from political contests. He was a member of the Protestant Episcopal Church, of deeply religious nature In his will he gave directions that his slaves should all be set free when his children had grown up. He died on his plantation, from a prevailing epidemic, on April 25, 1845, at the age of 52

AUTHORITIES

Miss L H Norfleet, MS. Letter, March, 1912

JAMES LANDON STARK, eldest child of Jedediah Hyde Stark, a lawyer of Salisbury, Connecticut, and grandson of Silas and Jerusha (Hyde) Stark, of Colchester, was born in Salisbury on October 12, 1792. His mother was

Abigail, daughter of James Camp, of Salisbury. Immediately after his birth the family removed to Halifax, in Vermont, near the Southern border. He was prepared for College by his pastor, the Rev. Thomas H. Wood (Williams Coll. 1799).

On graduation he began the study of law in his father's office, and on his admission to the bar he began practice in the same town, of which he continued a resident through life.

He was a representative in the Legislature in 1823, 1824, 1827, 1828, 1834, and 1839, and a Judge of the Windham County Court in 1823-24, 1826-31, and 1834. He also kept a country tavern in Halifax. The latter part of his life was devoted to agricultural pursuits, which were most congenial to his tastes.

He died in South Halifax on March 14, 1868, in his 76th year.

He was married on November 2, 1817, to Sibyl, daughter of Asa and Submit (Severance) Smith, of Halifax. Of his seven sons and two daughters, one daughter and three sons survived him; two sons died in infancy.

AUTHORITIES.

Hemenway, Vermont Hist. Gazetteer, v, pt. 2, 419. *Jed. Stark,* MS. Letter, June, 1868. *Walworth,* Hyde Genealogy, i, 515.

Heman Stebbins, son of Solomon Stebbins, of West Springfield, Massachusetts, and grandson of Benjamin and Sabra (Lyman) Stebbins, was born on June 3, 1791. His mother was Mahala, third daughter of Colonel Benjamin Day, of West Springfield, and sister of Benjamin Day (Yale 1768). He was prepared for College at Monson Academy under Levi Collins (Yale 1802).

He studied law after graduation, and on being admitted to the bar in the spring of 1819 settled in (South) Brookfield, where he practiced his profession for about fifteen years. He was also an expert land surveyor, and for the

45

last three years of his life he was employed as a civil engineer, in running the experimental lines for the location of the Western Railroad, which passed through Brookfield.

He died in Brookfield on November 9, 1838, in his 48th year.

He was a deacon in the Unitarian Church of South Brookfield.

He married on October 23, 1824, Sarah May, youngest child of Amos and Polly (Lyon) Paine, of (South) Woodstock, Connecticut, who removed to Providence after his death, and died there on October 23, 1881, aged 77 years.

Their children were one son and three daughters.

AUTHORITIES.

Rev L. T. Chamberlain, MS Letter, August, 1867 Paine Family Records, i, 187, ii, 66-67, 113 W. Springfield Centennial Celebration, 123

JOSEPH CLAY STILES, the second son of Joseph Stiles, a rice-planter of Savannah, Georgia, and grandson of Captain Samuel and Frances (Lightbourne) Stiles, of Bryan County, was born on December 6, 1795. His mother was Catharine, daughter of the Hon. Joseph and Ann (Legardere) Clay, of Savannah. A younger brother received an honorary M.A. degree at Yale in 1837. He was prepared for the Sophomore Class by the Rev. Samuel Whelpley in Newark, New Jersey

On graduation he enlisted at Savannah in the Chatham Artillery for the last year of the war. After this episode he studied law in the Litchfield Law School, and subsequently in Savannah under the Hon John M Berrien (Princeton Coll. 1796).

He began practice in his native city in partnership with William W Gordon, and on August 14, 1820, was married by the Rev. Nathaniel W. Taylor to Caroline, daughter of Captain Gad and Asenath (Osborn) Peck, of New Haven, who died on Green Island, the summer home of the Stiles family, on the coast near Savannah, about the 1st of September, 1821, after six days' illness, at the age of 19.

Greatly depressed by this event, he was brought under religious conviction, and began to preach to the negroes on his father's plantations. The result was that he abandoned his profession, and entered in 1822 the Andover Theological Seminary, but returned home after a little more than a year, owing to impaired eyesight. After a period of rest, he was licensed to preach by the Hopewell (now Augusta) Presbytery on April 3, 1825, and was ordained as an evangelist by the same body at Milledgeville, in August, 1826.

For three years he labored diligently in home missionary work.

On April 2, 1828, he was married, at Sunbury, in Liberty County, to Caroline Clifford, daughter of James and Sarah (Pelot, Gignilliat) Nephew, of McIntosh County, of Swiss Huguenot descent.

In 1829 he established his residence at Darien, in McIntosh County, and until 1835 he performed much effective labor at his own charges in the low country of Georgia and in Florida, acting also for a few months in 1830 as pastor of the First Presbyterian Church of Savannah.

Late in 1835 he removed to central Kentucky (largely with a view to the benefit of his slaves), and for some nine years his work lay mainly in Woodford County; he preached principally in Versailles and Midway, also in Harmony, Owen County, and for a short time in Cincinnati.

In 1844 he accepted a call from the Shockoe Hill (later Grace Street) Presbyterian Church of Richmond, Virginia, where he ministered for four years with devotion and success.

In 1848 he was called to the pastorate of the Mercer Street Presbyterian Church in New York City, but was obliged to resign after two years on account of ill health

He was then appointed Special Agent for the South of the American Bible Society, and during 1850–51 he traveled, chiefly in the South, preaching and soliciting contributions to the Society's funds.

Late in 1852 he took charge of the South Congregational Church in New Haven, which had been erected especially for him by Gerard Hallock, and to which he gave a part of his time until November, 1857. In October, 1853, he was appointed General Agent of the Southern Aid Society, for the assistance of feeble Southern churches; in 1857 the American Home Missionary Society withdrew aid from such churches, of which the members were slaveholders, and he labored with the more zeal in that office until the spring of 1861.

The honorary degree of Doctor of Divinity had been conferred on him by Transylvania University in 1846, and that of Doctor of Laws by Oglethorpe University in 1860.

On the outbreak of the Civil War, leaving his wife and daughters in New Haven, he returned to the South and gave himself to the religious welfare of the Southern soldiers, preaching almost constantly, under an appointment as evangelist from the Synod of Virginia. His labors were mostly in the command of Stonewall Jackson, with whom he was intimately associated and whom he greatly admired.

After the war he labored as an evangelist in Virginia, Alabama, Florida, Missouri, and Maryland, ceasing only when physically disabled. His last sermon was preached in West Virginia in June, 1874, and after months of prostration he died in Savannah, on March 27, 1875, in his 80th year

His widow died at her son-in-law's house in New Haven, on March 29, 1879, in her 69th year

Their children were four daughters, of whom one died in infancy, and three sons. The eldest daughter married Professor Hubert A. Newton (Yale 1850). The eldest son was graduated at Yale in 1859.

Dr. Stiles was a man of dignified and impressive presence, and an eloquent and impassioned preacher.

A brief memorial of him was printed for private distribution. A photograph is given in the *Stiles Family*.

He published:

1. A Sermon [from Eph. i, 11] on Predestination; preached in Milledgeville, August, 1826. Milledgeville, 1826. 8°, pp. 86. [*A. C. A. M. H. S.*

The same. Second edition. Charleston, 1827. 8°, pp. 60. [*Y. C.*

2. A Letter to Alexander Campbell, in reply to an article in the Millenial Harbinger. Lexington, 1838. 8°, pp. 57. [*A. A. S.*

Stiles and Campbell had had a public discussion in Versailles in October, 1837, on theological points.

3. Reply to an article in the June number of the Millenial Harbinger. Frankfort, 1838. 8°, pp. 56. [*A. A. S.*

4. Address, at the twenty-third anniversary of the American Home Missionary Society. [New York, 1849.] 8°, pp. 4. [*U. T. S.*

5. Speech on the Slavery Resolutions, delivered in the General Assembly which met in Detroit in May last. New-York, 1850. 8°, pp. 63.
[*A. A. S. B. Ath. B. Publ. Br. Mus. Harv. N. Y. Publ. U. S. U. T. S. Y. C.*

The same. Washington, 1850. 8°, pp. 48. [*B. Publ. N. Y. Publ. U. S.*

6. The Abrahamic Covenant and the New Testament Church. Philadelphia (Presbyterian Publication Committee). 12°, pp. 54. [*B. Publ. U. T. S. Y. C.*

A tract, advocating the doctrine of infant baptism.

7. Modern Reform Examined, or, the Union of North and South on the Subject of Slavery. Philadelphia, 1857 12°, pp 310.
[*A. A S. A C A. B. Publ. Br. Mus Harv M. H S. N. Y. Publ. U. T. S. Y C*

Occasioned by the action of the American Home Missionary Society, in taking a decided stand against slavery

8 Universalism
A tract.

9 The Enquirer instructed and examined.
A tract.

10 The National Controversy, or, the Voice of the Fathers upon the state of the country New York, 1861 12°, pp 108.
[*A A S A C A B Ath B Publ Harv N Y Publ. U. T S Y. C.*

11 National Rectitude the only true basis of National Prosperity: an Appeal to the Confederate States. Petersburg, 1863 8°, pp. 45 [*B Publ Harv. Y C.*

12. Capt Thomas E King; or, a word to the army and the country. Charleston (South Carolina Tract Society) 1864 16°, pp. 56 [*B. Ath N Y. Publ. Y. C.*

13 Address on the Life and Death of Rev. A. H H Boyd, D.D, of Winchester, Va. Richmond, 1866. 8°, pp. 27. [*U T S.*

14. Future Punishment discussed in a Letter to a Friend. Saint Louis, 1868 12°, pp 60 [*U T S*

AUTHORITIES

Bulloch, Habersham Family, 50–52 *R. Stiles,* Stiles Family, 678, 680–89 *Honeyman,* Nevius Family, 658 *H.*

William Lucius Storrs, the third son of Colonel Lemuel Storrs, of Middletown, Connecticut, and a brother of the Hon. Henry R. Storrs (Yale 1804), was born in Middletown on March 25, 1795. He was prepared for the Sophomore Class by Hezekiah Rudd (Yale 1806), at Bacon Academy, Colchester. In Senior year he was on the board of editors of the *Athenæum*

After graduation he studied law with his brother in Whitestown, New York, and after his admission to the bar of that State in 1817, returned to Connecticut, and began practice in his native city.

He was soon called into public service. In 1827, 1828, 1829, and 1834, he represented Middletown in the Legislature, and in the last year was Speaker of the House.

From 1829 to 1833 he was a Representative in Congress. In 1838 he was again elected, and served until June, 1840, when he resigned, on his appointment as a Judge of the Connecticut Supreme Court.

He remained upon the bench through life, being promoted in February, 1857, on the retirement of Henry M. Waite (Yale 1809), to the rank of Chief Justice.

From 1841 to 1846 he held the appointment of Professor of Law in the Wesleyan University, at Middletown.

In August, 1846, he was appointed a Professor in the Law Department of Yale College, having acted as the principal instructor in that Department during the preceding year. A year later, however, he resigned the office, on account of impaired health and the pressure of other duties. Two of the granddaughters of his only sister, the wife of Governor Joseph Trumbull (Yale 1801), established in 1889 a lectureship called by his name in the Law School.

He died in Hartford on June 25, 1861, after ten days' illness, from a bilious fever, terminating in typhoid, in his 67th year.

He was never married.

His leading characteristics as a lawyer and judge were keenness of discrimination, comprehension of view, fidelity to induction, rigid sequence of thought, and analytical strength.

The honorary degree of Doctor of Laws was conferred on him by Western Reserve College in 1846.

AUTHORITIES.

Conn. Reports, xxix, 608-11. Hist. Magazine, v, 256. Storrs Family, 417, 430-34. *Trowbridge*, Champion Genealogy, 290.

JOSEPH PLATT TAYLOR, son of Colonel Timothy Taylor, a merchant, of Danbury, Connecticut, was born in Danbury on August 9, 1794 His mother was Elizabeth, daughter of the Hon. Joseph Platt Cooke (Yale 1750), a sister married in 1805 Rev. Samuel Merwin (Yale 1802), of New Haven. Colonel Taylor died in 1802, and this son was prepared for College by Elias Starr (Yale 1803) in Danbury. In May of his Senior year his mother married Captain Henry Daggett (Yale 1771), of New Haven

He remained in New Haven as a graduate student until 1817, and then he spent two years in the Medical School

In the fall of 1821 he entered the Andover Theological Seminary, and was graduated there in 1824. He had just begun to preach, when he died in New Haven, on May 14, 1825, in his 31st year. He is buried beside his mother and step-father

---

JOHN TITSWORTH, son of William and Margaret (Middaugh) Titsworth, was born in the Clove, near Deckertown, in Wantage Township, Sussex County, New Jersey, on April 19, 1793.

He was prepared for the Sophomore Class by the Rev Jabez Munsell (Dartmouth Coll. 1794) in Newburgh, New York

In 1816 he entered the Yale Medical School, also studying privately with Dr. Eli Ives (Yale 1799); he had already attended one course in the College of Physicians and Surgeons at New York, and received his degree of M.D here in 1818

He then began practice in New Haven, in connection with the business of a druggist, and on May 31, 1819, was married to Abigail Allen, third daughter of Deacon Nathan Beers, of New Haven, and a sister of Dr. Timothy P. Beers (Yale 1808). She was about a year his junior.

In 1826, on account of failing health, he retired to his native place, and devoted himself to agriculture.

When his health was partially restored, he began to practice again, with much success, and so continued until about 1850. After that date his professional services were mainly rendered in the way of consultation.

He united with the County Medical Society in 1840, and served several times as its President, delivering on such occasions an address of more than ordinary merit. His last address to the Society, in 1866, on the Duties of Physicians, and their intercourse one with another, showed no decline in his mental faculties.

In 1833 he united with the First Presbyterian Church of Wantage, and he filled the position of Ruling Elder from about 1840 until his death.

He died very suddenly, while dressing, on February 1, 1873, in his 80th year.

His wife died before him. One of their two sons and an only daughter survived him.

Dr. Titsworth, while eccentric in disposition and habits, and fearless in expressing his own ideas, was a man of such varied knowledge and remarkable conversational powers, and of so much kindness of heart, that he was everywhere welcomed and esteemed.

AUTHORITIES.

N. J. Med. Society's Transactions, 1873, 119-20. Phelps Family, i, 306, 534.

Cornelius Tuthill, son of the Hon. Selah Tuthill, of Hopewell, a village in the present township of Crawford, Orange County, New York, was born in Hopewell on April 18, 1795. His father, who was a native of Blooming Grove, in the same county, removed later to New Paltz, in Ulster County, whence his son entered College, having been prepared in the Kingston Academy.

The father later removed to Newburgh, and was a member-elect of Congress at his death in 1821

On graduation he began the study of law in Kingston, and continued it in the Litchfield Law School. While in Litchfield his course was arrested by a new religious experience, which led him to begin the study of theology with President Dwight in October, 1815. He united with the College Church on profession of his faith in March, 1816. In September, 1816, he was invited to a tutorship in the College, but declined.

Late in May, 1817, he was married, by the Rev. Samuel Merwin, to Louisa Caroline, the youngest child of Ebenezer and Mary (Dickerman) Huggins, of New Haven, and on September 9 he was licensed to preach by the New Haven West Association of ministers. He was highly acceptable and popular as a preacher, and received a unanimous call to settle over the Congregational Church in Cheshire, which he declined

In June, 1818, he was seriously ill with typhus fever, and was left in such broken health that he was forbidden to resume preaching.

In June, 1819, he took charge of a school in New Haven, which he taught successfully until he began, in March, 1820, to edit the *Microscope,* a semi-weekly literary periodical which a few recent Yale graduates joined him in producing. This venture was brought to a close in September by the condition of his health.

By the advice of physicians he sailed (alone) for Europe on October 29; and after eight months' absence returned in improved health

In the summer of 1821 he instructed a few pupils, and in September was appointed Clerk of the Superior Court for the county.

For the years 1822 and 1823 he edited the *Christian Spectator,* a monthly magazine published in New Haven.

In the spring of 1823 he was elected a member of the State Legislature; but this addition to his engagements proved too much for his strength, and he was prostrated by a fresh attack of pulmonary disease.

In May, 1824, he was re-elected to the Legislature, and although feeble was able for most of the time to take part in their proceedings.

On the first of December, 1823, he had entered the law-office of Judge William Bristol (Yale 1798) as a student, and on November 25, 1824, he was admitted to practice. But after this date his health steadily declined, until the end came, in New Haven, on February 21, 1825, in his 30th year.

His wife survived him with one son and three daughters. She became somewhat widely known as a writer, especially of stories for the young. She died in Princeton, New Jersey, on June 1, 1879, in her 81st year.

His publications consisted entirely of anonymous contributions to periodicals. Of these may be mentioned:

Reflections on the Unitarian Mode of Treating the Scriptures. In the *Panoplist*, volume 13, pp. 154–57 (April, 1817).

In the *Christian Spectator:*

Review of Babington on Christian Education; in volume 1, pp. 355–62 (July, 1819).

The Idea of the Jews, respecting the Form of the Universe; in the same, pp. 400–01 (August, 1819).

On the veracity of God; in volume 2, pp. 292–94 (June, 1820).

On the promise of a Messiah, and on the evidence that Jesus is the Messiah, derived from the fact that the gospel is preached to the poor; in the same, pp. 397–99 (August, 1820).

Extract of a Letter from Paris, describing an interview with Lafayette; in volume 3, pp. 465–66 (September, 1821).

Review of the Judgment, a Vision; in the same, pp. 466–71.

A description of the Mausoleum of the Medici, at Florence; in the same, pp. 527–28 (October, 1821).

A Sermon on Hebrews vi, 19–20; in the same, pp. 622–27 (December, 1821).

On the character of the Apostle Peter; in volume 4, pp. 3–7 (January, 1822).

Exposition of Matthew v, 5; in the same, pp. 12–13.

Review of Foster on Popular Ignorance; in the same, pp. 33–42.

A Sermon from Isa. xlix, 16; in the same, pp. 61–66 (February, 1822).

An Account of Gibraltar; in the same, pp. 72–78.

Thoughts on the Reformation; in the same, pp. 142–44 (March, 1822).

An Extract from the Journal of an American Gentleman, while at Naples; in the same, pp. 189–92 (April, 1822).

A Sermon from John ix, 4; in the same, pp. 230–34 (May, 1822).

A Sermon from John xiii, 34; in the same, pp. 623–26 (December, 1822).

On the Proper Length of Public Religious Services; in the same, pp. 634–36.

On Warming Houses of Worship; in the same, pp. 640–42.

On Extemporaneous Preaching; in volume 6, pp. 131–39 (March, 1824).

Of his contributions to the *Microscope*, the following are identified:

In volume 1, Object and plan of the work, pp. 1–8, 22–23; Importance of early rising, 30–31; Dandies, 33–37, 81–85; Story of Olivia, 73–77; Use of superlatives, 175–76; Petition of the Ribs, 181–83; Sketch of a she-politician, 193–200.

In volume 2, Qualities of style, pp. 65–68; Great readers, 105–09; On music, 109–11; The mansion of blessedness, an allegory, 137–46; Valedictory, 193–97.

AUTHORITIES.

Christian Spectator, v, 225–34. Columbian Register, Feb. 26, 1825. Dickerman Family, 471. Tuttle Family, 166.

GEORGE AUGUSTUS WASSON, son of Captain John and Elizabeth (Bartram) Wasson, of Fairfield, Connecticut, was baptized in Fairfield by the Rev. Andrew Eliot on July 6, 1794. His father died in 1797. An elder sister married the Rev. Andrew Eliot, Junior (Yale 1799). He was prepared for College by Samuel J. Hitchcock (Yale 1809) in the Fairfield Academy.

From 1828 to 1832 he held the position of inspector in the New York Custom House.

Subsequently he was a merchant in New York, and held various important trusts, both public and private.

He died in New York on August 30, 1849, in his 56th year, and was buried in Fairfield. His wife, Charlotte Ann Wasson, survived him without children.

AUTHORITIES.

Schenck, Hist. of Fairfield, ii, 513.

John Bliss Watson, the eldest son of Colonel John Watson, a farmer and ship-builder of East Windsor, and grandson of John Watson (Yale 1764), and Anne (Bliss) Watson, of East Windsor, was born in 1795. His mother was Anne, only child of John and Alice (Stoughton) Bliss, of East Windsor, and her husband's first cousin.

He was prepared for College by John Brainard (Yale 1808).

He studied law and entered about 1819 on practice in East Windsor; but after five or six years he became a prominent business-man there and also noted for his enterprise in introducing improved breeds of horses, cattle, and sheep.

He married Ann Peck, of Hartford, and had one daughter.

About 1830 he removed to Hartford, where he was engaged in practice for about ten years.

He died at his residence in Hartford on December 25, 1843, aged 48 years.

AUTHORITIES.

Stiles, Hist. of Windsor, ii, 778. *Trumbull,* Hist. of Hartford County, i, 131; ii, 124.

Nathaniel Sheldon Wheaton, the eldest son of Sylvester Wheaton, of Marbledale, a village in the township of Washington, Connecticut, and grandson of Joseph Wheaton, one of the first Episcopalians among the settlers in that neighborhood, was born on August 20, 1792. His mother was Mercy, daughter of Gilead and Mercy (Boardman) Sperry, of New Milford He was a first cousin of the Rev. Dr. Salmon Wheaton (Yale 1805), and a second cousin of the Rev. Dr. Nathaniel W. Taylor (Yale 1807). He was prepared for College by the Rev Dr. Tillotson Bronson (Yale 1786) in the Cheshire Episcopal Academy.

After graduation he found employment as a teacher in Maryland, in the meantime studying theology, and was admitted to deacon's orders by Bishop Kemp on June 7, 1817. He was advanced to priest's orders before returning to Connecticut, where he was invited, on January 5, 1820, to become assistant to Bishop Brownell, as rector of Christ Church, Hartford.

He accepted this offer, and began his work in March, with an annual salary of $900. The Bishop soon removed to New Haven, and Mr. Wheaton was elected Rector on April 23, 1821, with a salary of $1,000.

He accepted the rectorship on June 5, and discharged his duties with marked efficiency for over ten years.

On the incorporation of Washington, now Trinity College, in May, 1823, he was named as one of the Trustees, and in September, as he was desirous to visit England for his health, he was commissioned to go and solicit gifts of books and philosophical apparatus for the College. This mission caused his absence from his parish until November, 1824.

He was an interested student of architecture, and made such good use of his opportunities while in England, that when in 1828 he brought his parish to the step of erecting a new stone church, he was able to furnish the design, in excellent Gothic, and to superintend its construction. His whole course as rector showed him as a man of piety, learning, high character, and administrative ability.

On October 4, 1831, he resigned his rectorship to succeed Bishop Brownell in the office of President of Washington College.

His exertions in the founding of the College had been of supreme importance, and his presidency was marked by a notable increase in the funds of the institution, and by a marked improvement in the embellishment and care of the College grounds.

He resigned on February 28, 1837, to accept a call to the rectorship of Christ Church, in New Orleans, a congregation which had been fostered by Bishop Brownell during his visits to the South for his health. He labored there with fidelity until his resignation in 1844. During the ravages of the yellow fever he was incessant in his devotion to the sufferers; and in consequence of an attack of the fever he contracted severe dyspepsia, which never left him.

He visited Europe in 1844, and after a year's absence returned to Connecticut in broken health. For a time he resided in Hartford, officiating for Christ Church during a vacancy in the rectorship, and occasionally elsewhere.

But disease increased upon him, and being a bachelor with ample means he retired to his native village, where he assisted, when health allowed, in the services of the parish church.

He died in Marbledale, after months of severe suffering, on March 18, 1862, in his 70th year.

He endowed the church in Marbledale with a parsonage and suitable grounds. To Trinity College he left his valuable library, ten thousand dollars towards the erection of a chapel, and a like amount for the general fund.

A copy of his portrait, preserved in Trinity College Library, is given in Russell's *History of Christ Church.* A memorial window was erected in the church in 1879.

He was an engaging preacher, extremely simple in manner, and clear and unaffected in style. Under a reserved and sometimes cold exterior, he carried a warm and generous heart.

Yale conferred on him the honorary degree of Doctor of Divinity in 1833.

He published:

1 Remarks on Washington College, and on the "Considerations" suggested by its establishment. Hartford, 1825 8°, pp 52 [*Y. C*

An anonymous reply to a pamphlet published in 1824, and attributed to Roger S. Baldwin (Yale 1811)

2. The Providence of God displayed in the rise and fall of Nations—A Sermon [from Jer. xviii, 7–10], delivered at the Annual Election, in Trinity Church, New-Haven, on Wednesday the 7th of May, 1828. New-Haven, 1828 8°, pp. 18.
[*A. C. A. Harv M. H. S U. S. U. T. S Y. C*

3 Address at the laying of the corner-stone of Christ Church, Hartford, on May 13, 1828.
In the *Episcopal Watchman*, volume 2, pp 69–70 (May, 1828)

4. Description of Christ Church, Hartford.
In the same, volume 3, pp 337–39 (January, 1830).

5 A Journal of a residence during several months in London, including excursions through various parts of England, and a short Tour in France and Scotland; in the years 1823 and 1824. Hartford, 1830. 12°, pp. 520
[*A. A. S. A. C. A. B. Ath. B. Publ. Br Mus Columbia Univ. Harv U. S*

Large portions of the work had been published in the *Episcopal Watchman*, volumes 1–3, Hartford, June, 1827–August, 1829, with title: Notes of a Traveller.

6 An Address delivered before the Hartford County Peace Society, in Christ Church, Hartford, October 12, 1834. Hartford, 1834 8°, pp. 24.
[*A. A S B Publ C. H S. N. Y Publ U S Y. C*

7. Happiness or misery the result of choice: a Sermon, from Gal. vi, 7–8.
In the *Protestant Episcopal Pulpit*, volume 4, pp 193–204. New York, December, 1834

8. A Discourse on St Paul's Epistle to Philemon; exhibiting the duty of citizens of the Northern States in regard to the Institution of Slavery; delivered in Christ Church Hartford, Dec 22, 1850 Hartford, 1851. 8°, pp 30
[*B. Ath B Publ Br Mus. Harv U. S. Y. C.*

Advocating obedience to the Fugitive Slave Law.

AUTHORITIES.

Amer. Quart. Church Review, xiv, 734. *Beardsley,* Hist. of the Episcopal Church in Conn., ii, 249–50, 276–77, 294, 313, 425–27. Boardman Genealogy, 274. *Professor J. Brocklesby,* MS. Letter, July, 1862. Conn. Diocesan Convention Proceedings, 1862, 15. *Orcutt,* Hist. of New Milford, 349, 634–35, 789. *Russell,* Hist. of Christ Church, Hartford, *passim.*

THOMAS SCUDDER WICKES, the eldest child and only son of the Hon. Eliphalet and Martha (Herriman) Wickes, of Jamaica, Long Island, and grandson of Major Thomas and Abigail (VanWyck) Wickes, of Huntington, was born in Jamaica on April 18, 1795. He was prepared for College by Lewis E. A. Eigenbrodt, at his Academy in Jamaica. His eldest sister married Dr. Alldis S. Allen (Yale 1827).

In 1816 he entered Princeton Theological Seminary, where he spent upwards of two years, though prevented by ill-health from completing the course. He was licensed to preach by the Presbytery of New York on April 21, 1819.

On September 7, 1819, he was married to Maria Punnett, of St. Thomas, West Indies.

For the most of the next three years he was engaged in missionary work in the Southern States.

Mrs. Wickes died on April 9, 1821.

He was ordained as an evangelist by the Presbytery of New York on September 9, 1822, and for most of the time for the next fourteen years was employed in supplying feeble churches in New York State, mostly at his own expense, as by reason of feeble health he would never consent to be installed as pastor. He was at West Farms, a suburb of New York City, in 1823–24, and was the first minister of the First Presbyterian Church in Greenbush (East Albany) from 1825 to 1830. On September 15, 1829, he was married to Julia, daughter of Sylvanus J. and Olive (Fitch) Penniman, of Albany.

From 1831 to 1836, he supplied the church in Sand Lake, Rensselaer County.

After this he resided in Albany for three or four years, and subsequently in Ballston, until 1851. For the rest of his life his home was in Poughkeepsie, where he died, of acute pneumonia, on November 30, 1876, in his 82d year.

By his first wife he had one son; and by his second wife six daughters and four sons. Mrs. Wickes, with three sons and three daughters, survived him. A grandson was graduated at Yale in 1874.

AUTHORITIES.

Weekes Genealogy, 240; pt. 2, 91. *Mrs. Thomas S. Wickes*, MS. Letter, April, 1877.

LEONARD WITHINGTON, son of Joseph Weeks Withington, of Dorchester, Massachusetts, and grandson of Philip and Abigail (Weeks) Withington, of Dorchester, was born in Dorchester on August 9, 1789. His mother was Elizabeth White, of Dorchester. His father died in January, 1801.

In 1804 he entered the printing-office of Thomas & Andrews in Boston, and he served an apprenticeship there until 1808, when he went to Phillips Andover Academy to prepare for College, with the purpose of becoming an editor. He entered Yale at the opening of Sophomore year. In Senior year he was one of the editors of the bi-weekly magazine published by the Class, the *Athenæum*.

While in College he decided to prepare for the ministry; and accordingly upon graduation he began theological studies under President Dwight, which he continued under his own pastor, the Rev. John Codman (Harvard 1802). In 1816 he spent a few months in the Andover Seminary.

He was ordained and installed as pastor of the First Church in Newbury, Massachusetts, on October 31, 1816, and the ordination sermon by the Rev. Dr. John Codman, of Dorchester, was printed.

On January 7, 1817, he was married in Dorchester to Sophia, daughter of the late William Sherburne, of Boston, and of Mehitabel (Aspinwall) Sherburne, who died on April 1, 1826, in her 40th year.

He was next married, on May 28, 1827, to Caroline, second daughter of Dr. Nathan Noyes (Dartmouth Coll. 1796) and Sarah (Niles) Noyes, of Dorchester, who died on August 5, 1860, at the age of 57.

Bowdoin College conferred on him in 1850 the honorary degree of Doctor of Divinity. He was a man of original thought and vigorous expression, and of extensive and unusual acquisitions.

After forty-two years of active service, while his powers were still in full play, he retired on the anniversary of his ordination, with the title of senior pastor; and his remaining years were passed in quiet content in the midst of a grateful people.

Having outlived all his classmates, he died in Newbury on April 22, 1885, in his 96th year.

His three children (sons) by his first marriage died before him. By his second wife he had five sons and four daughters; two of the sons and the daughters survived him.

He published:

1. Good Tidings of Great Joy: or the Doctrine of Universal Salvation, clearly stated, incontestably proved, and faithfully applied, in a Sermon [from Luke ii, 12], preached and published by a Doctor of the Sect. 12°, pp. 12. [*Y. C.*

An anonymous satire.

2. The Excellence of the Scriptures. A Sermon, from Ps. xix, 7-10.

In the *American Evangelist,* volume 1, pp. 25-42 (October, 1827).

3. The Final Tendency of the religious disputes of the present day, impartially considered.—By Old Experience. Boston, 1829. 12°, pp. 29. [*A. C. A. U. S. Y. C.*

Anonymous.

4 Take Warning—A Sermon [from Isa v, 12] delivered at Newbury (First Parish), August 22, and in the First Presbyterian Church in Newburyport, August 29, 1830 Newburyport, 1830. 8°, pp. 16

[*A. A. S. A C A. B. Ath. B. Publ. M. H. S. Y. C.*

5. A Sermon [from Titus ii, 15], preached at the Annual Election, May 25, 1831 Boston, 1831. 8°, pp 48

[*A. A S A C. A. B. Ath. B Publ Br. Mus. Harv. M H. S N. Y. Publ. U T. S Y. C.*

In defence of the clergy

6 The Soul of Man—A Sermon [from Gen ii, 7] preached at the Tabernacle Church, Salem, Mass, April 22, 1832 Salem, 1832. 8°, pp 22

[*A. A. S A. C A. B Ath. B. Publ. Br. Mus M. H. S. N. Y. Publ U T S Y. C*

7. Puritan Morals Defended—A Discourse [from Acts xxviii, 22] delivered at the Dedication of the Crombie Street Church in Salem, . and the Installation of the Rev William Williams, November 22, 1832 Salem, 1832 8°, pp. 36

[*A. C. A. B Ath B. Publ. Br. Mus. N. Y Publ. U T S Y C.*

An excellent and characteristic utterance

8. Lecture on Emulation in Schools

In *Lectures* delivered before the American Institute of Instruction, 1833, pp 129-52

9 The Puritan: a series of essays, critical, moral, and miscellaneous.—By John Oldbug, Esq. Boston, 1836 2 volumes. 12°, pp 248, 268

[*A. A. S A. C. A. B Ath. B. Publ Harv U T S Y. C*

A collection of homely essays, mainly reprinted from periodicals, and descriptive of New England life and character.

10. Cobwebs swept away. or some popular deceptions exposed—A Sermon [from John vii, 12] delivered on Fast Day, April 6th, 1837 At the First Church in Newbury. Newburyport, 1837. 8°, pp 25

[*A A S A. C. A B Ath B Publ Br. Mus Harv. M H S Y C.*

11. An Address before the Essex Agricultural Society at Topsfield, September 27, 1838, at their annual Cattle Show. Salem, 1839. 8°, pp. 25. [*B. Ath. B. Publ. M. H. S. U. S.*
From the *Transactions* of the Society for 1838.

12. A Review of the late Temperance Movements in Massachusetts. Boston, 1840. 8°, pp. 28.
[*A. A. S. B. Publ. Br. Mus. U. T. S. Y. C.*

The same. Second edition. Boston, 1840. 8°, pp. 28.
[*B. Publ. Y. C.*

13. The Belle of Zion. By the author of "The Puritan, or Lay-Essayist." Boston, 1840. 12°, pp. 243. [*Y. C.*
A collection of religious sketches.

14. Penitential Tears, or a Cry from the Dust, by "the Thirty-one," prostrated and pulverized by the hand of Horace Mann, Secretary, &c. Boston, 1845. 8°, pp. 59.
[*A. C. A. B. Ath. B. Publ. Harv. M. H. S. U. S. Y. C.*

15. A Sermon [from Ps. xcix, 8–9] for the two hundredth Anniversary of the standing of the First Church in Newbury, on its present site, October 20, 1846. Newburyport, 1846. 8°, pp. 20.
[*A. A. S. A. C. A. B. Publ. Br. Mus. Harv. M. H. S. U. S. Y. C.*

16. A Bundle of Myrrh.—Thanksgiving Sermon [from Solomon's Song, i, 13]: preached Nov. 28, 1850, at Newbury First Parish. Newburyport, 1850. 12°, pp. 24.
[*A. C. A. B. Publ. Br. Mus. M. H. S.*

The same. Second edition. Newburyport, 1851. 12°, pp. 24.
[*A. A. S. B. Ath. B. Publ. M. H. S. Y. C.*
Against the Fugitive Slave Law.

17. A Funeral Sermon [from Hebr. xii, 1], at the Interment of Mrs. Sarah E. Little, wife of Rev. Elbridge G. Little. Preached April 1, 1851. Newburyport, 1851. 8°, pp. 16.
[*A. C. A. Br. Mus.*

18. Loose then from earth, the grasp of fond desire.—Two Sermons [from I Kings xxii, 34, and Matth. xxiv, 40], preached in Newbury, the Sabbath after the death of Giles A. Noyes, who was killed in a remarkable manner in that town, October 19, 1852. Newburyport, 1852. 8°, pp. 20. [*A. A. S. Harv.*

19. The Blessings of our Institutions, and our obligations to continue them.—A Discourse [from Matth. x, 8], preached in the First Congregational Church, Newbury, Fast Day, April 7, 1853. Newburyport, 1853. 8°, pp. 16.

[*A. A. S. A. C. A. B. Publ. Harv. M. H. S. Y. C.*

20. Memorial of Rev. Luther Fraseur Dimmick, D.D., late pastor of the North Congregational Church, Newburyport. Boston, 1860. 8°, pp. 16. [*A. C. A. B. Publ.*

See, also, in part in the *Congregational Quarterly*, volume 2, pp. 370–75 (October, 1860).

21. Solomon's Song; translated and explained. .. Boston, 1861. sm. 8°, pp. v, 329.

[*A. C. A. B. Ath. Br. Mus. B. Publ. Harv. U. T. S.*

Treating the book as an allegory on divine love.

22. An Essay on Vibrations in Theology.

In Contributions to the Ecclesiastical History of Essex County, Mass. Boston, 1865. 8°, pp. 386–96.

23. The Substance of an Address delivered at the funeral of William Wheelwright, in the Old South Church, Newburyport, Mass., October 17, 1873. Boston, 1873. 8°, pp. 12.

[*A. C. A. B. Publ. N. Y. Publ.*

A very striking composition, especially in view of the author's age.

He contributed frequently to periodicals; the following articles may be specified:

In the (*Monthly*) *Christian Spectator:*

A Rhetorical Praxis on the first Eclogue of Virgil, volume 4, pp. 78–82 (February, 1822).

[Review.] Everett's Orations, volume 7, pp. 534–40 (October, 1825).

Varieties, volume 8, pp. 76–80, 136–39 (February–March, 1826).

In the (*Quarterly*) *Christian Spectator:*

The Present State of Metaphysics, volume 6, pp. 609–31 (December, 1834).

In the *Literary and Theological Review:*

Review of Channing's Works, volume 1, pp. 304–35 (June, 1834).

Gibbon's Infidelity, volume 2, pp. 38–57 (March, 1835).

Living on God, volume 3, pp. 98–103 (March, 1836).

Review of Burchard's Sermons, the same, pp. 228–36 (June, 1836). This was also twice reprinted in pamphlet form.

In the *Bibliotheca Sacra:*

[Review.] South's Sermons, volume 2, pp. 312–29 (May, 1845).

Observations on the Fourth Eclogue of Virgil, volume 3, pp. 37–50 (February, 1846).

A Phenomenon in Church History, the same, pp. 673–98 (November, 1846).

Shakespeare—the old and the new Criticism on him, volume 4, pp. 522–40 (August, 1847).

Remarks on a Sermon delivered by Dr. Emmons before the Norfolk Education Society, 1817, volume 5, pp. 625–33 (November, 1848).

Man and his Food, volume 11, pp. 139–55 (January, 1854).

Davus sum, non Oedipus, volume 14, pp. 770–84 (October, 1857).

Caprices and Laws of Literature, volume 15, pp. 805–24 (October, 1858).

Epistola ad Rusticum Apologetica, volume 18, pp. 324–38 (April, 1861).

Permanent Preaching for a Permanent Pastorate, volume 19, pp. 310–27 (April, 1862).

In the *New Englander:*

Visions of an Andover Student, volume xiii, pp. 234–41, 379–86, 553–61 (May–November, 1855).

He contributed to Sprague's *Annals of the American Pulpit* notices of the Rev. Dr. John Tucker, volume 1, pp. 451–54, the Rev. Dr. Elijah Parish, volume 2, pp. 270–72, the Rev. Samuel P. Williams, volume 4, pp. 372–73, and the Rev. Hosea Hildreth, volume 8, pp. 448–49.

At Commencement in 1821 he delivered a Poem before the Phi Beta Kappa Society at Yale, and in 1845 he delivered the annual Address before the Alumni in New Haven: but neither of these was printed.

A Dialogue which he wrote for exhibition at the Yale Commencement in 1814 is preserved in manuscript in the Yale Library.

AUTHORITIES.

Boston Record Commissioners' Reports, xxi. 204. Contributions to Ecclesiastical Hist. of Essex County, 134–36. *Kingsley,* Yale College, i, 340–41. N. E. Hist. and Geneal. Register, lix, 60. Noyes Genealogy, i, 94.

Annals, 1814-15

In April, 1815, the building previously rented for the Medical Institution was purchased from the Hon James Hillhouse for $12,500.

At Commencement in 1815 three Tutors retired,—Samuel J. Hitchcock, John Langdon, and Josiah W. Gibbs, all of the Class of 1809; and Alexander M. Fisher, Josiah Spalding, Denison Olmsted, Elisha Mitchell, and Frederick Morgan, all of the Class of 1813, were elected to that office.

The failing health of President Dwight was beginning to cause anxiety, and arrangements were authorized by the Corporation so that he might, if necessary, have some relief from his duties as Professor of Divinity during the coming year.

Sketches, Class of 1815

*Jahacobus Motte Alston *1818
*Stephanus Goodwin Austin, A.M. 1831 *1872
*Julius Steele Barnes, M.D. 1818 *1870
*Samuel Birdseye Beardsley *1873
*Johannes Gardiner Calkins Brainard *1828
*Levi Brooks *1878
*Jacobus Tredwell Burr *1831
*Edvardsius Clarke, A.M. Hamilt. 1818 *1868
*Johannes Middleton Clayton, LL.D. 1846, Rerumpubl. Foed. Sen. et Polit. Secr., Reip. Del. Secr. et Cur. Supr. Jurid. Princ. *1856
*Guilielmus Codman, A.M. 1819 *1848
*Georgius Cooke *1871
*Jacobus Davis *1822
*Georgius Pollock Devereux *1837
*Abrahamus Jahacobus Duryee, A.M. 1819, M.D. Coll. Med. et Chir. Nov. Ebor. 1819 *1822
*Henricus Edvinus Dwight, A.M. *1832
*Johannes Dicks Eccles *1856
*Edvardus Fellows Ensign *1865
*Elisaeus Rexford Fenn
**Orin Fowler,* A.M., e Congr. *1852
*Guilielmus Edgarus Gallaudet *1852
*Thomas Gray *1860
*Horatius Gridley, A.M. 1820, M.D. 1833, Socius ex officio *1864
*Carolus Henricus Hammond, A.M. *1850
*Edvardus Harleston *1871
*Elija Hartshorn, A.M. 1824 *1840
*Johannes Hastings *1886

Rogerus Conant Hatch, A.M. *1868
*Jeremias Hine *1838
**Carolus Jacobus Hinsdale,* A.M. 1822 *1871
*Isaacus Edvardus Holmes, e Congr. *1867
**Horatius Hooker,* A.M., Tutor *1864
*Josias Hooker, A M. *1870
**Andreas Huntington* *1872
*Guilielmus Jessup, LL.D. Hamilt. 1848 *1868
*Henricus Kellogg, A.M. Guil. 1824 *1873
*Simeon Terry Kibbe *1825
*Carolus Leavenworth *1829
*Johannes Sullivan Lee, A.M *1818
*Johannes Bassnett Legaré, A.M. *1826
*Johannes Berwick Legaré *1850
*Guilielmus Lockwood, A M. *1827
*Thomas Alexander Marshall, LL D. 1866, e Congr., Reip. Kentuck Cur. Supr. Jurid. Princ. *1871
*Jacobus Henricus Mitchell *1873
*Alfredus Shepard Monson, A M., M.D. Univ. Penns. 1819 *1870
*Georgius Washington Morris *1838
*Erasmus Norcross *1874
*Alexis Painter, A M. 1821 *1867
*Jacobus Gates Percival, M D. 1820, in Rerump. Foed. Acad Milit. Chem. Prof. *1856
*Johannes Pope *1865
*Guilielmus Smith Robert *1877
*Hubbard Rockwell, A M., Tutor *1871
*Johannes Sill Rogers *1860
*Guilielmus Sidney Rossiter *1852
*Ezekiel Sanford, A M. *1822
**Israel Shailer* *1869
*Nathanael Benedict Smith *1881
*Truman Smith, e Congr., Rerumpubl. Foed. Sen. *1884
**Guilielmus Buell Sprague,* A.M. 1819, S.T.D. Columb. 1828 et Harv. 1848, LL.D. Neo-Caes 1869 *1876

**Randolphus Stone,* A.M. 1821, in Univ. Ohion. Litt. Angl. et Hist. Prof. *184–
*Woodbridge Strong, M.D. 1818 *1861
*Aegidius Hallam Swan *184–
*Thomas Turner *1850
*Jahacobus VanBenthuysen *1846
*Guilielmus Courtney Wetmore *1880
*Fredericus White *1839
*Sims White *1855
*Edmundus Fanning Wickham *1843
**Josephus Dresser Wickham,* A.M., S.T.D. Mediob. 1861, Tutor *1891
*Jesse Smith Woodhull, A.M. 1822 *1841
*Josephus Youle *1820

Jacob Motte Alston, a brother of Alston of the last Class, was born on the family plantation, near Georgetown, South Carolina, in 1797. He entered with the Class of 1814, but left that Class towards the end of Sophomore year.

He returned home after graduation, and followed the life of a planter on the paternal estate.

In September, 1818, he was killed instantly in Georgetown District by a fall from his horse, in his 22d year. This was probably the first death in the Class.

AUTHORITIES.

Conn. Journal, Sept. 29, 1818. *Grover,* Alston Family, 80.

Stephen Goodwin Austin, the youngest of three sons of Joseph Austin, a farmer of Suffield, Connecticut, and grandson of Joseph and Abigail (Allen) Austin, of Suffield, was born in Suffield on October 28, 1791. His mother was Sarah, second daughter of Captain Stephen and Abigail (Gillet) Goodwin, of Goshen He was prepared for the Junior Class in the Westfield Academy.

After graduation he studied law with Daniel W. Lewis (Yale 1788), of Geneva, New York, and was admitted to practice in January, 1819

In the same year he settled in Buffalo, where he practiced extensively for nearly twenty-five years

He married on October 1, 1819, Lavinia, daughter of Jesse Hurd, of the village of Middle Haddam, in Chatham, Connecticut.

He devoted himself exclusively to his profession, declining all public office, except that of Justice of the Peace. He was an excellent lawyer, of quick perception and acute intellect, of sound judgment as a business man, of unremitting industry and exemplary character

He retired from active business about 1853, and died in Buffalo, with faculties unimpaired, on June 19, 1872, in his 81st year.

His children were four daughters, two of whom died in infancy.

His portrait is given in Comley's *History of New York.*

AUTHORITIES.

Comley, Hist of N Y State, 342–43 *Smith,* Hist of Buffalo, ii, pt. 2, 1–2 Goodwin Family, 451 *H P*

JULIUS STEELE BARNES, the second son of Jonathan Barnes (Yale 1784), of Tolland, Connecticut, was born in Tolland on February 23, 1792. His mother, Rachel Steele, was adopted by her uncle, the Rev. George Colton (Yale 1756), of Bolton, under whose instruction her son was prepared for Yale.

After graduation he taught school for a time, and then began the study of medicine in the Yale Medical School, where he received the degree of M.D. in 1818.

He soon began the practice of his profession in Southington, where he was married, on November 1, 1821, to Laura, elder daughter of Selah and Mary, or Polly (Carter) Lewis, of Southington, and sister of James Lewis (Yale 1824), who died on May 20, 1867, aged 65 years.

Dr. Barnes continued to practice in Southington until near the time of his death there, on November 12, 1870, in his 79th year.

He was noted as a skilful practitioner, and devoted to his calling, while he labored also for the social and moral well-being of the whole community. His interest in the leading questions of the day led him to be active in politics, and he served for one term (1839) in the State Senate. He was also Judge of Probate for the Southington district for a short time. He united with the Congregational Church in Southington in 1834, and was firm in his belief.

His children were five sons (of whom one died in infancy) and four daughters. The second son was graduated at Yale College in 1847, and followed his father's profession. The second daughter married the Rev. Guy B. Day (Yale 1845).

AUTHORITIES.

Dr. Lewis Barnes, MS. Letter, April, 1871. Conn. Med. Society's Proceedings, 1871, 492–94. *Timlow,* Hist. of Southington, 459, xxi–xxii, clx. *Trumbull,* Hist. of Hartford County, ii, 381.

Samuel Birdseye Beardsley, the youngest son of Samuel Beardsley, of Huntington, Connecticut, and grandson of Samuel and Ann (French) Beardsley, of Huntington, was born on January 12, 1795. His mother was Phebe, second daughter of Silas and Ruth (Birdseye) Curtiss. He was prepared for College by William Belden (Yale 1803) in the Staples Academy in Easton.

He taught school for three years after graduation on the Eastern shore of Maryland, and next in Bridgeport,

Connecticut. He then attempted the study of theology, but gave it up on account of the condition of his health.

For years he was in a state of nervous instability, and occupied himself with farming. As he became better he resumed teaching in Monroe (formerly a part of Huntington), having for many years a select family school.

He died in Monroe on September 27, 1873, in his 79th year.

He married Abigail McEwen, by whom he had a son who was graduated from the Yale Medical School in 1845. He also had a daughter, much younger.

AUTHORITIES.

Orcutt, Hist. of Stratford, ii, 1139.

JOHN GARDINER CALKINS BRAINARD, the youngest son of the Hon. Jeremiah G. Brainard (Yale 1779), of New London, Connecticut, was born in New London on October 21, 1796, and was prepared for College by his brother (Yale 1802).

On graduation he returned to New London, and pursued the study of law in his brother William's office. On admission to the bar, in 1819, he removed to Middletown, with a view to beginning practice; but he soon found that his sensitive temperament unfitted him for the contests of the courts, and he retired to his father's house.

In the winter of 1821–22 he removed to Hartford; but though nominally still an attorney, he had no business, and in March, 1822, he undertook the editorship of the *Connecticut Mirror,* a weekly newspaper of that city, of strong Federal sympathies, and a marked literary tone. He paid little attention to politics, but devoted himself to the literary part of the paper, publishing in it many ballads and other poetical pieces, which attracted wide attention.

He had always been delicate, and his declining health (from consumption) obliged him to give up work in the spring of 1827, when he retired to New London, though he did not formally resign his editorial post until January, 1828. He lingered until September 26, 1828, when he died in his father's house, in his 32d year. He united with the Congregational church during the last part of his illness. He was never married.

An engraved portrait, from an unfinished pencil sketch, was prefixed to his collected *Poems* in 1842, with a Memoir by the Rev. Royal Robbins (Yale 1806); and was reproduced in the *Connecticut Magazine*, volume 7 (1902); it first appeared in the *Token* for 1830, with a tribute to Brainard's memory by Mrs. Sigourney.

Brainard was small in person, retiring in manner, rather careless in dress, and peculiarly awkward in his walk His poetry was principally "occasional," and often hastily written, but showed a sincerity and depth of appreciation of natural beauty, which will preserve it in remembrance.

He published:

1. In the *Microscope*, New Haven, 1820· The memoirs of Gabriel Gap, volume 1, pp. 65–68, 97–100, 145–52; volume 2, pp. 169–72.

2 Occasional Pieces of Poetry. New-York, 1825. 16°, pp. 111. [*B. Publ. Y. C.*

Many of these pieces had appeared in the *Connecticut Mirror*.

After his death appeared:

3. Fugitive Tales, No I—Fort Braddock Letters. Washington, D. C., 1830. 16°, pp. 97. [*Y. C*

Originally published in the *Connecticut Mirror*.

4. Literary Remains, with a Sketch of his Life.—By J. G Whittier. Hartford [1832] 12°, pp 228 [*B. Ath. Br. Mus. Harv. Y C.*

This volume contains about fifty pieces more than that of 1825; these had mostly appeared in the *Connecticut Mirror* since 1825.

5. The Poems of J G C Brainard. A new and authentic collection, with an original Memoir of his life Hartford, 1842 16°, pp lxiv, 191 + pl. [*Br Mus. Harv. Y C.*

This collection contains only one or two more pieces than that of 1832, but is more carefully edited

AUTHORITIES.

Brainard, Brainerd-Brainard Genealogy, pt 1, 62–68 Conn Magazine, vii, 371–80 *Field*, Brainerd Genealogy, 20–35, Centennial Address, 108. *S G Goodrich*, Recollections of a Lifetime, ii, 143–60 Religious Intelligencer, xiii, 445. [*Robbins*], Memoir of Brainard

---

Levi Brooks, the eldest child of Levi Brooks, of West Springfield, Massachusetts, and grandson of Israel Brooks, of Springfield, was born in West Springfield on September 23, 1791. His mother was Persis, younger daughter of Simeon and Ruth Elizabeth (Hatch) Ely, of West Springfield. He was prepared for the Junior Class by the Rev. Timothy M. Cooley (Yale 1792), of East Granville.

After graduation he was employed as a private tutor in New York City, and then began the study of medicine there In 1818 he joined the Yale Medical School, and he received his license to practice from the Connecticut Medical Society in the spring of 1819

He then practiced his profession for three years in Catskill, New York, where he married Asenath, daughter of Judge Blanchard.

In 1822 he removed to Ohio, and soon settled in St. Clairsville, Belmont County, about ten miles west of Wheeling. He remained in practice there and elsewhere in the middle and northern parts of the State until about 1844, when he retired from professional labor.

About 1855 he settled in Cleveland, where his wife died on August 30, 1864 A year or two later he removed to the house of his eldest daughter, in Albion, Orleans County, New York, where he spent the rest of his life

He retained his faculties unimpaired until a few weeks before the end, when a slight stroke of paralysis left him speechless. He died in Albion on August 28, 1878, aged nearly 87 years.

Of nine children, five survived him.

AUTHORITIES.

Mrs. W. W. Beckwith, MS. Letter, March, 1881. Nathaniel Ely's Descendants, 66.

James Tredwell Burr, the only son of Isaac Burr, a merchant, of New York City, and grandson of Joseph and Hannah (Mabbett) Burr, of Hempstead, Long Island, was born about 1796. His mother was Elizabeth Tredwell, of Hempstead. He was prepared for College by the Rev. Edmund D. Barry at his school in New York.

He was in business in New York for some years before his death, in the firm of Burr & Seaman, merchants.

He died in Pensacola, Florida, on February 26, 1831, aged about 34 years. His will, dated in New York in December, 1830, was admitted to probate in June, 1831. He was never married.

AUTHORITIES.

Todd, Burr Family, 4th ed., 309.

Edwards Clarke, the younger son of the Hon. Jabez Clark, of Windham, Connecticut, and grandson of Dr. John Clark (Yale 1749), was born in Windham on February 24, 1796. His mother was Amie, daughter of Colonel Jedidiah Elderkin, of Windham, and sister of Captain Vine Elderkin (Yale 1763) and of Bela Elderkin (Yale 1767). He was prepared for College by his pastor, the Rev. William Andrews (Middlebury Coll. 1806).

After graduation he studied law in Utica, New York, with his uncle, Erastus Clark, and was admitted to the bar of that State in 1818. He soon after returned to

Windham, where he resided thenceforth, with the exception of two years (about 1845) which he spent in Michigan.

He was from 1836 to 1838 the chief Judge of the County Court, and also for a short time Judge of the Windham Probate District. He was a consistent member of the Congregational Church.

He married, on May 28, 1823, Hannah, younger daughter of Deacon Samuel Perkins (Yale 1785), of Windham,—her brother (Yale 1817) having already married Mr. Clarke's sister.

He died in Windham on March 8, 1868, aged 72 years. His widow died on May 11, 1873, aged 71 years.

Of their children three daughters and a son survived him; two sons and three daughters died in infancy.

AUTHORITIES.

Goodwin, Genealogical Notes, 28. Huntington Family Memoir, 98. Perkins Genealogy, pt. 3, 86–87. Tuttle Family, 361–62. *Rev. S. G. Willard,* MS. Letter, May, 1868.

JOHN MIDDLETON CLAYTON, the elder son of James Clayton, and grandson of James and Grace Clayton, was born in Dagsborough, near the southern border of Delaware, on July 24, 1796. His uncle, Dr. Joshua Clayton, was President of Delaware from 1789 to 1793, and the first Governor of the State, from 1793 to 1796. His mother was Sarah, daughter of Ignatius Middleton, of Annapolis, Maryland. In his youth the family removed to Milford, Delaware. At the Junior Exhibition of his Class, in May, 1814, he delivered an Oration on Military Glory.

After graduation he began the study of law in the office of his first cousin, Thomas Clayton of Newcastle, then a Member of Congress. From March, 1817, to November, 1818, he attended the Litchfield Law School, and after his return to Delaware finished his course of study at home, and was admitted to the bar in October, 1819. He began practice in Dover and rose almost at once to distinguished rank, especially as a jury lawyer.

In the meantime he had attracted notice by his promise, and was elected clerk of the State House of Representatives at the sessions of 1816, 1817, and 1819. In 1820, 1821, and 1822, he was Clerk of the State Senate. In 1821 he was appointed Auditor of Accounts by the Legislature,—an office of great responsibility, which he held until his resignation after two years.

On September 12, 1822, he was married by the Rev. Samuel Brincklé, at Middletown, Delaware, to Sally Ann, daughter of Dr. James Fisher, of Camden. She died in childbirth, leaving two sons, on February 18, 1825; the sons both died before their father without issue.

He was a member of the State House of Representatives in 1824, and in January, 1827, was appointed by Governor Paynter as Secretary of the State (to fill a vacancy).

In the Presidential campaign of 1828 he supported John Quincy Adams, and was then first recognized as an extraordinarily gifted popular orator. In consequence he was elected by the Legislature to the United States Senate for six years from March, 1829; and a year later, during the memorable debate on Foot's resolution, he made a speech which John Quincy Adams described as "one of the most powerful and eloquent orations ever delivered in either of the halls of Congress."

In November, 1831, he was a member of the convention to revise the constitution of Delaware.

In the succeeding session of Congress he came prominently before the public in his inquiry into the abuses in the Post-Office department.

Again, in February, 1833, he was conspicuous in promoting Clay's Compromise Tariff, and in that year was made chairman of the Senate's important Committee on the Judiciary.

In January, 1835, he announced his desire to retire from the Senate at the expiration of his term; but he was re-elected for a second term, and in deference to the wishes of his friends he remained in office until his resignation, in the fall of 1836, in order to provide more efficiently for the needs of those dependent on him.

The honorary degree of Doctor of Laws was conferred on him by Yale College in August, 1836.

He had only, however, just begun practice again when, in January, 1837, he accepted the office of Chief Justice of the State. This office he resigned in August, 1839, in order to be ready to take an active part in the next Presdential campaign.

In the spring of 1842 he removed his residence from Dover to Newcastle, where he practiced law to some extent, while continuing to take a deep interest in public affairs.

In January, 1845, he was again elected to the United States Senate, and he took his seat on March 4.

In the Presidential campaign of 1848 he supported General Taylor vigorously, and was selected in March, 1849, for the appointment of Secretary of State.

The most notable achievement of his term of office was the negotiation with the British government of what is known as the Clayton-Bulwer treaty, for the neutralization of the American isthmus.

On the death of President Taylor in July, 1850, he retired to private life, but was re-elected to the Senate in January, 1853, by a combined vote of both Whigs and Democrats, in order that he might have the opportunity to defend himself against charges brought by General Cass in relation to the Central-American treaty.

After several years of precarious health, he died in Dover, during the Congressional recess, on November 9, 1856, in his 61st year. In his last illness he united with the Presbyterian Church. He freed, long before his death, the slaves whom he had inherited.

His *Memoir* (1882) by the Hon. Joseph P. Comegys contains an engraving from his portrait; another portrait is given in *Harper's Magazine,* volume 59, 1879, and in the Obituary addresses published by Congress.

He had marked personal attractions, with fascinating manners and a musical voice. His powers as an advocate before a jury, and in debate, were of the very highest order.

He published:

1. Speech in the Senate of the United States, on the fourth day of March, in reply to Mr. Grundy of Tennessee, Mr. Woodbury of New Hampshire, and others; the Resolution of Mr. Foot, of Connecticut, being under consideration. Washington, 1830. 8°, pp. 56.
[*A. A. S. B. Ath. B. Publ. C. H. S. Columbia Univ. M. H. S. U. S. Y. C.*

2. Speech, in the Senate of the United States, Feb. 10, 1831, on the Resolution of Mr. Grundy to prohibit the Select Committee on the management of the Post Office Department, from investigating the principles upon which the removals have been made in that Department. Washington, 1831. 8°, pp. 32.
[*B. Ath. B. Publ. Harv.*

3. Speech on the Bill for the Apportionment of the Representation in Congress, delivered in the Senate .. April 25th, 1832. Washington, 1832. 8°, pp. 24.
[*A. A. S. B. Publ. Columbia Univ. Harv. M. H. S.*

4. Speech in Reply to Mr. Buchanan, of Pennsylvania and others, on Mr. Benton's Resolution relative to the National Defence. United States Senate, Feb. 8, 1836. Washington, 1836. 8°, pp. 32.
[*A. A. S. B. Ath. Harv. M. H. S.*

5. Speech, at the Delaware Whig Mass Convention, held at Wilmington, June 15, 1844. Washington, 1844. 8°, pp. 16.
[*Harv. N. Y. Publ.*

The same. Albany, 1844. 8°, pp. 15. [*A. A. S. Br. Mus.*

The same. [New York, 1844.] 8°, pp. 10.
[*N. Y. Publ. U. T. S.*

On protective duties.

6. Speech upon the Oregon question, delivered in the Senate of the United States, February 12, 1846. Washington, 1846. 8°, pp. 16. [*U. S.*

7. Speech on French Spoliations, delivered in the Senate .., April 23 and 24, 1846. Washington, 1846. 8°, pp. 35.
[*A. A. S. B. Publ. Columbia Univ. Harv. M. H. S.*

8. Speech on President Polk's Veto to the Bill "To provide for the ascertainment and satisfaction of claims of American citizens for spoliations committed by the French prior to the 31st day of July, 1801." Delivered in the Senate of the United States, August 10, 1846. Washington, 1846. 8°, pp. 16. [*Harv. U. S.*

9. Substance of the Argument for the United States, in the matter of the Pea Patch Island, before the Hon. John Sergeant, delivered in the Hall of American Independence, in the City of Philadelphia, on the second and third of December, 1847, containing a discussion of the title of the States of Delaware and New Jersey to the river Delaware and its islands. Philadelphia, 1848. 8°, pp. 34. [*A. A. S.*

One of his most elaborate and important efforts.

10. Speech in defence of Zachary Taylor.—Delivered in the Senate of the United States, July 5, 1848. Washington. [1848.] 8°, pp. 16. [*A. A. S. Harv. N. Y. Publ. Y. C.*

11. Address on the Life, Character, and Services of Com. Jacob Jones. Delivered in Wilmington, .. December 17, 1850. Wilmington, 1851. 8°, pp. 25. [*Br. Mus. N. Y. Publ.*

12. Speech, delivered at a public dinner given to him at Wilmington, on the 16th November, 1850, by the Whigs of Delaware. [1853.] 8°, pp. 44. [*U. S.*

13. Speech delivered in the Senate of the United States on the 8th of March, 1853, in vindication of the Central American Treaty concluded with Great Britain on the 19th of April, 1850. Washington, 1853. 8°, pp. 43. [*Harv. N. Y. Publ. U. S. Y. C.*

14. Speech in the Senate of the United States on the 14th of March, 1853, in reply to Mr. Mason, of Virginia, and Mr. Douglas,

of Illinois, in vindication of the Central American Treaty concluded with Great Britain on the 19th of April, 1850. Washington, 1853. 8°, pp. 22. [*Harv. Y. C.*

15. Treaty of Washington. Speech delivered in the Senate of the United States, January 12 and 16, 1854, in reply to Mr. Cass. [Washington, 1854.] 8°, pp. 24.
[*A. A. S. B. Ath. B. Publ. Harv.*

16. Speech on the Bill to organize territorial governments in Nebraska and Kansas; discussing the Missouri Compromise and the doctrine of non-intervention. Delivered in the Senate of the United States, March 1 and 2, 1854. Washington, 1854. 8°, pp. 22. [*B. Publ. Harv. Y. C.*

17. Speech on his amendment proposing to strike out that part of the Nebraska bill which allows foreigners to vote without naturalization in the territories of Nebraska and Kansas. Delivered in the Senate of the United States, May 25, 1854. [Washington, 1854.] 8°, pp. 8. [*B. Publ.*

18. Speech on the Veto Message of the President, on the Bill for the Benefit of the Indigent Insane. In the Senate of the United States, June 15, 1854. Washington, 1854. 8°, pp. 22.
[*A. A. S. B. Ath. B. Publ. Harv. M. H. S.*

19. Remarks of J. M. Clayton and others, on his motion to strike out the new tariff, inserted by the House of Representatives, in the civil and diplomatic appropriation Bill. In the Senate of the United States, March 1, 1855. Washington, 1855. 8°, pp. 12.
[*B. Publ.*

20. [Letter to James H. Causten.] Washington, March 4, 1855. 4°, pp. 2. [*Harv.*
On Causten's service as agent for the French spoliation claims.

21. Speech in regard to Captain S. F. Du Pont, U. S. N., in the Senate of the United States, March 11, 1856, in executive session. Washington, 1856. 8°, pp. 14.
[*A. A. S. B. Publ. Harv. N. Y. Publ. U. S. Y. C.*

22. Speech on the Central American Treaty of April 19, 1850; delivered in the Senate of the United States, March 17 and 19, 1856. Washington, 1856. 8°, pp. 21. [*N. Y. Publ.*

23 Speeches in the United States Senate, March 31, and April 1, 1856, in reply to Senator Houston, of Texas, and others, and in Defense of the Naval Board. Washington, 1856 8°, pp 22
[*A. A S. B Ath B Publ Harv M H S N Y Publ U S*

24. Speech on affairs in Kansas Territory Delivered in the Senate of the United States, June 16, 1856 Washington, 1856 8°, pp. 11 [*B. Ath. U S*

Large extracts from many of his speeches and official papers are reprinted in the *Memoir* by Comegys; and the *Congressional Record* has also many more.

AUTHORITIES

J Q Adams, Diary, viii, 213
Comegys, Memoir of J M Clayton
Hepburn, Clayton Family, 30, 32
Lewis, Great American Lawyers, iii, 405-32

WILLIAM CODMAN, son of William Codman, a merchant of New York City, and grandson of John and Abigail (Asbury) Codman, of Boston and Charlestown, Massachusetts, was born in New York on October 19, 1795. His mother was Susannah, daughter of Dr. Nathaniel and Eleanor (Foster) Coffin, of Portland, Maine The Rev. Dr. John Codman (Harvard 1802), of Dorchester, Massachusetts, was a first cousin. He was prepared for College by John Borland. At the Junior Exhibition of his Class, in May, 1814, he delivered the Latin Oration

He became a shipping merchant in New York City, and died there on November 17, 1848, in his 54th year.

He was married, on July 3, 1833, by the Rev. Dr. McElroy, to Martha Ann, the eldest daughter of the late William B. Gilley, a book publisher of New York, and Harriet (Eaglesfield) Gilley; she died very suddenly in New York City on March 5, 1875, in her 63d year. He left three daughters, two of whom died unmarried.

He is remembered as a very well-read and polished gentleman

George Cooke, a son of John Cooke, of New Haven, and grandson of John and Martha (Booth) Cooke, of New Haven, and great-grandson of the Rev. Samuel Cooke (Yale 1705), of Bridgeport, was born in New Haven on March 30, 1796. His father was the pioneer (1794) in the coach-making business in New Haven. His mother was Anne, daughter of William and Elizabeth (Maltby) Lyon, of New Haven. He was prepared for College by Alanson Hamlin (Yale, 1799) in Danbury.

He taught school at the South for two or three years after graduation; and was then for a few years engaged in business in New Canaan, Connecticut.

After this he entered into the carriage business in New York City, with his father and brother, in the firm of John Cooke & Sons, superintending also their extensive manufactory in New Haven.

About 1849 he removed his residence to New Haven, continuing in the same business.

He died in New Haven on May 30, 1871, in his 76th year. He was never married.

James Davis entered College from Smyrna, Delaware.

He studied law and settled in his native State.

He is said to have died by his own hand in Wilmington, Delaware, in June, 1822, at the age of 26 or 27.

George Pollock Devereux, the younger son of John and Frances (Pollock) Devereux, of Newbern, North Carolina, and a brother of Thomas P. Devereux (Yale 1813), was born in 1795. His youth was spent in Stratford, Connecticut, among his mother's relatives.

After graduation he studied law in the Litchfield Law School.

He was admitted to the bar in 1818, and for three years practiced law with his uncle, George Pollock, who intended to make him his heir, and in 1821 took him abroad for a European tour.

After his return he was married, on June 13, 1827, by the Rev. Edward Rutledge (Yale 1817) to his second cousin, Sarah Elizabeth, daughter of Judge Samuel William Johnson (Yale 1779), of Stratford; she was also a first cousin of his brother's wife.

He resided on a plantation near Raleigh, North Carolina, and died in Suffolk, in southeastern Virginia, while on his way to Stratford for the summer, on May 13, 1837, at the age of 42. His death, from a hemorrhage of the stomach, was the result of a fall from his horse some years before.

His widow made her home for some years in New Haven, and died at her youngest daughter's in Middletown, Connecticut, on March 10, 1867, in her 70th year.

Their children were five daughters, three of whom died in infancy. The youngest daughter married the Rev. John Townsend (Union Coll. 1851); and her older sister, Mrs. Lillie Devereux Blake, has had a conspicuous career as a lecturer and author.

AUTHORITIES.

Geneal. Hist. of Conn., i, 206, 210. N. C. Hist. and Geneal. Register, iii, 158. Tuttle Family, 425.

Abraham Jacob Duryee was a son of John and Jane Duryee, of Harlem, a suburb of New York City. His preparation was completed in the Hopkins Grammar School at New Haven, under Chauncey A. Goodrich (Yale 1810).

He studied medicine at the College of Physicians and Surgeons in New York City, receiving the degree of M.D. in 1819.

He settled in New York City for the practice of his profession, but died early, in March, 1822, aged about 27 years.

Henry Edwin Dwight, the youngest son of President Timothy Dwight (Yale 1769), was born in New Haven on April 19, 1797. He was prepared for College at the Hopkins Grammar School by Chauncey A. Goodrich.

Soon after graduation he went to New York City, as a clerk in the hardware store of his brother, Benjamin (Yale 1799); and later returned to New Haven to take a similar place with his eldest brother, Timothy.

In March, 1820, he joined with Tuthill of the preceding class in bringing out the brilliant, but short-lived periodical called the *Microscope*.

He had united with the College Church in May, 1819, and in the fall of 1821 he began the course of study in the Andover Theological Seminary. Towards the end of his second year there, over-exertion on a walking-trip to the White Mountains brought on a very severe cold, with bleeding at the lungs. This led to the abandonment of his course in the Seminary, and his departure for Europe, where he spent four years (1824 to 1828) in study at the Universities of Göttingen and Berlin.

In May, 1828, he joined with his brother Sereno (Yale 1803) in the establishment of a boarding-school for boys, called the New Haven Gymnasium, which had a highly successful career for three years, when the health of both principals gave way.

He was able, however, after this, to give some extempore lectures, on his European experiences, in New York and Philadelphia, which were received with favor; and he was contemplating another visit to Germany, for the further study of methods of education.

He died in New Haven, from a violent rheumatic attack, after an illness of two months, attended with severe suffering, on August 11, 1832, in his 36th year.

At the time of his last illness he was expecting to be married to Miss Salisbury, of Boston, who afterwards married his friend Nathaniel Chauncey (Yale 1806).

He had also been recently selected for a professorship in the contemplated New York University, in case his health should allow.

A Funeral Oration in his memory, by J. A. Pizarro, who had taught Spanish in his Gymnasium, was published, in an English translation, at Baltimore in 1834 (16°, pp. 18).

He published:

1. In the *Microscope,* New Haven, 1820:

Editorial note, volume 1, pp. 9–12.

On the character and writings of Dryden, pp. 17–21, 41–45, 129–32.

On angels in works of fiction, pp. 46–48.

The Vale of Death, an allegory, pp. 89–96.

A supposed destitution in Taste in American writers, pp. 105–09, 113–17.

Hume's theory respecting virtue, 121–26.

Letter from a traveler in Ohio, 137–41.

Story of Amelia and Alonzo, volume 2, pp. 9–16.

The Republic of Letters, an allegory, pp. 41–47.

Prospects of American Literature, pp. 81–86, 89–96.

The Happiness of Heaven, pp. 161–65.

2. Account of the Kaatskill Mountains. In the *American Journal of Science and Arts,* volume 2, pp. 11–29 (April, 1820).

3. Travels in the North of Germany, in the years 1825 and 1826. New-York, 1829. 8°, pp. iv, 454 + pl.
[*A. A. S. B. Ath. Br. Mus. Harv. N. Y. Publ. U. S. U. T. S. Y. C.*

AUTHORITIES.

Dwight Family, i, 171, 210–11. Relig. Intelligencer, xvii, 191, 255.

John Dicks Eccles was born in Fayetteville, North Carolina, on March 29, 1792. He delivered the valedictory Oration at graduation.

He returned home, and in 1816 entered the law office of Judge Thomas Ruffin (Princeton Coll. 1805), in Hillsboro. In 1819 he was admitted to the bar, and he settled in practice in Fayetteville.

In 1820 he married Elizabeth Pollock, daughter of Colonel Edward Jones, Solicitor General of the State.

He had an acute and brilliant intellect, and attained eminence as a lawyer; he confined himself in the main to his profession, serving, however, as a Whig Representative in the Legislature in 1827, 1828, and 1829.

In 1842 failing health compelled him to retire from active business, and he lived in invalid seclusion until his death at Ecclesford, near Fayetteville, after a lingering and very painful illness, on June 15, 1856, in his 65th year.

His wife survived him, with one son and three daughters, a younger son having died before him.

Edward Fellows Ensign was born in Sheffield, Massachusetts, and was prepared for College by William H. Maynard (Williams Coll. 1810).

He studied law, and was admitted to the bar in 1820, when he began practice in his native town.

He held many local offices, such as postmaster for many years, and sheriff.

He married late in life, and had children.

He died in 1865, aged about 71 years.

Elisha Rexford Fenn, the eldest child of Abijah Fenn, of Watertown, Connecticut, and grandson of Isaac and Mehitable (Humaston) Fenn, of Watertown, was born in Watertown on February 24, 1794. His mother was Ann (called Nancy) Abigail, daughter of the Rev. Elisha Rexford (Yale 1763) and Lydia (Munson) Rexford, of New Stratford Society, now Monroe. The family removed to Baltimore, Maryland, before his admission to College, but are not traced there after 1815.

He was prepared for Yale by the Rev. Daniel Parker (Yale 1798), of Ellsworth Society in Sharon.

He is believed to have died soon after graduation.

AUTHORITIES.

Anderson, Hist. of Waterbury, i, Appendix, 49.

ORIN FOWLER, the eldest son in a family of twelve children of Captain Amos Fowler, of Goshen Society in Lebanon, Connecticut, and grandson of Captain Dijah and Abigail (Bigelow) Fowler, of Lebanon, was born in Lebanon on July 29, 1791. His mother was Rebecca, daughter of John and Rhoda (Gillet) Dewey, of Lebanon. He was prepared for Williams College by his pastor, the Rev. William B. Ripley (Yale 1786), and entered in 1811. At the end of the first term he took a dismission, and after further study under Hezekiah Rudd (Yale 1806) in Bacon Academy, Colchester, he entered as Sophomore at Yale in the fall of 1812.

A few months before graduation he accepted the preceptorship of the Academy in Fairfield, and held the place with entire acceptance until the fall of 1816, when he resigned, to devote himself more fully to theological studies with the Rev. Heman Humphrey (Yale 1805), of Fairfield. He was licensed to preach by the Association of the Western District of Fairfield County, on October 14, 1817.

After some months of scattered employment, chiefly in Fairfield County, he decided in March, 1818, to go on a mission to the West in the employ of the Connecticut Missionary Society, and was ordained with a view to this work, in Farmington, on June 3, 1818, by the North Association of Hartford County.

After about a year, which he spent mostly in Indiana, he returned to Connecticut in the summer of 1819.

In the following winter he supplied the pulpit of the Congregational Church in Plainfield, and was installed there as pastor on March 1, 1820. The church, then consisting of four male and forty female members, was largely increased, and a season of prosperity followed. After some years an unfortunate lack of discretion on Mr. Fowler's part caused him to incur the ill-will of prominent persons in his church, who professed to believe reports derogatory to his character. Although the Windham Association of Ministers after a public investigation were satisfied with his explanations, a subsequent council agreed that the existing dissatisfaction rendered a separation expedient, and he was accordingly dismissed on January 27, 1831.

He went almost immediately to the Congregational Church in Fall River, Massachusetts, where he was installed on July 7.

In 1841 he delivered some discourses on the history of the town, which included a reference to the disputed boundary-line between Massachusetts and Rhode Island. In consequence he was not long after named on a committee to defend the interests of the town before the Commissioners of the two States. He performed this service, and subsequently, after his fellow-citizens objected to the decision, and he had appeared as their spokesman in the public press, he was chosen (in the fall of 1847) to the State Senate, and there contributed largely to a rejection of the Commissioners' Report by Massachusetts.

His useful career in the Legislature led in turn to his election to the United States Congress, as a Free-Soil Whig, in the fall of 1848. He continued to provide for the supply of his pulpit until the last of November, 1849, when he left for Washington. Agreeably to previous understanding, he was dismissed from his pastorate by the council which installed his successor in the spring of 1852. During his residence in Washington, he often supplied pulpits in that vicinity.

He was re-elected to Congress for a second term, but the labors of his position were too onerous, and he died in Washington, after a brief illness, on September 3, 1852, in his 62d year.

In his Congressional career he had shown himself an advocate of temperance laws and a strong opponent of slavery. He had also been an efficient promoter of cheap postage.

He was married, on October 16, 1821, to Amaryllis, fourth daughter of Deacon John H. Payson, of Pomfret, Connecticut, and a sister of the Rev. George Payson (Yale 1812), who survived him.

His only child died early, and he adopted two children of the Rev. Erastus Learned (Brown Univ. 1795), of Canterbury, Connecticut; the daughter married the Rev. President Samuel C. Bartlett (Dartmouth Coll. 1836), and the son was graduated at Amherst College in 1845.

Mr. Fowler was a man of admirable business habits, methodical, executive, accurate, and practical; as a minister he was most successful in pastoral labor.

He published:

1. Remarks on the State of Indiana.

In the *Christian Spectator,* volume 1, pp. 401–03, 463–67 (August-September, 1819).

2. The duty of distinction in preaching, explained and enforced.—A Sermon [from I Cor. xiv, 8] delivered March 9, 1825, at the Ordination of the Rev. Israel G. Rose, A.M., as pastor of the church in Westminster Society, Canterbury. Hartford, 1825. 8°, pp. 24.

[*A. C. A. Br. Mus. C. H. S. Harv. N. Y. H. S. Y. C.*

3. A Disquisition on the Evils of Using Tobacco, and the necessity of immediate and entire reformation.—Delivered before the Fall River Lyceum, on the evening of June 4th, 1833; and before the congregation to whom the author statedly ministers, on the evening of October 27th, 1833. Providence, 1833. 8°, pp. 26.

[*A. A. S. A. C. A. Y. C.*

The same. Second edition. Boston, 1835. 8°, pp. 24.

[*Br. Mus. Columbia Univ. N. Y. Publ. U. S. U. T. S.*

The same. Third edition. Boston, 1842. 8°, pp. 27.
[*B. Ath. M. H. S.*

4. The Mode and Subjects of Baptism.—Four Sabbath Evening Lectures on the Mode and Subjects of Baptism, preached in November and December, 1834, before the Church and Congregation to which the author ministers.—Published by request of the church. Boston, 1835. 8°, pp. 119. [*A. A. S. A. C. A. B. Publ. Harv.*

5. An historical sketch of Fall River, from 1620 to the present time; with notices of Freetown and Tiverton; in three discourses, delivered January 24, 1841. Fall River, 1841. 8°, pp. 66.
[*A. C. A. B. Publ. Harv. M. H. S. N. Y. H. S.*

Also, after his death,

The same, with title: History of Fall River, . . as published in 1841, together with a sketch of the life of Rev. O. Fowler, [etc.] . . . Fall River, 1862. 8°, pp. 100.
[*A. C. A. B. Ath. B. Publ. Harv. U. S. Y. C.*

6. Slavery in California and New Mexico.—Speech in the House of Representatives, March 11, 1850, in Committee of the whole on the state of the Union, on the President's message communicating the Constitution of California. [Washington, 1850.] 8°, pp. 15.
[*A. A. S. A. C. A. B. Ath. B. Publ. Harv. M. H. S. U. S. Y. C.*

7. Remarks on a motion to reduce postage on all letters to two cents.—Made in the House of Representatives of the United States, December 31, 1850. Washington, 1851. 8°, pp. 8.
[*B. Publ. U. S.*

An argument for two-cent postage.

8. Speech on the legislation of Massachusetts—our Government—the disposal of the public lands—the tariff—constitutional law—and our foreign relations.—Delivered in the House of Representatives of the United States, in Committee of the whole on the State of the Union, on the Bill for the Encouragement of Agriculture, Commerce, Manufactures, and other branches of Industry, March 31, 1852. [Washington, 1852.] 8°, pp. 16.
[*A. A. S. A. C. A. B. Ath. B. Publ. Harv. M. H. S. U. S. U. T. S. Y. C.*

9. Speech on the Wheeling Bridge case. Delivered in the House of Representatives of the United States, August 18, 1852. Washington, 1852. 8°, pp. 7. [*B. Publ.*

AUTHORITIES.

Congregational Quarterly, ii, 202-03. *Larned,* Hist. of Windham County, ii, 509. *Sprague,* Annals of the Amer. Pulpit, ii, 648-52. *Walworth,* Hyde Genealogy, ii, 710.

WILLIAM EDGAR GALLAUDET, son of Peter Wallace Gallaudet, of Philadelphia, and brother of Thomas Hopkins Gallaudet (Yale 1805), was born in Philadelphia on December 24, 1797. The family removed to Hartford, Connecticut, in his infancy, and he was prepared for the Junior Class by John Witter (Yale 1812) in the Plainfield Academy.

He became a clerk in New York and died in that city, after a few hours' illness, on April 8, 1821, in his 24th year.

AUTHORITIES.

N. Y. Geneal. and Biogr. Record, xix, 121.

THOMAS GRAY, the only son of Samuel Gray (Dartmouth Coll. 1771), of Windham, Connecticut, who was for over forty years Clerk of the Windham County Courts, and grandson of Samuel and Lydia (Dyer) Gray, of Windham, was born in Windham on September 3, 1794. His mother was Charlotte, youngest daughter of Colonel Jedediah and Anne (Wood) Elderkin, of Windham. Ebenezer Gray (Yale 1805) was his first cousin.

He studied law after graduation, and engaged to some extent in its practice in Windham, after his admission to the bar in 1819.

He was one of the representatives of the town in the State Legislature in 1828 and 1829.

He was Clerk or Assistant Clerk of the Superior Court for Windham County for the last five or six years of his life, and Judge of Probate for the Windham district for about three years before his death. He had previously been Clerk of the Probate Court for thirteen years, and Town Clerk for fourteen years.

He died while on a visit in Norwich, on August 29, 1860, aged 66 years.

He united with the Congregational Church in Windham in 1831, and his exemplary life won the high respect of his fellow-townsmen.

He was married on September 30, 1821, to Mary C., daughter of Henry Webb, of Windham, who died on March 16, 1823, aged 23 years. They had no children.

He next married on May 11, 1824, her sister Lucretia, by whom he had one son and three daughters.

AUTHORITIES.

Larned, Hist. of Windham County, ii, 518.

Horatio Gridley, the son of Amos Gridley, Junior, a thriving farmer of Kensington Society, in Berlin, Connecticut, and his wife, Drusilla Barrett, was born in Berlin, on September 10, 1792. His preparation for College was completed under the Rev. Joab Brace (Yale 1804), of Newington Society, in Wethersfield.

On graduation, though in feeble health, he entered the Andover Theological Seminary; but before the close of his first year, symptoms of pulmonary consumption obliged him to give up the course. The state of his health then led him to take a deep interest in medicine, and he began the study of that profession with Dr. Samuel B. Woodward, then of Wethersfield, attending also some lectures in the Yale Medical Department.

He began practice in Woodbury in 1820, and was married, on December 9, 1823, to Mary, eldest daughter of Leonard and Prudence (Robbins) Welles, of Wethersfield.

In 1826 he removed to his native town, where he remained for twenty-five years in the constant practice of his profession. The honorary degree of Doctor of Medicine was conferred on him by Yale in 1833. In 1843 he was a member of the State Senate, and *ex-officio* a Fellow of the College.

In 1851 he was obliged to give up work by an increasing general failure of muscular power, and he removed to Hartford, to make a home for his only surviving child, who was in business there. He died in Hartford from paralysis, after confinement to the house for nearly two years, on November 9, 1864, in his 73d year.

He was buried in Kensington. His wife survived him.

Their children were three sons and a daughter. The eldest son was graduated at this College in 1847, and at the Yale Medical School in 1850, but died on the threshold of his career.

As a physician, he was judicious, prudent, and very faithful; and a man of good judgment in all matters.

AUTHORITIES.

Conn. Med. Society's Proceedings, 1865, 160-61.

CHARLES HENRY HAMMOND was a son of Abijah Hammond, of New York City, and grandson of Captain Abijah and Mary (Saltmarsh) Hammond, of Boston. His mother was Catharine, daughter of the Hon. Abraham and Frances (Ludlow) Ogden, of Newark, New Jersey. He was born about 1795, and was prepared by William A. Whelpley (Yale 1807), in Morristown, New Jersey.

He settled in Bennington, Vermont, and in 1826 represented that town in the Legislature.

His death is reported to have occurred in Ohio, early in 1850. He was never married.

AUTHORITIES.

Wheeler, Ogden Family, 188.

Edward Harleston, the second son of Edward Harleston, of Charleston, South Carolina, and grandson of Captain John and Hannah (Child) Harleston, of Harleston, a suburb of Charleston, was born on December 25, 1794. His mother was Annabella, only daughter of the Hon. James Moultrie, Chief Justice of East Florida, and Cecilia (Staunton) Moultrie. He was prepared for College by the Rev. Christopher E. Gadsden (Yale 1804).

His life was passed in South Carolina, mainly as a planter of rice and cotton.

He married on March 3, 1818, Georgianna W. Doughty, who bore him one son and two daughters, all of whom died in infancy. He married secondly, on January 26, 1826, Anna Isabella Huger, of Charleston, by whom he had seven daughters and three sons.

He served in the State Legislature for several years.

He died in Charleston on February 11, 1871, in his 77th year.

AUTHORITIES.

S. C. Hist. and Geneal. Magazine, iii, 162–63.

Elijah Hartshorn, Junior, son of Dr. Elijah and Jerusha (Johnson) Hartshorn, of Franklin, Connecticut, was born in Franklin on November 30, 1790. He was prepared for College by his pastor, the Rev. Dr. Samuel Nott (Yale 1780).

After graduation he studied theology, probably with Dr. Nott, and was licensed to preach in 1820 by the New London Association of ministers.

He temporarily supplied many pulpits in the vicinity of Franklin, but was never ordained.

He died in Franklin on September 19, 1840, in his 50th year. He was never married.

AUTHORITIES.

Woodward, Franklin Church Hist., 71.

John Hastings, the second son of Dr. John and Sibyl (Dickinson) Hastings, of Hatfield, Massachusetts, and grandson of the Hon. John and Content (Little) Hastings, of Hatfield, was born on December 22, 1791. He was prepared for College by his pastor, the Rev. Dr. Joseph Lyman (Yale 1767).

He was married, on January 29, 1823, to Lucretia, daughter of Daniel and Damaris (Stevens) Ward, of Petersham.

He resided in Hatfield until about 1833, when he removed to Heath, on the northern border of the State, where he was occupied as a merchant and innkeeper.

In 1842 he removed to Onondaga Valley, a village near Syracuse, New York, where he remained until his death.

He was a member of the Presbyterian Church and held in high respect in the community.

He was active in politics, and retained his faculties to the last. He served as justice of the peace until he declined a re-election, and as town-clerk for twenty-eight years.

He died in Onondaga Valley on January 21, 1886, in his 95th year.

His wife died on June 27, 1873, in her 82d year. Their children, two sons, died before him, and his home in his last years was with his grandchildren.

AUTHORITIES.

Bond, Hist. of Watertown, 289. *Mrs. Lizzie G. Henderson,* MS. Letter, February, 1886. *Judd,* Hist. of Hadley, 2d ed., pt. 2, 67. Petersham Vital Records, 51, 105.

Roger Conant Hatch, the second child of Dr. Josiah Hatch, of Westfield Society in Middletown, Connecticut, a surgeon in the Revolution, was born in Middletown on October 20, 1784. His mother was Elizabeth Bronson, the widow of Dr. Roger Conant (Yale 1765). He was prepared for the Junior Class by the Rev. Timothy M. Cooley (Yale 1792), of East Granville, Massachusetts, whither his father had removed. He was in advance of all his classmates in age.

After graduation he studied theology for about a year with the Rev. Samuel Osgood (Dartmouth Coll. 1805), of Springfield, Massachusetts, and then spent some time as a missionary of the Young Men's Missionary Association of New York.

On October 21, 1818, he was ordained and installed as pastor of the Congregational Church in Hopkinton, near Concord, New Hampshire, where he remained, highly esteemed, until his dismission on June 26, 1832. During this period he admitted one hundred and forty-seven persons to his church.

During the next three years he supplied various vacant churches, as in Newfane and Hartford, Vermont, and in Greenfield and Swanzey, New Hampshire.

On December 23, 1835, he was settled over the Second Congregational (Orthodox) Church in Warwick, Franklin County, Massachusetts, where he ministered acceptably until his dismission on June 22, 1853.

His residence continued in Warwick until his death there, after a long period of disease, which had weakened both body and mind, on September 12, 1868, aged nearly 84 years.

He was married, on September 13, 1820, to Hannah, daughter of Benjamin and Beulah (Stow) Fay, of Westborough, Massachusetts, who died in Peoria, Illinois, on May 3, 1875, aged 79 years. They had four sons and four daughters; of these children all but two survived their father. The second son was graduated at Amherst College in 1849, and became a clergyman. The third daughter married the Hon. William Windom, of Minnesota.

Mr. Hatch was a man of dignified and stately manners, a model pastor and preacher, and in every way esteemed and revered.

AUTHORITIES

Blake, Hist of Warwick, 163 Congregational Quarterly, xi, 69-71 *Holland,* Hist of Western Mass, ii, 448 *Lawrence,* N Hampshire Churches, 393 *Lord,* Life and Times in Hopkinton, 402-04. *Packard,* Hist of Churches in Franklin County, Mass, 403 Westborough Vital Records, 168

JEREMIAH HINE, the eldest son of Charles Hine, a farmer of Woodbridge, Connecticut, and grandson of Charles and Lydia (Sperry) Hine, of Woodbridge, was born in Woodbridge on January 26, and was baptized on April 5, 1795. His mother was Anna, daughter of Henry and Lydia (Botsford) Baldwin, of Woodbridge. In his boyhood the family removed to South East, Putnam County, New York, where he was prepared for College by Russell J. Minor (Yale 1801)

After graduation he taught school in Lancaster County, Pennsylvania, for two years, at the same time beginning the study of law. He then continued his studies for two years longer, with Walker Todd (Yale 1810), in Carmel, the shire town of Putnam County, New York.

In 1819 he began practice in Carmel, and soon went into a partnership with Henry B. Cowles (Union Coll. 1816), which continued until Mr. Cowles removed to New York, about 1834.

In March, 1822, he was appointed Surrogate of Putnam County, and he retained the office until the close of 1832. He was also District Attorney of the same county from September, 1829, until his death.

In December, 1836, he was married to Zillah, daughter of Heman and Chloe Cole, of South East. He had only one child, who died in infancy.

For the last year of his life he was in quite poor health, and was at times very low-spirited In one of his fits of depression he took his own life, in Carmel, on August 24, 1838, in his 44th year.

His wife married again, and survived him for many years.

Mr. Hine was esteemed as a well-equipped and honest lawyer, thorough in all his work, very industrious, and very temperate in his habits, but not a fluent speaker.

AUTHORITIES.

George Hine, MS. Letter, February, 1866. Hine Genealogy, 89, 139. *Pelletreau,* Hist. of Putnam County, 288-29.

CHARLES JAMES HINSDALE, a son of Epaphras and Elizabeth (Bowen) Hinsdale, of New York City and grandson of Captain Barnabas and Magdalen (Seymour) Hinsdale, of Hartford, Connecticut, was born in New York on February 12, 1796. The family removed to Newark, New Jersey, in 1800, and he was prepared for the Sophomore Class by the Rev. Samuel Whelpley in Morristown.

He entered Andover Theological Seminary late in 1816, but after remaining there through half the course he transferred himself to the Seminary at Princeton, where he was graduated in 1819.

In 1820 he went to the South on a missionary tour, remaining about two years.

In September, 1822, he began preaching in the First Congregational Church in Meriden, Connecticut, and having been called in November to the pastorate, with a salary of five hundred and fifty dollars, he was ordained and installed there on June 15, 1823.

During his very successful ministry about fifty were added to the church, and the congregation increased largely. He was dismissed in December, 1833.

In 1835 he was called to the Congregational Church in Blandford, Massachusetts, where he was installed on January 20, 1836. He continued as the settled pastor of that church until dismissed at his own request in December, 1860, though he performed occasional ministerial duties up to his death. He was instantly killed, in Blandford, by being thrown from his carriage on October 17, 1871, in his 76th year.

He married on April 17, 1823, Catharine Banks, widow of Erastus Chittenden, who died in 1817, and the second daughter of Judge David D. and Martha (Banks) Crane, of Newark; she died on April 26, 1865, in her 73d year. They had four sons and three daughters, of whom the eldest son and eldest daughter died in infancy; two sons and two daughters survived them. One son was graduated at Yale in 1848.

He next married, in November, 1866, Mary A., widow of Henry Lloyd, of Blandford, who died on November 14, 1893, in her 86th year.

Mr. Hinsdale had an animated pulpit style, and was very social and engaging in his manners.

AUTHORITIES.

Andrews, Hinsdale Genealogy, 136, 232-33. *Davis,* Hist. of Wallingford, 231. 175th Anniversary of Congregational Church, Meriden, 25, 47, 59, 74.

ISAAC EDWARD HOLMES, the fourth son of John Bee Holmes, a Revolutionary officer, and grandson of Isaac and Rebecca (Bee) Holmes, was born in Charleston, South Carolina, on April 6, 1796. His mother was Elizabeth, daughter of John Edwards, an Englishman who had emigrated to South Carolina. His preparation for College was begun under his first cousin, the Rev. Christopher Edwards Gadsden (Yale 1804), in Charleston, and was completed at the Hopkins Grammar School in New Haven under Chauncey A. Goodrich (Yale 1810).

Returning home after graduation he began the study of the law, and was admitted to practice in 1818, about which time he married his cousin, Mary Holmes. He early acquired some literary reputation by the publication of a volume of essays, and in 1823 he appeared in print as an ardent advocate of slavery and State Rights. During the crisis of 1832-33 he was one of the leaders of the extremists, and is said to have originated the proposition that the State should nullify the tariff.

After a successful practice of his profession and service in the City Council and the State Legislature, he entered Congress in 1839, and retained his seat until 1850, when he removed to California. He had served as chairman of the House committee on commerce, and later of that on naval affairs, and had made a reputation for fervid eloquence.

He then resumed the practice of law in San Francisco, but was recalled to Charleston by his wife's illness in 1854.

After her death, which occurred in December, 1856, he returned to California, and resided there until January, 1861. On learning of the passage of the ordinance of secession, he started for South Carolina, and on his way home through Washington endeavored in several interviews with Secretary Seward and General Scott to avert war, and reached Charleston with the belief that he had been successful. Although a thorough state-rights man, of the Calhoun school, he deemed secession at that time inexpedient.

A few years after his return his health began to fail, and it was never fully restored. He died in Charleston on February 24, 1867, in his 71st year.

A portrait is given in Wheeler's *History of Congress,* volume 1.

He published:

1. Recreations of George Taletell. 1822.

2. Caroliniensis. [Charleston, 1823.] 12°, pp. 80. [*C. H. S.*

A collection of anonymous papers, republished from the *Charleston Mercury,* in criticism of the Opinion, in August, 1823, of Judge

William Johnson in the case of the arrest of a mulatto from Jamaica.

Robert J Turnbull is said to have assisted in this pamphlet.

3. Speech on the Annexation of Texas to the United States — Delivered in the House of Representatives, Jan. 14, 1845. [Washington, 1845.] 8°, pp. 7. [*B. Publ* *U. S.* *Y. C.*

4 Speech on the Civil and Diplomatic Appropriation Bill. delivered in the House of Representatives, U S, June 28, 1848. [Washington, 1848.] 8°, pp 8 [*Harv* *Y C.*

5. Speech on the Texas Boundary. In the House of Representatives, Sept 3, 1850 Washington, 1850. 8°, pp 7. [*B. Publ*

AUTHORITIES

J. Q. Adams, Diary, x, 532; xi, 487, xii, 146, 238 *James G Holmes,* MS Letter, February, 1868. Holmes Family Chart *Wheeler,* Hist of Congress, i, 9–30

Horace Hooker, the youngest of twelve children of Elijah Hooker (a farmer of Kensington Parish in Berlin, Connecticut), and a nephew of the Rev. John Hooker (Yale 1751), was born in Berlin on March 25, 1793. His mother was Susannah Judd, widow of Samuel Seymour, of Kensington. He was prepared for College by the Rev. Joab Brace (Yale 1804), of Newington Parish in Wethersfield.

After graduation he was for about two years Principal of the Grammar School in Hartford, from which he was called to a tutorship in College, which he held for four and a half years.

In the meantime he had studied theology under Professor Fitch, and had been licensed to preach by the New Haven West Association of Ministers, on February 29, 1820 In April, 1822, he was ordained and installed as pastor of the Congregational Church in Watertown; but he was compelled to resign in October, 1824, on account of ill-health.

He then returned to Hartford, and became the editor of the *Connecticut Observer*, a weekly religious paper, which he conducted with ability from its first number on January 1, 1825, to 1841. He also held the office of Secretary of the Missionary Society of Connecticut from 1826, and of its successor, the Connecticut Home Missionary Society, from 1831 until his death. In addition he preached much in neighboring churches.

In May, 1852, he began to act as Chaplain of the Retreat for the Insane in Hartford, and he performed the duties of that office until laid aside by a paralytic attack in August, 1862. For several years previous to 1856 he spent his leisure time in the preparation of books for children.

He was a clear thinker, and expressed his thoughts in a style remarkable for neatness and perspicuity.

He was married on July 17, 1822, by the Rev. Dr. Joel Hawes to Mary Ann, eldest daughter of William Brown (Yale 1784), of Hartford, a lady of considerable literary ability, who died on May 3, 1838, aged 42 years.

He was next married on November 22, 1843, by the Rev. Thomas H. Gallaudet (Yale 1805) to Harriet, daughter of the late Edward Watkinson, of Hartford, who survived him.

By his second marriage he had one son, who was graduated at Yale in 1864, and one daughter, who married Clarence L. Westcott, of the same class.

He published:

1. First Report of the Directors of the Hartford Auxiliary Bible Society; with an Address delivered at their annual meeting:—by H. Hooker. Hartford, 1817. 8°, pp. 15. [*Y. C.*

The address occupies pp. 5–12.

2. In 1820 he contributed to the *Microscope*, New Haven, the following articles:

Account of a Society for criticism on preaching, vol. 1, pp. 77–80; Reasons assigned for the inferiority of women, vol. 2, pp. 73–80; On indiscriminate praise and censure, pp. 97–101.

3 Review of Remains of the Rev. Carlos Wilcox
In the *Quarterly Christian Spectator*, volume 1, pp 52–78 (March, 1829); the article is in part by the Rev. Leonard Bacon (Yale 1820).

4 Lecture on the temporal benefits of the Sabbath
In Lectures originally delivered before the Goodrich Association Hartford, 1833 12°, pp. 67–111.

5 The Child's Book on the Sabbath American Tract Society, New-York [1835] 12°, pp 201 [*A. C. A B Publ Y. C*

6. Scripture Biography for the Young, volumes 7–10 American Tract Society.
The previous volumes of the series were written by Dr. Thomas H Gallaudet (Yale 1805).

7. The Farmer's Own Book of Intellectual and Moral Improvement. New York, 1839 12°, pp. 180
[*B. Publ. N Y. Publ. Watkinson Libr.*

8 The Practical Spelling Book, with Reading Lessons. By T. H. Gallaudet and H Hooker. Hartford. [1840.] 12°, pp. 166
[*B. Publ Br. Mus Harv.*

9 The School and Family Dictionary, and Illustrative Definer. By T H. Gallaudet, and H Hooker New York, 1841. 12°, pp 221 [*B. Publ. U. S.*

10 Psalms and Hymns, for Christian Use and Worship; prepared and set forth by the General Association of Connecticut New-Haven, 1845. 12°, pp 720 [*Y C.*
Edited by H. Hooker and O E Daggett.

11 Congregational Home Missions in Connecticut.
In Contributions to the Ecclesiastical History of Connecticut. New Haven, 1861 8°, pp. 163–79
He furnished in 1851 a brief notice of Dr. Thomas H. Gallaudet, which is printed in Sprague's *Annals of the American Pulpit*, volume 2, pp 613–15

AUTHORITIES

College Courant, xiii, 123 Descendants of Thomas Hooker, 58, 126–27.

JOSIAH HOOKER, the third son of Judge John Hooker (Yale 1782), of Springfield, Massachusetts, and a brother of George Hooker (Yale 1814), was born in Springfield on April 17, 1796. He was prepared for College by the Rev. Ezra Witter (Yale 1793), of Wilbraham.

He studied law after graduation, and at first opened an office in Pittsfield, but soon returned to Springfield, where he continued until his death. He was a member of the State Legislature in 1838. From 1846 until his death he was the President of the Springfield Institution for Savings. He took much interest in the schools of the city, and was for nearly twenty years a member-at-large of the school-committee. He was a man of deeply religious character, an excellent lawyer, and a very useful citizen, greatly esteemed for his sterling qualities.

After three or four years of invalidism, he died in Springfield on July 14, 1870, in his 75th year.

He married on October 23, 1849, Jane Wealthy, daughter of John Adams and Wealthy (Kingsley) Judd, of Westhampton, who survived him without children, and died in Springfield on January 27, 1901.

An engraving from his portrait is given in Chapin's *Old Springfield.*

AUTHORITIES.

Bates, Hist. Address, 67. *Chapin,* Old Springfield, 223. Descendants of Thomas Hooker, 121. Dwight Family, ii, 845.

ANDREW HUNTINGTON, the youngest of eleven children of Captain Andrew Huntington, of Goshen Society in Lebanon, Connecticut, and grandson of Simon and Sarah (Huntington) Huntington, of Lebanon, was born on May 31, 1791. His mother was Ruth, daughter of Elijah and Ruth (Tracy) Hyde, of Lebanon. He was prepared for College by his pastor, the Rev. William B. Ripley (Yale 1786).

Soon after graduation he began to teach in the Academy in Greenville, Greene County, New York, and while thus engaged was married, on May 1, 1819, to Mary, daughter of Barnabas Chipman, of Shoreham, Vermont.

In 1822 he removed to New York City, where he continued teaching, and was at the same time studying theology in a small class which was under the instruction of the Rev Gardiner Spring (Yale 1805), the Rev. Samuel H. Cox, and the Rev. Philip M. Whelpley.

He was licensed to preach in 1825 by the North River Presbytery.

About 1830 he became the principal of an academy in Pompey, Onondaga County, and while thus engaged he supplied for most of the time destitute Presbyterian churches in that vicinity. Later he taught in Hudson and elsewhere

About 1850 he gave up teaching and devoted himself to the work of the ministry in Chenango County. He was ordained as an evangelist on February 19, 1852, and was steadily employed, but declined all offers of settlement.

In 1862 he retired from further service. He died in Milan, Ohio, the home of his married daughter, on June 5, 1872, at the age of 81.

His wife survived him with one son (Yale 1843) and two daughters. A younger son died before him.

AUTHORITIES

Mrs Andrew Huntington, MS Letter, October, 1872 *E B. Huntington,* Huntington Family Memoir, 191–92, 281 *Walworth,* Hyde Genealogy, 1, 291–92

William Jessup, second son of Major Zebulon Jessup, of Southampton, Long Island, and grandson of Deacon John and Mehetabel Jessup, was born in Southampton on June 21, 1797. His mother was Zerviah, daughter of Samuel and Zerviah (Rhodes) Huntting, of Southampton.

He was prepared for College by the Rev. Dr. Aaron Woolworth (Yale 1784), of Bridgehampton.

In 1818 he removed from his home to Montrose, Pennsylvania, where he began the practice of the law. He was married, on July 4, 1820, to Amanda, daughter of Henry Harris, of Southampton.

In 1838 he was appointed Presiding Judge of the Eleventh Judicial District of Pennsylvania, which office he filled until the judiciary became elective, in 1851, when he was removed, being a Whig in a Democratic district.

For the rest of his active life he was engaged in practice, in connection with his eldest son.

The honorary degree of Doctor of Laws was conferred on him by Hamilton College in 1848. He was foremost in every good and benevolent enterprise, both in church and state, and occupied a prominent position in all the educational and temperance movements in the vicinity. He was an able advocate and eminent as a jurist.

During the last five years of his life he was laid aside from active duty by paralysis. He died in Montrose on September 11, 1868, in his 72d year.

His wife survived him. Their children were five daughters, one of whom died before him, and five sons. The first, second, and fifth sons were graduated here, in 1849, 1851, and 1864, respectively. His third son left the Class of 1860 at the end of the Sophomore year, to prepare himself more speedily for missionary work with his next older brother in Syria, but received the honorary degree of M.A. in 1863.

AUTHORITIES.

Howell, Hist. of Southampton, 2d ed., 282, 334. *H. G. Jesup*, Jessup Genealogy, 353-54. *W. H. Jessup*, MS. Letter, June, 1869.

HENRY KELLOGG, the youngest child of Daniel Kellogg, of Amherst, Massachusetts, and a nephew of Aaron Kellogg (Yale 1778), was born in Amherst on December 10,

1794. His mother was Mercy, third daughter of Joseph and Sarah (Ingram) Eastman, of Amherst. A brother was graduated at Williams College in 1810. When he was about nine years old he was placed in the family of his sister, who had married General Martin Field (Williams Coll. 1798), of Newfane, Vermont. His preparation for Yale was completed under the Rev. Nathan Perkins (Yale 1795), of Amherst.

After graduation he returned to Newfane and studied law with General Field. In 1818 he was admitted to practice and settled in Bennington, where he resided for half a century. He held the office of postmaster from 1832 to 1850, and was also clerk of the Supreme and County Courts.

He was married on January 27, 1825, to Margaret Ann Vanderspiegel, daughter of James and Margaret (Schenck) Hubbell, of Bennington.

After her death he married, on October 16, 1831, her sister, Anne Maria.

By his first wife he had one daughter, who never married; and by his second wife two daughters and six sons.

In 1868 he removed to the residence of one of his sons, in Troy, New York, where he died on November 4, 1873, aged nearly 79 years. His wife also died in 1873, aged 66 years.

AUTHORITIES.

Hubbell Family, 283, 330. *Judd*, Hist. of Hadley, 2d ed., pt. 2, 85. Kelloggs of the New World, i, 281, 626.

Simeon Terry Kibbe, the eldest child of William Kibbe (Yale 1787), of Enfield, Connecticut, was born in Enfield on August 3, 1794. His father removed in his boyhood to New York City, and he was prepared to enter Yale at the opening of Sophomore year by the Rev. Nehemiah Prudden (Yale 1775), of Enfield. During the Sophomore year his father removed to Canandaigua. He joined the

College Church on profession of faith in April of his Senior year.

In the fall of 1816 he was enrolled as a resident graduate at New Haven, but subsequently he studied law, and settled in practice in Canandaigua; but died there on January 20, 1825, in his 31st year.

He was married, on July 26, 1819, to his first cousin, Lucy Terry, eldest child of General William and Mehitabel (Terry) Barton, of Hartford, who next married, in October, 1826, Moses Chapin (Yale 1811), of Rochester, New York. His children were two sons, the younger of whom died in infancy.

AUTHORITIES.

Dwight Family, i, 289-90. Terry Families, 78.

Charles Leavenworth, the eldest child of Dr. David Leavenworth, of Canaan, Columbia County, New York, and grandson of Asa and Submit (Scott) Leavenworth, of Watertown, Connecticut, was born in Canaan on January 16, 1796. His mother was Lucinda, third child of Zachariah and Lucy (Gaylord) Mather, of Torringford, Connecticut. In his boyhood the family settled in Great Barrington, Massachusetts. A brother was graduated here in 1824. He was prepared for College by Russell J. Minor (Yale 1801), of South East, New York.

He studied law with Robert F. Barnard, of Sheffield, and settled in practice in 1819 in Egremont, adjoining Great Barrington.

He married at Green River, in Hillsdale township, Columbia County, New York, on April 2, 1825, Ernestine, sixth child of Calvin and Mary (Hogeboom) Kelsey, and a native of Alford, Massachusetts.

He was a good lawyer, but for some time after this he had led a dissipated life. Subsequently he reformed, and he died from consumption, in Egremont, on January 19,

1829, at the age of 33. He left one son, who was for a short time a member of the Class of 1849 at Yale.

His widow married in May, 1836, Warham Burt, of East Hampton, Massachusetts, whom she long survived.

AUTHORITIES.

[*Field*], Hist. of Berkshire county, 239. Loomis Female Genealogy, i, 218. Leavenworth Genealogy, 157, 580.

John Sullivan Lee, the eldest child of Dr. Samuel Holden Parsons Lee, of New London, Connecticut, and grandson of Captain Ezra and Deborah (Mather) Lee, was born in New London, on September 8, 1795. His mother was Elizabeth, younger daughter of John Sullivan, the purser of the *Cygnet,* a British vessel stationed at New London in 1764-67, and his wife Elizabeth Chapman. A brother was graduated from the Yale Medical School in 1823. He was prepared for College by Ebenezer Kellogg (Yale 1810), in the academy at New London.

On graduation he began the study of medicine in Philadelphia, and a year later came to New York City, where he continued his studies with Dr. David Hosack and in connection with the College of Physicians and Surgeons.

In the fall of 1817 he found his health so much impaired by threatened pulmonary disease that he undertook a voyage to Italy. He returned in 1818 with high hopes, but was again prostrated, and was advised to try another foreign voyage. While waiting in New York for the vessel in which he was to embark for Italy, to complete her preparations, he was attacked with hemorrhage of the lungs, and died there on December 19, 1818, at the age of 23. He was buried in New London.

AUTHORITIES.

N. Y. Spectator, Jan. 1, 1819. *Salisbury,* Family-Histories and Genealogies, iii, 60.

John Bassnett Legaré, the great-great-grandson of Solomon Legaré, the Huguenot emigrant, was born in Charleston, South Carolina, in 1794. He was a son of James and Mary (Wilkinson) Legaré, and grandson of Thomas and Eliza (Bassnett) Legaré, and a first cousin of his classmate, as well as of the distinguished Hon. Henry S. Legaré (College of S. C. 1814).

He entered Yale after the opening of Freshman year, from Phillips Academy, Andover.

He became a planter on John's Island, about six miles southwest from Charleston, but died unmarried, of country fever, on November 4, 1826, in his 33d year.

AUTHORITIES.

Miss I. DeSaussure, MS. Letter, Dec., 1911.

John Berwick Legaré was born in Charleston, South Carolina, in 1794, the son of Thomas and Ann Eliza (Berwick) Legaré, and a first cousin of the graduate last named.

He studied law, and after being admitted to the bar in Charleston in 1818, began practice in that city, and was distinguished in his profession.

He was at one time a partner of the Hon. Thomas S. Grimké (Yale 1810), who died in 1834.

In his later years he was the victim of the convivial habits of the day.

He died in Charleston on May 24, 1850, aged 56 years.

He married Miss Jones, of Charleston, who survived him a few years.

A son, bearing the same name, was graduated from the College of South Carolina in 1840.

WILLIAM LOCKWOOD, JUNIOR, the younger son of the Rev. William Lockwood (Yale 1774), of Milford, Connecticut, was born in Milford on September 9, 1792 His mother was a daughter of the Hon Jonathan Sturges (Yale 1759) In 1797 his father accepted a call to the Congregational Church in Glastonbury, where he prepared his son for admission to the Sophomore Class

After graduation he was employed as a tutor in the family of Josiah Sturges, a New York merchant. He there met in an intimate way his first cousin, Mary Ann, daughter of Barnabas Lothrop and Mary (Sturges) Sturges, of Fairfield, Connecticut, who was also a niece of his employer. The result of this intimacy was their marriage, in New York, by the Rev. Benjamin Mortimer, on April 22, 1818

He became a merchant in New York, in partnership with Ebenezer P Cady He died in New York City on December 6, 1827, in his 36th year.

His wife survived him, with their children, four sons, of whom the youngest only left descendants.

AUTHORITIES

Lockwood Family, 244, 380

THOMAS ALEXANDER MARSHALL, the younger son of the Hon. Humphrey Marshall, United States senator from Kentucky, and grandson of John and Jane (Guisenbury) Marshall, of Bourbon County, Kentucky, was born in Woodford County on January 15, 1794 His mother, who was her husband's first cousin, was a daughter of Colonel Thomas and Mary Randolph (Keith) Marshall, of Fauquier County, Virginia, and a sister of Chief Justice John Marshall The family removed to the neighborhood of Frankfort in his early boyhood His elder brother was graduated at Princeton College in 1806

He entered Yale in 1813, having completed his preparation under Josiah Spalding, of the graduating class of that year.

He studied law at home, and was married on November 26, 1816, to Eliza Price, of Lexington, whose mother was a daughter of Colonel Thomas Hart, and a sister of the wife of the Hon. Henry Clay.

In 1817 he began the practice of law in Frankfort, but family considerations induced him to remove in 1819 to Paris, in Bourbon County, where he devoted himself closely to his profession until his election to Congress.

He represented Bourbon County as a Whig in the Legislature in 1827 and 1828. He served in Congress from December, 1831, to March, 1835. He was then, on March 18, 1835, commissioned by Acting-Governor James T. Morehead as Judge of the court of appeals of Kentucky, and soon after removed to Lexington. From 1836 he was also a professor in the law school of Transylvania University, but he resigned the post in 1849, lest it should interfere with his judicial duties.

In August, 1856, he retired to private life, and removed to Frankfort in 1857, and thence to Louisville in 1859. He represented the latter city in the Legislature in 1863, 1864, and 1865.

In 1866 the honorary degree of Doctor of Laws was conferred on him by Yale.

In the same year he was appointed by Governor Thomas E. Bramlette to fill an unexpired term as Chief Justice for six months,—thus completing twenty-two years of service on the bench, for seven of them (1847–51, 1854–56, and 1866) as Chief Justice.

He died in Louisville, after a brief illness, on April 17, 1871, in his 78th year, and was buried in Lexington.

His widow died on November 17, 1875, in her 81st year. Their children were four sons and two daughters.

Judge Marshall was regarded as an erudite jurist, and

respected as an earnest Christian, of great purity of character

AUTHORITIES

Paxton, Marshall Family, 185

James Henry Mitchell, the only son of James Mitchell, of Wethersfield, Connecticut, and grandson of Captain James and Hannah (Warner) Mitchell, of Wethersfield, and grand-nephew of Judge Stephen Mix Mitchell (Yale 1763), was born on February 25, 1796. His mother was Mary, youngest daughter of Ezekiel and Anna (Wells) Fosdick, of Wethersfield.

After graduation he went to Ohio, and for about five years taught in Lebanon, about twenty-five miles north-east of Cincinnati. During this time he was married to Martha Skinner, of Lebanon

He removed thence to Dayton, about twenty miles to the northward, which was his home for the rest of his life His occupation was that of a civil engineer, and he had much to do with public improvements in Dayton.

His wife died on March 5, 1866, and he died on October 13, 1873, after an illness of eight months, from cirrhosis of the stomach, in his 78th year.

Of their nine children six survived him

AUTHORITIES

Stiles, Hist of Wethersfield, ii, 508

Alfred Shepard Monson, the eldest child of Dr. Æneas Monson (Yale 1780), of New Haven, was born in New Haven on September 23, 1795

For a year after graduation he taught in the South, and then began the study of medicine in the Yale Medical

School; he completed it at the University of Pennsylvania, receiving the degree of M.D. in 1819.

He then settled in practice in New Haven, and was married on May 22, 1822, to Mary Ann, daughter of Nathaniel Patten, of Hartford.

He retired before long from professional duty, but continued to reside in New Haven until his death. His house, on a part of his paternal estate, was removed for the erection of the Yale Gymnasium. He had a keen interest in the natural sciences, especially botany, and in agriculture.

Dr. Monson died in New Haven on May 22, 1870, in his 75th year, leaving a large estate.

His widow died in New Haven on April 28, 1887, in her 84th year.

They had five sons and one daughter, all of whom survived their father, except two sons. The eldest son was graduated from the Yale Medical School in 1847. Thomas Nelson Dale, a well-known geologist, is a grandson.

He published:

An Address delivered before the New Haven Horticultural Society, May 25, 1843: by A. S. Monson, President of the Society.—With the Transactions of the Society for the year 1842. New Haven, 1843. 8°, pp. 72. [*A. A. S. Harv. Y. C.*

Dr. Monson's Address occupies pp. 3–42.

The Yale Library owns Dr. Monson's manuscript Meteorological Record, from 1819 to 1869, with slight gaps.

AUTHORITIES.

Munson Record, ii, 788, 809–10.

George Washington Morris entered College at the opening of Sophomore year from New York City.

He lived in Paris for many years.

He died in 1838, aged about 42 years.

Erasmus Norcross, a son of William and Sarah (Marsh) Norcross, was born in Monson, Massachusetts, on July 22, 1794, and was prepared for College by Levi Collins (Yale 1802) in the Monson Academy

After graduation he studied law with the Hon. George Bliss (Yale 1784), of Springfield, and on his admission to the bar began practice in his native town

In 1822 he was married to Eliza Holbrook, of Springfield

In 1833 he retired from his profession, and soon after removed to New York City, where he resided until his death, except from 1842 to 1852, which years he spent in Boston.

His life was a quiet and happy one, with continued good health and in full possession of his faculties He usually passed his summers in the country, and thus in 1874 was boarding in Stratford, Connecticut, having chosen that neighborhood on account of its nearness to New Haven, where he attended the Commencement exercises in June. He died in Stratford, very suddenly, from apoplexy, on August 23, in his 81st year.

His wife survived him, with an only son.

AUTHORITIES

G C Norcross, MS Letter, May, 1875

Alexis Painter, the third son of Thomas Painter, a Revolutionary soldier of West Haven, Connecticut, and grandson of Joseph and Amy (Stevens) Painter, of West Haven, was born on November 24, 1794. His mother was Hannah, daughter of Samuel and Lydia (Sherman) Candee, of West Haven A sister married the Rev. Samuel Rich (Yale 1804). He was prepared for College by Chauncey A. Goodrich, in the New Haven Hopkins Grammar School.

He was enrolled as a graduate student in New Haven from 1815 to 1817, and he then studied law in the Litchfield Law School, and on being admitted to the bar began practice in Annapolis, Maryland.

He continued in practice long enough to gain his first and only case, and then abandoned the profession, mainly on account of conscientious scruples.

He then taught for a short time in Maryland, and after his return North he shipped as a sailor on a voyage to Liverpool, but found himself too old for such a vocation.

He then went to Westfield, Massachusetts, and engaged in mercantile business, and thence to Cummington as a manufacturer.

He was, however, unfortunate in business, and in 1837 he returned to his native place and resumed teaching.

About 1852 he relinquished this occupation on account of failing health, and after that time, although he recovered his health, he engaged in no professional pursuit, but lived a retired though useful life in West Haven.

He was an early, earnest, and steadfast friend and advocate of the anti-slavery cause, and a pioneer in the temperance reform. He was indeed in almost every respect a reformer and a radical; he was, however, not only a man of rigid moral principle, but an earnest believer in evangelical Christianity.

He died in West Haven on October 19, 1867, in his 73d year.

He was married in 1825 to Maria, daughter of Deacon Dobson Wheeler and Thalia (Hine) McMahon, of New Milford, who survived him, with five of their children. A son was graduated from the Yale Medical School in 1856, and a daughter married William H. W. Campbell (Yale 1856).

AUTHORITIES.

Baldwin, Candee Genealogy, 37. *W. H. W. Campbell,* MS. Letter, July, 1868. *Orcutt,* Hist. of N. Milford, 730.

James Gates Percival, the second of three sons of Dr. James Percival, of Kensington Society, in Berlin, Connecticut, and grandson of James and Dorothy (Gates) Percival, of East Haddam, was born in Kensington on September 15, 1795. His mother was Elizabeth, sister of the Rev. Seth Hart (Yale 1784), of Kensington. His father died suddenly in January, 1807, and he was prepared for College by his uncle and by the Rev. Joab Brace (Yale 1804), of Newington Parish in Wethersfield. He entered Yale with the Class of 1814, but withdrew in the spring of the Sophomore year, mainly from chagrin at the rejection of a volume of poems which he proposed to publish, and the consequent ridicule of his classmates. After a year's absence, he returned to the same standing. At the Junior Exhibition in 1814, he delivered an oration on Imagination, and at Commencement another on the comparative value of scientific and military reputation.

After graduation he made an attempt at the study of medicine in New Haven, and also at the study of law in Berlin; but finally went to Philadelphia as a tutor in the family of Charles Chauncey (Yale 1792), with whom he pursued legal studies, even to the point of admission to the bar.

In the fall of 1817 he returned to New Haven, and began the study of medicine with Dr. Eli Ives (Yale 1799), but a few months later went again to Philadelphia as private tutor in the family of Dr. Henry Neill. After a year thus spent he came and completed his medical course, and received the degree of M.D. from the Yale Medical School in the spring of 1820.

He had made remarkable acquisitions in various branches of medicine and in botany, and soon after taking his degree he was employed to give a course of lectures on anatomy at the Medical College. From New Haven he went back to Kensington Parish and undertook the practice of his profession, but speedily abandoned it.

Before this a number of his poems had been printed in the *Microscope,* a periodical issued at New Haven from March to September, 1820, and the favor with which they were received led him to publish in July, 1821, a volume of *Poems,* which commanded a hearing.

Later in the same year he was induced to go to Charleston, South Carolina, as an assistant to a traveling botanical lecturer; and when left stranded there, he gave a course of lectures on botany, and also prepared another volume of poetry, which was published in January, 1822.

He returned to New Haven in the late spring, and published a thin volume of poetry in August, and another in November.

As a means of support, he was induced in February, 1823, to assume the editorship of the *Connecticut Herald,* a weekly New Haven paper; but the failure of the proprietors ended this venture in the following June.

He then undertook the publication of a volume of his collected poems, which appeared in November, and was also republished in London.

Through the intercession of friends an appointment was procured for him, in March, 1824, as Assistant Surgeon in the United States army, and acting Professor of Chemistry, in the Military Academy at West Point. His morbid sensibility made every situation impossible, and he was transferred in July at his urgent request to the position of inspector of recruits in Boston. This also proved only temporary, and he resigned his commission on August 1, and resorted to literary labor.

Besides other minor tasks, he engaged in November, 1826, to prepare a revised edition of the English translation of Malte-Brun's Geography, and in 1827 to revise the manuscript for the quarto edition of Noah Webster's *Dictionary.* For these purposes he settled in New Haven.

The engagement on the Dictionary terminated in the early autumn of 1828, and about that time he bought a house in his native parish and removed his valuable library thither. But he returned to New Haven in 1829, and remained there for many years His pecuniary situation was distressing, and his employments varied. In 1834 he spent nearly five months in geological exploration of parts of Connecticut. In 1835 the Legislature made a small appropriation for a geological and mineralogical survey of the State, and Dr. Percival was appointed by Governor Henry W Edwards to undertake the geological portion. He spent most of his time for the next seven years on this duty, but withdrew abruptly from it, on account of fancied ill-treatment.

In 1843 he established himself in quarters in three rooms in the New Haven Hospital building, where he lived as a hermit.

In April, 1853, he was employed by a mining company to investigate certain lead mines, chiefly in Wisconsin, and was so occupied to the great advantage of the State for the rest of that year. In the meantime by his wish some of his New Haven friends arranged for the building of a tomb-like house for his use, on the eastern side of Park street, south of George, which was completed in November, 1854 In August, 1854, he was commissioned by Governor William A. Barstow as State Geologist of Wisconsin, and to the work of this office he devoted himself until his death.

While preparing his second report for publication, he died in Hazel Green, Wisconsin, after five months' illness, as the result of overwork and exposure, on May 22, 1856, in his 61st year. He was buried there, and a monument was erected over his grave in 1893, chiefly by friends in the East He was never married.

The Rev Julius H. Ward published in 1866 an exhaustive volume, *The Life and Letters of Percival.* Prefixed is an engraving from an excellent portrait by Francis Alexander, painted in 1825; another portrait by Samuel F B. Morse, in 1823, is in existence, as well as one painted by George A Flagg, in 1831

Percival's poetry has not retained the place assigned to it by his earlier contemporaries. Edward Everett, in the *North American Review,* volume 14 (1821), declared that the volume of *Poems* just published "contains the marks of an inspiration more lofty and genuine than any similar collection of fugitive pieces which has come to our notice from a native bard." A singularly just criticism by James Russell Lowell is given in the same *Review* for January, 1867.

He published:

1. In the *Microscope,* New Haven, April–September, 1820, twenty-seven poetical pieces, without his name, as follows:

Volume 1, pp. 48, 54–56, 70–72, 80, 103–04, 111–12, 119–20, 134–36, 143–44, 161–72, 192, 200; Volume 2, pp. 24, 30–32, 62–64, 86–88, 102–04, 111–12, 127–28, 144, 147–52, 172–75, 191–92.

2. Poems. New Haven, 1821. 16°, pp. 348.
[*Br. Mus. Watkinson Libr. Y. C.*

3. Clio.—No. I. Charleston, 1822. 12°, pp. 108.
[*B. Publ. Br. Mus. Harv. N. Y. Publ. Watkinson Libr. Y. C.*

4. Clio.—No. II. New-Haven, 1822. 12°, pp. 132.
[*B. Publ. Br. Mus. Watkinson Libr. Y. C.*

5. Oration delivered before the Φ. B. K. Society, September 10th, 1822, on some of the moral and political truths derivable from the study of history. New-Haven, 1822. 8°, pp. 19.
[*B. Ath. B. Publ. Br. Mus. Harv. N. Y. Publ. Y. C.*

6. Prometheus. Part II. with other Poems. New-Haven, 1822. 12°, pp. 108. [*Y. C.*

Part I is contained in No. 2, above.

7. Five pieces by Percival, gleaned from New Haven newspapers, are contained in Miscellanies selected from the Public Journals. Boston, 1822. 12°. [*Y. C.*

8. Poems. New-York, 1823. 8°, pp. iv, 396.
[*B. Ath. B. Publ. Br. Mus. Harv. N. Y. Publ. Y. C.*

The same. London, 1824. 2 volumes. 8°, pp. viii, 259; vi, 272. [*N. Y. Publ. Y. C.*

9. Poem delivered before the Connecticut Alpha of the Phi Beta Kappa Society, September 13, 1825. Boston, 1826. 8°, pp. 40.
[*B. Ath. B. Publ. Br. Mus. Harv. N. Y. Publ. Y. C.*

10. Clio.—No. III. New-York, 1827. 12°, pp. 204.
[*B. Publ. Br. Mus. Harv. N. Y. Publ. Watkinson Libr. Y. C.*

11. The New Haven Whig Song-Book: prepared for the New Haven County Mass Convention; Thursday, Oct. 8th, 1840. New Haven, 1840. 12°, pp. 21. [*N. H. Col. Hist. Soc.*
Anonymous.

12. Report on the Geology of the State of Connecticut. New Haven, 1842. 8°, pp. 495 + map.
[*B. Publ. Br. Mus. Harv. Y. C.*

13. The Dream of a Day, and other Poems. New Haven, 1843. 12°, pp. 264. [*B. Publ. Br. Mus. Harv. N. Y. Publ. Y. C.*

14. Geological Report on the Kensington Silver-Lead Mines, Berlin, Conn. New Haven, 1853. 8°, pp. 6. [*B. Publ.*

15. Geological Reports on the Middletown Silver-Lead Mines, Middletown, Connecticut. By J. G. Percival and W. H. Stevens. New York, 1853. 8°, pp. 11 + pl. [*N. H. Col. Hist. Soc.*
Percival's Report occupies pp. 5–8.

16. Annual Report on the Geological Survey of the State of Wisconsin. Madison, 1855. 8°, pp. 101 + map. [*B. Publ. Y. C.*

17. Report on the Iron of Dodge and Washington Counties, State of Wisconsin. .. Milwaukee, 1855. 8°, pp. 12 + pl.
[*B. Publ. Br. Mus. M. H. S.*

After his death appeared:

18. Annual Report of the Geological Survey of the State of Wisconsin. Madison, 1856. 8°, pp. 111.
[*B. Ath. Br. Mus. M. H. S. Y. C.*

Another edition of his Poetical Works, with a biographical sketch by Lucius W. Fitch (Yale 1840), was issued in 1859, in 2 volumes.

He contributed largely to various periodicals at different times. His most important scientific articles were the following, in the *American Journal of Science and the Arts:*

Notice of various mineral localities in Berlin, Conn., volume 5, pp. 42–45 (April, 1822).

Analysis of a Treatise on the Classification and distribution of fossile vegetables, by Ad. Brongniart, volume 7, pp. 178–85 (April, 1824).

Notices of the Geology and Mineralogy of Sicily, from F. Ferrara. Translated and condensed, volume 8, pp. 201–13; and

Analysis of a Memoir, "Sur les caracteres Zoologiques des Formations . ., par A. Brongniart," the same, pp. 213–18 (August, 1824).

Curious effect of Solar Light, volume 12, pp. 164–65, 180–81 (March, 1827).

His literary contributions were made, among other journals, to the weekly *Boston Spectator* (1825); the *United States Literary Gazette* (1825), twenty-one of which were also published in a volume of *Miscellaneous Poems* selected from the United States Literary Gazette, Boston, 1826, 12°; the *Sabbath School Herald* (1830); the *New England Magazine;* the *Knickerbocker Magazine;* the *Democratic Review.*

Among volumes edited or translated by him may be mentioned:

F. Magendie, Physiological and Chemical Researches on the use of the Prussic. .Acid in the treatment of diseases of the breast, 1820.

V. Knox, Elegant Extracts, 1826, 6 volumes.

J. Goldsmith, Geography illustrated on a Popular Plan; or a Geographical View of the World, 1829.

Malte-Brun, System of Universal Geography, 1834, 3 volumes.

C. C. Clarke, The Wonders of the World .. described and illustrated. 1836.

AUTHORITIES.

Atlantic Monthly, iv, 59–73. *C. C. Baldwin,* Diary, 227–29. *Mitchell,* Amer. Lands and Letters, i, 277–80. New Englander, xiii, 400–49. Putnam's Monthly Magazine, viii, 638–44. *Ward,* Life and Letters of Percival. Wisconsin State Hist. Society's Collections, iii, 66–79.

JOHN POPE, son of Colonel LeRoy Pope, a native of Amherst County, Virginia, was born in the now extinct town of Petersburg, at the junction of the Broad and Savannah Rivers, in Elbert County, Georgia, on July 16,

1794 His early education was gained in the famous academy of the Rev. Dr Moses Waddel, in Columbia County, but in the meantime his father removed to Huntsville, in northern Alabama, then part of the Mississippi Territory, and in 1811 he entered Cumberland College, in Nashville, Tennessee. A year later he joined the Sophomore Class at Yale. A brother was graduated here in 1823

On graduation he began the study of law; but soon after, having married Louisa Rembert, the daughter of a wealthy Georgia planter, he turned his attention to cotton planting, near Huntsville.

He served for several terms in the State Legislature, where he distinguished himself as the champion of a liberal system of internal improvements

His fondness for agricultural pursuits led him to abandon political life. Attracted by the undeveloped resources of West Tennessee, then an almost unbroken wilderness, he settled near Memphis, which was still little more than an Indian trading post, and devoted himself to raising cotton His success is shown by the fact that he obtained the premium for the best bale of short cotton exhibited at the World's Fair in London in 1851. He took a prominent part in the organization of the Shelby County Agricultural Society, of which he was for many years the President, and his contributions to the agricultural literature of the day were extensive and valuable

His services in the development of the valley of the Mississippi were recognized at the Southwestern Internal Improvement Convention, which met at Memphis in November, 1845, with John C. Calhoun in the chair, when Mr Pope was made chairman of the Committee on Agriculture

In 1832 he declined a nomination to the State Constitutional Convention

For some years before his death he was President of the Union Bank of Tennessee, and at a much earlier date he was prominently engaged in the preliminary work upon the Memphis and Charleston railroad.

He died at his residence near Memphis on March 27, 1865, in his 71st year.

His wife died in 1837, and he married a few years later Elizabeth Hemphill Jones, of Wilmington, Delaware, who also died before him.

One son survived him.

AUTHORITIES.

Hist of Elmwood Cemetery, Memphis, 143-44.

William Smith Robert, the fourth child of Dr. Daniel and Mary (Smith) Robert, of Mastic, in Brookhaven, Long Island, was born in Mastic on March 13, 1795. A brother was graduated here in 1810. He was prepared for College by the Rev. Dr. Aaron Woolworth (Yale 1784), of Bridgehampton.

His entire life after graduation was spent on his ancestral estate in Mastic, and he never was engaged in any business, or held office of any kind.

He was married, on February 8, 1831, to Caroline E. Smith, of Mastic, who died on August 16, 1850.

Three sons and three daughters survived him, one son having graduated here in the Class of 1862, and another having been for three years a member of the same class.

AUTHORITIES.

C. S. Robert, MS. Letter, February, 1862.

Hubbard Rockwell, the elder son of the Rev. Lathrop Rockwell (Dartmouth Coll. 1789), pastor of the Congregational church in Lyme, Connecticut, and grandson of Josiah and Lydia (Marsh) Rockwell, of Lebanon, was baptized by his father in Lyme on August 30, 1795. His mother was Olive (or Ruth?) Dutton, of Lebanon. The Rev. Dr. Warren B. Dutton (Yale 1829) and the Rev. Dr. Elijah F. Rockwell (Yale 1834) were his first cousins. He was prepared for College by Hezekiah Rudd (Yale 1806) at Bacon Academy in Colchester, and he held the second rank in his Class at Yale on graduation, delivering the Latin Salutatory Oration at Commencement.

He taught in New London after graduation, was a tutor in Yale from 1817 to 1819, and during the greater part of his life was a teacher in New York City, but shunned all society and even avoided communication with his relatives. He was regarded as, at times, not perfectly sound in mind.

After an old age of extreme poverty, he died very suddenly at his boarding-house in New York, on January 14, 1871, in his 76th year. As his relatives were at the time unknown, he was buried at the expense of the Collegiate Reformed Church, of which he was a member. He never married.

AUTHORITIES.

Loomis Female Genealogy, i, 328. *Rev. Dr. E. F. Rockwell*, MS. Letter, November, 1875. Rockwell Family, 178.

JOHN SILL ROGERS, son of Gideon and Lucy (Ackley) Rogers, of Lyme, Connecticut, was born in Lyme on April 15, 1796. He was prepared for College by Hezekiah Rudd (Yale 1806) in Bacon Academy, Colchester.

After graduation he studied medicine, in the Yale Medical School and elsewhere, and on February 10, 1822, he married Matilda, only daughter of Lynde and Mehitable (Marvin) Lord, of Lyme, and sister of Dr. Frederick W. Lord (Yale 1821).

He was a physician and farmer in Lyme, until 1837, when he removed to Rome, in Ashtabula County, northeastern Ohio.

He represented Lyme in the Lower House of the Connecticut Legislature in 1821, 1822, and 1832; and was a State Senator in 1835. In 1839 he represented Ashtabula County in the Ohio House.

He died in Rome on December 28, 1860, in his 65th year.

His widow died in 1867, aged 73 years. Their children were two daughters. Thomas W. Swan (Yale 1869) was a grandson.

AUTHORITIES.

Salisbury, Family-Histories and Genealogies, i, 320. *Walworth*, Hyde Family, ii, 736.

William Sidney Rossiter, third son of Nathaniel Rossiter (Yale 1785), of Guilford, Connecticut, was born in Guilford on March 7, 1798. A brother was graduated here in 1810. His father removed to New Haven in 1804, and he was prepared for College by Chauncey A. Goodrich (Yale 1810), in the Hopkins Grammar School. He was the youngest in his Class at graduation.

From 1815 to 1817 he was enrolled as a graduate student in College.

He remained in New Haven, and was employed as cashier of the Eagle Bank at the time of its disastrous failure in September, 1825. About 1830 he removed to Rochester, New York, and thence about 1840 to Brooklyn. From this time until his death he was a commission merchant in New York, having an extensive forwarding business between that city and the western portions of the State, and Pennsylvania, Ohio, and Indiana. He was not, however, of a commercial temperament, but distinctly literary and artistic; and his letters still preserved in the family are remarkable for their perfect and musical English. He was a man of distinguished appearance, with the courtly manners and grace of the old school. His portrait is preserved in the family.

He died of cholera in Brooklyn, on August 31, 1852, aged 54 years, and was buried in New Haven.

He married in 1821 Hannah, daughter of James and Mary (Miller) Murdock, of Schenectady, New York, who died on December 31, 1855, at the age of 52

Of their eight children, one son and four daughters grew to maturity

AUTHORITIES

W S Rossiter, MS Letter, November, 1911.

EZEKIEL SANFORD was born in Ridgefield, Connecticut, on February 12, 1796, the second son of Colonel Benjamin Sanford, of Ridgefield, and grandson of Captain Ezekiel and Sarah (Sturges) Sanford, of Redding. His mother was Sarah Ingersoll, eldest sister of Charles G. Olmsted (Yale 1809). In his infancy the family removed to Onondaga County, New York

He entered College at the opening of the Sophomore year from Manlius, in Onondaga County. At a later date his father removed to Philadelphia

He was enrolled as a graduate student at Yale in 1815–16. Later he studied law, and settled in Philadelphia. He edited there for a time the *Analectic Magazine,* and while engaged in the publication of a series of the *Works of the British Poets,* he was so much prostrated by consumption that he was obliged to seek a Southern climate.

He settled in 1820 in Columbia, South Carolina, where he was admitted to the bar He died there early in December, 1822, at the age of 26

He published:

1. A History of the United States before the Revolution· with some account of the Aborigines Philadelphia, 1819 8°, pp cxcii, 342.

[*A. A S. B Ath B Publ Harv U S. Watkinson Libr.*

The prefatory matter is pronounced by Field in his *Indian Bibliography* "a very excellent résumé of what is known of the aborigines"; the volume was severely criticized by Nathan Hale in the *North American Review* for September, 1819 (volume 9, pp. 356–76), and favorably noticed in the *Analectic Magazine* for April, 1819 (volume 13, pp. 304–15).

He also began to edit:

2. The Works of the British Poets, with Lives of the Authors. Philadelphia, 1819. 12°, volumes 1–17, 22. [*Br. Mus.*

The work was continued by Robert Walsh.

After his death appeared:

3. The Humours of Eutopia: a Tale of Colonial Times. By an Eutopian. Philadelphia, 1828. 2 volumes. 12°, pp. 230. [*B. Ath. B. Publ. U. S. Y. C.*

A satire on the manners of colonial times.

AUTHORITIES.

Thomas Sanford Family, i, 202.

Israel Shailer, son of Lieutenant Thomas and Anna (Fiske) Shailer, of Haddam, Connecticut, was born in Haddam on November 22, 1788, and was prepared for College by his pastor, the Rev. David Dudley Field (Yale 1802). He united with the College Church on profession of his faith in July of the Senior year.

After graduation he studied theology with the Rev. John Elliott (Yale 1786), of East Guilford, now Madison, and was licensed to preach by the Middlesex Association of Ministers on June 2, 1818.

He was ordained as an evangelist, at Millington, in East Haddam, on June 7, 1820, to serve as a missionary to the Western Reserve of Ohio, under the direction of the Missionary Society of Connecticut.

On April 25, 1821, he was installed as pastor of the Congregational Church in Richfield, near Hudson, in Summit County, and in 1823 he married Sophronia Mills, of Hudson. He subsequently became a member of the Presbytery of Huron, and remained in connection with the Presbyterian church for the rest of his life.

He was dismissed from his pastorate on August 17, 1830. While pastor he had spent half of his time as a missionary to other congregations, and after his retirement he continued to preach in neighboring churches, and later was employed as a colporteur for the circulation of religious literature

For the last five years of his life he was laid aside by blindness and infirmity.

He died in Richfield on July 2, 1869, in his 81st year His wife survived him, with one son and four daughters,—another son and three daughters having died previously.

AUTHORITIES

Rev J A McKinstry, MS Letter, August, 1869

NATHANIEL BENEDICT SMITH, the only child of the Hon Nathaniel Smith (honorary M.A. 1795), of Woodbury, Connecticut, Member of Congress, and afterwards Judge of the Supreme Court of the State, and grandson of Richard and Annis (Hurd) Smith, of Woodbury, was born in Woodbury on December 7, 1795 His mother was Ruth, the only daughter of the Rev. Noah Benedict (Princeton Coll 1757), pastor in Woodbury, and a sister of Judge Noah B Benedict (Yale 1788). He was prepared for College by the Rev. Dr. Azel Backus (Yale 1787), of Bethlehem, and spent the first half of the course with the Class of 1814.

On graduation he began the study of law with his uncle, Judge Benedict, and after an interval of graduate study in New Haven he completed his course in the Litchfield Law School On his admission to the bar in 1818, he began practice in New Haven, and was married, on February 22, 1819, to Mary Ann Wolcott, fifth daughter of the Rev Samuel Goodrich (Yale 1783), of Berlin, a lady of uncommon intellectual gifts.

He was soon obliged by his father's infirm health to return to Woodbury. His father died in March, 1822, and the care of his large landed property so engrossed him that he withdrew from his profession.

He represented the town in the General Assembly in 1828, and again in 1847. For four years from May, 1838, he served as Judge of Probate for the Woodbury District. But neither inclination nor ambition led him to seek public honors, and for the remainder of his life he was content to be interested in his farm, and to rest in the sincere esteem of his fellow-citizens.

He died suddenly in Woodbury on February 5, 1881, in his 86th year.

His wife died on January 20, 1872, in her 73d year.

His children, two daughters and a son, died before him. The son was a student in the Yale Divinity School in 1866–67, having previously served in the Civil War.

AUTHORITIES.

Benedict Genealogy, 372. *Cothren,* Hist. of Woodbury, i, 405, 677; ii, 1459–60. Goodrich Family, 129. *S. G. Goodrich,* Recollections of a Lifetime, i, 48–50. Tuttle Family, 109.

TRUMAN SMITH, the eldest child of Phineas and Deborah Ann Smith, of Roxbury, then part of Woodbury, Connecticut, and a first cousin of the preceding graduate, was born in Roxbury on November 29, 1791. His mother was a daughter of Joshua and Deborah (Leavenworth) Judson, of Roxbury. A brother was graduated in 1816.

He was brought up on his father's farm, and his preparation for College was completed under the Rev. Daniel Parker (Yale 1798), of Ellsworth Society in Sharon.

He was enrolled as a graduate student at Yale in 1815–16, and later studied law in the Litchfield Law School, and was admitted to the Litchfield county bar in March, 1818.

In the fall of 1818 he opened an office for the practice of his profession in Litchfield, which continued to be his home until 1854. At the time he began practice, an unusual number of the County bar were eminent for ability, so that his steady advancement was specially remarkable.

After some fifteen years' experience, he found himself possessed of the confidence of the community and of large political influence. In 1831, 1832, and 1834, he was a representative in the State Legislature. From 1839 to 1843 he served in the National House of Representatives, but declined a nomination for a third term. In 1844 he voted for Clay as a Presidential Elector from Connecticut.

He was again in Congress from 1845 to 1849, and in 1848 was the chairman of the Whig Committee in the campaign which resulted in the election of General Taylor to the presidency. At this date he and his classmate Clayton were undoubtedly the strongest leaders of their party in Congress.

Meantime he was elected to the United States Senate for a term of six years from March, 1849. Before he took his seat, he declined the offer of the Secretaryship of the Interior from President Taylor, lest the position should seem to be a reward for political activity.

He continued an active, honored, and efficient member of the Senate until May, 1854, when he resigned, being forced to resume practice by the state of his finances.

In the ensuing fall he removed his residence to Stamford, and opened a law office in New York City.

On the organization in 1862 of the Court for the trial of the cases of British or American vessels suspected of being engaged in the slave trade, President Lincoln appointed him as one of the judges, and he held the office until the existence of the Court was terminated in 1870.

He retired from business in the fall of 1872, and in his later years interested himself largely in benevolent and philanthropic movements.

He died at his residence in Stamford, after two years of failing health, on May 3, 1884, in his 93d year.

His portrait is given in the *American Whig Review*, volume 16 (1852), and in the *Genealogical History of Connecticut*.

He married, on June 2, 1832, Maria, daughter of Roger Cook, of Litchfield, by whom he had two daughters and a son.

She died on April 24, 1849, and he was next married, on November 7, 1850, to Mary A. Dickinson, by whom he had six sons.

One daughter by his first marriage, the wife of the Hon. Orville H. Platt, LL.D. (honorary Yale 1887), and three sons by his second marriage, survived him.

He published:

1. New Jersey Election.—Speech in opposition to the Proposition of Mr. C. Johnson, of Tennessee, to instruct the Committee on Election "to report forthwith which five of the ten individuals claiming seats from the State of New Jersey received the greatest number of votes," at the Election of 1838. .. —Delivered in the House of Representatives, February 25 and 26, 1840. Washington, 1840. 8°, pp. 21. [*B. Ath. M. H. S. Y. C.*

2. Speech on the Oregon Question.—Delivered in the House of Representatives, U. S., February 7th, 1846. Washington, 1846. 8°, pp. 19. [*A. A. S. B. Publ. Harv. M. H. S. Y. C.*

3. Speech in opposition to the Warehouse Bill, with considerations on "Wool and Woollens."—Delivered in the House of Representatives of the U. S., July 31, 1846. Washington, 1846. 8°, pp. 16. [*A. A. S. M. H. S. N. Y. Publ. Y. C.*

4. Speech on the physical character of the Northern States of Mexico, (including the disputed territory between the Nueces and the Rio Grande, also New Mexico and Upper California,) with a consideration of .. the condition of the inhabitants, .. with reference to their fitness to become citizens of the United States; and also of the consequences which must result from the admission of any or all of such States into the Union; and showing that the present war with Mexico has been prosecuted for objects and purposes

likely to prove in a high degree injurious to the American People.—Delivered in the House of Representatives U. States, March 2, 1848. [Washington, 1848.] 8°, pp. 31.

[*A. A. S. B. Publ. M. H. S. U. S. U. T. S. Y. C.*

5. Letter to the Hon. Daniel Gott, of the House of Representatives, on the importance of supporting the nomination of General Zachary Taylor for the Presidency, in reference to the past, present, and prospective political condition of the two Houses of Congress. [Washington, 1848.] 8°, pp. 4. [*U. S.*

6. Remarks on the imputations of N. B. Blunt, Esq., of the City of New York, on his course as a Delegate to the recent Whig National Convention, together with an exposition of the benefits which will result to the Country from the elevation of Gen. Zachary Taylor to the Presidency .. [Washington, 1848.] 8°, pp. 8.

[*Harv. N. H. Col. Hist. Soc. N. Y. Publ. U. S. U. T. S.*

Dated, June 20, 1848. A defence of the author's course, as a delegate, in preferring Taylor to Clay.

7. To the Public. [Washington, 1849.] 8°, pp. 3. [*U. S.*

A letter, giving his reasons for refusing the nomination of Secretary of the Home Department, should such a Department be established.

8. Speech on Removals and Appointments to office.—Delivered in the Senate of the United States, March 21 and 22, 1850. [Washington, 1850.] 8°, pp. 32.

[*A. A. S. B. Ath. B. Publ. M. H. S. N. Y. Publ. U. S. Y. C.*

A defence of President Taylor.

9. Speech on the Bill "to admit California into the Union—to establish territorial governments for Utah and New Mexico, making proposals to Texas for the establishment of the Western and Northern boundaries." ... Delivered in the Senate of the United States, July 8, 1850. Washington, 1850. 8°, pp. 32.

[*A. A. S. B. Ath. B. Publ. M. H. S. N. Y. Publ. U. T. S. Y. C.*

10. Speech on the French Spoliation Claims.—Delivered in the Senate of the United States, January 16 & 17, 1851. Washington, 1851. 8°, pp. 32.

[*A. A. S. B. Publ. Harv. M. H. S. U. S. Y. C.*

11. Speech on printing the returns of the Seventh Census, and on Congressional and departmental printing generally: delivered in the Senate of the United States, January 12, 1852. Washington, 1852. 8°, pp. 16. [*A. A. S. N. Y. Publ. Y. C.*

12. Second Speech on the Bill for the construction of a canal around the Sault Ste. Marie. Delivered in the Senate of the United States, August 17, 1852. [Washington, 1852.] 8°, pp. 8. [*N. Y. Publ.*

13. Speech on the proposition of Hon. Mr. Douglas, of Illinois, to authorize a levy of tonnage duties by the States for the improvement of rivers and harbors. Delivered in the Senate of the United States, August 23, 1852. Washington, 1852. 8°, pp. 16. [*N. Y. Publ.*

14. Speech in support of the Bill reported by the Hon. Mr. Rusk, of Texas, from a Select Committee, for the construction of a Railroad and Telegraph line from the Mississippi Valley to the Pacific Ocean, delivered in the United States Senate, February 17, 1853. [Washington, 1853.] 8°, pp. 8. [*B. Publ. Y. C.*

15. An Examination of the Question of Anæsthesia, arising on the Memorial of Charles Thomas Wells, presented to the United States Senate, Second Session, Thirty-second Congress, and referred to a Select Committee .. Washington, 1853. 8°.

I have not seen the above, which was probably anonymous.

A second edition, with the author's name. New York, 1858. 8°, pp. viii, 5–135. [*Harv. Surg. Gen'l's. Libr.*

The same; with Appendix, from the Journal of Commerce. New York, 1859. 8°, pp. viii, 5–154. [*Surg. Gen'l's. Libr. Y. C.*

16. The Appendix was also printed separately, with title: Anæsthesia! The greatest discovery of the age! Who is entitled to the credit of it? Let those read who desire to know the Truth. 8°, pp. 16. [*Surg. Gen'l's. Libr. Y. C.*

17. Speech on the Nebraska Question. Delivered in the Senate of the United States, February 10 and 11, 1854. Washington, 1854. 8°, pp. 23.

[*B. Ath. B. Publ. Br. Mus. Harv. M. H. S. U. T. S. Y. C.*

18. Anthracite Coal, and the proposed tax of fifteen cents per ton; the injustice and inexpediency of that tax examined and considered. Washington, 1862. 8°, pp. 7. [*A. A. S.*

By Mr. Smith, as representing the Pennsylvania Coal Company.

19. Considerations on the Slavery Question, addressed to the President of the United States. [Dated, New York, December 24th, 1862.] 8°, pp. 15. [*B. Ath. N. Y. Publ. Y. C.*

20. Anæsthesia. Who is entitled to the credit of making the great discovery? Wm. T. G. Morton and his designs on the U. S. Treasury. His letters patent null and void. New York, 1864. 8°, pp. 16. [*Surg. Gen'l's. Libr.*

21. An Inquiry into the origin of Modern Anæsthesia. Hartford, 1867. 8°, pp. 165 + pl.

[*Br. Mus. Harv. M. H. S. Surg. Gen'l's. Libr. U. S. Y. C.*

A reprint, with additions, of communications by "A Lover of Truth and Justice" to the *Medical and Surgical Reporter,* Philadelphia, 1864.

22. The Spirituous Liquor Traffic and its manifold evils in Connecticut; with considerations on the impracticability of the Prohibitory Act of 1854, and the Inadmissibility of the License Law of 1872: and proposing an intermediate policy... Hartford, 1873. 8°, pp. 45. [*A. A. S. B. Publ. Y. C.*

23. In the Matter of the Award made by the Senate of the United States in favor of the Choctaw Nation of Indians, under and by virtue of the Treaty between the said Nation, and the United States of June 22, 1855. 1875. 8°, pp. 14. [*U. S. Y. C.*

Dated Washington, Feb. 13, 1875, and signed by Mr. Smith as "Solicitor pro tem for the Choctaws."

24. The Spoils System the offspring of Modern Democracy, and the source of numberless evils to the country.—Crush it out! New York, 1876. 8°, pp. 16. [*A. A. S. B. Publ.*

A campaign document for Hayes.

25. Fragment of a Sermon [from Acts xxiii, 1–5] on the great American sin of speaking Evil of Rulers .. New Haven, 1879. 8°, pp. 7. [*M. H. S.*

In commendation of President Grant.

AUTHORITIES.

Cothren, Hist. of Woodbury, i, 463, 677. Geneal. Hist. of Conn., ii, 1054. Hist. of Litchfield County, 1881, 34-35. *Huntington,* Hist. of Stamford, 413. Leavenworth Genealogy, 84-88.

William Buell Sprague, the youngest son of Benjamin Sprague, of that part of Hebron which is now Andover, Connecticut, and grandson of Benjamin and Hannah (Hutchinson) Sprague, of Killingworth, was born in Andover on October 16, 1795. His mother was Sibyl, daughter of William and Sibyl (Post) Buell, of that part of Hebron which is now Marlborough. He was prepared for College by the Rev. Abiel Abbot (Harvard 1787), of Coventry.

During the year after graduation, he was a private tutor in the family of Major Lawrence Lewis, a nephew of Washington, at Woodlawn, near Mount Vernon. In the fall of 1816 he entered the Princeton Theological Seminary, where he spent three years.

On August 25, 1819, he was ordained and installed as colleague to the Rev. Dr. Joseph Lathrop (Yale 1754), pastor of the Congregational Church in West Springfield, Massachusetts.

Dr. Lathrop died on the last day of 1820, and Dr. Sprague continued in office for ten years. The honorary degree of Doctor of Divinity was conferred on him by Columbia College in 1828.

Having received a call in June, 1829, to Albany, New York, he resigned his charge in July, and on the 26th of the following month was installed as pastor of the Second Presbyterian Church in Albany, with which he remained for forty years. The degree of Doctor of Divinity was again given him by Harvard University in 1848, and that of Doctor of Laws by Princeton College in 1859.

On September 28, 1869, he resigned his pastorate, and in May, 1870, he removed to the residence of a son in

Flushing, Long Island, where he died on May 7, 1876, in his 81st year.

He was married, on September 5, 1820, to Charlotte, second daughter of General William Eaton (Dartmouth Coll. 1790) and Elizabeth (Sikes, Danielson) Eaton, of Brimfield, Massachusetts, who died suddenly on June 25, 1821, in her 26th year, leaving a daughter, who grew to maturity.

He was married, secondly, on August 2, 1824, to Mary, third daughter of the Hon. Samuel Lathrop (Yale 1792), and granddaughter of the Rev. Dr. Lathrop, of West Springfield. She died in Albany on September 16, 1837, after an illness of more than two months, in her 34th year; and he next married, on May 13, 1840, her younger sister, Henrietta Burnett Lathrop, who survived him.

By his second marriage he had three sons, one of whom died in infancy, and a daughter; and by his third marriage, four daughters, one of whom died in infancy, and a son. The last-named was graduated at Harvard in 1868.

Dr. Sprague wrote with great fluency, and was noted for his generous hospitality. He was called on for many occasional discourses, especially in commemoration of deceased friends.

His chief single literary labor was the compilation of the *Annals of the American Pulpit,* an invaluable biographical and historical work.

One of his principal recreations was the collection of autograph manuscripts. Early in life circumstances favored him with the acquisition of a considerable portion of Washington's private correspondence, and he made skilful use of all opportunities for adding to his accumulations.

Before his death he gave large collections of pamphlet literature to various libraries in which he was interested; thus, he presented to the Yale Library his valuable series of Massachusetts Election Sermons, to the New York State Library his bound collections on secular subjects, to

Princeton Theological Seminary his collections of religious pamphlets, in a thousand bound volumes; and to Union Theological Seminary, over eighty bound volumes of sermons.

He traveled in Europe in 1828 and again in 1836.

He was a member of many historical and other societies.

An engraving from his portrait is given in Munsell's *Historical Collections,* volume 4.

He published:

1. The duty of a Christian Minister explained and enforced: a Sermon [from I Cor. ii, 2], delivered at the Installation of the Rev. Orin Fowler, as pastor of the Congregational Church and Society in Plainfield; March 1, 1820. Hartford, 1820. 8°, pp. 32.
[*A. C. A. B. Publ. Br. Mus. C. H. S. N. Y. Publ. U. T. S. Y. C.*

The sermon occupies pp. 1–21. Mr. Fowler was a classmate.

2. A Sermon [from II Kings, ii, 12], preached January 3, 1821, at the Interment of the Reverend Joseph Lathrop, D.D. . . . Hartford, 1821. 8°, pp. 34.
[*A. C. A. B. Ath. B. Publ. Br. Mus. Harv. M. H. S. Y. C.*

3. A Sermon [from Job xiv, 10], preached May 15, 1821, at the Interment of Mrs. Elizabeth Lathrop, relict of the Rev. Joseph Lathrop, D.D. Springfield, 1821. 8°, pp. 24.
[*A. C. A. Br. Mus. M. H. S. Y. C.*

4. The Tribute of a Mourning Husband.—A Sermon [from Job xix, 21], delivered at West-Springfield, July 1, 1821, the Sabbath after the interment of Mrs. Charlotte E. Sprague, by her bereaved husband. New-York, 1821. 8°, pp. 27.
[*A. C. A. Br. Mus. C. H. S. Harv. Y. C.*

5. Letters on Practical Subjects, from a Clergyman of New-England, to his daughter. Hartford, 1822. 12°, pp. viii, 136.
[*B. Publ. Harv.*

The same, with the author's name, and the title: Letters on practical subjects, to a daughter. New York, 1831. 12°. [*Br. Mus.*

The same. London (Tract Society).

The same, anonymous unauthorized edition, with omissions, entitled: The Daughter's Own Book; or, Practical Hints from a Father to his Daughter. Glasgow, 1833.

The same. Boston, 1833. 12°, pp. 240 + pl. [*B. Publ.*

The same. Philadelphia, 1835. 16°, pp. 240. [*U. S.*

The same. (Author's) Third American edition. Revised and enlarged. New York, 1834. 12°, pp. 281. [*U. S. Y. C.*

6. The Danger of Evil Company: a Sermon [from I Cor. xv, 33], preached in West Springfield, March 30th, 1823. Boston, 1823. 8°, pp. 35. [*B. Publ. Harv. N. Y. Publ. U. T. S. Y. C.*

7. A Sermon [from John xii, 5], preached in Springfield, August 28, 1823; at the Annual Meeting of the Bible Society, the Foreign Missionary Society, and the Education Society, of the County of Hampden. Springfield, 1823. 8°, pp. 30.
[*A. A. S. A. C. A. B. Publ. C. H. S. Harv. U. T. S. Y. C.*

8. An Historical Discourse from [Deut. xxxii, 7], delivered at West Springfield, December 2, 1824, the day of the Annual Thanksgiving. Hartford, 1825. 8°, pp. 91.
[*A. A. S. B. Ath. B. Publ. Br. Mus. C. H. S. Harv. M. H. S. U. T. S. Y. C.*
Including a valuable historical appendix.

9. A Sermon [from Isa. lxiii, 1] delivered at the Ordination of the Rev. Wales Tileston, to the pastoral care of the Congregational Church in Charlemont, March 16, 1825. Hartford, 1825. 8°, pp. 24.
[*A. A. S. A. C. A. B. Publ. Br. Mus. C. H. S. N. Y. Publ. U. S. U. T. S.*

10. The Claims of Past and Future Generations on Civil Rulers.—A Sermon [from Luke xii, 48], preached at the Annual Election, May 25, 1825 ... Boston, 1825. 8°, pp. 36.
[*A. A. S. A. C. A. B. Ath. B. Publ. Br. Mus. C. H. S. Harv. M. H. S. U. T. S. Y. C.*

11. Wicked men ensnared by themselves.—A Sermon [from Ps. ix, 16] preached, December 16, 1825, in the Second Parish of West Springfield, at the Interment of Samuel Leonard and Mrs.

Harriet Leonard, his wife; the former of whom murdered the latter, and then committed suicide. ... Springfield, 1826. 8°, pp. 44.

[*A. A. S. A. C. A. B. Ath. B. Publ. Br. Mus. C. H. S. Harv. M. H. S. Y. C.*

12. The purpose of God in afflicting Ministers:—a Sermon [from II Cor. i, 6], preached at South Hadley, April 30, 1826, the Sabbath immediately succeeding the death of Mrs. Abigail E. Boies, wife of the Reverend Artemas Boies. Hartford, 1826. 8°, pp. 24.

[*A. C. A. B. Ath. B. Publ. Br. Mus. Harv. N. Y. Publ. Y. C.*

13. The Gospel the Wisdom of God.—A Sermon [from I Cor. ii, 7] preached at Salem, February 14, 1827, at the ordination of the Rev. John P. Cleaveland, as Pastor of the Tabernacle Church. Salem, 1827. 8°, pp. 40.

[*A. A. S. A. C. A. B. Ath. B. Publ. Br. Mus. Harv. M. H. S. N. Y. Publ. U. T. S. Y. C.*

14. Intemperance, a just cause for alarm and exertion.—A Sermon [from Ps. cxix, 158], preached at West Springfield, April 5, 1827, the day of the Annual Fast. New-York, 1827. 8°, pp. 26.

[*A. A. S. A. C. A. B. Ath. B. Publ. Br. Mus. Harv. M. H. S. Y. C.*

15. Character of Jesus Christ.—A Sermon [from Phil. ii, 6–11] delivered June 13, 1827, before the Hampden Association of Ministers. .. Hartford, 1827. 8°, pp. 31.

[*A. C. A. B. Ath. B. Publ. M. H. S. N. Y. Publ. U. T. S. Y. C.*

16. Religious Celebration of Independence.—A Discourse [from Ex. xiii, 3] delivered at Northampton, on the Fourth of July, 1827. Hartford, 1827. 8°, pp. 29.

[*A. C. A. Br. Mus. C. H. S. Harv. M. H. S. U. T. S. Y. C.*

17. Letters from Europe, in 1828; first published in the New-York Observer. New-York, 1828. 12°, pp. 136.

[*A. C. A. B. Publ. Br. Mus. N. Y. Publ. U. T. S.*

The author was in Europe from February to April, 1828; these letters were published in the *Observer* from May 17 to October 4. Also, reprinted in London.

18. A Sermon [from Ps. cxviii, 25] preached January 14, 1829, at the dedication of the new house for public worship, erected by the Evangelical Congregational Church and Society in Barre; and at the ordination of the Rev. John Storrs, as their pastor. Hartford, 1829. 8°, pp. 32.

[*A. A. S. A. C. A. B. Publ. Br. Mus. N. Y. Publ.*

19. Power of Divine Truth.—A Sermon [from Hebr. iv, 12] preached at Greenfield, January 21, 1829, at the Ordination of the Reverend Caleb Sprague Henry, as Pastor of the Second Congregational Church .. Hartford, 1829. 8°, pp. 30.

[*A. C. A. M. H. S. N. Y. Publ. U. T. S. Y. C.*

20. A Sermon [from II Cor. xiii, 11] preached at West Springfield, on the Resignation of the Author's pastoral charge, July 26, 1829. Boston, 1829. 8°, pp. 39.

[*A. C. A. B. Publ. Br. Mus. C. H. S. M. H. S. Y. C.*

21. Causes of an Unsuccessful Ministry: two Sermons [from Hebr. iv, 2], addressed to the Second Presbyterian Congregation in the City of Albany, August 30, 1829; the Sabbath immediately succeeding the author's induction as their pastor. Albany, 1829. 8°, pp. 49.

[*A. A. S. A. C. A. B. Ath. B. Publ. Br. Mus. U. T. S. Y. C.*

22. An Address delivered in the South Dutch Church, Albany, October 6, 1829, on the Anniversary of the County Sabbath School Union. Albany, 1829. 12°, pp. 21. [*A. C. A. Br. Mus.*

23. A Sermon [from John vi, 68], delivered in the Murray Street Church, New York, on Sabbath evening, April 11, 1830. New York, 1830. 8°, pp. 49. [*Br. Mus. N. Y. Publ. Y. C.*

The subject is, Revealed religion, the only source of true happiness.

24. A Discourse [from I Cor. x, 31] delivered at Castleton, May 27, 1830, at the opening of the Vermont Classical Seminary. Albany, 1830. 8°, pp. 28.

[*B. Publ. Br. Mus. Harv. M. H. S. Y. C.*

25. A Sermon [from Ps. cxliv, 15], addressed to the Second Presbyterian Congregation in Albany, on the fourth of July, 1830. Albany, 1830. 8°, pp. 17.

[*A. A. S. B. Publ. Br Mus. M. H. S. U. T. S. Y. C.*

26. A Sermon [from Ps. xlv, 4], addressed to the Second Congregational Society, in Greenwich, Connecticut, September 1, 1830, at the installation of the Reverend Joel Mann, as their pastor. Albany, 1830. 8°, pp. 26.

[*A. A. S. A. C. A. B. Ath. B. Publ. Br. Mus. U. T. S. Y. C.*

27. Lectures to young people. With an Introductory Address, by S. Miller, D.D. New-York, 1830. 12°, pp. xxi, 288.

[*B. Publ. Br. Mus. U. S.*

Several editions.

28. Lectures on Revivals of Religion: with an introductory essay by L. Woods, D.D. Also an Appendix, consisting of Letters ... Albany, 1832. 8°, pp. xxxii, 287 + 165.

[*A. C. A. Br. Mus. Y. C.*

Several later editions, both American and British.

29. A Discourse [from Prov. xvi, 22], delivered on Sabbath evening, March 17, 1833, in St. Peter's church, in aid of the Albany Apprentices' Library .. Albany, 1833. 8°, pp. 25.

[*A. A. S. A. C. A. B. Ath. B. Publ. Br. Mus. N. Y. Publ. Y. C.*

30. A Sermon [from Job xiv, 19] delivered in the Second Presbyterian church in the city of Albany, June 2, 1833, the Sabbath immediately succeeding the Death of Mr. John Bulkley, aged nineteen years, member of the Senior class in Amherst College. Albany, 1833. 8°, pp. 25. [*A. C. A. B. Publ. Br. Mus. Y. C.*

31. A Sermon [from Haggai ii, 9], preached at the Dedication of the New Congregational Church in Andover, Connecticut, October 28, 1833. Albany, 1833. 8°, pp. 26.

[*A. C. A. Br. Mus. M. H. S. Y. C.*

32. Hints designed to regulate the Intercourse of Christians. Albany, 1834. 12°, pp. vi, 269.

[*A. C. A. Br. Mus. U. T. S. Y. C.*

Several editions.

33. A Sermon [from Hebr. xiii, 3] preached in the Second Presbyterian Church, Albany, Sabbath evening, May 11, 1834 .. In behalf of the Polish Exiles lately arrived in this country. Albany, 1834. 8°, pp. 16.

[*A. A. S. A. C. A. B. Publ. Br. Mus. C. H. S. M. H. S. N. Y. Publ. U. T. S. Y. C.*

34. An Oration commemorative of the late General Lafayette, pronounced before the military and civic societies of the city of Albany, in the South Dutch Church, July 24, 1834. Albany, 1834. 8°, pp. 34.

[*A. C. A. B. Ath. B. Publ. Br. Mus. Harv. M. H. S. N. Y. Publ. U. S. Y. C.*

35. An Address to theological students on ministerial fidelity and prudence.

In the *Annual* of the Board of Education of the Presbyterian Church in the United States for 1835. Philadelphia, 1835. 16°, pp. 21–42. [*U. T. S. Y. C.*

36. Danger of being over wise. A Sermon [from Eccl. vii, 16] preached June 7th, 1835, in the Second Presbyterian church in Albany. Albany, 1835. 8°, pp. 27.

[*A. A. S. A. C. A. B. Publ. Br. Mus. N. Y. Publ. U. T. S. Y. C.*

Especially, on the exclusion of wine from the Lord's Supper.

37. Reply to Professor Stuart's Letter addressed to him through the American Temperance Intelligencer of August, 1835, relative to his late Sermon on the exclusion of wine from the Lord's Supper. Albany, 1835. 8°, pp. 29.

[*A. A. S. A. C. A. B. Publ. Br. Mus. Harv. N. Y. Publ. U. T. S. Y. C.*

38. Appeal to the Public in relation to the charges made against him in Zion's Herald . .—Originally published in the three Albany daily papers. Albany, 1835. 8°, pp. 12. [*A. C. A. Y. C.*

In reply to an attack on his character, in connection with No. 36.

39. Religious Ultraism: A Sermon [from Phil. iv, 5] delivered August 25, 1835, at the Installation of the Rev. John H. Hunter, as pastor of the First Congregational Church in West Springfield, Massachusetts. Albany, 1835. 8°, pp. 47.

[*A. A. S. A. C. A. B. Publ. Br. Mus. C. H. S. N. Y. Publ. U. T. S. Y. C.*

40. Correspondence, &c. between E. C. Delavan and the Rev. Dr. Sprague. [Albany, 1837.] 8°, pp. 8. [*B. Ath.*

Brief letters, in 1835–36, relating to the use of wine at the Lord's Supper.

41. A Sermon [from Phil. ii, 12–13], delivered March 22, 1837, at the Ordination and Installation of the Rev. Montgomery T. Good-

ale, as Pastor of the Presbyterian Church in Amsterdam Village. Albany, 1837. 8°, pp. 12. [*A. A. S. A. C. A. B. Publ. Br. Mus.*

42. A Sermon [from I Cor. xv, 41] addressed to the Second Presbyterian Congregation in Albany, April 23, 1837, the Sabbath after the interment of Mrs. Ruth Savage, wife of the Hon. John Savage .. Albany, 1837. 8°, pp. 20. [*B. Ath. B. Publ. Y. C.*

43. Tower of Babel: a Sermon [from Gen. xi, 9] addressed to the Second Presbyterian Congregation in Albany, May 11th, 1837. Albany, 1837. 8°, pp. 26. [*A. C. A. B. Publ. Br. Mus. Y. C.*

44. Lectures illustrating the contrast between True Christianity and various other systems. New-York, 1837. 12°, pp. viii, 386. [*Br. Mus. Harv. U. T. S.*

The same. London, 1838. 12°. [*Br. Mus.*

45. A Sermon [from I Tim. ii, 1–2] addressed to the Second Presbyterian Congregation in Albany, March 4, 1838, the Sabbath after intelligence was received that the Hon. Jonathan Cilley, Member of Congress from Maine, had been murdered in a duel with the Hon. William J. Graves, Member from Kentucky. Albany, 1838. 8°, pp. 15.

[*A. A. S. A. C. A. B. Ath. B. Publ. Br. Mus. Harv. M. H. S. N. Y. H. S. N. Y. Publ. U. T. S. Y. C.*

46. An Address delivered on the evening of December 4, 1838, before the Young Men's Association for mutual improvement in Albany, as introductory to their Annual Course of Lectures. Albany, 1838. 8°, pp. 30.

[*A. A. S. A. C. A. B. Publ. M. H. S. Y. C.*

On the rights of the mind.

47. A Sermon [from I Cor. xi, 1] delivered December 19, 1838, at the Ordination of the Rev. A. Augustus Wood, as pastor of the First Congregational Church, West-Springfield. Albany, 1839. 8°, pp. 31.

[*A. A. S. A. C. A. B. Publ. Br. Mus. U. T. S. Y. C.*

48. Religion and Rank: a Sermon [from Prov. viii, 11] addressed to the Second Presbyterian Congregation in Albany, February 3, 1839, the Sabbath immediately succeeding the funeral of the Hon. Stephen Van Rensselaer. Albany, 1839. 8°, pp. 33.

[*A. C. A. B. Ath. B. Publ. C. H. S. M. H. S. N. Y. Publ. Y. C.*

49. Memoir of Rev. Doctor Griffin. Prefixed to volume 1 of Sermons by the late Rev. Edward D. Griffin, D.D. New-York, 1839. 8°, pp. 1-270.

50. A Mind in Ruins.—A Sermon [from Job iii, 23] occasioned by the death of Richard Marvin, Esq., and addressed to the Second Presbyterian Congregation in Albany, August 23, 1840, the Sabbath immediately succeeding his interment. Albany, 1840. 8°, pp. 24.
[*A. C. A. B. Ath. M. H. S.*

51. Voice of the Rod: A Sermon [from Micah vi, 9], delivered at Albany, May 14, 1841, the day of the National Fast, occasioned by the death of the late William Henry Harrison, President of the United States. Albany, 1841. 8°, pp. 28.
[*A. C. A. B. Publ. Br. Mus. Harv. M. H. S. U. T. S.*

52. A Sermon [from Hebr. xiii, 7-8], addressed to the Fourth Presbyterian Congregation in Albany, on Sabbath evening, January 1, 1843, in consequence of the death of their pastor, Rev. Edward D. Allen. With the Addresses delivered at the funeral. Albany, 1843. 8°, pp. 62.
[*A. C. A. B. Ath. B. Publ. Br. Mus. Harv. M. H. S. N. Y. Publ. U. T. S. Y. C.*
The sermon occupies pp. 3-39.

53. A Sermon [from Acts xvi, 9] delivered in connection with the anniversary of the Foreign Evangelical Society, in the Reformed Dutch Church, Lafayette Place, New-York, on Sabbath evening, May 7, 1843; and subsequently repeated, by request of said Society, in Albany and Philadelphia. New-York, 1843. 8°, pp. 55.
[*A. A. S. A. C. A. B. Publ. Br. Mus. Harv. M. H. S. N. Y. Publ. U. T. S. Y. C.*

54. An Address delivered August 16, 1843, before the Society of Phi Beta Kappa in Yale College. New Haven, 1843. 8°, pp. 48.
[*A. C. A. B. Ath. B. Publ. Br. Mus. Harv. M. H. S. N. Y. Publ. U. T. S. Y. C.*
On the responsibilities, temptations, and rewards of men of letters; with tributes to Noah Webster, James Abraham Hillhouse, and Timothy Dwight.

55. A Sermon [from Isa. xliii, 1-2] addressed to the Second Presbyterian Congregation in Albany, November 26, 1843, in consequence of the death of James McClure, Esq. Albany, 1843. 8°, pp. 33. [*A. C. A. N. Y. Publ.*

56. A Discourse [from Gen. xlv, 5] on True Magnanimity, addressed particularly to Young Men, and delivered in the Second Presbyterian Church in Albany, February 25, 1844. Albany, 1844. 8°, pp. 56.

[*A. A. S. A. C. A. B. Publ. C. H. S. M. H. S. N. Y. Publ. U. T. S. Y. C.*

57. A Discourse [from Eccl. iii, 1] pronounced July 30, 1844, before the Philomathesian Society in Middlebury College. Albany, 1844. 8°, pp. 67.

[*B. Publ. Br. Mus. Harv. M. H. S. N. Y. Publ. Y. C.*

58. An Address delivered at the close of the annual examination of the Young Ladies' Institute, Pittsfield, Mass., September 28, 1844. Pittsfield, 1844. 8°, pp. 32.

[*A. A. S. A. C. A. Br. Mus. M. H. S. U. T. S. Y. C.*

59. A Sermon [from Rom. xii, 2] on the Danger of Political Strife, addressed to the Second Presbyterian Congregation, Albany, Oct. 13, 1844. Albany, 1844. 8°, pp. 23.

[*A. A. S. A. C. A. B. Publ. M. H. S. N. Y. H. S. Y. C.*

Preached shortly before a Presidential election.

60. Letters to Young Men, founded on the history of Joseph. Albany, 1844. 12°.

Several editions.

61. Life of Timothy Dwight, President of Yale College. In Sparks's *Library of American Biography,* second series, volume 4, pp. 223–364. Boston, 1845. 16°.

62. An Address, delivered April 11, 1845, in the Second Presbyterian Church, Albany, on occasion of the interment of Mr. William Davis, Misses Lucinda and Anna Wood, and Miss Mary Anne Torrey, who perished in the wreck of the Steam Boat Swallow, on the evening of the 7th. Albany, 1845. 8°, pp. 30.

[*M. H. S. N. Y. H. S. N. Y. Publ. Y. C.*

63. A Sermon [from Ps. xcvi, 6] delivered April 22, 1845, at the opening of the New Church, erected by the First Presbyterian Congregation, Lansingburgh. Lansingburgh, 1845. 8°, pp. 44.

[*A. C. A. C. H. S. Harv. U. T. S. Y. C.*

64. A Sermon [from Ps. xxxvi, 9] preached in the Second Presbyterian church, Albany, the Sabbath immediately succeeding the

Death of Mrs. Oliver S. Strong, of Jersey City, daughter of Archibald McIntyre, Esq., of Albany. Albany, 1845. 8°, pp. 32.
[*A. C. A. Br. Mus.*

65. A Discourse delivered on Sabbath evening, August 17, 1845, before the Mills Society of Inquiry, and the Theological Society of Williams College. Albany, 1845. 8°, pp. 58.
[*A. C. A. B. Publ. Br. Mus. M. H. S. U. T. S. Y. C.*
On Some of the dangers to which the ministry is exposed from the temptations incident to College life.

66. A Sermon [from Rev. i, 16] delivered August 27, 1845, at the Installation of the Rev. Malcolm N. McLaren, as pastor of the First Presbyterian Church, Rochester. Albany, 1845. 8°, pp. 51.
[*A. C. A. B. Publ. Br. Mus. C. H. S. N. Y. Publ. U. T. S. Y. C.*

67. A Discourse [from Eccl. viii, 11, and Matth. xxii, 37] on the Ruling Passion, delivered by request of the young men of the North Dutch Church, New York, on Sabbath evening, November 16, 1845. [Albany, 1845.] 8°, pp. 32.
[*A. C. A. B. Publ. U. T. S.*

68. A Sermon [from I Sam. vii, 12], delivered on Sabbath morning, Jan. 4, 1846, containing Sketches of the History of the Second Presbyterian Church and Congregation, Albany, during thirty years from the period of their organization. Albany, 1846. 8°, pp. 43.
[*A. A. S. A. C. A. B. Ath. B. Publ. Br. Mus. Harv. M. H. S. N. Y. H. S. U. T. S. Y. C.*

69. An Address delivered at the opening of the Brooklyn Female Academy, on Monday evening, May 4, 1846. Albany, 1846. 8°, pp. 26.
[*A. A. S. A. C. A. B. Publ. Br. Mus. Harv. M. H. S. N. Y. H. S. U. S. Y. C.*

70. A Discourse delivered on Sabbath evening, July 19, 1846, before the Theological Society of Union College. Albany, 1846. 8°, pp. 51. [*A. C. A. B. Publ. Br. Mus. Y. C.*
On Theological Science.

71. An Address delivered August 5, 1846, before the Hermean Society of Geneva College. Albany, 1846. 8°, pp. 38.
[*B. Publ. Br. Mus. M. H. S. N. Y. Publ. U. T. S. Y. C.*

72. An Address delivered on the evening of the twenty-second of February, 1847, before the Young Men's Association of the city of Albany. Albany, 1847. 8°, pp. 51.

[*A. A. S. A. C. A. B. Ath. B. Publ. Br. Mus. Harv. M. H. S. N. Y. H. S. N. Y. Publ. U. T. S. Y. C.*

On Washington's character, particularly as illustrated by his Farewell Address.

73. A Sermon [from Numb. xxiii, 23] delivered in connection with the anniversary of the American Society for Meliorating the Condition of the Jews, in the Presbyterian Church, Mercer Street, New York, on Sabbath evening, May 9, 1847. New-York, 1847. 8°, pp. 24.

[*A. C. A. B. Ath. B. Publ. Br. Mus. U. T. S. Y. C.*

74. A Discourse [from Matth. xxv, 15] commemorative of the Rev. Thomas Chalmers, D.D., delivered in the Second Presbyterian Church, Albany, on Sabbath evening, June 27, 1847. .. Albany, 1847. 8°, pp. 47.

[*A. C. A. B. Ath. B. Publ. Br. Mus. Harv. M. H. S. N. Y. H. S. N. Y. Publ. U. T. S. Y. C.*

Also in the *National Preacher* for August, 1847.

75. A Discourse [from Ps. cxlvi, 3–4] occasioned by the death of the Hon. Silas Wright, late Governor of the State of New-York; and delivered in the Second Presbyterian Church, Albany, Sept. 5, 1847. Albany, 1847. 8°, pp. 37.

[*A. C. A. B. Ath. B. Publ. Br. Mus. Harv. M. H. S. N. Y. Publ. U. T. S. Y. C.*

Two editions.

76. An Address delivered in Albany, at the Funeral of Mrs. Jane Wyckoff, Jan. 31, 1847. Albany, 1848. 8°, pp. 19.

[*A. C. A. B. Ath. B. Publ. Br. Mus. M. H. S. N. Y. H. S. N. Y. Publ.*

77. An Address, delivered before the Literary Societies of the Wesleyan University, Middletown, Connecticut, July 31, 1848. Albany, 1848. 8°, pp. 56.

[*A. C. A. B. Ath. B. Publ. Br. Mus. Harv. M. H. S. N. Y. H. S. N. Y. Publ. Y. C.*

On William Wilberforce.

78. An Address at the opening of the new edifice for the Howard Sunday School on Sabbath evening, September 10th, 1848 ... Philadelphia, 1848. 8°, pp. 48. [*B. Publ. Harv. U. S.*

79. Words to a young man's conscience. 1848.

80. A Discourse [from II Sam. iii, 38] commemorative of the late Ambrose Spencer, late Chief Justice of the State of New York: delivered in the Second Presbyterian Church, Albany, on Sabbath Evening, April 20, 1848. Albany, 1849. 8°, pp. 34.
[*B. Ath. B. Publ. Harv. M. H. S. N. Y. Publ. Y. C.*

81. An Address delivered at the Dedication of the Hinsdale Academy, January 11, 1849. Albany, 1849. 8°, pp. 30.
[*B. Ath. B. Publ. Br. Mus. Harv. M. H. S. U. T. S. Y. C.*

82. A Discourse [from Eccl. i, 4], delivered February 25, 1849, on the Completion of a Century from the Organization of the Congregational Church in Andover, Connecticut. Albany, 1849. 8°, pp. 32. [*A. C. A. B. Ath. B. Publ. Y. C.*

83. A Discourse [from Acts xi, 24] delivered on Sunday Evening, March 25, 1849, in the Second Presbyterian Church, Albany, in consequence of the death of Hon. Timothy S. Williams, late a member of the Senate of New-York. Albany, 1849. 8°, pp. 39.
[*A. C. A. B. Ath. B. Publ. Br. Mus. Harv. M. H. S. N. Y. H. S. N. Y. Publ. U. T. S. Y. C.*

84. An Address delivered July 24, 1849, before the United Literary Societies of Hamilton College. Albany, 1849. 8°, pp. 42.
[*A. C. A. B. Ath. B. Publ. Harv. M. H. S. U. T. S.*

85. Essay on the character of the Rev. James Richards, D.D. In Sermons by the late Rev. J. Richards, D.D. Albany, 1849. 12°, pp. 5-38. [*A. C. A. Harv. N. Y. H. S. N. Y. Publ.*

86. A Discourse [from II Kings ii, 12] commemorative of the Rev. Samuel Miller, D.D., late Professor in the Theological Seminary at Princeton, delivered in the Second Presbyterian Church, Albany, on Sabbath Evening, January 27, 1850. Albany, 1850. 8°, pp. 51.
[*A. A. S. A. C. A. B. Ath. B. Publ. Br. Mus. Harv. M. H. S. N. Y. Publ. U. T. S. Y. C.*

87. A Discourse, delivered September 3, 1850, before the Porter Rhetorical Society, in the Theological Seminary at Andover. Albany, 1850. 8°, pp. 49.
[*A. C. A. B. Ath. B. Publ. Br. Mus. Harv. M. H. S. N. Y. Publ. U. T. S. Y. C.*
On the aids of pulpit eloquence from models and from occasions.

88. A Discourse delivered before the Phi Beta Kappa Society of Bowdoin College, September 5, 1850. Albany, 1850. 8°, pp. 44.

[*A. C. A. B. Ath. B. Publ. Br. Mus. Harv. M. H. S. N. Y. Publ. U. T. S. Y. C.*

89. On the perpetuity of intellectual influence. A Discourse [from John xi, 11] occasioned by the death of Justin Ely, Esq., and delivered in the First Congregational Church, West Springfield, September 30, 1850. Albany, 1850. 8°, pp. 28.

[*A. C. A. M. H. S.*

90. An Oration pronounced before the Phi Beta Kappa Society of Harvard University, July 17, 1851. Albany, 1851. 8°, pp. 60.

[*A. C. A. B. Ath. B. Publ. Br. Mus. Harv. M. H. S. U. T. S. Y. C.*

On the American mind—her character and destiny.

91. A Sermon [from Acts x, 38] delivered October 12, 1851, the Sabbath Morning after the death of Daniel Campbell. Albany, 1851. 8°, pp. 34.

[*A. C. A. B. Ath. B. Publ. Br. Mus. Harv. M. H. S. U. T. S. Y. C.*

92. A Discourse [from Hebr. xi, 4] delivered by request of the Executive Committee of the Board of Foreign Missions, Sabbath Evening, May 2, 1852. In the Church on University Place, New York. New York, 1852. 8°, pp. 22.

[*A. A. S. A. C. A. B. Publ. M. H. S. U. T. S. Y. C.*

On the posthumous influence of foreign missionaries.

93. A Discourse [from Acts vii, 38], delivered at Montpelier, on the evening of October 20, 1852, the fortieth anniversary of the Vermont Bible Society. Albany, 1852. 8°, pp. 31.

[*A. A. S. A. C. A. B. Publ. Br. Mus. U. T. S. Y. C.*

94. A Sermon [from Prov. xvi, 31] preached on Sabbath afternoon, August 21, 1853, in connection with the funeral solemnities of John Boardman, Ruling Elder in the Second Presbyterian Church, Albany. Albany, 1853. 8°, pp. 33.

[*A. C. A. B. Ath. B. Publ. Br. Mus. Harv. M. H. S. U. T. S.*

95. A Sermon [from Isa. liii, 1–2] delivered at Dudley, Massachusetts, January 17, 1854, at the Funeral of the Rev. Joshua Bates, D.D. Albany, 1854. 8°, pp. 40.

[*A. C. A. B. Publ. Br. Mus. Harv. M. H. S. N. Y. Publ. U. T. S. Y. C.*

96. A Sermon [from Ps. xix, 7] delivered on Wednesday Evening, June 21, 1854, at the installation of the Rev. E. Smalley, D.D., as pastor of the Second Presbyterian Church in Troy. Troy, 1854. 8°, pp. 26.

[*A. A. S. A. C. A. B. Publ. Br. Mus. U. T. S. Y. C.*

97. A Sermon [from John xiii, 7] delivered in the Second Presbyterian Church, Albany, on Sabbath afternoon, July 20, 1854, immediately after the funeral of Mrs. Harriet Chapin .. Albany, 1854. 8°, pp. 32.

[*A. C. A. B. Ath. B. Publ. Br. Mus. M. H. S. U. T. S. Y. C.*

98. A Sermon [from Acts ix, 36–42] delivered in the Second Presbyterian Church, Albany, on Sabbath morning, August 20, 1854; commemorative of the character of Mrs. Christina Lee .. Albany, 1854. 8°, pp. 40.

[*A. C. A. B. Ath. B. Publ. Br. Mus. Harv. M. H. S. U. S. U. T. S. Y. C.*

99. A Sermon [from Acts xxvi, 22] addressed to the Second Presbyterian Congregation in Albany, Sunday Morning, August 27, 1854, on the completion of a Quarter of a Century from the commencement of the author's ministry among them. Albany, 1854. 8°, pp. 40.

[*A. A. S. A. C. A. B. Publ. Br. Mus. M. H. S. U. T. S. Y. C.*

100. A Sermon [from Ps. lxxi, 9] delivered in the Second Presbyterian Church, Albany, September 3, 1854, the Sabbath immediately succeeding the funeral of the Hon. John Townsend. Albany, 1854. 8°, pp. 26

[*A. C. A. B. Ath. B. Publ. Br. Mus. M. H. S. U. T. S. Y. C.*

101. A Sermon [from Daniel xii, 3] delivered at Johnstown, Nov. 3, 1854, at the Funeral of the Rev. Hugh Mair, D.D. Albany, 1854. 8°, pp. 29. [*A. C. A. B. Publ. M. H. S. U. T. S.*

102. A Sermon [from Rom. xi, 13] preached March 7, 1855, on occasion of the Ordination of the Rev. Theron H. Hawkes, and his Installation as Pastor of the First Congregational Church, in West Springfield, Mass. Albany, 1855. 8°, pp. 37.

[*A. A. S. A. C. A. B. Publ. Br. Mus. M. H. S. N. Y. Publ. U. T. S. Y. C.*

103. A Sermon [from James i, 5–6] preached on Sabbath morning, April 1, 1855, in the Second Presbyterian Church, Albany, on occasion of the death of Thomas Stamps, Esq. Printed for private distribution only. Albany, 1855. 8°, pp. 23.
[*A. C. A. B. Publ. N. Y. Publ. U. T. S. Y. C.*

104. A Sermon [from II Tim. ii, 15] preached on Wednesday evening, July 11, 1855, at the Installation of the Rev. Duncan Kennedy, D.D., as pastor of the Second Presbyterian Church, Troy. Albany, 1855. 8°, pp. 24.
[*A. A. S. A. C. A. Br. Mus. M. H. S. N. Y. Publ. U. T. S. Y. C.*

105. Monitory Letters to Church Members. 1855.

106. Visits to European Celebrities. Boston, 1855. 12°, pp. 305. [*A. C. A. B. Publ. Br. Mus. Harv. N. Y. Publ.*
Originally published as forty-two articles in the *Presbyterian*. Facsimiles of the autographs of the celebrities are given.

107. A Sermon [from I Cor. xv, 57] preached in the Second Presbyterian Church, Albany, April 27, 1856, on occasion of the death of Frederick J. Barnard, Jr. Albany, 1856. 8°, pp. 24.
[*B. Ath. B. Publ. Br. Mus. Harv. M. H. S. U. T. S. Y. C.*

108. A Sermon [from Ps. xxv, 21] preached in the Second Presbyterian Church, Albany, July 13, 1856, the Sabbath morning immediately succeeding the interment of John J. Boyd, and Archibald Campbell. Albany, 1856. 8°, pp. 29.
[*A. C. A. B. Ath. Br. Mus. M. H. S. U. T. S.*

109. An Address delivered in West Springfield, August 25, 1856, on occasion of the one hundredth anniversary of the ordination of the Rev. Joseph Lathrop, D.D. Albany, 1856. 8°, pp. 55.
[*B. Publ. Harv. Y. C.*

The same. With an Appendix. Springfield, 1856. 8°, pp. 102.
[*Br. Mus. M. H. S. Y. C.*

110. A Sermon [from Gen. v, 24] preached on Sabbath afternoon, January 25, 1857, with reference to the death of Nathaniel Davis, Ruling Elder in the Second Presbyterian Church, Albany. Albany, 1857. 8°, pp. 41.
[*A. C. A. B. Ath. Br. Mus. Harv. M. H. S. N. Y. Publ. U. T. S. Y. C.*

111. Annals of the American Pulpit; or commemorative notices of distinguished American Clergymen of various denominations, .. to the close of the year 1855. With historical introductions. New York, 1857–69. 9 volumes. 8°.

[*A. A. S. A. C. A. B. Ath. B. Publ. Harv. M. H. S. N. Y. Publ. U. S. U. T. S. Y. C.*

A work of great labor and of proportionate importance. The author left the material for a tenth volume, which is yet unpublished.

112. The Man of Business, considered in his various relations. In *Men of Business.* New York, 1857. 12°, 45 pp.

113. A Sermon [from Acts xx, 24, and II Tim. i, 12] preached in the Second Presbyterian Church, Albany, Sunday afternoon, September 21, 1857, on occasion of the death of the Rev. John Ludlow, D.D. ... Albany, 1857. 8°, pp. 31.

[*A. C. A. B. Publ. Br. Mus. M. H. S. N. Y. Publ. U. T. S. Y. C.*

114. A Sermon [from Prov. xxxi, 31] addressed to the Second Presbyterian Congregation, Albany, Sabbath morning, March 14, 1858, on occasion of the death of Mrs. Alexander Marvin. Printed .. for private distribution. Albany, 1858. 8°, pp. 30.

[*A. C. A. B. Ath. B. Publ. Y. C.*

115. A Sermon [from Job xlii, 17] addressed to the Second Presbyterian Congregation, Albany, Sunday afternoon, May 9, 1858, on occasion of the death of the Hon. Archibald McIntyre. Albany, 1858. 8°, pp. 37.

[*A. C. A. B. Ath. B. Publ. Harv. M. H. S. N. Y. Publ. U. T. S. Y. C.*

116. A Sermon [from Ps. lxxvii, 19] addressed to the Second Presbyterian Congregation, Albany, on Sunday morning, September 5, 1858, on the completion of the Atlantic Telegraph. Albany, 1858. 8°, pp. 32.

[*A. C. A. B. Publ. Br. Mus. Harv. M. H. S. N. Y. Publ. U. T. S.*

117. An Address delivered in the Mercer Street Church, New York, December 2, 1858, at the funeral of the Hon. Benjamin Franklin Butler, late Attorney General of the United States. New York, 1859. 8°, pp. 21. [*B. Publ. Harv. M. H. S. U. T. S.*

118. A Sermon [from Prov. iii, 35] delivered in the Second Presbyterian Church, Albany, April 10, 1859, on occasion of the death of Ebenezer Pemberton. Albany, 1859. 8°, pp. 23.
[*A. C. A. B. Ath. Br. Mus.*

119. A Sermon [from John xi, 38] delivered in the Second Presbyterian Church, Albany, Sunday morning, November 6, 1859, on occasion of the death of Mrs. Eliza McIntyre, wife of the late Hon. Archibald McIntyre. Albany, 1859. 8°, pp. 47.
[*A. C. A. B. Ath. B. Publ. Br. Mus. M. H. S. U. T. S. Y. C.*

120. A Sermon [from II Tim. iv, 6-8] preached at East Granville, Mass., on Friday, December 16, 1859, at the funeral of the Rev. Timothy Mather Cooley, D.D. Albany, 1860. 8°, pp. 38.
[*A. C. A. B. Publ. Br. Mus. Harv. M. H. S. N. Y. Publ. U. T. S. Y. C.*

Also in the *National Preacher,* for April, 1860.

121. Memoir of Mrs. John V. L. Pruyn. Albany, 1859 [1860]. 8°, pp. 29.
[*A. C. A. B. Ath. B. Publ. Br. Mus. N. Y. Publ. U. T. S. Y. C.*

122. Our Triennial Catalogue.—A Discourse, addressed to the Alumni of Yale College, at their annual meeting, July 25, 1860. Albany, 1860. 8°, pp. 76.
[*A. C. A. B. Ath. B. Publ. Br. Mus. Harv. N. Y. Publ. U. S. U. T. S. Y. C.*

123. A Sermon [from Luke xiv, 11] having some reference to the character of the late Rev. Cortlandt Van Rensselaer, D.D., preached in the Second Presbyterian Church, Albany, Sabbath morning, September 16, 1860. Albany, 1860. 8°, pp. 36.
[*A. C. A. B. Ath. B. Publ. M. H. S. N. Y. Publ. Y. C.*

123½. The close of a Sermon [from Rev. xxii, 14] preached on Sunday morning, December 9, 1860, with some reference to the death of Miss Ellie P. Frisbie, by her Pastor. Albany, 1860. 8°, pp. 10. [*A. C. A.*

124. A Discourse [from Isa. xxviii, 29] addressed to the First Presbyterian Congregation in Elizabeth, N. J., February 10, 1861, the Sunday morning immediately succeeding the death of the Rev. Nicholas Murray, D.D., their pastor. Albany, 1861. 8°, pp. 51.
[*A. C. A. B. Ath. B. Publ. Harv. M. H. S. U. T. S. Y. C.*

125. A Discourse [from Isa. lvii, 1] delivered Sunday morning, April 7, 1861, in the Second Presbyterian Church, Albany, in commemoration of the late Hon. John McLean, LL.D. ... Albany, 1861. 8°, pp. 34.

[*A. C. A. B. Ath. B. Publ. Br. Mus. Harv. M. H. S. U. S. U. T. S. Y. C.*

126. An Address delivered on occasion of the Raising of the National Flag, upon the Second Presbyterian Church, Albany, on Monday, June 17, 1861. Albany, 1861. 8°, pp. 8.

[*A. A. S. A. C. A. B. Publ. Harv. U. T. S. Y. C.*

127. The Founders: Chapter 6 in Memorial Volume of the First Fifty Years of the American Board of Commissioners for Foreign Missions. Boston, 1861, 8°, pp. 104–25.

128. Glorifying God in the Fires.—A Discourse [from Isa. xxiv, 15] delivered in the Second Presbyterian Church, Albany, November 28, 1861, the day of the Annual Thanksgiving, in the State of New York. Albany, 1861. 8°, pp. 58.

[*A. A. S. A. C. A. B. Ath. B. Publ. Br. Mus. Harv. U. T. S. Y. C.*

129. Memoir of the Life of the Rev. Oliver Bronson. In Bronson's *Sermons*. Albany, 1861. 12°. [*Br. Mus.*

130. A Discourse addressed to the Alumni of the Princeton Theological Seminary, April 30, 1862, on occasion of the completion of its first half century.—With an Appendix. .. Albany, 1862. 8°, pp. 72.

[*A. C. A. B. Ath. B. Publ. Harv. M. H. S. N. Y. Publ. U. S. U. T. S. Y. C.*

131. A Discourse [from Rev. vii, 15] delivered at Spencertown, N. Y., on Thursday, December 11, 1862, at the funeral of the Rev. Timothy Woodbridge, D.D., who, during his whole ministry, was the subject of total blindness. Albany, 1863. 8°, pp. 30.

[*A. C. A. B. Publ. Br. Mus. Harv. M. H. S. Y. C.*

132. A Discourse [from Acts xxiii, 1] delivered on Friday, December 12, 1862, at the funeral of the Rev. Samuel Osgood, D.D., ... in Springfield. Albany, 1863. 8°, pp. 42.

[*A. C. A. B. Ath. B. Publ. Br. Mus. Harv. M. H. S. N. Y. Publ. U. T. S. Y. C.*

133. A Discourse [from John iv, 34] commemorative of the late Rev. Robert Baird, D.D., delivered on occasion of the anniversary of the American and Foreign Christian Union, in the Reformed Dutch Church, corner of Fifth Avenue and Twenty-first Street, New York, on Sabbath evening, May 10, 1863. Albany, 1863. 8°, pp. 48.
[*A. C. A. B. Ath. Br. Mus. Harv. M. H. S. N. Y. Publ. U. T. S. Y. C.*

134. A Sermon [from John xix, 41] preached in the Second Presbyterian Church, Albany, October 18, 1863, the Sunday morning after the funeral of Joel Rathbone, Esq. .. Albany, 1863. 8°, pp. 24. [*A. C. A. B. Ath. B. Publ. Harv. Y. C.*

135. An Address delivered in the Evangelical Lutheran Ebenezer Church, Albany, on occasion of the Funeral of Mrs. Susan C. Pohlman, wife of the Rev. Henry N. Pohlman, D.D., November 10, 1863. Albany, 1863. 8°, pp. 18.
[*A. C. A. B. Ath. B. Publ. Br. Mus. Harv. M. H. S. Y. C.*

136. A Discourse [from II Tim. iv, 6] addressed to the United Presbyterian Congregation, Troy, February 21, 1864, the Sabbath morning immediately succeeding the funeral of the Rev. Peter Bullions, D.D., their pastor. Albany, 1864. 8°, pp. 32.
[*A. C. A. B. Publ. Br. Mus. Harv. M. H. S. N. Y. Publ. Y. C.*

137. An Address delivered, March 31, 1864, on occasion of the funeral of the Rev. John N. Campbell, D.D., late pastor of the First Presbyterian Church, Albany. Albany, 1864. 8°, pp. 27.
[*A. C. A. B. Publ. Br. Mus. Harv. M. H. S. U. T. S. Y. C.*

138. A Discourse [from Gen. v, 27] delivered August 2, 1864, in the Plymouth Church, Syracuse, on occasion of the funeral of the Reverend Daniel Waldo, who had nearly completed his one hundred and second year. New York, 1864. 8°, pp. 16.
[*A. C. A. B. Publ. Harv. M. H. S.*

139. Memoirs of the Rev. John McDowell, D.D., and the Rev. William A. McDowell, D.D. New York, 1864. 12°, pp. ix, 305 + pl. [*A. C. A. B. Ath. Br. Mus. Y. C.*

140. A Discourse [from Job xiv, 10] delivered in the Second Presbyterian Church, Albany, September 4, 1864, the Sunday morn-

ing after the funeral of Mr. Alexander Marvin. Albany, 1864. 8°, pp. 24. [*A. C. A. B. Ath. B. Publ. Harv. Y. C.*

141. A Discourse [from II Tim. iv, 7] addressed to the congregation in the Presbyterian Church on University Place, New York, Sabbath morning, October 23, 1864, commemorative of the Rev. George Potts, D.D., their late pastor. Albany, 1864. 8°, pp. 36.
[*A. C. A. B. Ath. B. Publ. Harv. M. H. S. N. Y. Publ. U. T. S. Y. C.*

142. A Sermon [from Col. iv, 14] addressed to the Second Presbyterian Congregation, Albany, Sunday morning, April 2, 1865, on occasion of the death of Sylvester D. Willard, M.D., Surgeon-General of the State of New-York. Albany, 1865. 8°, pp. 32.
[*A. C. A. B. Ath. B. Publ. Harv. N. Y. Publ. U. T. S. Y. C.*

143. A Discourse [from Joel ii, 2] delivered in the Second Presbyterian Church, Albany, April 16, 1865, the Sunday morning immediately succeeding the Assassination of the President of the United States. Albany, 1865. 12°, pp. 18.
[*A. C. A. Harv. Y. C.*

144. An Address, delivered on the 9th of August, 1865, before the Phrenakosmian Society of Pennsylvania College, Gettysburg. Albany, 1865. 8°, pp. 37.
[*A. C. A. B. Publ. Harv. M. H. S. N. Y. Publ. U. S. U. T. S. Y. C.*

On the Mission of the Educated Mind of our Country, as determined by the present National Crisis.

145. A Discourse [from John iv, 37], delivered Sabbath morning, September 3, 1865, on occasion of the Fiftieth Anniversary of the Dedication of the Second Presbyterian Church, Albany. Albany, 1865. 8°, pp. 41.
[*A. A. S. A. C. A. B. Ath. B. Publ. Harv. M. H. S. U. T. S. Y. C.*

146. A Discourse [from Job v, 26] delivered in the Second Presbyterian Church, Albany, December 3, 1865, on occasion of the death of Mrs. Jemima Prentice, widow of the late Sartell Prentice. Albany, 1865. 8°, pp. 33.
[*A. C. A. B. Ath. B. Publ. Br. Mus. Harv. M. H. S. N. Y. Publ. U. S. U. T. S. Y. C.*

147. Recollections of Dr. Daniel Dana. In W. C. Dana's *Life of D. Dana*. Boston, 1866. pp. 260–68. [*B. Publ. U. T. S.*

148. Tribute to the memory of Azariah E. Stimson. Albany, 1866. 8°, pp. 12. [*A. C. A. B. Ath. M. H. S.*
Signed with the author's initials.

149. A Discourse addressed to the First Presbyterian Congregation of Elizabeth, N. J., October 9, 1867, on occasion of the completion of its second century. Albany, 1867. 8°, pp. 43.
[*A. C. A. B. Publ. Harv. M. H. S. U. T. S. Y. C.*

150. A Discourse [from II Cor. vi, 1] commemorative of the late Rev. John M. Krebs, D.D., delivered in the Rutgers Presbyterian Church, .. New York, on Sabbath morning, October 27, 1867. Albany, 1867. 8°, pp. 37.
[*A. C. A. B. Ath. B. Publ. Harv. M. H. S. N. Y. Publ. U. T. S. Y. C.*

151. An Address delivered on occasion of the funeral of the Rev. William James, D.D., in the First Presbyterian Church, Albany, Wednesday, February 19, 1868. Albany, 1868. 8°, pp. 22.
[*A. C. A. B. Publ. Harv. M. H. S. U. T. S. Y. C.*

152. An Address delivered at the funeral of the Rev. Benjamin H. Pitman, in the Presbyterian Church of Guilderland, Wednesday, March 11th, 1868. Albany, 1868. 8°, pp. 16.
[*A. C. A. B. Publ. Y. C.*

153. A Discourse [from Ps. xci, 16] delivered in the First Congregational Church in Northampton, Mass., on the 26th of July, 1868, the Sabbath immediately succeeding the funeral of the Rev. William Allen, D.D.—With an Appendix ... Albany, 1868. 8°, pp. 35.
[*A. C. A. B. Ath. B. Publ. Br. Mus. Harv. M. H. S. N. Y. Publ. U. T. S. Y. C.*

154. Memorial of Samuel Henry Cook. Albany, 1869. 8°, pp. 24. [*A. C. A. Harv.*

155. An Address delivered on Tuesday evening, June 15, 1869, at the close of the anniversary exercises of the Young Ladies' Institute, Albany. Albany, 1869. 8°, pp. 12.
[*A. C. A. B. Publ. Harv. M. H. S. N. H. Col. Hist. Soc.*

156. A Discourse [from Zech. i, 5] delivered in the First Congregational Church in West Springfield, August 26, 1869, on the Com-

pletion of Fifty years from the commencement of the Author's ministry in that place. Albany, 1869. 8°, pp. 28.

[*A. C. A. B. Ath. B. Publ. M. H. S.*

157. A Discourse [from Deut. ii, 7] addressed to the Second Presbyterian Congregation, Albany, on Sunday morning, September 5, 1869, on occasion of the Fortieth Anniversary of the commencement of the author's ministry among them. Albany, 1869. 8°, pp. 32.

[*A. A. S. A. C. A. B. Publ. Harv. M. H. S. U. T. S. Y. C.*

158. An Address delivered Sunday, June 20th, 1869, in the First Presbyterian Church, Albany, on occasion of the funeral of Alden March, M.D., LL.D. Albany, 1870. 8°, pp. 15.

[*A. C. A. M. H. S.*

159. The Life of Jedidiah Morse, D.D. New York [1874]. 8°, pp. viii, 333 + pl.

[*A. C. A. B. Ath. Br. Mus. M. H. S. N. Y. Publ. U. T. S. Y. C.*

This was prepared in 1867, but publication was delayed, to include material by Dr. Morse's sons.

160. Biographical Sketches (Old School Branch): chapter 3 in Presbyterian Reunion Memorial Volume. New York, 1871. 8°, pp. 103–95.

He contributed frequently to periodicals: thus, To the *National Preacher*, volume 1, pp. 81–96, November, 1826, two Sermons, from Rom. viii, 34, on the Mediation of Christ, the ground of the believer's triumph.

Volume 5, pp. 177–92, May, 1831, a Sermon, from Rev. xx, 11, on the Probability of perdition inferred from present impenitence; and a Sermon, from Lam. i, 9, on the Wicked surprised by their own destruction.

Volume 7, pp. 97–112, December, 1832, a Sermon, from Ps. lxxxvi, 8, on the God of the Christian and the God of the infidel; and a Sermon, from Luke x, 42, on Choosing the good part.

Volume 12, pp. 81–96, June, 1838, a Sermon, from Luke xiv, 22, on the Abounding Grace of the Gospel; and a Sermon, from Prov. xiv, 12, on Destructive consequences of self-flattery.

Volume 13, pp. 129–44, September, 1839, a Sermon, from Job vii, 16, on I would not live alway; and a Sermon, from Rev. xix, 12, on the Crown of thorns and the many crowns.

Volume 21, pp. 173–89, August, 1847, a Sermon, from Matth. xxv, 15, on the Life and Death of Dr. Chalmers.

Volume 22, pp. 152–63, July, 1848, a Sermon, from I Tim. vi, 17–19, on the Uses and abuses of money.

Volume 25, pp. 17–28, January, 1851, a Sermon, from Phil. iv, 13, on the Power of Christianity.

Volume 26, pp. 110–20, May, 1852, a Sermon, from Ps. cvi, 19, on the Golden calf.

Volume 28, pp. 77–91, April, 1854, a Funeral Discourse on the Rev. Dr. Joshua Bates, from Isa. iii, 1–2.

Volume 34, pp. 114–28, April, 1860, a Sermon, from II Tim. iv, 6–8, in Memoriam of Rev. T. M. Cooley, D.D.

To the *Quarterly Christian Spectator,* volume 3, pp. 202–27, June, 1831, Review of the Works of the Rev. Robert Hall.

Volume 4, pp. 345–74, September, 1832, Character and Writings of Dr. Mason; and pp. 439–56, Dickinson's Prize Letters.

Volume 5, pp. 1–20, March, 1833, Character and Works of Jay.

To the *Biblical Repertory and Princeton Review:*

Volume 5, pp. 55–76, January, 1833, On the Deportment of candidates for the ministry, in a review of the Annual of the Board of Education; and pp. 417–39, October, 1833. Review of Cox on Quakerism.

Volume 6, pp. 181–213, April, 1834, The Bible the Christian's Standard; Decorum due to Public Worship; Reflections on the Life and Character of Balaam.

Volume 35, pp. 95–108, January, 1863, Review of Memoirs of Dr. Nicholas Murray.

To the *Presbyterian Preacher,* April, 1834:

A Sermon from I Cor. x, 15, on the Conduct of sinners tested by the worldly wisdom; and a Sermon, from Zech. iv, 10, on Conscientious objections against coming to the Lord's Table, answered.

To the *Literary and Theological Review:*

Volume 1, pp. 280–304, June, 1834, Review of the Memoirs of Matthew Henry; and pp. 595–613, December, 1834, Review of the Works of Rev. J. A. James.

To the *American Biblical Repository:*

Volume 21, pp. 164–77, January, 1843, Review of Life and Writings of Ebenezer Porter Mason.

To the *American Pulpit,* volume 2, pp. 51-70, July, 1846, a Sermon, from II Kings, xxii, 2, on the Character to which young men should aspire to meet the demands of the age; also in same volume, for December, a Sermon on the Deluge; and in volume 4, May, 1848, a Sermon on the death of John Quincy Adams.

To the *Evangelical Preacher,* Zanesville, Ohio, 1848:
The Love of Money.—A Discourse, from I Tim. vi, 10, pp. 16.

In the *Evangelical Review,* Gettysburg, Pa., volume 14, pp. 463-81 (1863), on the Undeveloped resources of the Church.

To the *New Englander:*
Volume 8, pp. 30-46, February, 1850, The Buckminsters, father and son.
Volume 9, pp. 44-57, February, 1851, Everett's Orations and Speeches.

He also furnished introductory or editorial matter to many volumes, as:
Remembrances of a Polish Exile by A. J. Philadelphia, 1835.
Sketches of the Life of the Rev. Lemuel Haynes, by T. M. Cooley. New York, 1837.
Women of the Old and New Testament. New York, 1850.
The Excellent Woman as described in the Book of Proverbs. Boston, 1852.
The World's Laconics, by Edward Berkeley [= Tryon Edwards]. New York, 1853.
The Christian's Present for all seasons, by D. A. Harsha. New York, 1866.
Mementos of Rev. Edward Payson, by E. L. Janes. New York, 1873.

His collection of original manuscripts and autographs was offered for sale after his death; a catalogue of the collection was printed for private distribution (New York, 1876. 8°, pp. 15). His library was sold at auction in June, 1870.

AUTHORITIES.

C. C. Baldwin, Diary, 297-98. Dwight Family, ii, 782-83. *Huntington,* Lathrop Family Memoir, 186-87. N. Y. Geneal. and Biogr. Record, viii, 1-8. *Munsell,* Hist. Collections of Albany, iv, 67-70. Princeton Review Index, 298-300. *Welles,* Buell Family, 65, 328.

RANDOLPH STONE was born about 1790, and came to College from Bristol, Connecticut. He was early left an orphan, and was prepared for the Sophomore Class by the Rev Daniel Parker (Yale 1798), of Ellsworth Society in Sharon. He had united with the church and was looking forward to the ministry before entering Yale. A brother was graduated in 1817.

On graduation he was appointed College Butler, and was the last person to hold that office. He also taught for a few months in the Hopkins Grammar School Later, he studied theology under Dr. Dwight's direction, and after being licensed to preach by the New Haven West Association on September 9, 1817, he went to the Western Reserve of Ohio as a missionary.

In the latter part of 1818 he was invited to settle in Cleveland, and also in Morgan, in Ashtabula County A little later a settlement was suggested to him as successor to the Rev Dr. Benjamin Trumbull (Yale 1759) in North Haven, Connecticut, and another in Warren, Trumbull County, Ohio.

He decided to accept the offer from Morgan, and was ordained and installed there, over a Presbyterian church of about thirty members, on May 19, 1819. He assisted in organizing the First Presbyterian Church in Cleveland in September, 1820, and for the first six months supplied their pulpit for one-third of the time.

He remained in Morgan until August, 1828, and was not again regularly installed over any church.

In the latter part of 1827 he became an editor of the *Ohio Observer,* a religious paper published in Cleveland or in Hudson, and continued in that relation until some time in 1830.

He then went back to the East, and spent about five years in the supply of vacant churches Thus, he was in charge of the Presbyterian Church in Warren, Pennsylvania, in 1832–33, and was in Dalton, Massachusetts, in 1834–35

In 1836 he was again preaching successfully in the Western Reserve,—at the close of that year in Willoughby in Lake County.

In 1838 he became Professor of History and English Literature in the Ohio University, at Athens, but retained the chair for only about a year.

In 1843 he is reported as living in Parma, near Cleveland. He probably died soon after.

The only publication of his that I have noticed is an Extract from a letter to a friend in New Haven, dated May 19, 1820, in the *Religious Intelligencer,* volume 5, pp. 57–60 (June 24, 1820).

AUTHORITIES.

Harvey, Reply to Parker, 9–10, 103–05. *Prof. H. M. Haydn,* MS. Letter, Dec., 1911. *Parker,* Proscription delineated, 40–45, 281–84.

WOODBRIDGE STRONG, the third son of the Rev. Joseph Strong (Yale 1784), of Heath, Massachusetts, and Sophia (Woodbridge) Strong, was born in Heath on August 24, 1794. His father was dismissed from his parish in Heath in 1803, and in 1806 was settled in East Glastonbury, Connecticut. He was prepared for College by the Rev. Ephraim T. Woodruff (Yale 1797), of North Coventry.

After graduation he studied medicine in the Yale Medical School, under the immediate instruction of Dr. Nathan Smith, and received the degree of M.D. in 1818.

He soon opened an office in Boston, where he resided and practiced continuously for over forty years.

He was married, on June 27, 1826, to Elizabeth Fanny, daughter of the Hon. Laban Wheaton (Harvard 1774) and Fanny (Morey) Wheaton, of Norton, who died on March 25, 1834, in her 39th year, leaving no children. Her father devoted the portion of his estate which was designed for her inheritance to the establishment of a Female Seminary in Norton, which has had a wide influence.

He was next married in Boston, on May 28, 1840, to Harriet Atwood, formerly of Pelham, New Hampshire, widow of M. C. Torrey, who died on December 28, 1851, aged 38 years. She left one daughter, who died in March, 1859.

In August, 1859, Dr. Strong, as a result of his grief for her loss, was attacked with a cerebral affection, from which he did not recover. He died in the Insane Hospital at Somerville, near Boston, on March 31, 1861, in his 67th year.

As a physician he was enthusiastic and skilful, but perhaps too self-reliant and independent to be generally popular. He was a man of superior intellectual powers, positive in his habits of thought and in his convictions of duty. He had been for many years a consistent member of the Park Street Congregational Church.

AUTHORITIES.

Boston Med. and Surg. Journal, lxiv, 231–32. *Dwight,* Strong Family, i, 362, 376. N. Y. Geneal. and Biogr. Record, ii, 136. Norton Vital Records, 335, 396. *Dr. Maltby Strong,* MS. Letter, June, 1861.

Giles Hallam Swan, the youngest child of George Swan, of North Stonington, Connecticut, and a brother of the Rev. Roswell R. Swan (Yale 1802), was born on April 29, 1793. He lost both parents in his infancy, and lived with his brother in Norwalk (after his marriage in 1807). He was prepared for College by William Belden (Yale 1803) at the Staples Academy in Easton.

After graduation, with a colony of other Norwalk settlers, he went to Ohio.

He settled on a farm in the new township of Norwalk, and died about 1843. His wife long survived him.

AUTHORITIES.

Wheeler, Hist. of Stonington, 614.

THOMAS TURNER, the eldest child of James Turner, of Warrenton, Warren County, North Carolina, and grandson of Thomas and Rebecca Turner, of Southampton County, Virginia, and Bute, then in Warren County, North Carolina, was born on June 14, 1794. His mother was Mary (or Polly) Anderson, of Warrenton. His father was Governor of the State in 1802–05, and United States Senator from 1805 to 1816. His preparation for Yale was completed in New Haven under Tutor Samuel J. Hitchcock (Yale 1809). A sister married George E. Badger (Yale 1813).

He married, on January 25, 1817, Nancy Baskerville, of Lombardy Grove, Mecklenburg County, Virginia, and settled on a farm in Granville County, North Carolina. He never entered public life, but was known and esteemed as a kindly, hospitable citizen.

He died on April 14, 1850, in his 56th year. He had four daughters and three sons. After his death his widow removed to Warrenton, where she died on November 2, 1859.

AUTHORITIES.

Hon. W. A. Montgomery, MS. Letter, Nov., 1911. *Mrs. Norfleet S. Smith*, MS. Letter, Febr., 1912. *Wheeler*, Hist. Sketches of N. C., ii, 439; Reminiscences, 455.

JACOB VANBENTHUYSEN was a son of John and Catharine VanBenthuysen, of Poughkeepsie, Duchess County, New York, and was prepared by Daniel H. Barnes (Union Coll. 1809) in the Poughkeepsie Academy for admission to the Sophomore Class.

He studied law in Poughkeepsie, and after his admission to the bar in 1825, he began practice there. He enjoyed the confidence of his fellow-citizens, and was universally liked for his habitual courtesy and sound judgment. He was for three years (1836–38) President of the Board of Trustees of the village.

He was appointed Postmaster of Poughkeepsie by President Jackson, soon after his accession in 1829, and held that office until his death there, very suddenly, at his boarding-house, the Poughkeepsie Hotel, from apoplexy, on July 19, 1846, at the age of 51. He was never married.

AUTHORITIES.

Miss H. W. Reynolds, MS. Letter, Jan., 1912.

WILLIAM COURTNEY WETMORE, the youngest son of Victory Wetmore, of Stratford, Connecticut, and a grandson of the Rev. Izrahiah Wetmore (Yale 1748), of Stratford, was born on October 12, 1796. His mother was Catharine Maria, younger daughter of Abijah and Catharine (Tomlinson) McEwen, of Stratford. He was prepared for College by Hezekiah G. Ufford (Yale 1806) in New York.

After graduation he studied law in the Litchfield Law School, and about 1818 entered the office of Messrs. Brackett & Clark in New York City, becoming subsequently a partner in the firm. From 1848 he was connected in business with Richard Bowne.

From the first he made a specialty of the law of real estate, and was occupied chiefly with conveyancing and the administration of trusts. He refused all offers of public position, except that for three years before his death he served as President of the Board of Commissioners of the Central Park.

He resided in New York City until about 1868, when he removed to Fordham, but returned to the city in October, 1879.

After some months of feebleness, he died in New York, from organic disease of the heart, on March 22, 1880, in his 84th year.

He was married to Elizabeth, daughter of Ezekiel and Hannah Lovejoy, of Stratford, who survived him with four sons and a daughter.

AUTHORITIES.

Wetmore Family, 121, 133.

FREDERICK WHITE was a native of Columbia, formerly part of Lebanon, Connecticut, and was prepared for admission to the Sophomore Class by the Rev. Ephraim T. Woodruff (Yale 1797), of North Coventry.

He studied law after graduation, but abandoned the profession, being at one time of dissipated habits, from which, however, he recovered.

He also taught for a time in New Jersey, but was attacked with consumption, and returned to his native place, only to die, on May 25, 1839, at the age of 45.

AUTHORITIES.

Rev. C. Little, MS. Letter, September, 1844.

SIMS WHITE, the eldest child of Christopher Gadsden and Martha (Walter) White, was born on July 9, 1796, at "Lifeland," his father's plantation in St. Stephen's Parish, forty miles north of Charleston, South Carolina. He was prepared for Yale by Alpheus Baker (Dartmouth Coll. 1801).

After graduation he studied law in the office of Judge Langdon Cheves, in Charleston, and was admitted to the bar in 1818.

On March 10, 1819, he married his first cousin, Jane Purcell White, by whom he had two children. After her death he married, on May 12, 1825, Anna Elinor Gaillard, a niece of Senator John Gaillard.

Of his twelve children ten reached maturity.

He did not remain long in practice in Charleston, preferring the life of a planter in the country, and devoting himself in part to the education of his children.

He died in Columbia on August 12, 1855, at the age of 59, and was buried in the family burying ground at Biggin Church, St. John's Parish, Berkeley County, about twenty miles north of Charleston.

His widow died on June 19, 1862, aged 57 years.

AUTHORITIES.

Miss I. DeSaussure, MS. Letter, Dec., 1911.

EDMUND FANNING WICKHAM, the second son of John Wickham, an eminent lawyer of Richmond, Virginia, and grandson of John and Hannah (Fanning) Wickham, of Cutchogue village, in Southold, Long Island, was born in Richmond on July 30, 1796. His mother was Mary Smith, only child of the Rev. William and Mary (Gray, Tazewell) Fanning, of Greenesville County, Virginia, and a first cousin of her husband.

He entered College at the opening of the Sophomore year.

He spent his life in Richmond, where he died on September 25, 1843, in his 48th year.

He married Lucy, daughter of Robert and Mary (Nelson) Carter, of Shirley, Charles City County, who died in January, 1835, at the age of 36.

Their children, four sons and two daughters, all grew to maturity. The eldest son became a surgeon in the United States army.

AUTHORITIES.

Brooks, Fanning Family, i, 153; ii, 659.

JOSEPH DRESSER WICKHAM, the eldest son of Daniel Hull Wickham, from Southold, Long Island, a country storekeeper in Thompson, Connecticut, was born in Thompson on April 4, 1797. His mother was Mary, daughter of Captain Jacob and Esther (Johnson) Dresser, of Thompson. The family removed to New York City in his infancy, and he was prepared for College by Azariah Scofield (Yale 1801).

For the year after graduation he served as amanuensis to President Dwight, and during the following year he was the Rector of the Hopkins Grammar School. From 1818 to 1820 he held a College Tutorship, at the same time studying theology under the direction of Professors Fitch and Goodrich. He was licensed to preach by the New Haven West Association on January 2, 1821.

In 1821 he engaged in service as a missionary on Long Island, and then spent some time in central New York under the employ of the Presbyterian Education Society.

In January, 1823, he began preaching in the Congregational Church in Oxford, Chenango County, where he was ordained as an evangelist on July 31.

He was married in Worcester, Massachusetts, on May 26, to Julia Ann, the only daughter of the late Hon. Jonathan Edwards Porter (Harvard 1786), of New Haven, and Fidelia (Dwight) Porter, and a niece of President Dwight.

In the spring of 1825 he removed to Westchester County, where he had charge for about three years of the Presbyterian churches in New Rochelle and West Farms.

In 1829 he joined George Washington Hall (Yale 1803) as one of the proprietors of the Washington Institute, a large boarding-school for boys in Thirteenth Street, New York.

His wife died in New York, after a protracted illness, on December 23, 1830, in her 38th year, and he was next married, on December 28, 1831, to Amy, third daughter of Colonel Moses and Amy (Colt) Porter, of South Hadley, Massachusetts, and a cousin of his first wife. She died on October 29, 1832, in her 32d year.

In 1834 the Washington Institute passed into the hands of Mr. Wickham's two brothers-in-law, Timothy Dwight Porter (Yale 1816) and Theodore Woolsey Porter (Yale 1819).

He married as his third wife, on October 12, 1834, Elizabeth Cooke, eldest daughter of the Rev. Samuel Merwin (Yale 1802), then of Wilton, Connecticut; and on the 16th of the following month he was installed over a recently organized Presbyterian church at Matteawan in Fishkill.

At the end of two years, being solicited to resume connection with the Education Society, he resigned his pastorate and then spent a laborious year among the churches of Northern and Western New York.

In December, 1837, he removed to Manchester, Vermont, to take charge of the Burr Seminary, a preparatory school of high character, with which he remained connected as principal until November, 1862, except that for the year 1853–54, he was the Treasurer of Middlebury College and acting Professor of Latin and Greek, and for the two following years was connected with the Collegiate Institute in Poughkeepsie, New York. He was a Trustee of Middlebury College from 1840 until his death; and received from it the honorary degree of Doctor of Divinity in 1861.

After retiring to private life in 1862, he continued to reside in Manchester, and served as president of the Board of Trustees of the Burr Seminary until the end.

He was the last survivor of his Class and of the graduates under President Dwight, and for three years the oldest living graduate of the College.

He died in Manchester, from old age, on May 12, 1891, in his 95th year.

His wife survived him. By his first marriage he had a daughter who died in infancy; and by his second marriage a daughter who survived him.

Dr. Wickham retained until the last remarkable physical and mental vigor, and a cheery and hopeful outlook.

While tutor he published several articles in the *Microscope,* New Haven, 1820. Five of these were poetical pieces, volume 1, pp. 104, 183–84; volume 2, pp. 32, 56, 175–76; the others were, The folly of indulgence in morbid sensibility, volume 2, pp. 49–53, and The story of Horatio, pp. 121–26, 129–35.

AUTHORITIES.

Dwight Family, i, 242–43. *Hotchkin,* Hist. of Western N. Y., 296.

JESSE SMITH WOODHULL, the only son of Judge Abraham Woodhull, of the village of Setauket, in Brookhaven, Long Island, and grandson of Justice Richard and Margaret (Smith) Woodhull, of Setauket, was born on February 5, 1796, and was prepared for College by Alanson Hamlin (Yale 1799) in Danbury, Connecticut. His mother was Mary, daughter of Obadiah Smith.

He settled on his ancestral farm in Setauket, and there married Ann Maria, daughter of Samuel Brewster, who died on September 30, 1824, at the age of 27.

He next married Charity, daughter of Woodhull Smith, of Smithtown, who survived him.

He died in Setauket, after a brief illness, on March 30, 1841, at the age of 45.

His only surviving child was a son by his first marriage.

AUTHORITIES.

N. Y. Geneal. and Biogr. Record, iv, 59, 125. Woodhull Genealogy, 87, 137.

JOSEPH YOULE, the eldest son of George Youle, a dry-goods merchant of New York City, was prepared for College by the Rev. Daniel Smith (Yale 1791), of Stamford, Connecticut.

He became deranged shortly before graduation, and on his partial restoration made a trip to Europe for the benefit of his health.

After his return he suffered a relapse, and in a fit of insanity threw himself from a third-story window of his father's house in New York, on January 6, 1820, and was instantly killed. He was in his 24th year.

APPENDIX

The present volume contains notices of 601 graduates.

The places of their birth may be classified as follows:—Connecticut, 357 (Fairfield County, 64; Hartford County, 62; Litchfield County, 60; New Haven County, 56; New London County, 50; Windham County, 30; Middlesex County, 22; Tolland County, 13); Massachusetts, 72; New York, 69; South Carolina, 40; Georgia, 10; North Carolina, 9; New Hampshire, 7; New Jersey and Virginia, 6 each; Pennsylvania, 5; Maryland and Vermont, 4 each; Rhode Island, 3; Delaware and Maine, 2 each; Kentucky, 1; outside of the United States, 4.

Their latest or principal places of residence were:—New York, 172; Connecticut, 166; Massachusetts, 53; South Carolina, 34; Ohio, 29; Pennsylvania, 21; Alabama, Illinois, and North Carolina, 10 each; Georgia, 8; Louisiana, 7; Indiana, New Jersey, Vermont, and Virginia, 6 each; Maine, Maryland, and Michigan, 4 each; Kentucky and Mississippi, 3 each; etc.

Their occupations may be thus summarized:—Lawyers, 191; Ministers, 108; Physicians, 71; Business men, 67; Teachers, 47; Farmers and Planters, 44; Editors and Authors, 12; etc.

ADDITIONS AND CORRECTIONS

Volume I.

Page 324, line 11 from bottom. Cornelius Bennet, son of Ebenezer and Esther Bennett, was born in Middleboro, Massachusetts, on July 9, 1703. He married, in Barnstable, on January 12, 1732, Ruth, daughter of Shubael and Puella (Hussey) Gorham, who died on September 2, 1792, in her 80th year. He died in Middleboro, on February 22, or 25, 1766. He is called "Dr." on his tombstone.

Page 342, line 13. John Whiting is here wrongly identified with the Colonel of the same name. The graduate first married, on December 3, 1729, Phebe, daughter of Edward Greenman, of Westerly, and widow of Amos Hallam, of Stonington. She died in 1763, and he married, on August 6, 1767, Mary, daughter of David and Sarah (Parish) Tracy, of Preston, and successively widow of James Clark, of Norwich, and James Luce, of Scotland Parish. She died on June 24, 1792, in her 74th year.

His elder daughter married Dr. Gideon Welles (Yale 1753), and the younger married Harding Jones.

Page 600, line 17. SETH DEAN's mother was the second daughter of John Smith, of Taunton, Massachusetts. He married, first, Mercy Fenner, on October 6, 1743; and secondly, on September 17, 1762, while of Plainfield, Lydia, widow of Isaac Allen, of Brooklyn, Connecticut, who died in 1776.

Page 680, line 21. JOSEPH LAMSON died on August 12, 1773.

VOLUME II.

Page 224, line 18. JOSIAH TOPPING became a physician, and settled in Granby, Connecticut, where he married, on November 15, 1756, Susanna, daughter of Lieutenant David Holcomb. His will, proved on March 3, 1794, names his wife, three sons and five daughters.

Page 417, line 14. HARDING JONES was the elder son of Frederick Jones, of Newbern, and grandson of Chief Justice Frederick and Jane (Harding) Jones, of Edenton. His mother, Mary, daughter of Jeremiah Vail, married secondly William Wilson, and thirdly Roger Moore. His widow married secondly Richard Ellis, and thirdly David Witherspoon.

Page 428, line 9 from bottom. ELNATHAN ROSSETER married Mercy, daughter of Judah and Prudence (Stanton) Coleman, and had three sons and three daughters.

VOLUME III.

Page 472, line 3 from bottom. BARUCH BECKWITH, youngest son of the Rev. George, was called to the pastorate of the Congregational Church in Oakham, Massachusetts, on July 23, 1778. He accepted the call, but died before his ordination, in Lancaster, of dysentery, on September 15, aged 26 years.

Page 530, line 9. TIMOTHY KIMBALL died on March 9, 1786.

Page 578, line 2. JAMES MORRIS had one daughter and four sons by this wife. He married again, on March 6, 1815, Rhoda, daughter of Gad and Jane (Bishop) Farnam, of Litchfield, by whom he had a daughter and a son.

Page 667, line 16. SAMUEL COGSWELL died on August 31, 1790.

VOLUME IV.

Page 97, line 21. WILLIAM BALDWIN's will is dated July 15, and proved October 23, 1818.

Page 527, line 9. AZEL BACKUS died on December 9, 1816.

Page 539, line 3 from bottom. EBENEZER DUTTON is said to have settled in Canandaigua, not Cazenovia. He married about 1813 his first cousin, Ruth Dutton, and had one son and one daughter.

Page 600, line 9. BENJAMIN GALE died in Troy in August, 1817, aged 51 years.

VOLUME V.

Page 88, line 7 from bottom. ICHABOD LORD SKINNER did not marry a second time. His wife Hannah died in Frostburg on March 6, 1843, in her 73d year.

Page 185, line 5 from bottom. JAMES CANTEY died in Liberty County in 1799. He married Elizabeth Blandford Inglesby, by whom he had one son.

Page 370, line 6 from bottom JEREMIAH OSBORN probably died early in 1827, his death is noticed in the newspapers of April.

Page 791, line 5 ELIHU SPENCER was born on January 26, 1785 His marriage as given in the text is incorrect He married on May 16, 1816, Sarah, daughter of Abner and Ruth (Ellsworth) Sage, of Chatham, Connecticut, who died in Middletown on October 8, 1863, in her 76th year A son was graduated at Wesleyan University in 1838

VOLUME VI

Page 76, line 11 WILLIAM F VAILL married, on December 28, 1808, Asenath, daughter of Colonel Richard Ely Selden, of Hadlyme, who died in Hadlyme on November 24, 1834, aged 49 years He next married Lucretia, daughter of Eleazar and Tirzah (Porter) Loomis, of Coventry, who died on March 25, 1867, aged 61 years

INDEX

Italics indicate the graduates of whom sketches are given.

THE TUTTLE, MOREHOUSE & TAYLOR PRESS, NEW HAVEN, CONN.

CPSIA information can be obtained at www.ICGtesting.com
Printed in the USA
LVOW11s1927040514

384389LV00006B/473/P